The Great West

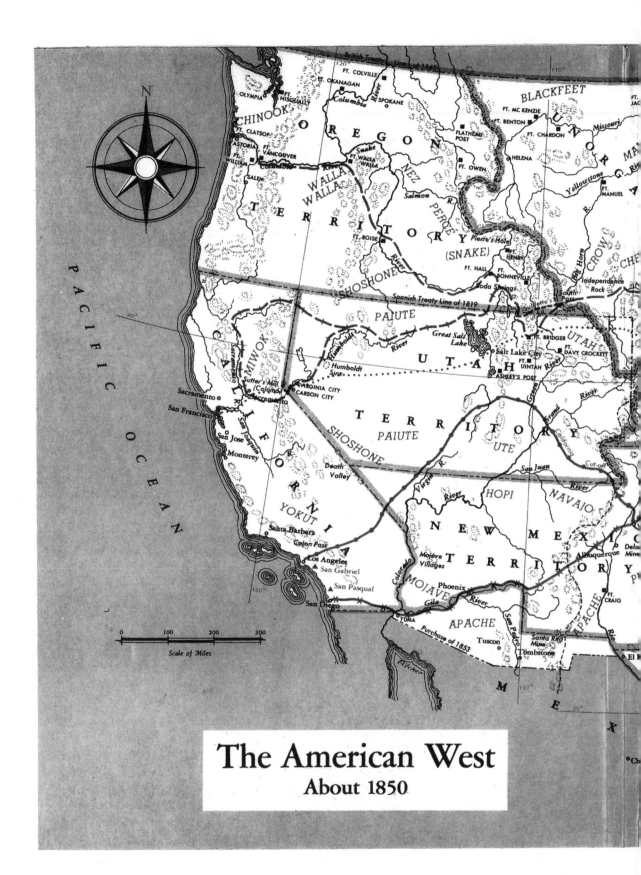

The American West
About 1850

Books by Charles Neider

FICTION

OVERFLIGHT

A VISIT TO YAZOO

MOZART AND THE ARCHBOOBY

NAKED EYE

THE AUTHENTIC DEATH OF HENDRY JONES

THE WHITE CITADEL

NONFICTION

BEYOND CAPE HORN: TRAVELS IN THE ANTARCTIC

EDGE OF THE WORLD: ROSS ISLAND, ANTARCTICA

SUSY: A CHILDHOOD

MARK TWAIN

THE FROZEN SEA: A STUDY OF FRANZ KAFKA

Some Books Edited by Charles Neider

THE COMPLETE TALES OF WASHINGTON IRVING

THE COMPLETE SHORT STORIES OF ROBERT LOUIS STEVENSON

THE COMPLETE HUMOROUS SKETCHES AND TALES OF MARK TWAIN

THE AUTOBIOGRAPHY OF MARK TWAIN

THE COMPLETE SHORT STORIES OF MARK TWAIN

SHORT NOVELS OF THE MASTERS

GREAT SHORT STORIES FROM THE WORLD'S LITERATURE

THE GREAT WEST: A TREASURY OF FIRSTHAND ACCOUNTS

THE COMPLETE ESSAYS OF MARK TWAIN

GEORGE WASHINGTON: A BIOGRAPHY BY WASHINGTON IRVING

Edited, with Introduction and Notes by

CHARLES
NEIDER

DA CAPO PRESS   NEW YORK

THE GREAT WEST

A Treasury of Firsthand Accounts

Library of Congress Cataloging-in-Publication Data

The great West: a treasury of firsthand accounts / edited, with introduction
and notes by Charles Neider.—1st Da Capo Press ed.
   p.   cm.
  ISBN 0-306-80761-0 (alk. paper)
  1. West (U.S.)—History—Sources. 2. West (U.S.)—Biography. I. Neider,
Charles, 1915– .
F591.G769 1997
978—dc21

                             96-45126
                                CIP

First Da Capo Press edition 1997

This Da Capo Press paperback edition of *The Great West* is an unabridged
republication of the edition first published in New York in 1958.
It is reprinted by arrangement with Charles Neider.

Published by Da Capo Press, Inc.
A Subsidiary of Plenum Publishing Corporation
233 Spring Street, New York, N.Y. 10013

To Bernie Breitbart

Contents

A Note on the Selections   9

Introduction   11

Part I — PATHFINDERS

The Search for the Seven Cities   FRANCISCO VAZQUEZ DE CORONADO   19

A Report from Monterey   SEBASTIAN VIZCAINO   29

Thomas Jefferson's Instructions to
    Meriwether Lewis   A DOCUMENT   31

A Remarkable Journey to the Pacific   MERIWETHER LEWIS
    AND WILLIAM CLARK   35

The Journey to Pike's Peak   ZEBULON MONTGOMERY PIKE   71

An Overland Journey to California   JEDEDIAH STRONG SMITH   86

A Visit to the San Gabriel Mission   HARRISON G. ROGERS   90

The Adventures of Zenas Leonard   ZENAS LEONARD   96

The Crossing of the Sierra Nevada   JOHN CHARLES FRÉMONT   121

Part II — HEROES AND VILLAINS

Adventures in the Wilderness   DAVID CROCKETT   133

James Bridger, Mountain Man   GRENVILLE M. DODGE   149

Notice of a Runaway Apprentice   A DOCUMENT   168

Kit Carson   JOHN CHARLES FRÉMONT   168

A Brush with Crow Indians   KIT CARSON   169

Narrow Escapes   KIT CARSON   171

Adventures with Frémont   KIT CARSON   174

Wild Bill, My Scout   GEORGE A. CUSTER   181

Interviewing Wild Bill   GEORGE WARD NICHOLS   183

The Killing of Wild Bill   J. W. BUEL   197

Indians!   GEORGE A. CUSTER   201

Orders to General Custer   GENERAL ALFRED H. TERRY   210

Report to General Sheridan   GENERAL ALFRED H. TERRY   211

General Custer's Last Fight   TWO MOON, AS RELATED TO
    HAMLIN GARLAND   212

Findings of a Court of Inquiry	A DOCUMENT	217
General Carr on Buffalo Bill Cody	E. A. CARR	219
Robbed by Danites	BUFFALO BILL CODY	221
Hard Times	BUFFALO BILL CODY	227
A Buffalo Killing Match	BUFFALO BILL CODY	233
Adventures Among the White Men	GERONIMO	238
The Surrender of Sitting Bull	E. H. ALLISON	248
The Capture of Tiburcio Vasquez	BEN C. TRUMAN	263
Wanted: Jesse James	A DOCUMENT	270
Some Exploits of the James Brothers	J. W. BUEL	272
The Tragedy in Detail	NEWSPAPER ACCOUNT	279
The Inquest	NEWSPAPER ACCOUNT	282
The Life and Adventures of Calamity Jane	HERSELF	287
The Death Warrant of Billy the Kid	A DOCUMENT	291
The Death Warrant Returned	A DOCUMENT	292
How I Killed Billy the Kid	PAT F. GARRETT	292
The Body of Billy the Kid	A DOCUMENT	300

Part III — OBSERVERS

Adventures on the Prairie	WASHINGTON IRVING	303
Ashore in California	RICHARD HENRY DANA	312
A Day with the Cow Column	JESSE APPLEGATE	318
A Buffalo Hunt	JOHN CHARLES FRÉMONT	326
The Golden Gate	JOHN CHARLES FRÉMONT	328
The Platte and the Desert	FRANCIS PARKMAN	331
The Black Hills	FRANCIS PARKMAN	338
The Diary of John Sutter	JOHN SUTTER	340
Looking for Gold	J. D. BORTHWICK	358
Miners' Law	J. D. BORTHWICK	365
Gold is Where You Find It	J. D. BORTHWICK	372
Western Characters	HORACE GREELEY	379
Portrait of a Desperado	MARK TWAIN	384
The Pony Express	MARK TWAIN	392
Virginia City Revisited	J. ROSS BROWNE	395
Hunting Big Redwoods	JOHN MUIR	408
The Emigrant Train	ROBERT LOUIS STEVENSON	426
The Yellowstone	RUDYARD KIPLING	435
The Round-Up	EMERSON HOUGH	441

A Note on the Selections

For the purposes of this volume I have regarded the American West as beginning geographically west of the Mississippi River and ending chronologically at the turn of the last century, approximately with the closing of the frontier.

Obviously, no single volume concerned with so vast a stage can hope to be either comprehensive or definitive.

Although I have tried, as always, to emphasize excellence of literary style, I have not hesitated in this instance to subordinate style whenever documentary value was of prime consideration. I have tried to suggest a panorama or pageant of the West in the words of the people who were actually there. It seems to me that no secondary materials can have the romance, the charm and the flavor of contemporary documents.

I have not emphasized novelty in my choice of accounts. Nothing could be easier than to make a show in this direction. The libraries are still full of materials which are barely known to scholars, let alone the general reader, for whom this book is designed. I have tried to touch the chief highlights, and those which have stirred the nation's imagination.

I am indebted, for many courtesies extended to me, to several institutions and their staffs in the preparation of this volume—the New York Public Library, the public libraries of Santa Monica and Monterey, California, the Huntington Library, the Bancroft Library of the University of California at Berkeley, the library of U. C. L. A., and the libraries of Stanford, Yale, and Columbia Universities. I am particularly indebted to Cass Canfield, Jr., my editor in this venture, for very valuable aid and counsel.

C. N.

Introduction

My experience of the American West was —and is—one of the prime experiences of my life. How it came about and with what consequences for me I should like to communicate to you, even if only in a feeble way. For the physical joy and mental serenity which the West inspires are part of our national heritage and deserve to be shared by those lucky enough to have encountered them keenly.

Admittedly it is a bit late in the day to be singing their praise. And yet the West is not merely the old West, as though it had not undergone changes, as though it were not changing even now. One's experience is in some ways new and new praise is justified. In addition, there are some things, fortunately, which deserve to be praised by each new pair of eyes that sees them.

Although I was born in Odessa and raised in Richmond and New York, my view of the United States was, until fairly recently, a parochial one. This was perhaps due more to circumstances beyond my control than to any inner inclination. I was poor, and travel, unhappily, required money. (But it is likely that such an explanation is insufficient. My European orientation and interests were probably the stronger cause.) Like most American boys I grew up with a great admiration for the West and its heroes, and identified in my daydreams with Buffalo Bill, Kit Carson, General Custer and all the others. I was proud of the fact that the West was a part of my general scene. It is true that I had local heroes—such as John Smith and Richard Byrd and Robert E. Lee and George Washington—and I could never forget that Virginia considered herself "the mother of presidents" and the heart of the Confederacy, or that many of the great pathfinders and trappers had been born and raised in Virginia. But the West was distant, romantic and grand; and—very important—it was the place of the good guys and the bad: the place where western films were made, where such modern heroes as Tom Mix lived, and where the action of certain thrilling paperbacks took place.

Somewhere between my boyhood and my youth I acquired new notions of the West, notions unfortunate for my earlier enthusiasm. The West, I now believed, had been tamed and was only a provincialized East. The frontier had closed and the country had become—or was quickly becoming—homogeneous. The West was a lonely sprinkling of cities and towns, all cut to the American pattern, with familiar streets, stores and faces. And the West was emotionally somewhat unstable, with a tendency to brag and to go in for glitter and fad. Just how or why I acquired these notions I do not know; or at any rate it would be a long and difficult process to try to put my finger on the reasons. The telling fact is that I acquired them not by traveling in the West but by hearsay, by reading or through some disillusion, some inner need. These notions stayed with me a long time, although with the passing of years I began to experience a longing to go and see for myself.

Several men of whom I thought highly had found happiness in the West and I

11

could not easily explain this fact away. D. H. Lawrence had described, with his surpassing genius in such things, the beauties of the New Mexico landscape around Taos. Thomas Mann, with whom I was proud to claim friendship, had likened the skies of southern California to those of Egypt and had worked well in that hilly, seaside part of Los Angeles known as Pacific Palisades. Igor Stravinsky was flourishing in California, as was Frank Lloyd Wright in Arizona. And, although in a fresher time, Robert Louis Stevenson, an early hero of mine, had described the charms of Monterey in an essay on the town which no modern writer could surpass, and had also described a trip across the plains with obvious admiration and zest. And Mark Twain had found a ruggednesss, a humor, a violence, a greatness in the West which had done much to expand and fulfill his genius.

Still, these cases did not seem to apply to mine, although what my case was, in precise terms, I did not know. Lawrence, being a tubercular, had had good reason to admire the climate around Taos, with its high altitude and dry sky. Besides, he had had a yen for travel and for exotic and primitive places. Mann had been unhappy in the academic and actual climate of Princeton and had found in southern California many compatriots—Arnold Schönberg, Bruno Walter, Viki Baum, Lion Feuchtwanger and others. And the neo-Egyptian skies had helped him to continue his Biblical epic of the story of Joseph. Stravinsky was someone remote and strange to me, with theatrical overtones, and I could not judge his needs. Wright had found particular inspiration in the contours and configurations of the western landscape. Stevenson had gone west to find a wife—Fanny Osbourne, of Monterey—and Mark Twain

had had specific reasons for going to Nevada, his brother having received an appointment as an official of the Territory. And so, despite such examples before me, and my growing longing to have a look at the West, I went there for the first time in a skeptical frame of mind, prepared to be disappointed.

My opportunity came as a lucky accident: the Hartford Foundation of Pacific Palisades invited me to live and work in its canyon for half a year. How enchanting that canyon was and how important the whole trip was going to be for me I could not possibly have imagined as I drove out of New York early in March of 1952 and headed south for Georgia and the snow-free route.

On entering Texas, I considered that I had begun my travels in the West itself. The difference between Texas and the parts of the South I had passed through became apparent the moment I crossed the state line. Highway U. S. 80 was perfectly graded and paved, and set down with ample measure. At Longview, where I stopped for the night, I was surprised to see mission architecture, many new buildings, a small skyscraper and shiny drugstores. Luxury goods were abundantly on display. Boys on the streets wore ten-gallon hats and fancy cowboy boots and swaggered as they walked. The churches, or some of them, were gaudy and ultramodern. I had no doubt that I had entered a new and prosperous world. My only question was: whether it was a world I cared to become a part of.

But the towns and cities were by no means all of Texas. Texas was the astonishing distances, dust storms, a free and easy gait and, in the western part, rocky deserts which awoke in me a sense of doom, a sense unpleasant then but surprisingly valuable in retrospect. It is useless to try to convey the experience of great space. You simply must have it for yourself to understand, just as you must experience the ocean to know what is meant by ocean. That experience is essential to knowing the West. As I lived through it it seemed to me that it was washing away some of the notions I had acquired about the West since my early boyhood. The stony mountains jutted into a moistureless sky, the great boulders were piled tremendously, and there were nothing but hard earth, cactus and the highway losing itself in the hills. Meeting a car in that space was a novel experience.

Western Texas was an introduction to New Mexico and Arizona. More of that same vastness, that burning blue air and that etched sun. And now there were mesas and buttes and much evidence of the Spanish influence and of the proximity of Mexico. By the time I reached California, with its tawny rippled desert, its Salton Sea and fertile Coachella Valley, I had been washed clean of all notions and was ready to have, or rather to accept, the new experience in all its dazzle and size and fertility. No doubt I was ready for the experience and no doubt I needed it. Without such a need and readiness even a visit to the Garden of Eden would probably be fruitless. But it was more than just a need. The landscape and the climate and the people had something rich to give, and to give it in abundance.

As I have already said, I had thought that the frontier had closed long ago. But during my stay in the West, which lengthened to the better part of a year, I began to sense what I had failed to foresee: that although the frontier had closed physically, its forces were still operating in a way of life which was sometimes strikingly different from that of the East. This was evidenced not only in a freer use of clothes for both men and women but in the easier human relations and the greater fluidity between classes of people, as well as the freer architecture, the greater mobility in space, and the conception of the good life as something within the possibility of everyone, and something to be molded out of tomorrow rather than to be crafted out of a contemplation of yesterday. It seemed to me that a sharper sense of democracy—democracy in practice—existed in the West than in the East. Finally, it was refreshing to think of Japan and Mexico as one's neighbors rather than of England and France. I began to be excited about an America which was partly the past and partly the present, partly legend and partly fact, and which moved me in such a way that I wished to write about it and to communicate my experiences and enthusiasms. And I constantly wished to learn more about it, about the immense spaces, serene skies, glowing colors, the wastelands, dry gulches, great valleys and firred mountains, and about the mixture of peoples, Mexicans, Indians, descendants of old Spanish families, and Americans from everywhere. Sometimes when I returned to these scenes after a stay in the East I wondered if my enthusiasm would wane and was delighted to find that it did not, that it could no more wane than my enthusiasm for good air and good water.

There used to be a legend among prospective emigrants to America that the United States was a land of gold, and some of the more naïve people perhaps really imagined the pavements to be laid with gold bricks. The West, and especially California, is now to the East what America used to be—and still is—to Europe. The time I spent in the California canyon was a rich one, spiritually and physically, for me. Using the canyon as a base, I traveled in various directions and was greatly impressed by what I saw. Speaking quite personally, I can say that the West rewarded me handsomely, not only in happiness but in literary inspiration. Once, while in Monterey, I had the good luck to turn up Fanny Stevenson's Samoan diary, which was lying in a glass case of Stevenson House, an adobe in which Robert Louis Stevenson is supposed to have lived in the fall of 1879.

While preparing the diary for publication at the request of its owner, the State of California, I had ample reason to poke into the resources of several western libraries and to understand what a gold mine for scholars and writers the literary history of the West contains. It was during this research, and in the pleasure of much collateral reading, that I came upon the idea for the present volume, as well as for the collection of Mark Twain's short stories which was recently published, and a completely revised edition of Mark Twain's autobiography, the manuscript of which resides in the Berkeley library of the University of California. And—most important of all for me—it was during this reading and this experience that I received the idea for my second novel, *The Authentic Death of Hendry Jones,* partially based on the story of Billy the Kid, but not so much on the actual story as the myth the folk imagination invented.*

In the American West legend has sometimes merged so well with fact that it is not always possible to separate the two.

*The Authentic Death of Hendry Jones, first published in 1956, was later made into the movie One-Eyed Jacks, starring Marlon Brando, who produced and directed as well.

From a literary point of view a separation is not always advisable. For example, the actual history of William Bonney, known as Billy the Kid, is confused, vague and sometimes artistically anticlimactic. But the stories told about him, like those about folk heroes and villains, are as satisfying as myths usually are. Billy the Kid as we know him is not so much an historical event as a folk invention. He is Robin Hood, a knight, the young killer as genius, Satan incarnate, the resurrected one, and so on. He was barely in his grave before it was claimed that it was not really he who had been killed and buried.

This process of myth making was particularly active in the West and came at a time when the eastern myths had begun to crystallize. Why the West was so creative in its legends I do not know, but it is probable that the fluid and primitive nature of its society, the great spaces, the Spanish and Indian influences, and the heroic level of some of its dramas were among the primary reasons. The West as a great myth is one of the most important artistic products of the American imagination, and yet it has been touched upon only superficially. Because the old West was raw, and an object of satire in the East; because many of its actors seemed childish to sophisticated easterners; and because those responsible for using western materials for artistic purposes are too often inadequate to the task: because of such reasons it is usually believed that western materials are adequate for gunman paperbacks and cowboy movies only, and that exceptions merely prove the rule. This is an error which can only be rectified by the production of superior art, and such art, in turn, can only be created out of a profound knowledge and feeling for the western materials and the western experience, materials such as the documents contained in the present book.

These are facts which western writers, perhaps too close to the scene, have on the whole overlooked, as they have overlooked such basic elements as the West's spaces. The western landscape is not the kind that one can easily cope with. Vast, with few signs of habitation in seemingly endless stretches, it can affect one like the rolling sea, or produce agoraphobia. A person sometimes feels drowned in it and, on reaching a town, may compensate for a feeling of ego exhaustion with swagger and defiance or a quiet efficient self-assertion. It is the sort of landscape which tends, I think, to encourage violence as well as eccentricity, and this was even more true in the days of horse travel than it is now. Few writers have tried to embody such effects, or rather such causes and their effects, in their western work.

It is interesting to take a glance at how semilegendary materials have been generally used. Using Billy the Kid as an example again, one sees that his contemporaries regarded him purely as a local phenomenon. Writers in the two generations following him portrayed him unvaryingly in penny-dreadful terms. No novel until recently claimed to treat him seriously, and almost all novels which treated him at all did so while suffering from the localisms and provincialisms which plague so many western writers, or writers of western books: dialect, cheap plot, thin characterization, and in general a failure to realize their materials in folkloristic and mythical ways. That it is possible to achieve a serious novel, high tragedy and perhaps even a work of art out of western materials I am entirely convinced of; but to do so requires a sophisticated literary intelligence. I believe that the western raw materials will be the basis of an important literature and

that this literature may well surpass in excellence that of other regions of our country. A renaissance of serious interest in the West has been strengthening for several years now.

The period of our western history which produced Billy the Kid and characters like him was strong in certain aspects: fatalism, courage and the ability to die unsentimentally. Such characters lived their lives the way they played their poker and made their entrances and exits with a shrug. Their conception of their destiny was quite simply their conception of their luck. When their luck ran out their destiny had come to its end. If you bucked your luck you bucked your destiny. This is similar to the Greek idea of *hubris*. All of these motifs can be better understood when one remembers the Spanish influence in our Southwest and West.

Among the Spanish-speaking peoples fatalism, courage and casualness in the face of death are symbolized in a national sport, the bullfight. There is good reason why a bullfighter like Manolete became a national hero. The bullfighter exposes himself to great risks, yet by courage and will power subdues his natural inclination to flee. In the very presence of death he performs an aesthetic act, and through him the spectators surmount their human frailties and fears and become superhuman with him. The western gunman as legend has created him is similar in some respects to the bullfighter. In the presence of death he remains cool and is able to subdue his fear in order to perform like a virtuoso with his gun.

I tried in my novel to dramatize the moment of death and to discard all the old euphemisms for death found in western novels, in which death seems to be only a stage death. Dying by the gun was often a vivid and cruel experience. I tried to portray it for what it was. I also tried to bring to bear upon western materials all of the sobriety and sharp focus of a highly developed realism, and to treat scene and character with a respect and care equal to those I would have employed if I had written a novel set in Boston or New York. But I do not mean to sound personal here, although to sound personal in this context is unavoidable. I mean only to suggest the great potentialities of the western materials, as well as to indicate the extent and intensity of one man's enthusiasm for the West and for its documents and legends.

At any rate, the West offered me infinitely more than I knew how to accept. Winter in Arizona, cool summer on the coast of California, spring in the deserts, fall in the Sierras; the sublime serene moments along the Pacific or under the great trees or on the trails of the Grand Canyon or in the lovely canyon in which I had the good fortune to live—such experiences are warranted to last a lifetime and to enhance the quality of one's life. The West still is a place of action, of life fulfilling and expressing itself through motion. In New York one internalizes much more, interiorizes; that is the usual form of expression and living there. Granted that life without it would be banal; but there comes a time when one wants to live through action as well as contemplation and thought; and when one is not afraid of the possibility of spending time in what one has heard is a cultural desert, for one has reached the point where either he can haul his cultural climate on his back or it is too late to worry about such things as a cultural climate.

When the years begin to run out (no: when the years begin to *seem* to run out) , the West is the place. And yet I regret that I did not experience the West in my boyhood and youth as well. Still, a boyhood in Virginia is nothing to run down either —or in New York for that matter. Speaking quite personally again, I can only thank my stars that I had my life to spend in this country. I say this not out of the native's self-confidence, which often takes the country for granted and looks abroad for greener pastures, but out of the knowledge that but for a fateful choice or lucky accident I might well have had to spend my life under the threatening sky and in the fetid air of a country unused to the traditions of political liberty and the individual's worth, those traditions which, granted a certain rawness and a certain violence, found—and still find—such strong expression in the American West.

CHARLES NEIDER

I. Pathfinders

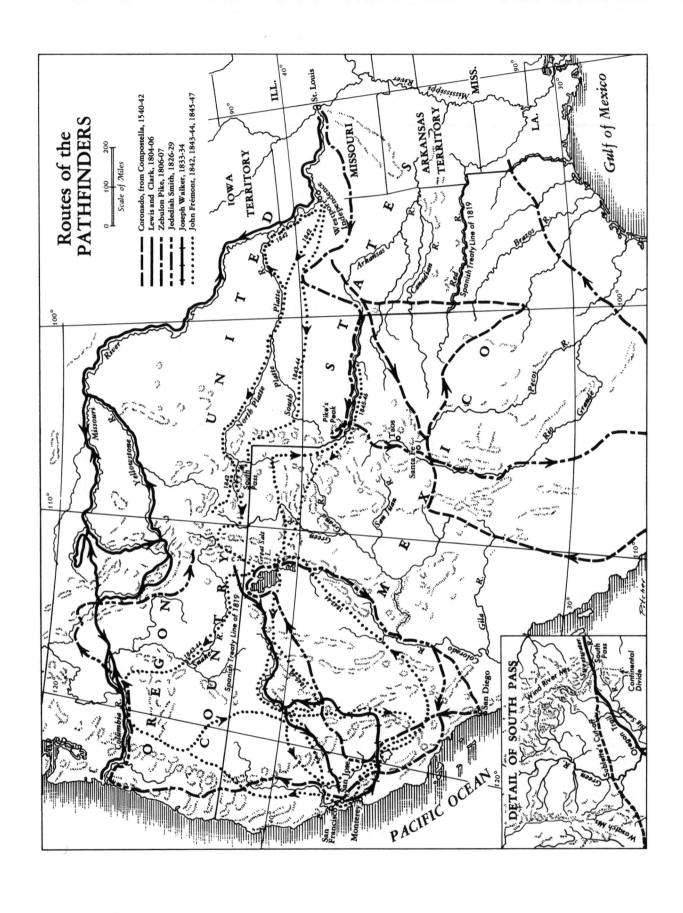

Routes of the PATHFINDERS

Coronado, from Compostella, 1540-42
Lewis and Clark, 1804-06
Zebulon Pike, 1806-07
Jedediah Smith, 1826-29
Joseph Walker, 1833-34
John Frémont, 1842, 1843-44, 1845-47

Scale of Miles
0   100   200

DETAIL OF SOUTH PASS

1. The Search for the Seven Cities

BY FRANCISCO VAZQUEZ DE CORONADO

EDITOR'S NOTE: Coronado's (c. 1500-1554) journey into the American Southwest remains one of the most remarkable explorations recorded in the annals of American history. It took place seventy-five years before the English were able to establish themselves on the northeastern coast of North America.

Coronado's goal was the fabled Seven Cities of Cibola, where he hoped to find much gold. But he did not discover the riches he sought, for the Seven Cities turned out to be, it is almost certain, the Zuñi pueblos of New Mexico. From the pueblos he wrote the following letter in August 1540 to Antonio de Mendoza, viceroy of New Spain, giving an account of his arduous journey from Mexico City, as well as a description of the Cities themselves. He had left Mexico City at the head of a band of Spaniards in February of the same year and was now in difficulties regarding supplies, as well as disappointed by the failure of his mission.

Instead of returning to Mexico City at this point, Coronado, still hoping to find gold, sent his men through Arizona, New Mexico, Texas and Kansas, discovering, as a by-product, the Grand Canyon. But his hopes were never realized. In the spring of 1542 he led a battered remnant of his army home, where he was considered incompetent and a failure.

Several accounts of the explorations were written by members of the expedition. Coronado's letter was translated by George Parker Winship from the Italian version in Ramusio's *Viaggi*, vol. 3 (ed. 1556). There is another English translation in Hakluyt's *Voyages*, vol. 3 (ed. 1600). I have omitted Winship's rather technical footnotes.

THE ACCOUNT GIVEN BY FRANCISCO VAZQUEZ DE CORONADO, CAPTAIN-GENERAL OF THE FORCE WHICH WAS SENT IN THE NAME OF HIS MAJESTY TO THE NEWLY DISCOVERED COUNTRY, OF WHAT HAPPENED TO THE EXPEDITION AFTER APRIL 22 OF THE YEAR MDXL, WHEN HE STARTED FORWARD FROM CULIACAN, AND OF WHAT HE FOUND IN THE COUNTRY THROUGH WHICH HE PASSED.

I

ON the 22d of the month of April last, I set out from the province of Culiacan with a part of the army, having made the arrangements of which I wrote to Your Lordship. Judging by the outcome, I feel sure that it was fortunate that I did not start the whole of the army on this undertaking, because the labors have been so very great and the lack of food such that I do not believe this undertaking could have been completed before the end of this year, and that there would be a great loss of life if it should be accomplished. For, as I wrote to Your Lordship, I spent eighty days in traveling to Culiacan, during which time I and the gentlemen of my company, who were horsemen, carried on our backs and on our horses a little food, in such wise that after leaving this place none of us carried any necessary effects weighing more than a pound. For all this, and although we took all possible care and forethought of the

19

small supply of provisions which we carried, it gave out. And this is not to be wondered at, because the road is rough and long, and what with our harquebuses, which had to be carried up the mountains and hills and in the passage of the rivers, the greater part of the corn was lost. And since I send Your Lordship a drawing of this route, I will say no more about it here.

Thirty leagues before reaching the place which the father provincial spoke so well of in his report, I sent Melchior Diaz forward with fifteen horsemen, ordering him to make but one day's journey out of two, so that he could examine everything there before I arrived. He traveled through some very rough mountains for four days, and did not find anything to live on, nor people, nor information about anything, except that he found two or three poor villages, with twenty or thirty huts apiece. From the people here he learned that there was nothing to be found in the country beyond except the mountains, which continued very rough, entirely uninhabited by people. And, because this was labor lost, I did not want to send Your Lordship an account of it. The whole company felt disturbed at this, that a thing so much praised, and about which the father had said so many things, should be found so very different; and they began to think that all the rest would be of the same sort.

When I noticed this, I tried to encourage them as well as I could, telling them that Your Lordship had always thought that this part of the trip would be a waste of effort, and that we ought to devote our attention to those Seven Cities and the other provinces about which we had information — that these should be the end of our enterprise. With this resolution and purpose, we all marched cheerfully along a very bad way, where it was impossible to pass without making a new road or repairing the one that was there, which troubled the soldiers not a little, considering that everything which the friar had said was found to be quite the reverse; because, among other things which the father had said and declared, he said that the way would be plain and good, and that there would be only one small hill of about half a league. And the truth is, that there are mountains where, however well the path might be fixed, they could not be crossed without there being great danger of the horses falling over them. And it was so bad that a large number of the animals which Your Lordship sent as provision for the army were lost along this part of the way, on account of the roughness of the rocks. The lambs and wethers lost their hoofs along the way, and I left the greater part of those which I brought from Culiacan at the river of Lachimi, because they were unable to travel, and so that they might proceed more slowly.

Four horsemen remained with them, who have just arrived. They have not brought more than 24 lambs and 4 wethers; the rest died from the toil, although they did not travel more than two leagues daily. I reached the Valley of Hearts at last, on the 26th day of the month of May, and rested there a number of days. Between Culiacan and this place I could sustain myself only by means of a large supply of corn bread, because I had to leave all the corn, as it was not yet ripe. In this Valley of Hearts we found more people than in any part of the country which we had left behind, and a large extent of tilled ground. There was no corn for food among them, but as I heard that there was some in another valley called Señora, which I did not wish to disturb by force, I sent Melchior Diaz with goods to exchange for it, so as to give this to the friendly Indians whom we brought with us, and to some who had lost their animals along the way and had not been able to carry the food which they had taken from Culiacan. By the favor of Our Lord, some little corn was obtained by this trading, which relieved the friendly Indians and some Spaniards. Ten or twelve of the horses had died of overwork by the time that we reached this Valley of Hearts, because they were unable to stand the strain of carrying heavy burdens and eating little. Some of our negroes and some of the Indians also died here, which was not a slight loss for the rest of the expedition. They told me that the Valley of Hearts is a long five-days' journey from the western sea. I sent to summon Indians from the coast in order to learn about their condition, and while I was waiting for these the horses rested. I stayed there four days, during which the Indians came from the sea, who told me that there were seven or eight islands two days' journey from that sea-coast, directly opposite, well populated with people, but poorly supplied with food, and the people were savages. They told me they had seen a ship pass not very far from the land. I do not know whether to think that it was the one which was sent to discover the country, or perhaps some Portuguese.

II

I SET out from the Hearts and kept near the seacoast as well as I could judge, but in fact I found myself continually farther off, so that when I reached Chichilticale I found that I was fifteen days' journey distant from the sea, although the father provincial had said that it was only 5 leagues distant and that he had seen it. We all became very distrustful, and felt great anxiety and dismay to see that everything was the reverse of what he had told Your Lordship. The Indians of Chichilticale say that when they go to the sea for fish, or for anything else that they need, they go across the country, and that it takes them ten days; and this information which I have recived from the Indians appears to me to be true. The sea turns toward the west directly opposite the Hearts for 10 or 12 leagues, where I learned that the ships of Your Lordship had been seen, which had gone in search of the port of Chichilticale, which the father said was on the thirty-fifth degree.

God knows what I have suffered, because I fear that they may have met with some mishap. If they follow the coast, as they said they would, as long as the food lasts which they took with them, of which I left them a supply in Culiacan, and if they have not been overtaken by some misfortune, I maintain my trust in God that they have already discovered something good, for which the delay which they have made may be pardoned. I rested for two days at Chichilticale, and there was good reason for staying longer, because we found that the horses were becoming so tired; but there was no chance to rest longer, because the food was giving out. I entered the borders of the wilderness region on Saint John's eve, and, for a change from our past labors, we found no grass during the first days, but a worse way through mountains and more dangerous passages than we had experienced previously. The horses were so tired that they were not equal to it, so that in this last desert we lost more horses than before; and some Indian allies and a Spaniard called Spinosa, besides two negroes. died from eating some herbs because the food had given out.

I sent the army-master, Don Garcia Lopez de Cardenas, with 15 horsemen, a day's march ahead of me, in order to explore the country and prepare the way, which he accomplished like the man that he is, and agreeably to the confidence which Your Lordship has had in him. I am the more certain that he did so, because, as I have said, the way is very bad for at least 30 leagues and more, through impassable mountains. But when we had passed these 30 leagues, we found fresh rivers and grass like that of Castile, and especially one sort like what we call *Scaramoio;* many nut and mulberry trees, but the leaves of the nut trees are different from those of Spain. There was a considerable amount of flax near the banks of one river, which was called on this account El Rio del Lino. No Indians were seen during the first day's march, after which four Indians came out with signs of peace, saying that they had been sent to that desert place to say that we were welcome, and that on the next day the tribe would provide the whole force with food. The army-master gave them a cross, telling them to say to the people in their city that they need not fear, and that they should have their people stay in their own houses, because I was coming in the name of His Majesty to defend and help them.

After this was done, Ferrando Alvarado came back to tell me that some Indians had met him peaceably, and that two of them were with the army-master waiting for me. I went to them forthwith and gave them some paternosters and some little cloaks, telling them to return to their city and say to the people there that they could stay quietly in their houses and that they need not fear. After this I ordered the army-master to go and see if there were any bad passages which the Indians might be able to defend, and to seize and hold any such until the next day, when I would come up. He went, and found a very bad place in our way where we might have received much harm. He immediately established himself there with the force which he was conducting. The Indians came that very night to occupy that place so as to defend it, and finding it taken, they assaulted our men. According to what I have been told, they attacked like valiant men, although in the end they had to retreat in flight, because the army-master was on the watch and kept his men in good order. The Indians sounded a little trumpet as a sign of retreat, and did not do any injury to the Spaniards. The army-master sent me notice of this the same night, so that on the next day I started with as good order as I could, for we were in such great need of food that I thought we should all die of hunger if we continued to be without provisions for another day, especially the Indians, since altogether we did not have two bushels of corn, and so I was obliged to hasten forward without delay. The Indians lighted their fires from point to point, and these were answered from a distance with as good understanding as we could have shown. Thus notice was given concerning how we went and where we had arrived.

As soon as I came within sight of this city, I sent the army-master, Don Garcia Lopez, Friar Daniel and Friar Luis, and Ferrando Vermizzo, with some horsemen, a little way ahead, so that they might find the Indians and tell them that we were not coming to do them any harm, but to defend them in the name of our lord the

Emperor. The summons, in the form which His Majesty commanded in his instructions, was made intelligible to the people of the country by an interpreter. But they, being a proud people, were little affected, because it seemed to them that we were few in number, and that they would not have any difficulty in conquering us. They pierced the gown of Friar Luis with an arrow, which, blessed be God, did him no harm. Meanwhile I arrived with all the rest of the horse and the footmen, and found a large body of the Indians on the plain, who began to shoot with their arrows. In obedience to the orders of Your Lordship and of the marquis, I did not wish my company, who were begging me for permission, to attack them, telling them that they ought not to offend them, and that what the enemy was doing was nothing, and that so few people ought not to be insulted. On the other hand, when the Indians saw that we did not move, they took greater courage, and grew so bold that they came up almost to the heels of our horses to shoot their arrows. On this account I saw that it was no longer time to hesitate, and as the priests approved the action, I charged them. There was little to do, because they suddenly took to flight, part running toward the city, which was near and well fortified, and others toward the plain, wherever chance led them. Some Indians were killed, and others might have been slain if I could have allowed them to be pursued. But I saw that there would be little advantage in this, because the Indians who were outside were few, and those who had retired to the city were numerous, besides many who had remained there in the first place.

As that was where the food was, of which we stood in such great need, I assembled my whole force and divided them as seemed to me best for the attack on the city, and surrounded it. The hunger which we suffered would not permit of any delay, and so I dismounted with some of these gentlemen and soldiers. I ordered the musketeers and crossbowmen to begin the attack and drive back the enemy from the defenses, so that they could not do us any injury. I assaulted the wall on one side, where I was told that there was a scaling ladder and that there was also a gate. But the crossbowmen broke all the strings of their crossbows and the musketeers could do nothing, because they had arrived so weak and feeble that they could scarcely stand on their feet. On this account the people who were on top were not prevented at all from defending themselves and doing us whatever injury they were able. Thus, for myself, they knocked me down to the ground twice with countless great stones which they threw down from above, and if I had not been protected by the very good headpiece which I wore, I think that the outcome would have been bad for me. They picked me up from the ground, however, with two small wounds in my face and an arrow in my foot, and with many bruises on my arms and legs, and in this condition I retired from the battle, very weak. I think that if Don Garcia Lopez de Cardenas had not come to my help, like a good cavalier, the second time that they knocked me to the ground, by placing his own body above mine, I should have been in much greater danger than I was. But, by the pleasure of God, these Indians surrendered, and their city was taken with the help of Our Lord, and a sufficient supply of corn was found there to relieve our necessities.

The army-master and Don Pedro de Tovar and Ferrando de Alvarado and Paulo

Coronado's March. *Frederick Remington*

de Melgosa, the infantry captain, sustained some bruises, although none of them were wounded. Agoniez Quarez was hit in the arm by an arrow, and one Torres, who lived in Panuco, in the face by another, and two other footmen received slight arrow wounds. They all directed their attack against me because my armor was gilded and glittered, and on this account I was hurt more than the rest, and not because I had done more or was farther in advance than the others; for all these gentlemen and soldiers bore themselves well, as was expected of them. I praise God that I am now well, although somewhat sore from the stones. Two or three other soldiers were hurt in the battle which we had on the plain, and three horses were killed — one that of Don Lopez and another that of Vigliega and the third that of Don Alfonso Manrich — and seven or eight other horses were wounded; but the men, as well as the horses, have now recovered and are well.

III

It now remains for me to tell about this city and kingdom and province, of which the Father Provincial gave Your Lordship an account. In brief, I can assure you that in reality he has not told the truth in a single thing that he said, but everything is the reverse of what he said, except the name of the city and the large stone houses. For, although they are not decorated with turquoises, nor made of lime nor of good bricks, nevertheless they are very good houses, with three and four and five stories, where there are very good apartments and good rooms with corridors, and some very good rooms under ground and paved, which are made for winter, and are something like a sort of hot baths. The ladders which they have for their houses are all movable and portable, which are taken up and placed wherever they please. They are made of two pieces of wood, with rounds like ours.

The Seven Cities are seven little villages, all having the kind of houses I have described. They are all within a radius of 5 leagues. They are all called the kingdom of Cevola, and each has its own name and no single one is called Cevola, but all together are called Cevola. This one which I have called a city I have named Granada, partly because it has some similarity to it, as well as out of regard for Your Lordship. In this place where I am now lodged there are perhaps 200 houses, all surrounded by a wall, and it seems to me that with the other houses, which are not so surrounded, there might be altogether 500 families. There is another town near by, which is one of the seven, but somewhat larger than this, and another of the same size as this, and the other four are somewhat smaller. I send them all to Your Lordship, painted with the route. The skin on which the painting is made was found here with other skins.

The people of the towns seem to me to be of ordinary size and intelligent, although I do not think that they have the judgment and intelligence which they ought to have to build these houses in the way in which they have, for most of them are entirely naked except the covering of their privy parts, and they have painted mantles like the one which I send to Your Lordship. They do not raise cotton, because the country is very cold, but they wear mantles, as may be seen by the exhibit which I send. It is also true that some cotton thread was found in their houses. They wear the hair on their heads like the Mexicans. They all have good figures, and are well bred. I

think that they have a quantity of turquoises, which they had removed with the rest of their goods, except the corn, when I arrived, because I did not find any women here nor any men under 15 years or over 60, except two or three old men who remained in command of all the other men and the warriors. Two points of emerald and some little broken stones which approach the color of rather poor garnets were found in a paper, besides other stone crystals, which I gave to one of my servants to keep until they could be sent to Your Lordship. He has lost them, as they tell me. We found fowls, but only a few, and yet there are some. The Indians tell me that they do not eat these in any of the seven villages, but that they keep them merely for the sake of procuring the feathers. I do not believe this, because they are very good, and better than those of Mexico.

The climate of this country and the temperature of the air is almost like that of Mexico, because it is sometimes hot and sometimes it rains. I have not yet seen it rain, however, except once when there fell a little shower with wind, such as often falls in Spain. The snow and the cold are usually very great, according to what the natives of the country all say. This may very probably be so, both because of the nature of the country and the sort of houses they build and the skins and other things which these people have to protect them from the cold. There are no kinds of fruit or fruit trees. The country is all level, and is nowhere shut in by high mountains, although there are some hills and rough passages. There are not many birds, probably because of the cold, and because there are no mountains near. There are no trees fit for firewood here, because they can bring enough for their needs from a clump of very small cedars 4 leagues distant. Very good grass is found a quarter of a league away, where there is pasturage for our horses as well as mowing for hay, of which we had great need, because our horses were so weak and feeble when they arrived.

The food which they eat in this country is corn, of which they have a great abundance, and beans and venison, which they probably eat (although they say that they do not), because we found many skins of deer and hares and rabbits. They make the best corn cakes I have ever seen anywhere, and this is what everybody ordinarily eats. They have the very best arrangement and machinery for grinding that was ever seen. One of these Indian women here will grind as much as four of the Mexicans. They have very good salt in crystals, which they bring from a lake a day's journey distant from here. No information can be obtained among them about the North sea or that on the west, nor do I know how to tell Your Lordship which we are nearest to. I should judge that it is nearer to the western, and 150 leagues is the nearest that it seems to me it can be thither. The North sea ought to be much farther away. Your Lordship may thus see how very wide the country is. They have many animals — bears, tigers, lions, porcupines, and some sheep as big as a horse, with very large horns and little tails. I have seen some of their horns the size of which was something to marvel at. There are also wild goats, whose heads I have seen, and the paws of the bears and the skins of the wild boars. For game they have deer, leopards, and very large deer, and every one thinks that some of them are larger than that animal which Your Lordship favored me with, which belonged to Juan Melaz. They inhabit some plains eight days' journey toward the north. They

have some of their skins here very well dressed, and they prepare and paint them where they kill the cows, according to what they tell me.

IV

THESE Indians say that the kingdom of Totonteac, which the father provincial praised so much, saying that it was something marvelous, and of such a very great size, and that cloth was made there, is a hot lake, on the edge of which there are five or six houses. There used to be some others, but these have been destroyed by war. The kingdom of Marata can not be found, nor do these Indians know anything about it. The kingdom of Acus is a single small city, where they raise cotton, and this is called Acucu. I say that this is the country, because Acus, with or without the aspiration, is not a word in this region; and because it seems to me that Acucu may be derived from Acus, I say that it is this town which has been converted into the kingdom of Acus. They tell me that there are some other small ones not far from this settlement, which are situated on a river which I have seen and of which the Indians have told me. God knows that I wish I had better news to write to Your Lordship, but I must give you the truth, and, as I wrote you from Culiacan, I must advise you of the good as well as of the bad. But you may be assured that if there had been all the riches and treasures of the world, I could not have done more in His Majesty's service and in that of Your Lordship than I have done, in coming here where you commanded me to go, carrying, both my companions and myself, our food on our backs for 300 leagues, and traveling on foot many days, making our way over hills and rough mountains, besides other labors which I refrain from mentioning. Nor do I think of stopping until my death, if it serves His Majesty or Your Lordship to have it so.

Three days after I captured this city, some of the Indians who lived here came to offer to make peace. They brought me some turquoises and poor mantles, and I received them in His Majesty's name with as good a speech as I could, making them understand the purpose of my coming to this country, which is, in the name of His Majesty and by the commands of Your Lordship, that they and all others in this province should become Christians and should know the true God for their Lord, and His Majesty for their king and earthly lord. After this they returned to their houses and suddenly, the next day, they packed up their goods and property, their women and children, and fled to the hills, leaving their towns deserted, with only some few remaining in them. Seeing this, I went to the town which I said was larger than this, eight or ten days later, when I had recovered from my wounds. I found a few of them there, whom I told that they ought not to feel any fear, and I asked them to summon their lord to me. By what I can find out or observe, however, none of these towns have any, since I have not seen any principal house by which any superiority over others could be shown. Afterward, an old man, who said he was their lord, came with a mantle made of many pieces, with whom I argued as long as he stayed with me. He said that he would come to see me with the rest of the chiefs of the country, three days later, in order to arrange the relations which should exist between us. He did so, and they brought me some little ragged mantles and some turquoises. I said that they ought to come down from their strongholds and return to their houses with their wives and children, and that they should become Christians, and recognize His Majesty as their king and lord. But they still remain in their strongholds, with their wives and all their property.

I commanded them to have a cloth painted for me, with all the animals that they know in that country, and although they are poor painters, they quickly painted two for me, one of the animals and the other of the birds and fishes. They say that they will bring their children so that our priests may instruct them, and that they desire to know our law. They declare that it was foretold among them more than fifty years ago that a people such as we are should come, and the direction they should come from, and that the whole country would be conquered. So far as I can find out, the water is what these Indians worship, because they say that it makes the corn grow and sustains their life, and that the only other reason they know is because their ancestors did so. I have tried in every way to find out from the natives of these settlements whether they know of any other peoples or provinces or cities. They tell me about seven cities which are at a considerable distance, which are like these, except that the houses there are not like these, but are made of earth [adobe], and small, and that they raise much cotton there. The first of these four places about which they know is called, they say, Tucano. They could not tell me much about the others. I do not believe that they tell me the truth, because they think that I shall soon have to depart from them and return home. But they will quickly find that they are deceived in this. I sent Don Pedro de Tobar there, with his company and some other horsemen, to see it. I would not have dispatched this packet to Your Lordship until I had learned what he found there, if I thought that I should have any news from him within twelve or fifteen days. However, as he will remain away at least thirty, and, considering that this information is of little importance and that the cold and the rains are approaching, it seemed to me that I ought to do as Your Lordship commanded me in your instructions, which is, that as soon as I arrived here, I should advise you thereof, and this I do, by sending you the plain narrative of what I have seen, which is bad enough, as you may perceive. I have determined to send throughout all the surrounding regions, in order to find out whether there is anything, and to suffer every extremity before I give up this enterprise, and to serve His Majesty, if I can find any way in which to do it, and not to lack in diligence until Your Lordship directs me as to what I ought to do.

We have great need of pasture, and you should know, also, that among all those who are here there is not one pound of raisins, nor sugar, nor oil, nor wine, except barely half a quart, which is saved to say mass, since everything is consumed, and part was lost on the way. Now, you can provide us with what appears best; but if you are thinking of sending us cattle, you should know that it will be necessary for them to spend at least a year on the road, because they can not come in any other way, nor any quicker. I would have liked to send to Your Lordship, with this dispatch, many samples of the things which they have in this country, but the trip is so long and rough that it is difficult for me to do so. However, I send you twelve small mantles, such as the people of this country ordinarily wear, and a garment which seems to me to be very well made. I kept it because it seemed to me to be of very good

workmanship, and because I do not think that anyone has ever seen in these Indies any work done with a needle, unless it were done since the Spaniards settled here. And I also send two cloths painted with the animals which they have in this country, although, as I said, the painting is very poorly done, because the artist did not spend more than one day in painting it. I have seen other paintings on the walls of these houses which have much better proportion and are done much better.

I send you a cow skin, some turquoises, and two earrings of the same, and fifteen of the Indian combs, and some plates decorated with these turquoises, and two baskets made of wicker, of which the Indians have a large supply. I also send two rolls, such as the women usually wear on their heads when they bring water from the spring, the same way that they do in Spain. One of these Indian women, with one of these rolls on her head, will carry a jar of water up a ladder without touching it with her hands. And, lastly, I send you samples of the weapons with which the natives of this country fight, a shield, a hammer, and a bow with some arrows, among which there are two with bone points, the like of which have never been seen, according to what these conquerors say. As far as I can judge, it does not appear to me that there is any hope of getting gold or silver, but I trust in God that, if there is any, we shall get our share of it, and it shall not escape us through any lack of diligence in the search. I am unable to give Your Lordship any certain information about the dress of the women, because the Indians keep them guarded so carefully that I have not seen any, except two old women. These had on two long skirts reaching down to their feet and open in front, and a girdle, and they are tied together with some cotton strings. I asked the Indians to give me one of those which they wore, to send to you, since they were not willing to show me the women. They brought me two mantles, which are these that I send, almost painted over. They have two tassels, like the women of Spain, which hang somewhat over their shoulders.

The death of the negro is perfectly certain, because many of the things which he wore have been found, and the Indians say that they killed him here because the Indians of Chichilticale said that he was a bad man, and not like the Christians, because the Christians never kill women, and he killed them, and because he assaulted their women, whom the Indians love better than themselves. Therefore they determined to kill him, but they did not do it in the way that was reported, because they did not kill any of the others who came with him, nor did they kill the lad from the province of Petatlan, who was with him, but they took him and kept him in safe custody until now. When I tried to secure him, they made excuses for not giving him to me, for two or three days, saying that he

was dead, and at other times that the Indians of Acucu had taken him away. But when I finally told them that I should be very angry if they did not give him to me, they gave him to me. He is an interpreter; for although he can not talk much, he understands very well.

Some gold and silver has been found in this place, which those who know about minerals say is not bad. I have not yet been able to learn from these people where they got it. I perceive that they refuse to tell me the truth in everything, because they think that I shall have to depart from here in a short time, as I have said. But I trust in God that they will not be able to avoid answering much longer. I beg Your Lordship to make a report of the success of this expedition to His Majesty, because there is nothing more than what I have already said. I shall not do so until it shall please God to grant that we find what we desire. Our Lord God protect and keep your most illustrious Lordship. From the province of Cevola, and this city of Granada, the 3d of August, 1540. Francisco Vazquez de Coronado kisses the hand of your most illustrious Lordship.

2. A Report from Monterey

BY SEBASTIAN VIZCAINO

EDITOR'S NOTE: Sebastian Vizcaino (c. 1550-1615), who discovered the bay of Monterey, was not the first to explore that section of the California coast. He followed Cabrillo, Ferrelo and Drake. But his voyage of 1602-03 is one of the most famous of the California explorations, as much for its hardships as for its discoveries; and for a century and a half

afterward little if anything was added to the world's knowledge of California.

A narrative of the voyage was written by Father Antonio de la Ascension, who accompanied the expedition. In it he told of their trials and of the terrors of scurvy. He described the Indians in some detail and gave an excellent description of Monterey harbor. On December 28, 1602 Vizcaino wrote the following report, in the form of a letter, which was sent to New Spain by the *Almiranta,* a ship under his command. I have not been able to determine to whom the letter was addressed. The present text was translated by George Butler Griffin.

YOUR HIGHNESS will have had notice of how the Count de Monte-Rey, viceroy of New Spain, in conformity with the orders which he has from His Majesty, charged me with the exploration of the harbors & bays of the coast of the South Sea from the port of Acapulco to Cape Mendocino, giving me for that purpose two ships, a lancha, & a barcoluengo, together with seamen & soldiers, arms & ammunition, and provisions for eleven months; that, in accordance with the orders given me for that end, I sailed from Acapulco on the 5th day of May of this year; that I have prosecuted said exploration, although with great difficulty & labor, because the navigation was unknown and head winds were constant, while the aid of providence and the good desire I have ever felt for serving His Majesty availed me little. I have discovered many harbors, bays and islands, as far as the port of Monterey, a harbor which is in thirty-seven degrees of latitude, surveying all & sounding, & noting the sailing-directions, according to the art of navigation, without neglecting any substantial thing concerning the same, and noting what the land and the numerous peoples dwelling therein seemingly promise. I send a copy to the said Count, in order that he may transmit the information to His Majesty and to Your Highness. As to what this harbor of Monterey is, in addition to being so well situated in point of latitude for that which His Majesty intends to do for the protection and security

of ships coming from the Philippines: In it may be repaired the damages which they may have sustained, for there is a great extent of pine forest from which to obtain masts and yards, even though the vessel be of a thousand tons burthen, live oaks & white oaks for shipbuilding, and this close to the seaside in great number. And the harbor is very secure against all winds. The land is thickly peopled by Indians and is very fertile, in its climate and the quality of the soil resembling Castile, and any seed sown there will give fruit, and there are extensive lands fit for pasturage, and many kinds of animals and birds — as is set forth in the report referred to.

I advise His Majesty concerning the great extent of this land and its numerous population, and what promise it holds forth, and what the Indians have given me to understand concerning the people of the interior, and of how gentle & affable the people are, so that they will receive readily, as I think, the holy gospel and will come into subjection to the royal crown; and, since His Majesty is lord and master of all, let him provide as may seem best to him. As to what it behooves me to do on my part, I will serve him till death.

With regard to my having delayed longer than the time which was thought necessary for this exploration: Because of the many difficulties of which I have spoken, the greater part of the provisions & ammunition which were furnished to me has been expended; while, owing to the great labors which my crews have gone through, a number of men have fallen ill and some have died — so that for making the exploration at this time, as well of the region of Cape Mendocino as of the entire littoral of the Californias, as is called for by my orders, I have met with obstacles to the completion of all the work without considerable succor in the way of provisions, people & ammunition, & speedy dispatch of these. Let the admiral be advised by the said Count of this, he asking him for what is necessary, & letting him know to what place and at what time he must dispatch these things to me (sending to him also the map, report & sailing-directions concerning all I have done in said exploration to the present time) so that Your Highness may order that the same be sent to me. I trust in God that I may do a great service to His Majesty and that I shall discover great realms and riches. Of all that may be done I shall advise Your Highness, as opportunities for doing this may present themselves, with truth and faithfully. May Our Lord guard Your Highness, a ward so necessary to the Christian. I am the servant of Your Highness.

Sebastian Vizcaino
28th December, 1602,
Harbor of Monterey.

3. Thomas Jefferson's Instructions to Meriwether Lewis

To Meriwether Lewis, esquire, Captain of the 1st regiment of infantry of the United States of America: Your situation as Secretary of the President of the United States has made you acquainted with the objects of my confidential message of Jan. 18, 1803, to the legislature. You have seen the act they passed, which, tho' expressed in general terms, was meant to sanction those objects, and you are appointed to carry them into execution.

Instruments for ascertaining by celestial observations the geography of the country thro' which you will pass, have already been provided. light articles for barter, & presents among the Indians, arms for your attendants, say for from 10 to 12 men, boats, tents, & other travelling apparatus, with ammunition, medicine, surgical instruments & provisions you will have prepared with such aids as the Secretary at War can yield in his department; & from him also you will receive authority to engage among our troops, by voluntary agreement, the number of attendants above mentioned, over whom you, as their commanding officer are invested with all the powers the laws give in such a case.

As your movements while within the limits of the U. S. will be better directed by occasional communications, adapted to circumstances as they arise, they will not be noticed here. what follows will respect your proceedings after your departure from the U. S.

Your mission has been communicated to the Ministers here from France, Spain & Great Britain, and through them to their governments: and such assurances given them as to it's objects as we trust will satisfy them. the country of Louisiana having been ceded by Spain to France, the passport you have from the Minister of France, the representative of the present soverign of the country, will be a protection with all it's subjects: And that from the Minister of England will entitle you to the friendly aid of any traders of that allegiance with whom you may happen to meet.

The object of your mission is to explore the Missouri river, & such principal stream of it, as, by it's course & communication with the waters of the Pacific Ocean, may offer the most direct & practicable water communication across this continent, for the purposes of commerce.

Beginning at the mouth of the Missouri, you will take observations of latitude & longitude, at all remarkable points on the river, & especially at the mouths of rivers, at rapids, at islands & other places & objects distinguished by such natural marks & characters of a durable kind, as that they may with certainty be recognized hereafter. the courses of the river between these points of observation may be supplied by the compass, the log-line & by time, corrected by the observations themselves. the variations of the compass too, in different places, should be noticed.

The interesting points of portage between the heads of the Missouri & the water offering the best communication with the Pacific Ocean should also be fixed by observation, & the course of that water to the ocean, in the same manner as that of the Missouri.

Your observations are to be taken with great pains & accuracy, to be entered distinctly, & intelligibly for others as well as yourself, to comprehend all the elements necessary, with the aid of the usual tables, to fix the latitude and longitude of the places at which they were taken, & are to be rendered to the war office, for the purpose of having the calculations made concurrently by proper persons within the

U. S. several copies of these, as well as your other notes, should be made at leisure times & put into the care of the most trustworthy of your attendants, to guard by mutiplying them, against the accidental losses to which they will be exposed. a further guard would be that one of these copies be written on the paper of the birch, as less liable to injury from damp than common paper.

The commerce which may be carried on with the people inhabiting the line you will pursue, renders a knolege of these people important. you will therefore endeavor to make yourself acquainted, as far as a diligent pursuit of your journey shall admit,

with the names of the nations & their numbers;
the extent & limits of their possessions;
their relations with other tribes or nations;
their language, traditions, monuments;
their ordinary occupations in agriculture, fishing, hunting, war, arts, & the implements for these;
their food, clothing, & domestic accomodations;
the diseases prevalent among them, & the remedies they use;
moral & physical circumstances which distinguish them from the tribes we know;
peculiarities in their laws, customs & dispositions;
and articles of commerce they may need or furnish, & to what extent.

And considering the interest which every nation has in extending & strengthening the authority of reason & justice among the people around them, it will be useful to acquire what knolege you can of the state of morality, religion & information among them, as it may better enable those who endeavor to civilize & instruct them, to adapt their measures to the existing notions & practises of those on whom they are to operate.

Other object worthy of notice will be

the soil & face of the country, it's growth & vegetable productions; especially those not of the U. S.

the animals of the country generally, & especially those not known in the U. S.

the remains and accounts of any which may deemed rare or extinct;

the mineral productions of every kind; but more particularly metals, limestone, pit coal & salpetre; salines & mineral waters, noting the temperature of the last, & such circumstances as may indicate their character.

Volcanic appearances.

climate as characterized by the thermometer, by the proportion of rainy, cloudy & clear days, by lightening, hail, snow, ice, by the access & recess of frost, by the winds prevailing at different seasons, the dates at which particular plants put forth or lose their flowers, or leaf, times of appearance of particular birds, reptiles or insects.

Altho' your route will be along the channel of the Missouri, yet you will endeavor to inform yourself, by inquiry, of the character & extent of the country watered by it's branches, & especially on it's southern side. the North river or Rio Bravo which runs into the gulph of Mexico, and the North river, or Rio colorado, which runs into the gulph of California, are understood to be the principal streams heading opposite to the waters of the Missouri, and running Southwardly. whether the dividing grounds between the Missouri & them are mountains or flatlands, what are their distance from the Missouri, the character of the intermediate country, & the people inhabiting it, are worthy of particular enquiry. The Northern waters of the Missouri are less to be enquired after, because they have been ascertained to a considerable degree, and are still in a course of ascertainment by English traders & travellers. but if you can learn anything certain of the most Northern source of the Missisipi, & of it's position relative to the lake of the woods, it will be interesting to us. some account too of the path of the Canadian traders from the Missisipi, at the mouth of the Ouisconsin river, to where it strikes the Missouri and of the soil & rivers in it's course, is desireable.

In all your intercourse with the natives treat them in the most friendly & conciliatory manner which their own conduct will admit; allay all jealousies as to the object of your journey, satisfy them of it's innocence, make them acquainted with the position, extent, character, peaceable & commercial dispositions of the U. S. of our wish to be neighborly, friendly & useful to them, & of our dispositions to a commercial intercourse with them; confer with them on the points most convenient as mutual emporiums, & the articles of most desireable interchange for them & us. if a few of their influential chiefs, within practicable distance, wish to visit us, arrange such a visit with them, and furnish them with authority to call on our officers, on their entering the U. S. to have them conveyed to this place at public expence. if any of them should wish to have some of their young people brought up with us, & taught such arts as may be useful to them, we will receive, instruct & take care of them. such a mission, whether of influential chiefs, or of young people, would give some security to your own party. carry with you some matter of the kinepox, inform those of them with whom you may be of it' efficacy as a preservative from the small-pox; and instruct & incourage them in the use of it. this may be especially done wherever you winter.

As it is impossible for us to foresee in what manner you will be recieved by those people, whether with hospitality or hostility, so is it impossible to prescribe the exact degree of perseverance with which you are to pursue your journey. we value too much the lives of citizens to offer them to probably destruction. your numbers will be sufficient to secure you against the unauthorised opposition of individuals, or of small parties: but if a superior force, authorised or not authorised, by a nation, should be arrayed against your further passage, & inflexibly determined to arrest it, you must decline it's further pursuit, and return. in the loss of yourselves, we should lose also the information you will have acquired. by returning safely with that, you may enable us to renew the essay with better calculated means. to your own discretion therefore must be left the degree of danger you may risk, & the point at which you should decline, only saying we wish you to err on the side of your safety, & bring back your party safe, even if it be with less information.

As far up the Missouri as the white settlements extend, an intercourse will probably be found to exist between them and the Spanish posts at St. Louis, opposite Cahokia, or Ste. Genevieve opposite Kaskaskia, from still farther up the river, the traders may furnish a conveyance for letters. beyond that you may perhaps be able to engage Indians to bring letters for the government to Cahokia or Kaskaskia, on promising that they shall there receive such special compensation as you shall have stipulated with them. avail yourself of these means to communicate to us, at seasonable intervals, a copy of your journal, notes & observations of every kind, putting into cypher whatever might do injury if betrayed.

Should you reach the Pacific ocean inform yourself of the circumstances which may decide whether the furs of those parts may not be collected as advantageously at the head of the Missouri (convenient as is supposed to the waters of the Colorado & Oregon or Columbia) as at Nootka sound or any other point of that coast; & that trade be consequently conducted through the Missouri & U. S. more beneficially than by the circumnavigation now practised.

On your arrival on that coast endeavor to learn if there be any port within your reach frequented by the sea-vessels of any nation, and to send two of your trusty people back by sea, in such way as shall appear practicable, with a copy of your notes. and should you be of opinion that the return of your party by the way they went will be eminently dangerous, then ship the whole, & return by sea by way of Cape Horn or the Cape of good Hope, as you shall be able. as you will be without money, clothes or provisions, you must endeavor to use the credit of the U. S. to obtain them; for which purpose open letters of credit shall be furnished you authorising you to draw on the Executive of the U. S. or any of its officers in any part of the world, on which drafts can be disposed of, and to apply with our recommendations to the Consuls, agents, merchants, or citizens of any nation with which we have intercourse, assuring them in our name that any aids they may furnish you, shall honorably repaid, and on demand. Our consuls Thomas Howes at Batavia in Java, William Buchanan on the isles of France and Bourbon, & John Elmslie at the Cape of good hope will be able to supply your necessities by draughts on us.

Should you find it safe to return by the way you go, after sending two of your party round by sea, or with your whole party, if no conveyance by sea can be found, do so; making such observations on your return as may serve to supply, correct or confirm those made on your outward journey.

In re-entering the U. S. and reaching a place of safety, discharge any of your attendants who may desire & deserve it, procuring for them immediate paiment of all arrears of pay & cloathing which may have incurred since their departure; & assure them that they shall be recommended to the liberality of the legislature for the grant of a soldier's portion of land each, as proposed in my message to Congress & repair yourself with your papers to the seat of government.

To provide, on the accident of your death, against anarchy, dispersion & the consequent danger to your party, and total failure of the enterprise, you are hereby authorised, by any instrument signed & written in your hand, to name the person among them who shall succeed to the command on your decease, & by like instruments to change the nomination from time to time, as further experience of the characters accompanying you shall point out superior fitness; and all the powers & authorities given to yourself are, in the event of your death, transferred to & vested in the successor so named, with further power to him, & his successors in like manner to name each his successor, who, on the death of his predecessor, shall be invested with all the powers & authorities given to yourself.

Given under my hand at the city of Washington, this 20th day of June 1803

Th. Jefferson
Pr. U. S. of America

4. A Remarkable Journey to the Pacific

BY MERIWETHER LEWIS AND WILLIAM CLARK

EDITOR'S NOTE: Meriwether Lewis (1774-1809) and William Clark (1770-1838) led the first United States expedition overland to the Pacific. The account of the journey has become a classic of American exploration. The expedition began at St. Louis, then a village, on May 14, 1804, and ended in the same village on September 23, 1806. Among the remarkable facts concerning the adventure was the one that, despite the hazards involved in a journey of some four thousand miles, only one member of the party died and only one deserted.

The text which follows is that of the 1893 edition, edited by Elliott Coues and based on the authorized history of the expedition, 1814, prepared by Nicholas Biddle from the original manuscripts of Lewis and Clark. I have selected sections to show the height of the journey as the party reached the Pacific. Many of Coues' footnotes are lengthy and technical and I have omitted all of them in this volume.

MONDAY, *October 21st, 1805.* The morning was cool, and the wind from the southwest. At 5½ miles we passed a small island; 1½ miles further, another in the middle of the river, which has some rapid water near its head; and opposite its lower extremity, eight cabins of Indians on the right side. We landed near them to breakfast; but such is the scarcity of wood, that last evening we had not been able to collect anything except dry willows, not more than barely sufficient to cook our supper, and this morning we could not find enough even to prepare breakfast. The Indians received us with great kindness, and examined everything they saw with much attention. In their appearance and employments, as well as in their language, they do not differ from those higher up the river. The dress is nearly the same; that of the men consisting of nothing but a short robe of deer- or goat-skin; while the women wear only a piece of dressed skin, falling from the neck so as to cover the front of the body as low as the waist, and a bandage tied round the body and passing between the legs, over which a short robe of deer- or antelope-skin is occasionally thrown. Here we saw two blankets of scarlet and one of blue cloth, and also a sailor's round jacket; but we obtained only a few pounded roots, and some fish, for which we of course paid them. Among other things we observed some acorns, the fruit of the white-oak. These they use as food either raw or roasted, and on inquiry informed us that they were procured from the Indians who live near the Great Falls. This place they designate by a name very commonly applied to it by the Indians and highly expressive, the word "Timm," which they pronounce so as to make it perfectly represent the sound of a distant cataract.

After breakfast we resumed our journey, and in the course of three miles passed a rapid [Owyhee] where large rocks were strewed across the river, and at the head of which on the right shore were two huts of Indians. We stopped here for the purpose of examining it, as we always do when any danger is to be apprehended, and send round by land all those who cannot swim. Five [?] miles further is another [Rock Creek] rapid, formed by large rocks projecting from each side, above which were five huts of Indians on the right side, occupied, like those we had already seen, in drying fish. One mile below this is the lower point of an island close to the right side, opposite which on that shore are two Indian huts.

On the left side of the river at this place are immense piles of rocks, which seem to have slipped from the cliffs under which they lie; they continue till, spreading still further into the river, at the distance of a mile from the island they occasion a very dangerous rapid [Squally Hook]; a little below which on the right side are five huts. For many miles the river is now narrow and obstructed with very large rocks thrown into its channel; the hills continue high and covered, as is very rarely the case, with a few low pine-trees on their tops. Between three and four miles below the last rapid occurs a second [Indian], which is also difficult, and three miles below it is a small river, which seems to rise in the open plains to the southeast, and falls in on the left. It is 40 yards wide at its mouth, but discharges only a small quantity of water at present. We gave it the name of Lepage's river, from [Baptiste] Lepage, one of our company. Near this little river [now known as the John Day] and immediately below it, we had to encounter a new rapid. The river is crowded in every direction with large rocks and small rocky islands; the passage is crooked and difficult, and for two miles we were obliged to wind with great care along the narrow channels and between the huge rocks. At the end of this rapid are four huts of Indians on the right, and two miles below five more huts on the same side. Here we landed and passed the night, after making 33 miles.

The inhabitants of these huts explained to us that they were the relations of those who live at the Great Falls. They appear to be of the same nation with those we have seen above, whom, indeed, they resemble in everything except that their language, though the same, has some words different. They all have pierced noses, and the men, when in full dress, wear a long tapering piece of shell or bead through the nose. These people did not, however, receive us with the same cordiality to which we have been accustomed. They were poor, but we were able to purchase from them some wood to make a fire for supper, though they have but little, which they say they bring from the Great Falls. The hills in this neighorhood are high and rugged; a few scattered trees, either small pine or scrubby white-oak, are occasionally seen on them. From the last rapids we also observed the conical mountain [Mt. Hood] toward the southwest, which the Indians say is not far to the [our] left of the Great Falls. From its vicinity to that place we called it the Timm or Falls mountain. The country through

Shoshone Crossing River. *Alfred Jacob Miller*

which we passed is furnished with several fine springs, which rise either high up the sides of the hills, or else in the river meadows, and discharge into the Columbia.

We could not help remarking that almost universally the fishing establishments of the Indians, both on the Columbia and the waters of Lewis' [Snake] river, are on the right bank. On inquiry we were led to believe that the reason may be found in their fear of the Snake Indians; between whom and themselves, considering the warlike temper of that people, and the peaceful habits of the river tribes, it is very natural that the latter should be anxious to interpose so good a barrier. These Indians are described as residing on a great river to the south, and always at war with the people of this neighborhood. One of our chiefs pointed out to-day a spot on the left where, not many years ago, a great battle was fought, in which numbers of both nations were killed.

We were agreeably surprised this evening by a present of some very good beer, made [by John Collins] out of the remains of bread composed of the pasheco-quamash, part of the stores we had laid in at the head of the Kooskooskee, which by frequent exposure had become sour and molded.

October 22d. The morning was fair and calm. We left our camp at nine o'clock, and after going on for six miles came to the head of an island and a very bad [Hellgate] rapid, where the rocks are scattered nearly across the river. Just above this and on the right are six huts of Indians. At the distance of two miles below are five more huts; the inhabitants of which are engaged in drying fish, and some of them are in their canoes killing fish with gigs. Opposite this establishment is a small island in a bend toward the right, on which there were such quanti-

ties of fish that we counted 20 stacks of dried and pounded salmon. This small island is at the upper point of one much larger, the sides of which are high uneven rocks, jutting over the water; here there is a bad rapid. The island continues for four miles, and at the middle of it is a large river, which appears to come from the southeast, and empties on the left. We landed just above its mouth in order to examine it, and soon found the route intercepted by a deep, narrow channel, running into the Columbia above the large entrance, so as to form a dry and rich island about 400 yards wide and 800 long. Here, as along the grounds of the river, the natives had been digging large quantities of roots, as the soil was turned up in many places. We reached this river about a quarter of a mile above its mouth, at a place where a large body of water is compressed within a channel about 200 yards wide, where it foams over rocks, many of which are above the surface of the water. These narrows are the end of a rapid which extends two miles back, where the river is closely confined between two high hills, below which it is divided by numbers of large rocks and small islands, covered with a low growth of timber. This river, which is called by the Indians Towahnahiooks, is 200 yards wide at its mouth, has a very rapid current, and contributes about one-fourth as much water as the Columbia possesses before the junction. Immediately at the entrance are three sand-islands, and near it the head of an island which runs parallel to the large rocky island.

We now returned to our boats, and passing the mouth of the Towahnahiooks went between the islands. At the distance of two miles we reached the lower end of this rocky island, where were eight huts of Indians. Here we saw some large logs of wood, which had been most probably rafted down the Towahnahiooks; and a mile below, on the right bank, were 16 lodges of Indians, with whom we stopped to smoke. Then, at the distance of about a mile, we passed six more huts on the same side, nearly opposite the lower extremity of the island, which has its upper end in the mouth of the Towahnahiooks. Two miles below we came to 17 huts [of Eneeshurs] on the right side of the river, situated at the commencement of the pitch which includes the Great Falls. Here we halted, and immediately on landing walked down, accompanied by an old Indian from the huts, in order to examine the falls and ascertain on which side we could make a portage most easily.

We soon discovered that the nearest route was on the right side, and therefore dropped down to the head of the rapid, unloaded the canoes, and took all the baggage over by land to the foot of the rapid. The distance is 1,200 yards. On setting out we crossed a solid rock, about one-third of the whole distance; then reached a space 200 yards wide, which forms a hollow, where the loose sand from the low grounds has been driven by the winds, is steep and loose, and therefore disagreeable to pass; the rest of the route is over firm and solid ground. The labor of crossing would have been very inconvenient if the Indians had not assisted us in carrying some of the heavy articles on their horses; but for this service they repaid themselves so adroitly that, on reaching the foot of the rapids, we formed a camp in a position which might secure us from the pilfering of the natives, which we apprehend much more than we do their hostilities.

Near our camp are five large huts of Indians engaged in drying fish and preparing it for the market. The manner of doing this is by first opening the fish and exposing it to the sun on scaffolds. When it is sufficiently dried it is pounded between two stones till it is pulverized, and is then placed in a basket about two feet long and one in diameter, neatly made of grass and rushes, and lined with the skin of a salmon stretched and dried for the purpose. Here the fish are pressed down as hard as possible, and the top is covered with fish-skins, which are secured by cords through the holes of the basket. These baskets are then placed in some dry situation, the corded part upward, seven being usually placed as close as they can be put together, and five on the top of these. The whole is then wrapped up in mats, and made fast by cords, over which mats are again thrown. Twelve of these baskets, each of which contains from 90 to 100 pounds, form a stack, which is left exposed till it is sent to market. The fish thus preserved keep sound and sweet for several years, and great quantities, they inform us, are sent to the Indians who live below the falls, whence it finds its way to the whites who visit the mouth of the Columbia. We observe, both near the lodges and on the rocks in the river, great numbers of stacks of these pounded fish.

Besides fish, these people supplied us with filberts and berries, and we purchased a dog for supper; but it was with much difficulty that we were able to buy wood enough to cook it. In the course of the day we were visited by many Indians, from whom we learned that the principal chiefs of the bands residing in this neighborhood are now hunting in the mountains toward the southwest. On that side of the river none of the Indians have any permanent habitations; and on inquiry we were confirmed in our belief that it was for fear of attacks from the Snake Indians, with whom they are at war. This nation they represent as very numerous and residing in a great number of villages on the Towahnahiooks, where they live principally on salmon. That river, they add, is not obstructed by rapids above its mouth, but there becomes large and reaches to a considerable distance; the first villages of the Snake Indians on that river being twelve days' journey on a course about southeast from this place.

October 23d. Having ascertained from the Indians, and by actual examination, the best mode of bringing down the canoes, it was found necessary, as the river was divided into several narrow channels by rocks and islands, to follow the route a-dopted by the Indians themselves. This operation Captain Clark began this morning, and, after crossing to the other side of the river, hauled the canoes over a point of land, to avoid the perpendicular fall of 20 feet. At the distance of 457 yards we reached the water, and embarked at a place where a long rocky island compresses the channel of the river within the space of 150 yards, so as to form nearly a semicircle. On leaving this rocky island the channel is somewhat wider; but a second and much larger island of hard black rock still divides it from the main stream, while on the left shore it is closely bordered by perpendicular rocks. Having descended in this way for a mile, we reached a pitch of the river, which being divided by two large rocks, descends with great rapidity down a fall eight feet in height. As the boats could not be navigated down this steep descent, we were obliged to land, and let them down as slowly as possible by strong ropes of elk-skin, which we had prepared for the purpose. They all passed in safety except one, which, being loosed by the breaking of the ropes, was driven down, but was recovered by the In-

dians below. With this rapid ends the first pitch of the Great Falls, which is not great in point of height, and remarkable only for the singular manner in which the rocks have divided its channel.

From the marks everywhere perceivable at the falls, it is obvious that in high floods, which must be in the spring, the water below the falls rises nearly to a level with that above them. Of this rise, which is occasioned by some obstructions which we do not as yet know, the salmon must avail themselves to pass up the river in such multitudes that this fish is almost the only one caught in great abundance above the falls; but below that place we observe the salmon-trout, and the heads of a species of trout smaller than the salmon-trout, which is in great quantities, and which they are now burying, to be used as their winter food. A hole of any size being dug, the sides and bottom are lined with straw, over which skins are laid; on these the fish, after being well dried, are laid, covered with other skins, and the hole is closed with a layer of earth 12 or 15 inches deep.

About three o'clock we reached the lower camp, but our joy at having accomplished this object was somewhat diminished by the persecution of a new acquaintance. On reaching the upper point of the portage, we found that the Indians had camped there not long since, and had left behind them multitudes of fleas. These sagacious animals were so pleased to exchange the straw and fish-skins, in which they had been living, for some better residence, that we were soon covered with them, and during the portage the men were obliged to strip to the skin in order to brush them from their bodies. They were not, however, so easily dislodged from our clothes, and accompanied us in great numbers to our camp.

We saw no game except a sea-otter which was shot in the narrow channel as we came down, but we could not get it. Having therefore scarcely any provisions, we purchased eight small fat dogs, a food to which we are now compelled to have recourse, for the Indians are very unwilling to sell us any of their good fish, which they reserve for the market below. Fortunately, however, the habit of using this animal has completely overcome the repugnance which we felt at first, and dog, if not a favorite dish, is always an acceptable one. The meridian altitude of to-day gives 45° 42′ 57″ 3‴ N. as the latitude of our camp.

On the beach near the Indian huts we observed two canoes of a different shape and size from any which we had hitherto seen. One of these we got in exchange for our smallest canoe, giving a hatchet and a few trinkets to the owner, who said he had purchased it from a white man below the falls, by giving him a horse. These canoes are very beautifully made; they are wide in the middle and tapering toward each end, with curious figures carved on the bow. They are thin, but being strengthened by cross-bars about an inch in diameter, which are tied with strong pieces of bark through holes in the sides, are able to bear very heavy burdens, and seem calculated to live in the roughest water.

A great number of Indians both from above and below the falls visited us to-day, and toward evening we were informed by one of the chiefs who had accompanied us that he had overheard that the Indians below intended to attack us as we went down the river. Being at all times ready for any attempt of that sort, we were not under greater apprehensions than usual at this intelligence. We therefore only re-examined our arms, and increased the ammunition to 100 rounds. Our chiefs, who had not the same motives of confidence, were by no means so much at their ease, and when at night they saw the Indians leave us earlier than usual, their suspicions of an intended attack were confirmed, and they were very much alarmed.

October 24th. The Indians approached us with apparent caution, and behaved with more than usual reserve. Our two chiefs, by whom these circumstances were not unobserved, now told us that they wished to return home; that they could be no longer of any service to us; that they could not understand the language of the people below the falls; that those people formed a different nation from their own; that the two people had been at war with each other; and that as the Indians had expressed a resolution to attack us, they would certainly kill them. We endeavored to quiet their fears, and requested them to stay two nights longer, in which time we would see the Indians below, and make a peace between the two nations. They replied that they were anxious to return and see their horses. We however insisted on their remaining with us, not only in hopes of bringing about an accommodation between them and their enemies, but because they might be able to detect any hostile designs against us, and also assist us in passing the next falls, which are not far off, and represented as very difficult. They at length agreed to stay with us two nights longer.

About nine o'clock we proceeded, and on leaving our camp near the lower fall, found the river about 400 yards wide, with a current more rapid than usual, though with no perceptible descent. At the distance of 2½ miles the river widened into a large bend or basin on the right, at the beginning of which were three huts of Indians. At the extremity of this basin stands a high black rock, which, rising perpendicularly from the right shore, seems to run wholly across the river; so totally indeed does it appear to stop the passage that we could not see where the water escaped, except that the current appeared to be drawn with more than usual velocity to the left of the rock, where was a great roaring. We landed at the huts of the Indians, who went with us to the top of this rock, from which we saw all the difficulties of the channel. We were no longer at a loss to account for the rising of the river at the falls, for this tremendous rock stretches across the river to meet the high hills of the left shore, leaving a channel only 45 yards wide, through which the whole body of the Columbia must press its way [*i.e.*, Short Narrows]. The water, thus forced into so narrow a channel, is thrown into whirls, and swells and boils in every part with the wildest agitation. But the alternative of carrying the boats over this high rock was almost impossible in our present situation; and as the chief danger seemed to be, not from any rocks in the channel, but from the great waves and whirlpools, we resolved to try the passage in our boats, in hopes of being able by dexterous steering to escape. This we attempted, and with great care were able to get through, to the astonishment of all the Indians of the huts we had just passed, who now collected to see us from the top of the rock. The channel continues thus confined for a space of about half a mile, when the rock ceased. We passed a single Indian hut at its foot, where the river again enlarges to the width of 200 yards, and at the distance of a mile and a half stopped to view a very bad rapid; this is formed by two rocky islands which divide the channel, the lower and larger of which is in the middle

of the river. The appearance of this place was so unpromising that we unloaded all the most valuable articles, such as guns, ammunition, our papers, etc., and sent them by land, with all the men that could not swim, to the extremity of these rapids. We then descended with the canoes, two at a time; though the canoes took in some water, we all went through safely; after which we made two miles, stopped in a deep bend of the river toward the right, and camped a little above a large [Echeloot] village of 21 houses. Here we landed; and as it was late before all the canoes joined us, we were obliged to remain this evening, the difficulties of the navigation having permitted us to make only six miles.

This village is situated at the extremity of a deep bend toward the right, immediately above a ledge of high rocks, 20 feet above the marks of the highest flood, but broken in several places, so as to form channels which are at present dry, extending nearly across the river; this forms the second fall, or the place most probably which the Indians indicate by the word "Timm." While the canoes were coming on, Captain Clark walked with two men down to examine the channels. On the rocks the Indians are accustomed to dry fish; and as the season for that purpose is now over, the poles which they use are tied up very securely in bundles, and placed on the scaffolds. The stock of fish dried and pounded was so abundant that he counted 107 of them, making more than 10,000 pounds of that provision. After examining the [Long] narrows as well as the lateness of the hour would permit, he returned to the village through a rocky, open country, infested with polecats [skunks].

This village, the residence of a tribe called the Echeloots, consists of 21 houses,

Lewis and Clark

scattered promiscuously over an elevated situation, near a mound about 30 feet above the common level, which has some remains of houses on it, and bears every appearance of being artificial. The houses, which are the first wooden buildings we have seen since leaving the Illinois country, are nearly equal in size, and exhibit a very singular appearance. A large hole, 20 feet wide and 30 in length, is dug to the depth of 6 feet. The sides are then lined with split pieces of timber, rising just above the surface of the ground, which are smoother to the same width by burning, or shaved with small iron axes. These timbers are secured in their erect position by a pole stretched along the side of the building near the eaves, and supported on a strong post fixed at each corner. The timbers at the gable ends rise gradually higher, the middle pieces being the broadest. At the top of

these is a sort of semicircle, made to receive a ridge-pole the whole length of the house, propped by an additional post in the middle and forming the top of the roof. From this ridgepole to the eaves of the house are placed a number of small poles or rafters, secured at each end by fibers of the cedar. On these poles, which are connected by small transverse bars of wood, is laid a covering of the white cedar, or arbor vitæ, kept on by the strands of the cedar fibers; but a small distance along the whole length of the ridge-pole is left uncovered for the purpose of lighting and permitting the smoke to pass through. The roof thus formed has a descent about equal to that common among us, and near the eaves is perforated with a number of small holes, made most probably to discharge arrows in case of an attack. The only entrance is by a small door at the gable end, cut out of the middle piece of timber, 29½ inches high, and 14 inches broad, reaching only 18 inches above the earth. Before this hole is hung a mat; on pushing it aside and crawling through, the descent is by a small wooden ladder, made in the form of those used among us. One-half of the inside is used as a place of deposit for dried fish, of which large quantities are stored away, and with a few baskets of berries form the only family provisions; the other half, adjoining the door, remains for the accommodation of the family. On each side are arranged near the walls small beds of mats placed on little scaffolds or bedsteads, raised from 18 inches to 3 feet from the ground; and in the middle of the vacant space is the fire, or sometimes two or three fires, when, as is usually the case, the house contains three families.

The inhabitants received us with great kindness, invited us to their houses, and in the evening, after our camp had been formed, came in great numbers to see us. Accompanying them was a principal chief and several of the warriors of the nation below the great narrows. We made use of this opportunity to attempt a reconciliation between them and our two chiefs, and to put an end to the war which had disturbed the two nations. By representing to the chiefs the evils which this war inflicted on them, and the wants and privations to which it subjects them, they soon became disposed to conciliate each other; and we had some reason to be satisfied with the sincerity of the mutual professions that the war should no longer continue, and that in future they would live in peace with each other. On concluding this negotiation we proceeded to invest the chief with the insignia of command, a medal, and some small articles of clothing; after which the violin [Cruzatte's]

was produced and our men danced, to the great delight of the Indians, who remained with us till a late hour.

October 25th. We walked down with several of the Indians to view that part of the [Long] narrows which they represented as most dangerous. We found it very difficult; but, as with our large canoes the portage was impracticable, we concluded to carry our most valuable articles by land, and then hazard the passage. We therefore returned to the village, and after sending some of the party with our best stores to make a portage, and fixing others on the rock to assist with ropes the canoes that might meet with any difficulty, we began the descent, in the presence of great numbers of Indians who had collected to witness this exploit. The channel for three miles is worn through a hard rough black rock from 50 to 100 yards wide, in which the water swells and boils in a tremendous manner. The first three canoes escaped very well; the fourth, however, had nearly filled with water; the fifth passed through with only a small quantity of water over her. At half a mile we had got through the worst part; and having reloaded our canoes went on very well for 2½ miles, except that one of the boats was nearly lost by running against a rock. At the end of this channel of three miles, in which the Indians inform us they catch as many salmon as they wish, we reached a deep basin or bend of the river toward the right, near the entrance of which are two rocks. We crossed this basin, which has a quiet and gentle current, and at the distance of a mile from its commencement, a little below where the river resumes its channel, reached a rock which divides it [above Holman's creek].

At this place we met our old chiefs, who, when we began the portage, had walked down to the village below to smoke a pipe of friendship on the renewal of peace. Just after our meeting we saw a chief of the village above, with a party who had been out hunting, and were then crossing the river with their horses on their way home. We landed to smoke with this chief, whom we found a bold-looking man of pleasing appearance, about 50 years of age, dressed in a war-jacket, a cap, leggings, and moccasins. We presented him with a medal and other small articles, and he gave us some meat, of which he had been able to procure but little; for on his route he had met with a war-party of Indians from the Towahnahiooks, with whom there was a battle. We here smoked a parting pipe with our two faithful friends, the chiefs who had accompanied us from the heads of the river, and who now had each bought a horse, intending to go home by land.

On leaving this rock the river is gentle, but strewed with a great number of rocks for a few miles, when it becomes a beautiful still stream about half a mile wide. At five miles from the large bend we came to the mouth of a [Mill] creek 20 yards wide, heading in the range of mountains which runs S.S.W. and S.W. for a long distance, and discharging a considerable quantity of water; it is called by the Indians Quenett. We halted below it under a high point of rocks on the left; and as it was necessary to make some celestial observations, we formed a [Fort Rock] camp on top of the rocks. This situation is perfectly well calculated for defense in case the Indians should incline to attack us, for the rocks form a sort of natural fortification, with the aid of the river and creek; it is also convenient to hunt along the foot of the mountains to the west and southwest, where there are several species of timber which form fine coverts for game.

From this rock the pinnacle of the round mountain covered with snow, which we had seen a short distance below the forks of the Columbia, and which we had called the Falls or Timm mountain, is S. 43° W., about 37 miles distant. The face of the country on both sides of the river, above and below the falls, is steep, rugged, and rocky, with a very small proportion of herbage, and no timber except a few bushes; the hills to the west, however, have some scattered pine, white-oak, and other kinds of trees. All the timber used by the people at the upper falls is rafted down the Towahnahiooks; and those who live at the head of the [Long] narrows we have just passed bring their wood in the same way from this creek to the lower part of these narrows, from which it is carried three miles by land to their habitations.

Both above and below, as well as in the narrows, we saw a great number of sea-otters or seals. This evening one deer was killed, and great signs of that animal were seen near the camp. In the creek we shot a goose, and saw much appearance of beaver. One of the party also saw a fish, which he took to be a drum-fish. Among the willows we found several snares set by the natives for the purpose of catching wolves.

October 26th. The morning was fine. We sent six men to hunt, and to collect rosin to pitch the canoes, which, by being frequently hauled over rocks, have become very leaky. The canoes were also brought out to dry, and on examination it was found that many of the articles had become spoiled by being repeatedly wet. We were occupied with the observations necessary to determine our longitude, and with conferences among the Indians, many of whom came on horseback to the opposite shore in the forepart of the day, and showed some anxiety to cross over to us. We did not, however, think it proper to send for them; but toward evening two chiefs, with 15 men, came over in a small canoe. They proved to be the two principal chiefs of the tribes at and above the falls, who had been absent on a hunting excursion as we passed their residence. Each of them on their arrival made us a present of deer's flesh, and small white cakes made of roots. Being anxious to ingratiate ourselves in their favor, so as to insure a friendly reception on our return, we treated them with all the kindness we could show; we acknowledged the chiefs, gave a medal of the small size, a red silk handkerchief, an armband, a knife, and a piece of paint to each chief, small presents to several of the party, and half a deer. These attentions were not lost on the Indians, who appeared very well pleased with them. At night a fire was made in the middle of our camp, and as the Indians sat round it our men danced to the music of the violin [Cruzatte's], which so delighted them that several resolved to remain with us all night; the rest crossed the river. All the tribes in this neighborhood are at war with the Snake Indians, whom they all describe as living on the Towahnahiooks [Des Chutes river], and whose nearest town is said to be four days' march from this place, in a direction nearly southwest. There has lately been a battle between these tribes, but we could not ascertain the loss on either side.

The water rose to-day eight inches — a rise which we could only ascribe to the circumstance of the wind's having been up the river for the last 24 hours, since the influence of the tide cannot be sensible here on account of the falls [Cascades] below. The hunters returned in the evening; they had seen the tracks of elk and bear in the mountains, and killed five deer, four very large gray squirrels, and a grouse; they inform us that the country off the river is broken, stony, and thinly timbered with pine and white-oak. Besides these delicacies one of the men killed with a gig a salmon-trout which, being fried in some bear's oil which had been given to us by the chief whom we met this morning below the narrows, furnished a dish of very delightful flavor. A number of white cranes were also seen flying in different directions, but at such a height that we could not procure any of them. The fleas, with which we had contracted an intimacy at the falls, are so unwilling to leave us that the men are obliged to throw off all their clothes in order to relieve themselves from their persecution.

Sunday, October 27th. The wind was high from the westward during last night and this morning, but the weather being fair we continued our celestial observations. The two chiefs who remained with us were joined by seven Indians, who came in a canoe from below. To these men we were very particular in our attentions; we smoked and eat with them; but some of them, who were tempted by the sight of our goods exposed to dry, wished to take liberties with them; to which we were under the necessity of putting an immediate check; which restraint displeased them so much that they returned down the river in very ill humor. The two chiefs, however, remained with us till the evening, when they crossed the river to their party.

Before they went we procured from them a vocabulary of the Echeloot, their native language, and on comparison were surprised at its difference from that of the Eneeshur tongue. In fact, though the Echeloots, who live at the Great Narrows, are not more than six miles from the Eneeshurs or residents at and above the Great Falls, the two people are separated by a broad distinction of language. The Eneeshurs are understood by all the tribes residing on the Columbia above the Falls; but at that place they meet with the unintelligible language of the Echeloots, which then descends the river to a considerable distance. Yet the variation may possibly be rather a deep shade of dialect than a radical difference, since among both [tribes] many words are the same, and the identity cannot be accounted for by supposing that their neighborhood has interwoven them into their daily conversations, because the same words are equally familiar among all the Flathead bands which we have passed. To all these tribes the strange clucking or guttural noise which first struck us is common. They also flatten the heads of their children in nearly the same manner; but we now begin to observe that the heads of males, as well as of the other sex, are subjected to this operation, whereas among the mountains custom has confined it almost to the females. The hunters brought home four deer, one grouse, and a squirrel.

October 28th. The morning was again cool and windy. Having dried our goods, we were about setting out, when three canoes came from above to visit us, and at the same time two others from below arrived for the same purpose. Among these last was an Indian who wore his hair in a cue and had on a round hat and a sailor's jacket, which he said he had obtained from the people below the great rapids, who bought them from the whites. This interview detained us till nine o'clock, when we proceeded down the river, which is now bordered with cliffs of loose dark colored rocks about 90 feet high, with a thin covering of pines and other small trees. At the distance of four miles we reached a small village of eight houses under some high rocks on the right [at or near Crate's Point], with a small [Cheneweth] creek on the opposite side of the river.

We landed and found the houses similar to those we had seen at the great narrows; on entering one of them we saw a British musket, a cutlass, and several brass tea-kettles, of which they seemed to be very fond. There were figures of men, birds, and different animals, which were cut and painted on the boards which form the sides of the room; though the workmanship of these uncouth figures was very rough, they were as highly estemed by the Indians as the finest frescoes of more civilized people. This tribe is called the Chilluckittequaw; their language, though somewhat different from that of the Echeloots, has many of the same words, and is sufficiently intelligible to the neighboring Indians. We procured from them a vocabulary, and then, after buying five small dogs, some dried berries and a white bread or cake made of roots, we left them. The wind, however, rose so high that we were obliged, after going one mile, to land on the left side, opposite a rocky island, and pass the day there. We formed our camp in a niche above a point of high rocks, as this was the only safe harbor we could find, and submitted to the inconvenience of lying on the sand exposed to the wind and rain during all the evening. The high wind, which obliged us to consult the safety of our boats by not venturing further, did not at all prevent the Indians from navigating the river.

We had not been long on shore before a canoe with a man, his wife, and two children came from below through the high waves with a few roots to sell; and soon after we were visited by many Indians from the village above, with whom we smoked and conversed. The canoes used by these people are like those already described, built of white cedar or pine, very light, wide in the middle and tapering toward the ends, the bow being raised and ornamented with carvings of the heads of animals. As the canoe is the vehicle of transportation, the Indians have acquired great dexterity in its management, and guide it safely over the highest waves. They have among their utensils bowls and baskets very neatly made of small bark and grass, in which they boil their provisions. The only game seen today were two deer, of which only one was killed; the other was wounded, but escaped.

October 29th. The morning was still cloudy and the wind from the west, but as it had abated its violence we set out at daylight. At the distance of four miles we passed a creek on the right [?], one mile below which is a village of seven houses on the same side. This is the residence of the principal chief of the Chilluckittequaw nation, whom we now found to be the same between whom and our two chiefs we had made a peace at the Echeloot village. He received us very kindly and set before us pounded fish, filberts, [and other] nuts, berries of the sacacommis, and white bread made of roots. We gave in return a bracelet of ribbon to each of the women of the house, with which they were very much pleased. The chief had several articles, such as scarlet and blue cloth, a sword, a jacket and a hat, which must have been procured from the whites; and on one side of the room were two wide split boards placed together [edge to edge], so as to make space [be wide enough] for a rude figure of a man cut and painted on them. On pointing to this and asking him what it meant, he said something, of which all we understood was

"good," and then stepped to the image and brought out his bow and quiver, which, with some other warlike instruments, were kept behind it.

The chief then directed his wife to hand him his medicinebag, from which he brought out 14 fore-fingers, which he told us had once belonged to the same number of his enemies whom he had killed in fighting with the nations to the southeast, to which place he pointed; alluding, no doubt, to the Snake Indians, the common enemy of the nations on the Columbia. This bag is about two feet in length, containing roots, pounded dirt, etc., which the Indians only know how to appreciate. It is suspended in the middle of the lodge, and it is supposed to be a species of sacrilege to be touched by any but the owner. It is an object of religious fear, and from its sanctity is the safest place to deposit their medals and their more valuable articles. The Indians have likewise small bags which they preserve in their great medicine-bag, whence they are taken and worn around their waists and necks, as amulets against real or imaginary evils. This was the first time we had ever known Indians to carry from the field any trophy except the scalp. The fingers were shown with great exultation, and after a harangue, which we were left to presume was in praise of his exploits, they were carefully replaced among the valuable contents of the red medicine-bag. This village being part of the same nation with the village we passed above, the language of the two is the same; their houses are of similar form and materials, and calculated to contain about 30 souls. The inhabitants were unusually hospitable and good-humored, so that we gave to the place the name of Friendly village.

We breakfasted here, and after purchasing twelve dogs, four sacks of fish, and a few dried berries, proceeded on our journey. The hills we passed are high, with steep rocky sides, some pine and white-oak, and an undergrowth of shrubs scattered over them. Four miles below this village is a small river [Klikitat] on the right side; immediately below is a village of Chilluck-ittequaws, consisting of 11 houses. Here we landed and smoked a pipe with the inhabitants, who were very cheerful and friendly. They as well as the people of the last village inform us that this river comes a considerable distance from the N.N.E.; that it has a great number of falls, which prevent the salmon from passing up, and that there are ten nations residing on it, who subsist on berries, or such game as they can procure with their bows and arrows. At its mouth the river is 60 yards wide, and has a deep and very rapid channel. From the number of falls of which the Indians spoke we gave it the name of Cataract river. We purchased four dogs, and then proceeded.

The country as we advance is more rocky and broken, and the pine and low white-oak on the hills increase in great quantity. Three miles below Cataract river we passed three large rocks in the river; that in the middle is large and longer than the rest, and from the circumstances of its having several square vaults on it, obtained the name of Sepulcher island [Klikitat name Memaloose Alahee—"Land of the Dead."] A short distance below are two huts of Indians on the right. The river now widens, and in three miles we came to two more houses on the right, one mile beyond which is a rocky island in a bend of the river toward the left. Within the next six miles we passed 14 huts of Indians scattered on the right bank, and then reached the entrance of a river on the left, which we called Labieshe's [Labiche's]

river, after Labieshe, one of our party. Just above this river is a low ground more thickly timbered than usual, and in front are four huts of Indians on the bank, which are the first we have seen on that side of the Columbia. The exception may be occasioned by this spot being more than usually protected from the approach of enemies by the creek and the thick wood behind.

We again embarked, and at the distance of a mile passed the mouth of a rapid creek on the right, 18 yards wide. In this creek the Indians whom we left take their fish, and from the number of canoes which were in it we called it Canoe creek. Opposite this creek is a large sand-bar, which continues for four miles along the left side of the river. Just below this a beautiful cascade falls in on the left, over a precipice of rock 100 feet in height. One mile further are four Indian huts in the low ground on the left, and two miles beyond this is a point of land on the right, where the mountains become high on both sides, and possess more timber and greater varieties of it than hitherto, while those on the left are covered with snow. One mile from this point we halted for the night at three Indian huts on the right [Skamania Co., Wash.], having made 32 miles.

On our first arrival they seemed surprised, but not alarmed, and we soon became intimate by means of smoking and our favorite entertainment for the Indians, the violin. They gave us fruit, roots, and root-bread, and we purchased from them three dogs. The houses of these people are similar to those of the Indians above, and their language is the same; their dress also, consisting of robes or skins of wolves, deer, elk, and wildcat, is made nearly after the same model; their hair is worn in plaits down each shoulder, and round their neck is put a strip of some skin with the tail of the animal hanging down over the breast; like the Indians above, they are fond of otter-skins, and give a great price for them. We here saw the skin of a mountain sheep, which they say lives among the rocks in the mountains; the skin was covered with white hair; the wool was long, thick, and coarse, with long coarse hair on the top of the neck and on the back, resembling somewhat the bristles of a goat. Immediately behind the village is a pond, in which were great numbers of small swan.

October 30th. A moderate rain fell during all last night, but the morning was cool; and, after taking a scanty breakfast of deer, we proceeded. The river is now about three-quarters of a mile wide, with a current so gentle that it does not exceed one mile and a half an hour; but its course is obstructed by the projection of large rocks, which seem to have fallen promiscuously from the mountains into the bed of the river. On the left side four different streams of water empty in cascades from the hills. What is, however, most singular is that there are stumps of pine-trees scattered for some distance in the river, which has the appearance of being dammed below and forced to encroach on the shore. These obstructions continued to the distance of twelve miles, when we came to the mouth of a river on the right, where we landed.

We found it 60 yards wide, and its banks possess two kinds of timber which we had not hitherto seen. One is a very large species of ash; the other resembles in its bark the beech, but the tree itself is smaller, as also are the leaves. We called this stream Crusatte's [or Cruzatte's] river, after Crusatte, one of our men. Opposite its mouth the Columbia widens to the distance of a mile, with a large sand-bar, and large stones and rocks scattered through the channel. We here saw several of the large buzzards, which are of the size of the largest eagle, with the under part of their wings white: we also shot a deer and three ducks, on part of which we dined, and then continued down the Columbia.

Above Crusatte's river the low grounds are about three-quarters of a mile wide, rising gradually to the hills, with a rich soil covered with grass, fern, and other small undergrowth; but below, the country rises with a steep ascent, and soon the mountains approach the river with steep rugged sides, covered with a very thick growth of pine, cedar, cottonwood, and oak. The river is still strewed with large rocks. At 2½ miles below Crusatte's river is a large creek on the right, with a small island in the mouth. Just below this creek we passed along the right side of three small islands on the right bank of the river, with a larger island on the opposite side, and landed on an island very near the right shore at the head of the Great Shoot, opposite two smaller islands at the fall or shoot itself. Just above the island on which we camped is a small village of eight large houses in a bend on the right, where the country, from having been very mountainous, becomes low for a short distance. We made 15 miles to-day, during all which time we were kept constantly wet with the rain; but as we were able to get on this island some of the ash, which we saw for the first time to-day, and which makes a tolerable fire, we were as comfortable as the moistness of the evening would permit.

As soon as we landed, Captain Lewis went with five men [up] to the village, which is situated near the river, with ponds in the low grounds behind. The greater part of the inhabitants were absent collecting roots down the river; the few, however, who were at home treated him very kindly, and gave him berries, nuts, and fish; in the house were a gun and several articles which must have been procured from the whites; but not being able to procure any information, he returned to the island. Captain Clark had in the meantime gone down to examine the shoot and discover the best route for a portage. He followed an Indian path which, at the distance of a mile, led to a village on an elevated situation, the houses of which had been large and built in a different form from any we had yet seen, but which had been lately abandoned, the greater part of the boards having been put into a pond near the village; this was most probably for the purpose of drowning the fleas, which were in immense quantities near the houses. After going about three miles the night obliged him to return to camp. He resumed his search in the morning,

October 31st, through the rain. At the extremity of the basin, in which is situated the island where we camped, several rocks and rocky islands are interspersed through the bed of the river. The rocks on each side have fallen down from the mountains; that on the left being high, and on the right the hill itself, which is lower, slipping into the river; so that the current is here compressed within a space of 150 yards. Within this narrow limit it runs for 400 yards with great rapidity, swelling over the rocks with a fall of about 20 feet; it then widens to 200 paces, and the current for a short distance becomes gentle; but at the distance of a mile and a half, opposite the old village mentioned yesterday, it is obstructed by a very bad rapid, where the waves are unusually high; the river being confined between large rocks, many of which are at the surface of the water. Captain Clark proceeded along the same path he had taken before, which led him through a thick wood and along a hillside, till 2½ miles below the shoots [chutes] he struck the river at the place whence the

Indians make their portage to the head of the shoot. He here sent Crusatte, the principal waterman, up the stream, to examine if it were practicable to bring the canoes down the water. In the meantime he, with Joseph Fields, continued his route down the river, along which the rapids seemed to stretch as far as he could see. At half a mile below the end of the portage he came to a house, the only remnant of a town which, from its appearance, must have been of great antiquity. The house was uninhabited; being old and decayed, he felt no disposition to encounter the fleas which abound in every situation of that kind, and therefore did not enter.

About half a mile below this house, in a very thick part of the woods, is an ancient burial place. It consists of eight vaults made of pine or cedar boards closely connected, about eight feet square and six in height; the top covered with wide boards sloping a little, so as to convey off the rain. The direction of all of these vaults is east and west, the door being on the eastern side, partially stopped with wide boards decorated with rude pictures of men and other animals. On entering he found in some of them four dead bodies, carefully wrapped in skins, tied with cords of grass and bark, lying on a mat, in a direction east and west. The other vaults contained only bones, which were in some of them piled to the height of four feet. On the tops of the vaults, and on poles attached to them, hung brass kettles and frying-pans with holes in their bottoms, baskets, bowls, sea-shells, skins, pieces of cloth, hair, bags of trinkets and small bones—the offerings of friendship or affection, which have been saved by a pious veneration from the ferocity of war, or the more dangerous temptations of individual gain. The whole of the walls as well as the door were decorated with strange figures cut and painted on them; and

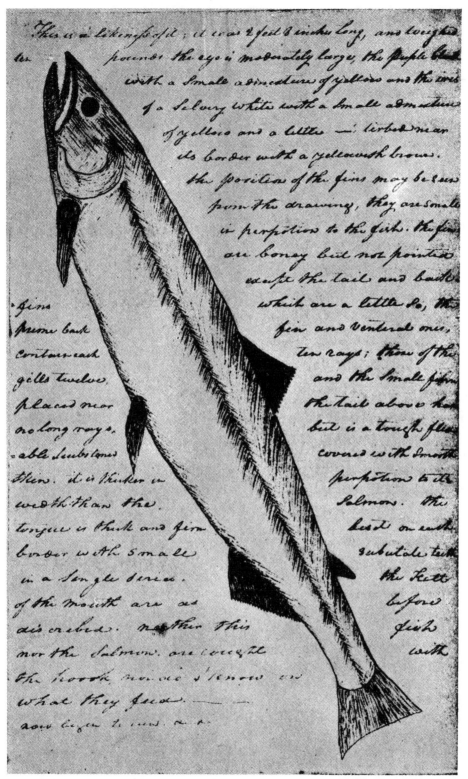

A Page from Clark's Diary—drawing and description of a white salmon trout

besides were several wooden images of men, some so old and decayed as to have almost lost their shape, which were all placed against the sides of the vaults. These images, as well as those in the houses we have lately seen, do not appear to be at all the objects of adoration; in this place they were most probably intended as resemblances of those whose decease they indicate; when we observe them in houses, they occupy the most conspicuous part, but are treated more like ornaments than objects of worship. Near the vaults which are standing are the remains of others on the ground completely rotted and covered with moss; and as they are formed of the most durable pine and cedar timber, there is every appearance that for a very long series of years this retired spot has been the depository for the Indians near this place.

After examining this place Captain Clark went on, and found the river as before strewed with large rocks, against which the water ran with great rapidity. Just below the vaults the mountain, which is but low on the right side, leaves the river, and is succeeded by an open stony level, which extends down the river, while on the left the mountain is still high and rugged. At two miles' distance he came to a village of four houses, which were now vacant and the doors barred up. On looking in he saw the usual quantity of utensils still remaining, from which he concluded that the inhabitants were at no great distance collecting roots or hunting, in order to lay in their supply of food for the winter. He left them and went on three miles to a difficult rocky rapid, which was the last in view. Here, on the right, are the remains of a large and ancient village, which could be plainly traced by the holes for the houses and the deposits for fish. After he had examined these rapids

and the neighboring country he returned to camp by the same route. The only game he obtained was a sand-hill crane.

In the meantime we had been occupied in preparations for making the portage, and in conference with the Indians, who came down from the village to visit us. Toward evening two canoes arrived from the village at the mouth of Cataract [Klikitat] river, loaded with fish and bear's grease for the market below. As soon as they landed they unloaded the canoes, turned them upside down on the beach, and camped under a shelving rock near our camp.

We had an opportunity of seeing to-day the hardihood of the Indians of the neighboring village. One of the men shot a goose, which fell into the river and was floating rapidly toward the great shoot, when an Indian observing it plunged in after it. The whole mass of the waters of the Columbia, just preparing to descend its narrow channel, carried the animal down with great rapidity. The Indian followed it fearlessly to within 150 feet of the rocks, where he would inevitably have been dashed to pieces; but seizing his prey he turned round and swam ashore with great composure. We very willingly relinquished our right to the bird in favor of the Indian who had thus saved it at the imminent hazard of his life; he immediately set to work and picked off about half the feathers, and then, without opening it, ran a stick through it and carried it off to roast.

Friday, November 1st, 1805. The morning was cool and the wind high from the northeast. The Indians who arrived last night took their empty canoes on their shoulders and carried them below the great shoot, where they put them in the water and brought them down the rapid, till at the distance of 2½ miles they stopped to take in their loading, which they had been afraid to trust in the last rapid, and had therefore carried by land from the head of the shoot. After their example we carried our small canoe and all the baggage across the slippery rocks to the foot of the shoot. The four large canoes were next brought down by slipping them along poles, placed from one rock to another, and in some places by using, partially, streams which escaped alongside of the river. We were not, however, able to bring them across without three of them receiving injuries which obliged us to stop at the end of the shoot to repair them. At this shoot we saw great numbers of sea-otters; but they are so shy that it is difficult to reach them with the musket; one of them that was wounded sunk and was lost. Having by this portage avoided the rapid and shoot of 400 yards in length, we re-embarked, passed at a mile and a half the bad rapid opposite the old village on the right, and making our way through the rocks saw the house just below the end of the portage, and the eight vaults near it; and at the distance of four miles from the head of the shoot reached a high rock, which forms the upper part of an island [Brant] near the left shore. Between this island and the right shore we proceeded, leaving at the distance of a mile and a half the village of four houses on our right, and a mile and a half lower came to the head of a rapid near the village on the right. Here we halted for the night, having made only seven miles from the head of the shoot. During the whole of the passage the river is very much obstructed by rocks. The island, which is about three miles long, reaches to the rapid which its lower extremity contributes to form. The meridian altitude of to-day gave us the latitude of 45° 44′ 3″ N.

As we passed the village of four houses, we found that the inhabitants had returned, and stopped to visit them. The houses are similar to those already described, but larger, from 35 to 50 feet long and 30 feet wide, being sunk in the ground about six feet, and raised the same height above. Their beds are raised about 4½ feet above the floor; the ascent is by a new painted ladder, with which every family is provided, and under them are stored their dried fish, while the space between the part of the bed on which they lie and the wall of the house is occupied by the nuts, roots, berries, and other provisions, which are spread on mats. The fireplace is about eight feet long and six feet wide, sunk a foot below the floor, secured by a frame, with mats placed around for the family to sit on. In all of the houses are images of men of different shapes, placed as ornaments in the parts of the house where they are most seen. They gave us nuts, berries, and some dried fish to eat, and we purchased, among other articles, a hat made after their own taste, such as they wear, without a brim. They ask high prices for all that they sell, observing that the whites below pay dearly for all which they carry there.

We cannot learn precisely the nature of the trade carried on by the Indians with the inhabitants below. But as their knowledge of the whites seems to be very imperfect, and as the only articles which they carry to market, such as pounded fish, bear-grass, and roots, cannot be an object of much foreign traffic, their intercourse appears to be an intermediate trade with the natives near the mouth of the Columbia. From them these people obtain, in exchange for their fish, roots, and bear-grass, blue and white beads, copper teakettles, brass armbands, some scarlet and blue robes, and a few articles of old European clothing. But their great object is to obtain beads, an article which holds the first place in their ideas of relative value, and to procure which they will sacrifice their last article of clothing or last mouthful of food. Independently of their fondness for them as an ornament, these beads are the medium of trade, by which they obtain from the Indians still higher up the river, robes, skins, chappelel [*sic*] bread, bear-grass, etc. Those Indians in turn employ them to procure from the Indians in the Rocky mountains, bear-grass, pachico-roots [*sic*], robes, etc.

These Indians are rather below the common size, with high cheek-bones; their noses are pierced, and in full dress ornamented with a tapering piece of white shell or wampum about two inches long. Their eyes are exceedingly sore and weak; many of them have only a single eye, and some are perfectly blind. Their teeth prematurely decay, and in frequent instances are altogether worn away. Their general health, however, seems to be good, the only disorder we have remarked being tumors in different parts of the body. The women are small and homely in their appearance, their legs and thighs much swelled, and their knees remarkably large—deformities which are no doubt owing to the manner in which they sit on their hams. They go nearly naked, having only a piece of leather tied round the breast, falling thence nearly as low as the waist; a small robe about three feet square, and a piece of leather, which ill supplies the place of a cover, tied between their legs. Their hair is suffered to hang loose in every direction, and in their persons, as well as in their cookery, they are filthy to a most disgusting degree. We here observe that the women universally have their heads flattened, and in many of the villages we have lately seen the female children undergoing this operation.

Saturday, November 2d, 1805. We now examined the rapid below more particularly, and the danger appearing to be too great for the loaded canoes, all those who could not swim were sent with the baggage by land. The canoes then passed safely, and were reloaded. At the foot of the rapid we took a meridian altitude of 59° 45′ 45″. Just as we were setting out seven squaws arrived across the portage, loaded with dried fish and bear-grass, neatly packed in bundles, and soon after four Indians came down the rapid in a large canoe. After breakfast we left our camp at one o'clock, passed the upper point of an island which is separated from the right shore by a narrow channel through which in high tides the water passes. But at present it contains no running water, and a creek [Hamilton] which falls into it from the mountains on the right is in the same dry condition, though it has the marks of discharging immense torrents at some seasons. The island thus made is three miles in length and about one in width; its situation is high and open; the land is rich, and at this time covered with grass and a great number of strawberry-vines from which we gave it the name of Strawberry island. In several places we observed that the Indians had been digging for roots; indeed the whole island bears every appearance of having been at some period in a state of cultivation. On the left side of the river the low ground is narrow and open.

The rapid we have just passed is the last of all the descents of the Columbia. At this place the first tide-water commences, and the river in consequence widens immediately below the rapid. As we descended we reached, at the distance of one mile from the rapid, a creek under a bluff on the left; at three miles is the lower point of Strawberry island. To this immediately succeed three small islands covered with wood. In the meadow to the right, at some distance from the hills, stands a perpendicular rock about 800 feet high and 400 yards around the base. This we called Beacon rock. Just below is an Indian village of nine houses, situated between two small creeks. At this village the river widens to nearly a mile in extent; the low grounds become wider, and they as well as the mountains on each side are covered with pine, spruce-pine, cotton-wood, a species of ash, and some alder. After being so long accustomed to the dreary na-kedness of the country above, the change is as grateful to the eye as it is useful in supply-ing us with fuel. Four miles from the village is a point of land on the right, where the hills become lower, but are still thickly timbered. The river is now about two miles wide, the current smooth and gentle, and the effect of the tide has been sensible since leav-ing the rapid. Six miles lower is a rock rising from the middle of the river to the height of 100 feet, and about 80 yards at its base. We continued six miles further, and halted for the night under a high projecting rock on the left side of the river, opposite the point of a large meadow.

The mountains, which, from the great shoot to this place, are high, rugged, and thickly covered with timber, chiefly of the pine species, here leave the river on each side; the river becomes 2½ miles in width; the low grounds are extensive and well sup-plied with wood. The Indians whom we left at the portage passed us on their way down the river, and seven others, who were de-scending in a canoe for the purpose of trad-ing below, camped with us. We had made from the foot of the great shoot 29 miles to-day. The ebb tide rose at our camp about nine inches; the flood must rise much higher. We saw great numbers of water-fowl, such as swan, geese, ducks of various kinds, gulls, plovers, and the white and gray brant, of which last we killed 18.

November 3d. We were detained until ten o'clock by a fog so thick that a man could not be discerned at the distance of 50 steps. As soon as it cleared off we set out in company with our new Indian acquaintances, who came from a village near the Great Falls. The low grounds along the river are cov-ered so thickly with rushes, vines, and other small growth that they are almost impass-able. At the distance of three miles we reached the mouth of a river on the left, which seemed to lose its waters in a sand-bar opposite, the stream itself being only a few inches in depth. But, on attempting to wade across, we discovered that the bed was a very bad quicksand, too deep to be passed on foot. We went up a mile and a half to ex-amine this river, and found it to be at this distance a very considerable stream, 120 yards wide at its narrowest part, with several small islands. Its character resembles very much that of the river Platte. It drives its quicksand over the low grounds with great impetuosity, and such is the quantity of coarse sand which it discharges that the accumulation has formed a large sand-bar or island, three miles long and a mile and a half wide, which divides the waters of the quicksand river into two channels. This sand-island compresses the Columbia within a space of half a mile, and throws its whole current against the right shore. Opposite this river, which we call Quicksand river, is a large creek, to which we give the name of Seal river. The first appears to pass through the low country, at the foot of the high range of mountains toward the southeast, while the second, as well as all the large creeks on the right side of the Columbia, rises in the same ridge of mountains N.N.E.

from this place. The mountain, which we have [rightly] supposed to be the Mount Hood of Vancouver, bears S. 85° E. about 47 miles from the mouth of the Quicksand river.

After dinner we proceeded, and at the distance of three miles reached the lower mouth of Quicksand river. On the opposite side a large creek falls in near the head of an island, which extends for 3½ miles down the river; it is a mile and a half in width, rocky at the upper end, and has some timber round its borders; but in the middle is open and has several ponds. Half a mile lower is another island in the middle of the river, to which, from its appearance, we gave the name of Diamond island. Here we met 15 Indians ascending the river in two canoes; but the only information we could procure from them was that they had seen three vessels, which we presume to be European, at the mouth of the Columbia. We went along its right side for three miles, and camped opposite it [at or near Fisher's Landing], after making to-day 13 miles.

A canoe soon after arrived from the village at the foot of the last rapid, with an Indian and his family, consisting of a wife, three children, and a woman who had been taken prisoner from the Snake Indians, living on a river from the south, which we afterward found to be the Multnomah. Sacajawea was immediately introduced to her, in hopes that, being a Snake Indian, they might understand each other; but their language was not sufficiently intelligible to permit them to converse together. The Indian had a gun with a brass barrel and cock, which he appeared to value highly.

Below Quicksand river the country is low, rich, and thickly wooded on each side of the river. The islands have less timber, but are furnished with a number of ponds near which are vast quantities of fowls, such as swan, geese, brants, cranes, storks, white gulls, cormorants, and plovers. The river is wide and contains a great number of sea-otters. In the evening the hunters brought in game for a sumptuous supper, which we shared with the Indians, both parties of whom spent the night with us.

November 4th. The weather was cloudy and cool, and the wind from the west. During the night the tide rose 18 inches near our camp. We set out about eight o'clock, and at the distance of three miles came to the lower end of Diamond island. It is six miles long, nearly three in width, and, like the other islands, thinly covered with timber; it has a number of ponds or small lakes scattered over its surface. Besides the animals already mentioned, we shot a deer on it this morning. Near the end of Diamond island are two others, separated by a narrow channel filled at high tide only, which continue on the right for the distance of three miles; and, like the adjacent low grounds, are thickly covered with pine. Just below the last we landed on the left bank of the river, at a village of 25 houses. All of these were thatched with straw and built of bark, except one which was about 50 feet long, built of boards in the form of those higher up the river; from which it differed, however, in being completely above ground and covered with broad split boards. This village contains about 200 men of the Skilloot nation, who seem well provided with canoes, of which there were at least 52, some of them very large, drawn up in front of the village.

On landing we found the Indian from above who had left us this morning, and who now invited us into a lodge of which he appeared to own a part. Here he treated us with a root, round in shape, and about the size of a small Irish potato, which they call wappatoo. This is the common arrowhead or sagittifolia, so much cultivated by the Chinese; when roasted in the embers till it becomes soft it has an agreeable taste, and is a very good substitute for bread.

After purchasing some more of this root, we resumed our journey, and at seven miles' distance came to the head of a large island near the left. On the right shore is a fine open prairie for about a mile, back of which the country rises and is supplied with timber, such as white-oak, pine of different kinds, wild crab, and several species of undergrowth, while along the borders of the river there are only a few cottonwood and ash trees. In this prairie were also signs of deer and elk.

When we landed for dinner, a number of Indians from the last village came down for the purpose, as we supposed, of paying us a friendly visit, as they had put on their favorite dresses. In addition to their usual covering they had scarlet and blue blankets, sailors' jackets and trousers, shirts and hats. They had all of them either war-axes, spears, and bows and arrows, or muskets and pistols, with tin powder-flasks. We smoked with them and endeavored to show them every attention, but we soon found them very assuming and disagreeable companions. While we were eating, they stole the pipe with which they were smoking, and the greatcoat of one of the men. We immediately searched them all, and discovered the coat stuffed under the root of a tree near where they were sitting; but the pipe we could not recover. Finding us determined not to suffer any imposition, and discontented with them, they showed their displeasure in the only way which they dared, by returning in an ill-humor to their village.

We then proceeded and soon met two canoes, with twelve men of the same Skilloot nation, who were on their way from below. The larger of the canoes was ornamented with the figure of a bear in the bow and a man in the stern, both nearly as large as life, both made of painted wood and very neatly fixed to the boat. In the same canoe were two Indians, finely dressed and with round hats. This circumstance induced us to give the name of Image-canoe to the large island, the lower end of which we now passed at the distance of nine miles from its head. We had seen two smaller islands to the right, and three more near its lower extremity. The Indians in the canoe here made signs that there was a village behind those islands, and indeed we presumed there was a channel on that [left] side of the river, for one of the canoes passed in that direction between the small islands; but we were anxious to press forward, and therefore did not stop to examine more minutely. The river was now about a mile and a half in width, with a gentle current; the bottoms were extensive and low, but not subject to be overflowed. Three miles below Image-canoe island we came to four large houses on the left side, at which place we had a full view of the mountain which we first saw on the 19th of October, from the Muscleshell rapid, and which we now find to be the Mount St. Helen of Vancouver. It bears N. 25° E., about 90 miles distant; it rises in the form of a sugar-loaf to a very great height, and is covered with snow. A mile lower we passed a single house on the left and another on the right. The Indians had now learnt so much of us that their curiosity was without any mixture of fear, and their visits became very frequent and troublesome. We therefore continued on till after night, in hopes of getting rid of them; but after passing a village on each side, which on account of the lateness of the hour we saw indistinctly, we found there was no escaping from their importunities. We therefore landed at the distance of seven miles below Image-canoe island, and camped near a single house of the right, having made during the day 29 miles.

The Skilloots whom we passed to-day speak a language somewhat different from that of the Echeloots or Chilluckittequaws near the long narrows. Their dress is similar, except that the Skilloots possess more articles procured from the white traders; and there is a further difference between them, inasmuch as the Skilloots, both males and females, have the head flattened. Their principal food is fish and wappatoo-roots, with some elk and deer, in killing which with their arrows they seem very expert; for during the short time we remained at the village three deer were brought in. We also observed there a tame brairo.

As soon as we landed we were visited by two canoes loaded with Indians, from whom we purchased a few roots. The grounds along the river continue low and rich, and among the shrubs which cover them is a large quantity of vines, resembling the raspberry. On the right the low grounds are terminated at the distance of five miles by a range of high hills covered with tall timber, and running southeast and northwest. The game as usual very abundant; among other birds we observe some white geese with a part of their wings black.

November 5th. Our choice of a camp had been very unfortunate; for on a sand-island opposite us were immense numbers of geese, swan, ducks, and other wild fowl, which during the whole night serenaded us with a confusion of noises which completely prevented our sleeping. During the latter part of the night it rained, and we therefore willingly left camp at an early hour. We passed at three miles a small prairie, where the river is only three-quarters of a mile in width, and soon after two houses on the left, half a mile distant from each other; from one of which three men came in a canoe merely to look at us, and having done so returned home. At eight miles we came to the lower point of an island [Bachelor's; Lewis' and Lake rivers empty here], separated from the right side by a narrow channel, on which, a short distance above the end of the island, is situated a large village. It is built more compactly than the generality of the Indian villages, and the front has 14 houses, which are ranged for a quarter of a mile along the channel. As soon as we were discovered seven canoes came out to see us, and after some traffic, during which they seemed well disposed and orderly, accompanied us a short distance below. The river here again widens to the space of a mile and a half. As we descended we soon observed, behind a sharp [Warrior] point of rocks, a channel [Willamette slough] a quarter of a mile wide, which we suppose must be the one taken by the canoes yesterday on leaving Image-canoe island. A mile below this channel are some low cliffs of rocks [left, between St. Helen's and Columbia City, Ore.], near which is a large island on the right side [shoals and jetty there now], and two small islands a little further on [Burke's and Martin's, below Maxwell's point]. Here we met two canoes ascending the river. At this place the shore on the right becomes bold and rocky, and the bank is bordered by a range of high hills covered with a thick growth of pine; on the other side is an extensive low [Deer] island, separated from the left side by a narrow channel [Deer Island slough].

Here we stopped to dine, and found the island open, with an abundant growth of grass, and a number of ponds well supplied with fowls; at the lower extremity are the remains of an old village. We procured a swan, several ducks, and a brant, and saw some deer on the island. Besides this island, the lower extremity of which is [less than] 17 miles from the channel just mentioned, we passed two or three smaller ones in the same distance [as already said]. Here the hills on the right retire from the river, leaving a high plain, between which, on the left bank, a range of high hills, running southeast and covered with pine, forms a bold and rocky shore. At the distance of six miles, however, these hills again return and close the river on both sides.

We proceeded on [past Kalama], and at four miles reached a creek on the right, about 20 yards in width, immediately below which is an old village. Three miles further, at the distance of 32 miles from our camp of last night, we halted under a point of highland, with thick pine trees, on the left bank of the river [opposite Carroll's bluff]. Before landing we met two canoes, the largest of which had at the bow the image of a bear, and that of a man on the stern. There were 26 Indians on board, but they all proceeded upward, and we were left, for the first time since we reached the waters of the Columbia, without any of the natives during the night. Besides the game already mentioned, we killed a grouse much larger than the common size, and observed along the shore a number of striped snakes.

The river is here deep, and about a mile and a half in width. Here too the ridge of low mountains [Coast range] running northwest and southeast crosses the river, and forms the western boundary of the plain through which we have just passed. This great plain or valley begins above the mouth of Quicksand river, and is about 60 miles wide in a straight line, while on the right and left it extends to a great distance. It is a fertile and delightful country, shaded by thick groves of tall timber, watered by small ponds, and running on both sides of the river. The soil is rich and capable of any species of culture; but in the present condition of the Indians, its chief production is the wappatoo-root, which grows spontaneously and exclusively in this region. Sheltered as it is on both sides, the temperature is much milder than that of the surrounding country; for even at this season of the year we observe very little appearance of frost. During its whole extent it is inhabited by numerous tribes of Indians, who either reside in it permanently, or visit its waters in quest of fish and wappatoo-roots. We gave it the name of the [Wappatoo or] Columbia valley.

November 6th. The morning was cool, wet, and rainy. We proceeded at an early hour between the high hills on both sides of the river, till at the distance of four miles we came to two tents of Indians in a small plain on the left [Rainier], where the hills on the right recede a few miles from the river, and a long narrow island stretches along the right shore. Behind this island is the mouth of a large river, 150 yards wide, called by the Indians Coweliske. We halted for dinner on the island, but the redwood and green-briar are so interwoven with pine, alder, ash, a species of beech, and other trees, that the woods form a thicket, which our hunters could not penetrate. Below the mouth of the Coweliske a very remarkable knob rises from the water's edge to the height of 80 feet, being 200 paces round the base; as it is in a low part of the island, at some distance from the high grounds, its appearance is very singular [Mt. Coffin].

On setting out after dinner we overtook two canoes going down to trade; one of the Indians, who spoke a few words of English,

Fur Traders on the Missouri Attacked by Indians

mentioned that the principal person who traded with them was a Mr. Haley; and he showed a bow of iron and several other things, which he said Mr. Haley had given him. Nine miles below that river is a creek on the same [side]; and between them are three smaller islands, one on the left shore, the other [Walker's] about the middle of the river, and a third [Fisher's] near the lower end of the long narrow island, opposite a high cliff of black rocks on the left, 16 miles from our camp. Here we were overtaken by the Indians from the two tents we passed in the morning, from whom we now purchased wappatoo-roots, salmon, trout, and two beaver-skins, for which last we gave five small fish-hooks. At these cliffs [Green's point] the mountains, which had continued high and rugged on the left, retired from the river, and as the hills on the other side had left the water at the Coweliske, a beautiful extensive plain now presented itself before us. For a few miles we passed alongside an island [Grim's] a mile in width and three miles long, below which is a smaller island [Gull]. Here the high rugged hills, thickly covered with timber, border the right bank of the river and terminate the low grounds. These were supplied with common rushes, grass, and nettles in the moister parts with the bulrushes and flags, and along the water's edge with willows. Here also were two ancient villages, now abandoned by their inhabitants, of whom no vestige remains, except two small dogs, almost starved, and a prodigious quantity of fleas. After crossing the plain and [thus] making five miles, we proceeded through the hills for eight miles [passing Wallace's island]. The river is about a mile in width, and the hills are so steep that we could not for several miles find a place sufficiently flat to suffer us to sleep in a level position; at length, by removing some large stones, we cleared a place fit for our purpose above the reach of the tide, and after a journey of 29 miles slept among the smaller stones under a mountain to the right [one mile below Cape Horn]. The weather was rainy during the whole day; we therefore made large fires to dry our bedding and to kill the fleas, which have accumulated upon us at every old village we have passed.

November 7th. The morning was rainy, and the fog so thick that we could not see across the river. We observed, however, opposite our camp, the upper point of an island [Puget's], between which and the steep hills on the right we proceeded for five miles [site of Cathlamet]. Three miles lower is the beginning of an island separated from the right shore by a narrow channel; down this we proceeded under the direction of some Indians, whom we had just met going up the river, and who returned in order to show us their village. It consists of four houses only, situated on this channel behind several marshy islands formed by two small creeks. On our arrival they gave us some fish, and we afterward purchased some wappatoo-roots, fish, three dogs, and two otter-skins, for which we gave fish-hooks chiefly, that being an article of which they are very fond.

These people seem to be of a different nation from those we have just passed; they are low in stature, ill shaped, and all have their heads flattened. They call themselves Wahkiacum, and their language differs from that of the tribes above, with whom they trade for wappatoo-roots. The houses are built in a different style, being raised entirely above ground, with the eaves about five feet high and the door at the corner. Near the end, opposite this door, is a single fireplace, round which are the beds, raised four feet from the floor of earth; over the fire are hung the fresh fish, which, when dried, are stowed away with the wappatoo-roots under the beds. The dress of the men is like that of the people above, but the women are clad in a peculiar manner, the robe not reaching lower than the hip, and the body being covered in cold weather by a sort of corset of fur, curiously plaited and reaching from the arms to the hip; added to this is a sort of petticoat, or rather tissue of white cedar bark, bruised or broken into small strands, and woven into a girdle by several cords of the same material. Being tied round the middle, these strands hang down as low as the knee in front, and to the mid-leg behind; they are of sufficient thickness to answer the purpose of concealment whilst the female stands in an erect position, but in any other attitude form but a very ineffectual defense. Sometimes the tissue is strings of silk-grass, twisted and knotted at the end.

After remaining with them about an hour, we proceeded down the channel with an Indian dressed in a sailor's jacket for our pilot, and on reaching the main channel were visited by some Indians who have a temporary residence on a marshy [Tenasillihee] island in the middle of the river, where is a great abundance of water-fowl. Here the mountainous country again approaches the river on the left, and a higher [Saddle] mountain is distinguished toward the southwest. At a distance of 20 miles from our camp we halted at a village of Wahkiacums, consisting of seven ill-looking houses, built in the same form with those above, and situated at the foot of the high hills on the right, behind two small marshy islands. We merely stopped to purchase some food and two beaver-skins, and then proceeded. Opposite to these islands the hills on the left retire, and the river widens into a kind of bay crowded with low islands, subject to be overflowed occasionally by the tide.

We had not gone far from this village when the fog cleared off, and we enjoyed the delightful prospect of the ocean—that ocean, the object of all our labors, the reward of all our anxieties. This cheering view exhilarated the spirits of all the party, who were still more delighted on hearing the distant roar of the breakers. We went on with great cheerfulness under the high mountainous country which continued along the right bank [passing Three Tree and Jim Crow points]; the shore was, however, so bold and rocky that we could not, until after going 14 miles from the last village, find any spot fit for a camp [opposite Pillar Rock]. At that distance, having made during the day 34 miles, we spread our mats on the ground, and passed the night in the rain. Here we were joined by our small canoe, which had been separated from us during the fog this morning. Two Indians from the last village also accompanied us to the camp; but, having detected them in stealing a knife, they were sent off.

November 8th. It rained this morning, and having changed the clothing which had been wet during yesterday's rain, we did not set out till nine o'clock. Immediately opposite our camp is a [Pillar] rock at the distance of [half] a mile in the river, about 20 feet in diameter and 50 in height; toward the southwest are some high mountains, one of which is covered with snow at the top. We proceeded past several low islands in the bay or bend to the left of the river, which is here five or six miles wide. We were here overtaken by three Indians in a canoe, who had salmon to sell. On the right side we passed an old village, and then, at the distance of three miles, entered an inlet [rounding Yellow bluffs], or niche, about six miles across, making a deep bend of nearly five miles into the hills on the right shore, where it receives the waters of several creeks. We coasted along this inlet, which, from its little depth, we called Shallow bay; and at the bottom of it halted to dine near the remains of an old village, from which, however, we kept at a cautious distance, as it was occupied by great numbers of fleas. At this place we observed a number of fowl, among which we killed a goose, and two ducks exactly resembling in appearance and flavor the canvasback duck of the Susquehannah. After dinner the three Indians left us. We then took advantage of the returning tide to go on about three miles to a point on the right, eight miles [direct] distant from our camp; but here the waves ran so high, and dashed about our canoes so much that several of the men became seasick. It was therefore judged imprudent to go on in the present state of the weather, and we landed at the point [Gray's; Cape Swell of Gass]. The situation was extremely uncomfortable; the high hills jutted in so closely that there was not room for us to lie level, or to secure our baggage free from the tide, and the water of the river was too salt to be used; but the waves increased every moment so much that we could not move from the spot with safety. We therefore fixed ourselves on the beach left by the ebb tide, and having raised the baggage on poles, passed a disagreeable night, the rain during the day having wet us completely, as indeed we have been for some days.

November 9th. Fortunately for us, the tide did not rise as high as our camp during the night; but being accompanied by high winds from the south, the canoes, which we could not place beyond its reach, were filled with water, and were saved with much difficulty. Our position was very uncomfortable, but as it was impossible to move from it, we waited for a change of weather. It rained, however, during the whole day, and at two o'clock in the afternoon the flood tide set in, accompanied by a high wind from the south, which, about four o'clock, shifted to the southwest and blew almost a gale directly from the sea. The immense waves now broke over the place where we were camped; the large trees, some of them five or six feet thick, which had lodged at the point, were drifted over our camp, and the utmost vigilance of every man could scarcely save our canoes from being crushed to pieces. We remained in the water, and drenched with rain, during the rest of the day, our only food being some dried fish and some rainwater which we caught. Yet, though wet and cold, and some of them sick from using salt water, the men were cheerful, and full of anxiety to see more of the ocean. The rain continued all night.

Sunday, November 10th. This morning the wind lulled, and the waves not being so high, we loaded our canoes and proceeded. The mountains on the right are high, covered with timber, chiefly pine, and descend in a bold and rocky shore to the water. We went through a deep niche and several inlets on the right [past Cementville and Cliff Point], while on the opposite side is a large bay, above which the hills are close on the river. At the distance of ten miles the wind rose from the northwest, and the waves became so high that we were forced to return for two miles to a place where we could with safety unload. Here we landed at the mouth of a small run, and, having placed our baggage on a pile of drifted logs, waited until low water. The river then appeared more calm; we therefore started, but after going a mile found the waves too high for our canoes, and were obliged to put to shore. We unloaded the canoes; and having placed the baggage on a rock above the reach of the tide, camped on some drift-logs, which formed the only place where we could lie, the hills rising steep over our heads to the height of 500 feet. All our baggage, as well as ourselves, were thoroughly wet with the rain, which did not cease during the day; it continued violently during the night, in the course of which the tide reached the logs on which we lay, and set them afloat.

November 11th. The wind was still high from the southwest, and drove the waves against the shore with great fury; the rain too fell in torrent, and not only drenched us to the skin, but loosened the stones on the hillside, which then came rolling down upon us. In this comfortless situation we remained all day, wet, cold, with nothing but dried fish to satisfy our hunger; the canoes in one place at the mercy of the waves, the baggage in another, and all the men scattered on floating logs, or sheltering themselves in the crevices of the rocks and hillsides. A hunter was dispatched in hopes of finding some fresh meat; but the hills were so steep, and so covered with undergrowth and fallen timber, that he could not penetrate them, and he was forced to return. About twelve o'clock we were visited by five Indians in a canoe; they came from [Warren's Landing] above this place, on the opposite side of the river; their language much resembles that of the Wahkiacums, and they call themselves Cathlamahs. In person they are small, ill made, and badly clothed; though one of them had on a sailor's round jacket and pantaloons, which, as he explained by signs, he had received from the whites below the point. We purchased from them 13 red char, a fish which we found very excellent. After some time they went aboard the boat and crossed the river, which is here five miles wide, through a very heavy sea.

November 12th. About three o'clock a tremendous gale of wind arose, accompanied with lightning, thunder, and hail; at six it became light for a short time, but a violent rain soon began and lasted during the day. During this storm one of our boats, secured by being sunk with great quantities of stone, got loose; but, drifting against a rock, was recovered without having received much injury. Our situation became now much more dangerous, for the waves were driven with fury against the rocks and trees, which till now had afforded us refuge. We therefore took advantage of a low tide, and moved about half a mile round a point to a small brook, which we had not observed till now on account of the thick bushes and driftwood which concealed its mouth. Here we were more safe; but still cold and wet, our clothes and bedding rotten as well as wet, our baggage at a distance, and the canoes—our only means of escape from this place—at the mercy of the waves. We were, however, fortunate enough to enjoy good health, and even had the luxury of getting some fresh salmon and three salmon-trout in the brook. Three of the men [Gibson, Bratton, Willard] attempted to go round a point in our small Indian canoe, but the high waves rendered her quite unmanageable—these boats requiring the seamanship of the natives themselves to make them live in so rough a sea.

November 13th. During the night we had short intervals of fair weather, but it began to rain in the morning and continued through the day. In order to obtain a view of the country below, Captain Clark followed up the course of the brook, and with much fatigue, after walking three miles, ascended the first spur of the mountains. The whole lower country was covered with almost impenetrable thickets of small pine,

with which is mixed a species of plant resembling arrow-wood, 12 or 15 feet high,
with a thorny stem, almost interwoven with
each other, and scattered among the fern
and fallen timber. There is also a red berry,
somewhat like the Solomon's seal, which is
called by the natives solme, and used as an
article of diet. This thick growth rendered
traveling almost impossible, and it was made
more fatiguing by the steepness of the mountain, which was so great as to oblige him to
draw himself up by means of the bushes.
The timber on the hills is chiefly of a large
tall species of pine, many of them 8 or 10
feet in diameter at the stump, and rising
sometimes more than 100 feet in height.
The hail which fell two nights since is still
to be seen on the mountains. There was no
game, and no trace of any, except some old
signs of elk. The cloudy weather prevented
his seeing to any distance; he therefore returned to camp, and sent three men in the
Indian canoe to try if they could double the
point [Ellice or Distress] and find some safer
harbor for our canoes. At every flood tide the
seas break in great swells against the rocks,
and drift the trees among our establishment,
so as to render it very insecure. We were confined as usual to dried fish, which is our last
resource.

November 14th. It rained without intermission during last night; to-day the wind
too was very high, and one of our canoes was
much injured by being dashed against rocks.
Five Indians from below came to us in a
canoe, and three of them, having landed, informed us that they had seen the men sent
down yesterday. At this moment one of them
[Colter] arrived, and informed us that these
Indians had stolen his gig and basket. We
therefore ordered the two women who remained in the canoe to restore them; but
this they refused, till we threatened to shoot,
when they gave back the articles, and we
then ordered them to leave us. They were of
the Wahkiacum nation. The man [Colter]
now informed us that they had gone round
the point as far as the high sea would suffer
them in the canoe, and then landed; that in
the night he had separated from his companions, who had gone further down, and
that at no great distance from where we are
is a beautiful sand-beach and a good harbor.
Captain Lewis concluded to examine more
minutely the lower part of the bay [Haley's];
taking one of the large canoes he was landed
at the point [Ellice], whence he proceeded
by land with four men, and the canoe returned nearly filled with water.

November 15th. It continued raining all
night, but in the morning the weather became calm and fair. We therefore began to
prepare for setting out; but before we were
ready a high wind sprang up from the southeast, and obliged us to remain. The sun
shone until one o'clock, and we were thus
enabled to dry our bedding and examine
our baggage. The rain, which has continued
for the last ten days without an interval of
more than two hours, has completely wet all
our merchandise, spoiled some of our fish,
destroyed the robes and rotted nearly half
of our few remaining articles of clothing,
particularly the leather dresses. About three
o'clock the wind fell; we instantly loaded the
canoes, and left the miserable spot to which
we have been confined the last six days. On
turning the point we came to the sand-
beach, through which runs a small stream
from the hills; at the mouth of this is an
ancient [Chinook] village of 36 houses,
which has at present no inhabitants except
fleas.

Here we met Shannon, who had been sent
back to meet us by Captain Lewis. The day
Shannon left us in the canoe, he and Willard

proceeded till they met a party of 20 Indians, who, having never heard of us, did not know where they [our men] came from; they, however, behaved with so much civility, and seemed so anxious that the men should go with them toward the sea, that their suspicions were excited, and they declined going on. The Indians, however, would not leave them; the men being confirmed in their suspicions, and fearful that if they went into the woods to sleep they would be cut to pieces in the night, thought it best to pass the night in the midst of the Indians. They therefore made a fire, and after talking with them to a late hour, laid down with their rifles under the heads. As they awoke that morning they found that the Indians had stolen and concealed their guns. Having demanded then in vain, Shannon seized a club, and was about assaulting one of the Indians, whom he suspected as a thief, when another Indian began to load a fowling-piece with the intention of shooting him. He therefore stopped, and explained by signs that if they did not give up the guns a large party would come down the river before the sun rose to such a height, and put every one of them to death. Fortunately, Captain Lewis and his party appeared at this time. The terrified Indians immediately brought the guns, and five of them came on with Shannon. To these men we declared that if ever anyone of their nation stole anything from us, he should be instantly shot. They reside to the north of this place, and speak a language different from that of the people higher up the river.

It was now apparent that the sea was at all times too rough for us to proceed further down the bay by water. We therefore landed, and having chosen the best spot we could select, made our camp of boards from

Chinook Indians. *George Catlin*

the old [Chinook] village. We were now situated comfortably, and being visited by four Wahkiacums with wappatoo-roots, were enabled to make an agreeable addition to our food.

November 16th. The morning was clear and beautiful. We therefore put out all our baggage to dry, and sent several of the party to hunt. Our camp is in full view of the ocean, on the bay laid down by Vancouver, which we distinguish by the name of Haley's bay, from a trader who visits the Indians here, and is a great favorite among them. The meridian altitude of this day gave 46° 19′ 11″ 7‴ as the latitude of our camp. The wind was strong from the southwest, and the waves were very high; yet the Indians were passing up and down the bay in canoes, and several of them camped near us. We smoked with them, but after our recent experience of their thievish disposition treated them with caution. Though so much exposed to the bad weather, none of the party have suffered, except one, who has a violent cold, in consequence of sleeping for several nights in wet leather. The hunters brought in two deer, a crane, some geese and ducks, and several brant, three of which [snow-geese] were white, except a black part of the wing, and much larger than the gray brant, which is itself a size beyond the duck.

Sunday, November 17th. A fair, cool morning and an easterly wind. The tide rises at this place 8½ feet, and rolls over the beach in great waves.

About one o'clock Captain Lewis returned, after having coasted down Haley's bay to Cape Disappointment, and some distance to the north along the seacoast. He was followed by several Chinnooks among whom were the principal chief and his family. They made us a present of a boiled root, very much like the common licorice in taste

and size, called culwhamo; in return we gave double the value of their present, and now learned the danger of accepting anything from them, since no return, even if ten times the value of their gift, can satisfy them. We were chiefly occupied in hunting, and were able to procure three deer, four brant, and two ducks, and also saw some signs of elk. Captain Clark now prepared for an excursion down the bay, and accordingly started [by land],

November 18th, accompanied by 11 men. He proceeded along the beach one mile to a point of rocks about 40 feet high, where the hills retire, leaving a wide beach [White's Point] and a number of ponds covered with water-fowl, between which and the mountain is a narrow bottom of alder and small balsam trees. Seven miles from the rocks is the entrance of a creek, or rather a drain, from the ponds and hills, where is a cabin of Chinnooks. The cabin contained some children, and four women, one of whom was in a most miserable state, covered with ulcers, proceeding, as we imagine, from venereal disease, with which several of the Chinnooks we have seen appear to be afflicted. We were taken across in a canoe by two squaws, to each of whom we gave a fish-hook, and then, coasting along the bay, passed at two miles the low bluff of a small hill, below which are the ruins of some old huts, and close to it the remains of a whale. The country is low, open, and marshy, interspersed with some high pine and a thick undergrowth. Five miles from the creek we came to a stream 40 yards wide at low water, which we called Chinnook river. The hills up this river and toward the bay are not high, but very thickly covered with large pine of several species; in many places pine trees, three or four feet in thickness, are seen growing on the bodies of large trees, which, though fallen and covered with moss, were in part sound. Here we dined on some brant and plover, killed as we came along, and after crossing in a boat lying in the sand near some old houses, proceeded along a bluff of yellow clay and soft stone to a little bay or harbor, into which a drain from some ponds empties. At this harbor the land is low, but as we went on it rose to hills of 80 or 90 feet above the water. At the distance of one mile is a second bay, and a mile beyond it a small, rocky island in a deep bend, which seems to afford a very good harbor, where the natives inform us European vessels anchor for the purpose of trading. We went on around another bay, in which is a second small island of rocks, and crossed a small stream, which rises in a pond near the seacoast, and after running through a low isthmus [Fort Canby here] empties into the bay. This narrow, low ground, about 200 or 300 yards wide, separates from the main hills a kind of peninsula, the extremity of which is two miles from the anchoring place.

This spot, which was called Cape Disappointment, is an elevated, circular knob, rising with a steep ascent 150 or 160 feet above the water, formed like the whole shore of the bay, as well as of the seacoast, and covered with thick timber on the inner side, but open and grassy in the exposure next to the sea. From this cape a high point of land bears S. 20° W., about 25 miles distant. In the range between these two eminences is the opposite point of the bay, a very low ground, which has been variously called Cape Rond by Lapeyrouse, and Point Adams by Vancouver. The water for a great distance off the mouth of the river appears very shallow, and within the mouth nearest to Point Adams is a large sand-bar, almost covered at high tide. We could not ascertain the direction of the deepest channel, for

the waves break with tremendous force the whole distance across the bay; but the Indians point nearer to the opposite side as the best passage. After remaining some time on this elevation, we descended across the low isthmus, and reached the ocean at the foot of a high hill [McKenzie head], about a mile in circumference, projecting into the sea. We crossed this hill, which is open and has a growth of high coarse grass, and camped on the north side of it, having made 19 miles. Besides the pounded fish and brant, we had for supper a flounder, which we picked up on the beach.

November 19th. In the night it began to rain and continued till eleven o'clock. Two hunters were sent on to kill something for breakfast, and the rest of the party, after drying their blankets, soon followed. At three miles we overtook the hunters and breakfasted on a small deer which they had been fortunate enough to kill. This, like all those we have seen on this coast, are much darker than our common deer. Their bodies, too, are deeper, their legs shorter, and their eyes larger. The branches of the horns are similar, but the upper part of the tail is black, from the root to the end; and they do not leap, but jump like sheep frightened.

We then continued over rugged hills and steep hollows near the sea, on a course about N. 20° W., in a direct line from the cape till at the distance of five miles we reached a point of high land; below which a sandy beach extends, in a direction N. 10° W., to another high point about twenty miles distant. This eminence we distinguished by the name of Point Lewis. It is there that the highlands, which at the commencement of the sandy beach recede toward Chinnook river, again approach the ocean. The intermediate country is low, with many small ponds, crowded with birds and watered by the Chinnook, on the borders of which resides the nation of the same name. We went four miles along the sandy beach to a small pine-tree, on which Captain Clark marked his name, with the year and day, and then returned to the foot of the hills, passing on the shore a sturgeon ten feet long, and several joints of the backbone of a whale, both of which seem to have been thrown ashore and foundered. After dining on the remains of the small deer, we crossed in a southeastern direction to the [Haley's] bay, where we arrived at the distance of two miles [at Ilwaco]; then we continued along the bay, crossed Chinnook [Wallacut] river, and camped on its upper side in a sandy bottom.

November 20th. It rained in the course of the night. A hunter [Labiche], dispatched early to kill some food, returned with eight ducks, of which we breakfasted, and then followed the course of the bay to the [present Chinook] creek or outlet of the ponds. It was now high tide, the stream 300 yards wide, and no person in the cabin to take us across. We therefore made a small raft, on which one of the men passed and brought a canoe to carry us over. As we went along the beach we were overtaken by several Indians, who gave us dried sturgeon and wappatoo-roots, and soon met several parties of Chinnooks returning from the camp. When we arrived there we found many Chinnooks; two of them being chiefs, we went through the ceremony of giving to each a medal, and to the most distinguished a flag. Their names were Comcommoly and Chil-

lahlawil. One of the Indians had a robe made of two sea-otter skins, the fur of which was the most beautiful we had ever seen. The owner at first resisted every temptation to part with it, but at length could not resist the offer of a belt of blue beads which Chaboneau's wife wore around her waist. During our absence the camp had been visited by many Indians, and the men who had been employed in hunting killed several deer and a variety of wild fowls.

November 21st. The morning was cloudy, and from noon till night it rained. The wind was high from the southeast, and the sea so rough that the water reached our camp. Most of the Chinnooks returned home; but we were visited in the course of the day by people of different bands in the neighborhood, among whom are the Chiltz, a nation residing on the seacoast near Point Lewis, and the Clatsops, who live immediately opposite [us], on the south side of the Columbia. A chief from the grand rapid also came to see us, and we gave him a medal. To each of our visitors we made a present of a small piece of ribbon, and purchased some cranberries and some articles of their manufacture, such as mats and household furniture, for all which we paid high prices. After we had been relieved from these Indians, we were surprised at a visit of a different kind. An old woman, the wife of a Chinnook chief, came with six young women, her daughters and nieces, and having deliberately camped near us, proceeded to cultivate an intimacy between our men and her fair wards.

5. The Journey to Pike's Peak

BY ZEBULON MONTGOMERY PIKE

EDITOR'S NOTE: Zebulon Montgomery Pike (1779-1813), the discoverer of Pike's Peak in Colorado, was twenty-six years old when he was chosen to lead an expedition to explore the upper Mississippi region of the Louisiana Purchase. On his return to St. Louis in April 1806 he was almost immediately sent to head a second expedition, this one to explore the territory west and southwest of St. Louis as far as the headwaters of the Arkansas and Red Rivers. This new expedition was required to move into Spanish territory, as is seen in the following account. The purpose of sending Pike into Spanish territory is not clear, although it has sometimes been surmised that his mission was to win the territory for the United States, as well as to treat with Indian tribes.

In the selection I have chosen from Pike's account of his expedition his party travels from a Pawnee village through Kansas and Colorado to Pike's Peak. Pike ascended the Arkansas River through the Royal Gorge and there first saw the mountain named in his honor, in November 1806. It was first climbed in 1819 by the exploring party under Major S. H. Long. Pike eventually made his way to the Rio Grande, where he became a prisoner of the Spanish for a while. They treated him with consideration. He was killed in the War of 1812 while leading an attack against Toronto (then known as York), Canada.

The account which follows is that of the standard edition of Pike's report, Elliott Coues' edition of 1895, based on the original edition of 1810. I have omitted Coues' footnotes.

WEDNESDAY, *Oct. 1st*. Paid a visit to town* and had a very long conversation with the chief, who urged everything in his power to induce us to turn back. Finally, he very candidly told us that the Spaniards wished to have gone further into our country, but he induced them to give up the idea; that they had listened to him and he wished us to do the same; that he had promised the Spaniards to act as he now did, and that we must proceed no further, or he must stop us by force of arms. My reply was, "that I had been sent out by our great father to explore the western country, to visit all his red children, to make peace between them, and turn them from shedding blood; that he might see how I had caused the Osage and Kans to meet to smoke the pipe of peace together, and take each other by the hand like brothers; that as yet my road had been smooth, with a blue sky over our heads. I had not seen any blood in our path; but he must know that the young warriors of his great American father were not women, to be turned back by words; that I should therefore proceed, and if he thought proper to stop me, he could attempt it; but we were men, well armed, and would sell our lives at a dear rate to his nation; that we knew our great father would send his young warriors there to gather our bones and revenge our deaths on his people, when our spirits would rejoice in hearing our exploits sung in the war-songs of our chiefs." I then left his lodge and returned to camp, in considerable perturbation of mind.

Oct. 2d. We received advice from our Kans that the chief had given publicity to his idea of stopping us by force of arms,

* Pawnee Village

which gave serious reflections to me, and was productive of many singular expressions from my brave lads, which called for my esteem at the same time that they excited my laughter. Attempted to trade for horses, but could not succeed. In the night we were alarmed by some savages coming near our camp at full speed; but they retreated equally rapidly, on being hailed with fierceness by our sentinels. This created some degree of indignation in my little band, as we had noticed that all the day had passed without any traders presenting themselves, which appeared as if all intercourse was interdicted. I wrote to the secretary at war, the general, etc.

Oct. 3d. The intercourse again commenced. Traded for some horses, and wrote for my express.

Oct. 4th. Two French traders arrived at the village in order to procure horses to transport their goods from the Missouri to the village. They gave us information that Captains Lewis and Clark, with all their people, had descended the river to St. Louis; this diffused general joy through our party. Our trade for horses advanced none this day.

Sunday, Oct. 5th. Buying horses. Preparing to march, and finishing my letters.

Oct. 6th. Marched my express. Purchasing horses and preparing to march on the morrow.

Oct. 7th. In the morning we found two of our newly purchased horses missing. Sent in search of them; the Indians brought in one pretty early. Struck our tents and commenced loading our horses. Finding there was no probability of our obtaining the other lost one, we marched at 2 p. m.; and as the chief had threatened to stop us by force of arms, we made every arrangement to make him pay as dearly for the at-

tempt as possible. The party was kept compact, and marched by a road round the village, in order that, if attacked, the savages would not have their houses to fly to for cover. I had given orders not to fire until within five or six paces, and then to charge with the bayonet and saber, when I believe it would have cost them at least 100 men to have exterminated us, which would have been necessary. The village appeared all to be in motion. I galloped up to the lodge of the chief, attended by my interpreter and one soldier, but soon saw there was no serious attempt to be made, although many young men were walking about with their bows, arrows, guns, and lances. After speaking to the chief with apparent indifference, I told him that I calculated on his justice in obtaining the horse, and that I should leave a man until the next day at twelve o'clock to bring him out. We then joined the party and pursued our route.

When I was once on the summit of the hill which overlooks the village, I felt my mind relieved from a heavy burden; yet all the evil I wished the Pawnees was that I might be the instrument, in the hands of our government, to open their ears and eyes with a strong hand, to convince them of our power.

Our party now consisted of two officers, one doctor, 18 soldiers, one interpreter, three Osage men, and one woman, making 25 warriors. We marched out and encamped on a small branch [of Rock creek], distant seven miles, on the same route we came in. Rain in the night.

Oct. 8th. I conceived it best to send Baroney back to the village with a present, to be offered for our horse, the chief having suggested the propriety of this measure; he met his son and the horse with Sparks. Marched at ten o'clock, and at four o'clock

Pawnee Indians. *George Catlin*

came to the place where the Spanish troops encamped the first night they left the Pawnee village. Their encampment was circular, having only small fires round the circle to cook by. We counted 59 fires; now if we allow six men to each fire, they must have been 354 in number. We encamped on a large branch of the second [Solomon's] fork on the Kans river. Distance 18 miles.

Oct. 9th. Marched at eight o'clock, being detained until that time by our horses being at a great distance. At eleven o'clock we found the forks of the Spanish and Pawnee roads, and when we halted at twelve o'clock, we were overtaken by the second chief, Iskatappe, and the American chief with one-third of the village. They presented us with a piece of bear-meat.

When we were about to march, we discovered that the dirk of the doctor had been stolen from behind the saddle. After march-ing the men, the doctor and myself, with the interpreter, went to the chief and demanded that he should cause a search to be made; it was done, but when the dirk was found, the possessor asserted that he had found it on the road. I told him that he did not speak the truth, and informed the chief that we never suffered a thing of ever so little value to be taken without liberty. At this time the prairie was covered with his men, who began to encircle us around, and Lieutenant Wilkinson with the troops had gained half a mile on the road. The Indian demanded a knife before he would give it up; but as we refused to give any, the chief took one from his belt and gave him, took the dirk and presented it to the doctor, who immediately returned it to the chief as a present, desired Baroney to inform him he now saw it was not the value of the article but the act we despised, and then galloped off.

In about a mile we discovered a herd of elk, which we pursued; they took back in sight of the Pawnees, who immediately mounted 50 or 60 young men and joined in the pursuit. Then, for the first time in my life, I saw animals slaughtered by the true savages with their original weapons, bows and arrows; they buried the arrow up to the plume in the animal. We took a piece of meat and pursued our party; we overtook them and encamped within the Grand or Solomon Fork, which we had crossed lower down on the 23d of September, on our route to the Pawnees. This was the Spanish encamping ground. Distance 18 miles.

In the evening two Pawnees came to our camp, who had not eaten for three days, two of which they had carried a sick companion whom they had left this day; we gave them for supper some meat and corn, and they immediately departed in order to carry their sick companion this seasonable supply. When they were coming into camp, the sentinel challenged, it being dark; they immediately, on seeing him bring his piece to the charge, supposing he was about to fire on them, advanced to give him their hands; he, however, not well discerning their motions, was on the point of firing; but being a cool, collected little fellow, called out that there were two Indians advancing on him, and asked if he should fire. This brought out the guard, when the poor affrighted savages were brought into camp, very much alarmed, for they had not heard of a white man's being in their country, and thought they were entering one of the camps of their own people.

Oct. 10th. Marched at seven o'clock and halted at twelve o'clock to dine. Were overtaken by the Pawnee chief whose party we left the day before, who informed us the hunting-party had taken another road, and that he had come to bid us good-by. We left a large ridge on our left, and at sundown crossed it. . . . From this place we had an extensive view of the southwest; we observed a creek at a distance, to which I meant to proceed. The doctor, interpreter, and myself arrived at eight o'clock at night; found water and wood, but had nothing to eat. Kindled a fire in order to guide the party; but they, not being able to find the route and not knowing the distance, encamped on the prairie without wood or water.

Oct. 11th. Ordered Baroney to return to find the party and conduct them to our camp. The doctor and myself went out to hunt, and on our return found all our people had arrived, except the rear-guard, which was in sight. Whilst we halted five Pawnees came to our camp and brought some bones of a horse which the Spanish troops had been obliged to eat at their encampment on this creek. We took up our line of march at twelve o'clock, and at sundown the party halted on the Saline. I was in pursuit of buffalo, and did not make the camp until near ten o'clock at night. Killed one buffalo. Distance 12 miles.

Sunday, Oct. 12th. Here Belle Oiseau and one Osage left us, and there remained only one man and woman of that nation. Their reason for leaving us was that our course bore too much west, and they desired to bear more for the hunting-ground of the Osage. In the morning we sent out to obtain the buffalo meat, and laid by until after breakfast. Proceeded at eleven o'clock; and crossing the [Grand Saline] river two or three times, we passed two camps where the Spanish troops had halted. Here they appeared to have remained some days, their roads being so much blended with the traces of the buffalo that we lost them entirely. This was a mortifying stroke, as we had reason to calculate that they had good guides, and were on the best route for wood and water. We took a southwest direction, and before night were fortunate enough to strike their roads on the left; and at dusk, much to our surprise, struck the east [Smoky Hill] fork of the Kans, or La Touche de la Cote Bucanieus. Killed one buffalo. Distance 18 miles.

Oct. 13th. The day being rainy, we did not march until two o'clock; when, it having an appearance of clearing off, we raised our camp [and crossed the Smoky Hill river]; after which we marched seven miles and encamped on the head of a branch of the river we had left. Had to go two miles for water. Killed one cabrie.

Oct. 14th. It having drizzled rain all night, and the atmosphere being entirely obscured, we did not march until a quarter past nine o'clock, and commenced crossing the dividing ridge between the Kans and Arkansaw rivers. Arrived on a branch of the latter at one o'clock; continued down it in search of water until after dusk, when we found a pond on the prairie, which induced us to halt. Sparks did not come up, being scarcely able to walk with rheumatic pains. Wounded several buffalo, but could not get one of them. Distance 24 miles.

Oct. 15th. In the morning rode out in search of the south trace, and crossed the low prairie [Cheyenne Bottoms], which was nearly all covered with ponds, but could not discover it. Finding Sparks did not arrive, sent two men in search of him, who arrived with him about eleven o'clock. At twelve o'clock we commenced our line of march, and at five o'clock Dr. Robinson and myself left the party at a large [Walnut] creek, having pointed out a distant wood

to Lieutenant Wilkinson for our encampment, in order to search some distance up it for the Spanish trace. Killed two buffalo and left part of our clothing with them to scare away the wolves. Went in pursuit of the party. On our arrival at the [Little Walnut] creek appointed for the encampment, did not find them. Proceeded down it for some miles, and not finding them, encamped, struck fire, and then supped on one of our buffalo tongues.

Oct. 16th. Early on horseback; proceeded up the [Little Walnut] creek some distance in search of our party, but at twelve o'clock crossed to our two buffaloes; found a great many wolves at them, notwithstanding the precautions taken to keep them off. Cooked some marrow-bones and again mounted our horses, and proceeded down the creek to

Zebulon Montgomery Pike

their junction. Finding nothing of the party, I began to be seriously alarmed for their safety. Killed two more buffalo, made our encampment, and feasted sumptuously on the marrow-bones. Rain in the night.

Oct. 17th. Rose early, determining to search the [Little Walnut] creek to its source. Very hard rain, accompanied by a cold northwester all day. Encamped near night without being able to discover any signs of the party. Our sensations now became excruciating, not only for their personal safety, but for fear of the failure of the national objects intended to be accomplished by the expedition. Our own situation was not the most agreeable, not having more than four rounds of ammunition each, and being 400 miles in the nearest direction from the first civilized inhabitants. We, however, concluded to search for the party on the morrow, and if we did not succeed in finding them, to strike the Arkansaw, where we were in hopes to discover some traces, if not cut off by the savages.

Oct. 18th. Commenced our route at a good time, and about ten o'clock discovered two men on horseback in search of us — one my waiter. They informed us the party was encamped on the Arkansaw, about three miles south of where we then were; this surprised us very much, as we had no conception of that river being so near. On our arrival we were met by Lieutenant Wilkinson, who, with all the party, was greatly concerned for our safety. The Arkansaw, on the party's arrival, had not water in it six inches deep, and the stream was not more than 20 feet wide; but the rain of the two days covered all the bottom of the river, which in this place is 450 yards from bank to bank. These are not more than four feet in height, bordered by a few cottonwood

trees; on the north side is a low swampy prairie; on the south, a sandy sterile desert at a small distance. In the afternoon the doctor and myself took our horses and crossed the Arkansaw, in order to search for some trees which might answer the purpose to make canoes; found but one, and returned at dusk. It commenced raining at twelve o'clock.

Sunday, Oct. 19th. Finding the river rising rapidly, I thought it best to secure our passage over [from the N. to the S. bank]; we consequently made it good by ten o'clock. Rain all day. Preparing our tools and arms for labor and the chase on the morrow.

Oct. 20th. Commenced our labor at two trees for canoes, but one proved too much doated. Killed two buffalo and one cabrie. Discharged our guns at a mark, the best shot a prize of one tent and a pair of shoes. Our only dog was standing at the root of the tree, in the grass; one of the balls struck him on the head and killed him. Ceased raining about twelve o'clock.

Oct. 21st. Dr. Robinson and myself mounted our horses, in order to go down the river to the entrance of the three last creeks we had crossed on our route; but meeting with buffalo, we killed four; also, one cabrie. Returned to the camp and sent for the meat.

Oct. 22d. Having sat up very late last evening, expecting the sergeant and party, who did not arrive, we were very anxious for them; but about ten o'clock Bradley arrived and informed us that they could not find the buffalo which we had killed on the prairie. They all arrived before noon. In the afternoon we scaffolded some meat, and nearly completed the frame of a skin canoe, which we concluded to build.

Overhauled my instruments and made some rectifications preparatory to taking an observation, etc.

Oct. 23d. Dr. Robinson and myself, accompanied by one man, ascended the river with an intention of searching for the Spanish trace; at the same time we dispatched Baroney and our two hunters to kill some buffalo, to obtain the skins for canoes. We ascended the river about 20 miles to a large branch [Pawnee fork] on the right. Just at dusk gave chase to a buffalo and were obliged to shoot 19 balls into him before we killed him. Encamped on the fork [at Larned, Pawnee Co.].

Oct. 24th. We ascended the right branch [Pawnee fork] about five miles [old Fort Larned], but could not see any sign of the Spanish trace; this is not surprising, as the river bears southwest, and they no doubt kept more to the west from the head of one branch to another. We returned and on our way killed some prairie-squirrels, or wishtonwishes, and nine large rattlesnakes, which frequent their villages. On our arrival, found the hunters had come in a boat, one hour before, with two buffalo and one elk skin.

The wishtonwish of the Indians, prairie-dogs of some travelers, or squirrels, as I should be inclined to denominate them, reside on the prairies of Louisiana in towns or villages, having an evident police established in their communities. The sites of their towns are generally on the brow of a hill, near some creek or pond, in order to be convenient to water, and that the high ground which they inhabit may not be subject to inundation. Their residence, being under ground, is burrowed out, and the earth, which answers the double purpose of keeping out the water and affording an elevated place in wet seasons to repose

on, and to give them a further and more distinct view of the country. Their holes descend in a spiral form; therefore I could never ascertain their depth; but I once had 140 kettles of water poured into one of them in order to drive out the occupant, without effect. In the circuit of the villages they clear off all the grass, and leave the earth bare of vegetation; but whether it is from an instinct they possess inducing them to keep the ground thus cleared, or whether they make use of the herbage as food, I cannot pretend to determine. The latter opinion I think entitled to a preference, as their teeth designate them to be of the graminivorous species, and I know of no other substance which is produced in the vicinity of their positions on which they could subsist; and they never extend their excursions more than half a mile from the burrows. They are of a dark brown color, except their bellies, which are white. Their tails are not so long as those of our gray squirrels, but are shaped precisely like theirs; their teeth, head, nails, and body are the perfect squirrel, except that they are generally fatter than that animal. Their villages sometimes extend over two and three miles square, in which there must be innumerable hosts of them, as there is generally a burrow every ten steps in which there are two or more, and you see new ones partly excavated on all the borders of the town. We killed great numbers of them with our rifles and found them excellent meat, after they were exposed a night or two to the frost, by which means the rankness acquired by their subterraneous dwelling is corrected. As you approach their towns, you are saluted on all sides by the cry of "wishtonwish," from which they derive their name with the Indians, uttered in a shrill and piercing manner. You then observe

Crow Indians Attacking Buffalo with Lances.   *Alfred Jacob Miller*

them all retreating to the entrance of their burrows, where they post themselves, and regard every, even the slightest, movement that you make. It requires a very nice shot with a rifle to kill them, as they must be killed dead, for as long as life exists they continue to work into their cells. It is extremely dangerous to pass through their towns, as they abound with rattlesnakes, both of the yellow and black species; and strange as it may appear, I have seen the wishtonwish, the rattlesnake, the horn frog, with which the prairie abounds (termed by the Spaniards the cammellion [camaeleon, *i. e.,* chameleon], from their taking no visible sustenance), and a land-tortoise, all take refuge in the same hole. I do not pretend to assert that it was their common place of resort; but I have witnessed the above facts more than in one instance.

Oct. 25th. Took an observation; passed the day in writing, and preparing for the departure of Lieutenant Wilkinson.

Sunday, Oct. 26th. Delivered out a ration of corn by way of distinction of the Sabbath. Preparing for our departure.

Oct. 27th. Delivered to Lieutenant Wilkinson letters for the general and our friends, with other papers, consisting of his instructions, traverse tables of our voyage, and a draught of our route to that place complete, in order that if we were lost, and he arrived in safety, we might not have made the tour without some benefit to our country. He took with him, in corn and meat, 21 days' provisions, and all the necessary tools to build canoes or cabins. Launched his canoes. We concluded we would separate in the morning, he to descend [the river], and we to ascend to the mountains.

Oct. 28th. As soon as possible all was in motion, my party crossing the river to the north side, and Lieutenant Wilkinson launching his canoes of skins and wood. We breakfasted together, and then filed off; but I suffered my party to march, while I remained to see Lieutenant Wilkinson sail. This he did at ten o'clock, having one skin canoe, made of four buffalo skins and two elk skins, which held three men besides himself and one Osage. In his wooden canoe were one soldier, one Osage, and their baggage; one other soldier marched on shore. We parted with "God bless you" from both parties; they appeared to sail very well. In the pursuit of our party, Dr. Robinson, Baroney, one soldier, and myself, killed a brelau [blaireau, badger,] and a buffalo; of the latter we took only his marrow-bones and liver. Arrived where our men had encamped, about dusk. Distance 14 miles.

Oct. 29th. Marched after breakfast and in the first hour's march passed two fires, where 21 Indians had recently encamped, in which party, by their paintings on the rocks, there were seven guns. Killed a buffalo, halted, made fire, and feasted on the choice pieces of meat. About noon discovered two horses feeding with a herd of buffalo; we attempted to surround them, but they soon cleared our fleetest coursers. One appeared to be an elegant horse. These were the first wild horses we had seen. Two or three hours before night struck the Spanish road; and, as it was snowing, halted and encamped the party at the first woods on the bank of the river. The doctor and myself then forded it, the ice running very thick, in order to discover the course the Spaniards took; but owing to the many buffalo roads, could not ascertain it. It evidently appeared that they had halted here some time, as the ground was covered with horse-dung for miles around. Returned to camp. The snow fell about two inches deep, and then it cleared up. Distance 12 miles.

Oct. 30th. In the morning sent out to kill a buffalo, to have his marrow-bones for breakfast, which was accomplished. After breakfast the party marched up on the north side; the doctor and myself crossed with considerable difficulty, on account of the ice, to the Spanish camp, where we took a large circuit in order to discover the Spanish trace, and came in at a point of woods south of the river, where we found our party encamped. We discovered also that the Spanish troops had marked the river up [*i. e.,* left an up-river trail], and that a party of savages had been there not more than three days before. Killed two buffalo. Distance 4 miles. [Opposite Garfield, Pawnee Co., where Big Coon creek falls in.]

Oct. 31st. Fine day; marched at three quarters past nine o'clock, on the Spanish road. Encamped, sun an hour high, after having made 16 miles [opposite Kinsley, Edwards Co.].

We observed this day a species of crystallization on the road, when the sun was high, in low places where there had been water settled; on tasting it found it to be salt; this gave in my mind some authenticity to the report of the prairie being covered for leagues. Discovered the trace of about 20 savages who had followed our road; and of horses going down the river. Killed one buffalo, one elk, one deer.

Nov. 1st. Marched early; just after commencing our line, heard a gun on our left. The doctor, Baroney, and myself being in advance, and lying on the ground waiting for the party, a band of cabrie came up among our horses, to satisfy their curiosity; we could not resist the temptation of killing two, although we had plenty of meat. At the report of the gun they appeared astonished, and stood still until we hallowed [hallooed] at them to drive them away. Encamped in the evening on an island.

Upon using my glass to observe the adjacent country, I observed on the prairie a herd of horses. Dr. Robinson and Baroney accompanied me to go and view them; when within a quarter of a mile they discovered us, and came immediately up near us, making the earth tremble under them; this brought to my recollection a charge of cavalry. They stopped and gave us an opportunity to view them; among them there were some very beautiful bays, blacks, and grays, and indeed of all colors. We fired at a black horse, with an idea of creasing him, but did not succeed; they flourished round and returned again to see us, when we returned to camp.

Sunday, Nov. 2d. In the morning, for the purpose of trying the experiment, we equipped six of our fleetest coursers with riders and ropes, to noose the wild horses, if in our power to come among the band. They stood until we came within forty yards of them, neighing and whinneying, when the chase began, which we continued about two miles, without success. Two of our horses ran up with them; but we could not take them. Returned to camp. I have since laughed at our folly; for taking wild horses in that manner is scarcely ever attempted, even with the fleetest horses and most expert ropers. See my account of wild horses and the manner of taking them, in my dissertation on the province of Texas. Marched late. Killed one buffalo. River turned to north by west. Hills changed to the north side. Distance 13½ miles.

Nov. 3d. Marched at ten o'clock. Passed numerous herds of buffalo, elk, some horses, etc., all traveling south. The river bottoms full of salt ponds; grass similar to our salt meadows. Killed one buffalo. Distance 25½ miles.

Nov. 4th. This day brought to our recollection the fate of our countrymen at Recovery, when defeated by the Indians, in the year 1791. In the afternoon discovered the north side of the river to be covered with animals; which, when we came to them, proved to be buffalo cows and calves. I do not think it an exaggeration to say there were 3,000 in one view. It is worthy of remark that in all the extent of country yet crossed, we never saw one cow, and that now the face of the earth appeared to be covered with them. Killed one buffalo. Distance 24½ miles.

Nov. 5th. Marched at our usual hour; at the end of two miles shot a buffalo and two deer, and halted, which detained us so long that we foolishly concluded to halt this day and kill some cows and calves, which lay on the opposite side of the river. I took post on a hill, and sent some horsemen over, when a scene took place which gave a lively representation of an engagement. The herd of buffalo being divided into separate bands covered the prairie with dust, and first charged on the one side, then to the other, as the pursuit of the horsemen impelled them; the report and smoke from the guns added to the pleasure of the scene, which in part compensated for our detention.

Nov. 6th. Marched early, but was detained two or three hours by the cows which we killed. The cow buffalo was equal to any meat I ever saw, and we feasted sumptuously on the choice morsels. I will not attempt to describe the droves of animals we now saw on our route; suffice it to say that the face of the prairie was covered with them, on each side of the river; their numbers exceeded imagination. Distance 16 miles.

Nov. 7th. Marched early. The herbage being very poor, concluded to lay by on the morrow, in order to recruit our horses. Killed three cow buffalo, one calf, two wolves, one brelaw. Distance 18 miles.

Nov. 8th. Our horses being very much jaded and our situation very eligible, we halted all day; jerked meat, mended mockinsons, etc.

Sunday, Nov. 9th. Marched early. At twelve o'clock struck the Spanish road, which had been on the outside of us, and which appeared to be considerably augmented. On our arrival at the camp, found it to consist of 96 fires, from which a reasonable conclusion might be drawn that there were from 600 to 700 men. We this day found the face of the country considerably changed, being hilly, with springs; passed numerous herds of buffalo and some horses. Distance 27 miles.

Nov. 10th. The hills increased; the banks of the river covered with groves of young cottonwood; the river itself much narrower and crooked. Our horses growing weak; two gave out; bring them along empty; cut down trees at night for them to browse on. Killed one buffalo. Distance 20 miles.

Nov. 11th. Marched at the usual hour. Passed two old camps, and one of last summer, which had belonged to the savages, and we supposed Tetaus. Passed a Spanish camp where it appeared they remained some days, as we conjectured, to lay up meat, previously to entering the Tetau country, as the buffalo evidently began to grow much less numerous. Finding the impossibility of performing the voyage in the time proposed, I determined to spare no pains to accomplish every object, even should it oblige me to spend another winter in the desert. Killed one buffalo, one brelaw. Distance 24 miles.

Nov. 12th. Was obliged to leave the two horses, which entirely gave out. Missed the Spanish road. Killed one buffalo. Distance 20 miles.

Nov. 13th. We marched at the usual hour. The riverbanks began to be entirely covered with woods on both sides, but no other species than cotton-wood. Discovered very fresh signs of Indians, and one of our hunters informed me he saw a man on horseback, ascending a ravine on our left. Discovered signs of war-parties ascending the river. Wounded several buffalo. Killed one turkey, the first we have seen since we left the Pawnees. [Supposed distance 12 miles.]

Nov. 14th. In the morning, Dr. Robinson, one man and myself, went up the ravine in which the man was supposed to have been seen, but could make no important discovery. Marched at two o'clock; passed a point of red rocks and one large creek. Distance 10 miles.

Nov. 15th. Marched early. Passed two deep creeks and many high points of rocks; also, large herds of buffalo.

At two o'clock in the afternoon I thought I could distinguish a mountain to our right, which appeared like a small blue cloud; viewed it with the spy glass, and was still more confirmed in my conjecture, yet only communicated it to Dr. Robinson, who was in front with me; but in half an hour they appeared in full view before us. When our small party arrived on the hill they with one accord gave three cheers to the Mexican mountains. Their appearance can easily be imagined by those who have crossed the Alleghenies; but their sides were whiter, as if covered with snow, or a white stone. Those were a spur of the grand western chain of mountains which divide the waters of the Pacific from those of the Atlantic ocean; and it [the spur] divides the waters which empty into the Bay of the Holy Spirit from those of the Mississippi, as the Alleghenies do those which discharge themselves into the latter river and the Atlantic. They appear to present a natural boundary between the province of Louisiana and New Mexico, and would be a defined and natural boundary.

Before evening we discovered a fork [Purgatory river] on the south side bearing S. 25° W.; and as the Spanish troops appeared to have borne up it, we encamped on its banks, about one mile from its confluence, that we might make further discoveries on the morrow. Killed three buffalo. Distance 24 miles.

Sunday, Nov. 16th. After ascertaining that the Spanish troops had ascended the right branch or main river, we marched at two o'clock. The Arkansaw appeared at this place to be much more navigable than below, where we first struck it; and for any impediment I have yet discovered in the river, I would not hesitate to embark in February at its mouth and ascend to the Mexican mountains, with crafts properly constructed. Distance 11½ miles.

Nov. 17th. Marched at our usual hour; pushed on with an idea of arriving at the mountains, but found at night no visible difference in their appearance from what we did yesterday. One of our horses gave out and was left in a ravine, not being able to ascend the hill; but I sent back for him and had him brought to the camp. Distance 23½ miles.

Nov. 18th. As we discovered fresh signs of the savages, we concluded it best to stop and kill some meat, for fear we should get into a country where we could not kill game. Sent out the hunters; walked myself to an eminence whence I took the courses to the different mountains, and a small sketch of their appearance. In the evening, found the hunters had killed without mercy, having slain 17 buffalo and wounded at least 20 more.

Nov. 19th. Having several buffalo brought in, gave out sufficient to last this month. I found it expedient to remain and dry the meat, as our horses were getting very weak, and the one died which was brought up on the 17th. Had a general feast of marrow-bones, 136 of them furnishing the repast.

Nov. 20th. Marched at our usual hour; but as our horses' loads were considerably augmented by the death of one horse and the addition of 900 lbs. of meat, we moved slowly and made only 18 miles. Killed two buffalo and took some choice pieces.

Nov. 21st. Marched at our usual hour; passed two Spanish camps, within three miles of each other. We again discovered the tracks of two men, who had ascended the river yesterday. This caused us to move with caution; but at the same time increased our anxiety to discover them. The river was certainly as navigable here, and I think much more so, than some hundred miles below; which I suppose arises from its flowing through a long course of sandy soil, which must absorb much of the water, and render it shoaler below than above, near the mountains. Distance 21 miles.

Nov. 22d. Marched at our usual hour, and with rather more caution than usual. After having marched about five miles on the prairie, we descended into the bottom — the front only; when Baroney cried out *"Voila un Savage!"* We observed a number running from the woods toward us; we advanced to them, and on turning my head to the left I observed several running on the hill, as it were to surround us; one with a stand of colors. This caused a momentary halt; but perceiving those in front reaching out their hands, and without arms, we again advanced; they met us with open arms, crowding round to touch and embrace us. They appeared so anxious that I dismounted from my horse; in a moment a fellow had mounted him and was off. I then observed that the doctor and Baroney were in the same predicament. The Indians were embracing the soldiers. After some time tranquillity was so far restored, they having returned our horses all safe, as to enable us to learn they were a war-party from the Grand Pawnees, who had been in search of the Tetaus; but not finding them, were now on their return. An unsuccessful war-party, on their return home, are always ready to embrace an opportunity of gratifying their disappointed vengeance on the first persons whom they meet.

Made for the woods and unloaded our horses, when the two partisans endeavored to arrange the party; it was with great difficulty that they got them tranquil, and not until there had been a bow or two bent on the occasion. When in some order, we found them to be 60 warriors, half with fire-arms, and half with bows, arrows, and lances. Our party was 16 total. In a short time they were arranged in a ring, and I took my seat between the two partisans; our colors were placed opposite each other; the utensils for smoking were paraded on a small seat before us; thus far all was well. I then ordered half a carrot of tobacco, one dozen knives, 60 fire steels, and 60 flints to be presented them. They demanded ammunition, corn, blankets, kettles, etc., all of which they were refused, notwithstanding the pressing instances of my interpreter to accord to some points. The pipes yet lay unmoved, as if they were undetermined whether to treat us as friends or enemies; but after some time we were presented with a kettle of water, drank, smoked, and ate together. During this time Dr. Robinson was standing up to observe their actions, in order that we might be ready to commence hostilities as soon as they. They now took their presents and commenced distributing them, but some malcontents threw them away, by way of contempt.

We began to load our horses, when they encircled us and commenced stealing everything they could. Finding it was difficult to preserve my pistols, I mounted my horse, when I found myself frequently surrounded; during which some were endeavoring to steal the pistols. The doctor was equally engaged in another quarter, and all the soldiers in their positions, in taking things from them. One having stolen my tomahawk, I informed the chief; but he paid no respect, except to reply that "they were pitiful." Finding this, I determined to protect ourselves, as far as was in my power, and the affair began to take a serious aspect. I ordered my men to take their arms and separate themselves from the savages; at the same time declaring to them that I would kill the first man who touched our baggage. On which they commenced filing off immediately; we marched about the same time, and found they had made out to steal one sword, tomahawk, broad-ax, five canteens, and sundry other small articles. After leaving them, when I reflected on the subject, I felt myself sincerely mortified, that the smallness of my number obliged me thus to submit to the insults of lawless banditti, it being the first time a savage ever took anything from me with the least appearance of force.

After encamping at night the doctor and myself went about one mile back, and waylaid the road, determined in case we discovered any of the rascals pursuing us to steal our horses, to kill two at least; but after waiting behind some logs until some time in the night, and discovering no person, we returned to camp. Killed two buffalo and one deer. Distance 17 miles.

Sunday, Nov. 23d. Marched at ten o'clock; at one o'clock came to the third fork [St. Charles river], on the south side, and encamped at night in the point of the grand forks [confluence of Fountain river]. As the river appeared to be dividing itself into many small branches, and of course must be near its extreme source, I concluded to put the party in a defensible situation, and ascend the north fork [Fountain river] to the high point [Pike's Peak] of the blue mountain [Front range], which we conceived would be one day's march, in order to be enabled, from its pinical [pinnacle], to lay down the various branches and positions of the country. Killed five buffalo. Distance 19 miles.

Nov. 24th. Early in the morning we cut down 14 logs, and put up a breast work, five feet high on three sides and the other thrown on the river. After giving the necessary orders for their government during my absence, in case of our not returning, we marched at one o'clock, with an idea of arriving at the foot of the mountain; but found ourselves obliged to take up our night's lodging under a single cedar which we found in the prairie, without water and extremely cold. Our party besides myself consisted of Dr. Robinson, and Privates Miller and Brown. Distance 12 miles.

Nov. 25th. Marched early, with an expectation of ascending the mountain, but was only able to encamp at its base, after passing over many small hills covered with

Indians Hunting Buffalo in the Snow

cedars and pitch-pines. Our encampment was on a [Turkey] creek, where we found no water for several miles from the mountain; but near its base, found spring sufficient. Took a meridional observation, and the altitude of the mountain. Killed two buffalo. Distance 22 miles.

Nov. 26th. Expecting to return to our camp the same evening, we left all our blankets and provisions at the foot of the [Cheyenne] mountain. Killed a deer of a new species, and hung his skin on a tree with some meat. We commenced ascending; found it very difficult, being obliged to climb up rocks, sometimes almost perpendicular; and after marching all day we encamped in a cave, without blankets, victuals, or water. We had a fine clear sky, while it was snowing at the bottom. On the side of the mountain we found only yellow and pitch-pine. Some distance up we found buffalo; higher still the new species of deer, and pheasants.

Nov. 27th. Arose hungry, dry, and extremely sore, from the inequality of the rocks on which we had lain all night, but were amply compensated for toil by the sublimity of the prospect below. The unbounded prairie was overhung with clouds, which appeared like the ocean in a storm, wave piled on wave and foaming, while the sky was perfectly clear where we were. Commenced our march up the mountain, and in about one hour arrived at the summit of this chain. Here we found the snow middle-deep; no sign of beast or bird inhabiting this region. The thermometer, which stood at 9° above zero at the foot of the mountain, here fell to 4° below zero. The summit of the Grand Peak, which was entirely bare of vegetation and covered with snow, now appeared at the distance of 15 or 16 miles from us. It was as high again as what we

had ascended, and it would have taken a whole day's march to arrive at its base, when I believe no human being could have ascended to its pinical. This, with the condition of my soldiers, who had only light overalls on, no stockings, and were in every way ill provided to endure the inclemency of the region; the bad prospect of killing anything to subsist on, with the further detention of two or three days which it must occasion, determined us to return. The clouds from below had now ascended the mountain and entirely enveloped the summit, on which rest eternal snows. We descended by a long, deep ravine, with much less difficulty than contemplated. Found all our baggage safe, but the provisions all destroyed. It began to snow, and we sought shelter under the side of a projecting rock, where we all four made a meal on one partridge and a piece of deer's ribs the ravens had left us, being the first we had eaten in that 48 hours.

Nov. 28th. Marched at nine o'clock. Kept straight on down the [Turkey] creek to avoid the hills. At half past one o'clock shot two buffalo, when we made the first full meal we had made in three days. Encamped in a valley under a shelving rock. The land here very rich, and covered with old Tetau [Comanche] camps.

Nov. 29th. Marched after a short repast, and arrived at our camp before night; found all well.

Sunday, Nov. 30th. Marched at eleven o'clock; it snowed very fast, but my impatience to be moving would not permit my lying still at that camp. The doctor, Baroney, and myself went to view a Tetau encampment, which appeared to be about two years old; and from their having cut down so large a quantity of trees to support their horses, we concluded there must have been at least 1,000 souls. Passed several more in the course of the day; also one Spanish camp. This day came to the first cedar and pine. Killed two deer. Distance 15 miles.

6. An Overland Journey to California

BY JEDEDIAH STRONG SMITH

EDITOR'S NOTE: Unlike most of his contemporaries in the fur trade, many of whom originated in the Southern states, particularly Virginia, Jedediah Smith (1798-1831) came of pioneer New England stock. A devout Methodist, he lived a life of danger and hardship, on several occasions narrowly escaping death when Indians pursued him. While still young he was finally killed by Comanche Indians on the Santa Fe trail.

He made many journeys over difficult territory in order to explore the fur possibilities of the Western country and to find, if possible, a Pacific outlet for the trade. In the spring of 1826 Smith embarked on the first stage of a journey which was to take him from the Mississippi to the Pacific over the midland route. He was the first white man to take this route, over great mountain passes and stretches of desert, and therefore the first American to enter California by the overland route. Starting from the Great Salt Lake in August 1826, with a party of fifteen men, he went southwest to the Colorado River, then west by the Santa Fe–Los Angeles trail, reaching San Diego. From San Diego he proceeded north to the San Gabriel Mission, then north and east across the Sierra Nevadas, and across Nevada and Utah to the Salt Lake, where he arrived in June of 1827. The following year Smith again went to California, and then up to Oregon in the first California–Oregon overland expedition by a white man.

Although the documentary literature of the old West is a substantial one, it is not surprising to find various omissions in it. One of the very unfortunate omissions is the scarcity of manuscripts of Jedediah Smith. It has been generally assumed that his notes and journals were lost in a St. Louis fire. Fortunately the following letter, describing his first journey to California, has survived, but one wishes it were more detailed. However, one of Smith's company, Harrison Rogers, kept a journal, and I have included part of it to help highlight Smith's historic journey.

LITTLE LAKE OF BEAR RIVER, July 17th 1827. Genl. Wm. Clark, Supt. of Indian Affairs

Sir, My situation in this country has enabled me to collect information respecting a section of the country which has hitherto been measurably veiled in obscurity to the citizens of the United States. I allude to the country S.W. of the *Great Salt Lake* west of the Rocky mountains.

I started about the 22d of August 1826, from the Great Salt Lake, with a party of fifteen men, for the purpose of exploring the country S.W. which was entirely unknown to me, and of which I could collect no satisfactory information from the Indians who inhabit this country on its N.E. borders.

My general course on leaving the Salt Lake was S.W. and W. Passing the Little Uta Lake and ascending Ashley's river, which empties into the Little Uta Lake.

Jedediah Strong Smith

themselves *Pa-Ulches* (those Indians as well as those last mentioned, wear rabbit skin robes) who raise some little corn and pumpkins. The country is nearly destitute of game of any description, except a few hares. Here (about ten days march down it) the river turns to the South East. On the S.W. side of the river there is a *cave*, and entrance of which is about 10 or 15 feet high, and 5 or 6 feet in width; after descending about 15 feet, a room opens out from 25 to 30 in length and 15 to 20 feet in width; the roof, sides and floor are solid rock salt, a sample of which I send you, with some other articles which will be hereafter described. I here found a kind of plant of the prickly pear kind, which I called the cabbage pear, the largest of which grows about two feet and a half high and 1½ feet in diameter; upon examination I found it to be nearly of the substance of a turnip, altho' by no means palatable; its form was similar to that of an egg, being smaller at the ground and top that in the middle; it is covered with pricks similar to the prickly pear with which you are acquainted.

There are here also a number of shrubs and small trees with which I was not acquainted previous to my route there, and which I cannot at present describe satisfactorily, as it would take more space than I can here allot.

The *Pa Ulches* have a number of marble pipes, one of which I obtained and send you, altho it has been broken since I have had it in my possession; they told me there was a quantity of the same material in their country. I also obtained of them a knife of *flint,* which I send you, but it has likewise been broken by accident.

I followed Adams river two days further to where it empties into the Seedekeeden a South East course. I crossed the Seeds-

From this lake I found no more signs of buffalo; there are a few antelope and mountain sheep, and an abundance of *black tailed hares*. On Ashley's river, I found a nation of Indians who call themselves *Sampatch;* they were friendly disposed towards us. I passed over a range of mountains running S.E. and N.W. and struck a river running S.W. which I called *Adams River,* in compliment to our President. The water is of a muddy cast, and is a little brackish. The country is mountainous to East; towards the West there are sandy plains and detached rocky hills.

Passing down this river some distance, I fell in with a nation of Indians who call keeder, and went down it four days a south east course; I here found the country remarkably barren, rocky, and mountainous; there are a good many rapids in the river, but at this place a valley opens out about 5 to 15 miles in width, which on the river banks is timbered and fertile. I here found a nation of Indians who call themselves *Ammuchabas;* they cultivate the soil, and raise corn, beans, pumpkins, watermelons and muskmelons in abundance, and also a little wheat and cotton. I was now nearly destitute of horses, and had learned what it was to do without food; I therefore remained there fifteen days and recruited my men, and I was enabled also to exchange my horses and purchase a few more of a few runaway Indians who stole some horses of the Spaniards. I here got information of the Spanish country (the Californias) and obtained two guides, recrossed the Seeds-kadeer, which I afterwards found emptied into the Gulf of California about 80 miles from this place by the name of the Collar-ado; many render the river *Gild* from the East.

I travelled a west course fifteen days over a country of complete barrens, generally travelling from morning until night without water. I crossed a Salt plain about 20 miles long and 8 wide; on the surface was a crust of beautiful white salt, quite thin. Under this surface there is a layer of salt from a half to one and a half inches in depth; between this and the upper layer there is about four inches of yellowish sand.

On my arrival in the province of Upper California, I was looked upon with suspicion, and was compelled to appear in presence of the Governor of the Californias residing at San Diego, where, by the assistance of some American gentlemen (especially Capt. W. H. Cunningham of the ship Cour-

ier from Boston) I was enabled to obtain permission to return with my men the route I came, and purchased such supplies as I stood in want of. The Governor would not allow me to trade up the Sea coast towards Bodaga. I returned to my party and purchased such articles as were necessary, and went Eastward of the Spanish settlements on the route I had come in. I then steered my course N.W. keeping from 150 miles to 200 miles from the sea coast. A very high range of mountains lay on the East. After travelling three hundred miles in that direction through a country somewhat fertile, in which there was a great many Indians, mostly naked and destitute of arms, with the exception of a few Bows and Arrows and what is very singular amongst Indians, they cut their hair to the length of three inches; they proved to be friendly; their manner of living is on fish, roots, a-corns and grass.

On my arrival at the river which I named the *Wimmul-che* (named after a tribe of Indians which resides on it, of that name) I found a few beaver, and elk, deer, and antelope in abundance. I here made a small hunt, and attempted to take my party across the [mountain] which I before mentioned, and which I called *Mount Joseph,* to come on and join my partners at the Great Salt Lake. I found the snow so deep on Mount Joseph that I could not cross my horses, five of which starved to death; I was compelled therefore to return to the valley which I had left, and there, leaving my party, I started with two men, seven horses and two mules, which I loaded with hay for the horses and provisions for ourselves, and started on the 20th of May, and succeeded in crossing it in eight days, having lost only two horses and one mule. I found the snow on the top of this mountain from

An Indian Trapper. *Frederick Remington*

4 to 8 feet deep, but it was so consolidated by the heat of the sun that my horses only sunk from half a foot to one foot deep.

After travelling twenty days from the east side of Mount Joseph, I struck the S.W. corner of the Great Salt Lake, travelling over a country completely barren and destitute of game. We frequently travelled without water sometimes for two days over sandy deserts, where there was no sign of vegetation and when we found water in some of the rocky hills, we most generally found some Indians who appeared the most miserable of the human race having nothing

to subsist on (nor any clothing) except grass seed, grass-hoppers, etc. When we arrived at the Salt Lake, we had but one horse and one mule remaining, which were so feeble and poor that they could scarce carry the little camp equipage which I had along; the balance of my horses I was compelled to eat as they gave out.

The company are now starting, and therefore must close my communication. Yours respectfully,

Jedediah S. Smith,
of the firm of
Smith, Jackson and Sublette.

7. A Visit to the San Gabriel Mission

BY HARRISON G. ROGERS

EDITOR'S NOTE: During Jedediah Smith's sojourn in California, Harrison G. Rogers, the clerk of Smith's small company, kept a record of daily occurrences, fragments of which have survived, and from which I have selected an excerpt, written in 1826. The mission of San Gabriel was the fourth of the Alta California missions and was originally established on San Pedro Bay in 1771. It was subsequently moved inland to the site near Los Angeles.

[MONDAY, NOVEMBER] 27TH. We got ready as early as possible and started a W. course, and traveled 14 m. and enc. for the day, we passed innumerable herds of cattle, horses and some hundred of sheep; we passed 4 or 5 Ind. lodges, that their Inds. acts as herdsmen. There came an old Ind. to us that speaks good Spanish, and took us with him to his mansion, which consisted

of 2 rows of large and lengthy buildings, after the Spanish mode, thay remind me of the British Barracks. So soon as we enc. there was plenty prepared to eat, a fine young cow killed, and a plenty of corn meal given us; pretty soon after the 2 commandants of the missionary establishment come to us and had the appearance of gentlemen. Mr. S. went with them to the Mansion and I stay with the company, there was great feasting among the men as they were pretty hungry not having any good meat for some time.

28TH. Mr. S. wrote me a note in the morning, stating that he was received as a gentleman and treated as such, and that he wished me to go back and look for a pistol that was lost, and send the company on to the missionary establishment. I complied with his request, went back, and found the pistol, and arrived late in the evening, was received very politely, and showed into a room and my arms taken from me. About 10 o'clock at night supper was served, and Mr. S. and myself sent for. I was introduced to the 2 priests over a glass of good old whiskey and found them to be very joval friendly gentlemen, the supper consisted of a number of different dishes, served different from any table I ever was at. Plenty of good wine during supper, before the cloth was removed sigars was introduced. Mr. S. has wrote to the governor, and I expect we shall remain here some days.

29TH. Still at the mansion. We was sent for about sunrise to drink a cup of tea, and eat some bread and cheese. They all appear friendly and treat us well, although they are Catholicks by profession, they allow us the liberty of conscience, and treat us as they do their own countrymen, or brethren.

About 11 o'clock, dinner was ready, and the priest come after us to go and dine; we were invited into the office, and invited to take a glass of gin and water and eat some bread and cheese; directly after we were seated at dinner, and every thing went on in style, both the priests being pretty merry, the clerk and one other gentleman, who speaks some English. They all appear to be gentlemen of the first class, both in manners and habbits. The Mansion, or Mission, consist of 4 rows of houses forming a complete square, where there is all kinds of macanicks at work; the church faces the east and the guard house the west; the N. and S. line comprises the work shops. They have large vineyards, apple and peach orchards, and some orrange and some fig trees. They manufacture blankets, and sundry other articles; they distill whiskey and grind their own grain, having a water mill, of a tolerable quality; they have upwards of 1,000 persons employed, men, women, and

children, Inds. of different nations. The situation is very handsome, pretty streams of water running through from all quarters, some thousands of acres of rich and fertile land as level as a die in view, and a part under cultivation, surrounded on the N. with a high and lofty mou., handsomely timbered with pine, and cedar, and on the S. with low mou, covered with grass. Cattle — this Mission has upwards of 30,000 head of cattle, and horses, sheep, hogs, etc. in proportion. I intend visiting the iner apartments to-morrow if life is spared. I am quite unwell to-day but have been engaged in writing letters for the men and drawing a map of my travels for the priests. Mr. Smith, as well as myself, have been engaged in the same business. They slaughter at this place from 2 to 3,000 head of cattle at a time; the mission lives on the profits. Saint Gabriel is in north latitude 34 degrees and 30 minutes. It still continues warm; the thermometer stands at 65 and 70 degrees.

30TH. Still at Saint Gabriel; everything goes on well; only the men is on a scanty allowance, as yet. There was a wedding in this place today, and Mr. S. and myself invited; the bell was rang a little before sun rise, and the morning service performed; then the musick commenced serranading, the soldiers firing, etc., about 7 oclock tea and bread served, and about 11, dinner and musick. The ceremony and dinner was held at the priests; they had an ellegant dinner, consisting of a number of dishes, boiled and roast meat and fowl, wine and brandy or ogadent, grapes brought as a dessert after dinner. Mr. S. and myself acted quite independent, knot understanding there language, nor they ours; we endeavored to appoligise, being very dirty and not in a situation to shift our clothing, but no excuse would be taken, we must be present, as we have been served at there table ever since we arrived at this place; they treat [us] as gentlemen in every sense of the word, although our apparel is so indifferent, and we not being in circumstances at this time to help ourselves, being about 800 m. on a direct line from the place of our deposit. Mr. S. spoke to the commandant this evening respecting the rations of his men; they were immediately removed into another apartment, and furnished with cooking utensils and plenty of provisions, they say, for 3 or 4 days. Our 2 Ind. guides were imprisoned in the guard house the 2nd. day after we arrived at the missionary establishment and remain confined as yet. Mr. S has wrote to the commandant of the province, and we do not know the result as yet, or where we shall go from this place, but I expect to the N.W. I intended visiting the iner apartments to-day, but have been engaged in assisting Mr. S. in making a map for the priest and attending the ceremonies of the wedding.

DECEMBER 1ST, 1826. We still remain at the mansion of St. Gabriel; things going on as usual; all friendship and peace. Mr. S. set his black-smiths, James Reed and Silas Gobel, to work in the B. S. Shop, to make a bear trap for the priest, agreeable to promise yesterday. Mr. S. and the interpreter went in the evening to the next mission, which is 9 m. distance from St. Gab. and called St. Pedro, a Spanish gentleman from that Mission having sent his servant with horses for them. There came an Itallian gentleman from Port Sandeago today by the name of John Battis Bonafast who speaks good English, and acts as interpreter for all the American and English vessels that arrives in ports on the coast, quite a smart and intelligent man, The men all appear satisfied since there was new regu-

lations made about eating. Mr. S. informed me this morning that he had to give Read a little floggin yesterday evening, on account of some of his impertinence; he appeared more complasant to-day than usual. Our fare at table much the same as at first, a plenty of everything good to eat and drink.

2ND. Much the same to-day as yesterday, both being what the Catholicks call fast days; in the morning after sun rise, or about that time, you have tea, bread and cheese, at dinner fish and fowl, beans, peas, potatoes and other kinds of sauce, grapes as a desert, wine, gin and water plenty at dinner. I could see a great deal of satisfaction here if I could talk there language, but, as it is, I feel great diffidence in being among them, knot knowing the topic of there conversation, still every attention is paid to me by all that is present, especially the old priest. I must say he is a very fine man and a very much of a gentleman. Mr. S. has not returned from the other Mission as yet. This province is called the Province of New California; this mission ships to Europe annually from 20 to 25 thousand dollars worth of hides and tallow, and about 20 thousand dollars worth of soap. There vineyards are extensive; they make there own wine, and brandy; they have orranges and limes growing here. The Inds. appear to be much altered from the wild Indians in the mou. that we have passed. They are kept in great fear; for the least offense they are corrected; they are compleat slaves in every sense of the word. Mr. S and Laplant returned late in the evening, and represents there treatment to be good at the other mission. Mr. S. tells me that Mr. Francisco, the Spanish gentleman that he went to visit, promises him as many horses and mules as he wants.

DECEMBER 3RD., SUNDAY. About 6 o'clock the bell rang for mass, and they poured into church from all quarters, men, women and children; there was none of us invited therefore we all remained at our lodgings. The fare to-day at table as usual; there was an additional cup of tea in the afternoon. The Inds. play bandy with sticks, it being the only game I have seen as yet among them. They play before the priests door. I am told they dance, both Spanyards and Inds., in the course of the evening.

4TH. Still at St. Gabriel; things much as usual The priest presented Mr. S. with two pieces of shirting containing 64 yards for to make the men shirts, all being nearly naked. Mr. Smith gives each man 3½ yards and kept the same number for himself, each man getting enough to make a shirt. The weather still continues to be moderate, the thermometer stands at 60 and 63 in the day, and 50-53 in the night. The Thermometer hangs within doors, etc.

5TH. We are still remaining at the mansion of St. Gabriel, waiting the result of the Governor's answer to a letter that Mr. S. addressed him on the 27th of November. We expect the courier some time today with letters. It still continues moderate.

6TH. Early this morning I presented the old priest with my buffalo robe and he brought me a very large blankett and presented me, in return, about ten o'clock. Nothing new. Things going on as they have been heretofore; no answer from the governor as yet; we are waiting with patience to hear from the governor.

11TH [7TH]. No answer as yet from the governor of the province. Mr. S. and all hands getting impatient. There was a Spanish gentleman arrived yesterday evening named Francis Martinnis, a very intelligent man, who speaks pretty good English, and appears very friendly; he advises Mr. S. to go an see the governor in case he does not

receive an answer in a few days. He is a man of business and is well aware that men on expenses and business of importance should be presservering; he appears anxious as respects our well fare. Mr. S. has some idea of going in company with him to Sandiego, the residence of the governor.

8TH. Nothing of importance has taken place today. Mr. S. was sent for to go to Sandiego to see the governor. Capt. Cunningham, commanding the ship Courier, now lying in port at Sandiego, arrived here late this evening. The captain is a Bostonian, and has been trading on the coast for hides and tallow since June last; he informs me that he is rather under the impression that he shall be obliged to remain untill some time in the suceeding summer in consequence of so much opposition, as there is a number of vessels on the coast trading for the same kind of articles. He says that money is very scarce, amongst the most of the people, Mr. Martinas tells me that there is between 16 and 17,000 natives that is converted over to the Catholic faith and under the control of the different Missions; the white population he estimates at 6,000, making 22 or 23,000 thousand souls in the province of New Callifornia.

9TH. Mr. Smith and one of the men, in company with Capt. Cunningham, left San Gabriel, this morning for Sandiego, the governor's place of residence. I expect he will be absent for eight or ten days. The weather still keeps moderate, things much the same, friendship and peace as yet.

10TH. SUNDAY. There was five Inds. brought to the mission by two other Inds, who act as constables, or overseers, and sentenced to be whiped for not going to work when ordered.

Each received from 12 to 14 lashes on their bare posteriors; they were all old men, say from 50 to 60 years of age, the commandant standing by with his sword to see that the Ind. who flogged them done his duty. Things in other respects similar to the last Sabbath.

11TH. Nothing of consequence has taken place today more than usual, only the band of musick consisting of two small violins, one bass violin, a trumpet and triangle was played for 2 hours in the evening before the priests door by Inds. They made tolerable good music, the most in imitation to whites that [I] ever heard. Directly after the musick would cease, there was several rounds of cannon fired by the soldiers in commemoration of some great saints day or feast day. They keep at this place 4 small field pieces, 2 6-pounders and 2 2-pounders to protect them from the Inds. in case they should rebel, and, from the best information I can get from the soldiers, they appear at times some what alarmed, for fear the Inds. will rise and destroy the Mission.

12TH. About sun rise, the bell rang and mass called; men women and children attended church; they discharged a number of small arms and some cannon while the morning service were performing. There main church is upwards of 200 feet in length and about 140 in breadth made of stone and brick, a number of different apartments in it. They hold meeting in the large church every Sunday; the Spanyards first attend and then the Inds. They have a room in the iner apartment of the Mission to hold church on their feast days. There religion appears to be a form more than a reality. I am in hopes we shall be able to leave here in five or six days at most, as all hands appear to be anxious to move on to the North. Things in other respects much the same; the weather still continues to be good. In the evening there was a kind of procession,

amongst both Spanyards and Inds. I enquired the reason, I was told by a Mr. David Philips, an Englishman, that this day, a year ago, the Virgin Mary appeared to an Ind. and told him that the 12th day of December should always be kept as a feast day and likewise a holliday among them and both Spaniards and Inds. believe it.

13TH. I walked through the work shops; I saw some Inds. blacksmithing, some carpentering, others making the wood work of ploughs, others employed in making spining wheels for the squaws to spin on. There is upwards 60 women employed in spining yarn and others weaving. Things much the same, cloudy and some rain to-day. Our black smith[s] have been employed for several days making horse and nails for our own use when we leave here.

14TH. I was asked by the priest to let our black smiths make a large trap for him to set in his orrange garden, to catch the Inds. in when they come up at night to rob his orchard. The weather clear and warm. Things in other respects much the same as they have been heretofore; friendship and peace prevail with us and the Spanyards. Our own men are contentious and quarrelsome amongst themselves and have been ever since we started the expedition. Last night at supper for the first time the priest questioned me as respected my religion. I very frankly informed him that I was brought up under the Calvinist doctrine, and did not believe that it was in the power of man to forgive sins. God only had that power, and when I was under the necessity of confessing my sins, I confessed them unto God in prayer and supplication, not to man; I further informed him that it was my opinion, that men ought to possess as well as profess religion to constitute the Christian; he said that when he was in his church and his robe on, he then believed he was equal unto God, and had the power to forgive any sin, that man was guilty of, and openly confessed unto him, but when he was out of church and his common waring apparel on he was as other men, divested of all power of forgiving sins.

15TH. I went out fowling with the commandant of the Mission. I killed 7 brant and one duck, and the commandant killed 2 brants and a duck; the priest furnished me with shot. Two of our men went to work today, Arthur Black and John Gaiter; they are to get a horse a piece for 3 days work. Times much the same as they have been some time back; nothing new occurs.

16TH. Late this morning a Mr. Henry, owner of a brig now lying in port, arrived at the Mission; he appears to be a very much of a gentleman, and quite intelligent. His business here is to buy hides, tallow and soap, from the priest. Nothing new has taken place. Things much the same about the Mission; the priest administered the sacrament to a sick Indian today, and he thinks he will die.

17TH. The sick Indian that the priest administered the sacrament too yesterday, died last night, and was entered in there graveyard this evening; the proceeding in church similar to the last Sabbath. Sunday appears to be the day that the most business is transacted at this Mission; the priest plays at cards both Sunday a[nd] weak a days, when he has company that can play pretty expert.

18TH. I received a letter from Mr. S. informing me that he rather was under the impression that he would be detained for some time yet, as the general did [not] like to take the responsibility on himself to let us pass until he received instructions from the general in Mexico; under those circum-

stances I am fearful we will have to remain here some time yet. Our men have been employed fitting out a cargo of hides, tallow, and soap for a Mr. Henry Edwards, a German by birth, and the most intelligent man that I have met with since I arrived at this place; he is what they term here a Mexican trader.

Mr. S. also wrote to me for eight beaver skins, to present to the Spanish officers to face there cloaks with; I complied with his request, and selected eight of the Best and sent to him.

19TH. Still remaining at San Gabriel; things much the same. I went out with my gun to amuse myself, killed some black birds and ducks. The express left here this morning for Sandiego. I sent the eight beaver skins to Mr. Smith to present to the Spanish officers to face their cloaks, by him. The old father continues his frindship to me; it does not appear to abate in the least. I still eat at his table. This Mission, if properly managed, would be equal to [a] mine of silver or gold; there farms is extensive; they raise from 3 to 4000 bushels of wheat annually, and sell to shippers for $3. per bushel. There annual income, situated as it is and managed so badly by the Inds., is worth in hides, tallow, soap, wine, ogadent, wheat, and corn from 55 to 60,000 dollars.

20TH. Nothing new has taken place; all peace and friendship. I expect an answer from Mr. Smith in six or eight days if he does not get permission to pass on. My situation is a very delicate one, as I have to be amongst the grandees of the country every day. My clothes are [illegible] the clothing of blanketts [illegible] pantaloons, two shirts and [illegible] read cap. I make a very grotesque appearance when seated at table amongst the dandys with there ruffles, silks, and broad clothes, and I am

8. The Adventures of Zenas Leonard

BY ZENAS LEONARD

EDITOR'S NOTE: Zenas Leonard (1809-1858) left his parental home in Clearfield, Pa., in the spring of 1830, spent a year in a mercantile house in Pittsburgh, then joined an expedition to the Rocky Mountains in the capacity of clerk. Until the summer of 1833 he was a free fur trapper, after which time he entered the employ of Captain B. L. E. de Bonneville. In that year Bonneville ordered one of his lieutenants, Joseph Reddeford Walker, to explore the country between Green River, Wyoming, and the Pacific with a view to seeing what beaver he could find. Leonard joined Walker's expedition as a clerk and kept a journal of events.

The expedition was one of the earliest to reach the Pacific by the midland route, following Jedediah Smith's historic achievement by only seven years. In addition to broadening the scope of the fur trade it was of considerable geographical importance, being credited with the discovery of both Yosemite Valley and the giant redwoods of California. Little is known of the Walker expedition, and Leonard's narrative of his adventures is therefore of some importance.

Walker's party of forty men skirted the Great Salt Lake and followed the Humboldt River to the Sierra Nevada mountains which they crossed, emerging into the San Joaquin valley. They pushed on to San Francisco and then to Monterey where they spent the winter of 1833-34. Walker and his party arrived back in Green River in the summer of 1834, having crossed the Sierras further south and marched north through Owens Valley, thence back along the Humboldt.

Leonard continued in Bonneville's employ until the summer of 1835. In the autumn of the same year he made his way back to Clearfield. He wrote his story down for a local paper, basing it on the journals he had kept. It appeared as a book in Clearfield in 1839. I have included something less than one-quarter of Leonard's account.

The Rickarees are a powerful nation, consisting of about 1000 warriors. Their principal chief is called Highbacked Wolf. Some twelve or fifteen years since, they were very friendly with the whites. This friendship was interrupted by the following circumstance:—About eight or ten years since, Mr. Mackenzie took a chief from three different nations (one of which was a Rickaree,) to Washington city, and while taking them back to their native wilds through Virginia, the Rickaree chief took sick and died in the city of Richmond. Mackenzie returned with the other two, Asnaboin and Mandan. While passing the Rickaree village, (which was then situated on the Missouri river, from whence they have since removed to this country,) Mackenzie stopped and informed them of the fate of their chief—which they disbelieved, and immediately declared war against the whites. They were much enraged, and made a violent attack upon the boats containing the merchandize of Mr. Mackenzie—a great part of which they destroyed, and have since been the cause of the death of numbers of white men.

April 10th. Having lost all hope of being rejoined by our lost man, who we concluded had been captured by the Indians, we resumed our journey with 14 men.—Beaver we found in abundance—catching more or less every day, and every thing seemed to

Rickaree Indians. *George Catlin*

promise a profitable business, until the 7th day of May—a day which will ever be remembered by each of us. Having encamped the night previous on a small creek in the Black Hills, or on the head waters of the river Platte, without timber or any thing to shelter ourselves, in case of an attack by the Indians, within 80 or 100 yards. We this evening again turned our horses loose to graze, which is not by any means customary and much less prudent, while travelling through a country infested with hostile savages, as they are always hovering around the encampment, ready to lay hands on any thing which they fancy. But on the present occasion we thought ourselves secure, as we had not seen nor met with any Indians for several days. On the following morning our horses were in sight on a hill a little above the encampment. About 9 o'clock three of us started to bring them down preparatory

to our start. As there was no danger apprehended, neither of us took our guns. When we got to the top of the hill the horses were not to be seen—having descended the hill on the other side. The other two men soon found their horses and started with them to camp. After searching a while I found mine with several others. The horses appeared much frightened, and I began to apprehend some danger. Whilst leading my horse towards the camp, an Indian, armed with a bow and arrow, came rushing upon me.— I made several attempts to mount, but as often failed, for as I would spring to get on he would jump from under me. The savage now approached within about fifteen steps of me, and signified that he would slay me unless I stopped and delivered up my horse. I sprang behind a bunch of bushes, which afforded me a tolerable shelter. He then made signs to me that if I would deliver myself up he would not hurt me. But this I refused. My only weapon was a large knife, which I carried in a scabbard at my waist. I drew this out and proposed to meet him. He then gave me to understand, that if I would lay down the knife he would lay down the bow and arrow, and we would meet and be friends. This I also refused to do.—He made use of various inducements to get me from behind the bush, but I heeded them not, for I knew his intention was to kill me if it was in his power. He still advanced slowly toward me. I had been in several dangerous situations with the Indians and wild beasts,—in some of which I had almost despaired. But none seemed to cause the same feeling as did my present predicament. Alone, and unarmed—my situation was distressing indeed. I had no chance of escaping, and an immediate and cruel death I knew would be my fate if I surrendered. Whilst reflecting on what to do, and looking at him through an aperture in the bush, he shot an arrow at me, which fortunately missed its aim, and struck a branch within a few inches of my face, and fell harmless to the ground. By this time he had got quite close and being below me on the hill side, the thought struck me that I might despatch him with a stone—for which purpose I stooped down to get one, and carelessly let my body move from the shelter afforded by the brush, and at that instant I felt the pointed arrow pierce my side. I jirked the weapon out immediately, and started to run, still holding to my horse. I expected every moment as I ran quartering past the Indian to receive another, which I most certainly would have done, if the savage had been in the possession of any more; and to run to the brush for those he had already discharged at me, would only be giving me time to escape. He then pursued me. After running a short distance I thought that my horse might be the means of saving my life, if I would leave him for the Indian, and accordingly I released my hold; but the Indian disregarded the horse and followed me. By this time, owing to the loss of blood from my wound, and the great excitement I was under, I began to grow weak and faint, for I thought that every moment would be my last, as I heard the Indian puffing & blowing in my rear. We were now within sight of our camp, and were fortunately discovered by the men then there, who immediately ran to my relief. When I seen the face of my companions, I lost all my strength and fell prostrate to the ground. The Indian, foiled in his design on my life, retreated for the purpose of making sure of my horse, but in this he was also mistaken, for in turn he was pursued by my companions as hotly as he had chased me. When my mind again resumed its sway, I found myself in the camp carefully attended by my companions.

On entering into conversation with my companions, I found that I was not the only one who had encountered the Indians. I was ignorant of any more Indians being in the neighborhood than the one above alluded to, but it appeared by their story that, when the two men who started out with me, were returning with the horses, they came across a large body of Indians, supposed to be about 200, who, after a sharp engagement, in which one of our men, named Gillam, of Illinois, was killed, and two wounded, succeeded in taking all our horses except two. Whilst I was listening to this lamentable story, our spies came running to the camp, bringing the unwelcome tidings that the Indians were again approaching with great speed, determined to ride over us. Each man now gathered a robe, blanket, guns, and such things as he could not do without, & carried the wounded into the brush at the foot of the hill, where we immediately commenced building a fort. The Indians approached and surrounded our encampment very cautiously, thinking that they would take us by surprise, and capture man, beast and baggage without any difficulty—but they were outrageous when they found that there was no body at home. They made the best of their victory however, and took every thing we had left. —When they had completed the pillage, which was only done when they could no longer find any thing on which to lay their hands, they started off with their booty.— After they had travelled some distance they halted and collected in a circle, within plain view of where we were, and smoked to the Sun, or Great Spirit. While going through this ceremony, some of them happened to discover us. On this, they quit smoking, left their horses and came on foot within 30 or 40 steps of us,—but on seeing our fort, which was only partly built, they turned away and left us, without making any attack. We remained in this situation until morning— those who were able, being occupied in completing our fort. Soon after daylight the Indians again made their appearance, and approached within a stones throw of the fort, and on reconnoitering our situation they concluded that we were too well defended for them to gain any advantage over us,—and the second time they left us without giving us a chance of trying our strength.

This morning I felt very weak and feeble from my wound, and began to fear that it was more serious than was at first supposed. About 10 o'clock the company was ready for the move, and I was packed between two horses. After travelling two or three miles

we halted to rest near some brush—but not without having sentinels stationed for the purpose of keeping a vigilant look-out, for we still expected an attack from the Indians. Not long after we halted our sentinels informed us that the savages were again approaching. We immediately went into the brush and commenced throwing up a fort. They this time approached very cautiously, & seemed determined to put an end to our lives. When they observed that we were defended by a breast work, they halted, reconnoitered on every side, and finally gave up and left us. These Indians who had hung round our path so long, robbed us of so much necessary property, killed one and wounded three of us, and came so nigh exterminating our whole company, we found out, belonged to the Rickaree tribe —the same who frightened us in the sink hole, on Platte river.

It was now that we had leisure to contemplate our situation. Some of us had laboured hard, encountered one danger only to be eclipsed by another. We had at times endured the most excruciating suffering from hunger and fatigue—living in constant communion with the terrors of a wilderness studded with savages and no less dangerous beasts of prey, for two long years, and now left destitute of every thing except an old greasy blanket, a rifle and a few loads of ammunition, some thousands of miles from our paternal homes. To reflect on our present situation was enough to fill every heart with all the horrors of remorse. In fact, we felt a disposition about this time to do that which would not have been right, had an opportunity afforded. When we first embarked in this business it was with the expectation that to ensure a fortune in the fur trade only required a little perseverance and industry. We were not told that

Setting Traps for Beaver at Night.   *Alfred Jacob Miller*

we were to be constantly annoyed by the Indians, but that it only required the observance of a peaceful disposition on our par*, to secure their friendship and even supp ort. Some of the Indians with whom we had intercourse, it is true, had been of great advantage to us in our trapping expeditions; but then it would be of short duration,—for, if they would not render themselves obnoxious by their own treachery, our friendship with them would be sure to meet with an interruption through some ingenious artifice of a neighbouring jealous tribe. Such had been the life we had led, and such the reward.

Our situation was not at all suited for sober calculation. Some appeared altogether careless what would become of them—seeming to have a willingness to turn in with and live the life of a savage; some two or three were anxious to leave the wilderness and return to the States as empty as when we left them. But this was rejected by nearly all, for we still had a distant hope of having better luck.

Some of our men were acquainted with the situation of the rendezvous of a company of traders on the head waters of the Colerado, trading under the firm of B. L. E. Bowville,* & Co. and it was proposed to start for this post immediately. After much debate and persuasion, it was agreed that we should make the attempt. We got every thing ready—the wounded having entirely recovered—and started on our long and tedious journey. As we travelled along we killed plenty of various kinds of game—met with nothing to interrupt our journey, and on the 25th of July arrived at the camp of Bowville, which at this time consisted of 195 men, together with a small company belonging to Mackenzie, from the Missouri river, of 60 men. We were well received by these men, most of whom had been in the woods for several years, and experienced many hardships and privations, similar to what we had suffered. They seemed to sympathize with us about our loss, and all appeared anxious that we should turn in with them and restore our lost fortunes. After we had become thoroughly rested from the fatigue of our long tramp to this post, most of our men hired in different ways with this company. These men had been engaged in trapping in the vicinity of this rendezvous for a long time, & had caught nearly all the beaver, and were thinking about moving to some other section of country. There was a large tract of land laying to the South West of this, extending to the Columbia river on the North, and to the Pacific ocean and Gulph of Calafornia on the West and South, which was said to abound with beaver, and otherwise suited as a trading country. As our company was now very large, the officers concluded on dividing it into three divisions. Accordingly Capt. Bowville was left here with a considerable force to watch the movements of the Indians, and to do what he could at trapping; as this had been a great harbor for beaver, it was thought that there might be still some more to be caught. A Mr. Cerren with a few men was sent back to St. Lewis, with 4000 lbs. of beaver fur, with instructions to return and meet Capt. Bowville at the Great Salt Lake in the following summer, with a supply of provisions to do the company, for the two following years. The other division, under the command of a Mr. Walker, was ordered to steer through an unknown country, towards the Pacific, and if he did not find beaver, he should return to the Great S. L. in the following summer. Mr. Walker was a man

* Bonneville

A Mountain Hunter. *Frederick Remington*

well calculated to undertake a business of this kind. He was well hardened to the hardships of the wilderness—understood the character of the Indians very well—was kind and affable to his men, but at the same time at liberty to command without giving offence,—and to explore unknown regions was his chief delight. I was anxious to go to the coast of the Pacific, and for that purpose hired with Mr. Walker as clerk, for a certain sum per year. The 20th of Aug. was fixed as the day for each company to take its departure.* When the day arrived every thing was in readiness,—each man provided with four horses, and an equal share of blankets, buffaloe robes, provisions, and every article necessary for the comfort of men engaged in an expedition of this kind. As we travelled along each man appeared in better spirits, and more lively than on any other similar occasion,—and I some-

times thought that we were now on an expedition from which we would realize some profit. On the fourth day of our journey we arrived at the huts of some Bawnack Indians. These Indians appear to live very poor and in the most forlorn condition. They generally make but one visit to the buffaloe country during the year, where they remain until they jirk as much meat as their females can lug home on their backs. They then quit the mountains and return to the plains, where they subsist on fish and small game the remainder of the year. They keep no horses, & are always an easy prey for other Indians provided with guns and horses. On telling these Indians the route we intended to take, they told us we must provide ourselves with meat enough to subsist upon for many days— which we found to be very good advice. We now set to work laying in a stock of provision, and in a few days each man was provided with about 60 pounds of substantial meat, which was packed upon our horses, and we set sail in good cheer.

On the 4th of September we killed our last buffaloe on the West side of the Salt Lake. We still continued along the margin of the Lake, with the intention of leaving it when we got to the extreme west side of it. About the 12th we found the country very poor, and almost without game, except goats and some few rabbits. On the 13th we left the Lake and took a westerly course into the most extensive & barren plains I ever seen. This day we came to a spring, where we found some Indians encamped, who were on their way up to the buffaloe country, to lay in their winters supply of meat. These Indians appear to be more wealthy, and exercise more ingenuity in providing for themselves than those we had

* The correct date is July 24, 1833.

met with a few days ago. They have paths beat from one spring or hole of water to another, and by observing these paths, they told us, we would be enabled to find water without much trouble. The chief of this tribe, further told us, that after travelling so many days South-west, (the course we were now about to take,) we would come to a high mountain which was covered with snow at the top the whole year round, and on each side of which we would find a large river to head, and descend into the sandy plains below, forming innumerable small lakes, and sinks into the earth and disappears. Some distance further down these plains, he said, we would come to another mountain, much larger than the first, which he had never been across. In all this space, he said, there was no game; but that near this latter mountain we would come across a tribe of poor Indians, whom he supposed would not be friendly.

On the next morning we left these Indians, and pursued our course Northwest. Our men, who were in such fine spirits when we left the rendezvous, began to show symptoms of fatigue, & were no longer so full of sport. We travelled along these paths according to the directions of the Indians, now and then meeting with a few straggling natives, who were in a manner naked, on the trail of the main body to the buffaloe country.—Some of these straggling Indians showed us some lumps of salt, which was the most white, clear and beautiful I ever seen.

On the 30th we arrived at a considerable hill, which, in appearance, is similar to a smooth rock,—where we encamped for the night, and let our horses loose to graze— which we thought might now be done with safety, as we were no longer beset by the murderous Rickarees. While laying about

resting ourselves, some of the men observed the horses very eagerly licking the stones which lay on the surface of the ground, near the spring. This circumstance caused the men to examine the stones, which we found to be salt, and had been carried here from the hill by the Indians. Their surface was covered with moss or rust, but on breaking them, or rubbing off the rust, the salt is seen in its purity. This hill runs North and South, and is from one to three miles across, and produces no kind of vegetation, whatever except a little grass which grows in holes or gutters around its base, formed by water descending from the hill during the rainy season. This country appeared the most like a desert of any I had yet seen. It is so dry and sandy that there is scarcely any vegetation to be found—not even a spear of grass, except around the springs. The water in some of these springs, too, is so salt that it is impossible to drink it. The Indians say that it never rains, only in the spring of the year. Every thing here seems to declare that, here man shall not dwell.

After travelling a few days longer thro' these barren plains; we came to the mountain described by the Indian as having its peak covered with snow. It presents a most singular appearance—being entirely unconnected with any other chain. It is surrounded on either side by level plains, and rises abruptly to a great highth, rugged, and hard to ascend. To take a view of the surrounding country from this mountain, the eye meets with nothing but a smooth, sandy, level plain. On the whole, this mountain may be set down as one of the most remarkable phenomenas of nature. Its top is covered with the pinone tree, bearing a kind of mast, which the natives are very fond of, and which they collect for winter provision. This hill is nearly round, and looks like a hill or mound, such as may be met with in the prairies on the east side of the mountain.

Not far from our encampment we found the source of the river mentioned by the Indian. After we all got tired gazing at this mountain and the adjacent curiosities, we left it and followed down the river, in order to find water and grass for our horses. On this stream we found old signs of beaver, and we supposed that, as game was scarce in this country, the Indians had caught them for provision. The natives which we occasionally met with, still continued to be of the most poor and dejected kind—being entirely naked and very filthy. We came to the hut of one of these Indians who happened to have a considerable quantity of fur collected.—At this hut we obtained a large robe composed of beaver skins fastened together, in exchange for two awls and one fish-hook. This robe was worth from 30 to 40 dollars. We continued travelling down this river, now and then catching a few beaver. But, as we continued to extend our acquaintance with the natives, they began to practice their national failing of stealing. So eager were they to possess themselves of our traps, that we were forced to quit trapping in this vicinity and make for some other quarter. The great annoyance we sustained in this respect greatly displeased some of our men, and they were for taking vengeance before we left the country—but this was not the disposition of Captain Walker. These discontents being out hunting one day, fell in with a few Indians, two or three of whom they killed, and then returned to camp, not daring to let the Captain know it. The next day while hunting, they repeated the same violation—but this time not quite so successful, for the Captain found it out, and immediately took measures for its effectual suppression.

At this place, all the branches of this stream is collected from the mountain into the main channel, which forms quite a large stream; and to which we gave the name of Barren River*—a name which we thought would be quite appropriate, as the country, natives and every thing belonging to it, justly deserves the name.—You may travel for many days on the banks of this river, without finding a stick large enough to make a walking cane.—While we were on its margin, we were compelled to do without fire, unless we chanced to come across some drift that had collected together on the beach. As we proceeded down the river we found that the trails of the Indians began to look as if their numbers were increasing, ever since our men had killed some of their brethren. The further we descended the river, the more promising the country began to appear, although it still retained its dry, sandy nature. We had now arrived within view of a cluster of hills or mounds, which presented the appearance, from a distance, of a number of beautiful cities built up together. Here we had the pleasure of seeing timber, which grew in very sparing quantities some places along the river beach.

On the 4th of September we arrived at some lakes, formed by this river, which we supposed to be those mentioned by the Indian chief whom we met at the Great Salt Lake. Here the country is low and swampy, producing an abundance of very fine grass —which was very acceptable to our horses, as it was the first good grazing they had been in for a long time—and here, on the borders of one of these lakes, we encamped, for the purpose of spending the night, and

* The Humboldt River, otherwise known as the Ogden, after Peter Skene Ogden, and the Mary's, after Ogden's Indian wife.

letting our horses have their satisfaction. A little before sun-set, on taking a view of the surrounding waste with a spy-glass, we discovered smoke issuing from the high grass in every direction. This was sufficient to convince us that we were in the midst of a large body of Indians; but as we could see no timber to go to, we concluded that it would be as well to remain in our present situation, and defend ourselves as well as we could. We readily guessed that these Indians were in arms to revenge the death of those which our men had killed up the river; & if they could succeed in getting any advantage over us, we had no expectation that they would give us any quarter. Our first care, therefore, was to secure our horses, which we did by fastening them all together, and then hitching them to pickets drove into the ground. This done, we commenced constructing something for our own safety. The lake was immediately in our rear, and piling up all our baggage in front, we had quite a substantial breast work—which would have been as impregnable to the Indian arrows, as were the cotton-bags to the British bullets at New Orleans in 1815. Before we had got every thing completed, however, the Indians issued from their hiding places in the grass, to the number, as near as I could guess, of 8 or 900, and marched straight towards us, dancing and singing in the greatest glee. When within about 150 yards of us, they all sat down on the ground, and despatched five of their chiefs to our camp to inquire whether their people might come in and smoke with us. This request Capt. Walker very prudently refused, as they evidently had no good intentions, but told them that he was willing to meet them half way between our breast work, and where their people were then sitting. This appeared to displease them

very much, and they went back not the least bit pleased with the reception they had met with.

After the five deputies related the result of their visit to their constituents, a part of them rose up and signed to us, (which was the only mode of communicating with them) that they were coming to our camp. At this 10 or 12 of our men mounted the breast work and made signs to them that if they advanced a step further it was at the peril of their lives. They wanted to know in what way we would do it. Our guns were exhibited as the weapons of death. This they seemed to discredit and only laughed at us. They then wanted to see what effect our guns would have on some ducks that were then swimming in the lake, not far from the shore. We then fired at the ducks—thinking by this means to strike terrour into the savages and drive them away. The ducks were killed, which astonished the Indians a good deal, though not so much as the noise of the guns—which caused them to fall flat to the ground. After this they put up a beaver skin on a bank for us to shoot at for their gratification—when they left us for the night. This night we stationed a strong guard, but no Indians made their appearance, and were permitted to pass the night in pleasant dreams.

Early in the morning we resumed our journey along the lakes, without seeing any signs of the Indians until after sunrise, when we discovered them issuing from the high grass in front, rear, and on either side of us. This created great alarm among our men, at first, as we thought they had surrounded us on purpose, but it appeared that we had only *happened* amongst them, and they were as much frightened as us. From this we turned our course from the border of the lake into the plain. We had not travelled far until the Indians began to move after us—first in small numbers, but presently in large companies.—They did not approach near until we had travelled in this way for several hours, when they began to send small parties in advance, who would solicit us most earnestly to stop and smoke with them. After they had repeated this several times, we began to understand their motive —which was to detain us in order to let their whole force come up and surround us, or to get into close quarters with us, when their bows and arrows would be as fatal and more effective than our firearms. We now began to be a little stern with them, and gave them to understand, that if they continued to trouble us, they would do it at their own risk. In this manner we were teased until a party of 80 or 100 came forward, who appeared more saucy and bold than any others. This greatly excited Capt. Walker, who was naturally of a very cool temperament, and he gave orders for the charge, saying that there was nothing equal to a good start in such a case. This was sufficient. A number of our men had never been engaged in any fighting with the Indians, and were anxious to try their skill. When our commander gave his consent to chastise these Indians, and give them an idea of our strength, 32 of us dismounted and prepared ourselves to give a severe blow. We tied our extra horses to some shrubs and left them with the main body of our company, and then selected each a choice steed, mounted and surrounded this party of Indians. We closed in on them and fired, leaving thirty-nine dead on the field —which was nearly the half—the remainder were overwhelmed with dismay—running into the high grass in every direction, howling in the most lamentable manner.

Capt. Walker then gave orders to some of the men to take the bows of the fallen Indians and put the wounded out of misery. The severity with which we dealt with these Indians may be revolting to the heart of the philanthropist; but the circumstances of the case altogether atones for the cruelty. It must be borne in mind, that we were far removed from the hope of any succour in case we were surrounded, and that the country that we were in was swarming with hostile savages, sufficiently numerous to devour us. Our object was to strike a decisive blow. This we did—even to a greater extent than we had intended.

These Indians are totally naked—both male and female—with the exception of a shield of grass, which they wear around their loins. They are generally small and weak, and some of them very hairy. They subsist upon grass-seed, frogs, fish, &c.— Fish, however, are very scarce—their manner of catching which, is somewhat novel and singular. They take the leg-bone of a sand-hill crane, which is generally about 18 inches long, this is fastened in the end of a pole—they then, by means of a raft made of rushes, which are very plenty—float along the surface of these lakes, and spear the fish. They exhibit great dexterity with this simple stucture—sometimes killing a fish with it at a great distance. They also have a kind of hook by which they sometimes are very successful, but it does not afford them as much sport as the spear. This hook is formed of a small bone, ground down on a sand-stone, and a double beard cut in it with a flint—they then have a line made of wild flax. This line is tied nearest the beard end of the hook, by pulling the line the sharp end with the beard, catches, and turns the bone crossways in its mouth.

These lakes are all joined together by means of the river which passes from one to another, until it reaches the largest,* which has no out-let. The water in this lake becomes stagnant and very disagreeable—its surface being covered with a green substance, similar to a stagnant frog pond. In warm weather there is a fly, about the size and similar to a grain of wheat, on this lake, in great numbers.—When the wind rolls the waters onto the shore, these flies are left on the beach—the female Indians then carefully gather them into baskets made of willow branches, and lay them exposed to the sun until they become perfectly dry, when they are laid away for winter provender. These flies, together with grass seed, and a few rabbits, is their principal food during the winter season.

Their habitations are formed of a round hole dug in the ground, over which sticks are placed, giving it the shape of a potatoe hole—this is covered with grass & earth—the door at one side and the fire at the other. They cook in a pot made of stiff mud, which they lay upon the fire & burn; but from the sandy nature of the mud, after cooking a few times, it falls to pieces, when they make a new one.

These Indians call themselves Shoeshocoes; and the Lakes have been named Battle Lakes.

On the 10th of October we left these Indians and built rafts out of rushes to convey us across the river, when we left the Lakes and continued our course in the direction of a large mountain, which was in sight, and which we could see was covered with snow on the summit. In the evening we encamped on the margin of a large Lake formed by a river which heads in this mountain.** This lake, likewise, has no outlet for the water, except that which sinks into the ground. The water in this lake is similar to lie, and tastes much like pearlash. If this

river was in the vicinity of some city, it would be of inestimable value, as it is admirably calculated to wash clothes without soap, and no doubt could be appropriated to many valuable uses. There is also a great quantity of pummice stone floating on the surface of the water, and the shore is covered with them. The next day we travelled up this river towards the mountain, where we encamped for the night. This mountain is very high, as the snow extends down the side nearly half way—the mountain runs North and South.

In the morning we despatched hunters to the mountain on search of game and also to look out for a pass over the mountain, as our provisions were getting scarce—our dried buffaloe meat being almost done. After prowling about all day, our hunters returned in the evening, bringing the unwelcome tidings that they had not seen any signs of game in all their ramblings, and what was equally discouraging, that they had seen no practicable place for crossing the mountain. They, however, had with them a young colt and camel, which they secured by the natives taking fright and running off, when the hunters came in sight. The next morning, having eaten the last of our dried buffaloe meat, it was decided that the colt should be killed and divided equally to each man. Our situation was growing worse every hour, and something required to be done to extricate ourselves. Our horses were reduced very much from the fatigues of our journey and light food, having travelled through a poor, sandy country extending from the buffaloe country of the Rocky Mountains, to our present encampment, a distance of about 1200 miles, without encountering a single

* Humboldt Lake.
** Apparently Carson Lake.

hill of any consequence, (with the exception of the one in which Barren river heads, and that we went around,) and so poor and bare that nothing can subsist on it with the exception of rabbits—these being the only game we had met with since we had left the buffaloe country, with the exception of one or two antelopes. Notwithstanding these plains forbids the support of animals of every description, yet I do not believe that we passed a single day without seeing Indians, or fresh signs, and some days hundreds of them. Today we sent out several scouting parties to search out a pass over the mountain. Capt. Walker, Nidever and myself started out together. After getting part of the way up the mountain we came to a grove of timber, where the mountain was too steep for our horses, and we left them, and travelled on foot. Nidever was separated from us, when two Indians made their appearance, but as soon as they saw us, they took to flight and run directly towards Nidever, who as once supposed they had been committing some mischief with us, fired, and, as they were running one behind the other, killed them both at one shot. After this unpleasant circumstance we went back to our horses, and from thence to camp. Mr. Nidever was very sorry when he discovered what he had done. In the evening the balance of our scouting party returned, but none of them had killed any game. One of them had found an Indian path, which they thought led over the mountain—whereupon it was resolved that in the morning we would take this path, as it seemed to be our only prospect of preservation. Accordingly, at an early hour the next morning we started on our journey along the foot of the mountain in search of the path discovered on the previous day, and found it. On examination we found

that horses travelled it, and must of course come from the west. This gave us great encouragement, as we were very fearful we would not be able to get our horses over at all. Here we encamped for the night. In the morning we started on our toilsome journey. Ascending the mountain we found to be very difficult from the rocks and its steepness. This day we made but poor speed, and encamped on the side of the mountain.

Oct. 16. Continued our course until in the afternoon, when we arrived at what we took for the top, where we again encamped, but without any thing to eat for our horses, as the ground was covered with a deep snow, which from appearance, lays on the North side of the peaks, the whole year around. These peaks are generally covered with rocks and sand,—totally incapable of vegetation; except on the South side, where grows a kind of Juniper or Gin shrub, bearing a berry tasting similar to gin. Here we passed the night without anything to eat except these gin berries, and some of the insects from the lake described above, which our men had got from the Indians. We had not suffered much from cold for several months previous to this; but this night, surrounded as we were with the everlasting snows on the summit of this mountain, the cold was felt with three fold severity.

In taking a view the next morning of the extensive plains through which we had travelled, its appearance is awfully sublime. As far as the eye can reach, you can see nothing but an unbroken level, tiresome to the eye to behold. To the East the aspect is truly wonderful. The sight meets with nothing but a poor sandy plain, extending from the base of the Rocky mountains to the level below—interposed with several rivers winding their way, here and there forming innumerable lakes, having their margins thinly adorned with a few withering and fading cottonwood trees—where the water ceases to flow, and sinks into the sand. But this is not all. The rivers which head in this mountain, all lead towards the East, as if to meet those from the Rocky mountains, and likewise empty into the lakes. The next morning it was with no cheerful prospect that each man prepared himself for travelling, as we had nothing to eat worth mentioning. As we advanced, in the hollows sometimes we would encounter prodigious quantities of snow. When we would come to such places, a certain portion of the men would be appointed alternately to go forward and break the road, to enable our horses to get through; and if any of the horses would get swamped, these same men were to get them out. In this tedious and tiresome man-

ner we spent the whole day without going more than 8 or 10 miles. In some of these ravines where the snow is drifted from the peaks, it never entirely melts, and may be found at this season of the year, from ten to one hundred feet deep. From appearance it never melts on the top, but in warm weather the heap sinks by that part melting which lays next the ground. This day's travel was very severe on our horses, as they had not a particle to eat. They began to grow stupid and stiff, and we began to despair of getting them over the mountain. We encamped this night on the south side of one of these peaks or ridges without any thing to eat, and almost without fire. To add to the troubles and fatigues which we encountered in the day time, in getting over the rocks and through the snow, we had the mortification this evening to find that some of our men had become almost

Trappers Dancing Around the Campfire. *Alfred Jacob Miller*

unmanageable, and were desirous of turning back and retracing our steps to the buffaloe country! The voice of the majority,
which always directs the movements of
such a company, would not pacify them;
nor had the earnest appeals of our captain
any effect. The distance was too great for
them to undertake without being well
provided, and the only way they could be
prevented, was by not letting them have any
of the horses or ammunition. Two of our
horses were so much reduced that it was
thought they would not be able to travel in
the morning at all, whereupon it was agreed
that they should be butchered for the use
of the men. This gave our men fresh courage, and we went to bed this night in better
spirits than we had done for a long time.
Some of the men had fasted so long, and
were so much in want of nourishment, that
they did not know when they had satisfied
the demands of nature, and eat as much and
as eagerly of this black, tough, lean, horse
flesh, as if it had been the choicest piece of
beef steak.

In the morning, after freely partaking
of the horse meat, and sharing the remainder to each man, we renewed our journey,
now and then coming onto an Indian path,
but as they did not lead in the direction
we were going, we did not follow them—
but the most of the distance we this day
travelled, we had to encounter hills, rocks
and deep snows. The snow in most of the
hollows we this day passed through, looks as
if it had remained here all summer, as eight
or ten inches from the top it was packed
close and firm—the top being loose and
light, having fell only a day or two previous.
About the middle of the afternoon we arrived at a small Lake or pond, where we
concluded to encamp, as at this pond we
found a small quantity of very indifferent

grass, but which our horses cropped off
with great eagerness. Here we spent the
night, having yet seen nothing to create a
hope that we had arrived near the opposite
side of the mountain—and what was equally
as melancholy, having yet discovered no
signs of game.

The next morning we resumed our labour, fortunately finding less snow and
more timber, besides a number of small
lakes, and some prospect of getting into a
country that produced some kind of vegetation. The timber is principally pine,
cedar and red wood, mostly of a scrubby
and knotty quality. After travelling a few
miles, further however, than any other day
since we had reached the top of the mountain, we again encamped on the margin of
another small lake, where we also had the
good fortune to find some pasture for our
horses. This evening it was again decided
to kill three more of our horses which had
grown entirely worthless from severe travelling and little food. The next morning
several parties were despatched on search
of a pass over the mountain, and to make
search for game; but they all returned in
the evening without finding either. The
prospect at this time began to grow somewhat gloomy and threaten us with hard
times again. We were at a complete stand.
No one was acquainted with the country,
nor no person knew how wide the summit
of this mountain was.—We had travelled
for five days since we arrived at what we
supposed to be the summit—were now still
surrounded with snow and rugged peaks—
the vigour of every man almost exhausted
—nothing to give our poor horses, which
were no longer any assistance to us in travelling, but a burthen, for we had to help the
most of them along as we would an old and
feeble man.

This mountain must be near as high as the main chain of the Rocky mountains— at least a person would judge so from the vast quantity of snow with which it is covered, and the coldness of the air. The descent from the Rocky mountains to this is but trifling, and supposed by all the company not to be greater than we had ascended this mountain from the plain—though we had no means of ascertaining the fact. It is true, however, that the vast plain through which we had travelled was almost perfectly level, on part of which the water gradually descended to the West, and on the other towards the East.

Our situation was growing more distressing every hour, and all we now thought of, was to extricate ourselves from this inhospitable region; and, as we were perfectly aware, that to travel on foot was the only way of succeeding, we spent no time in idleness—scarcely stopping in our journey to view an occasional specimen of the wonders of nature's handy-work. We travelled a few miles every day, still on the top of the mountain, and our course continually obstructed with snow hills and rocks. Here we began to encounter in our path, many small streams which would shoot out from under these high snow-banks, and after running a short distance in deep chasms which they have through ages cut in the rocks, precipitate themselves from one lofty precipice to another, until they are exhausted in rain below.—Some of these precipices appeared to us to be more than a mile high. Some of the men thought that if we could succeed in descending one of these precipices to the bottom, we might thus work our way into the valley below— but on making several attempts we found it utterly impossible for a man to descend, to say nothing of our horses. We were then obliged to keep along the top of the dividing ridge between two of these chasms which seemed to lead pretty near in the direction we were going—which was West, —in passing over the mountain, supposing it to run north & south. In this manner we continued until the 25th, without any particular occurrence, except that of our horses dying daily—the flesh of which we preserved for food. Our course was very rough & tiresome, having to encounter one hill of snow and one ledge of rocks after another. On the 25th every man appeared to be more discouraged and down-spirited than ever, and I thought that our situation would soon be beyond hope if no prospect of getting from the mountain would now be discovered. This day we sent out several parties on discoveries, who returned in the evening without bringing the least good news, except one man, who was last coming, having separated from his companions, brought a basket full of acorns to camp. These were the first acorns we had seen since we left the State of Missouri. These nuts our hunter had got from an Indian who had them on his back travelling as though he was on a journey across the mountain, to the East side.—When the Indian seen our hunter he dropped his basket of provision and run for life. These nuts caused no little rejoicing in our camp, not only on account of their value as food, but because they gave us the gratifying evidence that a country mild and salubrious enough to produce acorns was not far distant, which must be vastly different from any we had passed through for a long time. We now felt agreeably surprised that we had succeeded so far and so prosperously, in a region of many miles in extent where a native Indian could find nothing to eat in traversing the same route, but acorns. These nuts are quite different from those in Missouri—being much larger and more palatable. They are from 1½ to 3 inches in length, and about ¾ in diameter, and when roasted in the ashes or broiled, are superior to any chestnuts I ever eat— (though a person subsisting upon very lean horse meat for several days is hardly capable of judging with precision in a case of this kind.)

The next morning we resumed our journey somewhat revived with the strong expectation that after a few days more tedious travelling, we would find ourselves in a country producing some kind of game by which we might recruit our languid frames, and pasture to resuscitate the famished condition of our horses. We still found snow in abundance, but our course was not so much obstructed with rocks as formerly. In two or three days we arrived at the brink of the mountain. This at first was a happy sight, but when we approached close, it seemed to be so near perpendicular that it would be folly to attempt a descent. In looking on the plain below with the naked eye, you have one of the most singular prospects in nature; from the great height of the mountain the plain presents a dim yellow appearance;—but on taking a view with the spy glass we found it to be a beautiful plain stretched out towards the west until the horizon presents a barrier to the sight. From the spot where we stood to the plain beneath, must at least be a distance of three miles, as it is almost perpendicular, a person cannot look down without feeling as if he was wafted to and fro in the air, from the giddy height. A great many were the surmises as to the distance and direction to the nearest point of the Pacific. Captain Walker, who was a man well acquainted with geography, was of the opinion that it was not much further than we could see

with the aid of our glass, as the plain had the appearance of a sea shore. Here we encamped for the night, and sent men out to discover some convenient passage down towards the plain—who returned after an absence of a few hours and reported that they had discovered a pass or Indian trail which they thought would answer our purpose, and also some signs of deer and bear, which was equally as joyful news—as we longed to have a taste of some palatable food. The next morning after pursuing our course a few miles along the edge of the mountain top we arrived at the path discovered by our men, and immediately commenced the descent, gladly leaving the cold and famished region of snow behind. The mountain was extremely steep and difficult to descend, and the only way we could come any speed was by taking a zigzag direction, first climbing along one side and then turning to the other, until we arrived at a ledge or precipice of rocks, of great height, and extending eight or ten miles along the mountain—where we halted and sent men in each direction to ascertain if there was any possibility of getting over this obstruction. In the afternoon of the same day our men returned without finding any safe passage thro' the rocks—but one man had succeeded in killing a small deer, which he carried all the way to camp on his back— this was dressed, cooked and eat in less time than a hungry wolf would devour a lamb.

This was the first game larger than a rabbit we had killed since the 4th of August when we killed the last buffaloe near the Great Salt Lake, and the first we had eat since our dried meat was exhausted, (being 14 days,) during which we lived on stale and forbidden horse flesh. I was conscious that it was not such meat as a dog would feast on, but we were driven to extremes and had either to do this or die. It was the most unwholesome as well as the most unpleasant food I ever eat or ever expect to eat—and I hope that no other person will ever be compelled to go through the same. It seemed to be the greatest cruelty to take your rifle, when your horse sinks to the ground from starvation, but still manifests a desire and willingness to follow you, to shoot him in the head and then cut him up & take such parts of their flesh as extreme hunger alone will render it possible for a human being to eat. This we done several times, and it was the only thing that saved us from death. 24 of our horses died since we arrived on top of the mountain—17 of which we eat the best parts.

When our men returned without finding any passage over the rocks, we searched for a place that was as smooth and gradual in the descent as possible, and after finding one we brought our horses, and by fastening ropes round them let them down one at a time without doing them any injury. After we got our horses and baggage all over the rocks we continued our course down the mountain, which still continued very steep and difficult. The circumstance of one of our men killing a deer greatly cheered the languid spirits of our hunters, and after we got safely over the rocks several of the men started out on search of game, although it was then near night. The main body continued on down until we arrived at some green oak bushes, where we encamped for the night, to wait for our hunters,—who returned soon after dark well paid for their labour, having killed two large black tailed deer and a black bear, and all very fat and in good eating order. This night we passed more cheerful and in better heart than any we had spent for a long time. Our meat was dressed and

well cooked, and every man felt in good order to partake of it.

In descending the mountain this far we have found but little snow, and began to emerge into a country which had some signs of vegetation—having passed thro' several groves of green oak bushes, &c. The principal timber which we came across, is Red-Wood, White Cedar and the Balsom tree. We continued down the side of the mountain at our leisure, finding the timber much larger and better, game more abundant and the soil more fertile. Here we found plenty of oak timber, bearing a large quantity of acorns, though of a different kind from those taken from the Indian on the mountain top. In the evening of the 30th we arrived at the foot or base of this mountain—having spent almost a month in crossing over. Along the base of this mountain it is quite romantic—the soil is very productive—the timber is immensely large and plenty, and game, such as deer, elk, grizzly bear and antelopes are remarkably plenty.—From the mountain out to the plain, a distance varying from 10 to 20 miles, the timber stands as thick as it could grow, and the land is well watered by a number of small streams rising here and there along the mountain. In the last two days travelling we have found some trees of the Red-wood species, incredibly large—some of which would measure from 16 to 18 fathoms round the trunk at the height of a man's head from the ground.

On the 31st we pursued our course towards the plain in a western direction.— Now, that we had reached a country thickly filled with almost all kinds of game, our men and particularly those fond of hunting, were in fine spirits. This day our company was much scattered, and we could hardly tell which was the main body, as the men

Valley of the Yosemite.   *Albert Bierstadt*

were stretched over a large space of ground, all moving within each others hearing towards the plain. After a walk of about fifteen miles we arrived at the margin of the woods, where we concluded to spend the remainder of the day and night. When our men all gathered together it was astonishing to see the quantity of game which they had collected—principally deer and bear. Our hunters complained very much because there was no buffaloe here—as killing these animals afford the hunter such fine sport; and they would not believe any thing else than that buffaloe inhabited this region until they had made several unsuccessful hunts—as the climate and soil is about the same, the grass equally as good and plenty, and the prairies and forests as extensive as those of the region of the Rocky Mountains. But none of these animals have ever been found west of the Great Salt Lake, which is about three hundred miles west of the summit of the Rocky mountains.

On the following morning we directed our course across or rather along the plain, until we came to a large river heading in the mountain and wending its way through the plain. This river presents more wonderful curiosities than any other stream we passed. Its bed lays very deep forming very high banks, even in smooth and level parts of the country; but where there is rocks its appearance is beyond doubt the most remarkable of any other water course. Some places the rocks are piled up perpendicular to such a height that a man on top, viewed from the bed of the river, does not look larger than a small child. From the appearance of these precipices it is not exaggerating to state that they may be found from a quarter to half a mile high—and many of them no wider at the top than at the bottom. Through such places the river forces its

way with great rapidity, tossing pitching & foaming to such a degree that no Indian has the courage to attempt to navigate it with his canoe.—When the water passes through these *narrows* it spreads out in a beautiful deep bay as if to repose after its turbulent dashing against the rocks immediately above, until it reaches the next rapids, when it again pitches forward. This plain is well watered and is quite productive, as we found a large quantity of wild pumpkins and wild oats.

This night it was decided that we should forthwith commence trapping for furs and make this expedition as profitable as possible, for, as yet we had spent much time and toil, and lost many horses, without realizing any profit whatever—although every man expressed himself fully compensated for his labour, by the many natural curiosities which we had discovered. According to the arrangements made on the evening previous, we all the next morning commenced travelling down the river at a slow rate, carefully examining for beaver signs, and recruiting our horses, which they had much need of, as we found them to be much more injured in crossing the mountains than we had at first supposed—many of them being sprained and stiffened almost beyond recovery, and certainly beyond present use. We laid up a large supply of deer, elk, and bear meat, of the best kind. These animals are the fattest of the kind I had ever eat. Here we found a large quantity of acorns, such as those taken from the Indian. These acorns compose the principal food of the wild animals in this section,—the bear, I believe, solely subsists upon them, and where acorns are scarce, the game is both poor and scarce.

The country here appears to be in many respects similar to the east side of the Rocky mountains. The land is generally smooth and level, and the plains or prairies are very extensive, stretching toward the setting sun as far as the eye can reach; whilst a number of beautiful rivers, all heading in this rugged mountain, running parallel with each other thro' the plain, also to the west, with their banks handsomely adorned with flourishing timber of different kinds, such as Blackwalnut, Hickory, Oak, Elm, Mulbery, Hackberry, Alder, Shoemack, &c. This grove of timber may be found along the river at any point, and generally extends about four miles into the plain. Between this grove of timber, and the forest extending from the foot of the mountain, there is a level prairie of the richest soil, producing grass in abundance of the most delightful and valuable quality.

These prairies are in many places swarming with wild Horses, some of which are quite docile, particularly the males, on seeing our horses. They are all very fat, and can be seen of all colors, from spotted or white, to jet black; and here, as in the land of civilization, they are the most beautiful and noble, as well as the most valuable of the whole brute creation.

Since we left the mountain we have seen many signs of Indians, such as moccasin tracks, and smoke rising from the prairies in different places, but as yet we had not succeeded in getting in company with any. At this season of the year, when the grass in these plains is dry, if a fire should be started it presents a spectacle truly grand—and if the flame is assisted with a favorable wind, it will advance with such speed that the wild horses and other animals are sometimes puzzled to get out of the road, and every thing looks overwhelmed with consternation. We continued travelling down the river until the 7th of November, when we arrived at five Indian huts, containing 15 or 20 Indians male and female. When they first beheld the approach of beings so mysterious as we were to them, they exhibited the most unbounded alarm and fear. But it was not long till we succeeded in calming their terror, and convincing them that they had no reason to apprehend any danger, by showing a willingness to smoke, (this being the first token of friendship with all Indians,) which they at once understood and immediately became reconciled, and we commenced gathering all the information from them that our limited means would afford—each being entirely ignorant of the others language, and the Indians being extremely awkward both in making and understanding signs—which is the principal method of conversation with the different tribes in this region. After making many efforts to get some information from them with reference to the Big Water, white people, beaver, &c., without receiving any further satisfaction by way of answer to our inquiries, than a grunt similar to that of a hog, we concluded to spend the night with them for further trial. Towards night whilst passing through their camp, some of our men found two blankets and a knife, which convinced us at once that they had some communication with white people. When the blankets were held up to them they pronounced in tolerable distinctness, the word *Spanish,* and pointed to the west—from which circumstance we inferred that the Spanish settlement could not be far distant.

The next morning our Indian hosts bro't some horses to the camp for the purpose of trading, which were marked with a Spanish brand. After trading for five of the best of their horses, for which we gave one yard of scarlet cloth and two knives, we left these

Indians and continued down the river in search of beaver, which are very scarce. These Indians are quite small, & much darker than those of the buffaloe country, as well as more indolent & slothful. They generally run naked with the exception of a few, who wear shields made of some kind of skins. Their huts are composed of dry poles or logs set upon end, and their bedding consists of grass. Their food is composed principally of horse meat and acorns —the latter are very large and of a good quality, which they manufacture into a kind of mush. Their method of manufacturing this is as follows:—They go to a large log and build a fire upon it and burn it half or two-thirds of the way through, which is done by keeping the log wet except about a foot in diameter, where the fire is kept up until the hole is deep enough, and of the proper shape. After the hole is burnt deep enough they extinguish the fire, scrape out the coals and ashes, and have a tolerably well shaped *hopper.* When this is done they get a long stone which is rounded at one end, and put the acorns in and commence mashing them fine, which is easily done as they are always previously dried by fire or the sun. The meal thus made is then taken out & mixed with water in a basket made almost water-tight—which they broil by making stones red hot and throwing them into the basket. By this process they make a kind of mush with which any hungry man would be glad to satiate his appetite.

These Indians also appear very delicate and feeble—which they attribute to eating acorns. To-day, whilst some of our hunters were searching for beaver signs along the river beach, they found the carcases of four Indians, two of which were partly consumed by Grizzly bears. They appeared as if they had died natural deaths, and been laid there by their friends according to their custom of disposing of the dead, as two of them were well wrapped up in beaver skins. This day our course lay through a large prairie covered with wild oats—which at this season of the year when nothing but the stock remains, has much the appearance of common oats.—This plain lays on the South side of the river, to which we gave the name of Oat Plain. The grizzly bear and wild horses appeared more numerous in the country through which we this day passed, than I had ever before known them. In the evening just before sunset we came across the carcase of another Indian, which was also partly eaten by the wild beasts. From the numerous signs we were led to the belief that the country through which we were now travelling was thickly inhabited with Indians, but notwithstanding we kept watch both night and day we were unable to discover any but those we had left in the morning; nor could we find any of their habitations, although we would sometimes come across a trail that looked as if it was traversed by hundreds at a time. We also discovered some signs of white people, as we would occasionally come across a tree or log chopped with an axe as if done by trappers and hunters. At this place the river is from two to three hundred yards wide, as the country is generally level the water moves gently forward, being quite deep, clear and smooth. This night we encamped on the bank of the river in a very beautiful situation. Soon after the men went to rest and the camp had became quieted, we were startled by a loud distant noise similar to that of thunder. Whilst lying close to the ground this noise could be distinctly heard for a considerable length of time without intermission. When it was at first observed some of our men were much alarmed, as they readily supposed it was occasioned by an earthquake, and they began to fear that we would all be swallowed up in the bowels of the earth; and others judged it to be the noise of a neighboring cataract. Capt. Walker, however, suggested a more plausible cause, which allayed the fears of the most timid. He supposed that the noise origined by the Pacific rolling and dashing her boisterous waves against the rocky shore. Had any of us ever before been at the coast, we would have readily accounted for the mysterious noise.

The idea of being within hearing of the *end* of the *Far West* inspired the heart of every member of our company with a patriotic feeling for his country's honor, and all were eager to lose no time until they should behold what they had heard. We felt as if all our previous hardships and privations would be adequately compensated, if we would be spared to return in safety to the homes of our kindred and have it to say that we had stood upon the extreme end of the great west. The two next days we travelled very fast, without meeting with any thing to impede our progress. On the night of the 12th our men were again thrown into great consternation by the singular appearance of the heavens. Soon after dark the air appeared to be completely thickened with meteors falling towards the earth, some of which would explode in the air and others would be dashed to pieces on the ground, frightening our horses so much that it required the most active vigilance of the whole company to keep them together. This was altogether a mystery to some of the men who probably had never before seen or heard of anything of the kind, but after an explanation from Capt. Walker, they were satisfied that no danger need be apprehended from the falling of the stars, as they were termed.

After travelling a few miles the next morning we arrived at the head of tide water, which convinced us that the noise we had heard a few days previous was created by the ocean. We continued down the river until we arrived at the bay, where it mingles its water with the briny ocean. The country here lays very low, & looks as if it was subject to being overflowed. Here we found difficult travelling owing to the ground being wet and swampy. In the vicinity of this bay we found a great many Indians, who were mostly occupied in fishing—which are very plenty. These Indians appeared friendly enough, but then they manifested a kind of careless indifference, whether they treated us well or ill, that we did not like, and we therefore concluded to leave this place and make for the main coast as soon as possible,—and accordingly we started in a southern direction and after travelling a day and a half the broad Pacific burst forth to view on the 20th. The first night we encamped quite close to the beach near a spring of delightful water. The scenes which we could now contemplate was quite different from those we had beheld and dwelt amidst for months back. Here was a smooth unbroken sheet of water stretched out far beyond the reach of the eye—altogether different from mountains, rocks, snows & the toilsome plains we had traversed. Here we occasionally found the traces of white men, and as the Indians still appeared to act so strange, we began to think that the Spaniards had the Indians under complete subjection, and that they could, if so disposed, set them on us and give us trouble. It was therefore thought best to find out the whereabouts of the Spaniards and cultivate their friendship.

The Indians here practice fishing to a great extent; indeed it seems to be the only thing they do.—They have many methods of catching them—but the principle process is by spearing them with bones made sharp, and some have proper instruments of Spanish manufacture, in which they are very expert.—The principal fish in the river we came down, and which has the principal Indian fisheries, are shad and salmon. We did not find out the name of this tribe, or whether they consider themselves distinct from any other tribe. Most all of the natives we met with since crossing the last mountain, seem to belong to the same nation, as they were about the same colour and size—spoke the same language for any thing we could discover to the contrary, and all appeared equally ignorant and dillatory—and most of them entirely naked. They have no particular place of residence but claim the whole of the country stretching from the mountain to the sea shore as their own. In some parts the natives raise a small quantity of corn, pumpkins, melons, &c., the soil being so very strong and mellow, that it requires but little labour to raise good crops.

21st. This morning the ocean was not so calm as it was the previous evening.—All its sleeping energies were lashed into fury, and the mountain waves of the great deep would roll and dash against the shore, producing the most deafening sound. In the course of the day a detachment of our company was despatched to make discoveries, who returned in the evening and stated that they had discovered many signs of white people, whom they supposed to be Spaniards, but they were unable to come up with them. This same party also found the carcase of a whale which was ninety feet long—the tusks weighing 4½ pounds.

About noon of the third day after we arrived here, the attention of the company was directed to an object which could be dimly seen at a distance riding on the water, which was immediately judged to be a ship, but no one knew from whence it came, where it belonged or where going. It was now our curiosity to know more of this singular object and if possible to attract their attention and bring them to shore. Accordingly we fastened two white blankets together and hoisted them into the air on a pole. This had the desired effect. It was not long until we could tell that the distance between us was fast diminishing, and our joy and surprise may be imagined when we beheld the broad stripes and bright stars of the American flag waving majestically in the air at the mast head. The ship anchored some distance from the shore and the boats were despatched to see what nation we belonged to, and what our business was. Their astonishment was equally as great as ours when they ascertained that we were children of the same nation of themselves. On making this discovery, and a signal to that effect being given by the boats, the ship fired several salutes of cannon in honor of our meeting, which made the welkin ring. —On further acquaintance we ascertained this ship (the Lagoda) to belong to Boston, commanded by Capt. Baggshaw. After exchanging civilities by shaking hands all round, Capt. Baggshaw strongly insisted on us going on board and partaking of the ships fare, stating that he had a few casks of untapped Coneac. This was an invitation that none of us had the least desire to refuse, and accordingly 45 of us went on board the Lagoda, leaving the remainder to take care of the camp, &c. When arriving on the ship Capt. B., had a table spread with the choicest of liquors & best fare the ship would afford, which was immediately surrounded with hungry Capt's. Mates, Clerks, Sailors and greasy trappers—after eating, the glass was passed around in quick succession, first drinking after the fashion of brave Jack Tars, and afterwards in the mountain style, mixed with something of the manners of the natives, in order to amuse the sailors.

After we got on board, the sea became very rough, causing the vessel to pitch and plunge a great deal as she lay at anchor, and consequently I was compelled to return to shore from sea sickness. The balance remained and kept up the celebration until daylight the next morning, when they all returned to land, accompanied by the ships crew to taper off on the harder fare of the trapper and hunter. The feast on the vessel was far superior to anything we could give them, although they appeared perfectly satisfied with the reception they met with from us, as it was a long time since they had tasted any fresh meat, or any thing but salted victuals; and theirs was the first bread, butter, cheese, &c., that we had seen for more than two years.

After the feasting was at an end, Capt. Baggshaw gave us a description of the country to enable us to lay our plans accordingly. He said the nearest settlement was the town of St. Francisco, about forty miles north of our present encampment, situated on the south side of the Francisco Bay, formed by the river which we descended, which he calls Two Laries, or Bush river. It is about three-fourths of a mile wide at its mouth, and is considered a safe harbor for almost any quantity of vessels; and within 60 or 70 miles South of us is the town of Monterey, also Spanish, the capital of this province, & which is called Upper Calafornia. He also informed us that about

60 or 70 miles north of St. Francisco, and about 100 miles from our present position was a Russian settlement; which consists of about 150 families who settled in this country a few years ago for the purpose of catching sea otter, which are of great value, on account of the quality of the fur. They also cultivate the ground to a considerable extent. Captain Baggshaw went and examined the carcase of the whale which our men had found, and pronounced it to be the Sperm whale, the oil of which is of the most valuable kind. He supposed it had been washed here when the sea was rough during a storm, and was unable to make its way back over the sand bars. From him we also learned some further particulars concerning the mountain which had caused us so many hardships in crossing, parts of which was visible from the ocean, particularly the snow covered peaks. This he called the Calafornia mountain, as it runs parallel with the coast for a great distance, commencing at the mouth of the Columbia river, and extending along the coast to the mouth of Red river, or Gulf of Calafornia, forming a beautiful country from the sea shore to the base of the mountain, and extending north and south a distance of about 6 or 700 miles of rich soil, well timbered and abundantly watered by innumerable small streams heading in the mountain and flowing toward the Father of Waters.

Most of this vast waste of territory belongs to the Republic of the United States. What a theme to contemplate its settlement and civilization. Will the jurisdiction of the federal government ever succeed in civilizing the thousands of savages now roaming over these plains, and her hardy freeborn population here plant their homes, build their towns and cities, and say here shall the arts and sciences of civilization take root and flourish? yes, here, even in this remote part of the great west before many years, will these hills and valleys be greeted with the enlivening sound, of the workman's hammer, and the merry whistle of the plough-boy. But this is left undone by the government, and will only be seen when too late to apply the remedy. The Spaniards are making inroads on the South —the Russians are encroaching with impunity along the sea shore to the North,

and further North-east the British are pushing their stations into the very heart of our territory, which, even at this day, more resemble military forts to resist invasion, than trading stations. Our government should be vigilant. She should assert her claim by taking possession of the whole territory as soon as possible—for we have good reason to suppose that the territory *west* of the mountain will some day be equally as important to a nation as that on the *east*.

9. The Crossing of the Sierra Nevada

BY JOHN CHARLES FRÉMONT

EDITOR'S NOTE: John Charles Frémont (1813-1890), explorer, soldier and nominee for President, had a long and colorful life. He made his fame by his Western explorations, often in company with Kit Carson, who acted as his guide. He was involved in California's rebellion against Mexico; made a great fortune when gold was discovered on his vast California estate; and lost the fortune trying to build a railroad by the southern route to the Pacific. In 1856 he was nominated for President by the newly formed Republican party. He lost to Buchanan.

One of his most daring exploits was leading an entire expedition in an extremely dangerous and perhaps rash crossing of the Sierra Nevada in midwinter. His report of the expedition was widely read and added greatly to his fame. The following excerpt, selected from *Memoirs of My Life* (1887), describes the crossing. The year is 1844.

January 28th.—To-day we went through the pass with all the camp, and, after a hard day's journey of twelve miles, en-

camped on a high point where the snow had been blown off, and the exposed grass afforded a scanty pasture for the animals. Snow and broken country together made our travelling difficult; we were often compelled to make large circuits, and ascend the highest and most exposed ridges, in order to avoid snow, which in other places was banked up to a great depth.

During the day a few Indians were seen circling around us on snowshoes, and skimming along like birds; but we could not bring them within speaking distance.

Godey, who was a little distance from the camp, had sat down to tie his moccasins, when he heard a low whistle near, and looking up, saw two Indians half-hiding behind a rock about forty yards distant; they would not allow him to approach, but breaking into a laugh, skimmed off over the snow, seeming to have no idea of the power of fire-arms, and thinking themselves perfectly safe when beyond arm's length.

To-night we did not succeed in getting

the howitzer into camp. This was the most laborious day we had yet passed through; the steep ascents and deep snow exhausting both men and animals. Our single chronometer had stopped during the day, and its error in time occasioned the loss of an eclipse of a satellite this evening. It had not preserved the rate with which we started from the Dalles, and this will account for the absence of longitudes along this interval of our journey.

January 29th.—From this height we could see, at a considerable distance below, yellow spots in the valley, which indicated that there was not much snow. One of these places we expected to reach to-night; and some time being required to bring up the gun, I went ahead with Mr. Fitzpatrick and a few men, leaving the camp to follow in charge of Mr. Preuss.

We followed a trail down a hollow where

John C. Frémont

the Indians had descended, the snow being so deep that we never came near the ground; but this only made our descent the easier, and when we reached a little affluent to the river at the bottom, we suddenly found ourselves in presence of eight or ten Indians. They seemed to be watching our motions, and like the others, at first were indisposed to let us approach, ranging themselves like birds on a fallen log on the hill-side above our heads, where, being out of reach, they thought themselves safe. Our friendly demeanor reconciled them, and when we got near enough, they immediately stretched out to us handfuls of pine-nuts, which seemed an exercise of hospitality. We made them a few presents, and telling us that their village was a few miles below, they went on to let their people know what we were.

The principal stream still running through an impracticable cañon, we ascended a very steep hill, which proved afterward the last and fatal obstacle to our little howitzer, which was finally abandoned at this place. We passed through a small meadow a few miles below, crossing the river, which depth, swift current, and rock made it difficult to ford; and after a few more miles of very difficult trail, issued into a larger prairie bottom, at the farther end of which we encamped, in a position rendered strong by rocks and trees. The lower parts of the mountain were covered with the nut-pine.

Several Indians appeared on the hill-side, reconnoitering the camp, and were induced to come in; others came in during the afternoon; and in the evening we held a council. They immediately made it clear that the water on which we were also belonged to the Great Basin, in the edge of which we had been since December 17th; and it became evident that we had still the great ridge on the left to cross before we could reach the Pacific waters.

We explained to the Indians that we were endeavoring to find a passage across the mountains into the country of the whites, whom we were going to see; and told them that we wished them to bring us a guide, to whom we would give presents of scarlet cloth and other articles, which were shown to them. They looked at the reward we offered, and conferred with each other, but pointed to the snow on the mountain, and drew their hands across their necks, and raised them above their heads, to show the depth; and signified that it was impossible for us to get through. They made signs that we must go to the southward, over a pass through a lower range, which they pointed out; there, they said, at the end of one day's travel, we would find people who lived near a pass in the great mountain; and to that point they engaged to furnish us a guide. They appeared to have a confused idea, from report, of whites who lived on the other side of the mountain; and once, they told us, about two years ago, a party of twelve men, like ourselves, had ascended their river, and crossed to the other waters. They pointed out to us where they had crossed; but then, they said, it was summer time; now it would be impossible.

I believe that this was a party led by Mr. Chiles, one of the only two men whom I know to have passed through the California mountains from the interior of the Basin—Walker being the other; and both were engaged upward of twenty days, in the summer time, in getting over. Chiles's destination was the Bay of San Francisco, to which he descended by the Stanislaus River; and Walker subsequently informed me that, like myself, descending to the southward on a more eastern line, day after day he was searching for the Buenaventura, thinking that he had found it with every new stream, until, like me, he abandoned all idea of its existence, and turning abruptly to the right, crossed the great chain. These were both Western men, animated with the spirit of exploratory enterprise which characterizes that people.

The Indians brought in during the evening an abundant supply of pine-nuts, which we traded from them. When roasted, their pleasant flavor made them an agreeable addition to our now scanty store of provisions, which were reduced to a very low ebb. Our principal stock was in peas, which it is not necessary to say contain scarcely any nutriment. We had still a little flour left, some coffee, and a quantity of sugar, which I reserved as a defence against starvation.

The Indians informed us that at certain seasons they have fish in their waters, which we supposed to be salmon-trout; for the remainder of the year they live upon the pine-nuts, which form their great winter subsistence—a portion being always at hand, shut up in the natural storehouse of the cones. At present they were presented to us as a whole people living upon this simple vegetable.

The other division of the party did not come in to-night, but encamped in the upper meadow, and arrived the next morning. They had not succeeded in getting the howitzer beyond the place mentioned, and where it had been left by Mr. Preuss in obedience to my orders; and, in anticipation of the snow-banks and snow-fields still ahead, foreseeing the inevitable detention to which it would subject us, I reluctantly determined to leave it there for the time. It was of the kind invented by the French for the mountain part of their war in Algiers; and the distance it had come with us proved how well it was adapted to its purpose. We left it, to the great sorrow of the whole party, who were grieved to part with a companion which had made the whole distance from St. Louis, and commanded respect for us on some critical occasions, and which might be needed for the same purpose again.

January 30th.—Our guide, who was a young man, joined us this morning; and leaving our encampment late in the day, we descended the river, which immediately opened out into a broad valley, furnishing good travelling ground. In a short distance we passed the village, a collection of straw huts; and a few miles below the guide pointed out the place where the whites had been encamped before they entered the mountain.

With our late start we made but ten miles, and encamped on the low river bottom, where there was no snow, but a great deal of ice; and we cut piles of long grass to lay under our blankets, and fires were made of large dry willows, groves of which wooded the stream. The river took here a northeasterly direction, and through a spur from the mountains on the left was the gap where we were to pass the next day.

January 31st.—We took our way over a gently rising ground, the dividing ridge being tolerably low; and travelling easily along a broad trail, in twelve or fourteen miles reached the upper part of the pass, when it began to snow heavily, with very cold weather. The Indians had only the usual scanty covering, and appeared to suffer greatly from the cold. All left us except our guide. Half-hidden by the storm, the mountains looked dreary; and, as night began to approach, the guide showed great

reluctance to go forward. I placed him between two rifles, for the way began to be difficult. Travelling a little farther, we struck a ravine, which the Indian said would conduct us to the river; and as the poor fellow suffered greatly, shivering in the snow which fell upon his naked skin, I would not detain him any longer; and he ran off to the mountain, where, he said, there was a hut near by. He had kept the blue and scarlet cloth I had given him tightly rolled up, preferring rather to endure the cold than to get them wet.

In the course of the afternoon, one of the men had a foot frost-bitten; and about dark we had the satisfaction of reaching the bottoms of a stream timbered with large trees, among which we found a sheltered camp, with an abundance of such grass as the season afforded for the animals. We saw before us, in descending from the pass, a great continuous range, along which stretched the valley of the river; the lower parts steep, and dark with pines, while, above, it was hidden in clouds of snow. This we felt instantly satisfied was the central ridge of the Sierra Nevada, the great California Mountain, which only now intervened between us and the waters of the bay. We had made a forced march of twenty-six miles, and three mules had given out on the road. Up to this point, with the exception of two stolen by Indians, we had lost none of the horses which had been brought from the Columbia River, and a number of these were still strong and in tolerably good order. We had now sixty-seven animals in the band.

We had scarcely lighted our fires, when the camp was crowded with nearly naked Indians; some of them were furnished with long nets in addition to bows and appeared to have been out on the sage hills to hunt rabbits. These nets were, perhaps, thirty to forty feet long, kept upright in the ground by slight sticks at intervals, and were made from a kind of wild hemp, very much resembling, in manufacture, those common among the Indians of the Sacramento Valley. They came among us without any fear, and scattered themselves about the fires, mainly occupied in gratifying their astonishment. I was struck by the singular appearance of a row of about a dozen, who were sitting on their haunches perched on a log near one of the fires, with their quick sharp eyes following every motion.

We gathered together a few of the most intelligent of the Indians, and held this evening an interesting council. I explained to them my intentions. I told them that we had come from a very far country, having been travelling now nearly a year, and that we were desirous simply to go across the mountain into the country of the other whites. There were two who appeared particularly intelligent—one, a somewhat old man. He told me that, before the snows fell, it was six sleeps to the place where the whites lived, but that now it was impossible to cross the mountain on account of the deep snow; and showing us, as the others had done, that it was over our heads, he urged us strongly to follow the course of the river, which he said would conduct us to a lake in which there were many large fish. There, he said, were many people; there was no snow on the ground, and we might remain there until the spring.

From their descriptions we were enabled to judge that we had encamped on the upper water of the Salmon Trout River. It is hardly necessary to say that our communication was only by signs, as we understood nothing of their language; but they spoke, notwithstanding, rapidly and vehemently, explaining what they considered the folly of our intentions, and urging us to go down to the lake. *Táh-ve,* a word signifying snow, we very soon learned to know, from its frequent repetition. I told him that the men and the horses were strong, and that we would break a road through the snow; and spreading before him our bales of scarlet cloth, and trinkets, showed him what we would give for a guide. It was necessary to obtain one, if possible; for I had determined here to attempt the passage of the mountain.

Pulling a bunch of grass from the ground, after a short discussion among themselves, the old man made us comprehend that if we could break through the snow, at the end of three days we would come down upon grass, which he showed us would be about six inches high, and where the ground was entirely free. So far, he said, he had been in hunting for elk; but beyond that (and he closed his eyes) he had seen nothing; but there was one among them who had been to the whites, and, going out of the lodge, he returned with a young man of very intelligent appearance. Here, said he, is a young man who has seen the whites with his own eyes; and he swore, first by the sky, and then by the ground, that what he said was true. With a large present of goods we prevailed upon this young man to be our guide, and he acquired among us the name Mélo—a word signifying friend, which they used very frequently. He was thinly clad, and nearly barefoot; his moccasins being about worn out. We gave him skins to make a new pair, and to enable him to perform his undertaking to us. The Indians remained in the camp during the night, and we kept the guide and two others to sleep in the lodge with us—Carson lying across the door, and having made them comprehend the use of our fire-arms.

The snow, which had intermitted in the evening, commenced falling again in the course of the night, and it snowed steadily all day. In the morning I acquainted the men with my decision, and explained to them that necessity required us to make a great effort to clear the mountains. I reminded them of the beautiful Valley of the Sacramento, with which they were familiar from the descriptions of Carson, who had been there some fifteen years ago, and who, in our late privations, had delighted us in speaking of its rich pastures and abounding game, and drew a vivid contrast between its summer climate, less than a hundred miles distant, and the falling snow around us. I informed them (and long experience had given them confidence in my observations and good instruments) that almost directly west, and only about seventy miles distant, was the great farming establishment of Captain Sutter—a gentleman who had formerly lived in Missouri, and, emigrating to this country, had become the possessor of a principality. I assured them that, from the heights of the mountain before us, we should doubtless see the Valley of the Sacramento River, and with one effort place ourselves in the midst of plenty.

The people received this decision with the cheerful obedience which had always characterized them; and the day was immediately devoted to the preparations necessary to enable us to carry it into effect. Leggings, moccasins, clothing—all were put into the best state to resist the cold. Our guide was not neglected. Extremity of suffering might make him desert; we therefore did the best we could for him. Leggings, moccasins, some articles of clothing, and a large green blanket, in addition to the blue and scarlet cloth, were lavished upon him, and to his great and evident contentment. He arrayed himself in all his colors; and, clad in green, blue, and scarlet, he made a gay-looking Indian; and, with his various presents, was probably richer and better clothed than any of his tribe had ever been before.

I have already said that our provisions were very low; we had neither tallow nor grease of any kind remaining, and the want of salt became one of our greatest privations. The poor dog which had been found in the Bear River Valley, and which had been a *compagnon de voyage* ever since, had now become fat, and the mess to which it belonged requested permission to kill it. Leave was granted. Spread out on the snow, the meat looked very good; and it made a strengthening meal for the greater part of the camp. Indians brought in two or three rabbits during the day, which were purchased from them.

The river was forty to seventy feet wide, and now entirely frozen over. It was wooded with large cotton-wood, willow, and *grains de bœuf*. By observation, the latitude of this encampment was 38° 37′ 18″.

February 2d.—It had ceased snowing, and this morning the lower air was clear and frosty; and six or seven thousand feet above, the peaks of the Sierra now and then appeared among the rolling clouds, which were rapidly dispersing before the sun. Our Indian shook his head as he pointed to the icy pinnacles shooting high up into the sky, and seeming almost immediately above us. Crossing the river on the ice, and leaving it immediately, we commenced the ascent of the mountain along the valley of a tributary stream. The people were unusually silent; for every man knew that our enterprise was hazardous, and the issue doubtful.

The snow deepened rapidly, and it soon became necessary to break a road. For this service, a party of ten was formed, mounted on the strongest horses; each man in succession opening the road on foot, or on horseback, until himself and his horse became fatigued, when he stepped aside; and, the remaining number passing ahead, he took his station in the rear. Leaving this stream, and pursuing a very direct course, we passed over an intervening ridge to the river we had left.

On the way we passed two low huts entirely covered with snow, which might very easily have escaped observation. A family was living in each; and the only trail I saw in the neighborhood was from the door hole to a nut-pine tree near, which supplied them with food and fuel. We found two similar huts on the creek where we next arrived; and, travelling a little higher up, encamped on its banks in about four feet depth of snow. Carson found near, an open hill-side, where the wind and the sun had melted the snow, leaving exposed sufficient bunch-grass for the animals to-night.

The nut-pines were now giving way to heavy timber, and there were some immense pines on the bottom, around the roots of which the sun had melted away the snow; and here we made our camps and built huge fires. To-day we had travelled sixteen miles, and our elevation above the sea was six thousand seven hundred and sixty feet.

February 3d.—Turning our faces directly toward the main chain, we ascended an open hollow along a small tributary to the river, which, according to the Indians, issues from a mountain to the south. The snow was so deep in the hollow, that we were obliged to travel along the steep hillsides, and over spurs, where wind and sun

had in places lessened the snow, and where the grass, which appeared to be in good quality along the sides of the mountains, was exposed.

We opened our road in the same way as yesterday, but made only seven miles; and encamped by some springs at the foot of a high and steep hill, by which the hollow ascended to another basin in the mountain. The little stream below was entirely buried in snow. The springs were shaded by the boughs of a lofty cedar, which here made its first appearance; the usual height was one hundred and twenty to one hundred and thirty feet, and one that was measured near by was six feet it diameter.

There being no grass exposed here, the horses were sent back to that which we had seen a few miles below. We occupied the remainder of the day in beating down a road to the foot of the hill, a mile or two distant; the snow being beaten down when moist, in the warm part of the day, and then hard frozen at night, made a foundation that would bear the weight of the animals the next morning. During the day several Indians joined us on snow-shoes. These were made of a circular hoop, about a foot in diameter, the interior space being filled with an open network of bark.

February 4th.—I went ahead early with two or three men, each with a led horse, to break the road. We were obliged to abandon the hollow entirely, and work along the mountain-side, which was very steep, and the snow covered with an icy crust. We cut a footing as we advanced, and trampled a road through for the animals; but occasionally one plunged outside the trail, and slid along the field to the bottom, a hundred yards below.

Late in the day we reached another bench in the hollow, where in summer the stream passed over a small precipice. Here was a short distance of dividing ground between the two ridges, and beyond an open basin, some ten miles across, whose bottom presented a field of snow. At the further or western side rose the middle crest of the mountain, a dark-looking ridge of volcanic rock.

The summit line presented a range of naked peaks, apparently destitute of snow and vegetation; but below, the face of the whole country was covered with timber of extraordinary size. The view given of this ridge is from a camp on the western side of the basin.

Toward a pass which the guide indicated here, we attempted in the afternoon to force a road; but after a laborious plunging through two or three hundred yards, our best horses gave out, entirely refusing to make any further effort; and, for the time, we were brought to a stand. The guide informed us that we were entering the deep snow, and here began the difficulties of the mountain; and to him, and almost to all, our enterprise seemed hopeless. I returned a short distance back, to the break in the hollow, where I met Mr. Fitzpatrick.

The camp had been all the day occupied in endeavoring to ascend the hill, but only the best horses had succeeded. The animals, generally, not having sufficient strength to bring themselves up without the packs; and all the line of road between this and the springs was strewed with camp stores and equipage, and horses floundering in snow.

I therefore immediately encamped on the ground with my own mess, which was in advance, and directed Mr. Fitzpatrick to encamp at the springs, and send all the animals in charge of Tableau, with a strong guard, back to the place where they had been pastured the night before. Here was

A French-Canadian Trapper.
Frederick Remington

a small spot of level ground, protected on one side by the mountain, and on the other sheltered by a little ridge of rock. It was an open grove of pines, which assimilated in size to the grandeur of the mountain, being frequently six feet in diameter.

To-night we had no shelter, but we made a large fire around the trunk of one of the huge pines; and covering the snow with small boughs, on which we spread our blankets, soon made ourselves comfortable. The night was very bright and clear, and though the thermometer was only down to 10°, a strong wind which sprang up at sundown, made it intensely cold; and this was one of the bitterest nights during the journey.

Two Indians joined our party here; and one of them, an old man, immediately began to harangue us, saying that ourselves and animals would perish in the snow, and that if we would go back, he would show us another and a better way across the mountain. He spoke in a very loud voice, and there was a singular repetition of phrases and arrangement of words which rendered his speech striking and not unmusical.

We had now begun to understand some words, and, with the aid of signs, easily comprehended the old man's simple ideas. "Rock upon rock—rock upon rock—snow upon snow—snow upon snow," said he; "even if you get over the snow, you will not be able to get down from the mountains." He made us the sign of precipices, and showed us how the feet of the horses would slip, and throw them off from the narrow trails which led along their sides.

Our Chinook, who comprehended even more readily than ourselves, and believed our situation hopeless, covered his head with his blanket, and began to weep and lament. "I wanted to see the whites," said he; "I came away from my own people to see the whites, and I wouldn't care to die among them; but here"—and he looked around into the cold night and gloomy forest, and, drawing his blanket over his head, began again to lament.

Seated around the tree, the fire illuminating the rocks and the tall bolls of **the** pines round about, and the old Indian haranguing, we presented a group of very serious faces.

February 5th.—The night had been too cold to sleep, and we were up very early. Our guide was standing by the fire with all his finery on; and seeing him shiver in the cold, I threw on his shoulders one of my blankets. We missed him a few minutes afterward, and never saw him again. He had deserted. His bad faith and treachery were in perfect keeping with the estimate of Indian character which a long intercourse with this people had gradually forced upon my mind.

While a portion of the camp were occupied in bringing up the baggage to this point, the remainder were busied in making sledges and snow-shoes. I had determined to explore the mountain ahead, and the sledges were to be used in transporting the baggage.

The mountains here consisted wholly of a white micaceous granite.

The day was perfectly clear, and while the sun was in the sky, warm and pleasant.

By observation, our latitude was 38° 42′ 26″; and elevation, by the boiling-point, seven thousand four hundred feet.

February 6th.—Accompanied by Mr. Fitzpatrick, I set out to-day with a reconnoitering party, on snow-shoes. We marched all in single file, trampling the snow as heavily as we could. Crossing the open basin, in a march of about ten miles we reached the top of one of the peaks, to the left of the pass indicated by our guide.

Far below us, dimmed by the distance, was a large snowless valley, bounded on the western side, at the distance of about a hundred miles, by a low range of mountains, which Carson recognized with delight as the mountains bordering the coast. "There," said he, "is the little mountain—it is fifteen years ago since I saw it; but I am just as sure as if I had seen it yesterday." Between us, then, and this low coast range, was the Valley of the Sacramento; and no one who had not accompanied us through the incidents of our life for the last few months, could realize the delight with which at last we looked down upon it. At the distance of apparently thirty miles beyond us were distinguished spots of prairie;

and a dark line, which could be traced with the glass, was imagined to be the course of the river; but we were evidently at a great height above the valley, and between us and the plains extended miles of snowy fields, and broken ridges of pine-covered mountains.

It was late in the day when we turned toward the camp; and it grew rapidly cold as it drew toward night.

II. Heroes and Villains

10. Adventures in the Wilderness

BY DAVID CROCKETT

EDITOR'S NOTE: Although Davy Crockett (1786-1836) was born in and spent most of his life in Tennessee, I have included him in this collection because his name is always remembered in connection with the defense of Texas against Mexico. Frontiersman, humorist, Congressman, he was a legend in his lifetime — for his exploits in the wilderness as a marksman and trapper, and for his eccentric manners and salty wit. After losing his seat in the House of Representatives a second time in 1835 he emigrated in anger to Texas, where he lost his life in defending the Alamo at San Antonio, March 6, 1836. His autobiography (1834), from which I have selected the present account, is undoubtedly genuine. It reflects the crude and broad humor of the frontier.

David Crockett

HAVING returned from the Legislature, I determined to make another move, and so I took my eldest son with me, and a young man by the name of Abram Henry, and cut out for the Obion. I selected a spot when I got there, where I determined to settle; and the nearest house to it was seven miles, the next nearest was fifteen, and so on to twenty. It was a complete wilderness, and full of Indians who were hunting. Game was plenty of almost every kind, which suited me exactly, as I was always fond of hunting. The house which was nearest me, and which, as I have already stated, was seven miles off, and on the different side of the Obion river, belonged to a man by the name of Owens; and I started to go there. I had taken one horse along, to pack our provision, and when I got to the water I hobbled him out to graze, until I got back; as there was no boat to cross the river in, and it was so high that it had overflowed all the bottoms and low country near it.

We now took water like so many beavers, notwithstanding it was mighty cold, and waded on. The water would sometimes be up to our necks, and at others not so deep; but I went, of course, before, and carried a pole, with which I would feel along before me, to see how deep it was, and to

133

guard against falling into a slough, as there was many in our way. When I would come to one, I would take out my tomahawk and cut a small tree across it, and then go ahead again. Frequently my little son would have to swim, even where myself and the young man could wade; but we worked on till at last we got to the channel of the river, which made it about half a mile we had waded from where we took water. I saw a large tree that had fallen into the river from the other side, but it didn't reach across. One stood on the same bank where we were, that I thought I could fall, so as to reach the other; and so at it we went with my tomahawk, cutting away till we got it down; and, as good luck would have it, it fell right, and made us a way that we could pass. When we got over this, it was still a sea of water as far as our eyes could reach. We took into it again, and went ahead, for about a mile, hardly ever seeing a single spot of land, and sometimes very deep, At last we come in sight of land, which was a very pleasing thing; and when we got out, we went but a little way, before we came in sight of the house, which was more pleasing than ever; for we were wet all over, and mighty cold. I felt mighty sorry when I would look at my little boy, and see him shaking like he had the worst sort of an ague, for there was no time for fever then. As we got near the house, we saw Mr. Owens and several men that were with him, just starting away. They saw us, and stop'd, but looked much astonished until we got up to them, and I made myself known. The men who were with him were the owners of a boat which was the first that ever went that far up the Obion river; and some hands he had hired to carry it about a hundred miles still further up, by

water, tho' it was only about thirty by land, as the river is very crooked.

They all turned back to the house with me, where I found Mrs. Owens, a fine, friendly old woman; and her kindness to my little boy did me ten times as much good as any thing she could have done for me, if she had tried her best. The old gentleman set out his bottle to us, and I concluded that if a horn wasn't good then, there was no use for its invention. So I swig'd off about a half pint, and the young man was by no means bashful in such a case; he took a strong pull at it too. I then gave my boy some, and in a little time we felt pretty well. We dried ourselves by the fire, and were asked to go on board of the boat that evening. I agreed to do so, but left my son with the old lady, and myself and my young man went to the boat with Mr. Owens and the others. The boat was loaded with whiskey, flour, sugar, coffee, salt, castings, and other articles suitable for the country; and they were to receive five hundred dollars to land the load at M'Lemore's Bluff, besides the profit they could make on their load. This was merely to show that boats could get up to that point. We staid all night with them, and had a high night of it, as I took steam enough to drive out all the cold that was in me, and about three times as much more. In the morning we concluded to go on with the boat to where a great *harricane* had crossed the river, and blowed all the timber down into it. When we got there, we found the river was falling fast, and concluded we couldn't get through the timber without more rise; so we drop'd down opposite Mr. Owens' again, where they determined to wait for more water.

The next day it rained rip-roriously, and the river rose pretty considerable, but not enough yet. And so I got the boatsmen all to go out with me to where I was going to settle, and we slap'd up a cabin in little or no time. I got from the boat four barrels of meal, and one of salt, and about ten gallons of whiskey.

To pay for these, I agreed to go with the boat up the river to their landing place. I got also a large middling of bacon, and killed a fine deer, and left them for my young man and my little boy, who were to stay at my cabin till I got back; which I expected would be in six or seven days. We cut out, and moved up to the harricane, where we stop'd for the night. In the morning I started about daylight, intending to kill a deer, as I had no thought they would get the boat through the timber that day. I had gone but a little way before I killed a fine buck, and started to go back to the boat; but on the way I came on the tracks of a large gang of elks, and so I took after them. I had followed them only a little distance when I saw them, and directly after I saw two large bucks. I shot one down, and the other wouldn't leave him; so I loaded my gun, and shot him down too. I hung them up, and went ahead again after my elks. I pursued on till after the middle of the day before I saw them again; but they took the hint before I got in shooting distance, and run off. I still pushed on till late in the evening, when I found I was about four miles from where I had left the boat, and as hungry as a wolf, for I hadn't eaten a bite that day.

I started down the edge of the river low grounds, giving out the pursuit of my elks, and hadn't gone hardly any distance at all, before I saw two more bucks, very large fellows too. I took a blizzard at one of them, and up he tumbled. The other ran off a few jumps and stop'd; and stood there till

I loaded again, and fired at him. I knock'd his trotters from under him, and then I hung them both up. I pushed on again; and about sunset I saw three other bucks. I down'd with one of them, and the other two ran off. I hung this one up also, having now killed six that day. I then pushed on till I got to the harricane, and at the lower edge of it, about where I expected the boat was. Here I hollered as hard as I could roar, but could get no answer. I fired off my gun, and the men on the boat fired one too, but quite contrary to my expectation, they had got through the timber, and were about two miles above me. It was now dark, and I had to crawl through the fallen timber the best way I could; and if the reader don't know it was bad enough, I am sure I do. For the vines and briers had grown all through it, and so thick, that a good fat coon couldn't much more than get along. I got through at last, and went on near to where I had killed my last deer, and once more fired off my gun, which was again answered from the boat, which was still a little above me. I moved on as fast as I could, but soon came to water, and not knowing how deep it was, I halted and hollered till they came to me with a skiff. I now got to the boat, without further difficulty; but the brier had worked on me at such a rate, that I felt like I wanted sewing up, all over. I took a pretty stiff horn, which soon made me feel much better; but I was so tired that I could hardly work my jaws to eat.

In the morning, myself and a young man started and brought in the first buck I had killed; and after breakfast we went and brought in the last one. The boat then started, but we again went and got the two I had killed just as I turned down the river in the evening; and we then pushed on and o'ertook the boat, leaving the other two hanging in the woods, as we had now as much as we wanted.

We got up the river very well, but quite slowly; and we landed, on the eleventh day, at the place the load was to be delivered at. They here gave me their skiff, and myself and a young man by the name of Flavius Harris, who had determined to go and live with me, cut out down the river for my cabin, which we reached safely enough.

We turned in and cleared a field, and planted our corn; but it was so late in the spring, we had no time to make rails, and therefore we put no fence around our field. There was no stock, however, nor any thing else to disturb our corn, except the wild *varments,* and the old serpent himself, with a fence to help him, couldn't keep them out. I made corn enough to do me, and during that spring I killed ten bears, and a great abundance of deer. But in all this time, we saw the face of no white person in that country, except Mr. Owens' family, and a very few passengers, who went out there, looking at the country. Indians, though, were still plenty enough. Having laid by my crap, I went home, which was a distance of about a hundred and fifty miles; and when I got there, I was met by an order to attend a call-session of our Legislature. I attended it, and served out my time, and then returned, and took my family and what little plunder I had, and moved to where I had built my cabin, and made my crap.

I gathered my corn, and then set out for my Fall's hunt. This was in the last of October, 1822. I found bear very plenty, and, indeed, all sorts of game and wild varments, except buffalo. There was none of them. I hunted on till Christmass, having supplied my family very well all along with wild meat, at which time my powder gave

out; and I had none either to fire Christmass guns, which is very common in that country, or to hunt with. I had a brother-in-law who had now moved out and settled about six miles west of me, on the opposite side of Rutherford's fork of the Obion river, and he had bought me a keg of powder, but I had never gotten it home. There had just been another of Noah's freshes, and the low grounds were flooded all over with water. I know'd the stream was at least a mile wide which I would have to cross, as the water was from hill to hill, and yet I determined to go on over in some way or other, so as to get my powder. I told this to my wife, and she immediately opposed it with all her might. I still insisted, telling her we had no powder for Christmass, and, worse than all, we were out of meat. She said, we had as well starve as for me to freeze to death or to get drowned, and one or the other was certain if I attempted to go.

But I didn't believe the half of this; and so I took my woolen wrappers, and a pair of mockasins, and put them on, and tied up some dry clothes and a pair of shoes and stockings, and started. But I didn't before know how much any body could suffer and not die. This, and some of my other experiments in water, learned me something about it, and I therefore relate them.

The snow was about four inches deep when I started; and when I got to the water, which was only about a quarter of a mile off, it look'd like an ocean. I put in, and waded on till I come to the channel, where I crossed that on a high log. I then took water again, having my gun and all my hunting tools along, and waded till I came to a deep slough, that was wider than the river itself. I had crossed it often on a log; but, behold, when I got there, no log was to be seen. I knowed of an island in the slough, and a sapling stood on it close to the side of that log, which was now entirely under water. I knowed further, that the water was about eight or ten feet deep under the log, and I judged it to be about three feet deep over it. After studying a little what I should do, I determined to cut a forked sapling, which stood near me, so as to lodge it against the one that stood on the island, in which I succeeded very well. I then cut me a pole, and crawled along on my sapling till I got to the one it was lodged against, which was about six feet above the water. I then felt about with my pole till I found the log, which was just about as deep under the water as I had judged. I then crawled back and got my gun, which I had left at the stump of the sapling I had cut, and again made my way to the place of lodgement, and then climb'd down the other sapling so as to get on the log. I then felt my way along with my feet, in the water, about waist deep, but it was a mighty ticklish business. However, I got over, and by this time I had very little feeling in my feet and legs, as I had been all the time in the water, except what time I was crossing the high log over the river, and climbing my lodged sapling.

I went but a short distance before I came to another slough, over which there was a log, but it was floating on the water. I thought I could walk it, and so I mounted on it; but when I had got about the middle of the deep water, somehow or somehow else, it turned over, and in I went up to my head. I waded out of this deep water, and went ahead till I came to the high-land, where I stop'd to pull off my wet clothes, and put on the others, which I had held up with my gun, above the water, when I fell in. I got them on, but my flesh had no feeling in it, I was so cold. I tied up the wet ones, and hung them up in a bush. I now thought I would run, so as to warm myself a little, but I couldn't raise a trot for some time; indeed, I couldn't step more than half the length of my foot. After a while I got better, and went on five miles to the house of my brother-in-law, having not even smelt fire from the time I started. I got there late in the evening, and he was much astonished at seeing me at such a time. I staid all night, and the next morning was most piercing cold, and so they persuaded me not to go home that day. I agreed, and turned out and killed him two deer; but the weather still got worse and colder, instead of better. I staid that night, and in the morning they still insisted I couldn't get home. I knowed the water would be frozen over, but not hard enough to bear me, and so I agreed to stay that day. I went out hunting again, and pursued a big *he-bear* all day, but didn't kill him. The next morning was bitter cold, but I knowed my family was without meat, and I determined to get home to them, or die a-trying.

I took my keg of powder, and all my hunting tools, and cut out. When I got to the water, it was a sheet of ice as far as I could see. I put on to it, but hadn't got far before it broke through with me; and so I took out my tomahawk, and broke my way along before me for a considerable distance. At last I got to where the ice would bear me for a short distance, and I mounted on it, and went ahead; but it soon broke in again, and I had to wade on till I came to my floating log. I found it so tight this time, that I know'd it couldn't give me another fall, as it was frozen in with the ice. I crossed over it without much difficulty, and worked along till I got to my lodged sapling, and my log under the water. The swiftness of the current prevented the water from freezing over it, and so I had to wade, just as I did when I crossed it before. When I got to my sapling, I left my gun and climbed out with my powder keg first, and then went back· and got my gun. By this time I was nearly frozen to death, but I saw all along before me, where the ice and been fresh broke, and I thought it must be a bear straggling about in the water. I, therefore, fresh primed my gun, and, cold as I was, I was determined to make war on him, if we met. But I followed the trail till it led me home, and I then found it had been made by my young man that lived with me, who had been sent by my distressed wife to see, if he could, what had become of me, for they all believed that I was dead. When I got home I wasn't quite dead, but mighty nigh it; but I had my powder, and that was what I went for.

THAT night there fell a heavy rain, and it turned to a sleet. In the morning all hands turned out hunting. My young man, and a brother-in-law who had lately settled close by me, went down the river to hunt for turkeys; but I was for larger game. I told them, I had dreamed the night before of having a hard fight with a big black nigger, and I knowed it was a sign that I was to have a battle with a bear; for in a bear country, I never know'd such a dream to fail. So I started to go up above the harricane, determined to have a bear. I had two pretty good dogs, and an old hound, all of which I took along. I had gone about six miles up the river, and it was then about four miles across to the main Obion; so I determined to strike across to that, as I had found nothing yet to kill. I got on to the river, and turned down it; but the sleet was still getting worse and worse. The bushes were all bent down, and locked together with ice, so that it was almost impossible to get along. In a little time my dogs started a large gang of old turkey goblers, and I killed two of them, of the biggest sort. I shouldered them up, and moved on, until I got through the harricane, when I was so tired I laid my goblers down to rest, as they were confounded heavy, and I was mighty tired. While I was resting, my old hound went to a log, and smelt it awhile, and then raised his eyes toward the sky, and cried out. Away he went, and my other dogs with him, and I shouldered up my turkeys again, and followed on as hard as I could drive. They were soon out of sight, and in a very little time I heard them begin to bark. When I got to them, they were barking up a tree, but there was no game there. I concluded it had been a turkey, and that it had flew away.

When they saw me coming, away they went again; and, after a little time, began to bark as before. When I got near them, I found they were barking up the wrong tree again, as there was no game there. They served me in this way three or four times, until I was so infernal mad, that I determined, if I could get near enough, to shoot the old hound at least. With this intention I pushed on the harder, till I came to the edge of an open parara*, and looking on before my dogs, I saw in and about the biggest bear that ever was seen in America. He looked, at the distance he was from me, like a large black bull. My dogs were afraid to attack him, and that was the reason they had stop'd so often, that I might overtake them. They were now almost up with him, and I took my goblers from by back and hung them up in a sapling, and broke like a quarter horse after my bear, for the sight

* Prairie.

of him had put new springs in me. I soon got near to them, but they were just getting into a roaring thicket, and so I couldn't run through it, but had to pick my way along, and had close work even at that.

In a little time I saw the bear climbing up a large black oak-tree, and I crawled on till I got within about eighty yards of him. He was setting with his breast to me; and so I put fresh priming in my gun, and fired at him. At this he raised one of his paws and snorted loudly. I loaded again as quick as I could, and fired as near the same place in his breast as possible. At the crack of my gun he came tumbling down; and the moment he touched the ground, I heard one of my best dogs cry out. I took my tomahawk in one hand, and my big butcher-knife in the other, and run up within four or five paces of him, at which he let my dog go, and fixed his eyes on me. I got back in all sorts of a hurry, for I know'd if he got hold of me, he would hug me altogether too close for comfort. I went to my gun and hastily loaded her again, and shot him the third time, which killed him good.

I now began to think about getting him home, but I didn't know how far it was. So I left him and started; and in order to find him again, I would blaze a sapling every little distance, which would show me the way back. I continued this till I got within about a mile of home, for there I know'd very well where I was, and that I could easily find the way back to my blazes. When I got home, I took my brother-in-law and my young man, and four horses, and went back. We got there just before dark, and struck up a fire, and commenced butchering my bear. It was some time in the night before we finished it; and I can assert, on my honour, that I believed he would have weighed six hundred pounds. It was the

second largest I ever saw. I killed one, a few years after, that weighed six hundred and seventeen pounds. I now felt fully compensated for my sufferings in going after my powder; and well satisfied that a dog might sometimes be doing a good business, even when he seemed to be *barking up the wrong tree*. We got our meat home, and I had the pleasure to know that we now had plenty, and that of the best; and I continued through the winter to supply my family abundantly with bear-meat and venison from the woods.

I HAD on hand a great many skins, and so, in the month of February, I packed a horse with them, and taking my eldest son along with me, cut out for a little town called Jackson, situated about forty miles off. We got there well enough, and I sold my skins, and bought me some coffee, and sugar, powder, lead, and salt. I packed them all up in readiness for a start, which I intended to make early next morning. Morning came, but I concluded, before I started, I would go and take a horn with some of my old fellow-soldiers that I had met with at Jackson.

I did so; and while we were engaged in this, I met with three candidates for the Legislature; a Doctor Butler, who was, by marriage, a nephew to General Jackson, a Major Lynn, and a Mr. McEver, all first-rate men. We all took a horn together, and some person present said to me, "Crockett, you must offer for the Legislature." I told him I lived at least forty miles from any white settlement, and had no thought of becoming a candidate at that time. So we all parted and I and my little boy went on home.

It was about a week or two after this, that a man came to my house and told me I was a candidate. I told him not so. But he took out a newspaper from his pocket, and show'd me where I was announced. I said to my wife that this was all a burlesque on me, but I was determined to make it cost the man who had put it there at least the value of the printing, and of the fun he wanted at my expense. So I hired a young man to work in my place on my farm, and turned out myself electioneering. I hadn't been out long, before I found the people began to talk very much about the bear hunter, the man from the cane; and the three gentlemen, who I have already named, soon found it necessary to enter into an agreement to have a sort of caucus at their March court, to determine which of them was the strongest, and the other two was to withdraw and support him. As the court came on, each one of them spread himself, to secure the nomination; but it fell on Dr. Butler, and the rest backed out. The doctor was a clever fellow, and I have often said he was the most talented man I ever run against for any office. His being related to Gen'l. Jackson àlso helped him on very much; but I was in for it, and I was determined to push ahead and go through, or stick. Their meeting was held in Madison county, which was the strongest in the representative district, which was composed of eleven counties, and they seemed bent on having the member from there.

At this time Col. Alexander was a candidate for Congress, and attending one of his public meetings one day, I walked to where he was treating the people, and he gave me an introduction to several of his acquaintances, and informed them that I was out electioneering. In a little time my competitor, Doctor Butler, came along; he passed by without noticing me, and I suppose, indeed, he did not recognise me. But I hailed him, as I was for all sorts of fun; and when he turned to me, I said to him, "Well, doctor, I suppose they have weighed you out to me; but I should like to know why they fixed your election for *March* instead of *August?* This is," said I, "a branfire new way of doing business, if a caucus is to make a representative for the people!" He now discovered who I was, and cried out, "D—n it, Crockett, is that you?"—"Be sure it is," said I, "but I don't want it understood that I have come electioneering. I have just crept out of the cane, to see what discoveries I could make among the white folks." I told him that when I set out electioneering, I would go prepared to put every man on as good footing when I left him as I found him on. I would therefore have me a large buckskin hunting-shirt made, with a couple of pockets holding about a peck each; and that in one I would carry a great big twist of tobacco, and in the other my bottle of liquor; for I knowed when I met a man and offered him a dram, he would throw out his quid of tobacco to take one, and after he had taken his horn, I would out with my twist and give him another chaw. And in this way he would not be worse off then when I found him; and I would be sure to leave him in a first-rate humour. He said I could beat him electioneering all hollow. I told him I would give him better evidence of that before August, notwithstanding he had many advantages over me, and particularly in the way of money; but I told him that I would go on the products of the country; that I had industrious children, and the best of coon dogs, and they would hunt every night till midnight to support my election; and when the coon fur wa'n't good, I would myself go a wolfing, and shoot down a wolf, and skin his head, and his scalp would be good to me for three dollars, in our state treasury money; and in this way I would get along on the big string. He stood like he was both amused and astonished, and the whole crowd was in a roar of laughter. From this place I returned home, leaving the people in a first-rate way; and I was sure I would do a good business among them. At any rate, I was determined to stand up to my lick-log, salt or no salt.

In a short time there came out two other candidates, a Mr. Shaw and a Mr. Brown. We all ran the race through; and when the election was over, it turned out that I beat them all by a majority of two hundred and forty-seven votes, and was again returned as a member to the Legislature from a new region of the country, without losing a session. This reminded me of the old saying—"A fool for luck, and a poor man for children."

I now served two years in that body from my new district, which was the years 1823 and '24. At the session of 1823, I had a small trial of my independence, and whether I would forsake principle for party, or for the purpose of following after big men.

The term of Col. John Williams had expired, who was a senator in Congress from the state of Tennessee. He was a candidate for another election, and was opposed by Pleasant M. Miller, Esq., who, it was believed, would not be able to beat the colonel. Some two or three others were spoken of, but it was at last concluded that the only man who could beat him was the present "government," General Jackson. So, a few days before the election was to come on, he was sent for to come and run for the senate. He was then in nomination for the presidency; but sure enough he came, and did run as the opponent of

Colonel Williams, and beat him too, but not by my vote. The vote was, for Jackson, *thirty-five;* for Williams, *twenty-five.* I thought the colonel had honestly discharged his duty, and even the mighty name of Jackson couldn't make me vote against him.

But voting against the old chief was found a mighty uphill business to all of them except myself. I never would, nor never did, acknowledge I had voted wrong; and I am more certain now that I was right than ever.

I told the people it was the best vote I ever gave; that I had supported the public interest, and cleared my conscience in giving it, instead of gratifying the private ambition of a man.

I let the people know as early as then, that I wouldn't take a collar around my neck with the letters engraved on it,

---

MY DOG.

ANDREW JACKSON.

During these two sessions of the Legislature, nothing else turned up which I think it worth while to mention; and, indeed, I am fearful that I am too particular about many small matters; but if so, my apology is, that I want the world to understand my true history, and how I worked along to rise from a cane-brake to my present station in life.

Col. Alexander was the representative in Congress of the district I lived in, and his vote on the tariff law of 1824 gave a mighty heap of dissatisfaction to his people. They therefore began to talk pretty strong of running me for Congress against him. At last I was called on by a good many to be a candidate. I told the people that I couldn't stand that; it was a step above my knowledge, and I know'd nothing about Congress matters.

However, I was obliged to agree to run, and myself and two other gentlemen came out. But Providence was a little against two of us this hunt, for it was the year that cotton brought twenty-five dollars a hundred; and so Colonel Alexander would get up and tell the people, it was all the good effect of this tariff law; that it had raised the price of their cotton, and that it would raise the price of everything else they made to sell. I might as well have sung *salms* over a dead horse, as to try to make the people believe otherwise; for they knowed their cotton had raised, sure enough, and if the colonel hadn't done it, they didn't know what had. So he rather made a mash of me this time as he beat me exactly *two* votes, as they counted the polls, though I have always believed that many other things had been as fairly done as that same count.

He went on, and served out his term, and at the end of it cotton was down to *six* or *eight* dollars a hundred again; and I concluded I would try him once more, and see how it would go with cotton at the common price, and so I became a candidate.

BUT the reader, I expect, would have no objection to know a little about my employment during the two years while my competitor was in Congress. In this space I had some pretty tuff times, and will relate some few things that happened to me. So here goes, as the boy said when he run by himself.

In the fall of 1825, I concluded I would build two large boats, and load them with pipe staves for market. So I went down to the lake, which was about twenty-five miles

from where I lived, and hired some hands to assist me, and went to work; some at boat building, and others to getting staves. I worked on with my hands till the bears got fat, and then I turned out to hunting, to lay in a supply of meat. I soon killed and salted down as many as were necessary for my family; but about this time one of my old neighbours, who had settled down on the lake about twenty-five miles from me, came to my house and told me he wanted me to go down and kill some bears about in his parts. He said they were extremely fat, and very plenty. I know'd that when they were fat, they were easily taken, for a fat bear can't run fast or long. But I asked a bear no favours, no way, further than civility, for I now had *eight* large dogs, and as fierce as painters; so that a bear stood no chance at all to get away from them. So I went home with him, and then went on down toward the Mississippi, and commenced hunting.

We were out two weeks, and in that time killed fifteen bears. Having now supplied my friend with plenty of meat, I engaged occasionally again with my hands in our boat building, and getting staves. But I at length couldn't stand it any longer without another hunt. So I concluded to take my little son, and cross over the lake, and take a hunt there. We got over, and that evening turned out and killed three bears, in little or no time. The next morning we drove up four forks, and made a sort of scaffold, on which we salted up our meat, so as to have it out of the reach of the wolves, for as soon as we would leave our camp, they would take possession. We had just eat our breakfast, when a company of hunters came to our camp, who had fourteen dogs, but all so poor, that when they would bark they would almost have to lean up against a tree and take a rest. I told them their dogs couldn't run in smell of a bear, and they had better stay at my camp, and feed them on the bones I had cut out of my meat. I left them there, and cut out; but I hadn't gone far, when my dogs took a first-rate start after a very large fat old *he-bear,* which run right plump towards my camp. I pursued on, but my other hunters had heard my dogs coming, and met them, and killed the bear before I got up with him. I gave him to them, and cut out again for a creek called Big Clover, which wa'n't very far off. Just as I got there, and was entering a cane brake, my dogs all broke and went ahead, and, in a little time, they raised a fuss in a cane, and seemed to be going every way. I listened a while, and found my dogs was in two companies, and that both was in a snorting fight. I sent my little son to one, and I broke for t'other. I got to mine first, and found my dogs had a two-year-old bear down, a wooling away on him; so I just took out my big butcher, and went up and slap'd it into him, and killed him without shooting. There was five of the dogs in my company. In a short time, I heard my little son fire at his bear; when I went to him he had killed it too. He had two dogs in his team. Just at this moment we heard my other dog barking a short distance off, and all the rest immediately broke to him. We pushed on too, and when we got there, we found he had still a larger bear than either of them we had killed, treed by himself. We killed that one also, which made three we had killed in less than half an hour. We turned in and butchered them, and then started to hunt for water, and a good place to camp. But we had no sooner started, than our dogs took a start after another one, and away they went like a thunder-gust, and was out of hearing in a minute. We

followed the way they had gone for some time, but at length we gave up the hope of finding them, and turned back. As we were going back, I came to where a poor fellow was grubbing, and he looked like the very picture of hard times. I asked him what he was doing away there in the woods by himself? He said he was grubbing for a man who intended to settle there; and the reason why he did it was, that he had no meat for his family, and he was working for a little.

I was mighty sorry for the poor fellow, for it was not only a hard, but a very slow way to get meat for a hungry family; so I told him if he would go with me, I would give him more meat than he could get by grubbing in a month. I intended to supply him with meat, and also to get him to assist my little boy in packing in and salting up my bears. He had never seen a bear killed in his life. I told him I had six killed then, and my dogs were hard after another. He went off to his little cabin, which was a short distance in the brush, and his wife was very anxious he should go with me. So we started and went to where I had left my three bears, and made a camp. We then gathered my meat and salted, and scaffled* it, as I had done the other. Night now came on, but no word from my dogs yet. I afterwards found they had treed the bear about five miles off, near to a man's house, and had barked at it the whole enduring night. Poor fellows! many a time they looked for me, and wondered why I didn't come, for they knowed there was no mistake in me, and I know'd they were as good as ever fluttered. In the morning, as soon as it was light enough to see, the man took his gun and went to them, and shot the bear, and killed it. My dogs, however, wouldn't have

* Scaffolded.

any thing to say to this stranger; so they left him, and came early in the morning back to me.

We got our breakfast, and cut out again; and we killed four large and very fat bears that day. We hunted out the week, and in that time we killed seventeen, all of them first-rate. When we closed our hunt, I gave the man over a thousand weight of fine fat bear-meat, which pleased him mightily, and made him feel as rich as a Jew. I saw him the next fall, and he told me he had plenty of meat to do him the whole year from his week's hunt. My son and me now went home. This was the week between Christmass and New-year that we made this hunt.

When I got home, one of my neighbours was out of meat and wanted me to go back, and let him go with me, to take another hunt. I couldn't refuse; but I told him I was afraid the bear had taken to house by that time, for after they get very fat in the fall and early part of the winter, they go into their holes, in large hollow trees, or into hollow logs, or their cane-houses, or the harricanes; and lie there till spring, like frozen snakes. And one thing about this will seem mighty stange to many people. From about the first of January to about the last of April, these varments lie in their holes altogether. In all that time they have no food to eat; and yet when they come out, they are not an ounce lighter than when they went to house. I don't know the cause of this, and still I know it is a fact; and I leave it for others who have more learning than myself to account for it. They have not a particle of food with them, but they just lie and suck the bottom of their paw all the time. I have killed many of them in their trees, which enables me to speak positively on this subject. However, my

neighbour, whose name was McDaniel, and my little son and me, went on down to the lake to my second camp, where I had killed my seventeen bears the week before, and turned out to hunting. But we hunted hard all day without getting a single start. We had carried but little provisions with us, and the next morning was entirely out of meat. I sent my son about three miles off, to the house of an old friend, to get some. The old gentleman was much pleased to hear I was hunting in those parts, for the year before the bears had killed a great many of his hogs. He was that day killing his bacon hogs, and so he gave my son some meat, and sent word to me that I must come in to his house that evening, that he would have plenty of feed for my dogs, and some accommodations for ourselves; but before my son got back, we had gone out hunting, and in a large cane brake my dogs found a big bear in a cane-house, which he had fixed for his winter-quarters, as they sometimes do.

When my lead dog found him, and raised the yell, all the rest broke to him, but none of them entered his house until we got up. I encouraged my dogs, and they knowed me so well, that I could have made them seize the old serpent himself, with all his horns and heads, and cloven foot and ugliness into the bargain, if he would only have come to light, so that they could have seen him. They bulged in, and in an instant the bear followed them out, and I told my friend to shoot him, as he was mighty wrathy to kill a bear. He did so, and killed him prime. We carried him to our camp, by which time my son had returned; and after we got our dinners we packed up, and cut for the house of my old friend, whose name was Davidson.

We got there, and staid with him that

night; and the next morning, having salted up our meat, we left it with him, and started to take a hunt between the Obion lake and the Red-foot lake; as there had been a dreadful harricane, which passed between them, and I was sure there must be a heap of bears in the fallen timber. We had gone about five miles without seeing any sign at all; but at length we got on some high cany ridges, and, as we rode along, I saw a hole in a large black oak, and on examining more closely, I discovered that a bear had clomb the tree. I could see his tracks going up, but none coming down, and so I was sure he was in there. A person who is acquainted with bear-hunting, can tell easy enough when the varment is in the hollow; for as they go up they don't slip a bit, but as they come down they make long scratches with their nails.

My friend was a little ahead of me, but I called him back, and told him there was a bear in that tree, and I must have him out. So we lit from our horses, and I found a small tree which I thought I could fall so as to lodge against my bear tree, and we fell to work chopping it with our tomahawks. I intended, when we lodged the tree against the other, to let my little son go up, and look into the hole, for he could climb like a squirrel. We had chop'd on a little time and stop'd to rest, when I heard my dogs barking mighty severe at some distance from us, and I told my friend I knowed they had a bear; for it is the nature of a dog, when he finds you are hunting bears, to hunt for nothing else; he becomes fond of the meat, and considers other game as "not worth a notice," as old Johnson said of the devil.

We concluded to leave our tree a bit, and went to my dogs, and when we got there, sure enough they had an eternal great big fat bear up a tree, just ready for shooting. My friend again petitioned me for libery to shoot this one also. I had a little rather not, as the bear was so big, but I couldn't refuse; and so he blazed away, and down came the old fellow like some great log had fell. I now missed one of my dogs, the same that I before spoke of as having treed the bear by himself sometime before, when I had started the three in the cane break. I told my friend that my missing dog had a bear somewhere, just as sure as fate; so I left them to butcher the one we had just killed, and I went up on a piece of high ground to listen for my dog. I heard him barking with all his might some distance off, and I pushed ahead for him. My other dogs hearing him broke to him, and when I got there, sure enough again he had another bear ready treed; if he hadn't, I wish I may be shot. I fired on him, and brought him down; and then went back, and help'd finish butchering the one at which I had left my friend. We then packed both to our tree where we had left my boy. By this time, the little fellow had cut the tree down that we intended to lodge, but it fell the wrong way; he had then feather'd in on the big tree, to cut that, and had found that it was nothing but a shell on the outside, and all doted* in the middle, as too many of our big men are in these days, having only an outside appearance. My friend and my son cut away on it, and I went off about a hundred yards with my dogs to keep them from running under the tree when it should fall. On looking back at the hole, I saw the bear's head out of it, looking down at them as they were cutting. I hollered to them to look up, and they did so; and McDaniel catched up his gun, but by this time the bear was out, and coming

* Decayed.

down the tree. He fired at it, and as soon as it touch'd ground the dogs were all round it, and they had a roll-and-tumble fight to the foot of the hill, where they stop'd him. I ran up, and putting my gun against the bear, fired and killed him. We now had three, and so we made our scaffold and salted them up.

In the morning I left my son at the camp, and we started on towards the harricane; and when we had went about a mile, we started a very large bear, but we got along mighty slow on account of the cracks in the earth occasioned by the earthquakes. We, however, made out to keep in hearing of the dogs for about three miles, and then we come to the harricane. Here we had to quit our horses, as old Nick himself couldn't have got through it without sneaking it along in the form that he put on, to make a fool of our old grandmother Eve. By this time several of my dogs had got tired and come back; but we went ahead on foot for some little time in the harricane, when we met a bear coming straight to us, and not more than twenty or thirty yards off. I started my tired dogs after him, and Mc-Daniel pursued them, and I went on to where my other dogs were. I had seen the track of the bear they were after, and I knowed he was a screamer. I followed on to about the middle of the harricane, but my dogs pursued him so close, that they made him climb an old stump about twenty feet high. I got in shooting distance of him and fired, but I was all over in such a flutter from fatigue and running, that I couldn't hold steady; but, however, I broke his shoulder, and he fell. I run up and loaded my gun as quick as possible, and shot him again and killed him. When I went to take out my knife to butcher him, I found I

had lost it in coming through the harricane. The vines and briers was so thick that I would sometimes have to get down and crawl like a varment to get through at all; and a vine had, as I supposed, caught in the handle and pulled it out. While I was standing and studying what to do, my friend came to me. He had followed my trail through the harricane, and had found my knife, which was mighty good news to me; as a hunter hates the worst in the world to lose a good dog, or any part of his hunting-tools. I now left McDaniel to butcher the bear, and I went after our horses, and brought them as near as the nature of case would allow. I then took our bags, and went back to where he was; and when we had skin'd the bear, we fleeced off the fat and carried it to our horses at several loads. We then packed it up on our horses, and had a heavy pack of it on each one. We now started and went on till about sunset, when I concluded we must be near our camp; so I hollered and my son answered me, and we moved on in that direction to the camp. We had gone but a little way when I heard my dogs make a warm start again; and I jumped down from my horse and gave him up to my friend, and told him I would follow them. He went on to the camp, and I went ahead after my dogs with all my might for a considerable distance, till at last night came on. The woods were very rough and hilly, and all covered over with cane.

I now was compel'd to move on more slowly; and was frequently falling over logs, and into the cracks made by the earth-quakes, so that I was very much afraid I would break my gun. However I went on about three miles, when I came to a good big creek, which I waded. It was very cold, and the creek was about knee-deep; but I felt no great inconvenience from it just then, as I was all over wet with sweat from running, and I felt hot enough. After I got over the creek and out of the cane, which was very thick on all our creeks, I listened for my dogs. I found they had either treed or brought the bear to a stop, as they continued barking in the same place. I pushed on as near in the direction to the noise as I could, till I found the hill was too steep for me to climb, and so I backed and went down the creek some distance till I came to a hollow, and then took up that, till I come to a place where I could climb up the hill. It was mighty dark, and was difficult to see my way or any thing else. When I got up the hill, I found I had passed the dogs; and so I turned and went to them. I found, when I got there, they had treed the bear in a large forked poplar, and it was setting in the fork.

I could see the lump, but not plain enough to shoot with any certainty, as there was no moonlight; and so I set in to hunting for some dry brush to make me a light; but I could find none, though I could find that the ground was torn mightily to pieces by the cracks.

At last I thought I could shoot by guess, and kill him; so I pointed as near the lump as I could, and fired away. But the bear didn't come; he only clomb up higher, and got out on a limb, which helped me to see him better. I now loaded up again and fired, but this time he didn't move at all. I commenced loading for a third fire, but the first thing I knowed, the bear was down among my dogs, and they were fighting all around me. I had my big butcher in my belt, and I had a pair of dressed buckskin breeches on. So I took out my knife, and stood, determined, if he should get hold of me, to defend myself in the best way I could. I stood there for some time, and could now and then see a white dog I had, but the rest of them, and the bear, which were dark coloured, I couldn't see at all, it was so miserable dark. They still fought around me, and sometimes within three feet of me; but, at last, the bear got down into one of the cracks, that the earthquakes had made in the ground, about four feet deep, and I could tell the biting end of him by the hollering of my doogs. So I took my gun and pushed the muzzle of it about, till I tought I had it against the main part of his body, and fired; but it happened to be only the fleshy part of his foreleg. With this, he jumped out of the crack, and he and the dogs had another hard fight around me, as before. At last, however, they forced him back into the crack again, as he was when I had shot.

I had laid down my gun in the dark, and I now began to hunt for it; and, while hunting, I got hold of a pole, and I concluded I would punch him awhile with that. I did so, and when I would punch him, the dogs would jump in on him, when he would bite them badly, and they would jump out again. I concluded, as he would take punching so patiently, it might be that he would lie still enough for me to get down in the crack, and feel slowly along till I could find the right place to give him a dig with my butcher. So I got down, and my dogs got in before him and kept his head towards them, till I got along easily up to him; and placing my hand on his rump, felt for his shoulder, just behind which I intended to stick him. I made a lounge with my long knife, and fortunately stuck him right through the heart; at which he just sank down, and I crawled out in a hurry. In a little time my dogs all come out too, and seemed satisfied, which was the way they always had of telling me that they had finished him.

I suffered very much that night with cold, as my leather breeches, and every thing else I had on, was wet and frozen. But I managed to get my bear out of this crack after several hard trials, and so I butchered him, and laid down to try to sleep. But my fire was very bad, and I couldn't find any thing that would burn well to make it any better; and I concluded I should freeze, if I didn't warm myself in some way by exercise. So I got up, and hollered a while, and then I would just jump up and down with all my might, and throw myself into all sorts of motions. But all this wouldn't do; for my blood was now getting cold, and the chills coming all over me. I was so tired, too, that I could hardly walk; but I thought I would do the best I could to save my life, and then, if I died, nobody would be to blame. So I went to a tree about two feet through, and not a limb on it for thirty feet, and I would climb up it to the limbs, and then lock my arms together around it, and slide down to the bottom again. This would make the insides of my legs and arms feel mighty warm and good. I continued this till daylight in the morning, and how often I clomb up my tree and slid down I don't know, but I reckon at least a hundred times.

In the morning I got my bear hung up so as to be safe, and then set out to hunt for my camp. I found it after a while, and McDaniel and my son were very much rejoiced to see me get back, for they were about to give me up for lost. We got our breakfasts, and then secured our meat by building a high scaffold, and covering it over. We had no fear of its spoiling, for the weather was so cold that it couldn't.

We now started after my other bear,

which had caused me so much trouble and suffering; and before we got him, we got a start after another, and took him also. We went on to the creek I had crossed the night before and camped, and then went to where my bear was, that I had killed in the crack. When we examined the place, McDaniel said he wouldn't have gone into it, as I did, for all the bears in the woods.

We took the meat down to our camp and salted it, and also the last one we had killed; intending, in the morning, to make a hunt in the harricane again.

We prepared for resting that night, and I can assure the reader I was in need of it. We had laid down by our fire, and about ten o'clock there came a most terrible earthquake, which shook the earth so, that we were rocked about like we had been in a cradle. We were very much alarmed; for though we were accustomed to feel earthquakes, we were now right in the region which had been torn to pieces by them in 1812, and we thought it might take a notion and swallow us up, like the big fish did Jonah.

In the morning we packed up and moved to the harricane, where we made another camp, and turned out that evening and killed a very large bear, which made *eight* we had now killed in this hunt.

The next morning we entered the harricane again, and in little or no time my dogs were in full cry. We pursued them, and soon came to a thick cane-brake, in which they had stop'd their bear. We got up close to him, as the cane was so thick that we couldn't see more than a few feet. Here I made my friend hold the cane a little open with his gun till I shot the bear, which was a mighty large one. I killed him dead in his tracks. We got him out and butchered him, and in a little time started another and killed him, which now made *ten* we had killed; and we know'd we couldn't pack any more home, as we had only five horses along; therefore we returned to the camp and salted up all our meat, to be ready for a start homeward next morning.

The morning came, and we packed our horses with the meat, and had as much as they could possibly carry, and sure enough cut out for home. It was about thirty miles, and we reached home the second day. I

had now accommodated my neighbour with meat enough to do him, and had killed in all, up to that time, fifty-eight bears, during the fall and winter.

As soon as the time come for them to quit their houses and come out again in the spring, I took a notion to hunt a little more, and in about one month I killed forty-seven more, which made one hundred and five bears I had killed in less than one year from that time.

11. James Bridger, Mountain Man

BY GRENVILLE M. DODGE

EDITOR'S NOTE: James Bridger (1804-1881) was one of the greatest, if not the greatest, of the mountain men. As the historian Allan Nevins has so well said, "It was Bridger who once remarked that for seventeen years he had never tasted bread; who carried an Indian arrowhead embedded in his back for three years, until Marcus Whitman cut it out; who, when asked whether another grave wound he received would not suppurate, replied carelessly, 'In the mountains meat never spoils.' It was Bridger who with a piece of charcoal or stick could scratch on the ground a map of the Far West more correct than any made by cartographers; who discovered many of the principal landmarks between the Rockies and Sierras; who, in 1824 the first white man to see the Great Salt Lake, spat out a mouthful of its water with the exclamation, 'Hell, we are on the shores of the Pacific.' It was he who knew more about the Indians, their habits, minds and desires, than any other white man; who was seen by Captain Stansbury of the Army keeping a large circle of Sioux spellbound for an hour by a long narrative in sign language (the group fre-quently bursting into choruses of surprise or laughter); who summed up the experience of years with 'hostiles' in the remark, 'Where there ain't no Indians, there you find them thickest!' It was Bridger who bought a copy of Shakespeare with a yoke of cattle worth $125 and hired a wagon boy at $40 a month to read it to him, but gave up in the middle of *Richard III* with the ejaculation, 'I won't listen any more to the talk of a man who was mean enough to kill his mother.' "

Major General Grenville M. Dodge, who wrote this tribute to Bridger, made several surveys for the Union Pacific and also took part in the Indian Wars in 1865-66. Bridger acted as a guide for General Dodge during this time.

At this late day it is a very difficult undertaking to attempt to write a connected history of a man who spent a long life on the plains and in the mountains, performing deeds and rendering services of inestimable value to this country, but who, withal, was so modest that he has not bequeathed

James Bridger

to his descendants one written word concerning the stirring events which filled his active and useful life.

It is both a duty and pleasure to make public such information as I possess and have been able to gather concerning James Bridger, and it is eminently proper and appropriate that this information should be published at the time when his remains are removed to the beautiful spot where they will forever rest, and a simple monument erected that posterity may know something of the remarkable man whose body lies beside it.

James Bridger was born in Richmond, Virginia, March 17, 1804. He was the son of James and Schloe Bridger. The father at one time kept a hotel in Richmond, and also had a large farm in Virginia. In 1812 he emigrated to St. Louis and settled on Six Mile Prairie. He was a surveyor, working in St. Louis and Illinois. His business kept him continually from home, and when his wife died in 1816 he was away from home at the time, and three little children were left alone. One, a son, soon died, the second—a daughter, and the third—the subject of this sketch. The father had a sister, who took charge of the children and farm. In the fall of 1817 the father died, leaving the two children entirely alone with their aunt on the farm. They were of Scotch descent. Their father's sister married John Tyler, who was afterwards President of the United States, and was, therefore, uncle by marriage to James Bridger.

After the death of his father and mother Bridger had to support himself and sister. He got money enough together to buy a flatboat ferry, and when ten years of age made a living by running that ferry at St. Louis. When he was thirteen years old he was apprenticed to Phil Cromer to learn the blacksmith's trade. Becoming tired of this, in 1822 he hired out to a party of trappers under General Ashley, who were en route to the mountains. As a boy he was shrewd, had keen faculties of observation, and said when he went with the trappers that the money he earned would go to his sister.

The Rocky Mountain Fur Company was organized by General W. H. Ashley in 1822, and commanded by Andrew Henry. It left St. Louis in April, 1822, and it was with this party that Bridger enlisted.

Andrew Henry moved to the mouth of the Yellowstone, going by the Missouri River. They lost one of their boats which was loaded with goods worth $10,000, and while his land force was moving up parallel with his boats the Indians, under the guise of friendship, obtained his horses. This forced him to halt and build a fort for the winter at the mouth of the Yellowstone, and they trapped and explored in this locality until the spring of 1823.

Ashley, having returned to St. Louis in the fall of 1822, arrived with his second expedition in front of the Aricara villages on May 10, 1823, where he was defeated in battle by the Indians, losing one-half his men, his horses and baggage. He then sent a courier across country to Henry, who went down the Missouri River with his force, and joined Ashley near the mouth of the Cheyenne. The United States forces under General Atkinson were then coming up the Missouri Valley to quell the Indian troubles, and Ashley and Henry expected to remain and meet them, and their party joined this force under Colonel Leavenworth.

After this campaign was over, Henry, with eighty men, including Bridger, moved in August, 1823, to his fort at the mouth of the Yellowstone, and in crossing the country lost two men in a fight with the Indians. He arrived at the fort August 23, 1823, and found that 22 of his horses had been stolen by the Indians. He abandoned the fort, and moved by the Yellowstone to near the Mouth of the Powder River. Meeting a band of Crows, he purchased 47 horses. He then divided his party, and in the autumn of 1823 dispatched the new party under Etienne Prevost, a noted trapper and trader. They moved by the Big Horn and Wind Rivers to Green River.

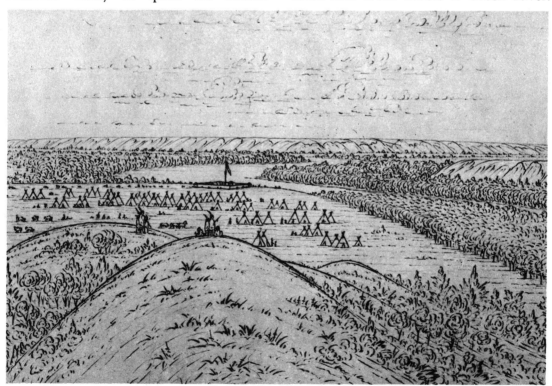

Mouth of the Yellowstone. *George Catlin*

With this party was Bridger, and no doubt it was this party that late in the fall of 1823 discovered the South Pass. The South Pass is the southern end of the Wind River mountains, and all the country there gives down into a level valley until the Medicine Bow range is reached, some one hundred and fifty miles southeast. It forms a natural depression through the continent, and it is through this depression that the Union Pacific Railroad was built. In those days the pass was known to the trappers in the Wind River valley as the southern route. This depression is a basin, smaller than Salt Lake, but has no water in it. It is known as the Red Desert, and extends about one hundred miles east and west, and sixty or seventy miles north and south. The east and west rims of this basin make two divides of the continent.

This party trapped on Wind, Green and other rivers, and in 1823 to 1824 wintered in Cache Valley on Bear River. So far as we have any proof, Bridger was the first white man positively known to see Salt Lake. It is claimed that a Spanish Missionary, Friar Escalante, of Santa Fe, visited the lake in 1776. To settle a wager as to the course of Bear River, Bridger followed the stream to Great Salt Lake and found the water salt. He returned to his party and reported what he had learned, and they concluded it was an arm of the Pacific Ocean. In the spring of 1825 four men in skin boats explored the shore line, and found it had no outlet.

Andrew Henry was in charge of the Rocky Mountain Fur Company until the fall of 1824, when Jedediah S. Smith took the place, and remained Ashley's partner until 1826. Ashley sold the Rocky Mountain Fur Company to Smith, Jackson and Sublette in July, 1826. Bridger trapped in the interest of these men until 1829, Christopher Carson being with him this year. The winter of 1829-30 Bridger spent on Powder River with Smith and Jackson, and in April, 1830, went with Smith by the way of the Yellowstone to the upper Missouri and to the Judith Basin, and then to the yearly rendezvous on Wind River, near the mouth of the Porporgie.

Sublette left St. Louis April 10, 1830, with eighty-one men and ten wagons, with five mules to each wagon, and these were the first wagons to be used over what was known as the Oregon trail. They reached the Wind River rendezvous on July 16.

On August 4, 1830, Smith, Jackson and Sublette sold out the company to Milton G. Sublette, Henry Frack, John B. Gervais and James Bridger. The new firm was called the Rocky Mountain Fur Company, and under these people was the only time the company operated under its own name. The trappers divided and occupied different sections of the country. Bridger, with Fitzpatrick and Sublette, took two hundred men, went into the Big Horn Basin, crossed the Yellowstone, then north to the great falls of the Missouri, ascended the Missouri to the three forks, went by the Jefferson to the divide, then south several hundred miles to Salt Lake. Here they obtained the furs collected by Peter Skeen Ogden, of the Hudson Bay Company. They then covered the country to the eastward, and reached the valley of Powder River by the first of winter, traveling in all about 1,200 miles. Here they spent the winter. It is probable that during this trip Bridger first saw Yellowstone Lake and Geysers, and he was probably the first fur trader to make known the wonders of Yellowstone Park. He talked to me a great deal about it in the fifties, and his description of it was of such a nature that it was considered to be a great exaggeration, but the development of the park in later years shows that he did not exaggerate its beauties and wonders. Bridger was evidently well acquainted with its wonderful features. Captain Chittenden, in his "The Yellowstone National Park," quotes from Gunnison's "History of the Mormons," giving Bridger's description of the park as follows: "A lake, sixty miles long, cold and pelucid, lies embosomed among high precipitous mountains. On the west side is a sloping plain, several miles wide, with clumps of trees and groves of pines. The ground resounds with the tread of horses. Geysers spout up seventy feet high, with a terrific, hissing noise, at regular intervals. Water falls are sparkling, leaping and thundering down the precipices, and collect in the pools below. The river issues from this lake, and for fifteen miles roars through the perpendicular canon at the outlet. In this section are the 'Great Springs,' so hot that meat is readily cooked in them, and, as they descend on the successive terraces, afford at length delightful baths. On the other side is an acid spring, which gushes out in a river torrent; and below is a cave, which supplies vermillion for the savages in abundance. In this admirable summary we readily discover the Yellowstone Lake, the Grand Canon, the falls, the geyser basins, the mammoth springs and Cinnebar Mountain."

Bridger talked about the Yellowstone Lake and its surroundings to everyone he met, and it was not his fault that the country was not explored and better known until in the sixties.

A small lake near the headwaters of the Yellowstone has been named Bridger Lake.

In the spring of 1831 Bridger and Sublette started for the Blackfoot country, where they met a band of the Crows who stole all their horses. Bridger led a party of his men in pursuit and recaptured all these horses as well as taking all the ponies of the Crows.

Fitzpatrick had gone to St. Louis to bring out the winter supplies. Bridger and Sublette followed nearly their previous year's route in their hunting, and in the fall reached the rendezvous on Green River, where they met Gervais and Frack, who were at the head of another party of the Rocky Mountain Fur Company.

After leaving St. Louis, Fitzpatrick came out with his supplies by the way of Santa Fe, and was so long in reaching the rendezvous on Green River that Sublette and Bridger returned to the Powder River to winter, and here they first met the competition of the American Fur Company, which finally drove the Rocky Mountain Fur Company out of the business. Fitzpatrick and Frack joined Bridger here on Powder River, but becoming disgusted with the movements of the American Fur Company, under Vandenburg and Dripps, Fitzpatrick and Bridger with their entire outfit moved west some four hundred miles to Pierre's Hole, near the forks of the Snake River. In the spring of 1832 they moved up Snake to Salt, up that stream and across to John Day River, up that river to its head, and across to Bear River in the Great Salt Lake Basin. Here they again met the American Fur Company, with Vandenburg and Dripps. They struck off into a different country, and finally rendezvoused again at Pierre's Hole, waiting for the supplies from the States being brought out by William L. Sublette. At their rendezvous concentrated this summer the Rocky Mountain Fur Company, the American Fur Company, under Vandenburg and Dripps; Arthur J.

View from the Wind River Mountains, Wyoming.   *Albert Bierstadt*

Wyeth with a new party coming mostly from the New England States, a large number of free traders and trappers and numerous bands of Indians, and here occurred the celebrated battle of Pierre's Hole, with the Gros Ventre Indians, which was one of the hardest battles fought in an early day on the plains, the losses being very heavy.

The battle of Pierre's Hole, or the Teton Basin, was fought July 13, 1832. Of the different fur companies and free traders there were present some three hundred men and several hundred Indians of the Nez Perces and Flathead tribes. The Gros Ventres, about one hundred and fifty strong, always hostile to the whites, were returning from a visit to their kindred, the Arapahoes. They carried a British flag captured from Hudson Bay Company trappers.

When the Indians saw the band of trappers, who were some eight miles from the main rendezvous at Pierre's Hole, the Indians made signs of peace, but they were known to be so treacherous that no confidence was placed in their signs. However, Antoine Godin, whose father had been killed by this tribe, and a Flathead chief, whose nation had suffered untold wrongs from them, advanced to meet them. The Gros Ventre chief came forward, and when Godin grasped his hand in friendship the Flathead shot him dead. The Gros Ventres immediately retired to a grove of timber, and commenced piling up logs and intrenching. The trappers sent word to the rendezvous, and when Sublette and Campbell brought reinforcements the battle opened, the trappers charging the Indians, and finally tried to burn them out, but did not succeed. The Gros Ventres, through their interpreter, made the trappers believe that a large portion of their tribe, some

800, were attacking the rendezvous. Upon learning this the trappers immediately left for its defense and found the story was a lie, but by this ruse the Indians were able to escape. The whites lost five killed and six wounded. The loss of the Gros Ventres was never fully known. They left nine killed, with twenty-five horses and all their baggage, and admitted a loss of twenty-six warriors. The Indians escaped during the night and effected a junction with their tribe.

In 1832 the American Fur Company, operated by Vandenburg and Dripps, came into the territory of the Rocky Mountain Fur Company, which was under Fitzpatrick and Bridger, and undertook to follow their parties, knowing that their trapping grounds yielded a great many furs. They followed them to the headwaters of the Missouri and down the Jefferson. Fitzpatrick and Bridger thought they would get rid of them by going right into the Blackfoot nation, which was very hostile. Finally Vandenburg and Dripps located on the Madison Fork on October 14, 1832, and near this place the Blackfeet killed Vandenburg and two of his men, and drove his party out. The Blackfeet also attacked Bridger and his party, and in his "American Fur Traders" Chittenden gives this account of the wounding of Bridger:

"One day they saw a body of Blackfeet in the open plain, though near some rocks which could be resorted to in case of need. They made pacific overtures, which were reciprocated by the whites. A few men advanced from each party, a circle was formed and the pipe of peace was smoked. It is related by Irving that while the ceremony was going on a young Mexican named Loretto, a free trapper accompanying Bridger's band, who had previously ransomed from the Crows a beautiful Blackfoot girl, and made her his wife, was then present looking on. The girl recognized her brother among the Indians. Instantly leaving her infant with Loretto she rushed into her brother's arms, and was recognized with the greatest warmth and affection.

"Bridger now rode forward to where the peace ceremonies were enacting. His rifle lay across his saddle. The Blackfoot chief came forward to meet him. Through some apparent distrust Bridger cocked his rifle as if about to fire. The chief seized the barrel and pushed it downward so that its contents were discharged into the ground. This precipitated a melee. Bridger received two arrow shots in the back, and the chief felled him to the earth with a blow from the gun, which he had wrenched from Bridger's hand. The chief then leaped into Bridger's saddle, and the whole party made for the cover of the rocks, where a desultory fire was kept up for some time. The Indian girl had been carried along with her people, and in spite of her pitiful entreaties was not allowed to return. Loretto, witnessing her grief, seized the child and ran to her, greatly to the amazement of the Indians. He was cautioned to depart if he wanted to save his life, and at his wife's earnest insistence he did so. Sometime afterwards he closed his account with the Rocky Mountain Fur Company and rejoined his wife among her own people. It is said that he was later employed as an interpreter at the fort below the falls of the Missouri."

One of the arrow heads which Bridger received in his back on this occasion remained there for nearly three years, or until the middle of August, 1835.

At that time Dr. Marcus Whitman was at the rendezvous on Green River en route to Oregon. Bridger was also there, and Dr.

Whitman extracted the arrow from his back. The operation was a difficult one, because the arrow was hooked at the point by striking a large bone, and a cartilaginous substance had grown around it. The doctor pursued the operation with great self-possession and perserverance, and his patient manifested equal firmness. The Indians looked on meantime with countenances indicating wonder, and in their own peculiar manner expressed great astonishment when it was extracted. The arrow was of iron and about three inches long."

In the early thirties Bridger discovered the "Two Oceans Pass," the most remarkable pass, probably, in the world. It is 8,150 feet above the level of the sea. Its length about one mile, and width nearly the same. From the north a stream comes from the canon and divides in the pass, part following to the Atlantic waters by the Yellowstone and part to the Pacific by the Snake River, the two minor streams bearing the names of Atlantic and Pacific Creeks. A stream also comes from the south and makes the same divergence. Fish by these streams pass from one water to the other. Bridger used to tell the story of this river and fish passing through it, but no one believed it until in later years it was discovered to be true, and it is now one of the curiosities of Yellowstone Park.

The first great highway across the plains was no doubt developed by Bridger, and his trappers and traders, in their travels, as the most feasible route to obtain wood, water and grass. Its avoidance of mountains and difficult streams to cross was soon made patent to them. It was known in an early day as the Overland Trail, and later on as the Oregon Trail. It was established by the natural formation of the country. It was first used by the wild animals, who followed the present trail very closely in their wanderings, especially the buffalo. Next came the Indians, who in their travels followed it as being the most feasible method of crossing from the Missouri River to the mountains. Following them came the trappers and hunters, then their supply trains, first by pack and later by wagons. The first wheeled vehicle known to have passed over the trail was a six pound cannon taken out by General Ashley to his posts on Utah Lake in the summer of 1826, and the first carts to pass over it were those taken out by Benneville. Then came the immigration to Oregon, which gave the route the name of the Oregon Trail. Next came the Mormons, and following them the great immigration to California from 1849 on.

In his "American Fur Trade" Captain Chittenden gives this description of the Overland Trail:

"As a highway of travel the Oregon Trail is the most remarkable known to history. Considering that it originated with the spontaneous use of travelers; that no transit ever located a foot of it; that no level established its grades; that no engineer sought out the fords or built any bridges, or surveyed the mountain passes; that there was no grading to speak of, nor any attempt at metalling the roadbed, and the general good quality of this two thousand miles of highway will seem most extraordinary. Father DeSmet, who was born in Belgium, the home of good roads, pronounced the Oregon Trail one of the finest highways in the world. At the proper season of the year this was undoubtedly true. Before the prairies became too dry, the natural turf formed the best roadway for horses to travel on that has probably ever been known. It was amply hard to sustain traffic, yet soft

enough to be easier to the feet even than the most perfect asphalt pavement. Over such road, winding ribbon-like through the verdant prairies amid the profusion of spring flowers, with grass so plentiful that the animal reveled on its abundance, and game everywhere greeted the hunter's rifle, and, finally, with pure water in the streams, the traveler sped his way with a feeling of joy and exhiliration. But not so when the prairies became dry and parched, the road filled with stifling dust, the stream beds mere dry ravines, or carrying only alkaline waters which could not be used, the game all gone to more hospitable sections, and the summer sun pouring down its heat with torrid intensity. It was then that the Trail became a highway of desolation, strewn with abandoned property, the skeletons of horses, mules and oxen, and alas! too often, with freshly made mounds and head-boards that told the pitiful tale of sufferings too great to be endured. If the Trail was the scene of romance, adventure, pleasure and excitement, so it was marked in every mile of its course by human misery, tragedy and death.

The immense travel which in later years passed over the Trail carved it into a deep furrow, often with several wide parallel tracks, making a total width of a hundred feet or more. It was an astonishing spectacle even to white men when seen for the first time.

Captain Raynolds, of the Corps of Engineers, United States Army, tells a good story on himself in this connection.

In the fall of 1859 he came south from the Yellowstone River along the eastern base of the Bighorn Mountains and struck the trail somewhere above the first ford of the North Platte. Before reaching it he innocently asked his guide, Bridger, if there was any danger of their crossing the trail "without seeing it." Bridger answered him only with a look of contemptuous amazement.

It may be easily imagined how great an impression the sight of this road must have made upon the minds of the Indians.

Father DeSmet has recorded some interesting observations upon this point.

In 1851 he traveled in company with a large number of Indians from the Missouri and Yellowstone Rivers to Fort Laramie, where a great council was held in that year to form treaties with the several tribes. Most of these Indians had not been in that section before, and were quite unprepared for what they saw. "Our Indian companions," says Father DeSmet, "who had never seen but the narrow hunting paths by which they transport themselves and their lodges, were filled with admiration on seeing this noble highway, which is as smooth as a bare floor swept by the winds, and not a blade of grass can shoot up on it on account of the continual passing. They conceived a high idea of the 'Countless White Nation,' as they express it. They fancied that all had gone over that road, and that an immense void must exist in the land of the rising sun. Their countenances testified evident incredulity when I told them that their exit was in no wise perceived in the land of the whites. They styled the route the 'Great Medicine Road of the Whites.' "

From 1833 to 1840 Bridger conducted trapping parties in the interest of the American Fur Company through the country west of the Big Horn River, reaching to the Snake, and had many fights with and hairbreadth escapes from hostile Indians.

In 1840 he was associated with Benito Vasquez in charge of an extensive outfit, which they conducted in person until 1843, when Bridger and Vasquez built Fort Brid-

ger, which seems to have terminated Bridger's individual trapping, and his experience as the head of trapping outfits.

In 1842 the Cheyennes and other Indians attacked the Shoshones near the site of Bridger's Fort and got away with the stock. Bridger at the head of the trappers and Snakes followed them, killing many of the Indians, and recapturing part of the stock. However, the Indians got away with several of the horses. On July 8 Mr. Preuss, of Fremont's expedition, met Bridger's party on the North Platte, near the mouth of the Medicine Bow. Writing of this meeting, he says:

"July 8th. Our road to-day was a solitary one. No game made its appearance — not even a buffalo or stray antelope; and nothing occurred to break the monotony until about 5 o'clock, when the caravan made a sudden halt. There was a galloping in of scout and horsemen from every side — a hurrying to and fro in noisy confusion; rifles were taken from their cover; bullet-pouches examined; in short, there was a cry of 'Indians' hear again. I had become so accustomed to these alarms that now they made but little impression on me; and before I had time to become excited the newcomers were ascertained to be whites. It was a large party of traders and trappers, conducted by Mr. Bridger, a man well known in the history of the country. As the sun was low, and there was a fine grass patch not far ahead, they turned back and encamped for the night with us.

"Mr. Bridger was invited to supper, and, after the table-cloth was removed, we listened with eager interest to an account of their adventures. What they had met we would be likely to encounter; the chances which had befallen them would likely happen to us; and we looked upon their life as a picture of our own. He informed us that the condition of the country had become exceedingly dangerous. The Sioux, who had been badly disposed, had broken out into open hostility, and in the preceding autumn his party had encountered them in a severe engagement, in which a number of lives had been lost on both sides. United with the Cheyenne and Gros Ventre Indians, they were scouring the upper country in war parties of great force, and were at this time in the neighborhood of the Red Buttes, a famous landmark, which was directly on our path. They had declared war upon every living thing which should be found westward of that point; though their main object was to attack a large camp of whites and Snake Indians who had a rendezvous in the Sweet Water Valley. Availing himself of his intimate knowledge of the country, he had reached Laramie by an unusual route through the Black Hills, and avoided coming in contact with any of the scattered parties.

"This gentleman offered his services to accompany us so far as the head of the Sweet Water, but in the absence of our leader, which was deeply regretted by us all, it was impossible for us to enter upon such an arrangement."

Fort Bridger, located in latitude 41 degrees 18 minutes 12 seconds and longitude 110 degrees 18 minutes 38 seconds, is 1,070 miles west of the Missouri River by wagon road, and 886 miles by railroad. Bridger selected this spot on account of its being on the overland emigrant and Mormon trail, whether by the North or South Platte routes, as both came together at or near Bridger.

The land on which Fort Bridger is located was obtained by Bridger from the Mexican Government before any of the country was ceded by Mexico to the United States. He lived there in undisputed possession until

he leased the property in 1857 to the United States by formal written lease signed by Albert Sidney Johnston's quartermaster. The rental value was $600 per year, which was never paid by the Government. After thirty years the Government finally paid Bridger $6,000 for the improvements on the land, but nothing for the land. A bill is now pending in Congress to pay his estate for the value of the land. The improvements were worth a great deal more money, but after the Government took possession it seemed to have virtually ignored the rights of Bridger.

The fort occupied a space of perhaps two acres, surrounded by a stockade. Timbers were set in the ground and elevated eight or ten feet above the surface. Inside this stockade Bridger had his residence on one side, and his trading post in the corner directly across from it. It had swinging gates in the center of the front, through which teams and cattle could be driven safe from Indians and renegade white thieves. He owned a large number of cattle, horses and mules, and his place was so situated that he enjoyed a large trade with the Mormons, gold hunters, mountaineers, and Indians.

In a letter Bridger wrote to Pierre Chotau, of St. Louis, on December 10, 1843, he says: "I have established a small fort, with blacksmith shop and a supply of iron, in the road of the immigrants on Black Fork of Green River, which promises fairly. In coming out here they are generally well supplied with money, but by the time they get here they are in need of all kinds of supplies, horses, provisions, smith-work, etc. They bring ready cash from the States, and should I receive the goods ordered will have considerable business in that way with them, and establish trade with the Indians in the neighborhood, who have a good number of

"I took ye for an Injin."   *Frederick Remington*

beaver among them. The fort is a beautiful location in the Black Fork of Green River, receiving fine, fresh water from the snow on the Uintah range. The streams are alive with mountain trout. It passes through the fort in several channels, each lined with trees, kept alive by the moisture of the soil."

It was a veritable oasis in the desert, and its selection showed good judgment on the part of the founder.

In 1856 Bridger had trouble with the Mormons. They threatened him with death

and the confiscation of all his property at Fort Bridger, and he was robbed of all his stock, merchandise, and, in fact, of everything he possessed, which he claimed was worth $100,000. The buildings at the fort were destroyed by fire, and Bridger barely escaped with his life. This brought on what was known as the Utah Expedition, under Albert Sidney Johnston, Bridger piloted the army out there, taking it through by what is known as the Southern Route, which he had discovered, which runs by the South Platte, up the Lodge Pole, over Cheyenne Pass, by old Fort Halleck, and across the continental divide at Bridger's Pass at the head of the Muddy, follows down Bitter Creek to Green River, crosses that river, and then up Black Fork to Fort Bridger.

As the troops had made no arrangements for winter, and shelter for the stock was not to be found in the vicinity of Salt Lake, Bridger tendered to them the use of Fort Bridger and the adjoining property, which offer was accepted by Johnston, who wintered his army there. It was at this time that the Government purchased from Bridger his Mexican Grant of Fort Bridger, but, as heretofore mentioned, never paid him for the property, merely paying the rental, and claiming that Bridger's title was not perfect. This was a great injustice to Bridger. His title was one of possession. He had established here a trading post that had been of great benefit to the Government and the overland immigration, and he was entitled to all he claimed. The fort was the rendezvous of all the trade and travel, of the Indians, trappers and voyagers of all that section of the country.

Concerning his claim against the Government, under date of October 27, 1873, Bridger wrote to General B. F. Butler, U. S. Senator, as follows:

" * * * You are probably aware that I am one of the earliest and oldest explorers and trappers of the Great West now alive. Many years prior to the Mexican War, the time Fort Bridger and adjoining territories became the property of the United States, and for ten years thereafter (1857) I was in peaceable possession of my old trading post, Fort Bridger, occupied it as such, and resided thereat, a fact well known to the Government, as well as the public in general.

"Shortly before the so-called Utah Expedition, and before the Government troops under General A. S. Johnston arrived near Salt Lake City, I was robbed and threatened with death by the Mormons, by the direction of Brigham Young, of all my merchandise, stock — in fact everything I possessed, amounting to more than $100,000 worth — the buildings in the fort practically destroyed by fire, and I barely escaped with my life.

"I was with and piloted the army under said General Johnston out there, and since the approach of winter no convenient shelter for the troops and stock could be found in the vicinity of Salt Lake, I tendered to them my so-called fort (Fort Bridger), with the adjoining shelter, affording rally for winter quarters. My offer being accepted, a written contract was entered into between myself and Captain Dickerson of the Quartermaster's Department, in behalf of the United States, approved by General A. S. Johnston, and more, so signed by various officers on the general's staff such as Major Fitz-John Porter, Drs. Madison, Mills and Bailey; Lieutenant Rich, Colonel Weight, and others, a copy of which is now on file in the War Department at Washington. I also was furnished with a copy thereof, which was unfortunately destroyed during the war.

* * * * *

"I am now getting old and feeble and am a poor man and consequently unable to prosecute my claim as it probably should be done. For that reason I respectfully apply to you with the desire of entrusting the matter into your hands, authorizing you for me to use such means as you may deem proper for the successful prosecution of this claim. I would further state that I have been strictly loyal during the later rebellion, and during the most of the time in the war in the employment of the Government.

"Trusting confidently that you will do me the favor of taking the matter in hand or furnish me with your advice in the matter, I have the honor, etc."

On July 4, 1849, Bridger's second wife, a Ute, died. He had been for some time considering the movement of his family to the States, where his children could be educated, intending to devote his own time to the trading post at Fort Bridger. He went to the States in 1850, taking with him his third wife, a Snake woman, and settled upon a little farm near Little Santa Fe, Jackson County, Mo. Bridger usually spent the summers on the plains and went home winters.

In the spring of 1862 Bridger was at his home in Little Santa Fe, when the Government called him onto the plains to guide the troops in the Indian campaigns. I found him there when I took charge of that country in January, 1865, and placed him as guide of the Eleventh Ohio Cavalry in its march from Fort Riley to Fort Laramie. Bridger remained with them at Fort Laramie as their guide, and took part with them in the many encounters they had with the Indians, and his services to them were invaluable.

In the Indian campaign of 1865-6 Bridger guided General Conner's column that marched from Fort Laramie to Tongue River, and took part in the battle on Tongue River.

Captain H. E. Palmer, Eleventh Kansas Cavalry, Acting Asst. Adjt. Genl. to General P. E. Conner, gives this description of the Indian camp on Tongue River, August 26, 1865:

"Left Piney Fork at 6:45 a. m. Traveled north over a beautiful country until about 8 a. m., when our advance reached the top of the ridge dividing the waters of the Powder from that of the Tongue River. I was riding in the extreme advance in company with Major Bridger. We were 2,000 yards at least ahead of the General and his staff; our Pawnee scouts were on each flank and a little in advance; at that time there was no advance guard immediately in front. As the Major and myself reached the top of the hill we voluntarily halted our steeds. I raised my field glass to my eyes and took in the grandest view that I had ever seen. I could see the north end of the Big Horn range, and away beyond the faint outline of the mountains beyond the Yellowstone. Away to the northeast the Wolf Mountain range was distinctly visible. Immediately before us lay the valley of Peneau creek, now called Prairie Dog creek, and beyond the Little Goose, Big Goose and Tongue River valleys, and many other tributary streams. The morning was clear and bright, with not a breath of air stirring. The old Major, sitting upon his horse with his eyes shaded with his hands, had been telling me for an hour or more about his Indian life — his forty years' experience on the plains, telling me how to trail Indians and distinguish the tracks of different tribes; how every spear of grass, every tree and shrub and stone was a compass to the experienced trapper and hunter — a subject that I had discussed with him nearly every day. During the winter of 1863 I had contributed to help Mrs. Bridger and the rest of the family, all of which facts the Major had been acquainted with, which induced him to treat me as an old-time friend.

As I lowered my glass the Major said: 'Do you see those ere columns of smoke over yonder?' I replied: 'Where, Major?' to which he answered: 'Over there by that ere saddle,' meaning a depression in the hills not unlike the shape of a saddle, pointing at the same time to a point nearly fifty miles away. I again raised my glass to my eyes and took a long, earnest look, and for the life of me could not see any column of smoke, even with a strong field glass. The Major was looking without any artificial help. The atmosphere appeared to be slightly hazy in the long distance, like smoke, but there were no distinct columns of smoke in sight. As soon as the General with his staff arrived I called his attention to Major Bridger's discovery. The General raised his field glass and scanned the horizon closely. After a long look, he remarked that there were no columns of smoke to be seen. The Major quietly mounted his horse and rode on. I asked the General to look again; that the Major was very confident that he could see columns of smoke, which, of course, indicated an Indian village. The General made another examination and again asserted that there was no column of smoke. However, to satisfy curiosity and to give our guides no chance to claim that they had shown us an Indian village and we would not attack it, he suggested to Captain Frank North, who was riding with his staff, that he go with seven of his Indians in the direction indicated to reconnoitre and to report to us on Peneau Creek or Tongue River, down which we were to march. I galloped on and overtook the Major, and as I came up to him overheard him remark about 'these damn paper collar soldiers' telling him there was no columns of smoke. The old man was very indignant at our doubting his ability to outsee us, with the aid of field glasses even. Just after sunset on August 27 two of the Pawnees who went out with Captain North towards Bridger's column of smoke two days previous came into camp with the information that Captain North had discovered an Indian village."

It was this village that Conner captured the next day, the fight being known as the Battle of Tongue River.

In May, 1869, Captain Raynolds was assigned to the exploration of the country surrounding Yellowstone Park, and I have no doubt it was from hearing of Bridger's knowledge of that park and its surroundings that caused him to engage Bridger for his guide. Bridger was with him about a year and a half, but they failed on this trip to enter the park, being stopped by the heavy snows in the passes, but they explored and mapped the country surrounding the park.

In 1860 Ned Buntline, the great short story romance writer, hunted up Bridger at his home in Weston, and Bridger gave him enough adventures to keep him writing the balance of his life. Bridger took a liking to Buntline, and took him across the plains with him on a scouting trip. After a while Buntline returned to the East, and not long afterwards the Jim Bridger stories commenced to be published. One of these was printed every week, and Bridger's companions used to save them up and read them to him. Buntline made Bridger famous, and carried him through more hairbreadth escapes than any man ever had.

Bridger's first wife was the daughter of a Flathead chief. She died in 1846. Her children were Felix and Josephine, both of whom were sent to school at St. Louis. Felix enlisted in the spring of 1863 in Company L, Second Missouri Artillery, under General Totten. He served throughout the Civil War, and later was with Custer in his Indian campaigns in Texas and Indian Territory. He died in 1876 on the farm near Little Santa Fe, Mo., having returned there from Dallas, Texas.

Bridger's second wife was a Ute, who died July 4, 1849, at the birth of her first child, now Mrs. Virginia K. Waschman. Bridger brought this child up on buffalo's milk. When she was 5 years old she was sent to

Robert Campbell in St. Louis, and two years later joined her sister Josephine in the convent.

When Virginia was about 10 years old she obtained from Mrs. Robert Campbell a daguerreotype of her father which was taken in 1843. She colored or painted this picture, and in 1902 presented it to me, saying: "I am most sure you will be pleased with it as a gift from me, and it will remind you of the great old times that you and father had when you were out in the mountains among the wild Indians. I have often heard my father speak of you, and have wanted to see you and tell you a great many things that happened when I was a child at Fort Bridger. Before my father's death he was very anxious to see you regarding old Fort Bridger, but could not find you."

In 1850 Bridger took as his third wife a Snake woman. He bought a little farm near Santa Fe, Mo., and moved his family there from Fort Bridger that year. Mary was born in 1853. William was born in 1857, and died from consumption in 1892. In 1858 his wife died and was buried in Boone cemetery, near Waldo Station, Mo. Bridger was on the plains at the time of her death, but returned to Missouri in the spring of 1859, soon after he heard of her death, and remained on the farm until 1862. This year he rented the farm to a man named Brooks, and bought the Colonel A. G. Boone house in Westport. He left his family there in charge of a Mr. London and his wife, and on the call of the Government in the spring of 1862 he left for the mountains to guide the troops on the plains. He remained on the plains until late in 1869 or 1870. In the spring of 1871 he moved back to his farm near Little Santa Fe.

Of his life from this time until his death, his daughter, Mrs. Waschman, writes me the following:

"In 1873 father's health began to fail him, and his eyes were very bad, so that he could not see good, and the only way that father could distinguish any person was by the sound of their voices, but all who had the privilege of knowing him were aware of his wonderful state of health at that time, but later, in 1874, father's eyesight was leaving him very fast, and this worried him so much. He has often-times wished that he could see you. At times father would get very nervous, and wanted to be on the go. I had to watch after him and lead him around to please him, never still one moment.

"I got father a good old gentle horse, so that he could ride around and have something to pass away time, so one day he named his old horse 'Ruff.' We also had a dog that went with father; he named this old, faithful dog 'Sultan.' Sometimes father would call me and say: 'I wish you would go and saddle old Ruff for me; I feel like riding around the farm,' and the faithful old dog would go along. Father could not see very well, but the old faithful horse would guide him along, but at times father would draw the lines wrong, and the horse would go wrong, and then they would get lost in the woods. The strange part of it was the old, faithful dog, Sultan, would come home and let us know that father was lost. The dog would bark and whine until I would go out and look for him, and lead him and the old horse home on the main road. Sometimes father wanted to take a walk out to the fields with old Sultan by his side, and cane in hand to guide his way out to the wheat field, would want to know how high the wheat was, and then father would go down on his knees and reach out his hands to feel for the wheat, and that was the way he passed away his time.

"Father at times wished that he could see,

and only have his eyesight back again, so that he could go back out to see the mountains. I know he at times would feel lonesome, and long to see some of his old mountain friends to have a good chat of olden times away back in the fifties.

"Father often spoke of you, and would say, 'I wonder if General Dodge is alive or not; I would give anything in the world if I could see some of the old army officers once more to have a talk with them of olden times, but I know I will not be able to see any of my old-time mountain friends any more. I know that my time is near. I feel that my health is failing me very fast, and see that I am not the same man I used to be.' "

Bridger was 77 years old when he died, and was buried on the Stubbins Watts farm, a mile north of Dallas, not far south of Westport. His two sons, William and Felix, were buried beside him.

On Bridger's grave-stone is the following:

"James Bridger, born March 17, 1804; died July 17, 1881.

We miss thee in the circle around the fireside,
We miss thee in devotion at peaceful eventide.
The memory of your nature so full of truth and love,
Shall lead our thoughts to seek thee among the best above."

At the time of his death Bridger's home was a long, two story house, not far from where he is buried, with big chimneys at each end. It is now abandoned and dilapidated, with windows all broken. It is about one mile south of Dallas. He had 160 acres of land. No one has lived in the house for

Trappers Setting Out for the Hunt. *Albert Jacob Miller*

years. The neighbors say it is haunted, and will not go near it.

One of his wives is buried in a grave-yard several miles east of his grave.

I found Bridger a very companionable man. In person he was over six feet tall, spare, straight as an arrow, agile, rawboned and of powerful frame, eyes gray, hair brown and abundant even in old age, expression mild and manners agreeable. He was hospitable and generous, and was always trusted and respected. He possessed in a high degree the confidence of the Indians. He was one of the most noted hunters and trappers on the plains. Naturally shrewd, and possessing keen facilities of observation, he carefully studied the habits of all the animals, especially the beaver, and, profiting from the knowledge obtained from the Indians, with whom he chiefly associated, and with whom he became a great favorite, he soon became one of the most expert hunters and trappers in the mountains. The beaver at first abounded in every mountain stream in the country, but, at length, by being constantly pursued, they began to grow more wary and diminish in numbers, until it became necessary for trappers to extend their researches to more distant streams. Eager to gratify his curiosity, and with a natural fondness for mountain scenery, he traversed the country in every direction, sometimes accompanied by an Indian, but oftener alone. He familiarized himself with every mountain peak, every deep gorge, every hill and every landmark in the country. Having arrived upon the banks of some before undiscovered stream, and finding signs of his favorite game, he would immediately proceed to his traps, and then take his gun and wander over the hills in quest of game, the meat of which formed the only diet of the trapper at that early day. When a stream afforded

game it was trapped to its source, and never left as long as beaver could be caught.

While engaged in this thorough system of trapping, no object of interest escaped his scrutiny, and when once known it was ever after remembered. He could describe with the minutest accuracy places that perhaps he had visited but once, and that many years before, and he could travel in almost a direct line from one point to another in the greatest distances, with certainty of always making his goal. He pursued his trapping expeditions north to the British possessions, south far into New Mexico and west to the Pacific Ocean, and in this way became acquainted with all the Indian tribes in the country, and by long intercourse with them learned their languages, and became familiar with all their signs. He adopted their habits, conformed to their customs, became imbued with all their superstitions, and at length excelled them in strategy.

He was a great favorite with the Crow nation, and was at one time elected and became their chief.

Bridger was also a great Indian fighter, and I have heard two things said of him by the best plainsmen of his time; that he did not know what fear was, and that he never once lost his bearings, either on the plains or in the mountains.

In those days Bridger was rich. He was at the head of great trapping parties, and two great fur companies — the Rocky Mountain Fur Company and Northwestern Fur Company. When he became older he spent his winters in Westport, and in the summer was a scout and guide for Government troops, getting ten dollars a day in gold.

Unquestionably Bridger's claims to remembrance rest upon the extraordinary part he bore in the explorations of the West. As a guide he was without an equal, and this is the testimony of everyone who ever employed him. He was a born topographer; the whole West was mapped out in his mind, and such was his instinctive sense of locality and direction that it used to be said of him that he could smell his way where he could not see it. He was a complete master of plains and woodcraft, equal to any emergency, full of resources to overcome any obstacle, and I came to learn gradually how it was that for months such men could live without food except what the country afforded in that wild region. In a few hours they would put together a bull-boat and put us across any stream. Nothing escaped their vision, the dropping of a stick or breaking of a twig, the turning of the growing grass, all brought knowledge to them, and they could tell who or what had done it. A single horse or Indian could not cross the trail but that they discovered it, and could tell how long since they passed. Their methods of hunting game were perfect, and we were never out of meat. Herbs, roots, berries, bark of trees and everything that was edible they knew. They could minister to the sick, dress wounds — in fact in all my experience I never saw Bridger or the other voyagers of the plains and mountains meet any obstacle they could not overcome.

While Bridger was not an educated man, still any country that he had ever seen he could fully and intelligently describe, and could make a very correct estimate of the country surrounding it. He could make a map of any country he had ever traveled over, mark out its streams and mountains and the obstacles in it correctly, so that there was no trouble in following it and fully understanding it. He never claimed knowledge that he did not have of the country, or its history and surroundings, and was positive in his statements in relation to it. He was a

good judge of human nature. His comments upon people that he had met and been with were always intelligent and seldom critical. He always spoke of their good parts, and was universally respected by the mountain men, and looked upon as a leader, also by all the Indians. He was careful to never give his word without fulfilling it. He understood thoroughly the Indian character, their peculiarities and superstitions. He felt very keenly any loss of confidence in him or his judgment, especially when acting as guide, and when he struck a country or trail he was not familiar with he would frankly say so, but would often say he could take our party up to the point we wanted to reach. As a guide I do not think he had his equal upon the plains.

So remarkable a man should not be lost to history and the country, and his work allowed to be forgotten, and for this reason I have compiled this sketch and raised a simple monument to his memory, reciting upon it briefly the principal facts of his life and work. It bears this inscription:

1804—JAMES BRIDGER—1881.

Celebrated as a hunter, trapper, fur trader and guide. Discovered Great Salt Lake 1824, the South Pass 1827. Visited Yellowstone Lake and Geysers 1830. Founded Fort Bridger 1843. Opened Overland Route by Bridger's Pass to Great Salt Lake. Was guide for U. S. exploring expeditions, Albert Sidney Johnstons' army in 1857, and G. M. Dodge in U. P. surveys and Indian campaigns 1865-66.

This monument is erected as a tribute to his pioneer work by Maj. Gen. G. M. Dodge.

12. Notice of a Runaway Apprentice

EDITOR'S NOTE: Just as Daniel Boone was the foremost frontiersman of the East, so was Christopher Carson (1809-1868) the foremost of the West. Boone is remembered in connection with the pioneering advance across the Appalachians, Carson with the advance across the Rockies. A great legend in his own time, Carson's reputation made him seem a huge man. Actually he was of middle height and mild and taciturn. Hunter, scout, trapper, guide, he was born in Kentucky and raised on the Missouri frontier. He spent his last years as an Indian agent at Taos. During that time he dictated the brief account which is his autobiography, and from which I have selected several typical passages.

NOTICE: To whom it may concern: That Christopher Carson, a boy about sixteen years old, small of his age, but thickset, light hair, ran away from the subscriber, living in Franklin, Howard County, Mo., to whom he had been bound to learn the saddler's trade, on or about the first day of September last. He is supposed to have made his way toward the upper part of the state. All persons are notified not to harbor, support, or subsist said boy under penalty of the law. One cent reward will be given to any person who will bring back the said boy.

      (signed)   DAVID WORKMAN

FRANKLIN, *Oct.* 6, 1826

* From the Missouri Intelligencer.

13. Kit Carson

BY JOHN CHARLES FRÉMONT

On the boat I met Kit Carson. He was returning from putting his little daughter in a convent-school at St. Louis. I was pleased with him and his manner of address at this first meeting. He was a man of medium height, broad-shouldered and deep-chested, with a clear steady blue eye and frank speech and address; quiet and unassuming.

It will be anticipating to speak here of Carson in connection with after-events, but I give one incident to illustrate the simple honesty of his character.

He had gone to Washington with despatches from me in 1847, and was staying at the house of Senator Benton, welcomed there as my friend. Mr. Benton was in the

Kit Carson

168

West, but Carson's modesty and gentleness quickly made him a place in the regard of the family, to whom he gave back a lasting attachment. At one time during his stay he was seen to be troubled in mind, and our young friend, Midshipman Beale, being asked to find what had quenched Carsons' good spirits, ascertained that he felt it was wrong to be among such ladies when they might not like to associate with him if they knew he had had an Indian wife. "She was a good wife to me. I never came in from hunting that she did not have the warm water ready for my feet." She had died long since, and he was now married to a daughter of Beaubien. But his straightforward nature would not let him rest while there was anything concealed which he thought ought to be known to the family who were receiving him as a friend. It was the child of his Indian wife that he had just placed in the shelter of the St. Louis convent-school when we first met.

I had expected to engage as guide an old mountaineer, Captain Drips, but I was so much pleased with Carson that when he asked to go with me I was glad to take him.

* From *Memoirs of My Life,* by Frémont.

14. A Brush With Crow Indians

BY KIT CARSON

In January, 1833, a party of men who had been out hunting returned about dark. Their horses were very poor, having been fed during the winter on cottonwood bark, and they turned them out to gather such nourishment as they could find. That night a party of about fifty Crow Indians came to our camp and stole nine of the horses that were loose. In the morning we discovered sign of the Indians and twelve of us took the trail and traveled about forty miles. It was getting late. Our animals were fatigued for the snow was deep, and the passing of many herds of buffaloes during the day caused us a great deal of difficulty in keeping the trail. At length we saw a grove of timber at a distance of two or three miles. Taking into consideration the condition of our animals, we concluded to make for it and camp for the night. On our arrival, however, we saw fires about four miles ahead of us. We tied our animals to trees, and as soon as it became dark, took a circuitous route for the Indian camp.

We planned to come upon the Indians from the direction in which they were traveling. It took us some time to get close enough to the camp to discover their strength, as we had to crawl, and use all the means that we were aware of to elude detection. After maneuvering in this direction for some time, we came within about one hundred yards of their camp. The Indians were in two forts of about equal strength. They were dancing and singing, and passing the night jovially in honor of their robbery of the whites. We spied our horses, which were tied near the entrance of one of the forts. Let come what would, we were bound to get them. We remained concealed in the brush, suffering severely from the cold, until the Indians laid down to sleep.

When we thought they were all asleep, six of us crawled towards our animals, the rest remaining where they were as a reserve for us to fall back on in case we did not meet with success. We hid behind logs and crawled silently towards the fort, the snow being of great service to us for when crawling we were not liable to make any noise. We finally reached the horses, cut the ropes, and by throwing snow balls at them drove them to where our reserve was stationed. We then held a council, taking the views of each in regard to what had best be done. Some were in favor of retiring; having recovered their property and received no damage, they were willing to return to camp. Not so with those that had lost no animals. They wanted satisfaction for the trouble and hardships they

had gone through while in pursuit of the thieves. Myself and two others were the only ones that had not lost horses and we were determined to have satisfaction, let the consequences be ever so fatal. The peace party could not get a convert to their side. Seeing us so determined to fight (there is always a brotherly affection existing among trappers and the side of danger is always their choice), it was not long before all agreed to join us in our perilous enterprise.

We started the horses that had been retaken to the place where we had tied our other animals, with three of our men acting as an escort. We then marched directly for the fort from which we had taken our horses. When we were within a few paces of it, a dog discovered us and began to bark. The Indians were alarmed and commenced to get up, when we opened a deadly fire, each

Crow Indian. *George Catlin*

ball taking its victim. We killed nearly every Indian in the fort. The few that remained were wounded and made their escape to the other fort, whose inmates commenced firing on us, but without any effect, since we kept concealed behind trees, firing only when we were sure of our object. It was now near day, and the Indians could see our force, which was so weak they concluded to charge on us. We received them calmly, and when they got very close fired on them, killing five, and the balance returned to their fort. After some deliberation among themselves, they finally made another attempt, which met with greater success. We had to retreat, but there was much timber in the vicinity, and we had but little difficulty in making our camp, where, being reinforced by the three men with the horses, we awaited the approach of the enemy. Since they did not attack us, we started for our main camp and arrived there in the evening. During our pursuit of the lost animals we suffered considerably, but in the success of recovering our horses and sending many a redskin to his long home, our sufferings were soon forgotten. We remained in our camp without any further molestation until spring, when we started for Laramie River on another trapping expedition.

15. Narrow Escapes

BY KIT CARSON

The snow was now commencing to fall and we concluded to go into winter quarters. We found a place at the mouth of the Winty that answered every purpose. During the winter a California Indian of Mr. Robidoux's party ran off with six animals, some of them being worth two hundred dollars per head. Robidoux came to me and requested that I should pursue him. I spoke to Captain Lee and he informed me that I might use my pleasure. There was a Utah village close by, and I got one of the Indians to accompany me. We were furnished with two fine animals and took the trail of the runaway, who had gone down the river, his object being to reach California.

After traveling about one hundred miles the animal of the Indian gave out and he would not accompany me any farther. I was determined not to give up the chase and continued the pursuit and in thirty miles overtook the Indian with the horses. Seeing me by myself, he showed fight and I was under the necessity of killing him. I recovered the horses, and returned to our camp, arriving in a few days without any further trouble.

Some trappers came to our camp and informed us that Fitzpatrick and Bridger were encamped on the Snake River. In March, 1834, we struck out for the purpose of finding their camp, and in fifteen days succeeded. Captain Lee sold his goods to Fitzpatrick and agreed to accept his pay in beaver. Lee then started for Taos, and I joined Fitzpatrick and remained with him one month. He had a great many men in his employ, and I thought it best to take three of them and go on a hunt by ourselves. We passed the summer trapping on the head of the Laramie and its tributaries, keeping to the mountains, our party being too weak to venture on the plains.

One evening when we were en route to rejoin Bridger's party, after I had selected the camp for the night, I gave my horse to one of the men and started on foot to kill something for supper, not having a particle of anything eatable on hand. I had gone about a mile when I discovered some elk on the side of a ridge. I shot one and immediately after the discharge of my gun I heard a noise in my rear. I turned around and saw two very large grizzly bears making for me. My gun was unloaded and I could not possibly reload it in time to fire. There were some trees at a short distance, and I made for them, the bears after me. As I got to one of them, I had to drop my gun, and make all haste to ascend it. I got up some ten or fifteen feet, where I had to remain till the bears found it convenient to leave. One remained but a short while, the other stayed for some time and with his paws nearly uprooted the small aspen trees that grew around the tree which I had ascended. He made several attempts at the tree in which I was perched, but as he could do no damage, he finally concluded to leave. I was heartily pleased at this, never having been so badly scared in my life. I remained in the tree for some time longer, and when I considered the bears far enough off, I descended and made for my camp as rapidly as possible. It was dark when I arrived and I could not send for the elk which I had killed, so we had to pass the night without anything to eat. During the night we trapped some beaver, so we had something for breakfast.

We remained in this place some ten or fifteen days, when Bridger appeared, on his way to the summer rendezvous. We joined him and went to Green River, the place of rendezvous, where two camps were established. I think there were two hundred trappers encamped, awaiting the arrival of supplies from St. Louis. We had to dispose of our beaver to procure the necessities of life. Coffee and sugar were two dollars a pint, powder the same, lead one dollar a bar, and common blankets from fifteen to twenty-five dollars apiece.

We remained in the rendezvous during the month of August, 1834. In September, camp was broken up and we divided into parties of convenient size and started on our fall hunt. The party of which I was a member consisted of fifty men. We set out for the country of the Blackfoot Indians, on the headwaters of the Missouri. We made a very poor hunt as the Indians were very troublesome. Five of our men were killed. A trapper could hardly go a mile from camp without being fired upon. As we found that we could do but little in this country, we started for winter quarters.

In November we got to the Big Snake River, where we again encamped. Nothing of moment transpired till February, 1835, when the Blackfeet came and stole eighteen of our horses. Twelve of us followed them about fifty miles before we caught up with them. They had traveled as far as they could, being delayed by the snow. In endeavoring to get the horses we fired some shots at them but could not approach near enough to do any great damage. They had snow shoes, we had none; they could travel over the snow without difficulty, while we would sink in it up to our waists.

The horses were on the side of a hill where there was but little snow, and our only object now was to get them. We asked for a parley, and the Indians agreed. One man from each side was to proceed half of the

A Brush with Indians. *Frederick Remington*

distance that separated us and have a talk. This was done, and we talked for some time, the Indians saying that they had thought we were Snake Indians and that they did not want to steal from the Whites. We replied that if they were friendly they would lay down their arms and have a friendly talk and smoke with us. They agreed to do this, and each party left one man to guard the arms. We then met at the place where the first two men were talking, and talked and smoked.

The Indians were thirty strong. They sent for our horses, but returned with only five of the worst and said they would not give up any more. We broke for our arms and they for theirs, and the fight commenced. A man named Markhead and I were in the advance, and overtook two In-dians who had remained in the rear of their party, concealed behind two trees. I approached one, and Markhead the other. Markhead was not paying sufficient attention to his Indian who, I noticed, raised his gun to fire. I forgot entirely the danger in which I myself was and neglected my Indian for Markhead's opponent. As the latter was about to fire on Markhead, I raised my gun and took sight. He saw me and endeavored to conceal himself, but he was too late. I fired and he fell. The moment I fired I remembered the Indian that I was after. I looked and saw him sighting for my breast. As I could not load in time, I commenced dodging about as well as I could. He fired, and the ball grazed my neck and passed through my shoulder.

We then drew off for about a mile and encamped for the night. It was very cold and we could not make any fires for fear the Indians might approach and fire on us. We had no covering but our saddle blankets, and I passed a miserable night from the pain of the wound, it having bled freely and the blood having frozen. In the morning we found that the Indians were in the same place. We were not strong enough to attack them, so we started for camp. On our arrival Bridger took thirty men and started for the place where we had left the Indians, but when we got there they had gone to the plains. So we only recovered the five stolen animals which they had given us.

In a few days we set out on our spring hunt. We trapped the waters of the Snake and the Green rivers, made a very good hunt, and then went into summer quarters on Green River. Shortly after we reached the rendezvous our equipment arrived. We disposed of our beaver to the traders that came up with it, remaining in summer quarters till September, 1835.

There was a large Frenchman in the party of Captain Drips, an overbearing kind of man, and very strong. He made a practice of whipping every man that he was displeased with — and that was nearly all. One day, after he had beaten two or three men, he said he had no trouble to flog Frenchmen, and as for Americans, he would take a switch and switch them. I did not like such talk from any man, so I told him that I was the worst American in camp. There were many who could thrash him but for the fact that they were afraid, and that if he used such expressions any more, I would rip his guts.

He said nothing but started for his rifle, mounted his horse, and made his appearance in front of the camp. As soon as I saw this, I mounted my horse also, seized the first weapon I could get hold of, which was a pistol, and galloped up to him and demanded if I was the one he intended to shoot. Our horses were touching. He said no, drawing his gun at the same time so he could have a fair shot at me. I was prepared and allowed him to draw his gun. We both fired at the same time, and all present said that but one report was heard. I shot him through the arm and his ball passed my head, cutting my hair and the powder burning my eye, the muzzle of his gun being near my head when he fired. During the remainder of our stay in camp we had no more bother with this French bully.

16. Adventures With Frémont

BY KIT CARSON

The year before, I had promised Frémont that I would join him in case he should return for the purpose of making any further exploration. About the first of August, 1845, he reached Bent's Fort, where he inquired for me and learned that I was on the Cimarron. He sent an express to me, and Owens and I sold our improvement for about half its worth and joined Frémont, who employed both of us.

We went up the Arkansas to the point where it comes out of the mountains, thence to the Balla Salado, thence to the Arkansas above the cañon, and up to its headwaters. From here we crossed over to Piney River, and descended to within twenty-five miles of its mouth; then to Grand River, which we crossed; then to the head of White River. We went down White River almost to its junction with Green River, crossed the latter stream and went on to the Winty, then up the latter almost to the mountains, which we crossed to Provost Fork. This river was named for a party of trappers led by a man named Provost, who were defeated on it by a band of Indians, all of the party but four being killed.

We traveled down the Provost to Little Utah Lake and followed its outlet almost to Great Salt Lake. Here Frémont made his camp, some distance south of our former encampment. In our front was a large island, the largest in the lake. We were informed by the Indians that there was an abundance of fresh water on it and plenty of antelope. Frémont went to explore it, taking me and a few more men along. We found good grass, water, and timber, and plenty of game. We remained there two days, killing game and exploring the island, which was about fifteen miles long and five miles in breadth. In going to the island we rode on horseback over salt from the thickness of a wafer to twelve inches.

We returned to our camp and remained a day on the south side of the lake near the

Frémont Addressing the Indians at Fort Laramie

last fresh water. From here Frémont sent Maxwell, Archambeau, Lajenesse, and myself to cross the desert, which I have often heard had never before been crossed by white men. Old trappers would speak of the impossibility of crossing it, saying that water could not be found, nor grass for the animals. But Frémont was determined to cross. Nothing his explorations required was impossible for him to perform.

Before we started it was arranged that at a certain hour of the next day he would ascend the mountain near his camp with his telescope, so that we could be seen by him, and if we found grass or water we should make a smoke as a signal to him to advance. We traveled about sixty miles, found neither water nor grass, nor a particle of vegetation, with the ground as level and bare as a barn floor, before we struck the mountains on the west side of the lake. There we found water and grass in abundance, and kindled the signal fire. Frémont saw it, and moved on with his party. Archambeau went back and met him when he was about half way across the desert. He camped one night, and the next evening at dark he completed the crossing, having lost only a few of his animals.

We now separated again. Mr. Talbot took charge of the camp with a man named Walker as his guide. He was ordered to strike for Mary's River and follow it down to where it is lost in the Basin. Meanwhile Frémont, with fifteen men, was to pass south of Mary's River, and both parties were to meet at the lake made by Carson River.

We passed over a fine country, abounding in wood, grass, and water, having only about forty miles to travel without water before reaching the Lake. We at length arrived, and awaited the coming of Talbot. In two or three days his party came in. Here we again **separated**, Talbot and Walker to go

through a pass to our south, and cross the Sierra Nevadas to the waters of San Joaquin. Meanwhile we went up the Carson River, and having crossed the Sierra Nevada, arrived safely at Sutter's Fort. Captain Sutter was happy to see us and furnished us everything we wanted.

We remained at the fort a few days, purchasing about forty head of cattle and a few horses, and then started to find our camp. We went up the San Joaquin Valley, crossed it where it comes out of the mountain, and then on to King's River and up to its headwaters. During our march, our cattle had become very tender-footed from traveling over the snow and rocks. From the head of King's River we started back for the prairie but when we arrived we had no cattle left, as they had all given out and we had to leave behind all except those we killed for meat. As we were leaving the mountains, some Indians crawled into our camp during the night, and killed two of our mules.

Next morning we started back for the fort. Through some mistake we had not found our camp, and as we had lost nearly all of our animals, it became necessary to return. The same evening we came upon a party of Indians. We killed five of them, and continued on to the fort. All of us were afoot, having lived principally on the meat of wild horses that we killed on the march. We now started for San Jose, where we remained only a few days to recruit. We procured a few animals there, and crossed the Coast Range to see if we could hear anything of our party under Talbot. At San Jose we heard that they were on the San Joaquin, and Frémont sent me with two men to meet them. We found them and guided them to San Jose.

After we had all got together again we started for Monterey to procure an outfit. When we were about thirty miles from

Monterey, Frémont received a very impertinent order from General Castro, commanding him to leave the country immediately, and saying that if he did not do so, he would be driven out. We packed up at dark and moved back about ten miles to a little mountain, where we found a good place and made camp. General Castro followed us with several hundred men and established his headquarters near us. He would fire his big guns frequently to scare us, thinking by such demonstrations he could make us leave.

We had about forty men in our party armed with rifles, while Castro had several hundred soldiers, artillery, cavalry, and infantry. Frémont had received expresses from the Americans in Monterey advising him to leave, as the Mexicans were strong and would surely attack us. He replied that he had done nothing to anger the Mexican commander, that he was performing a duty, and regardless of the consequences he would not retreat.

We remained in our position on the mountain for three days, and became tired of waiting for the attack of the valiant Mexican General. We then started for the Sacramento River, and ascended it to Peter Lawson's, where Frémont intended to obtain his outfit for the homeward trip.

We remained here ten days. During our stay, some Americans who were settled near-by came in with the report that there were about 1000 Indians in the vicinity making preparations to attack the settlements, and requested assistance of Frémont to drive them back. He started for the Indian encampment with his party and some few Americans near-by. We found them to be in great force, as had been stated. We attacked them, and although I do not know how many we killed, it was a perfect butchery. The survivors fled in all directions and

we returned to Lawson's, having accomplished our purpose and given the Indians such a chastisement that it would be long before they would again think of attacking the settlements.

We received the best of treatment at Lawson's, and finished our outfit. We then set out for the Columbia River, going up the Sacramento and passing near the Shasta Butte. We traveled on without any molestation till we reached the upper end of Klamath Lake.

A few days after we left, information was received in California that war had been declared between the United States and Mexico, and Lieutenant Gillespie of the U. S. Marines and six men were sent after us to have us come back. After he had traveled about three hundred miles his animals began to give out, and he had but poor hopes of overtaking us. He then concluded to mount two men on his best animals and send them on in advance. These men caught up with us on the lake, and gave the communications they bore to Frémont. Having but poor faith in the good will of the Klamath Indians, and fearing for the safety of Lieutenant Gillespie's party, Frémont concluded to go and meet him. He took ten picked men, traveled about sixty miles and came upon him encamped for the night.

He sat up till twelve or one o'clock reading the letters which he had received from the States. Owens and myself were lying near the fire, rolled in our saddle blankets, the night being cold. Shortly after Frémont lay down I heard a noise like the stroke of an axe. Jumping up, I saw that there were Indians in camp, and gave the alarm. They had already tomahawked two men, Basil Lajenesse and a Delaware, and were advancing to the fire, where four Delawares were sleeping. They heard the alarm in

Fort Union.   *Charles Bodmer*

A Fur-Trader in the Council Tepee.   *Frederick Remington*

time, and one of them named Crane got up and seized a gun. Unfortunately it was not his own gun and was not loaded. He did not know this, and kept standing erect trying to fire. He fell with five arrows in his breast, four of the wounds proving mortal.

The evening before I had fired off my gun for the purpose of cleaning it. In doing so I had accidentally broken the tube, and now had nothing but my pistol. I rushed upon the leader, and fired, cutting the string that held his tomahawk. Having no other weapon, I was now compelled to retire. Maxwell next fired on him, hitting him in the leg. As he was turning around, Step fired; the ball struck him in the back, passing near the heart, and he fell. The balance of his party then ran. He was the bravest Indian I ever saw. If his men had been as brave as himself we surely would all have been killed. We had three men killed and one slightly wounded. If we had not gone to meet Gillespie, he and his party would have been murdered, and the Indians were evidently on his trail for that purpose. We apprehended no danger that night and as the men were much fatigued no guard was posted. It was the first and last time we neglected to post a guard. Of the three men killed, Lajenesse was particularly regretted. He had been with us on every trip that had been made. But all of them were brave, good men. The only consolation we had for their loss was the reflection that if we had not arrived, Gillespie and his four men would have been killed. We lost but three, so two lives had been saved.

After the Indians left, each of us took a tree, expecting that they would return and attack us. We remained at our posts until daylight, when we packed up, and taking the bodies of the dead with us, started for the camp of our main party. We had proceeded about ten miles, when we found we could not possibly carry the bodies of our comrades any farther. We went back from the trail about half a mile and interred them, covering the graves with logs and brush, so that there was but little probability of their being discovered. We would have taken the bodies to our camp, but the timber was so thick that they knocked against the trees, and becoming much bruised, we concluded to bury them. We reached our camp that same evening and found that the men had received orders to follow our trail. We camped for the night, and the next morning we moved on a few miles, leaving fifteen men concealed in our old camp for the purpose of discovering the movements of the Indians. We had not been gone more than half an hour when two Indians appeared. They were quickly killed and their scalps taken.

Frémont concluded to return to California but decided to take a different route from that by which we had last entered the country, taking a trail that led around the opposite side of the lake. We were now located on a tributary of the lake nearly opposite to the place where we were encamped when we had the three men killed. In the morning I was sent ahead with ten chosen men, with orders to send back word, if I discovered any large village of Indians, and in case I should be seen by them for me to act as I thought best.

I had not gone more than ten miles when I discovered a large village of about fifty lodges, and at the same time I knew by the commotion in their camp that they had seen us. Considering it useless to send for reinforcements, I determined to attack them. I charged on them, and we fought for some time; we killed a number of them and the remainder fled.

Their houses were built of flag, beautifully woven. They had evidently been fishing for they had about ten wagon loads of fish in their houses. All their fishing tackle, camp equipage, etc. was also there. I wished to do them as much damage as I could, and directed their houses to be set on fire. The flag being dry, the fire was a beautiful sight. The Indians had commenced the war with us without cause. I thought they should be chastised in a summary manner, and they were severely punished.

Frémont saw the fire at a distance, and knowing that we were engaged, hurried forward to join us, but he arrived too late to share in the sport. We moved on about two miles from where the Indian village had been, and camped for the night. After encamping, Owens and twenty men were sent back to watch for Indians. In an hour he sent us word that fifty Indians had returned to camp, I suppose to hunt their lost and bury their dead.

As soon as this information was received, Frémont and six men started to join him, taking a route different from that which Owens had taken, so as to keep concealed. As we neared the camp we saw only one Indian, and immediately charged him. I was in advance. When I got within ten feet of him my gun snapped and he drew his bow to fire on me. I threw myself on one side of my horse to save myself. Frémont saw the danger I was in, and ran his horse over the Indian, throwing him on the ground. Before he could recover he was shot. I consider that Frémont saved my life on this occasion, for, in all probability, if he had not run over the Indian as he did, I would have been killed. We could find no more Indians, and fearing that the party seen by Owens had returned

to attack our camp, we returned to it, but the Indians did not again appear.

Next morning we struck out for the valley of the Sacramento, distant about four days' march. Maxwell and Archambeau were traveling parallel with the party, about three miles distant, engaged in hunting, when they saw an Indian coming towards them. As soon as he saw them he took from his quiver some young crows that were tied thereon, concealed them in the grass, and continued approaching. When he was within forty yards he commenced firing. They did not intend to hurt him, wishing to talk with him, but as he kept up a continuous fire on them and his shots were coming rather close, they were compelled to return his fire in self-defense. At the very first shot he fell, and was immediately scalped.

We continued our march until we struck the Sacramento. In passing down this river we discovered a deep and narrow cañon ahead of us. Supposing that we would go through it, the Indians had placed themselves on each side for the purpose of attacking us as we passed. But we crossed the river and continued on our way by a different route and did not go into the cañon at all. Godey, myself, and another man, whom I have forgotten, went in pursuit of the Indians, but we were mounted on mules and they could not be caught. One man, braver than the rest, hid himself behind a large rock and awaited our approach. We rode up quite close to him before he came from his hiding place and commenced firing arrows at us very rapidly. We had to retreat, and were kept so busy dodging arrows that we were unable to fire at him. After we had retreated beyond the range of his arrows, I dismounted and taking deliberate aim, fired at him. The shot took effect, and he was quickly scalped. He had a fine bow and a beautiful quiver full of arrows, which I afterwards presented to Lieutenant Gilles-pie. He was a brave Indian and deserved a better fate, but unfortunately he had placed himself on the wrong path.

17. Wild Bill, My Scout

BY GEORGE A. CUSTER

EDITOR'S NOTE: If we are to believe contemporary reports, James Butler Hickok (1837-1876), widely known as Wild Bill, was the greatest pistol shot of his time and possibly of all time, as well as one of the two greatest peace officers of the old West, the other being Wyatt Earp. He was born in Illinois. In 1855 he went to Kansas, and later became a stage driver on the Santa Fe trail. He also undertook various odd jobs. He was almost killed in a fight with a cinnamon bear, which he finally finished off with his knife. He was extremely strong, tall, with flowing blond hair and a quiet but commanding manner. On July 12, 1861, he engaged in one of the most famous fights of the West. Attacked by the McCanles gang at Rock Creek Station, Nebraska, he killed McCanles and two of his men. In the Civil War he was a sharpshooter, scout and spy for the Union Army. Later he was a scout for Generals Custer, Hancock and Sheridan and a U. S. marshal at Hays City and at Abilene, Kansas. He was murdered in Deadwood, Dakota Territory, on August 2, 1876.

Wild Bill

In addition to the regularly organized companies of soldiers which made up the pursuing column, I had with me a detachment of white scouts or Plainsmen, and one of friendly Indians, the latter belonging to the tribe of Delawares, once so famous in Indian wars. Of the Indians one only could speak English; he acted as interpreter for the party. Among the white scouts were numbered some of the most noted of their class. The most prominent man among them was "Wild Bill," whose highly varied career was made the subject of an illustrated sketch in one of the popular monthly periodicals a few years ago. "Wild Bill" was a strange character, just the one which a novelist might gloat over. He was a Plainsman in every sense of the word, yet unlike any other of his class. In person he was about six feet one in height, straight as the straightest of the warriors whose implacable foe he was; broad shoulders, well-formed chest and limbs, and a face strikingly handsome; a sharp, clear, blue eye, which stared you straight in the face when in conversation; a finely-shaped nose, inclined to be aquiline; a well-turned mouth, with lips only partially concealed by a handsome moustache. His hair and complexion were those of the perfect blond. The former was worn in uncut ringlets falling carelessly over his powerfully formed shoulders. Add to this figure a costume blending the immaculate neatness of the dandy with the extravagant taste and style of the frontiersman, and you have Wild Bill, then as now the most famous scout on the Plains. Whether on foot or on horseback, he was one of the most perfect types of physical manhood I ever saw. Of his courage there could be no question; it had been brought to the test on too many occasions to admit of a doubt. His skill in the use of the rifle and pistol was unerring; while his deportment was exactly the opposite of what might be expected from a man of his surroundings. It was entirely free from all bluster or bravado. He seldom spoke of himself unless requested to do so. His conversation, strange to say, never bordered either on the vulgar or blasphemous. His influence among the frontiersmen was unbounded, his word was law; and many are the personal quarrels and disturbances which he has checked among his comrades by his simple announcement that "this has gone far enough," if need be followed by the ominous warning

that when persisted in or renewed the quarreller "must settle it with me." "Wild Bill" is anything but a quarrelsome man; yet no one but himself can enumerate the many conflicts in which he has been engaged, and which have almost invariably resulted in the death of his adversary. I have a personal knowledge of at least half a dozen men whom he has at various times killed, one of these being at the time a member of my command. Others have been severely wounded, yet he always escapes unhurt.

On the Plains every man openly carries his belt with its invariable appendages, knife and revolver, often two of the latter. Wild Bill always carried two handsome ivory-handled revolvers of the large size; he was never seen without them. Where this is the common custom, brawls or personal difficulties are seldom if ever settled by blows. The quarrel is not from a word to a blow, but from a word to the revolver, and he who can draw and fire first is the best man. No civil law reaches him; none is applied for. In fact there is no law recognized beyond the frontier but that of "might makes right." Should death result from the quarrel, as it usually does, no coroner's jury is impanelled to learn the cause of death, and the survivor is not arrested. But instead of these old-fashioned proceedings, a meeting of citizens takes place, the survivor is *requested* to be present when the circumstances of the homicide are inquired into, and the unfailing verdict of "justifiable," "self-defence," etc., is pronounced, and the law stands vindicated. That justice is often deprived to a victim there is not a doubt. Yet in all of the many affairs of this kind in which "Wild Bill" has performed a part, and which have come to my knowledge, there is not a single instance in which the verdict of

From *My Life on The Plains,* by Custer.

twelve fair-minded men would not be pronounced in his favor. That the even tenor of his way continues to be disturbed by little events of this description may be inferred from an item which has been floating lately through the columns of the press, and which states that "the funeral of 'Jim Bludso,' who was killed the other day by 'Wild Bill,' took place to-day." It then adds: "The funeral expenses were borne by 'Wild Bill.'" What could be more thoughtful than this? Not only to send a fellow mortal out of the world, but to pay the expenses of the transit.

18. Interviewing Wild Bill

BY GEORGE WARD NICHOLS

Whenever I had met an officer or soldier who had served in the Southwest I heard of Wild Bill and his exploits, until these stories became so frequent and of such an extraordinary character as quite to outstrip personal knowledge of adventure by camp and field; and the hero of these strange tales took shape in my mind as did Jack the Giant Killer or Sinbad the Sailor in childhood's days. As then, I now had the most implicit faith in the existence of the individual; but how one man could accomplish such prodigies of strength and feats of daring was a continued wonder.

In order to give the reader a clearer understanding of the condition of this neighborhood, which could have permitted the duel mentioned above, and whose history will be given hereafter in detail, I will describe the situation at the time of which I am writing, which was late in the summer of 1865, premising that this section of country would not to-day be selected as a model example of modern civilization.

At that time peace and comparative quiet had succeeded the perils and tumult of war in all the more Southern States. The people of Georgia and the Carolinas were glad to enforce order in their midst; and it would have been safe for a Union officer to have ridden unattended through the land.

In Southwest Missouri there were old scores to be settled up. During the three days occupied by General Smith — who commanded the Department and was on a tour of inspection — in crossing the country between Rolla and Springfield, a distance of 120 miles, five men were killed or wounded on the public road. Two were murdered a short distance from Rolla — by whom we could not ascertain. Another was instantly killed and two were wounded at a meeting of a band of "Regulators," who were in the service of the State, but were paid by the United States Government. It should be said here that their method of "regulation" was slightly informal, their war-cry was, "A swift bullet and a short rope for returned rebels!"

I was informed by General Smith that during the six months preceding not less than 4000 returned Confederates had been summarily disposed of by shooting or hanging. This statement seems incredible; but there is the record, and I have no doubt of its truth. History shows few parallels to this relentless destruction of human life in time of peace. It can be explained only upon the ground that, before the war, this region was inhabited by lawless people. In the outset of the rebellion the merest suspicion of loyalty to the Union cost the patriot his life; and thus large numbers fled the land, giving up home and every material interest. As soon as the Federal armies occupied the country these refugees returned. Once securely fixed in their old homes they resolved that their former persecutors should not live in their midst. Revenge for the past and security for the future knotted many a nerve and sped many a deadly bullet.

Wild Bill did not belong to the Regulators. Indeed, he was one of the law and order party. He said:

"When the war closed I buried the hatchet, and I won't fight now unless I'm put upon."

Bill was born of Northern parents in the State of Illinois. He ran away from home when a boy, and wandered out upon the plains and into the mountains. For fifteen years he lived with the trappers, hunting and fishing. When the war broke out he returned to the States and entered the Union service. No man probably was ever better fitted for scouting than he. Joined to his tremendous strength he was an unequaled horseman; he was a perfect marksman; he had a keen sight, and a constitution which had no limit of endurance. He was cool to audacity, brave to rashness, always possessed of himself under the most critical circumstances; and, above all, was such a master in the knowledge of woodcraft that it might have been termed a science with him — a knowledge which, with the soldier, is priceless beyond description. Some of Bill's adventures during the war will be related hereafter.

The main features of the story of the deal was told me by Captain Honesty, who was unprejudiced, if it is possible to find an unbiased mind in a town of 3000 people after a fight has taken place. I will give the story in his words:

"They say Bill's wild. Now he isn't any sich thing. I've known him goin on ter ten year, and he's as civil a disposed person as you'll find he-e-arabouts. But he won't be put upon."

"I'll tell yer how it happened. But come inter the office; thar's a good many round hy'ar as sides with Tutt — the man that's shot. But I tell yer 'twas a far fight. Take some whisky? No! Well, I will, if yer'l excuse me.

"You see," continued the Captain, setting the empty glass on the table in an emphatic way, "Bill was up in his room a-playin seven-up, or four-hand, or some of them pesky games. Bill refused ter play with Tutt, who was a professional gambler. Yer see, Bill was a scout on our side durin the war, and Tutt was a reb scout. Bill had killed Dave Tutt's mate, and, atween one thing and another, there war an onusual hard feelin atwixt 'em.

"Ever sin Dave came back he had tried to pick a row with Bill; so Bill wouldn't play cards with him any more. But Dave stood over the man who was gambling with Bill and lent the feller money. Bill won bout two hundred dollars, which made Tutt spiteful mad. Bime-by, he says to Bill:

" 'Bill, you've got plenty of money — pay me that forty dollars yer owe me in that horse trade.'

"And Bill paid him. Then he said:

" 'Yer owe me thirty-five dollars more; yer lost it playing with me t'other night.'

"Dave's style was right provoking; but Bill answered him perfectly gentlemanly:

" 'I think yer wrong, Dave. It's only twen-

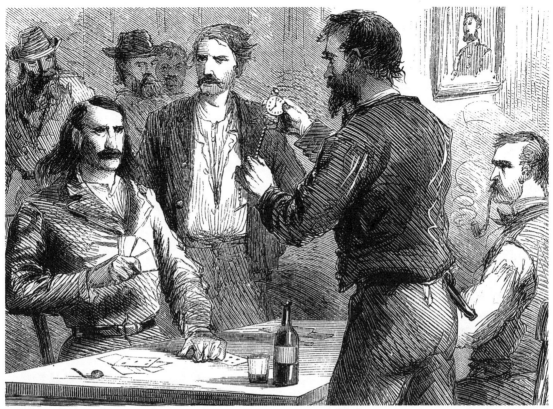

Putting Upon Him. *Harper's Magazine*

ty-five dollars. I have a memorandum of it in my pocket down stairs. Ef it's thirty-five dollars I'll give it yer.'

"Now Bill's watch was lying on the table. Dave took up the watch, put it in his pocket, and said: 'I'll keep this yere watch till yer pay me that thirty-five dollars.'

"This made Bill shooting mad; fur, don't yer see, Colonel, it was a-doubting his honor like, so he got up and looked Dave in the eyes, and said to him: 'I don't want ter make a row in this house. It's a decent house, and I don't want ter injure the keeper. You'd better put that watch back on the table.'

"But Dave grinned at Bill mighty ugly, and walked off with the watch, and kept it several days. All this time Dave's friends were spurring Bill on ter fight; there was no end ter the talk. They blackguarded him in an underhand sort of a way, and tried ter get up a scrimmage, and then they thought they could lay him out. Yer see Bill has enemies all about. He's settled the accounts of a heap of men who lived round here. This is about the only place in Missouri whar a reb can come back and live, and ter tell yer the truth, Colonel—" and the Captain, with an involuntary movement, hitched up his revolver-belt, as he said, with expressive significance, "they don't stay long round here!

"Well, as I was saying, these rebs don't

From Harpers Magazine, February 1867. Either Nichols exaggerated the facts (for example, in the McCanles fight) or Wild Bill pulled his leg.

like ter see a man walking round town who they knew in the reb army as one of their men, who they now know was on our side, all the time he was sending us information, sometimes from Pap Price's own head-quarters. But they couldn't provoke Bill inter a row, for he's afeard of hisself when he gits *awful* mad; and he allers left his shootin irons in his room when he went out. One day these cusses drew their pistols on him and dared him to fight, and then they told him that Tutt was a-goin ter pack that watch across the squar next day at noon.

"I heard of this, for every body was talk-ing about it on the street, and so I went after Bill, and found him in his room cleaning and greasing and loading his revolvers.

" 'Now, Bill,' says I, 'you're goin ter git inter a fight.'

" 'Don't you bother yerself, Captain,' says he. 'It's not the first time I have been in a fight; and these d—d hounds have put on me long enough. You don't want me ter give up my honor, do yer?'

" 'No, Bill,' says I, 'yer must keep yer honor.'

"Next day, about noon, Bill went down on the squar. He had said that Dave Tutt shouldn't pack that watch across the squar unless dead men could walk.

"When Bill got onter the squar he found a crowd stanin in the corner of the street by which he entered the squar, which is from the south, yer know. In this crowd he saw

Are You Satisfied?   *Harper's Magazine*

a lot of Tutt's friends; some were cousins of his'n, just back from the reb army; and they jeered him, and boasted that Dave was a-goin to pack that watch across the squar as he promised.

"Then Bill saw Tutt stanin near the courthouse, which yer remember is on the west side, so that the crowd war behind Bill.

"Just then Tutt, who war alone, started from the court-house and walked out into the squar, and Bill moved away from the crowd toward the west side of the squar. Bout fifteen paces brought them opposite to each other, and bout fifty yards apart. Tutt then showed his pistol. Bill had kept a sharp eye on him, and before Tutt could pint it Bill had his'n out.

"At that moment you could have heard a pin drop in that squar. Both Tutt and Bill fired, but one discharge followed the other so quick that it's hard to say which went off first. Tutt was a famous shot, but he missed this time; the ball from his pistol went over Bill's head. The instant Bill fired, without waitin ter see ef he had hit Tutt, he wheeled on his heels and pointed his pistol at Tutt's friends, who had already drawn their weepons.

"'Aren't yer satisfied, gentlemen?' cried Bill, as cool as an alligator. 'Put up your shootin-irons, or there'll be more dead men here.' And they put 'em up, and said it war a far fight."

"What became of Tutt?" I asked of the Captain, who had stopped at this point of his story, and was very deliberately engaged in refilling his empty glass.

"Oh! Dave? He was as plucky a feller as ever drew trigger; but, Lord bless yer! it was no use. Bill never shoots twice at the same man, and his ball went through Dave's heart. He stood stock-still for a second or two, then raised his arm as if ter fire again,

then he swayed a little, staggered three or four steps, and then fell dead.

"Bill and his friends wanted ter have the thing done regular, so we went up ter the Justice, and Bill delivered himself up. A jury was drawn; Bill was tried and cleared the next day. It was proved that it was a case of self-defense. Don't yer see, Colonel?"

I answered that I was afraid that I did not see that point very clearly.

"Well, well!" he replied, with an air of compassion, "you haven't drunk any whisky, that's what's the matter with yer." And then, putting his hand on my shoulder with a half-mysterious half-conscious look in his face, he muttered, in a whisper:

"*The fact is, thar was an undercurrent of a woman in that fight!*"

The story of the duel was yet fresh from the lips of the Captain when its hero appeared in the manner already described. After a few moments' conversation Bill excused himself, saying:

"I am going out on the prarer a piece to see the sick wife of my mate. I should be glad to meet yer at the hotel this afternoon, Kernel."

"I will go there to meet you," I replied.

"Good-day, gentlemen," said the scout, as he saluted the party; and mounting the black horse who had been standing quiet, unhitched, he waved his hand over the animal's head. Responsive to the signal, she shot forward as the arrow leaves the bow, and they both disappeared up the road in a cloud of dust.

"That man is the most remarkable character I have met in four years' active service," said a lieutenant of cavalry, as the party resumed their seats. "He and his mate — the man who scouted with him —attempted the most daring feat that I ever heard of."

As there appeared to be no business on

hand at the moment the party urged the lieutenant to tell the story.

"I can't tell the thing as it was," said the young officer. "It was beyond description. One could only hold their breath and feel. It happened when our regiment was attached to Curtis's command, in the expedition down into Arkansas. One day we were in the advance, and began to feel the enemy, who appeared in greater strength than at any time before. We were all rather uneasy, for there were rumors that Kirby Smith had come up from Texas with all his force; and as we were only a strong reconnoitring party a fight just then might have been bad for us. We made a big noise with a light battery, and stretched our cavalry out in the open and opposite to the rebel cavalry, who were drawn up in line of battle on the slope of the prairie about a thousand yards away. There we sat for half an hour, now and then banging at each other, but both parties keeping pretty well their line of battle. They waited for us to pitch in. We were waiting until more of our infantry should come.

"It was getting to be stupid work, however, and we were all hoping something would turn up, when we noticed two men ride out from the centre of their line and move toward us. At the first instant we paid little heed to them, supposing it some act of rebel bravado, when we saw quite a commotion all along the enemy's front, and then they commenced firing at the two riders, and then their line was all enveloped with smoke, out of which horsemen dashed in pursuit. The two riders kept well together, coming straight for us. Then we knew they were trying to escape, and the Colonel deployed our company as skirmishers to assist them. There wasn't time to do much, although, as I watched the pursued and their pursuers, and found the two men had halted

at what I could now see was a deep wide ditch, the moments seemed to be hours; and when they turned I thought they were going to give themselves up. But no; in the face of that awful fire they deliberately turned back to get space for a good run at the ditch. This gave time for two of their pursuers to get within a few yards of them, when they stopped, evidently in doubt as to the meaning of this retrograde movement. But they did not remain long in doubt, for the two men turned again, and, with a shout, rushed for the ditch, and then we were near enough to see that they were Wild Bill and his mate. Bill's companion never reached the ditch. He and his horse must have been shot at the same time, for they went down together and did not rise again.

"Bill did not get a scratch. He spoke to Black Nell, the mare we saw just now, who knew as well as her master that there was life and death in that twenty feet of ditch, and that she must jump it; and at it she went with a big rush. I never saw a more magnificent sight. Bill gave the mare her head, and turning in his saddle fired twice, killing both of his pursuers, who were within a few lengths of him. They went out of their saddles like stones, just as Black Nell flew into the air and landed safely on our side of the ditch. In a moment both the daring scout and the brave mare were in our midst, while our men cheered and yelled like mad.

"We asked Bill why he ran such a risk, when he could have stolen into our lines during the night?

"'Oh,' said he, 'mate and I wanted to show them cussed rebs what a Union soldier could do. We've been with them now for more than a month, and heard nothing but brag. We thought we'd take it out of them. But'—and Bill looked across the green-sward to where his companion still lay motionless

—'if they have killed my mate they shall pay a big price for it.'

"Bill must have brought valuable information," continued the lieutenant, "for he was at once sent to the General, and in an hour we had changed position, and foiled a flank movement of the rebels."

I went to the hotel during the afternoon to keep the scout's appointment. The large room of the hotel in Springfield is perhaps the central point of attraction in the city. It fronted on the street, and served in several capacities. It was a sort of exchange for those who had nothing better to do than to go there. It was reception-room, parlor, and office; but its distinguished and most fascinating characteristic was the bar, which occupied one entire end of the apartment. Technically, the "bar" is the counter upon which the polite official places his viands. Practically, the bar is represented in the long rows of bottles, and cut-glass decanters, and the glasses and goblets of all shapes and sizes suited to the various liquors to be imbibed. What a charming and artistic display it was of elongated transparent vessels containing every known drinkable fluid, from native Bourbon to imported Lacryma Christi!

The room, in its way, was a temple of art. All sorts of pictures budded and blossomed and blushed from the walls. Sixpenny portraits of the Presidents encoffined in pinewood frames; Mazeppa appeared in the four phases of his celebrated one-horse act; while a lithograph of "Mary Ann" smiled and simpered in spite of the stains of tobacco-juice which had been unsparingly bestowed upon her originally encarmined countenance. But the hanging committee of this undesigned academy seemed to have been prejudiced—as all hanging committees of good taste might well be—in favor of *Harper's Weekly;* for the walls of the room were well covered with wood-cuts cut from that journal. Portraits of noted generals and statesmen, knaves and politicians, with bounteous illustrations of battles and skirmishes, from Bull Run number one to Dinwiddie Court House. And the simple-hearted comers and goers of Springfield looked upon, wondered, and admired these pictorial descriptions fully as much as if they had been the master-pieces of a Yvon or Vernet.

A billiard-table, old and out of use, where caroms seemed to have been made quite as often with lead as ivory balls, stood in the centre of the room. A dozen chairs filled up the complement of the furniture. The appearance of the party of men assembled there, who sat with their slovenly shod feet dangling over the arms of the chairs or hung about the porch outside, was in perfect harmony with the time and place. All of them religiously obeyed the two before-mentioned characteristics of the people of the city—their hair was long and tangled, and each man fulfilled the most exalted requirement of laziness.

I was taking a mental inventory of all this when a cry and murmur drew my attention to the outside of the house, when I saw Wild Bill riding up the street at a swift gallop. Arrived opposite to the hotel, he swung his right arm around with a circular motion. Black Nell instantly stopped and dropped to the ground as if a cannon-ball had knocked life out of her. Bill left her there, stretched upon the ground, and joined the group of observers on the porch.

"Black Nell hasn't forgot her old tricks," said one of them.

"No," answered the scout. "God bless her! she is wiser and truer than most men I know on. That mare will do any thing for me. Won't you, Nelly?"

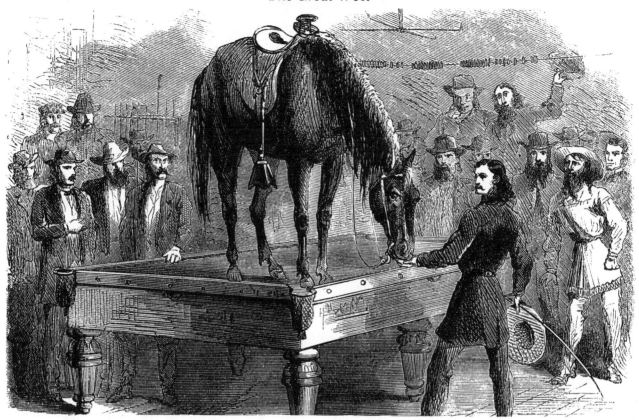

Black Nell. *Harper's Magazine*

The mare winked affirmatively the only eye we could see.

"Wise!" continued her master; "why, she knows more than a judge. I'll bet the drinks for the party that she'll walk up these steps and into the room and climb up on the billiard-table and lie down."

The bet was taken at once, not because any one doubted the capabilities of the mare but there was excitement in the thing without exercise.

Bill whistled in a low tone. Nell instantly scrambled to her feet, walked toward him, put her nose affectionately under his arm, followed him into the room, and to my extreme wonderment climbed upon the billiard-table, to the extreme astonishment of the table no doubt, for it groaned under the weight of the four-legged animal and several of those who were simply bifurcated, and whom Nell permitted to sit upon her. When she got down from the table, which was as graceful a performance as might be expected under the circumstances, Bill sprang upon her back, dashed through the high wide doorway, and at a single bound cleared the flight of steps and landed in the middle of the street. The scout then dismounted, snapped his riding-whip, and the noble beast bounded off down the street, rearing and plunging to her own intense satisfaction. A kindly-disposed individual, who must have been a stranger, supposing the mare was running away, tried to catch her, when she stopped, and as if she resented his impertinence, let fly her heels at him and then quietly trotted to her stable.

"Black Nell has carried me along through many a tight place," said the scout, as we walked toward my quarters. "She trains easier than any animal I ever saw. That trick of dropping quick which you saw has saved my life time and again. When I have been out scouting on the prarer or in the woods I have come across parties of rebels, and have dropped out of sight in the tall grass before they saw us. One day a gang of rebs who had been hunting for me, and thought they had my track, halted for half an hour within fifty yards of us. Nell laid as close as a rabbit, and didn't even whisk her tail to keep the flies off, until the rebs moved off, supposing they were on the wrong scent. The mare will come at my whistle and foller me about just like a dog. She won't mind any one else, nor allow them to mount her, and will kick a harness and wagon all ter pieces ef you try to hitch her in one. And she's right, Kernel," added Bill, with the enthusiasm of a true lover of a horse sparkling in his eyes. "A hoss is too noble a beast to be degraded by such toggery. Harness mules and oxen, but give a hoss a chance ter run."

I had a curiosity, which was not an idle one, to hear what this man had to say about his duel with Tutt, and I asked him:

"Do you not regret killing Tutt? You surely do not like to kill men?"

"As ter killing men," he replied, "I never thought much about it. The most of the men I have killed it was one or t'other of us, and at sich times you don't stop to think; and what's the use after it's all over? As for Tutt, I had rather not have killed him, for I want ter settle down quiet here now. But thar's been hard feeling between us for a long while. I wanted ter keep out of that fight; but he tried to degrade me, and I couldn't stand that, you know, for I am a fighting man, you know."

A cloud passed over the speaker's face for a moment as he continued:

"And there was a cause of quarrel between us which people round here don't know about. One of us had to die; and the secret died with him."

"Why did you not wait to see if your ball had hit him? Why did you turn round so quickly?"

The scout fixed his gray eyes on mine, striking his leg with his riding-whip, as he answered,

"I *knew* he was a dead man. I never miss a shot. I turned on the crowd because I was sure they would shoot me if they saw him fall."

"The people about here tell me you are a quiet, civil man. How is it you get into these fights?"

"D—d if I can tell," he replied, with a puzzled look which at once gave place to a proud, defiant expression as he continued—"but you know a man must defend his honor."

"Yes," I admitted, with some hesitation, remembering that I was not in Boston but on the border, and that the code of honor and mode of redress differ slightly in the one place from those of the other.

One of the reasons for my desire to make the acquaintance of Wild Bill was to obtain from his own lips a true account of some of the adventures related of him. It was not an easy matter. It was hard to overcome the reticence which marks men who have lived the wild mountain life, and which was one of his valuable qualifications as a scout. Finally he said:

"I hardly know where to begin. Pretty near all these stories are true. I was at it all the war. That affair of my swimming the river took place on that long scout of mine when I was with the rebels five months, when I was sent by General Curtis to Price's army. Things had come pretty close at that time, and it wasn't safe to go straight inter their lines. Every body was suspected who came from these parts. So I started off and went way up to Kansas City. I bought a horse there and struck out onto the plains, and then went down through Southern Kansas into Arkansas. I knew a rebel named Barnes, who was killed at Pea Ridge. He was from near Austin in Texas. So I called myself his brother and enlisted in a regiment of mounted rangers.

"General Price was just then getting ready for a raid into Missouri. It was sometime before we got into the campaign, and it was mighty hard work for me. The men of our regiment were awful. They didn't mind killing a man no more than a hog. The officers had no command over them. They were afraid of their own men, and let them do what they liked; so they would rob and sometimes murder their own people. It was right hard for me to keep up with them, and not do as they did. I never let on that I was a good shot. I kept that back for big occasions; but ef you'd heard me swear and cuss the blue-bellies, you'd a-thought me one of the wickedest of the whole crew. So it went on until we came near Curtis's army. Bimeby they were on one side Sandy River and we were on t'other. All the time I had been getting information until I knew every regiment and its strength; how much cavalry there was, and how many guns the artillery had.

"You see 'twas time for me to go, but it wasn't easy to git out, for the river was close picketed on both sides. One day when I was on picket our men and the rebels got talking

and cussin each other, as you know they used to do. After a while one of the Union men offered to exchange some coffee for tobacco. So we went out onto a little island which was neutral ground like. The minute I saw the other party, who belonged to the Missouri cavalry, we recognized each other. I was awful afraid they'd let on. So I blurted out:

"'Now, Yanks, let's see yer coffee — no burnt beans, mind yer — but the genuine stuff. We know the real article if we is Texans.'

"The boys kept mum, and we separated. Half an hour afterward General Curtis knew I was with the rebs. But how to git across the river was what stumped me. After that, when I was on the picket, I didn't trouble myself about being shot. I used to fire at our boys, and they'd bang away at me, each of us taking good care to shoot wide. But how to git over the river was the bother. At last, after thinking a heap about it, I came to the conclusion that I always did, that the boldest plan is the best and safest.

"We had a big sargent in our company who was allus a-braggin that he could stump any man in the regiment. He swore he had killed more Yanks than any man in the army, and that he could do more daring things than any others. So one day when he was talking loud I took him up, and offered to bet horse for horse that I would ride out into the open, and nearer to the Yankees than he. He tried to back out of this, but the men raised a row, calling him a funk, and a bragger, and all that; so he had to go. Well, we mounted our horses, but before we came within shootin distance of the Union soldiers I made my horse kick and rear so that they could see who I was. Then we rode slowly to the river bank, side by side.

"There must have been ten thousand men watching us; for, besides the rebs who wouldn't have cried about it if we had both been killed, our boys saw something was up, and without being seen thousands of them came down to the river. Their pickets kept firing at the sargent; but whether or not they were afraid of putting a ball through me I don't know, but nary a shot hit him. He was a plucky feller all the same, for the bullets zitted about in every direction.

"Bime-by we got right close ter the river, when one of the Yankee soldiers yelled out, 'Bully for Wild Bill!'

"Then the sargent suspicioned me, for he turned on me and growled out, 'By God, I believe yer a Yank! And he onst drew his revolver; but he was too late, for the minute he drew his pistol I put a ball through him. I mightn't have killed him if he hadn't suspicioned me. I had to do it then.

"As he rolled out of the saddle I took his

horse by the bit, and dashed into the water as quick as I could. The minute I shot the sargent our boys set up a tremendous shout, and opened a smashing fire on the rebs who had commenced popping at me. But I had got into deep water, and had slipped off my horse over his back, and steered him for the opposite bank by holding onto his tail with one hand, while I held the bridle rein of the sargent's horse in the other hand. It was the hottest bath I ever took. Whew! For about two minutes how the bullets zitted and skipped on the water. I thought I was hit again and again, but the reb sharp-shooters were bothered by the splash we made, and in a little while our boys drove them to cover, and after some tumbling at the bank got into the brush with my two horses without a scratch.

"It is a fact," said the scout, while he ca-

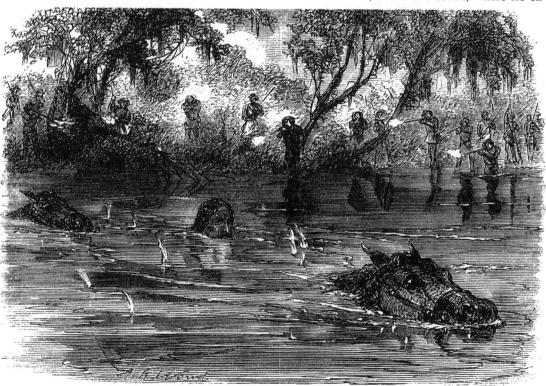

Taking to the Water. *Harper's Magazine*

ressed his long hair, "I felt sort of proud when the boys took me into camp, and General Curtis thanked me before a heap of generals.

"But I never tried that thing over again; nor I didn't go a scouting openly in Price's army after that. They all knew me too well, and you see 'twouldn't a been healthy to have been caught."

The scout's story of swimming the river ought, perhaps, to have satisfied my curiosity; but I was especially desirous to hear him relate the history of a sanguinary fight which he had with a party of ruffians in the early part of the war, when, single-handed, he fought and killed ten men. I had heard the story as it came from an officer of the regular army who, an hour after the affair, saw Bill and the ten dead men—some killed with bullets, others hacked and slashed to death with a knife.

As I write out the details of this terrible tale from notes which I took as the words fell from the scout's lips, I am conscious of its extreme improbability; but while I listened to him I remembered the story in the Bible, where we are told that Samson "with the jawbone of an ass slew a thousand men," and as I looked upon the magnificent example of human strength and daring, he appeared to me to realize the powers of a Samson and Hercules combined, and I should not have been inclined to place any limit upon his achievements. Besides this, one who has lived for four years in the presence of such grand heroism and deeds of prowess as was seen during the war is in what might be called a "receptive" mood. Be the story true or not, in part, or in whole, I believed then every word Wild Bill uttered, and I believe it to-day.

"I don't like to talk about that M'Kandlas

affair," said Bill, in answer to my question. "It gives me a queer shiver whenever I think of it, and sometimes I dream about it, and wake up in a cold sweat.

"You see this M'Kandlas was the Captain of a gang of desperadoes, horse-thieves, murderers, regular cut-throats, who were the terror of every body on the border, and who kept us in the mountains in hot water whenever they were around. I knew them all in the mountains, where they pretended to be trapping, but they were there hiding from the hangman. M'Kandlas was the biggest scoundrel and bully of them all, and was allers a-braggin of what he could do. One day I beat him shootin at a mark, and then threw him at the back-holt. And I didn't drop him as soft as you would a baby, you may be sure. Well, he got savage mad about it, and swore he would have his revenge on me some time.

"This was just before the war broke out, and we were already takin sides in the mountains either for the South or the Union. M'Kandlas and his gang were border-ruffians in the Kansas row, and of course they went with the rebs. Bime-by he clar'd out, and I shouldn't have thought of the feller agin ef he hadn't crossed my path. It 'pears he didn't forget me.

"It was in '61, when I guided a detachment of cavalry who were comin in from Camp Floyd. We had nearly reached the Kansas line, and were in South Nebraska, when one afternoon I went out of camp to go to the cabin of an old friend of mine, a Mrs. Waltman. I took only one of my revolvers with me, for although the war had broke out I didn't think it necessary to carry both my pistols, and, in all or'nary scrimmages, one is better than a dozen, ef you shoot straight. I saw some wild turkeys on the road as I was goin down, and popped one of 'em over, thinking he'd be just the thing for supper.

"Well, I rode up to Mrs. Waltman's, jumped off my horse, and went into the cabin, which is like most of the cabins on the prarer, with only one room, and that had two doors, one opening in front and t'other on a yard, like.

"How are you, Mrs. Waltman?' I said, feeling as jolly as you please.

"The minute she saw me she turned as white as a sheet and screamed: 'Is that you, Bill? Oh, my God! they will kill you! Run! run! They will kill you!'

" 'Who's a-goin to kill me?' said I. 'There's two can play at that game.'

" 'It's M'Kandlas and his gang. There's ten of them, and you've no chance. They've jes gone down the road to the corn-rack. They came up here only five minutes ago. M'Kandlas was draggin poor Parson Shipley on the ground with a lariat round his neck. The preacher was most dead with choking and the horses stamping on him. M'Kandlas knows yer bringin in that party of Yankee cavalry, and he swears he'll cut yer heart out. Run, Bill, run! — But it's too late; they're comin up the lane.'

"While she was a-talkin I remembered I had but one revolver, and a load gone out of that. On the table there was a horn of powder and some little bars of lead. I poured some powder into the empty chamber and rammed the lead after it by hammering the barrel on the table, and had just capped the pistol when I heard M'Kandlas shout:

" 'There's that d—d Yank Wild Bill's horse; he's here; and we'll skin him alive!'

"If I had thought of runnin before it war too late now, and the house was my best holt —a sort of fortress, like. I never thought I should leave that room alive."

The scout stopped in his story, rose from his seat, and strode back and forward in a state of great excitement.

"I tell you what it is, Kernel," he resumed, after a while, "I don't mind a scrimmage with these fellers round here. Shoot one or two of them and the rest run away. But all of M'Kandlas's gang were reckless, blood-thirsty devils, who would fight as long as they had strength to pull a trigger. I have been in tight places, but that's one of the few times I said my prayers.

" 'Surround the house and give him no quarter!' yelled M'Kandlas. When I heard that I felt as quiet and cool as if I was a-goin to church. I looked round the room and saw a Hawkins rifle hangin over the bed.

" 'Is that loaded?' said I to Mrs. Waltman.

" 'Yes,' the poor thing whispered. She was so frightened she couldn't speak out loud.

" 'Are you sure?' said I, as I jumped to the bed and caught it from its hooks. Although my eye did not leave the door, yet I could see she nodded 'Yes' again. I put the revolver on the bed, and just then M'Kandlas poked his head inside the doorway, but jumped back when he saw me with the rifle in my hand.

" 'Come in here, you cowardly dog!' I shouted. 'Come in here, and fight me!'

"M'Kandlas was no coward, if he was a bully. He jumped inside the room with his gun leveled to shoot; but he was not quick enough. My rifle-ball went through his heart. He fell back outside the house, where he was found afterward holding tight to his rifle, which had fallen over his head.

"His disappearance was followed by a yell from his gang, and then there was a dead silence. I put down the rifle and took the revolver, and I said to myself: 'Only six shots and nine men to kill. Save your powder, Bill, for the death-hug's a-comin!' I don't know why it was, Kernel," continued Bill, looking at me inquiringly, "but at that moment things seemed clear and sharp. I could think strong.

"There was a few seconds of that awful stillness, and then the ruffians came rushing in at both doors. How wild they looked with their red, drunken faces and inflamed eyes, shouting and cussing! But I never aimed more deliberately in my life.

"One—two—three—four; and four men fell dead.

"That didn't stop the rest. Two of them fired their bird-guns at me. And then I felt a sting run all over me. The room was full of smoke. Two got in close to me, their eyes glaring out of the clouds. One I knocked down with my fist. 'You are out of the way for a while,' I thought. The second I shot dead. The other three clutched me and crowded me onto the bed. I fought hard. I broke with my hand one man's arm. He had his fingers round my throat. Before I could get to my feet I was struck across the breast with the stock of a rifle, and I felt the blood rushing out of my nose and mouth. Then I got ugly, and I remember that I got hold of a knife, and then it was all cloudy like, and I was wild, and I struck savage blows, following the devils up from one side to the other side of the room and into the corners, striking and slashing until I knew that every one was dead.

"All of a sudden it seemed as if my heart was on fire. I was bleeding every where. I rushed out to the well and drank from the bucket, and then tumbled down in a faint."

Breathless with the intense interest with which I had followed this strange story, all the more thrilling and weird when its hero, seeming to live over again the bloody events of that day, gave way to its terrible spirit with wild, savage gestures. I saw then—what

my scrutiny of the morning had failed to discover—the tiger which lay concealed beneath that gentle exterior.

"You must have been hurt almost to death," I said.

"There were eleven buck-shot in me. I carry some of them now. I was cut in thirteen places. All of them bad enough to have let out the life of a man. But that blessed old Dr. Mills pulled me safe through it, after a bed siege of many a long week."

"That prayer of yours, Bill, may have been more potent for your safety than you think. You should thank God for your deliverance."

"To tell you the truth, Kernel," responded the scout with a certain solemnity in his grave face, "I don't talk about sich things ter the people round here, but I allers feel sort of thankful when I get out of a bad scrape."

"In all your wild, perilous adventures," I asked him, "have you ever been afraid? Do you know what the sensation is? I am sure you will not misunderstand the question, for I take it we soldiers comprehend justly that there is no higher courage than that which shows itself when the consciousness of danger is keen but where moral strength overcomes the weakness of the body."

"I think I know what you mean, Sir, and I'm not ashamed to say that I have been so frightened that it 'peared as if all the strength and blood had gone out of my body, and my face was as white as chalk. It was at the Wilme Creek fight. I had fired more than fifty cartridges, and I think fetched my man every time. I was on the skirmish line, and was working up closer to the rebs, when all of a sudden a battery opened fire right in front of me, and it sounded as if forty thousand guns were firing, and every shot and shell screeched within six inches of my head. It was the first time I was ever under artillery fire, and I was so frightened that I couldn't move for a minute or so, and when I did go back the boys asked me if I had seen a ghost? They may shoot bullets at me by the dozen, and it's rather exciting if I can shoot back, but I am always sort of nervous when the big guns go off."

"I would like to see you shoot."

"Would yer?" replied the scout, drawing his revolver; and approaching the window, he pointed to a letter O in a sign-board which was fixed to the stone-wall of a building on the other side of the way.

"That sign is more than fifty yards away. I will put these six balls into the inside of the circle, which isn't bigger than a man's heart."

In an off-hand way, and without sighting the pistol with his eye, he discharged the six shots of his revolver. I afterward saw that all the bullets had entered the circle.

As Bill proceeded to reload his pistol, he said to me with a naïveté of manner which was meant to be assuring:

"Whenever you get into a row be sure and not shoot too quick. Take time. I've known many a feller slip up for shootin' in a hurry."

It would be easy to fill a volume with the adventures of that remarkable man. My object here has been to make a slight record of one who is one of the best — perhaps the very best — example of a class who more than any other encountered perils and privations in defense of our nationality.

One afternoon as General Smith and I mounted our horses to start upon our journey toward the East, Wild Bill came to shake hands goodby, and I said to him:

"If you have no objection I will write out for publication an account of a few of your adventures."

"Certainly you may," he replied. "I'm sort of public property. But, Kernel," he continued, leaning upon my saddle-bow, while there was a tremulous softness in his voice and a strange moisture in his averted eyes, "I have a mother back there in Illinois who is old and feeble. I haven't seen her this many a year, and haven't been a good son to her, yet I love her better than any thing in this life. It don't matter much what they say about me here. But I'm not a cut-throat and vagabond, and I'd like the old woman to know what'll make her proud. I'd like her to hear that her runaway boy has fought through the war for the Union like a true man."

[William Hitchcock — called *Wild Bill, the Scout of the Plains* — shall have his wish. I have told his story precisely as it was told to me, confirmed in all important points by many witnesses; and I have no doubt of its truth.—G.W.N.]

19. The Killing of Wild Bill

BY J. W. BUEL

On the 2d day of August, 1876, Wild Bill was in Lewis & Mann's saloon, playing a game of poker with Capt. Massey, a Missouri river pilot, Charley Rich, and Cool Mann, one of the proprietors of the saloon. The game had been in progress nearly three hours, when about 4 o'clock, P. M., a man was seen to enter the door and pass up to the bar. Bill was sitting on a stool with the back of his head towards and about five feet from the bar. When the man entered, Bill had just picked up the cards dealt him, and was looking at his "hand," and therefore took no notice of the newcomer. The man, who proved to be Jack McCall, alias Bill Sutherland, after approaching the bar, turned, and drawing a large navy revolver, placed the muzzle within two inches of Bill's head and fired. The bullet entered the base of the brain, tore through the head, and made its exit at the right cheek, between the upper and lower jaw-bones, breaking off several teeth and carrying away a large piece of the cerebellum through the wound. The bullet struck Capt. Massey, who sat opposite Bill, in the right arm and broke the bone. At the instant the pistol was discharged, the cards fell from Bill's hands and he dropped sideways off the stool without uttering a sound. His companions were so horrified that several moments elapsed before it was discovered that Capt. Massey was wounded.

The assassin turned upon the crowd and compelled them to file out of the saloon before him. After reaching the street he defied arrest, but at five o'clock he gave himself up and asked for an immediate trial. Deadwood was, at that time, so primitive that it had no city officers, and there was no one legally competent to take charge of or try the prisoner. During the same evening, however, a coroner was chosen, who impaneled a jury and returned a verdict to the effect that J. B. Hickok (Wild Bill) came to his death from a wound resulting from a shot fired from a pistol by John McCall, alias Bill Sutherland.

Having proceeded thus far, it was determined to elect a judge, sheriff and prosecuting attorney to try McCall on the following day. Languishe, the lessee of McDaniel's

theatre, offered the use of the theatre for the purposes of the trial, which was arranged to take place at 9 o'clock on the following morning. Three men were sent out in different directions to notify the miners in the neighborhood of the murder, and to request their attendance at the trial.

Promptly at the time appointed, the improvised court convened, and Joseph Brown, who had been chosen sheriff, produced the prisoner. F. J. Kuykendall, the *pro tempore* judge, then addressed the crowd in a very appropriate manner, reminding those present that the court was purely a self-constituted one, but that in the discharge of his duty he would be governed by justice, and trust to them for a ratification of his acts. His remarks were greeted with hand-clappings of approval. The prisoner was then led forward and conducted to a seat on the stage to the right of the judge.

Never did a more forbidding countenance face a court than that of Jack McCall; his head, which was covered with a thick crop of chestnut hair, was very narrow as to the parts occupied by the intellectual portion of the brain, while the animal development was exceedingly large. A small, sandy moustache covered a sensual mouth, and the coarse double-chin was partially hid by a stiff goatee. The nose was what is commonly called "snub;" he had cross eyes and a florid complexion, which completed a more repulsive picture than Dore could conceive. He was clad in a blue flannel shirt, brown overalls, heavy shoes, and, as he sat in a stooping position, with his arms folded across his breast, he evidently assumed a nonchalance and bravado which were foreign to his feelings, and betrayed by the spasmodic heavings of his heart.

The selection of a jury consumed all the

Buel was a St. Louis newspaperman of the time.

forenoon, as it was next to impossible to select a man who had not formed or expressed an opinion concerning the murder, although but few who were in the panel had heard of the tragedy until a few hours before. A hundred names were selected, written upon separate scraps of paper, and placed in a hat. They were then well shaken, and the committee appointed for the purpose drew from the hat one name at a time. The party answering to the name then came forward and was examined by the judge touching his fitness to serve as an impartial juror. Ninety-two names were called from the panel before the jury was made up. Following are those who were selected and served: J. J. Bumfs, L. D. Brokow, J. H. Thompson, C. Whitehead, Geo. S. Hopkins, J. F. Cooper, Alexander Travis, K. F. Towle, John E. Thompson, L. A. Judd, Edward Burke and John Mann. The jurors being sworn, they took their seats, and testimony for the prosecution was begun.

The first witness called was Charles Rich, who said that he was in the saloon kept by Lewis & Mann on the afternoon of the 2d, and was seated at a table playing a game of poker with Wild Bill and several others, when the prisoner, whom he identified, came into the room, walked deliberately up to Wild Bill, placed a pistol to the back of the deceased, and fired, saying: "Take that!" Bill fell from the stool upon which he had been seated without uttering a word.

Samuel Young testified that he was engaged in the saloon; that he had just delivered $15 worth of pocket checks to the deceased, and was returning to his place behind the bar when he heard the report of a pistol shot; turning around, he saw the prisoner at the back of Wild Bill with a pistol in his hand which he had just discharged; heard him say, "Take that!"

Carl Mann was one of the proprietors of the saloon in which Wild Bill was killed; was in the poker game; noticed a commotion; saw the prisoner (whom he identified) shoot Wild Bill.

The defense called for the first witness, P. H. Smith, who said he had been in the employ of McCall four months; that he was not a man of quarrelsome disposition; that he had always considered him a man of good character; that he (the witness) had been introduced to Wild Bill in Cheyenne, and drank with him; that the deceased had a bad reputation, and had been the terror of every place in which he had resided.

H. H. Pickens said that he had known defendant four years, and believed him to be a quiet and peaceable man. Wild Bill's reputation as a "shootist" was very hard; he was quick in using the pistol and never missed his man, and had killed quite a number of persons in different parts of the country.

Ira Ford had known the defendant about one year; "like a great many others, he would go upon a spree like the rest of the boys." Wild Bill had the reputation of being a brave man, who could and would shoot quicker than any man in the Western country, and who always "got away" with his antagonist.

The defense called several others, the tenor of whose evidence was but a repetition of the foregoing. No attempt was made to show that Wild Bill had ever seen the prisoner.

The prisoner was called upon to make a statement. He came down from the stage into the auditorium of the theatre, and with his right hand in the bosom of his shirt, his head thrown back, in a harsh, loud and repulsive voice, with a bull-dog sort of bravado, said: "Well, men, I have but a few words to say. Wild Bill threatened to kill me if I crossed his path. I am not sorry for what I have done. I would do the same thing over again." The prisoner then returned to his place on the stage.

The prosecution then adduced testimony to prove that Wild Bill was a much abused man; that he never imposed on any one, and that in every instance where he had slain men he had done so either in the discharge of his duty as an officer of the law or in self-defense.

The case having been placed in the hands of the jury, the theatre was cleared, with the understanding that the verdict should be made known in the saloon where the murder was committed. The prisoner was remanded to the house where he had been imprisoned during the night. At 9 o'clock the following verdict was read to the prisoner:

DEADWOOD CITY, Aug. 3, 1876.—We, the jurors, find the prisoner, Mr. John McCall, not guilty.
CHARLES WHITEHEAD, Foreman.

The prisoner was at once liberated, and several of the model jurymen who had played their parts in this burlesque upon justice, and who had turned their blood-thirsty tiger loose upon the community, indulged in a sickening cheer which grated harshly upon the ears of those who heard it. The first vote taken by the jury resulted in eleven for acquittal and one for conviction, and the single man who desired justice was so intimidated by his fellow-jurors that he was induced to sanction the iniquitous verdict. It was even proposed by one of the jurymen that the prisoner be fined fifteen or twenty dollars and set free.

After the inquest the body of the deceased was placed upon a litter made of two poles and some boards; then a procession was formed, and the remains were carried to Charley Utter's camp, across the creek. Charles Utter, better known as Colorado Charley, had been the intimate friend of the deceased for fifteen years, and with that liberality which is a feature among mountaineers, had always shared his purse with him. Charley was much affected by the death of his friend, and incensed at the villain who had murdered him. A tepee was pitched at the foot of one of the giant trees which rise so majestically above Charley's camp. Preparations were at once made for the funeral. The following notice was printed and sent out:

"FUNERAL NOTICE.—Died in Deadwood, Black Hills, Aug. 2, 1876, from the effects of a pistol shot, J. B. Hickok (Wild Bill,) formerly of Cheyenne, Wyoming. Funeral services will be held at Charley Utter's camp, on Thursday afternoon, Aug. 3, 1876, at 3 o'clock. All are respectfully invited to attend."

At the time appointed a number of people gathered at the camp — Charley Utter had gone to a great deal of expense to make the funeral as fine as could be had in that country. Under the tepee, in a handsome coffin, covered with black cloth and richly mounted with silver ornaments, lay Wild Bill, a picture of perfect repose. His long chestnut hair, evenly parted over his marble brow, hung in waving ringlets over the broad shoulders; his face was cleanly shaved excepting the drooping moustache, which shaded a mouth that in death almost seemed to smile, but in life was unusually grave; the arms were folded over the stilled breast, which inclosed a heart that had beat with regular pulsation amid the most startling scenes of blood and violence. The corpse was clad in complete dress-suit of black broadcloth, new underclothing and white

Wild Bill

in the bright sunlight, the air redolent with the perfume of sweet flowers, the birds sweetly singing, and all nature smiling, the solemn cortege wended its way and deposited the mortal remains of Wild Bill.

After the farcical termination of the trial, and the burial of Wild Bill, several friends of the deceased ·met at Charley Utter's ranche and determined to avenge the cowardly assassination of their friend. McCall, unfortunately, heard of the meeting and its purposes and lost no time in getting out of the country. He roamed around in the far West, and finally settled at Yankton. In the following year a United States court was established in Dakotah Territory at Yankton, and Jack McCall was again apprehended and put upon trial. George Shingle, now a resident of Sturgis City, eighteen miles south of Deadwood, was an eye-witness of the shooting, but left Deadwood to escape the excitement on the same evening Bill was killed, and therefore did not appear as a witness at the original trial, but appeared in answer to the summons which called him to Yankton, and there told the story of the murder. The result of this trial was the conviction of McCall, and in July, 1877, he expiated his cowardly crime on the gallows at Yankton.

linen shirt; beside him in the coffin lay his trusty rifle, which the deceased prized above all other things, and which was to be buried with him in compliance with an often expressed desire.

A clergyman read an impressive funeral service, that was attentively listened to by the audience, after which the coffin-lid hid the well-known face ·of Wild Bill from the prying gaze of the world.

A grave had been prepared on the mountain side toward the east, and to that place

20. Indians!

BY GEORGE A. CUSTER

EDITOR'S NOTE: As almost every American schoolboy knows, General George Armstrong Custer (1839-1876) was a handsome, youthful and daring cavalry officer who emerged with a brilliant reputation from the Civil War. He had everything he wanted out of life, or so

it seemed. During several leisurely years he wrote *My Life on the Plains* (1874), from which the following account is drawn. In 1876 Custer and the Seventh Regiment were ordered against the Sioux in Montana and Dakota. Custer arrived at the junction of the Big

Horn and Little Big Horn rivers in Montana Territory on June 24th. On the 25th he advanced in three columns to surround a supposedly small force of hostile Indians and was attacked by the enemy's full force — a disaster caused largely by faulty intelligence. Custer and the center column rode into the midst of the Indians and were slaughtered — 265 of them — in what came to be known as Custer's Last Stand. This tragedy has elicited a great deal of speculation and analysis. I have selected eyewitness reports as well as military documents to give a sense of immediacy to events which are now almost legendary as well as historic.

The march from camp to Beaver Creek was made without incident. Here the combined forces of Colonel West and Lieuten-

Portrait of General Custer.
By Brady or assistant

ant Robbins encamped together during the night. Next morning at early dawn Lieutenant Robbins's party, having the train in charge, continued the march toward Fort Wallace, while Colonel West sent out scouting parties up and down the stream to search for Indians.

As yet none of their party were aware of the hostile attitude assumed by the Indians within the past few hours, and Colonel West's instructions contemplated a friendly meeting between his forces and the Indians should the latter be discovered. The march of the train and escort was made to Fort Wallace without interruption. The only incident worthy of remark was an observation of Comstock's, which proved how thoroughly he was familiar with the Indian and his customs.

The escort was moving over a beautifully level plateau. Not a mound or hillock disturbed the evenness of the surface for miles in either direction. To an unpracticed eye there seemed no recess or obstruction in or behind which an enemy might be concealed, but everything appeared open to the view for miles and miles, look in what direction one might. Yet such was not the case. Ravines of greater or less extent, though not perceptible at a glance, might have been discovered if searched for, extending almost to the trail over which the party was moving. These ravines, if followed, would be found to grow deeper and deeper, until, after running their course for an indefinite extent, they would terminate in the valley of some running stream. These were the natural hiding places of Indian war parties, waiting their opportunities to dash upon unsuspecting victims. These ravines serve the same purpose to the Indians of the timberless plains that the ambush did to those Indians of the Eastern States accustomed to fighting in the forests and everglades. Comstock's keen eyes took in all at a glance, and he remarked to Colonel Cook and Lieutenant Robbins, as the three rode together at the head of the column, that "If the Injuns strike us at all, it will be just about the time we are comin' along back over this very spot. Now mind what I tell ye all." We shall see how correct Comstock's prophecy was.

Arriving at the fort, no time was lost in loading up the wagons with fresh supplies, obtaining the mail intended for the command, and preparing to set out on the return to camp the following day. No late news regarding Indian movements was obtained. Fortunately, my letter from Fort McPherson to Mrs. Custer, asking her to come to Fort Wallace, miscarried, and she did not undertake a journey which in all probability would have imperiled her life, if not terminated it in a most tragic manner.

On the following morning Colonel Cook and Lieutenant Robbins began their return march. They had advanced one half the distance which separated them from Colonel West's camp without the slightest occurrence to disturb the monotony of their march, and had reached the point where, on passing before, Comstock had indulged in his prognostication regarding Indians; yet nothing had been seen to excite suspicion or alarm.

Comstock, always on the alert and with eyes as quick as those of an Indian, had been scanning the horizon in all directions. Suddenly he perceived, or thought he perceived, strange figures, resembling human heads, peering over the crest of a hill far away to the right. Hastily leveling his field glass, he pronounced the strange figures, which were scarcely perceptible, to be neither more nor less than Indians. The officers brought into requisition their glasses, and were soon convinced of the correctness of Comstock's report. It was some time before the Indians perceived that they were discovered. Concealment then being no longer possible, they boldly rode to the crest and exposed themselves to full view. At first but twenty or thirty made their appearance; gradually their number became augmented, until about a hundred warriors could be seen.

It may readily be imagined that the appearance of so considerable a body of Indians produced no little excitement and speculation in the minds of the people with the train. The speculation was as to the intentions of the Indians, whether hostile or friendly. Upon this subject all doubts were soon dispelled. The Indians continued to receive accessions to their numbers, the reinforcements coming from beyond the crest of the hill on which their presence was first discovered. Finally, seeming confident in their superior numbers, the warriors, all of whom were mounted, advanced leisurely down the slope leading in the direction of the train and its escort. By the aid of field glasses, Comstock and the two officers were able to determine fully the character of the party now approaching them. The last doubt was thus removed. It was clearly to be seen that the Indians were arrayed in full war costume, their heads adorned by the brilliantly colored war bonnets, their faces, arms, and bodies painted in various colors, rendering their naturally repulsive appearance even more hideous. As they approached nearer they assumed a certain order in the manner of their advance. Some were to be seen carrying the long glistening lance with its pennant of bright colors; while upon the left arm hung the round shield, almost bullet-proof, and ornamented with paint and feathers according to the taste of the wearer.

War Path.   *Alfred Jacob Miller*

Nearly all were armed with carbines and one or two revolvers, while many in addition to these weapons carried the bow and arrow.

When the entire band had defiled down the inclined slope, Comstock and the officers were able to estimate roughly the full strength of the party. They were astonished to perceive that between six and seven hundred warriors were bearing down upon them, and in a few minutes would undoubtedly commence the attack. Against such odds, and upon ground so favorable for the Indian mode of warfare, it seemed unreasonable to hope for a favorable result. Yet the entire escort, officers and men, entered upon their defense with the determination to sell their lives as dearly as possible.

As the coming engagement, so far as the cavalry was concerned, was to be a purely defensive one, Lieutenant Robbins at once set about preparing to receive his unwelcome visitors. Colonel Cook formed the train in two parallel columns, leaving ample space between for the horses of the cavalry. Lieutenant Robbins then dismounted his men and prepared to fight on foot. The led horses, under charge of the fourth trooper, were placed between the two columns of wagons, and were thus in a measure protected from the assaults which the officers had every reason to believe would be made for their capture. The dismounted cavalrymen were thus formed in a regular circle enclosing the train and horses. Colonel Cook took command of one flank, Lieutenant Robbins of the other, while Comstock, who as well as the two officers remained mounted, galloped from point to point wherever his presence was most valuable. These dispositions being perfected, the march was resumed in this order, and the attack of the savages calmly awaited.

The Indians, who were interested spectators of these preparations for their reception, continued to approach, but seemed willing to delay their attack until the plain became a little more favorable for their operations. Finally, the desired moment seemed to have arrived. The Indians had approached to within easy range, yet not a shot had been fired, the cavalrymen having been instructed by their officers to reserve their fire for close quarters. Suddenly, with a wild ringing war whoop, the entire band of warriors bore down upon the train and its little party of defenders.

On came the savages, filling the air with their terrible yells. Their first object, evidently, was to stampede the horses and draft animals of the train; then, in the excitement and consternation which would follow, to massacre the escort and drivers. The wagon master in immediate charge of the train had been ordered to keep his two columns of wagons constantly moving forward and well closed up. This last injunction was hardly necessary, as the frightened teamsters, glancing at the approaching warriors and hearing their savage shouts, were sufficiently anxious to keep well closed upon their leaders.

The first onslaught of the Indians was made on the flank which was superintended by Colonel Cook. They rode boldly forward as if to dash over the mere handful of cavalrymen, who stood in skirmishing order in a circle about the train. Not a soldier faltered as the enemy came thundering upon them,

but waiting until the Indians were within short rifle range of the train, the cavalrymen dropped upon their knees, and taking deliberate aim poured a volley from their Spencer carbines into the ranks of the savages, which seemed to put a sudden check upon the ardor of their movements and forced them to wheel off to the right. Several of the warriors were seen to reel in their saddles, while the ponies of others were brought down or wounded by the effectual fire of the cavalrymen.

Those of the savages who were shot from their saddles were scarcely permitted to fall to the ground before a score or more of their comrades dashed to their rescue and bore their bodies beyond the possible reach of our men. This is in accordance with the Indian custom in battle. They will risk the lives of a dozen of their best warriors to prevent the body of any one of their number from falling into the white man's possession. The reason for this is the belief, which generally prevails among all the tribes, that if a warrior loses his scalp he forfeits his hope of ever reaching the happy hunting ground.

As the Indians were being driven back by the well-directed volley of the cavalrymen, the latter, overjoyed at their first success, became reassured, and sent up a cheer of exultation, while Comstock, who had not been idle in the fight, called out to the retreating Indians in their native tongue, taunting them with their unsuccessful assault.

The Indians withdrew to a point beyond the range of our carbines, and there seemed to engage in a parley. Comstock, who had closely watched every movement, remarked that "There's no sich good luck for us as to think them Injuns mean to give it up so. Six hundred red devils ain't agoin' to let fifty men stop them from gettin' at the coffee and sugar that is in these wagons. And they ain't agoin' to be satisfied until they get some of our scalps to pay for the bucks we popped out of their saddles a bit ago."

It was probable that the Indians were satisfied that they could not dash through the train and stampede the animals. Their recent attempt had convinced them that some other method of attack must be resorted to. Nothing but their greater superiority in numbers had induced them to risk so much in a charge.

The officers passed along the line of skirmishers — for this in reality was all their line consisted of—and cautioned the men against wasting their ammunition. It was yet early in the afternoon, and should the conflict be prolonged until night, there was great danger of exhausting the supply of ammunition.

The Indians seemed to have thought of this, and the change in their method of attack encouraged such a result.

But little time was spent at the parley. Again the entire band of warriors, except those already disabled, prepared to renew the attack, and advanced as before — this time, however, with greater caution, evidently desiring to avoid a reception similar to the first. When sufficiently near to the troops the Indians developed their new plan of attack. It was not to advance *en masse*, as before, but fight as individuals, each warrior selecting his own time and method of attack. This is the habitual manner of fighting among all Indians of the Plains, and is termed "circling." First the chiefs led off, followed at regular intervals by the warriors, until the entire six or seven hundred were to be seen riding in single

Sioux Indians.   *George Catlin*   COURTESY NEW YORK HISTORICAL SOCIETY

file as rapidly as their fleet-footed ponies would carry them. Preserving this order, and keeping up their savage chorus of yells, war whoops, and taunting epithets, this long line of mounted barbarians was guided in such manner as to envelop the train and escort, and make the latter appear like a small circle within a larger one.

The Indians gradually contracted their circle, although maintaining the full speed of their ponies, until sufficiently close to open fire upon the soldiers. At first the shots were scattering wide of their mark; but, emboldened by the silence of their few but determined opponents, they rode nearer and fought with greater impetuosity. Forced now to defend themselves to the uttermost, the cavalrymen opened fire from their carbines, with most gratifying results. The Indians, however, moving at such a rapid gait and in single file, presented a most uncertain target. To add to this uncertainty, the savages availed themselves of their superior—almost marvelous—powers of horsemanship. Throwing themselves upon the sides of their well-trained ponies, they left no part of their persons exposed to the aim of the troopers except the head and one foot, and in this posture they were able to aim the weapons either over or under the necks of their ponies, thus using the bodies of the latter as an effective shield against the bullets of their adversaries.

At no time were the Indians able to force the train and its escort to come to a halt. The march was continued at an uninterrupted gait. This successful defense against the Indians was in a great measure due to the presence of the wagons, which, arranged in the order described, formed a complete barrier to the charges and assaults of the savages; and, as a last resort, the wagons could have been halted and used as a breastwork, be-

hind which the cavalry, dismounted, would have been almost invincible against their more numerous enemies. There is nothing an Indian dislikes more in warfare than to attack a foe, however weak, behind breastworks of any kind. Any contrivance which is an obstacle to his pony is a most serious obstacle to the warrior.

The attack of the Indians, aggravated by their losses in warriors and ponies, as many of the latter had been shot down, was continued without cessation for three hours. The supply of ammunition of the cavalry was running low. The "fourth troopers," who had remained in charge of the led horses between the two columns of wagons, were now replaced from the skirmishers, and the former were added to the list of active combatants. If the Indians should maintain the fight much longer, there was serious ground for apprehension regarding the limited supply of ammunition.

If only night or reinforcements would come! was the prayerful hope of those who contended so gallantly against such heavy odds. Night was still too far off to promise much encouragement; while as to reinforcements, their coming would be purely accidental — at least so argued those most interested in their arrival. Yet reinforcements were at that moment striving to reach them. Comrades were in the saddle and spurring forward to their relief. The Indians, although apparently turning all their attention to the little band inside, had omitted no precaution to guard against interference from outside parties. In this instance, perhaps, they were more than ordinarily watchful, and had posted some of their keen-eyed warriors on the high line of bluffs which ran almost parallel to the trail over which the combatants moved. From these bluffs not only a good view of the fight could be obtained, but the country for miles in either direction was spread out beneath them, and enabled the scouts to discern the approach of any hostile party which might be advancing. Fortunate for the savages that this precaution had not been neglected, or the contest in which they were engaged might have become one of more equal numbers. To the careless eye nothing could have been seen to excite suspicion. But the warriors on the lookout were not long in discovering something which occasioned them no little anxiety. Dismounting from their ponies and concealing the latter in a ravine, they prepared to investigate more fully the cause of their alarm.

That which they saw was as yet but a faint dark line on the surface of the plain, almost against the horizon. So faint was it that no one but an Indian or practiced frontiersman would have observed it. It was fully ten miles from them and directly in their line of march. The ordinary observer would have pronounced it a break or irregularity in the ground, or perhaps the shadow of a cloud, and its apparent permanency of location would have dispelled any fear as to its dangerous character. But was it stationary? Apparently, yes. The Indians discovered otherwise. By close watching, the long faint line could be seen moving along, as if creeping stealthily upon an unconscious foe. Slowly it assumed a more definite shape, until what appeared to be a mere stationary dark line drawn upon the green surface of the plain developed itself to the searching eyes of the red man into a column of cavalry moving at a rapid gait toward the very point they were then occupying.

Convinced of this fact, one of the scouts leaped upon his pony and flew with almost the speed of the wind to impart this knowledge to the chiefs in command on the plain

below. True, the approaching cavalry, being still several miles distant, could not arrive for nearly two hours; but the question to be considered by the Indians was, whether it would be prudent for them to continue their attack on the train—their ponies already becoming exhausted by the three hours' hard riding given them—until the arrival of the fresh detachment of the enemy, whose horses might be in condition favorable to a rapid pursuit, and thereby enable them to overtake those of the Indians whose ponies were exhausted. Unwilling to incur this new risk, and seeing no prospect of overcoming their present adversaries by a sudden or combined dash, the chiefs decided to withdraw from the attack, and make their escape while the advantage was yet in their favor.

The surprise of the cavalrymen may be imagined at seeing the Indians, after pouring a shower of bullets and arrows into the train, withdraw to the bluffs, and immediately after continue their retreat until lost to view.

The victory for the troopers, although so unexpected, was none the less welcome. The Indians contrived to carry away with them their killed and wounded. Five of their bravest warriors were known to have been sent to the happy hunting ground, while the list of their wounded was much larger.

After the Indians had withdrawn and left the cavalrymen masters of the field, our wounded, of whom there were comparatively few, received every possible care and attention. Those of the detachment who had escaped unharmed were busily engaged in exchanging congratulations and relating incidents of the fight.

In this manner nearly an hour had been whiled away, when far in the distance, in their immediate front, fresh cause for anxiety was discovered. At first the general opinion was that it was the Indians again, determined to contest their progress. Field glasses were again called into requisition, and revealed, not Indians, but the familiar blue blouses of the cavalry. Never was the sight more welcome. The next moment Colonel Cook, with Comstock and a few troopers, applied spurs to their horses and were soon dashing forward to meet their comrades.

The approaching party was none other than Colonel West's detachment, hastening to the relief of the train and its gallant little escort. A few words explained all, and told the heroes of the recent fight how it happened that reinforcements were sent to their assistance; and then was explained why the Indians had so suddenly concluded to abandon their attack and seek safety in quietly withdrawing from the field.

Sioux Camp—Skin Lodges

21. Orders to General Custer

BY GENERAL ALFRED H. TERRY

Camp at the Mouth of
Rosebud River,
June 22, 1876.

The Brigadier General commanding directs that as soon as your regiment can be made ready for the march, you proceed up the Rosebud in pursuit of the Indians whose trail was discovered by Major Reno a few days ago. It is, of course, impossible to give you any definite instructions in regard to this movement, and were it not impossible to do so, the Department commander places too much confidence in your zeal, energy and ability to wish to impose upon you precise orders which might hamper your action when nearly in contact with the enemy.

He will, however, indicate to you his own views of what your action should be, and he desires that you should conform to them unless you shall see sufficient reason for departing from them. He thinks that you should proceed up the Rosebud until you ascertain definitely the direction in which the trail above spoken of leads. Should it be found, as it appears to be almost certain that it will be found, to turn toward the Little Big Horn he thinks that you should still proceed southward, perhaps as far as the headwaters of the Tongue, and then turn toward the Little Big Horn, feeling constantly however, to your left so as to preclude the possibility of the escape of the Indians to the south or southeast by passing around your left flank.

The column of Col. Gibbon is now in motion for the mouth of the Big Horn. As soon as it reaches that point it will cross the Yellowstone and move up at least as far as the forks of the Big and Little Big Horn. Of course its future movements must be controlled by circumstances as they may arise; but it is hoped that the Indians, if upon the Little Big Horn, may be so nearly enclosed by the two columns that their escape will be impossible.

The Department Commander desires that on your way up the Rosebud you should thoroughly examine the upper part of Tullocks Creek, and that you should endeavor to send a scout through to Col. Gibbon's column with information of the result of your examination. The lower part of this creek will be examined by a detachment from Col. Gibbon's command.

The supply steamer will be pushed up the Big Horn as far as the forks of the river are found to be navigable for that space, and the Department Commander, who will accompany the column of Col. Gibbon, desires you to report to him there not later than the expiration of the time for which your troops are rationed, unless in the meantime you receive further orders.

Respectfully,

E. W. SMITH,
Capt. 18th Infantry,
Acting Asst. Adjt. Genl.

210

22. Report to General Sheridan

BY GENERAL ALFRED H. TERRY

I think I owe it to myself to put you more fully in possession of the facts of the late operations. While at the mouth of the Rosebud I submitted my plan to Genl. Gibbon and to General Custer. They approved it heartily. It was that Custer with his whole regiment should move up the Rosebud till he should meet a trail which Reno had discovered a few days before but that he should not follow it directly to the Little Big Horn; that he should send scouts over it and keep his main force further to the south so as to prevent the Indians from slipping in between himself and the mountains. He was also to examine the headwaters of Tullock's creek as he passed it and send me word of what he found there. A scout was furnished him for the purpose of crossing the country to me. We calculated it would take Gibbon's column until the twenty-sixth to reach the mouth of the Little Big Horn and that the wide sweep which I had proposed Custer should make would require so much time that Gibbon would be able to coöperate with him in attacking any Indians that might be found on that stream. I asked Custer how long his marches would be. He said they would be at first about thirty miles a day. Measurements were made and calculation based on that rate of progress. I talked with him about his strength and at one time suggested that perhaps it would be well for me to take Gibbon's cavalry and go with him. To this suggestion he replied that without reference to the command he would prefer his own regiment alone. As a homogeneous body, as much could be done with it as with the two combined and he ex-

pressed the utmost confidence that he had all the force that he could need, and I shared his confidence. The plan adopted was the only one that promised to bring the Infantry into action and I desired to make sure of things by getting up every available man. I offered Custer the battery of Gatling guns but he declined it saying that it might embarrass him: that he was strong enough without it. The movements proposed for Genl. Gibbon's column were carried out to the letter and had the attack been deferred until it was up I cannot doubt that we should have been successful. The Indians had evidently nerved themselves for a stand, but as I learn from Capt. Benteen, on the twenty-second the cavalry marched twelve miles; on the twenty-third, thirty-five miles; from five A. M. till eight P. M. on the twenty-fourth, forty-five miles and then after night ten miles further; then after resting but without unsaddling, twenty-three miles to the battlefield. The proposed route was not taken but as soon as the trail was struck it was followed. I cannot learn that any examination of Tullock's creek was made. I do not tell you this to cast any reflection upon Custer. For whatever errors he may have committed he has paid the penalty and you cannot regret his loss more than I do, but I feel that our plan must have been successful had it been carried out, and I desire you to know the facts. In the action itself, so far as I can make out, Custer acted under a misapprehension. He thought, I am confident, that the Indians were running. For fear that they might get away he attacked without getting all his men up and divided his command so that they were beaten in detail. I do not at all propose to give the thing up here but I think that my troops require a little time and in view of the strength which the Indians have developed I propose to bring up what little reinforcement I can get. I should be glad of any that you can send me. I can take two companies of Indians from Powder River and there are a few recruits and detached men whom I can get for the cavalry. I ought to have a larger mounted force than I now have but I fear cannot be obtained. I hear nothing from General Crook's operations. If I could hear I should be able to form plans for the future much more intelligently.

I should very much like instructions from you, or if not instructions, your views of the situation based as they might be on what has taken place elsewhere as well as here.

I shall refit as rapidly as possible and if at any time I should get information showing that I can act in conjunction with General Crook, or independently, with good results, I shall leave at once.

I send in another dispatch a copy of my written orders to Custer, but these were supplemented by the distinct understanding that Gibbon could not get to the Little Big Horn before the evening of the 26th.

ALFRED H. TERRY,
Brigadier General.

23. General Custer's Last Fight

BY TWO MOON, AS RELATED TO HAMLIN GARLAND

As we topped the low, pine-clad ridge and looked into the hot, dry valley, Wolf Voice, my Cheyenne interpreter, pointed at a little log cabin, toward the green line of alders wherein the Rosebud ran, and said:

"His house—Two Moon."

As we drew near we came to a puzzling fork in the road. The left branch skirted a corner of a wire fence, the right turned into a field. We started to the left, but the waving of a blanket in the hands of a man at the cabin door directed us to the right. As we drew nearer we perceived Two Moon spreading blankets in the scant shade of his low cabin. Some young Cheyennes were grinding a sickle. A couple of children were playing about the little log stables. The barn-yard and buildings were like those of a

white settler on the new and arid sod. It was all barren and unlovely—the home of poverty.

As we dismounted at the door Two Moon came out to meet us with hand outstretched. "How?" he said, with the heartiest, long-drawn note of welcome. He motioned us to be seated on the blankets which he had spread for us upon seeing our approach. Nothing could exceed the dignity and sincerity of his greeting.

As we took seats he brought out tobacco and a pipe. He was a tall old man, of a fine, clear brown complexion, big-chested, erect, and martial of bearing. His smiling face was broadly benignant, and his manners were courteous and manly.

While he cut his tobacco Wolf Voice interpreted my wishes to him. I said, "Two Moon, I have come to hear your story of the Custer battle, for they tell me you were a chief there. After you tell me the story, I want to take some photographs of you. I want you to signal with a blanket as the great chiefs used to do in fight."

Wolf Voice made this known to him, delivering also a message from the agents, and at every pause Two Moon uttered deep-voiced notes of comprehension. "Ai," "A-ah," "Hoh,"—these sounds are commonly called "grunts," but they were low, long-drawn expulsions of breath, very expressive.

Then a long silence intervened. The old man mused. It required time to go from the silence of the hot valley, the shadow of his little cabin, and the wire fence of his pasture, back to the days of his youth. When he began to speak, it was with great deliberation. His face became each moment graver and his eyes more introspective.

"Two Moon does not like to talk about the days of fighting; but since you are to make a book, and the agent says you are a friend to Grinnell,* I will tell you about it—the truth. It is now a long time ago, and my words do not come quickly.

"That spring [1876] I was camped on Powder River with fifty lodges of my people —Cheyennes. The place is near what is now Fort McKenney. One morning soldiers charged my camp. They were in command of Three Fingers [Colonel McKenzie]. We were surprised and scattered, leaving our ponies. The soldiers ran all our horses off. That night the soldiers slept, leaving the horses one side; so we crept up and stole them back again, and then we went away.

"We traveled far, and one day we met a big camp of Sioux at Charcoal Butte. We camped with the Sioux, and had a good time, plenty grass, plenty game, good water. Crazy Horse was head chief of the camp. Sitting Bull was camped a little ways below, on the Little Missouri River.

"Crazy Horse said to me, 'I'm glad you are come. We are going to fight the white man again.'

"The camp was already full of wounded men, women, and children.

"I said to Crazy Horse, 'All right. I am ready to fight. I have fought already. My people have been killed, my horses stolen; I am satisfied to fight.' "

Here the old man paused a moment, and his face took on a lofty and somber expression.

"I believed at that time the Great Spirits had made Sioux, put them there,"—he drew a circle to the right—"and white men and Cheyennes here,"—indicating two places to the left—"expecting them to fight. The Great Spirits I thought liked to see the fight; it was to them all the same like playing. So I thought then about fighting." As he said this, he made me feel for one moment the power of a sardonic god whose drama was the wars of men.

"About May, when the grass was tall and the horses strong, we broke camp and started across the country to the mouth of the Tongue River. Then Sitting Bull and Crazy Horse and all went up the Rosebud. There we had a big fight with General Crook, and whipped him. Many soldiers were killed— few Indians. It was a great fight, much smoke and dust.

"From there we all went over the divide, and camped in the valley of Little Horn. Everybody thought, 'Now we are out of the white man's country. He can live there, we will live here.' After a few days, one morning

From *McClure's Magazine*, September, 1898.
* George B. Grinnell, whom the Cheyennes, Blackfeet, and Gros Ventres love and honor.

The Sioux War.   General Crook's Battle on the Rosebud River

when I was in camp north of Sitting Bull, a Sioux messenger rode up and said, 'Let everybody paint up, cook, and get ready for a big dance.'

"Cheyennes then went to work to cook, cut up tobacco, and get ready. We all thought to dance all day. We were very glad to think we were far away from the white man.

"I went to water my horses at the creek, and washed them off with cool water, then took a swim myself. I came back to the camp afoot. When I got near my lodge, I looked up the Little Horn towards Sitting Bull's camp. I saw a great dust rising. It looked like a whirlwind. Soon Sioux horseman came

rushing into camp shouting: 'Soldiers come! Plenty white soldiers.'

"I ran into my lodge, and said to my brother-in-law, 'Get your horses; the white man is coming. Everybody run for horses.'

"Outside, far up the valley, I heard a battle cry, *Hay-ay, hay-ay!* I heard shooting, too, this way [clapping his hands very fast]. I couldn't see any Indians. Everybody was getting horses and saddles. After I had caught my horse, a Sioux warrior came again and said, 'Many soldiers are coming.'

"Then he said to the women, 'Get out of the way, we are going to have hard fight.'

"I said, 'All right, I am ready.'

"I got on my horse, and rode out into my

camp. I called out to the people all running about: 'I am Two Moon, your chief. Don't run away. Stay here and fight. You must stay and fight the white soldiers. I shall stay even if I am to be killed.'

"I rode swiftly toward Sitting Bull's camp. There I saw the white soldiers fighting in a line [Reno's men]. Indians covered the flat. They began to drive the soldiers all mixed up—Sioux, then soldiers, then more Sioux, and all shooting. The air was full of smoke and dust. I saw the soldiers fall back and drop into the river-bed like buffalo fleeing. They had no time to look for a crossing. The Sioux chased them up the hill, where they met more soldiers in wagons, and then messengers came saying more soldiers were going to kill the women, and the Sioux turned back. Chief Gall was there fighting, Crazy Horse also.

"I then rode toward my camp, and stopped squaws from carrying off lodges. While I was sitting on my horse I saw flags come up over the hill to the east like that [he raised his finger-tips]. Then the soldiers rose all at once, all on horses, like this [he put his fingers behind each other to indicate that Custer appeared marching in columns of fours]. They formed into three bunches [squadrons] with a little ways between. Then a bugle sounded, and they all got off horses, and some soldiers led the horses back over the hill.

"Then the Sioux rode up the ridge on all sides, riding very fast. The Cheyennes went up the left way. Then the shooting was quick, quick. Pop—pop—pop very fast. Some of the soldiers were down on their knees, some standing. Officers all in front. The smoke was like a great cloud, and every-

Custer's Last Stand

where the Sioux went the dust rose like smoke. We circled all round him—swirling like water round a stone. We shoot, we ride fast, we shoot again. Soldiers drop, and horses fall on them. Soldiers in line drop, but one man rides up and down the line—all the time shouting. He rode a sorrel horse with white face and white fore-legs. I don't know who he was. He was a brave man.

"Indians keep swirling round and round, and the soldiers killed only a few. Many soldiers fell. At last all horses killed but five. Once in a while some man would break out and run toward the river, but he would fall. At last about a hundred men and five horsemen stood on the hill all bunched together. All along the bugler kept blowing his commands. He was very brave too. Then a chief was killed. I hear it was Long Hair [Custer], I don't know; and then five horsemen and the bunch of men, may be so forty, started toward the river. The man on the sorrel horse led them, shouting all the time.* He wore a buckskin shirt, and had long black hair and mustache. He fought hard with a big knife. His men were all covered with white dust. I couldn't tell whether they were officers or not. One man all alone ran far down toward the river, then round up over the hill. I thought he was going to escape, but a Sioux fired and hit him in the head. He was the last man. He wore braid on his arms [sergeant].

"All the soldiers were now killed, and the bodies were stripped. After that no one could tell which were officers. The bodies were left where they fell. We had no dance that night. We were sorrowful.

"Next day four Sioux chiefs and two Cheyennes and I, Two Moon, went upon the battlefield to count the dead. One man carried a little bundle of sticks. When we came to dead men, we took a little stick and gave it to another man, so we counted the dead. There were 388. There were thirty-nine Sioux and seven Cheyennes killed, and about a hundred wounded.

"Some white soldiers were cut with knives, to make sure they were dead; and the war women had mangled some. Most of them were left just where they fell. We came to the man with big mustache; he lay down the hills toward the river.** The Indians did not take his buckskin shirt. The Sioux said, 'That is a big chief. That is Long Hair.' I don't know. I had never seen him. The man on the white-faced horse was the bravest man.

"That day as the sun was getting low our young men came up the Little Horn riding hard. Many white soldiers were coming in a big boat, and when we looked we could see the smoke rising. I called my people together, and we hurried up the Little Horn, into Rotten Grass Valley. We camped there three days, and then rode swiftly back over our old trail to the east. Sitting Bull went back into the Rosebud and down the Yellowstone, and away to the north. I did not see him again."***

The old man paused and filled his pipe. His story was done. His mind came back to his poor people on the barren land where the rain seldom falls.

"That was a long time ago. I am now old, and my mind has changed. I would rather see my people living in houses and singing and dancing. You have talked with me about fighting, and I have told you of the time long ago. All that is past. I think of these things now: First, that our reservation shall be fenced and the white settlers kept out and

---

* This man's identity is in dispute. He was apparently a scout.
** Custer fell up higher on the ridge.
*** This was a wonderful retreat.

our young men kept in. Then there will be no trouble. Second, I want to see my people raising cattle and making butter. Last, I want to see my people going to school to learn the white man's way. That is all."

There was something placid and powerful in the lines of the chief's broad brow, and his gestures were dramatic and noble in sweep. His extended arm, his musing eyes, his deep voice combined to express a meditative solemnity profoundly impressive. There was no anger in his voice, and no reminiscent ferocity. All that was strong and fine and distinctive in the Cheyenne character came out in the old man's talk. He seemed the leader and the thoughtful man he really is—patient under injustice, courteous even to his enemies.

24. Findings of a Court of Inquiry

General Orders No. 17. } HEADQUARTERS OF THE ARMY,
Adjutant General's Office,
Washington, March 11 1879.

1. The Court of Inquiry of which Colonel John H. King, 9th Infantry, is President, instituted by direction of the President, in Special Orders No. 255, Headquarters of the Army, Adjutant General's Office, November 25, 1878, on the application of Major Marcus A. Reno, 7th Cavalry, for the purpose of inquiring into Major Reno's conduct at the battle of the Little Big Horn River, on the 25th and 26th days of June, 1876, has reported the following facts and opinions, viz:—

First. On the morning of the 25th of June 1876, the 7th Cavalry, Lieutenant Colonel G. A. Custer commanding, operating against the hostile Indians in Montana Territory, near the Little Big Horn River, was divided into four battalions, two of which were commanded by Colonel Custer in person, with the exception of one company in charge of the pack-train; one by Major Reno and one by Captain Benteen. This division took place from about twelve (12) to fifteen (15) miles from the scene of the battle or battles afterwards fought. The column under Captain Benteen received orders to move to the left for an indefinite distance (to the first and second valleys) hunting Indians, with orders to charge any it might meet with. The battalion under Major Reno received orders to draw out of the column, and doing so marched parallel [with] and only a short distance from, the column commanded by Colonel Custer.

Second. About three or four miles from what afterwards was found to be the Little Big Horn River, where the fighting took place, Major Reno received orders to move forward as rapidly as he thought prudent, until coming up with the Indians, who were reported fleeing, he would charge them and drive everything before him, and would receive the support of the column under Colonel Custer.

Third. In obedience to the orders given him by Colonel Custer, Captain Benteen marched to the left (south), at an angle of about forty-five degrees, but, meeting an impracticable country, was forced by it to march more to his right than the angle above indicated and nearer approaching a parallel route to that trail followed by the rest of the command.

Fourth. Major Reno, in obedience to the orders given him, moved on at a fast trot on the main Indian trail until reaching the Little Big Horn River, which he forded, and halted for a few minutes to re-form his battalion. After re-forming, he marched the battalion forward towards the Indian village, down stream or in a northerly direction, two companies in line of battle and one in support, until about half way to the point where he finally halted, when he brought the company in reserve forward to the line of battle, continuing the movement at a fast trot or gallop until after passing over a distance of about two miles, when he halted and dismounted to fight on foot at a point of timber upon which the right flank of his battalion rested. After fighting in this formation for less than half an hour, the Indians passing to his left rear and appearing in his front, the skirmish line was withdrawn to the timber, and the fight continued for a short time—half an hour or forty-five minutes in all—when the command, or nearly all of it, was mounted, formed, and, at a rapid gait, was withdrawn to a hill on the opposite side of the river. In this movement one officer and about sixteen soldiers and citizens were left in the woods, besides one wounded man or more, two citizens and thirteen soldiers rejoining the command afterwards. In this retreat Major Reno's battalion lost some twenty-nine men in killed and wounded, and three officers, including Doctor De Wolf, killed.

Fifth. In the meantime Captain Benteen, having carried out, as far as was practicable, the spirit of his orders, turned in the direction of the route taken by the remainder of the regiment, and reaching the trail, followed it to near the crossing of the Little

Big Horn, reaching there about the same time Reno's command was crossing the river in retreat lower down, and finally joined his battalion with that of Reno, on the hill. Forty minutes or one hour later the pack-train, which had been left behind on the trail by the rapid movement of the command and the delays incident to its march, joined the united command, which then consisted of seven companies, together with about thirty (30) or thirty-five (35) men belonging to the companies under Colonel Custer.

Sixth. After detaching Benteen's columns Colonel Custer moved with his immediate command, on the trail followed by Reno, to a point within about one mile of the river, where he diverged to the right (or northward), following the general direction of the river to a point about four miles below that (afterward taken by Major Reno) where he and his command were destroyed by the hostiles. The last living witness of this march, Trumpeter Martin, left Colonel Custer's command when it was about two miles distant from the field where it afterwards met its fate. There is nothing more in evidence as to this command, save that firing was heard proceeding from its direction from about the time Reno retreated from the bottom up to the time the pack-train was approaching the position on the hill. All firing which indicated fighting was concluded before the final preparations [were made] in Major Reno's command for the movement which was afterwards attempted.

Seventh. After the distribution of ammunition and a proper provision for the wounded men, Major Reno's entire command moved down the river in the direction it was thought Custer's column had taken, and in which it was known General Terry's command was to be found. This movement was carried sufficiently far to discover that its continuance would imperil the entire command, upon which it returned to the position formerly occupied, and made a successful resistance till succor reached it. The defense of the position on the hill was a heroic one against fearful odds.

The conduct of the officers throughout was excellent, and while subordinates, in some instances, did more for the safety of the command by brilliant displays of courage than did Major Reno, there was nothing in his conduct which requires animadversion from this Court.

OPINION

It is the conclusion of this Court, in view of all the facts in evidence, that no further proceedings are necessary in this case, and it expresses this opinion in compliance with the concluding clause of the order convening the Court.

II. The proceedings and opinion of the Court of Inquiry in the foregoing case of Major Marcus A. Reno, 7th Cavalry, are approved by order of the President.

III. By direction of the Secretary of War, the Court of Inquiry of which Colonel John H. King, 9th Infantry, is President is hereby dissolved.

By command of General Sherman:

E. D. TOWNSEND,
Adjutant General.

Official.

25. General Carr on Buffalo Bill Cody

EDITOR'S NOTE: William Frederick Cody (1846-1917), better known as Buffalo Bill, was reputedly the greatest killer of buffaloes whom the old West produced. By his own count he killed 4,280 buffaloes in seventeen months, using a 50-calibre breech-loading Springfield rifle. He is also widely remembered as a frontiersman, scout and successful showman. While in the employ of General Custer he killed and scalped Chief Yellow Hand, a Sioux Indian, in a duel. During his long life he was also a horse wrangler, prospector, Pony Express rider, and a scout for the Union army in the Civil War. In 1883 he organized his Wild West Show, which was very successful both in the United States and in Europe. He was a friend of Wild Bill Hickok and employed him for several months in his show.

"I first met Mr. Cody, October 22d, 1868, at Buffalo Station, on the Kansas Pacific railroad, in Kansas. He was scout and guide for the seven companies of the Fifth Cavalry, then under Colonel Royal, and of which I was ordered to take the command. * * * *

"From his services with my command, steadily in the field for nine months, from October, 1868, to July, 1869, and at subsequent times, I am qualified to bear testimony to his qualities and character.

"He was very modest and unassuming. I did not know for a long time how good a title he had to the appellation, 'Buffalo Bill.' I am apt to discount the claims of scouts, as they will occasionally exaggerate; and when I found one who said nothing about himself, I did not think much of him, till I had proved him. He is a natural gentleman in his manners as well as in character, and has none of the roughness of the typical frontiersman. He can take his own part when required, but I have never heard of his using a knife or a pistol, or engaging in a quarrel where it could be avoided. His personal strength and activity are such that he can hardly meet a man whom he cannot handle, and his temper and disposition are so good that no one has reason to quarrel with him.

"His eye-sight is better than a good field glass; he is the best trailer I ever heard of; and also the best judge of the 'lay of country,' —that is, he is able to tell what kind of country is ahead, so as to know how to act. He is a perfect judge of distance, and always ready to tell correctly how many miles it is to water, or to any place, or how many miles have been marched. * * * *

"Mr. Cody seemed never to tire and was always ready to go, in the darkest night or the worst weather, and usually volunteered, knowing what the emergency required. His trailing, when following Indians or looking for stray animals or game, is simply wonderful. He is a most extraordinary hunter. I could not believe that a man could be certain to shoot antelope running till I had seen him do it so often.

"In a fight Mr. Cody is never noisy, obstreperous or excited. In fact, I never hardly noticed him in a fight, unless I happened to want him, or he had something to report, when he was always in the right place, and his information was always valuable and reliable.

"During the winter of 1868, we encountered hardships and exposure in terrific snow storms, sleet, etc, etc. On one occasion, that winter, Mr. Cody showed his quality by quietly offering to go with some dispatches to General Sheridan, across a dangerous region, where another principal scout was reluctant to risk himself.

"On the 13th of May, 1869, he was in the fight at Elephant Rock, Kansas, and trailed the Indians till the 16th, when we got another fight out of them on Spring Creek, in Nebraska, and scattered them after following them one hundred and fifty miles in three days. It was at Spring Creek where Cody was ahead of the command about three miles, with the advance guard of forty men, when two hundred Indians suddenly surrounded them. Our men dismounted and formed in a circle, holding their horses, firing and slowly retreating. They all, to this day, speak of Cody's coolness and bravery. This was the Dog Soldier band which captured Mrs. Alderdice and Mrs. Weichel in Kansas. They strangled Mrs. Alderdice's baby, killed Mrs. Weichel's husband, and took a great deal of property and stock from different persons. We got on their trail again, June 28th, and followed it nearly two hundred miles, till we struck the Indians on Sunday, July 11, 1869, at Summit Spring. The Indians, as soon as they saw us coming, killed Mrs. Alderdice with a hatchet, and shot Mrs. Weichel, but fortunately not fatally, and she was saved.

"Mr. Cody has since served with me as post guide and scout at Fort McPherson, where he frequently distinguished himself. * * * *

"In the summer of 1876, Cody went with me to the Black Hills region, where he killed Yellow-Hand. Afterwards he was with the Big Horn and Yellowstone expedition. I consider that his services to the country and the army by trailing, finding and fighting Indians, and thus protecting the frontier settlers, and by guiding commands over the best and most practicable routes, have been far beyond the compensation he has received. His friends of the Fifth Cavalry are all glad that he is in a lucrative business, and hope that he may live long and prosper. Personally, I feel under obligations to him for assistance in my campaigns which no

other man could, or would, have rendered. Of course I wish him, and his, every success.

FORT McPHERSON, NEBRASKA,)
July 3d, 1878 (
E. A. CARR, Lt. Col. 5th Cav.,
Brev. Maj. Gen'l U.S. Army.

26. Robbed by Danites

BY BUFFALO BILL CODY

In the summer of 1857, Russell, Majors & Waddell were sending a great many trains across the plains to Salt Lake with supplies for General Johnston's army. Men were in great demand, and the company was paying teamsters forty dollars per month in gold. An old and reliable wagon-master, named Lewis Simpson — who had taken a great fancy to me, and who, by the way, was one of the best wagon-masters that ever ran a bull train—was loading a train for the company, and was about to start out with it for Salt Lake. He asked me to go along as an "extra hand." The high wages that were being paid were a great inducement to me, and the position of an "extra hand" was a pleasant one. All that I would have to do would be to take the place of any man who became sick, and drive his wagon until he recovered. I would have my own mule to ride, and to a certain extent I would be a minor boss.

My mother was very much opposed to my taking this long trip, as I would be absent nearly a year, and there was a possibility that something might arise to prevent me from ever coming back, as we could not then

tell how the Mormon difficulty would terminate. Then again, owing to the Indians, a journey over the plains in those days was a perilous undertaking. She said that as I had recently returned from the plains, and had had a narrow escape from death at the hands of the Indians, she did not want me to risk my life a second time. I told her that inasmuch as I had determined to follow the plains for an occupation, nothing could now stop me from going on this trip, and if it became necessary I would run away.

Seeing that it was impossible to keep me at home, she reluctantly gave her consent, but not until she had called upon Mr. Russell and Mr. Simpson in regard to the matter, and had obtained from the latter gentleman his promise that I should be well taken care of, if we had to winter in the mountains. She did not like the appearance of Simpson, and upon inquiry she learned, to her dismay, that he was a desperate character, and that on nearly every trip he had made across the plains he had killed some one. Such a man, she thought, was not a fit master or companion for her son, and she was very anxious to have me go with some other wagon-master; but I still insisted upon remaining with Simpson.

"Madam, I can assure you that Lew. Simpson is one of the most reliable wagon-masters on the plains," said Mr. Russell, "and he has taken a great fancy to Billy. If your boy is bound to go, he can go with no better man. No one will dare to impose on him while he is with Lew. Simpson, whom I will instruct to take good care of the boy. Upon reaching Fort Laramie, Billy can, if he wishes, exchange places with some fresh man coming back on a returning train, and thus come home without making the whole trip."

This seemed to satisfy mother, and then she had a long talk with Simpson himself, imploring him not to forget his promise to take good care of her precious boy. He promised everything that she asked. Thus, after much trouble, I became one of the members of Simpson's train. Before taking our departure, I arranged with Russell, Majors & Waddell that when my pay should fall due it should be paid over to mother.

As a matter of interest to the general reader, it may be well in this connection to give a brief description of a freight train. The wagons used in those days by Russell, Majors & Waddell were known as the "J. Murphy wagons," made at St. Louis specially for the plains business. They were very large and were strongly built, being capable of carrying seven thousand pounds of freight each. The wagon-boxes were very commodious—being as large as the rooms of an ordinary house—and were covered with two heavy canvas sheets to protect the merchandise from the rain. These wagons were generally sent out from Leavenworth, each loaded with six thousand pounds of freight, and each drawn by several yokes of oxen in charge of one driver. A train consisted of twenty-five wagons, all in charge of one man, who was known as the wagon-master. The second man in command was the assistant wagon-master; then came the "extra hand," next the night herder; and lastly, the cavallard driver, whose duty it was to drive the lame and loose cattle. There were thirty-one men all told in a train. The men did their own cooking, being divided into messes of seven. One man cooked, another brought wood and water, another stood guard, and so on, each having some duty to perform while getting meals. All were heavily armed with Colt's pistols and Mississippi yagers, and every one always had his weapons handy so as to be prepared for any emergency.

The wagon-master, in the language of the plains, was called the "bull-wagon boss"; the

A Bullwhacker

teamsters were known as "bull-whackers"; and the whole train was denominated a "bull-outfit." Everything at that time was called an "outfit." The men of the plains were always full of droll humor and exciting stories of their own experiences, and many an hour I spent in listening to the recitals of thrilling adventures and hair-breadth escapes.

Russell, Majors & Waddell had in their employ two hundred and fifty trains, composed of 6,250 wagons, 75,000 oxen, and about eight thousand men; their business reaching to all the government frontier posts in the north and west, to which they transported supplies, and they also carried freight as far south as New Mexico.

The trail to Salt Lake ran through Kansas to the northwest, crossing the Big Blue river, then over the Big and Little Sandy, coming into Nebraska near the Big Sandy. The next stream of any importance was the Little Blue, along which the trail ran for sixty miles; then crossed a range of sand-hills and struck the Platte river ten miles below Old Fort Kearney; thence the course lay up the South Platte to the old Ash Hollow Crossing, thence eighteen miles across to the North Platte — near the mouth of the Blue Water, where General Harney had his great battle in 1855 with the Sioux and Cheyenne Indians. From this point the North Platte was followed, passing Court House Rock, Chimney Rock and Scott's Bluffs, and then on to Fort Laramie, where the Laramie River was crossed. Still following the North Platte for some considerable distance, the trail crossed this river at old Richard's Bridge, and followed it up to the celebrated Red Buttes—crossing the Willow creeks to the Sweet Water, passing the great Independence Rock and the Devil's gate, up to the Three Crossings of the Sweet Water, thence

past the Cold Springs, where, three feet under the sod, on the hottest day of summer, ice can be found; thence to the Hot Springs and the Rocky Ridge, and through the Rocky Mountains and Echo Canon, and thence on to the Great Salt Lake valley.

We had started on our trip with everything in good shape, following the above described trail. During the first week or two out, I became well acquainted with most of the train men, and with one in particular, who became a life-long and intimate friend of mine. His real name was James B. Hickok; he afterwards became famous as "Wild Bill, the Scout of the Plains"—though why he was so called I never could ascertain—and from this time forward I shall refer to him by his popular nickname. He was ten years my senior—a tall, handsome, magnificently built and powerful young fellow, who could out-run, out-jump and out-fight any man in the train. He was generally admitted to be the best man physically, in the employ of Russell, Majors & Waddell; and of his bravery there was not a doubt.

The circumstances under which I first made his acquaintance and learned to know him well and to appreciate his manly character and kind-heartedness, were these. One of the teamsters in Lew. Simpson's train was a surly, overbearing fellow, and took particular delight in bullying and tyrannizing over me, and one day while we were at dinner he asked me to do something for him. I did not start at once, and he gave me a slap in the face with the back of his hand, — knocking me off an ox-yoke on which I was sitting, and sending me sprawling on the ground. Jumping to my feet I picked up a camp kettle full of boiling coffee which was setting on the fire, and threw it at him. I hit him in the face, and the hot coffee gave him a severe scalding. He sprang for me with the ferocity of a tiger, and would undoubtedly have torn me to pieces, had it not been for the timely interference of my new-found friend, Wild Bill, who knocked the man down. As soon as he recovered himself, he demanded of Wild Bill what business it was of his that he should "put in his oar." "It's my business to protect that boy, or anybody else, from being unmercifully abused, kicked and cuffed, and I'll whip any man who tries it on," said Wild Bill; "and if you ever again lay a hand on that boy—little Billy there—I'll give you such a pounding that you won't get over it for a month of Sundays." From that time forward Wild Bill was my protector and intimate friend, and the friendship thus begun continued until his death.

Nothing transpired on the trip to delay or give us any trouble whatever, until the train struck the South Platte river. One day we camped on the same ground where the Indians had surprised the cattle herd, in charge of the McCarty brothers. It was with difficulty that we discovered any traces of anybody ever having camped there before, the only landmark being the single grave, now covered with grass, in which we had buried the three men who had been killed. The country was alive with buffaloes. Vast herds of these monarchs of the plains were roaming all around us, and we laid over one day for a grand hunt. Besides killing quite a number of buffaloes, and having a day of rare sport, we captured ten or twelve head of cattle, they being a portion of the herd which had been stampeded by the Indians, two months before. The next day we pulled out of camp, and the train was strung out to a considerable length along the road which ran near the foot of the sand-hills, two miles from the river. Between the road and the river we saw a large herd of buffaloes grazing quietly, they having been down to the stream for a drink.

Just at this time we observed a party of returning Californians coming from the West. They, too, noticed the buffalo herd, and in another moment they were dashing down upon them, urging their steeds to the greatest speed. The buffalo herd stampeded at once, and broke for the hills; so hotly were they pursued by the hunters that about five hundred of them rushed through our train pell-mell, frightening both men and oxen. Some of the wagons were turned clear round, and many of the terrified oxen attempted to run to the hills, with the heavy wagons attached to them. Others turned around so short that they broke the wagon tongues off. Nearly all the teams got entangled in their gearing, and became wild and unruly, so that the perplexed drivers were unable to manage them.

The buffaloes, the cattle, and the drivers, were soon running in every direction, and the excitement upset nearly everybody and everything. Many of the cattle broke their yokes and stampeded. One big buffalo bull became entangled in one of the heavy wagon-chains, and it is a fact that in his desperate efforts to free himself, he not only actually snapped the strong chain in two, but broke the ox-yoke to which it was attached, and the last seen of him he was running towards the hills with it hanging from his horns. A dozen other equally remarkable incidents happened during the short time that the frantic buffaloes were playing havoc with our train, and when they had got through and left us, our outfit was very badly crippled and scattered. This caused us to go into camp and spend a day in replacing the broken tongues, and repairing other damages, and gathering up our scattered ox-teams.

The next day we rolled out of camp, and proceeded on our way towards the setting sun. Everything ran along smoothly with us from that point until we came within about eighteen miles of Green river, in the Rocky mountains—where we camped at noon. At this place we had to drive our cattle about a mile and a half to a creek to water them. Simpson, his assistant, George Woods and myself, accompanied by the usual number of guards, drove the cattle over to the creek, and while on our way back to camp, we suddenly observed a party of twenty horsemen rapidly approaching us. We were not yet in view of our wagons, as a rise of ground intervened, and therefore we could not signal the train-men in case of any unexpected danger befalling us. We had no suspicion, however, that we were about to be trapped, as the strangers were white men. When they had come up to us, one of the party, who evidently was the leader, rode out in front and said:

"How are you, Mr. Simpson?"

"You've got the best of me, sir," said Simpson, who did not know him.

"Well, I rather think I have," coolly replied the stranger, whose words conveyed a double meaning, as we soon learned. We had all come to a halt by this time, and the strange horsemen had surrounded us. They were all armed with double-barreled shot guns, rifles and revolvers. We also were armed with revolvers, but we had had no idea of danger, and these men, much to our surprise, had "got the drop" on us, and had covered us with their weapons, so that we were completely at their mercy. The whole movement of corraling us was done so quietly and quickly that it was accomplished before we knew it.

"I'll trouble you for your six shooters, gentlemen," now said the leader.

"I'll give 'em to you in a way you don't want," replied Simpson.

The next moment three guns were leveled at Simpson. "If you make a move you're a dead man," said the leader.

Simpson saw that he was taken at a great disadvantage, and thinking it advisable not to risk the lives of the party by any rash act on his part, he said: "I see now that you have the best of me, but who are you, anyhow?"

"I am Joe Smith," was the reply.

"What! the leader of the Danites?" asked Simpson.

"You are correct," said Smith, for he it was.

"Yes," said Simpson, "I know you now; you are a spying scoundrel."

Simpson had good reason for calling him this and applying to him a much more approbrious epithet, for only a short time before this, Joe Smith had visited our train in the disguise of a teamster, and had remained with us two days. He suddenly disappeared, no one knowing where he had gone or why he had come among us. But it was all explained to us now that he had returned with his Mormon Danites. After they had disarmed us, Simpson asked, "Well, Smith, what are you going to do with us?"

"Ride back with us and I'll soon show you," said Smith.

We had no idea of the surprise which awaited us. As we came upon the top of the ridge, from which we could view our camp, we were astonished to see the remainder of the train men disarmed and stationed in a group and surrounded by another squad of Danites, while other Mormons were searching our wagons for such articles as they wanted.

"How is this?" inquired Simpson. "How

did you surprise my camp without a struggle? I can't understand it."

"Easily enough," said Smith; "your men were all asleep under the wagons, except the cooks, who saw us coming and took us for returning Californians or emigrants, and paid no attention to us until we rode up and surrounded your train. With our arms covering the men, we woke them up, and told them that all they had to do was to walk out and drop their pistols—which they saw was the best thing they could do under the circumstances over which they had no control—and you can just bet they did it."

"And what do you propose to do with us now?" asked Simpson.

"I intend to burn your train," said he; "you are loaded with supplies and ammunition for Sidney Johnson, and as I have no way to convey the stuff to my own people, I'll see that it does not reach the United States troops."

"Are you going to turn us adrift here?" asked Simpson, who was anxious to learn what was to become of himself and his men.

"No; I hardly am as bad as that. I'll give you enough provisions to last you until you can reach Fort Bridger," replied Smith; "and as soon as your cooks can get the stuff out of the wagons, you can start."

"On foot?" was the laconic inquiry of Simpson.

"Yes sir," was the equally short reply.

"Smith, that's too rough on us men. Put yourself in our place and see how you would like it," said Simpson; "you can well afford to give us at least one wagon and six yokes of oxen to convey us and our clothing and provisions to Fort Bridger. You're a brute if you don't do this."

"Well," said Smith, after consulting a

minute or two with some of his company, "I'll do that much for you."

The cattle and the wagon were brought up according to his orders, and the clothing and provisions were loaded on.

"Now you can go," said Smith, after everything had been arranged.

"Joe Smith, I think you are a mean coward to set us afloat in a hostile country, without giving us our arms," said Simpson, who had once before asked for the weapons, and had had his request denied.

Smith, after further consulation with his comrades, said: "Simpson, you are too brave a man to be turned adrift here without any means of defense. You shall have your revolvers and guns." Our weapons were accordingly handed over to Simpson, and we at once started for Fort Bridger, knowing that it would be useless to attempt the recapture of our train.

When we had traveled about two miles we saw the smoke arising from our old camp. The Mormons after taking what goods they wanted and could carry off, had set fire to the wagons, many of which were loaded with bacon, lard, hard-tack, and other provisions, which made a very hot, fierce fire, and the smoke to roll up in dense clouds. Some of the wagons were loaded with ammunition, and it was not long before loud explosions followed in rapid succession. We waited and witnessed the burning of the train, and then pushed on to Fort Bridger. Arriving at this post, we learned that two other trains had been captured and destroyed in the same way, by the Mormons. This made seventy-five wagon loads, or 450,000 pounds of supplies, mostly provisions, which never reached General Johnson's command, to which they had been consigned.

27. Hard Times

BY BUFFALO BILL CODY

As it was getting very late in the fall, we were compelled to winter at Fort Bridger; and a long, tedious winter it was. There were a great many troops there, and about four hundred of Russell, Majors & Waddell's employeés. These men were all organized into militia companies, which were officered by the wagon-masters. Some lived in tents, others in cabins. It was known that our supplies would run short during the winter, and so all the men at the post were put on three-quarter rations to begin with; before long they were reduced to one-half rations, and finally to one-quarter rations. We were forced to kill our poor worn-out cattle for beef. They were actually so poor that we had to prop them up to shoot them down. At last we fell back on the mules, which were killed and served up in good style. Many a poor, unsuspecting government mule passed in his chips that winter in order to keep the soldiers and bullwhackers from starvation.

Here They Come!

It was really a serious state of affairs. The wood for the post was obtained from the mountains, but having no longer any cattle or mules to transport it, the men were obliged to haul it themselves. Long lariats were tied to the wagons, and twenty men manning each, they were pulled to and from the mountains. Notwithstanding all these hardships, the men seemed to be contented and to enjoy themselves.

The winter finally passed away, and early in the spring, as soon as we could travel, the civil employeés of the government, with the teamsters and freighters, started for the Missouri river; the Johnson expedition having been abandoned.

On the way down we stopped at Fort Laramie, and there met a supply train bound westward. Of course we all had a square meal once more, consisting of hard tack, bacon, coffee and beans. I can honestly say that I thought it was the best meal I had ever eaten; at least I relished it more than any other, and I think the rest of the party did the same.

On leaving Fort Laramie, Simpson was made brigade wagon-master, and was put in charge of two large trains, with about four hundred extra men, who were bound for Fort Leavenworth. When we came to Ash Hollow, instead of taking the usual trail over to the South Platte, Simpson concluded to follow the North Platte down to its junction with the South Platte. The two trains were traveling about fifteen miles apart, when one morning while Simpson was with the rear train, he told his assistant wagon-master, George Woods and myself to saddle up our mules, as he wanted us to go with him and overtake the head train.

We started off at about eleven o'clock, and had ridden about seven miles when—while we were on a big plateau, back of Cedar Bluffs—we suddenly discovered a band of Indians coming out of the head of a ravine, half a mile distant, and charging down upon us at full speed. I thought that our end had come this time, sure. Simpson, however, took in the situation in a moment, and knowing that it would be impossible to escape by running our played-out mules, he adopted a bolder and much better plan. He jumped from his own mule, and told us to dismount also. He then shot the three animals, and as they fell to the ground he cut their throats to stop their kicking. He then jerked them into the shape of a triangle, and ordered us inside of the barricade.

All this was but the work of a few moments, yet it was not done any too soon, for the Indians had got within three hundred yards of us, and were still advancing, and uttering their demoniacal yells or war-whoops. There were forty of the red-skins and only three of us. We were each armed with a Mississippi yager and two Colt's revolvers.

"Get ready for them with your guns, and when they come within fifty yards, aim low, blaze away and bring down your man!"

Such was the quick command of Simpson. The words had hardly escaped from his mouth, when the three yagers almost simultaneously belched forth their contents. We then seized our revolvers and opened a lively fire on the enemy, at short range, which checked their advance. Then we looked over our little barricade to ascertain what effect our fire had produced, and were much gratified at seeing three dead Indians

and one horse lying on the ground. Only two or three of the Indians, it seemed, had fire-arms. It must be remembered that in those days every Indian did not own a needle gun or a Winchester rifle, as they now do. Their principal weapons were their bows and arrows.

Seeing that they could not take our little fortification, or drive us from it, they circled around us several times, shooting their arrows at us. One of the arrows struck George Wood in the left shoulder, inflicting only a slight wound, however, and several lodged in the bodies of the dead mules; otherwise they did us no harm.

The Indians finally galloped off to a safe distance, where our bullets could not reach them, and seemed to be holding a council. This was a lucky move for us, for it gave us an opportunity to reload our guns and pistols, and prepare for the next charge of the enemy. During the brief cessation of hostilities, Simpson extracted the arrow from Wood's shoulder, and put an immense quid of tobacco on the wound. Wood was then ready for business again.

The Indians did not give us a very long rest, for with another desperate charge, as if to ride over us, they came dashing towards the mule barricade. We gave them a hot reception from our yagers and revolvers. They could not stand, or understand, the rapidly repeating fire of the revolvers, and we again checked them. They circled around us once more and gave us a few parting shots as they rode off, leaving behind them another dead Indian and a horse.

For two hours afterwards they did not seem to be doing anything but holding a council. We made good use of this time by digging up the ground inside the barricade with our knives and throwing the loose earth around and over the mules, and we

Standing Off Indians. *Frederick Remington*

soon had a very respectable fortification. We were not troubled any more that day, but during the night the cunning rascals tried to burn us out by setting fire to the prairie. The buffalo grass was so short that the fire did not trouble us much, but the smoke concealed the Indians from our view, and they thought that they could approach close to us without being seen. We were aware of this, and kept a sharp look-out, being prepared all the time to receive them. They finally abandoned the idea of surprising us.

Next morning, bright and early, they gave us one more grand charge, and again we "stood them off." They then rode away half a mile or so, and formed a circle around us. Each man dismounted and sat down, as if to wait and starve us out. They had evidently seen the advance train pass on the morning of the previous day, and believed that we belonged to that outfit and were trying to overtake it; they had no idea that another train was on its way after us.

Our hopes of escape from this unpleasant and perilous situation now depended upon the arrival of the rear train, and when we saw the Indians were going to besiege us instead of renewing their attacks, we felt rather confident of receiving timely assistance. We had expected that the train would be along late in the afternoon of the previous day, and as the morning wore away we were somewhat anxious and uneasy, at its non-arrival.

At last, about ten o'clock, we began to hear in the distance the loud and sharp reports of the big bull-whips, which were handled with great dexterity by the teamsters, and cracked like rifle shots. These were as welcome sounds to us as were the notes of the bag-pipes to the beseiged garrison at Lucknow, when the reinforcements were coming up and the pipers were heard playing, "The Campbells are Coming." In a few moments we saw the lead or head wagon coming slowly over the ridge, which had concealed the train from our view, and soon the whole outfit made its appearance. The Indians observed the approaching train, and assembling in a group they held a short consultation. They then charged upon us once more, for the last time, and as they turned and dashed away over the prairie, we sent our farewell shots rattling after them. The teamsters, seeing the Indians and hearing the shots, came rushing forward to our assistance, but by the time they reached us the red-skins had almost disappeared from view. The teamsters eagerly asked us a hundred questions concerning our fight, admired our fort and praised our pluck. Simpson's remarkable presence of mind in planning the defense was the general topic of conversation among all the men.

When the teams came up we obtained some water and bandages with which to dress Wood's wound, which had become quite inflamed and painful, and we then put him into one of the wagons. Simpson and myself obtained a remount, bade goodbye to our dead mules which had served us so well, and after collecting the ornaments and other plunder from the dead Indians, we left their bodies and bones to bleach on the prairie. The train moved on again and we had no other adventures, except several exciting buffalo hunts on the South Platte, near Plum Creek.

We arrived at Fort Leavenworth about the middle of July, 1858, when I immediately visited home. I found mother in very poor health, as she was suffering from asth-

ma. My oldest sister, Martha, had, during my absence, been married to John Crane, and was living at Leavenworth.

During the winter at Fort Bridger I had frequently talked with Wild Bill about my family, and as I had become greatly attached to him I asked him to come and make a visit at our house, which he promised to do. So one day, shortly after our return from Fort Bridger, he accompanied me home from Leavenworth. My mother and sisters, who had heard so much about him from me, were delighted to see him and he spent several weeks at our place. They did everything possible to repay him for his kindness to me. Ever afterwards, when he was at or near Leavenworth, Wild Bill came out to our house to see the family, whether I was at home or not, and he always received a most cordial reception. His mother and sisters lived in Illinois, and he used to call our house his home, as he did not have one of his own.

I had been home only about a month, after returning from Fort Bridger, when I again started out with another train, going this time as assistant wagon-master under Buck Bomer. We went safely through to Fort Laramie, which was our destination, and from there we were ordered to take a load of supplies to a new post called Fort Wallach, which was being established at Cheyenne Pass. We made this trip and got back to Fort Laramie about November 1st. I then quit the employ of Russell, Majors & Waddell, and joined a party of trappers who were sent out by the post trader, Mr. Ward, to trap on the streams of the Chugwater and Laramie for beaver, otter, and other fur animals, and also to poison wolves for their pelts. We were out two months, but as the expedition did not prove very profitable, and was rather dangerous on account of the Indians, we abandoned the enterprise and came into Fort Laramie in the latter part of December.

Being anxious to return to the Missouri river, I joined with two others, named Scott and Charley, who were also desirous of going East on a visit, bought three ponies and a pack-mule, and we started out together. We made rapid progress on our journey, and nothing worthy of note happened until one afternoon, along the banks of the Little Blue River, we spied a band of Indians hunting on the opposite side of the stream, three miles away. We did not escape their notice, and they gave us a lively chase for two hours, but they could find no good crossing, and as evening came on we finally got away from them.

We traveled until late in the night; when upon discovering a low, deep ravine which we thought would make a comfortable and safe camping-place, we stopped for a rest. In searching for a good place to make our beds, I found a hole, and I called to my companions that I had found a fine place for a nest. One of the party was to stand guard while the others slept. Scott took the first watch, while Charley and I made a bed in the hole.

While clearing out the place we felt something rough, but as it was dark we could not make out what it was. At any rate we concluded that it was bones or sticks of wood; we thought perhaps it might be the bones of some animal which had fallen in there and died. These bones, for such they really proved to be, we pushed one side and then we lay down. But Charley, being an inveterate smoker, could not resist the temptation of indulging in a smoke before going to sleep. So he sat up and struck a match to light his old pipe. Our subterranean bed-chamber was thus illuminated for a mo-

ment or two; I sprang to my feet in an instant for a ghastly and horrifying sight was revealed to us. Eight or ten human skeletons lay scattered upon the ground.

The light of the match died out, but we had seen enough to convince us that we were in a large grave, into which, perhaps, some unfortunate emigrants, who had been killed by the Indians, had been thrown; or, perhaps, seeking refuge there, they had been corraled and then killed on the spot. If such was the case, they had met the fate of thousands of others, whose friends have never heard of them since they left their eastern homes to seek their fortunes in the Far West. However, we did not care to investigate this mystery any further, but we hustled out of that chamber of death and informed Scott of our discovery. Most of the plains-men are very superstitious, and we were no exception to the general rule. We surely thought that this incident was an evil omen, and that we would be killed if we remained there any longer.

"Let us dig out of here quicker than we can say Jack Robinson," said Scott; and we began to "dig out" at once. We saddled our animals and hurriedly pushed forward through the darkness, traveling several miles before we again went into camp. Next morning it was snowing fiercely, but we proceeded as best we could, and that night we succeeded in reaching Oak Grove ranch, which had been built during the summer. We here obtained comfortable accommodations and plenty to eat and drink—especially the latter.

Scott and Charley were great lovers and consumers of "tanglefoot," and they soon got gloriously drunk, keeping it up for three days, during which time they gambled with the ranchmen, who got away with all their money; but little they cared for that, as they had their spree. They finally sobered up, and we resumed our journey, urging our jaded animals as much as they could stand, until we struck Marysville, on the Big Blue. From this place to Leavenworth we secured first-rate accommodations along the road, as the country had become pretty well settled.

It was in February, 1859, that I got home. As there was now a good school in the neighborhood, taught by Mr. Divinny, my mother wished me to attend it, and I did so for two months and a half—the longest period of schooling that I ever recived at any one time in my life. As soon as the spring came and the grass began growing, I became uneasy and discontented, and again longed for the free and open life of the plains.

The Pike's Peak gold excitement was then at its height, and everybody was rushing to the new gold diggings. I caught the gold-fever myself, and joined a party bound for the new town of Auraria, on Cherry Creek, afterwards called Denver, in honor of the then governor of Kansas. On arriving at Auraria we pushed on to the gold streams in the mountains, passing up through Golden Gate, and over Guy Hill, and thence on to Black Hawk. We prospected for two months, but as none of us knew anything about mining we met with very poor success, and we finally concluded that prospecting for gold was not our forte. We accordingly abandoned the enterprise and turned our faces eastward once more.

When we struck the Platte River, the happy thought of constructing a small raft —which would float us clear to the Missouri and thence down to Leavenworth—entered our heads, and we accordingly carried out the plan. Upon the completion of the raft we stocked it with provisions, and "set sail" down the stream. It was a light craft and a jolly crew, and all was smooth sailing for four or five days.

When we got near old Julesburg, we met with a serious mishap. Our raft ran into an eddy, and quick as lightning went to pieces, throwing us all into the stream, which was so deep that we had to swim ashore. We lost everything we had, which greatly discouraged us, and we thereupon abandoned the idea of rafting it any farther. We then walked over to Julesburg, which was only a few miles distant. This ranch, which became a somewhat famous spot, had been established by "Old Jules," a Frenchman, who was afterwards killed by the notorious Alf. Slade.

The great pony express, about which so much has been said and written, was at that time just being started. The line was being stocked with horses and put into good running condition. At Julesburg I met Mr. George Chrisman, the leading wagon-master of Russell, Majors & Waddell, who had always been a good friend to me. He had bought out "Old Jules," and was then the owner of Julesburg ranch, and the agent of the pony express line. He hired me at once as a pony express rider, but as I was so young he thought I would not be able to stand the fierce riding which was required of the messengers. He knew, however, that I had been raised in the saddle—that I felt more at home there than in any other place—and as he saw that I was confident that I could stand the racket, and could ride as far and endure it as well as some of the older riders, he gave me a short route of forty-five miles, with the stations fifteen miles apart, and three changes of horses. I was required to make fifteen miles an hour, including the changes of horses. I was fortunate in getting well-broken animals, and being so light, I easily made my forty-five miles on time on my first trip out, and ever afterwards.

I wrote to mother and told her how well I liked the exciting life of a pony express rider. She replied, and begged of me to give it up, as it would surely kill me. She was right about this, as fifteen miles an hour on horseback would, in a short time, shake any man "all to pieces"; and there were but very few, if any, riders who could stand it for any great length of time. Nevertheless, I stuck to it for two months, and then, upon receiving a letter informing me that my mother was very sick, I gave it up and went back to the old home in Salt Creek Valley.

28. A Buffalo Killing Match

BY BUFFALO BILL CODY

SHORTLY after the adventures mentioned in the preceding chapter, I had my celebrated buffalo hunt with Billy Comstock, a noted scout, guide and interpreter, who was then chief of scouts at Fort Wallace, Kansas. Comstock had the reputation, for a long time, of being a most successful buffalo hunter, and the officers in particular, who had seen him kill buffaloes, were very desirous of backing him in a match against me. It was accordingly arranged that I should shoot him a buffalo-killing match, and the preliminaries were easily and satisfactorily agreed upon. We were to hunt one day of eight hours, beginning at eight o'clock in the morning, and closing at four o'clock in the afternoon. The wager was five hundred dollars a side, and the man who should kill the greater number of buffaloes from on horseback was to be declared the winner.

The hunt took place about twenty miles east of Sheridan, and as it had been pretty well advertised and noised abroad, a large crowd witnessed the interesting and exciting scene. An excursion party, mostly from St. Louis, consisting of about a hundred gentlemen and ladies, came out on a special train to view the sport, and among the number was my wife, with little baby Arta, who had come to remain with me for a while.

The buffaloes were quite plenty, and it was agreed that we should go into the same herd at the same time and "make a run," as we called it, each one killing as many as possible. A referee was to follow each of us on horseback when we entered the herd, and count the buffaloes killed by each man. The St. Louis excursionists, as well as the other spectators, rode out to the vicinity of the hunting grounds in wagons and on horseback, keeping well out of sight of the buffaloes, so as not to frighten them, until the time came for us to dash into the herd; when they were to come up as near as they pleased and witness the chase.

We were fortunate in the first run in getting good ground. Comstock was mounted on one of his favorite horses, while I rode old Brigham. I felt confident that I had the advantage of Comstock in two things—first, I had the best buffalo horse that ever made a track; and second, I was using what was known at that time as the needle-gun, a breech-loading Springfield rifle—calibre 50, —it was my favorite old "Lucretia," which has already been introduced to the notice of the reader; while Comstock was armed with a Henry rifle, and although he could fire a few shots quicker than I could, yet I was pretty certain that it did not carry powder and lead enough to do execution equal to my calibre 50.

At last the time came to begin the match. Comstock and I dashed into a herd, followed by the referees. The buffaloes separated; Comstock took the left bunch and I the right. My great *forte* in killing buffaloes from horseback was to get them circling by riding my horse at the head of the herd, shooting the leaders, thus crowding their followers to the left, till they would finally circle round and round.

On this morning the buffaloes were very accommodating, and I soon had them running in a beautiful circle, when I dropped them thick and fast, until I had killed thirty-eight; which finished my run.

Comstock began shooting at the rear of the herd, which he was chasing, and they kept straight on. He succeeded, however, in killing twenty-three, but they were scattered over a distance of three miles, while mine lay close together. I had "nursed" my buffaloes, as a billiard-player does the balls when he makes a big run.

After the result of the first run had been duly announced, our St. Louis excursion friends—who had approached to the place where we had stopped—set out a lot of

Hunting Buffalo

champagne, which they had brought with them, and which proved a good drink on a Kansas prairie, and a buffalo hunter was a good man to get away with it.

While taking a short rest, we suddenly spied another herd of buffaloes coming toward us. It was only a small drove, and we at once prepared to give the animals a lively reception. They proved to be a herd of cows and calves—which, by the way, are quicker in their movements than the bulls. We charged in among them, and I concluded my run with a score of eighteen, while Comstock killed fourteen. The score now stood fifty-six to thirty-seven, in my favor.

Again the excursion party approached, and once more the champagne was tapped. After we had eaten a lunch which was spread for us, we resumed the hunt. Striking out for a distance of three miles, we came up close to another herd. As I was so far ahead of my competitor in the number killed, I thought I could afford to give an extra exhibition of my skill. I had told the ladies that I would, on the next run, ride my horse without saddle or bridle. This had raised the excitement to fever heat among the excursionists, and I remember one fair lady who endeavored to prevail upon me not to attempt it.

"That's nothing at all," said I; "I have done it many a time, and old Brigham knows as well as I what I am doing, and sometimes a great deal better."

So, leaving my saddle and bridle with the wagons, we rode to the windward of the buffaloes, as usual, and when within a few hundred yards of them we dashed into the herd. I soon had thirteen laid out on the ground, the last one of which I had driven down close to the wagons, where the ladies were. It frightened some of the tender creatures to see the buffalo coming at full speed

directly toward them; but when he had got within fifty yards of one of the wagons, I shot him dead in his tracks. This made my sixty-ninth buffalo, and finished my third and last run, Comstock having killed forty-six.

As it was now late in the afternoon, Comstock and his backers gave up the idea that he could beat me, and thereupon the referees declared me the winner of the match, as well as the champion buffalo-hunter of the plains.*

On our way back to camp, we took with us some of the choice meat and finest heads. In this connection it will not be out of place to state that during the time I was hunting for the Kansas Pacific, I always brought into camp the best buffalo heads, and turned them over to the company, who found a very good use for them. They had them mounted in the best possible manner, and sent them to all the principal cities and railroad centers in the country, having them placed in prominent positions at the leading hotels, depots, and other public buildings, as a sort of trade-mark, or advertisement, of the Kansas Pacific Railroad; and to-day they attract the attention of the traveler almost everywhere. Whenever I am traveling over the country and see one of these trade-marks, I feel pretty certain that I was the cause of

* Poor Billy Comstock was afterwards treacherously murdered by the Indians. He and Sharpe Grover visited a village of Indians, supposed to be peaceably inclined, near Big Spring Station, in Western Kansas; and after spending several hours with the redskins in friendly conversation, they prepared to depart, having declined an invitation to pass the night there. It appears that Comstock's beautiful white-handled revolver had attracted the attention of the Indians, who overtook him and his companion when they had gone about half a mile. After surrounding the two men they suddenly attacked them. They killed, scalped and robbed Comstock; but Grover, although severely wounded, made his escape, owing to the fleetness of the excellent horse which he was riding. This sad event occurred August 27, 1868.

the death of the old fellow whose body it once ornamented, and many a wild and exciting hunt is thus called to mind.

The end of the track finally reached Sheridan, in the month of May, 1868, and as the road was not to be built any farther just then, my services as a hunter were not any longer required. At this time there was a general Indian war raging all along the western borders. General Sheridan had taken up his headquarters at Fort Hayes, in order to be in the field to superintend the campaign in person. As scouts and guides were in great demand, I concluded once more to take up my old avocation of scouting and guiding for the army.

Having no suitable place in which to leave my old and faithful buffalo-hunter Brigham, and not wishing to kill him by scouting, I determined to dispose of him. I was very reluctant to part with him, but I consoled myself with the thought that he would not be likely to receive harder usage in other hands than he had in mine. I had several good offers to sell him; but at the suggestion of some gentlemen in Sheridan, all of whom were anxious to obtain possession of the horse, I put him up at a raffle, in order to give them all an equal chance of becoming the owner of the famous steed. There were ten chances at thirty dollars each, and they were all quickly taken.

Old Brigham was won by a gentleman—Mr. Ike Bonham,—who took him to Wyandotte, Kansas, where he soon added new laurels to his already brilliant record. Although I am getting ahead of my story, I must now follow Brigham for a while. A grand tournament came off four miles from Wyandotte, and Brigham took part in it. As has already been stated, his appearance was not very prepossessing, and nobody suspected him of being anything but the most

ordinary kind of a plug. The friends of the rider laughed at him for being mounted on such a dizzy-looking steed. When the exercises—which were of a very tame character, being more for style than speed—were over, and just as the crowd were about to return to the city, a purse of $250 was made up, to be given to the horse that could first reach Wyandotte, four miles distant. The arrangement was carried out, and Brigham was entered as one of the contestants for the purse. Everybody laughed at Mr. Bonham when it became known that he was to ride that poky-looking plug against the five thoroughbreds which were to take part in the race.

When all the preliminaries had been arranged, the signal was given, and off went the horses for Wyandotte. For the first half-mile several of the horses led Brigham, but on the second mile he began passing them one after the other, and on the third mile he was in advance of them all, and was showing them all the road at a lively rate. On the fourth mile his rider let him out, and arrived at the hotel—the home-station—in Wyandotte a long way ahead of his fastest competitor.

Everybody was surprised, as well as disgusted, that such a homely "critter" should be the winner. Brigham, of course, had already acquired a wide reputation, and his name and exploits had often appeared in the newspapers, and when it was learned that this "critter" was none other than the identical buffalo-hunting Brigham, nearly the whole crowd admitted that they had heard of him before, and had they known him in the first place they certainly would have ruled him out.

I finally lost track of Brigham, and for several years I did not know what had become of him. Three years ago, while I was at Memphis, Tennessee, I met a Mr. Wilcox,

Buffalo Hunters Camp

who had been one of the superintendents of construction of the Kansas Pacific Railroad, and he informed me that he owned Brigham, and that he was at that time on his farm, only a few miles out of town. The next day I rode out with Mr. Wilcox and took a look at the gallant old horse. He was comfortably cared for in Mr. Wilcox's stable, and looked the same clever pony that he always was. It seemed as if he almost remembered me, and I put my arms around his neck, as though he had been a long-lost child. Mr. Wilcox bought the horse at Wyandotte, from the gentleman who had won him at the raffle, and he intends to keep him as long as he lives. I am grateful that he is

in such good hands, and whenever I again visit Memphis I shall surely go and see Brigham if he is still alive.

But to return to the thread of my narrative, from which I have wandered. Having received the appointment of guide and scout, and having been ordered to report at Fort Larned, then commanded by Captain Dangerfield Parker, I saw it was necessary to take my family—who had remained with me at Sheridan, after the buffalo-hunting match—to Leavenworth, and there leave them. This I did at once, and after providing them with a comfortable little home, I returned and reported for duty at Fort Larned.

29. Adventures Among the White Men

BY GERONIMO

EDITOR'S NOTE: Geronimo (c. 1829-1909), an extremely cunning, courageous and determined Indian warrior, was the leader of an Apache Indian band known as Chiricahuas. His mother, wife and children were massacred by Mexicans in 1858. Thereafter Geronimo led many raids of vengeance against the Mexicans, as well as against white settlers in Arizona and New Mexico. The U. S. Army put him and other Indians on reservations, but in 1876 he fled to Mexico, and for the next decade led many raids against American settlers. He surrendered in 1886 to General George F. Cook, but later escaped. General Nelson A. Miles finally captured him after a campaign lasting eighteen months and involving five thousand troops and five hundred Indian auxiliaries. Geronimo's band consisted of thirty-five men, eight boys and 101 women. Contrary to terms agreed upon by General Miles, President Grover Cleveland ordered Geronimo and fourteen companions to be placed under military confinement. He was imprisoned at Fort Sill, Oklahoma, where he was allowed to carry on stock raising and farming. Near the end of his life, while at Fort Sill, he dictated his autobiography to S. M. Barrett, superintendent of education at Lawton, Oklahoma. After encountering refusals from local authorities, Barrett secured permission from President Theodore Roosevelt to collect and publish the autobiography. He had the services of an educated Indian as interpreter. Barrett wrote:

"Geronimo refused to talk when a stenographer was present, or to wait for corrections or questions when telling the story. Each day he had in mind what he would tell and told it in a very clear, brief manner. . . . On the day that he first gave any portion of his autobiography he would not be questioned about any details, nor would he add another word, but simply said, 'Write what I have spoken,' and left us to remember and write the story without one bit of assistance. He would agree, however, to come on another day to my study, or any place designated by me, and listen to the reproduction (in Apache) of what had been told, and at such times would answer all questions or add information wherever he could be convinced that it was necessary."

About the time of the massacre of "Kaskiyeh" (1858) we heard that some white men were measuring land to the south of us. In company with a number of other warriors, I went to visit them. We could not understand them very well, for we had no interpreter, but we made a treaty with them by shaking hands and promising to be brothers. Then we made our camp near their camp, and they came to trade with us. We gave them buckskin, blankets, and ponies in exchange for shirts and provisions. We also brought them game, for which they gave us some money. We did not know the value of this money, but we kept it and later learned from the Navajo Indians that it was very valuable.

Every day they measured land with curious instruments and put down marks which we could not understand. They were good men, and we were sorry when they had gone on into the west. They were not soldiers. These were the first white men I ever saw.

About ten years later some more white men came. These were all warriors. They made their camp on the Gila River south of

---

Hot Springs. At first they were friendly and we did not dislike them, but they were not as good as those who came first.

After about a year some trouble arose between them and the Indians, and I took the warpath as a warrior, not as a chief.* I had not been wronged, but some of my people had been, and I fought with my tribe; for the soldiers and not the Indians were at fault.

Not long after this some of the officers of the United States troops invited our leaders to hold a conference at Apache Pass (Fort Bowie). Just before noon the Indians were shown into a tent and told that they would be given something to eat. When in the tent they were attacked by soldiers. Our chief, Mangus-Colorado, and several other warriors, by cutting through the tent, escaped; but most of the warriors were killed or captured. Among the Bedonkohe Apaches killed at this time were Sanza, Kladetahe, Niyokahe, and Gopi. After this treachery the Indians went back to the mountains and left the fort entirely alone. I do not think that the agent had anything to do with planning this, for he had always treated us well. I believe it was entirely planned by the soldiers.

From the very first the soldiers sent out to our western country, and the officers in charge of them, did not hesitate to wrong the Indians. They never explained to the Government when an Indian was wronged, but always reported the misdeeds of the Indians. Much that was done by mean white men was reported at Washington as the deeds of my people.

The Indians always tried to live peaceably with the white soldiers and settlers. One day during the time that the soldiers were stationed at Apache Pass I made a treaty with the post. This was done by shak-

Geronimo photographed after his last surrender   COURTESY NATIONAL ARCHIVES

ing hands and promising to be brothers. Cochise and Mangus-Colorado did likewise. I do not know the name of the officer in command, but this was the first regiment that ever came to Apache Pass. This treaty was made about a year before we were attacked in a tent, as above related. In a few

* As a tribe they would fight under their tribal chief, Mangus-Colorado. If several tribes had been called out, the war chief, Geronimo, would have commanded.

days after the attack at Apache Pass we organized in the mountains and returned to
fight the soldiers. There were two tribes—
the Bedonkohe and the Chokonen Apaches,
both commanded by Cochise. After a few
days' skirmishing we attacked a freight train
that was coming in with supplies for the
Fort. We killed some of the men and captured the others. These prisoners our chief
offered to trade for the Indians whom the
soldiers had captured at the massacre in the
tent. This the officers refused, so we killed
our prisoners, disbanded, and went into hiding in the mountains. Of those who took
part in this affair I am the only one now
living.

In a few days troops were sent out to
search for us, but as we were disbanded, it
was, of course, impossible for them to locate
any hostile camp. During the time they were
searching for us many of our warriors (who
were thought by the soldiers to be peaceable
Indians) talked to the officers and men, advising them where they might find the camp
they sought, and while they searched we
watched them from our hiding places and
laughed at their failures.

After this trouble all of the Indians agreed
not to be friendly with the white men any
more. There was no general engagement,
but a long struggle followed. Sometimes we
attacked the white men—sometimes they attacked us. First a few Indians would be
killed and then a few soldiers. I think the
killing was about equal on each side. The
number killed in these troubles did not
amount to much, but this treachery on the
part of the soldiers had angered the Indians
and revived memories of other wrongs, so
that we never again trusted the United
States troops.

Perhaps the greatest wrong ever done to
the Indians was the treatment received by
our tribe from the United States troops
about 1863. The chief of our tribe, Mangus-
Colorado, went to make a treaty of peace
for our people with the white settlement
at Apache Tejo, New Mexico. It had been
reported to us that the white men in this
settlement were more friendly and more reliable than those in Arizona, that they would
live up to their treaties and would not
wrong the Indians.

Mangus-Colorado, with three other warriors, went to Apache Tejo and held a council with these citizens and soldiers. They
told him that if he would come with his tribe
and live near them, they would issue to him,
from the Government, blankets, flour, provisions, beef, and all manner of supplies.
Our chief promised to return to Apache
Tejo within two weeks. When he came back
to our settlement he assembled the whole
tribe in council. I did not believe that the
people at Apache Tejo would do as they
said and therefore I opposed the plan, but
it was decided that with part of the tribe
Mangus-Colorado should return to Apache
Tejo and receive an issue of rations and supplies. If they were as represented, and if
these white men would keep the treaty faithfully, the remainder of the tribe would join
him and we would make our permanent
home at Apache Tejo. I was to remain in
charge of that portion of the tribe which
stayed in Arizona. We gave almost all of our
arms and ammunition to the party going to
Apache Tejo, so that in case there should
be treachery they would be prepared for
any surprise. Mangus-Colorado and about
half of our people went to New Mexico,
happy that now they had found white men
who would be kind to them, and with whom
they could live in peace and plenty.

No word ever came to us from them.

From other sources, however, we heard that they had been treacherously captured and slain. In this dilemma we did not know just exactly what to do, but fearing that the troops who had captured them would attack us, we retreated into the mountains near Apache Pass.

During the weeks that followed the departure of our people we had been in suspense, and failing to provide more supplies, had exhausted all of our store of provisions. This was another reason for moving camp. On this retreat, while passing through the mountains, we discovered four men with a herd of cattle. Two of the men were in front in a buggy and two were behind on horseback. We killed all four, but did not scalp them; they were not warriors. We drove the cattle back into the mountains, made a camp, and began to kill the cattle and pack the meat.

Before we had finished this work we were surprised and attacked by United States troops, who killed in all seven Indians—one warrior, three women, and three children. The Government troops were mounted and so were we, but we were poorly armed, having given most of our weapons to the division of our tribe that had gone to Apache Tejo, so we fought mainly with spears, bows, and arrows. At first I had a spear, a bow, and a few arrows; but in a short time my spear and all my arrows were gone. Once I was surrounded, but by dodging from side to side of my horse as he ran I escaped. It was necessary during this fight for many of the warriors to leave their horses and escape on foot. But my horse was trained to come at call, and as soon as I reached a safe place, if not too closely pursued, I would call him to me. During this fight we scattered in all directions and two days later reassembled at

Early Dawn Attack. *Charles Schreyvogel*

our appointed place of rendezvous, about fifty miles from the scene of this battle.

About ten days later the same United States troops attacked our new camp at sunrise. The fight lasted all day, but our arrows and spears were all gone before ten o'clock, and for the remainder of the day we had only rocks and clubs with which to fight. We could do little damage with these weapons, and at night we moved our camp about four miles back into the mountains where it would be hard for the cavalry to follow us. The next day our scouts, who had been left behind to observe the movements of the soldiers, returned, saying that the troops had gone back toward San Carlos Reservation.

A few days after this we were again attacked by another company of United States troops. Just before this fight we had been joined by a band of Chokonen Indians under Cochise, who took command of both divisions. We were repulsed, and decided to disband.

After we had disbanded our tribe the Bedonkohe Apaches reassembled near their old camp vainly waiting for the return of Mangus-Colorado and our kinsmen. No tidings came save that they had all been treacherously slain*. Then a council was held, and as it was believed that Mangus-Colorado was dead, I was elected Tribal Chief.

For a long time we had no trouble with anyone. It was more than a year after I had been made Tribal Chief that United States troops surprised and attacked our camp. They killed seven children, five women, and four warriors, captured all our supplies, blankets, horses, and clothing, and destroyed our tepees. We had nothing left; winter was beginning, and it was the coldest winter I ever knew. After the soldiers withdrew I took three warriors and trailed them. Their trail led back toward San Carlos.

While returning from trailing the Government troops we saw two men, a Mexican and a white man, and shot them off their horses. With these two horses we returned and moved our camp. My people were suffering much and it was deemed advisable to go where we could get more provisions. Game was scarce in our range then, and since I had been Tribal Chief I had not asked for rations from the Government, nor did I care to do so, but we did not wish to starve.

We had heard that Chief Victoria of the Chihenne (Oje Caliente) Apaches was holding a council with the white men near Hot Springs in New Mexico, and that he had plenty of provisions. We had always been on friendly terms with this tribe, and Victoria was especially kind to my people. With the help of the two horses we had captured, to carry our sick with us, we went to Hot Springs. We easily found Victoria and his band, and they gave us supplies for the winter. We stayed with them for about a year, and during this stay we had perfect peace. We had not the least trouble with Mexicans, white men, or Indians. When we had stayed as long as we should, and had again accumulated some supplies, we decided to leave Victoria's band. When I told him that we were going to leave he said that we should have a feast and dance before we separated.

The festivities were held about two miles above Hot Springs, and lasted for four days. There were about four hundred Indians at

* General Miles telegraphed from Whipple Barracks, Arizona, Sept. 24, 1886, relative to the surrender of the Apaches. Among other things he said: "Mangus-Colorado had years ago been foully murdered after he had surrendered."

this celebration. I do not think we ever spent a more pleasant time than upon this occasion. No one ever treated our tribe more kindly than Victoria and his band. We are still proud to say that he and his people were our friends.

When I went to Apache Pass (Fort Bowie) I found General Howard in command, and made a treaty with him. This treaty lasted until long after General Howard had left our country. He always kept his word with us and treated us as brothers. We never had so good a friend among the United States officers as General Howard. We could have lived forever at peace with him. If there is any pure, honest white man in the United States army, that man is General Howard. All the Indians respect him, and even to this day frequently talk of the happy times when General Howard was in command of our Post. After he went away he placed an agent at Apache Pass who issued to us from the Government clothing, rations, and supplies, as General Howard directed. When beef was issued to the Indians I got twelve steers for my tribe, and Cochise got twelve steers for his tribe. Rations were issued about once a month, but if we ran out we only had to ask and we were supplied. Now, as prisoners of war in this Reservation, we do not get such good rations.

Out on the prairie away from Apache Pass a man kept a store and saloon. Some time after General Howard went away a band of outlawed Indians killed this man, and took away many of the supplies from his store. On the very next day after this some Indians at the Post were drunk on "tiswin," which they had made from corn. They fought among themselves and four of them were killed. There had been quarrels and feuds among them for some time, and

after this trouble we deemed it impossible to keep the different bands together in peace. Therefore we separated, each leader taking his own band. Some of them went to San Carlos and some to Old Mexico, but I took my tribe back to Hot Springs and rejoined Victoria's band.

Soon after we arrived in New Mexico two companies of scouts were sent from San Carlos. When they came to Hot Springs they sent word for me and Victoria to come to town. The messengers did not say what they wanted with us, but as they seemed friendly we thought they wanted a council, and rode in to meet the officers. As soon as we arrived in town soldiers met us, disarmed us, and took us both to headquarters where we were tried by court-martial. They asked us only a few questions and then Victoria was released and I was sentenced to the guardhouse. Scouts conducted me to the guardhouse and put me in chains. When I asked them why they did this they said it was because I had left Apache Pass.

I do not think that I ever belonged to those soldiers at Apache Pass, or that I should have asked them where I might go. Our bands could no longer live in peace* together, and so we had quietly withdrawn, expecting to live with Victoria's band, where we thought we would not be molested. They also sentenced seven other Apaches to chains in the guardhouse.

I do not know why this was done, for these Indians had simply followed me from Apache Pass to Hot Springs. If it was wrong (and I do not think it was wrong) for us to go to Hot Springs, I alone was to blame.

* Victoria, chief of the Hot Spring Apaches, met his death in opposing the forcible removal of his band to a reservation, because having previously tried and failed he felt it impossible for separate bands of Apaches to live at peace under such arrangement.

They asked the soldiers in charge why they were imprisoned and chained, but received no answer.

I was kept a prisoner for four months, during which time I was transferred to San Carlos. Then I think I had another trial, although I was not present. In fact I do not know that I had another trial, but I was told that I had, and at any rate I was released.

After this we had no more trouble with the soldiers, but I never felt at ease any longer at the Post. We were allowed to live above San Carlos at a place now called Geronimo. A man whom the Indians called "Nick Golee" was agent at this place. All went well here for a period of two years, but we were not satisfied.

In the summer of 1883 a rumor was current that the officers were again planning to imprison our leaders. This rumor served to revive the memory of all our past wrongs —the massacre in the tent at Apache Pass, the fate of Mangus-Colorado, and my own unjust imprisonment, which might easily have been death to me. Just at this time we were told that the officers wanted us to come up the river above Geronimo to a fort (Fort Thomas) to hold a council with them. We did not believe that any good would come of this conference, or that there was any need of it; so we held a council ourselves, and fearing treachery, decided to leave the reservation. We thought it more manly to die on the warpath than to be killed in prison.

There were in all about 250 Indians, chiefly the Bedonkohe and Nedni Apaches, led by myself and Whoa. We went through Apache Pass and just west of there had a fight with the United States troops. In this battle we killed three soldiers and lost none.

We went on toward Old Mexico, but on the second day after this United States soldiers overtook us about three o'clock in the afternoon and we fought until dark. The ground where we were attacked was very rough, which was to our advantage, for the troops were compelled to dismount in order to fight us. I do not know how many soldiers we killed, but we lost only one warrior and three children. We had plenty of guns and ammunition at this time. Many of the guns and much ammunition we had accumulated while living in the reservation, and the remainder we had obtained from the White Mountain Apaches when we left the reservation.

Troops did not follow us any longer, so we went south almost to Casa Grande and camped in the Sierra de Sahuaripa Mountains. We ranged in the mountains of Old Mexico for about a year, then returned to San Carlos, taking with us a herd of cattle and horses.

Soon after we arrived at San Carlos the officer in charge, General Crook, took the horses and cattle away from us. I told him that these were not white men's cattle, but belonged to us, for we had taken them from the Mexicans during our wars. I also told him that we did not intend to kill these animals, but that we wished to keep them and raise stock on our range. He would not listen to me, but took the stock. I went up near Forth Apache and General Crook ordered officers, soldiers, and scouts to see that I was arrested; if I offered resistance they were instructed to kill me.

This information was brought to me by the Indians. When I learned of this proposed action I left for Old Mexico, and about four hundred Indians went with me. They were the Bedonkohe, Chokonen, and Nedni Apaches. At this time Whoa was dead, and Naiche was the only chief with me. We went south into Sonora and camped in the mountains. Troops followed us, but did not attack us until we were camped in the mountains west of Casa Grande. Here we were attacked by Government Indian scouts. One boy was killed and nearly all of our women and children were captured.

After this battle we went south of Casa Grande and made a camp, but within a few days this camp was attacked by Mexican soldiers. We skirmished with them all day, killing a few Mexicans, but sustaining no loss ourselves.

That night we went east into the foothills of the Sierra Madre Mountains and made another camp. Mexican troops trailed us, and after a few days attacked our camp again. This time the Mexicans had a very large army, and we avoided a general engagement. It is senseless to fight when you cannot hope to win.

That night we held a council of war; our scouts had reported bands of United States and Mexican troops at many points in the mountains. We estimated that about two thousand soldiers were ranging these mountains seeking to capture us.

General Crook had come down into Mexico with the United States troops. They were camped in the Sierra de Antunez Mountains. Scouts told me that General Crook wished to see me and I went to his camp. When I arrived General Crook said to me, "Why did you leave the reservation?" I said: "You told me that I might live in the reservation the same as white people lived. One year I raised a crop of corn, and gathered and stored it, and the next year I put in a crop of oats, and when the crop was almost ready to harvest, you told your soldiers to put me in prison, and if I resisted to kill me. If I had been let alone I would now have been in good circumstances, but instead of that you and the Mexicans are hunting me with soldiers." He said: "I never

gave any such orders; the troops at Fort Apache, who spread this report, knew that it was untrue." Then I agreed to go back with him to San Carlos.

It was hard for me to believe him at that time. Now I know that what he said was untrue, and I firmly believe that he did issue the orders for me to be put in prison, or to be killed in case I offered resistance.

We started with all our tribe to go with General Crook back to the United States, but I feared treachery and decided to remain in Mexico. We were not under any guard at this time. The United States troops marched in front and the Indians followed, and when we became suspicious, we turned back. I do not know how far the United States army went after myself, and some warriors turned back before we were missed, and I do not care.

I have suffered much from such unjust orders as those of General Crook. Such acts have caused much distress to my people. I think that General Crook's death was sent by the Almighty as a punishment for the many evil deeds he committed.

Soon General Miles was made commander of all the western posts, and troops trailed us continually. They were led by Captain Lawton, who had good scouts. The Mexican soldiers also became more active and more numerous. We had skirmishes almost every day, and so we finally decided to break up into small bands. With six men and four women I made for the range of mountains near Hot Springs, New Mexico. We passed many cattle ranches, but had no trouble with the cowboys. We killed cattle to eat whenever we were in need of food, but we frequently suffered greatly for water. At one time we had no water for two days and nights and our horses almost died from thirst. We ranged in the mountains of New Mexico for some time, then thinking that perhaps the troops had left Mexico, we returned. On our return through Old Mexico we attacked every Mexican found, even if for no other reason than to kill. We believed they had asked the United States troops to come down to Mexico to fight us.

South of Casa Grande, near a place called by the Indians Gosoda, there was a road leading out from the town. There was much freighting carried on by the Mexicans over this road. Where the road ran through a mountain pass we stayed in hiding, and whenever Mexican freighters passed we killed them, took what supplies we wanted, and destroyed the remainder. We were reckless of our lives, because we felt that every man's hand was against us. If we returned to the reservation we would be put in prison and killed; if we stayed in Mexico they would continue to send soldiers to fight us; so we gave no quarter to anyone and asked no favors.

After some time we left Gosoda and soon were reunited with our tribe in the Sierra de Antunez Mountains.

Contrary to our expectations the United States soldiers had not left the mountains in Mexico, and were soon trailing us and skirmishing with us almost every day. Four or five times they surpised our camp. One time they surprised us about nine o'clock in the morning, and captured all our horses (nineteen in number) and secured our store of dried meats. We also lost three Indians in this encounter. About the middle of the afternoon of the same day we attacked them from the rear as they were passing through a prairie—killed one soldier, but lost none ourselves. In this skirmish we recovered all our horses except three that belonged to me. The three horses that we did not recover were the best riding horses we had.

Soon after this we made a treaty with the Mexican troops. They told us that the United States troops were the real cause of these wars, and agreed not to fight any more with us provided we would return to the United States. This we agreed to do, and resumed our march, expecting to try to make a treaty with the United States soldiers and return to Arizona. There seemed to be no other course to pursue.

Soon after this scouts from Captain Lawton's troops told us that he wished to make a treaty with us; but I knew that General

The Trooper.   *Frederick Remington*

Miles was the chief of the American troops, and I decided to treat with him.

We continued to move our camp northward, and the American troops also moved northward, keeping at no great distance from us, but not attacking us.

I sent my brother Porico (White Horse) with Mr. George Wratton on to Fort Bowie to see General Miles, and to tell him that we wished to return to Arizona; but before these messengers returned I met two Indian scouts—Kayitah, a Chokonen Apache, and Marteen, a Nedni Apache. They were serving as scouts for Captain Lawton's troops. They told me that General Miles had come and had sent them to ask me to meet him. So I went to the camp of the United States troops to meet General Miles.

When I arrived at their camp I went directly to General Miles and told him how I had been wronged, and that I wanted to return to the United States with my people, as we wished to see our families, who had been captured and taken away from us.

General Miles said to me: "The President of the United States has sent me to speak to you. He has heard of your trouble with the white men, and says that if you will agree to a few words of treaty we need have no more trouble. Geronimo, if you will agree to a few words of treaty all will be satisfactorily arranged."

So General Miles told me how we could be brothers to each other. We raised our hands to heaven and said that the treaty was not to be broken. We took an oath not to do any wrong to each other or to scheme against each other.

Then he talked with me for a long time and told me what he would do for me in the future if I would agree to the treaty. I did not greatly believe General Miles, but because the President of the United States had sent me word I agreed to make the treaty, and to keep it. General Miles said to me: "I will take you under Government protection; I will build you a house; I will fence you much land; I will give you cattle, horses, mules, and farming implements. You will be furnished with men to work the farm, for you yourself will not have to work. In the fall I will send you blankets and clothing so that you will not suffer from cold in the winter time.

"There is plenty of timber, water, and grass in the land to which I will send you. You will live with your tribe and with your family. If you agree to this treaty you shall see your family within five days."

I said to General Miles: "All the officers that have been in charge of the Indians have talked that way, and it sounds like a story to me; I hardly believe you."

He said: "This time it is the truth."

I said: "General Miles, I do not know the laws of the white man, nor of this new country where you are to send me, and I might break their laws."

He said: "While I live you will not be arrested."

Then I agreed to make the treaty. (Since I have been a prisoner of war I have been arrested and placed in the guardhouse twice for drinking whisky.)

We stood between his troopers and my warriors. We placed a large stone on the blanket before us. Our treaty was made by this stone, and it was to last until the stone should crumble to dust; so we made the treaty, and bound each other with an oath.

I do not believe that I have ever violated that treaty; but General Miles never fulfilled his promises.

When we had made the treaty General Miles said to me: "My brother, you have in your mind how you are going to kill men, and other thoughts of war; I want you to put that out of your mind, and change your thoughts to peace."

Then I agreed and gave up my arms. I said: "I will quit the warpath and live at peace hereafter."

Then General Miles swept a spot of ground clear with his hand, and said: "Your past deeds shall be wiped out like this and you will start a new life."

30. The Surrender of Sitting Bull

BY E. H. ALLISON

EDITOR'S NOTE: One of the most famous (or notorious) Indians of the Prairie Sioux tribe was Sitting Bull (c. 1831-1890). A shrewd and daring chief, he led attacks against United States troops invading his hunting grounds in 1864-68. Although he made peace with the whites, his failure to remain on a reservation led to the campaign against him in which General Custer was killed. Several years later he surrendered, and after 1883 lived at the Standing Rock agency. In 1890, in the midst of much excitement among his tribe because it was believed an Indian messiah was shortly coming, Sitting Bull was arrested by Indian police and U. S. soldiers and killed while his warriors tried to rescue him. E. H. Allison was a scout in the employ of the U. S. army. He was chosen to conduct the negotiations for the surrender of Sitting Bull.

It was about the 25th of October, 1880, when we pulled out from Buford, reaching Camp Poplar Creek in two days, where I was met by an Indian runner from Bull's Camp, sent with a message to me from Chief Gall, to the effect that I would find him, with the entire camp, at the mouth of Frenchman's Creek, on the Milk River,

about one hundred and fifty miles from Poplar Creek. Accompanied by the runner, whose name was Strong Hand, we proceeded on our journey, making only about twenty miles a day. When we had reached within about six miles of the camp, we came upon a lone tepee, erected on a small mound near the trail; an old squaw stood near, observing our approach. Riding up to her, I learned that her son, who was in the tepee, had, the day before, quarreled with another Indian in the camp, over a horse trade, and that her son had killed the other Indian, and he was now, in compliance with the Indian custom, when guilty of the shedding of blood, performing an act of purification. She also informed me that during the preceding night, their Indian enemies, the Blackfeet, had made an attack on the camp, and had succeeded in running off twenty-six head of horses, without, however, doing any other damage, and that a war party was on their trail. This was most unwelcome news. The camp was sure to be in an uproar, and the warriors in a frame of mind, anything but favorable to my purpose; but this was mild intelligence compared with what we were about to witness in the next

Scalp Dance of the Sioux Indians.   *George Catlin*

forty-eight hours. About three o'clock, p. m., we reached the camp, which was on the west bank and near the mouth of Frenchman's Creek, when I was rather agreeably surprised, and somewhat puzzled, by receiving a pressing invitation, which could easily be construed into a command, to make my home at Sitting Bull's lodge, as long as I stayed in the camp. I accepted the invitation, but stipulated that Chief Gall should superintend the distribution of the provisions which I had brought them. To this Sitting Bull readily acceded, and notwithstanding the turbulent condition of the camp, I was soon comfortably housed, together with the soldier, in the tepee of the great Indian Priest and Prophet Sitting Bull. After an early supper, I sought and obtained a private interview with Chief Gall, who informed me that he had resolved to effect the surrender of the entire band,

Sitting Bull and all, but to accomplish this, more time would be required than he had first anticipated. He must first go back to Canada, to enable Sitting Bull to keep an engagement to meet Major Walsh, of the Dominion forces, in a council, at the Woody Mountain Trading Post. And to insure success, and expedite matters, he advised that I should meet him again at Woody Mountain, as soon as possible, after reporting to Major Brotherton, at Fort Buford. Considering the circumstances, I deemed it best to acquiesce in his plans. Yet I was anxious to make some kind of a showing on this trip, that would encourage Major Brotherton, and reward him for the confidence he had placed in me. I explained this to Chief Gall, who told me to remain in the camp two days, to rest my mules, and by that time he would have twenty families ready to send in with me; but he cautioned me not to let Sitting Bull know their real purpose, but to lead him to suppose they were only going in to the Agency on a visit to their friends.

Perfectly satisfied with these arrangements, I returned, a little after dark, to Sitting Bull's lodge, where the soldier, who could not speak a word of the Indian language, was having rather a lonesome time of it, and was growing somewhat anxious for my safety. We were both very tired, and soon lay down to rest, while I engaged the old Chief in conversation. Sitting Bull's family at that time consisted of his two wives, (sisters) two daughters and three sons, the eldest being a daughter of seventeen, the other daughter being next, about fourteen, the eldest son, Crow Foot, since dead, seven years old, and the two youngest boys were twins, born about three weeks before the battle of the Little Big Horn, and were, therefore, not more than four and a half years old; one of the twins was named Ih-pe-ya-na-pa-pi, from the fact that his mother "fled and abandoned" him in the tepee, at the time of the battle.

I continued in conversation with Sitting Bull until about midnight, when I fell asleep. I must have been asleep less than an hour, when I was awakened by the sharp crack of a rifle ringing out on the still night air, and the simultaneous war whoop of contending savages. The camp was instantly in a state of the wildest confusion. Indian women, seizing their babes, fled, screaming, they knew not whither, for safety; warriors suddenly awakened from their slumbers, seized their arms and flew with the speed of the wind to the aid of their comrades, who were already engaged in conflict with an enemy, whose presence could not be determined by the sharp report and flashes of fire from their guns, as they fired in the

darkness upon the Sioux camp. Here was an opportunity for the soldier and myself to prove our friendship, by aiding the Sioux warriors in their defence of the camp, which we proceeded to do, by seizing our rifles and hastily joining the warriors, who, by this time, had turned the enemy, whose firing soon ceased altogether, and we all returned to the camp, where comparative quiet was restored; but no one slept any more that night. The fact that myself and companion took part in the defence of the camp, was favorably commented on by all, and in all probability saved our lives, for the Indians are very superstitious, and their blood was up; something was wrong; in fact, things had been going wrong for several days. There must be a "Jonah" in the camp, and how easy it would be to find a pair of "Jonahs" in the persons of the two white men in camp; but our prompt action had made a most favorable impression, and diverted their thoughts from the subject of "Jonahs," and I improved the opportunity by comparing their uncertain, hunted existence with the happy life of their friends at the Agencies in Dakota, whose wives and little ones were even then sleeping peacefully in their beds, without fear of being disturbed by prowling bands of Indian foes.

A number of warriors followed cautiously after the retreating Blackfeet, but failed to come up with them. They returned to camp about ten in the borning, and reported finding blood-stained bandages on the trail, so there must have been some of the enemy wounded. Among the Sioux, no one was hurt, nor did they loose any horses on this occasion. But danger was yet lurking near. About two in the afternoon, a warrior came into camp, and reported the discovery of a small herd of buffalo, about four miles from camp. About thirty warriors mounted their horses and went out to kill them; among the number was Scarlet Plume, a popular young brave, who was a favorite with every one. The warriors approached the buffalo under cover, till they were within easy rifle range, when they opened fire and killed all but one, which struck out across the plain, seemingly unhurt. Young Scarlet Plume alone gave chase, following the animal and finally killing it near the head of a ravine running up from the Milk River which at that point was densely studded with timber. He had killed his last buffalo. He was alone and more than a mile from his companions. A party of Blackfeet braves, concealed in the timber, had been watching his movements, and now while he was busily engaged skinning the buffalo, they approached, under cover of the ravine, shot him, took his scalp, and made good their escape. His body was found by his father, Old Scarlet Thunder, and was brought by him into camp, a little before sunset that evening. Then indeed, there was weeping and wailing in that camp. Language utterly fails me when I try to describe the scene that followed. His old mother, his five sisters, and scores of friends and relatives tore their hair, slashed their limbs with knives, till the ground where they stood was wet with hot human gore, rent their garments, calling in a loud wailing voice upon the name of the lost son and brother.

2

It was no time for negotiations. Not a time for anything, in fact, but silence and obscurity on my part; so, with my companion, I sought the seclusion of Sitting Bull's tepee, where we spent the night in fitful and unrefreshing slumber. Early in the morning, at the first faint dawn of day, I

was awakened by a call from Chief Gall, whom I joined in a walk about the camp. He informed me that the twenty lodges he had promised me had silently taken their departure during the night, and that I would find them in the evening, encamped about twenty miles down the Milk River. He said that five women and nine children belonging to the party, but who had no horses, had remained behind, and desired to ride in my wagon. He also informed me that Strong Hand would return with me to Poplar Creek. Accordingly, as soon as breakfast was over, we hitched up the mules, and were only too glad to get away from a place, where, to say the least, our experience had been very unpleasant. Strong hand was returning afoot, and at his suggestion, I loaned him my horse, to enable him to traverse the river bottoms in quest of deer. The women and children climbed into the wagon with their meagre effects, and we began moving out of the camp, Strong Hand riding just in advance of the mules, while I occupied a seat with the driver. We had reached the outskirts of the camp, and were nearing the crossing of Frenchman's Creek, which was bordered on either side by a dense growth of willows, when I saw a number of warriors rapidly approaching us from the camp, each one carrying, in addition to his rifle, a stout club. From this I knew that they were what they call soldiers, corresponding to our police. They called to Strong Hand to halt, but instead of obeying, he put whip to his horse and quickly disappeared through the willows at the crossing, but not before one of the Indians, a son of the noted Chief, Black Moon, had raised his rifle and sent a bullet flying after him. My soldier friend, being unacquainted with Indian customs, supposed that we were sure enough attacked, and for an instant, lost his presence of mind, and was about to lash the mules into a run, in the mad hope of escaping from the savages in a ponderous government wagon, drawn by four equally ponderous draught mules. I snatched the lines from his hand, and reined in the mules, in the meantime begging Day not to get excited, and to put down that whip. He recovered himself instantly, when I handed him the lines and told him to hold the mules, and jumping to the ground, I ran directly to the brave who had fired the shot. I assumed a fearless demeanor which I did not feel, and demanded what was the matter. He waved me angrily away, repeating, "It is not you! It is not you!" "That man on your horse I wanted. He is himself a soldier of our band, and long ago he broke my arm with a blow from his club, when I had broken one of our customs by flushing a herd of buffalo; now he has broken a law by leaving camp without our consent, and I proposed to retaliate, but he is gone, and now you go!" I obeyed with alacrity, while the warriors turned slowly back to their camp. We were clear of them at last, and right glad we were to know it.

It was nearly dark when we came up with the twenty lodges sent on ahead by Chief Gall. Strong Hand was there with plenty of good venison, and laughing heartily at the morning episode, which he explained more fully, and acknowledged that the principle reason for borrowing my horse was now apparent. We returned in safety to Fort Buford, where, I hope, with a pardonable degree of pride, I turned over to Major Brotherton the first fruits of my labor, twenty lodges of the hostile Sioux, and submitted an official report to be forwarded to General Terry, of this, my second visit to the camp of Sitting Bull.

3

I remained in Buford five days, preparing for my third trip, and believing the work to have progressed to a period where I might find it necessary to extend, indefinitely, my stay in the camp, I determined to take with me some one to act in the capacity of courier, which would enable me to send a report back to Major Brotherton. For this purpose I chose the Post Interpreter, George Mulligan, with whom I started on about the 20th of November, reaching Camp Poplar Creek, sixty-five miles west of Buford, in two days. At this place is situated, beside the small garrison of troops, the Fort Peck, or Poplar Creek Agency for the Yanktonia Sioux, who, at that time, numbered, all told, about two thousand five hundred. These were professedly friendly Indians, who belonged properly to the Agencies on the lower Missouri, in Dakota. There is a bit of history connected with the location of these Indians in Montana, that I intend to make the subject of a chapter in a work that I expect to publish in the near future. From these people I received important information, to the effect that an Indian had arrived from Sitting Bull's Camp, who reported that an open rupture had occurred between Chief Gall and Sitting Bull, occasioned by the discovery by some of the adherents of Sitting Bull, that Chief Gall had instigated the desertion of the twenty lodges, who had gone with me to Buford, and concealment being no longer possible, Chief Gall, characteristically prompt in action, had leaped into the midst of the camp, and publicly called upon all who acknowledged him as their Chief, to separate themselves from the followers of Sitting Bull, and prepare immediately to follow him to Fort Buford. It was a bold thing to do, and the

The Prisoner

first time in the history of the reign of Sitting Bull, that his authority had been set at defiance. It was clearly a test of supremacy, and Chief Gall came off victorious, taking away from Sitting Bull fully two-thirds of the entire band, with whom he proceeded direct to Poplar Creek, where I awaited his arrival, which took place on the 25th. Sitting Bull was now left with only about three hundred lodges, altogether too small a force to expect to successfully defend themselves against even their Indian enemies. I, therefore, after a long talk with Chief Gall, determined to push right on to Woody Mountain and press negotiations while circumstances seemed to promise success. There were grave uncertainties, however, as to how I would be received. Their troubles, not the least of which, in the estimation of his adherents, was the decline of Sitting Bull's power, might all be dated from my first visit to their camp, and my friend, the Gall, would not be there to protect me from the vengeance of the desperate savages. One thing was certain, Sitting Bull had by this time divined my real purpose, and any attempt at concealment would be futile. But the work could not be done by proxy, so *I had to go on,* or sneak back to Buford and own up that I was afraid to go on with the work, and subject myself to the tantalizing "I told you so" of the knowing one, whose name is legion, and whose home is everywhere. Accordingly, after arranging with The Gall to remain with his band at Poplar Creek till my return, and sending a report to Major Brotherton, by an Indian, I continued, accompanied by Mulligan, to Woody Mountain. Winter had already set in, and we had a cold ride across the hundred and ten mile prairie, reaching the Woody Mountain Trading Post on the 27th of November, where we learned that Sitting Bull's camp was distant only eighteen miles. Major Crozier of the Dominion forces, was in command of the small garrison of Mounted Police, stationed at the Trading Post, and at his suggestion, I remained at the Post, and sent word, by an Indian, to Sitting Bull, to meet me there with all of his leading warriors, and with a view to putting them in good humor, I purchased from the trader a large quantity of provisions, which I had cooked, and prepared a sumptuous feast for them, which fact being conveyed to them by the Indian courier they were not slow to respond. Sitting Bull met me with a slight exhibition of friendliness, evidently reluctantly assumed. Being deprived of the counsel and support of Chief Gall, he was at a loss what to do. Constitutionally a coward, fears for his own personal safety caused him to waver and withhold his consent to come in with me at once, and then, too, he was only human, and doubtless, coward though he was, his mind was stirred with other considerations than personal fear. His exalted position as Patriarch of a people, who, in his opinion, were the greatest nation on earth, was fast slipping away from him. It had been the boast of his life that he would never be dependent upon the hated white man. Time and again he had met them in battle, and had always been the victor. Must he at last, in this tame, humiliating manner, surrender himself, and become a prisoner in the hands of an hereditary foe? Who can tell how fierce the struggle of that moment? The mental anguish endured, while he revolved these, to him mighty questions, in his mind? What wonder that he hesitated, and asked a few more days to think and talk with his people about it? I explained to him fully, that his surrender must be virtually unconditional; the only thing guaranteed was that their lives should be spared. I was free, however, to express my opinion that they would be eventually treated as other Agency Indians, and promising to wait ten days for a decision, and apprehending that Mulligan was doing too much talking on his own account, I dispatched him, with a report of progress, to Major Brotherton. During the following ten days, from the first to the tenth of December, I visited the camp three times, staying over night the first time with Sitting Bull, the second time with No Neck, and the third time with Black Bull, using every argument and pursuasion at my command, to induce them to return with me to Buford, and having a better command of the Sioux than I have of English, I do believe I waxed really eloquent, for while talking to a small assembly in Black Bull's lodge, that Chief confessed that my words, while describing their distressed, hunted condition, and the hopelessness of their children's future, had moved him to tears, something never before accomplished by a white man.

On the morning of the tenth, I made an appointment to meet Sitting Bull and his warriors in the Trader's Store, at Woody Mountain, there to receive his final decision. Accordingly, about noon they were assembled and ready for the council, at which, by my request, Major Crozier was present, and gave me all the aid in his power; but not till he withdrew from the council, did I finally succeed, about two o'clock p. m., in getting a promise from Sitting Bull and all of his followers, to raise camp the next morning, the 11th of December, 1880, and move with me toward the Missouri River. As soon as they had thus decided, most of them departed at once for their camp, to prepare for the morning's march, Sitting Bull among the number; I having promised

to follow in time to reach the camp that night, and sleep in Bull's lodge. Five or six of the warriors remained in the store to do some trading. One of them was Black Bull, or as he was called by the Indians, Lame Brule, a chief noted for bravery, another was the son of Black Moon, who, on the occasion of my second visit to the camp, had fired a shot at Strong Hand.

After purchasing as much food as I could conveniently pack on my horse, and sending a dispatch by a Cree half-breed to Major Brotherton, I started on Sitting Bull's trail to the camp, eighteen miles away. The snow was deep, and the temperature unusually cold, but my horse was too heavily burdened to admit of fast riding, so I was jogging along at an easy pace, and keeping a sharp lookout from force of habit, and had gone about nine miles, when I discovered an Indian following after me, at the highest rate of speed, and frantically beckoning me to stop. I halted, and awaited his approach. It was Black Bull; he had brought me a dispatch, signed by Fred. Cadd, the trader, and endorsed by Major Crozier, which read as follows:

"Your life is threatened; return at once! Black Bull will explain;" which he did, by informing me that soon after I had left the store, perhaps forty-five minutes, Black Moon's son gave the trader a deer skin, in exchange for which he asked for a quantity of flour, sugar and coffee. The same having been weighed out to him, he was dissatisfied with the trade, claiming that he was being cheated, (which was doubtless true,) and the trader refusing, either to give him more or return the deer skin, he flew into a rage and attempted to shoot the trader on the spot: but being frustrated in his purpose, (Black Bull modestly refrained from stating the fact, which I afterwards learned, that it was he who had saved the trader's life,) he declared that though they had cheated him out of his deer skin, and prevented his killing the trader, they could not cheat him of vengeance, for he knew of one white man who was in his power, and whose hot blood should melt the frozen snow, before the sun went down, and leaving the store, he mounted his horse and rode furiously away by a trail nearly parallel with the one taken by me, and the natural conclusion reached by all, was that he meant me, and this was the opinion of Black Bull, who urged me to return with him to the Trading Post, believing, he said, that I would be waylaid and murdered before I reached the camp. This was perplexing; success apparently almost within my grasp, and now this unexpected difficulty presents itself. What should I do? I had given my word to be in camp that night, and I had the promise of Sitting Bull and all his leading warriors to start for the American lines in the morning. If I failed to reach the camp that night, they, of course, would fail to move in the morning, and our agreement would be void, and total failure would probably result. Better to go ahead and be killed, than go back and be laughed at.

Penciling on the back of the dispatch my determination to go on at all hazard, I sent Black Bull back with it, while I slowly and thoughtfully pursued my way to the camp, closely scanning every ravine and bunch of poplars or sage bush, that might serve as a hiding place for the enraged warrior; but nothing unusual occurred, and I reached the camp in safety. Supper was waiting me in Sitting Bull's lodge, which was to be my home for the next ten days. While smoking a pipe with the Chief, after supper, I told him what I had heard of the difficulty at the trader's store. He said that a little while

before my arrival, the Black Moon's son had returned to the camp, his horse wet with sweat and apparently exhausted, which fact was noticed and commented on by several, but having made no statement, they had supposed that the proposed movement in the morning was all that agitated his mind. While we were yet discussing the matter, a little girl came into the tepee, and said that her father wanted me to come to his lodge, and immediately went out again, when Sitting Bull told me that that was Black Moon's son's little daughter. Then it was the enraged warrior himself who wanted to see me. What for? There was no use trying to evade a meeting; I might as well go and take my medicine at once, and be done with it; so taking my rifle, I followed the little girl to her father's lodge. Going in, I found the warrior apparently in the best of good humor, filling a pipe preparatory to a smoke. He motioned me to a seat, where his squaw served me with a large hot pancake and a cup of coffee, and while I was eating, supposing that I knew nothing of his encounter with the trader, he told me all about it, evidently with a desire to conceal nothing, not even his threat of vengeance, and concluded exultingly, while his countenance actually glowed with savage satisfaction, that *he had kept his word.*

While my heart was saddened by the thought that someone's life had been sacrificed to the avaricious greed of an Indian trader, yet I was certainly rejoiced to know that after all he had not chosen me as the object of his vengeance.

Several weeks afterwards, I learned that the mail, due in Woody Mountain that evening, had failed to arrive, and that some days later, fragments of human remains dragged around and scattered about by wolves, with shreds of clothing, revealed the fact that the mail carrier had been killed.

The warrior then explained that he had sent for me to tell me these things himself, and assure me that I need have no fears for my own safety, as far as he was concerned. It was his turn to be surprised, when I told him how I had heard all about it before I got to the camp, and when I mentioned the name of Black Bull, as being the one who brought me the dispatch, he gnashed his teeth as he said, "Only for him, *I would have got the real offender."*

4

Early the next morning found us moving toward the Missouri River; Black Bull and the others having returned from the Trading Post during the night.

Having barely horses enough to pack their effects, nearly all the able bodied warriors and squaws were afoot. The order of march being, First, three mounted warriors, who moved out about one hour in advance of the main body of warriors, one keeping to the proposed line of march, the other two acting as flankers, observing a distance of about one mile from the center guide; next in line of march, and immediately preceding the main body, were about fifty warriors afoot, and armed for action, who moved, however, without any more display of military order than would a herd of so many cattle. Then followed the camp proper, the squaws leading and driving ponies, all heavily laden with camp equipage, not even the little colts were exempt from burden, and all in an indescribable state of disorder. Bringing up the rear, was a guard of about seventy-five mounted warriors. From this company, at intervals of about a mile, all along the line of march, small detachments of five or six were sent ahead, riding rapidly on either flank, until

they reached a point a mile or two in advance of the main column, when, taking a position on some convenient hill, they would dismount, sit down in the snow, and fill a pipe for a smoke, while their horses were free to forage in the snow for the nutritious buffalo grass. Here they would remain until the rear guard came up, when they would rejoin them. In the mean time, another party of flankers had gone out, and so on, all day long. Our progress was necessarily slow, and we made only about an average of twelve miles a day. As to myself, I rode at will, sometimes with the advance guard, and sometimes with the main body, and again with the rear guard; always speaking words of encouragement to the feeble, and cheering the little ones with a prospect of good things, when we should get to Fort Buford. The weather was not cold for the first week, so there was but little suffering from that source; but we found no game, save an occasional jack rabbit, and the scant supply of food was nearly exhausted, and there was consequent suffering from hunger, and like the Israelites of old, they began to murmer. On our third day's march, I was riding by the side of Sitting Bull, just in the rear of the main body, when my name was called by a young warrior, a member of a flanking party, who were resting on a little hill by the wayside, who stoop up and beckoned me to come to him. Sitting Bull rode with me to the group, where we halted, and I asked the young man what he wanted. He seemed embarassed, and stood for nearly a minute, without replying, holding the muzzle of his rifle in his hands, while the butt rested on the ground. At last he said, looking at me, while his lips quivered and his voice trembled with savage emotion, "Where are you taking these people to?" "To Fort Buford," (O-kee-ja-ta) I replied.

"Then why don't you feed them, don't you know that they are hungry?" said he. I was about to reply, but Sitting Bull, realizing the situation, adroitly placed himself between me and the speaker, and while indicating by signs, that I should move on, he himself engaged the young man in conversation, and when a little later, he overtook me, he simply said, "The young man's heart is bad; his little sister is crying for food." Only for the intervention of Sitting Bull, I have no doubt but the young man would have attempted my life. On other occasions, I narrowly escaped death at the hands of the turbulent and ungovernable savages; but as this is not intended as a history of my own adventures, but the surrender of Sitting Bull, I will hasten on.

Our course was down the Rock Creek Valley for the first seven days, when we turned east and crossed over to the Porcupine Creek, which we followed for three days, to its confluence with the Milk River, distant only three miles from the great Missouri. Here we found buffalo in great numbers; there being within a radius of thirty miles, no less than thirty-five thousand. Here I determined to improve the opportunity for getting in a good supply of food and robes for the destitute Indians, and accordingly advised the head men to choose a camping ground, with a view to greater security against their Indian enemies.

That evening, after we had gone into camp, and everybody had satisfied their hunger by a bounteous supply of buffalo meat, I called a council of the chiefs, and asked them to select three braves to go at once with me as delegates, on a visit to Fort Buford, my object being, as I told them,

The Last Drop. *Charles Schreyvogel*

to convince them that their treatment by Major Brotherton would be good. I desired, also, that they receive confirmation from the lips of Major Brotherton himself, of all the representations that I had made them, concerning their surrender. Sitting Bull then called for three volunteers to go with me; but for a long time there was no response. Finally, after the assembled warriors had smoked their pipes in silence for full twenty minutes, causing a feeling of portentous gloom to pervade the atmosphere of the council lodge, suddenly, a tall, athletic warrior sprang to his feet, and taking a position in the center of the lodge, and facing me, gesticulating excitedly, he said: "I am the Patriarch Crow! My kinsmen, you all know me; you have never known me as the friend of the white man; you know that I have always hastened into the thickest of the fight, when the white man was our foe, nor did I withhold my hand when they cried for mercy, and the fact that we are now on our way to Fort Buford, so sue for peace, was not of my choosing; but when, eleven days ago, the chiefs of this band decided upon this course, that day I forgot that the white man was my enemy; that day, Patriarch Crow, the white man's enemy, died, and to-day, Patriarch Crow, the white man's friend lives, and he it is who speaks these words, and since volunteers were never lacking for deeds of war, neither shall they be lacking when called for a mission of peace. I go with my friend to Buford. Who will be the next to speak?" He then advanced, and shaking hands with me, sat down by my side, great drops of sweat rolling off his face. Though a leading warrior, and always foremost in battle, he was never before known to make a public speech, and I had his assurance that I was the first white man with whom he had ever shaken hands. He afterwards proved of invaluable service, but has since died at Standing Rock Agency, Dakota, where he was known, through the misinterpretation of his name, as the Crow King. Two others immediately volunteered, and the next morning, leaving the camp, where they were, for the first time in five years, in the midst of buffalo, I started with them for Buford, where we arrived on Christmas Eve, December 24, 1880.

5

On our way we had stopped at Poplar Creek, where I had an interview with Chief Gall, who informed me that many of his followers were becoming demoralized through the machinations of some of the so-called friendly Chiefs at the Agency, who wanted them not to go to Fort Buford to surrender, but to be enrolled as members of their bands at that Agency; dwelling upon the fact, as an inducement, that the Poplar Creek Agency was much nearer the buffalo range than the Agencies below in Dakota. He further informed me, that unless measures were taken to restrict the Agency Chiefs, when the time came to continue the march to Buford, many of his band would refuse to leave Poplar Creek. All these facts I reported to Major Brotherton, and advised that the two companies stationed at Poplar Creek, be re-enforced by at least five companies, which was accordingly done. Three companies being sent from Fort Keogh, Montana, and two from Buford, and all commanded by Major Guido Ilges.

My object in having the garrison at Poplar Creek re-enforced, was to overawe the Agency Chiefs and prevent their interference with the hostiles; but being detained with the delegates longer in Buford than I had anticipated, Major Ilges, with the re-enforcements, reached Camp Poplar Creek ahead of me, and immediately undertook a little work on his own account, and for his own glory, which, only for the prompt decided action, first, of Chief Gall, and afterwards of Patriarch Crow, would have undone all the work that I had thus far accomplished. He demanded the immediate and unconditional surrender of Chief Gall and his band. This was in the afternoon of about the ninth day of January, 1881, and I reached Poplar Creek with the Patriarch Crow and his two companions that night. Chief Gall heard of my return, and early in the morning, came over from his camp, which was situated in the woods across the Missouri River, crossing on the ice, to see me, and as he said, to present me with the pony he rode, a splendid black mare. He was proceeding to tell me how Major Ilges had ordered his surrender, when looking toward the military camp, we saw the entire command mounted, and in line with two pieces of artillery, and moving toward the river, in the direction of Gall's camp. Here was a splendid opportunity for a repetition of the Custer Massacre. Not more than four hundred soldiers going out to do battle with fully that many Indians, who had the advantage of being afoot, and protected by heavy timber and dense underbrush, while the soldiers had to advance, mounted, in plain view of the Indians, across an open field of ice.

"Quick! Mount and go!" said I. "You must reach your camp before those soldiers are within rifle range, and no matter what happens, don't you allow one of your warriors to lift a gun! And as soon as possible, display a white flag, and surrender. I will take you to Buford, nevertheless." He threw himself on to the back of the beautiful black pony and was away with the swiftness of a deer. Calling Patriarch Crow, who had been standing a little way off, I climbed with him to the top of the trader's store, from which point we could watch the movement of the troops, and had a plain view of the timber in which the Indians were encamped. Our interest was centered on the movements of Chief Gall, for everything depended on his ability to reach the camp, which was only about a mile and a half distant, before the Indians were aroused by the approach of the troops. Fortunately for the troops, he got there in time, but none too soon, for he had no sooner disappeared in the timber that hid the camp, than the troops formed in line of battle, wheeled the two pieces of artillery into position, and without making any attempt whatever to hold a parly with the Indians, with a view to a peaceful surrender, immediately opened fire on the camp, firing volley after volley into the camp, from the small arms, and at the same time shelling the woods with the field pieces. I have never ceased to wonder at the almost superhuman power exerted by Chief Gall over his people, which enabled him to hold them from returning the attack, and I wonder more that he restrained himself; but he is a man of strong determination, and having made up his mind to quit the war path, nothing could turn him from his purpose. He soon appeared, emerging from the timber, in the very face of the troops, waving a piece of white muslin at the end of a pole, when the firing ceased, and the soldiers took possession of the camp. Not a shot had been fired by the Indians, and though repeated volleys had been fired into the camp by the soldiers, only one squaw was killed and one warrior wounded. When the news reached the States, it was a battle, and Major Ilges got his full mead of praise.

Sioux Village Moving.   *George Catlin*

The attack upon the camp was made early in the morning, at a time when many of the warriors were taking their ponies out into the hills to graze. These heard the heavy firing and attempted to return, but finding the camp in the possession of the troops, fled westwardly, up the Missouri Valley, in the direction of Sitting Bull's camp. Our position on the roof of the store, enabled us to see the fugitives, as, one after another, they flew past the openings in the timber that skirted the banks of the river. This was an important discovery. These Indians would undoubtedly go to Sitting Bull's camp, and being ignorant of the real situation, their report would certainly stampede the entire outfit, and they would all go back across the Canadian border, in which case I might abandon all hope of effecting their surrender. Prompt and ener-getic action alone would avert the threat-ened misfortune.

Patriarch Crow, by the kind treatment he had received at Fort Buford, was com-pletely won over to the side of the Govern-ment, and I knew that I could rely on him in this emergency; and he proved himself worthy of my confidence. He saw the diffi-culty, and understood as well as I, what the result would be, unless something was done, and, therefore, when I urged him to fly to the camp and do all he could to prevent a stampede, he was ready to go, and though he was evidently indignant at the action of the troops, immediately mounted his horse, and after receiving an assurance from me, that I would follow as soon as circumstances would permit, he departed, saying, that I would either find the camp or his dead body at the mouth of Milk River.

6

I remained three days at Poplar Creek, assisting in the removal of Gall's band to Fort Buford, transportation having been provided by an order from General Terry. The weather becoming intensely cold, there was much suffering among the women and children, many of them having their feet, hands and faces frozen; but all received most excellent care as soon as they arrived at Buford, and were placed under the care of Major Brotherton.

When I started again for Sitting Bull's camp, I went in a government sleigh, with the dauntless Day again as teamster, and this time I was accompanied by Mr. Charles Deihl, of the *Chicago Times*.

On the evening of the second day out from Poplar Creek, we stopped for the night in a deserted cabin in the woods by the river. Near by, I found encamped three or four families, who had the day before left Sitting Bull's camp, from whom I received important information. They said that the fugitives had reached the camp and spread the news of the attack by the troops at Poplar Creek, alarming the Indians, who, with Sitting Bull in the lead, began a hasty retreat to the north, so that the whole tribe was in motion, when Patriarch Crow rode furiously into their midst, calling loudly for his four brothers and their friends to rally around him. He was quickly surrounded by an eager multitude, anxious to hear what he would say. He declared to them that the fugitives were cowards who had run without reason; that they had fled before they knew what the firing was about. He denounced them all for allowing their fears to get the better of their reason, and sarcastically inquired how many of them were wounded, and how many had been slain, defending the camp. He then declared that since not one of them had had the courage to protest against this unreasonable, cowardly flight, therefore, not one of them was worthy of chieftainship. That whoever he might be, who had heretofore assumed that honor, he must now, and forever after, be silent; for the time had now come when the voice of the Patriarch Crow should be heard, and that he would be obeyed, none who know him would doubt, and then calling upon all in whose hearts his words had found lodgment to follow him. He then rode rapidly to the head of the flying column, followed by all the warriors who had heard him and together, they compelled everyone to come back and re-occupy the camp they had so recently deserted.

The next act of Patriach Crow, I suspect was promted by his ambition to succeed permanently to the chieftainship, and believing that this could be more easily accomplished by destroying entirely the influence of Sitting Bull, and driving him back to Canada, which would leave him, Patriarch Crow, without a rival in that division of the tribe. Be that as it may, I could not be otherwise than well pleased with what he did, considering all the circumstances.

Early the next morning, the Patriarch Crow compelled Sitting Bull to remove his tepee to a small opening in the timber, three hundred yards away from the main camp, which being done, he then mounted his horse, and riding up and down through the camp, he called on all who were cowards, to remove their tepees to the opening, with Sitting Bull, but those who were not cowards, should remain where they were. Forty-three-families, all told, took their place in the opening, leaving about three hundred with Patriarch Crow, who then told Sitting Bull to go, and not to halt until he had crossed the Canadian border; and he went, and soon disappeared in the wind driven snows of the north. Patriarch Crow then commanded the initial movement toward Fort Buford, and encamped, where I met him in the evening, about three miles below the mouth of Milk River, they having made only about six miles on the first days' march under the new, self-appointed chief.

The march from that point to Fort Buford was uninterrupted, but was necessarily slow, in consequence of the deep snows and extreme cold weather. At a point thirty miles west of Wolf Point, I was met by a train of thirty government wagons and sleighs, sent out by Major Brotherton. These proved of valuable service, and greatly expedited our march, enabling us to reach Buford on about the tenth of February, where the hostiles under the Patriarch Crow, formally surrendered to Major Brotherton, and were placed, with the Chief Gall's band, in winter camp, to await transportation in the spring to Standing Rock Agency.

I now proposed to make one more trip to Woody Mountain, for Sitting Bull, but General Terry regarded the work as completed. All of the hostiles, with the exception of the small number of forty-three families, having surrendered, Sitting Bull was left without a following, and his power for evil being entirely destroyed, it was a matter of indifference to our government if he himself never came in, and this view was also held by General Sheridan. Therefore, no further steps were taken to induce him to surrender, save that I sent him word by an Indian, that he could follow his people to Fort Buford, where he would receive the same treatment received by them, and that I would be glad to have him do so, and this he finally did, arriving in Fort Buford in July, with about thirty-five families, a few families having remained, and still remain, in Canada; among the number, the intrepid Black Bull, and my old friend, The Lung, who chose to cast their fortunes with the Red River Half-Breeds of the north.

The other hostiles had previously been removed to Standing Rock, to which place we followed with Sitting Bull, whose subsequent history is a matter with which the public are acquainted.

31. The Capture of Tiburcio Vasquez

BY BEN C. TRUMAN

EDITOR'S NOTE: California had her share of bandits in the wild days, among whom Tiburcio Vasquez (1835-1875) and Joaquin Murietta were the most notorious. The following is an account of the capture of Vasquez which appeared in the Los Angeles *Star* on May 16, 1874. The *Star* also published interviews with the bandit. The author was the editor of the *Star* at that time. Vasquez was hanged in San Jose in 1875.

As the clerk of the City Council was about to read the last communication to that body yesterday, about 4.30 P. M., an unusual stir about the front attracted some attention, and in a moment more, City Fathers, City Clerk, City Surveyor, City Reporters, and everybody else in the room, were making for the front door. Instinctively we supposed Vasquez had something to do with the fuss. We were right. Vasquez was lying pale and bloody in a light wagon, in front of the entrance to the city jail. A surging crowd was gathering around. Two men who were taken in his company, at the time of the capture, were taken into jail and locked up. In a moment after Vasquez himself was lifted from the wagon and was borne into the city prison. Dr. Wise presented himself; and, assisted by several medical gentlemen of this city, rendered the wounded robber such surgical services as he required. The result of the examination showed a buck-shot in his left arm, one in the left leg, one in left side of head, one in front of the pectoral region, passing out under the left arm, and one in the left arm. The balls were extracted, the wounds pronounced not dangerous, and opinion expressed that he would be well in a few days.

During the time referred to, Mr. Miles, who lent Vasquez his watch out in the San Gabriel region, last April, came into the room. He was at once recognized by the wounded man—in fact, the recognition was mutual. Mr. Hartley, the Chief of Police, had taken Mr. Miles' watch into his keeping. It was returned to the proper owner. Mr. M.'s chain was missing, however; Vasquez said nothing about it at the time, but after Dr. Wise and his associates had dressed his wounds, he requested Dr. Wise to take his porte-monnaie from his pocket. It was done, and Vasquez opened it, and handed the missing chain to Dr. W., and requested him to return it to its rightful owner. He remarked, "it belongs to him *now*," emphasizing the last word, as much as to say, "he

might have whistled for it if they had not caught me." While his wounds were dressed, Mr. B. F. Hartley, Chief of Police, one of his captors, asked him why he (Vasquez) had asked him (Hartley) what his name was. Quoth Vasquez, "Usted es un hombre valiente lo mismo que yo." (You are a brave man like myself.) He bore the probing and opening of his wounds without a murmur. In personal appearance this robber chief is anything but remarkable. Take away the expression of his eye, furtive, snaky, and cunning, and he would pass unnoticed in a crowd. Not more than five feet seven inches in height, and of very spare build, he looks little like a man who could create a reign of terror. His forehead is low and slightly retreating to where it is joined by a thick mass of raven black and very coarse hair; his mustache is by no means luxuriant, his chin whiskers passably full; but his sunken cheeks are only lightly sprinkled with beard; his lips are thin and bloodless, his teeth white, even and firm; his left eye is slightly sunken. He always dresses neatly and well, most commonly wearing a black sack coat, white shirt, and narrow rimmed "nobby" hat. He has small and elegantly shaped feet, which he encases in fine boots. His feet and hands are small. Perhaps 130 pounds is as much as he weighs. His light build made it an easy task for the horse that bore him to perform forced marches.

Such is a brief sketch of the bandit. He is caged now, and will doubtless answer for his crimes. The reign of terror which he has been answerable for is at an end. No attempt was made to interfere with the law by the crowd which surrounded the jail. A feeling more of relief than of revenge or exultation seemed to be uppermost in the minds of all. If we interpret it rightly, it arose from a firm belief that, if convicted of the offenses with which he stands charged, he will receive just punishment. Woe be, however, to the man who names himself as his successor, and endeavors to emulate his deeds of violence. The people of this part of the State will stand no more brigandage. Now that the leader is captured, we are at liberty to say that for weeks we have been told time and again, by men who seldom counsel violence, that the taking of human life again by Vasquez and his gang would be the signal for retaliatory measures, which would be fearful in their consequences. Chaves, and the fugitive members of Vasquez' gang, may well pause before they seek revenge, or perpetrate any more robberies. The history of the capture of Vasquez forms one of the most interesting chapters in criminal matters that has ever been written. The captured robber has defied pursuit, mocked at strategy, and eluded for months the skill of the bravest and most celebrated detectives on the coast. We do not believe that, once afoot or on horseback, with three hours the start of his pursuers, Cuban bloodhounds would have compassed his capture. A sudden, well arranged surprise was the only chance to secure him. It has been effected, and in the manner hereinafter related.

After the futile pursuit of the robber up the Tejunga Pass, and over the ground described by the *Star,* in its full account of the chase inaugurated after the Repetto robbery, Mr. Wm. Rowland, Sheriff of this county, came to the conclusion that any further prosecution of the quest in that manner and direction was a waste of time, energy and money. His subordinates were ordered to desist, and many and loud were the complaints lodged against him for inaction and inefficiency.

Mr. Rowland, however, kept on the even tenor of his way; and availing himself of every possible source of information, at length became satisfied that the long-sought-for prize was within his grasp, and he quietly arranged for his capture. On Wednesday night he received positive information of the whereabouts of Tiburcio Vasquez. He had kept for some time a list of names from which to choose a party to undertake the arrest. He organized his party as follows: Mr. Albert Johnson, Under Sheriff; Major H. M. Mitchell, attorney-at-law of this city; Mr. J. S. Bryant, City Constable; Mr. E. Harris, policeman; Mr. W. E. Rogers, of the Palace Saloon; Mr. D. K. Smith, a citizen of this county; Mr. B. F. Hartley, Chief of Police and Deputy City Marshal, and Mr. Beers, of San Francisco, the special correspondent of the San Francisco *Chronicle.* Sheriff Rowland intended to accompany the party, but his informant told him emphatically if he left the city and was not seen early in the morning, unless Vasquez was captured at the earliest hour, the game would break cover and be over the hills and far away. The sequel, as shown by the arrest of Greek George, which we will refer to again, proved the soundness of the advice. The horses for the pursuing party were sent one by one on Wednesday evening to the corral of Mr. Jones, on Spring street, near Seventh. One by one the above party met at the rendezvous; and at 1:30 A. M. on Thursday the party of eight were in the saddle and on their way to the spot, which for many years will be pointed out as the scene of the capture.

Greek George's ranch lies about ten miles due west from Los Angeles. It is situated at the base of a mountain, one of a series of semi-detached spurs, between which there are a dozen trails, known only to the *habitués* of that section, which afford egress to the San Fernando plains. The dwelling-house on the ranch is an old adobe, forming a letter L, the foot of the letter facing the mountain range, the shank lying north and south. Behind the house, and but a short distance from it, runs a comparatively disused road, leading from the San Vincente through La Brea rancho, and thence to this city, behind this road the mountains, and in front of the house a small monte of willows grown up around a spring, and beyond these a rolling plain stretching to the ocean. At the northern end of the building was a room used by the robber as a store room and as a lookout. A window facing the north, afforded him an outlook for miles to the east (toward this city), and for a good distance west. No chance for an ordinary surprise for armed horsemen from either direction. The middle section of the western part (the shank), of the house, was used as a dining-room, where the bandit was eating when surprised, surrounded, and captured. A small apartment at the south end was used as a kitchen, in which was a small opening through which Vasquez made a leap for life, when he found himself in the toils. His horse was staked out a few rods to the northwest of the building when the event occurred. Let us see how the capture was effected.

As before stated, the party left Los Angeles at 1:30, Thursday morning. About 4 A. M., they arrived at the bee ranch of Major Mitchell, one of the party. There they took breakfast, and held a council of war. The bee ranch is up a small cañon, off the usual lines of travel, visited occasionally by neighboring ranchmen for wood. After consultation, Messrs. Albert Johnson, Mitchell, and Sam Bryant left the party and followed a mountain road about one mile and a half, until they came to a point opposite Greek George's ranch. Turning square north they

climbed to a point where, with a field glass, they could obtain an unobstructed view of the covert. A heavy fog rendered satisfactory observations impracticable for hours. When it lifted they saw enough to convince them that their game was at the very point designated. A horse answering the description of that ridden by the outlaw was picketed out as above stated. Twice they saw a man answering the description of Vasquez, leading him to the Monte, and returning, picket him out as before. Another man on horseback went in pursuit of a white horse which tallied with the description given of a horse belonging to the gang. Various plans for the capture of Vasquez were discussed by the trio, but finally it was decided that Mr. Johnson should return to the bee ranch and marshal his forces, while Mitchell and Smith went in pursuit of the horseman referred to, they believing him to be Chaves, the Lieutenant of Vasquez.

Arrived there, unexpectedly, and it almost seems providentally sent allies presented themselves. A wagon driven by a Californian, and in which there was another man (also a native), was driven up, from the direction of Greek George's. It was a box wagon. It was not long before the plan of capture was decided upon. Six of the party remained. The extra man with the wagon made seven. Mr. Hartley, who speaks Spanish fluently, was instructed to inform the driver that he was to turn his horses' heads, allow all six of the party and his extra man to lie down in the wagon bed, and then drive back to Greek George's, and as close to the house as possible; that if he gave a sign or made an alarm, his life would pay the forfeit. In due time the house was reached. In a moment the party were out of the wagon and on their feet with shot guns and rifles cocked and ready for what might offer. Mr.

Hartley and Mr. Beers went to the west side of the house, the other four to the southern, passing round the eastern end. The foremost of the party had hardly reached the door opening into the dining room, when a woman opened it partly. Seeing the armed party of four approaching, she gave an exclamation of fright, and attempted to close it. The party burst in, Mr. Harris leading the way, and seeing the retreating form of the prize they sought leaving the table, and plunging through the door leading into the kitchen.

Harris was close upon his heels, and Vasquez, with the agility of a mountain cat, had jumped through the narrow window, or rather opening which admitted the light, when Harris fired at the vanishing form with his Henry rifle, exclaiming, "There he goes through the window." The party left the house as precipitately as they entered it. Vasquez stood for a second of time irresolute. Whether to seek cover in the monte or rush for his horse, seemed the all important question. He seemed to decide for the horse —doubtless he would have given ten kingdoms if he had had them, to be astride of him—and started, when Mr. Harris fired; turning, he sought another direction, when one after another, shot after shot, showed him the utter hopelessness of escape. He had already been wounded, just how severely we have already told. He had fallen, but recovered himself; blood was spouting from his shoulder and streaming from his wounds. He threw up his hands, approached the party, and said with a cold, passionate smile wreathing his thin lips, "Boys you have done well; I have been a d—d fool; but it is all my own fault." He was taken to the courtyard on the southern side of the house, and laid upon an extemporized pallet. Not a murmur, scarce a contortion of the visage, be-

spoke either pain, remorse, or any other emotion of the mind or soul. Mr. Beers says: "While looking for his wounds, I placed my hand over his heart, and found its pulsations gave no signs of excitement. His eye was bright, and there was a pleasant smile on his face, and no tremor in his voice. He was polite and thankful for every attention. Although he thought and said that he was about to die—"Gone up," as he expressed it —his expression of countenance was one of admiration of our determined attack and our good luck.

The house was entered, and a young man, whose name is supposed to be Labrado, was captured in the north room before described. This was the arsenal of the robber gang. Three Henry rifles and one Spencer, all of the latest patterns and finest workmanship, besides other arms, were found there and taken possession of. Major Mitchell and Mr. Smith overhauled the party they went in pursuit of, and brought him back. His name is given as Reales, but he protests against the idea of his complicity with the bandits. How long the associates of the captured robber will baffle pursuit cannot be known. They are known, and their arrest is but a matter of time. It is to be regretted that Major Mitchell, who has been indefatigable in the pursuit of Vasquez, was deprived of the satisfaction of being in at the surrender. We stated that it was well that Mr. Rowland did not start out with the party. Greek George, whose real name we are informed is George Allen, was designated as the party who was harboring Vasquez. Vasquez was found there, that is certain. Allen was in town Wednesday night, and while he supposed he was watching Rowland's movements, he was being watched with a degree of wide-awakefulness he could hardly conceive of. He was solicitously attended in his

peregrinations throughout the city yesterday. Had he attempted to revisit his sub-
urban home before the consummation of
Sheriff Rowland's plans, he would have
learned the meaning of a writ of *ne exeat*
which would unquestionably have been extemporized for the occasion.

As it was, when his distinguished sometime guest had been, by the physicians in
attendance, prepared to receive visitors, Mr.
Allen was brought into his presence by
Sheriff Rowland. He was so much affected
by the sight that he forgot to express his sympathy. Had Mr. Rowland not been seen by
Mr. Allen yesterday, the latter would probably have remembered something which
required his presence at the ranch. His
mayor domo will have to look after things
at Greek George's until that gentleman ex-
plains how it came to pass that his house was
turned into a rendezvous for cut-throats and
robbers. Too much praise cannot be
awarded to our Sheriff for the quiet but effective manner in which he has carried out
his well-conceived plans. It would simply be
invidious to attempt to particularize any
member of the capturing party. All that we
have been able to learn upon the subject,
from any and every source, goes to show that
each man acted with consummate courage,
coolness and discretion. To all intents and
purposes the approach to the house where
the capture was effected was a deliberate approach to a masked battery. That Vasquez
was there, was a matter which admitted of
no doubt. How many of his fellow desperadoes were with him, no man of the party
could know. How well he was prepared to
"welcome them with bloody hands to hospitable graves," nobody could know; but
determined to capture him, if possible, they
"went for him," and got him.

His coolness in the hour of capture, the
fortitude and the uncomplaining stoicism
with which he bore his wounds, all go to
show that whatever opinion as to his bravery
may have become current with the public,
he is a man who would have sold his life
dearly if he had had a ghost of a show. We
verily believe that if he had had a knife or
pistol on his person he would have sought
and found death rather than capture. No
posse of armed men could have approached
the well chosen fastness which he had selected. Strategy and a fortunate concur-
rence of circumstances placed him in the
power of the law.

While being brought into town he exchanged notes with Major Mitchell relative
to the Tejunga Pass pursuit. He told the
Major that twice during the pursuit he was
near enough to kill him and his party if he
had desired so to do, and convinced Major
Mitchell of the truth of his assertion. Vasquez protested that he had never killed a
man; that the murders at Tres Pinos were
committed before his arrival; but he admitted that he led the party who committed the
outrages away from that point. After his capture he inquired who was the leader of the
party, and upon being told that Mr. Albert
Johnson was, he delivered to him his memorandum book, and commenced to make a
statement to him, not knowing at the time
but that his wounds were mortal.

His first declaration related to his two
children, when the preparations for the
march to the city being completed, the record was abruptly brought to a close. He
showed Mr. Johnson the photographs of the
children, and enclosed in the same envelope
with them was a wavy tress of black and silky
hair, bound in a blue ribbon. This he requested Mr. Johnson to preserve carefully
and return to him when he should require
or demand it. What secret heart history is

bound up with this mute memorial of days when perhaps the outlaw had his dream of home and all that makes life beautiful, no one can tell.

At a late hour we visited him in prison. Lying upon his pallet, to all human appearances a doomed man, a price set upon his head, an outlaw and an outcast, he received us and a number of other visitors with an ease and grace and elegance which would have done no discredit to any gentleman in the land, reclining upon his *fauteil* in his dressing-room. After answering quietly and politely a number of questions, he requested those present to retire, as he had something to communicate to the Sheriff relative to certain stolen property, excepting us, however, as a member of the press. We did not remain, however, to hear his disclosures. His memorandum book, among many other things, contained a great many extracts, clipped from the *Star, La Cronica* and other papers, containing accounts of his various exploits. They went to show conclusively that he has been furnished regularly by confederates with everything that could interest him or keep him informed of the measures set on foot to effect his capture.

On a small scrap of paper, dated April the 3d, was a memorandum in the Spanish language, in which the name of Repetto occurred. Whether it was a reminder of his intended visit to that gentleman, or a credit for the amount of the forced loan he exacted from him, we do not know. Now, that Vasquez is safely lodged in jail, all will doubtless agree that Sheriff Rowland and the actual captors of the bandit, the cool-headed and intrepid Albert Johnson, Under Sheriff, and his brave, energetic, and fearless associates, officers Hartley, Harris, and Bryant, Major Mitchell, and Messrs. Rogers, Smith, and Beers, are entitled to great cred-

it. They have been unceasing in their efforts to effect the capture of Vasquez from the time of the Repetto outrage, and the result is told as above.

William Rowland, Sheriff of Los Angeles County, is a native of this county; is about thirty-three years of age, and is now serving his second term. We presume that his successful organization of the hunt for Vasquez will not materially interfere with his prospects for re-election, if he should desire again to become a candidate.

Albert Johnston, Under Sheriff, is a New Yorker by birth, a brother of G. A. Johnston, of San Diego, and has been a resident of Los Angeles for about five years, having held the office of Under Sheriff ever since Mr. Rowland was elected. He came to this State when a mere youth, and went back to the East and remained several years, but like all good Californians had to come back. He is of about the same age as his principal.

Officer Harris is thirty-two years old; is well-known in this city, where he has lived for six years, and has been on the police force here for four years. He has detective qualities second to no man in the State; is brave, cool, and energetic, and just the man to have associated in such a hazardous undertaking.

Officer Hartley is a brave, modest gentleman, about thirty-seven years old, and a model member of our police force, upon which he has served efficiently and faithfully for two years. He has resided in Los Angeles for five years, and is very much respected.

Constable Sam Bryant is also one of the best officers Los Angeles has ever had. He, too, is a modest, brave, and efficient officer, about thirty-five years of age.

Major Mitchell, soldier, lawyer, miner, apiarist, and journalist, is a young man of talent and education. With what valor and intrepidity he followed the flag of the Southern confederacy may be seen in his persistent and unrivaled pursuit of the robber chief, from the Repetto event until the achievement yesterday.

Mr. W. E. Rogers is a young man of thirty-two years of age, twenty-four of which he lived in San Francisco. He has been associated with the Sheriff's party from the start, and he is as brave as he is genteel and unostentatious. He is part proprietor of the Palace saloon, and has made hosts of friends here since he took up his residence among us.

Mr. Smith is, we believe, a farmer, and resides outside of the city. When Mr. Smith

went to Greek George's house, a few days ago, to inquire if he wanted any barley cut, the latter not in the least suspected that the would-be hay maker was taking a survey of the premises for Mr. Rowland, so that, when the time arrived for the attack, it could be made without confusion and without loss of life, if possible, to the besieging party.

Mr. Beers, the correspondent of the Chronicle, is represented as being as gallant as his fellows, and marched up to the scene of attack with rifle in hand, prepared for any emergency.

Thus endeth the chapter of the pursuit and capture of TIBURCIO VASQUEZ!

32. Wanted: Jesse James

EDITOR'S NOTE: One of America's most notorious outlaws, Jesse Woodson James (1847-1882) at fifteen joined the guerrilla forces of C. W. Quantrell for the Confederacy. At the war's end, after surrendering he was treacherously shot and badly wounded. In the following year he became an outlaw, and in 1867 became the undisputed leader of a gang of bank and train robbers. As a result of the offer of $10,000 for his capture dead or alive, two members of his gang, Robert and Charles Ford, shot and killed him in his home at St. Joseph, Missouri, on April 3, 1882. Jesse's brother, Frank, a member of the gang, surrendered shortly after Jesse's death but was never brought to trial.

PROCLAMATION OF THE GOVERNOR
OF MISSOURI
REWARDS FOR THE ARREST OF
EXPRESS AND TRAIN ROBBERS.
State of Missouri
Executive Department.

WHEREAS, It has been made known to me, as the Governor of the State of Missouri, that certain parties, whose names are to me unknown, have confederated and banded themselves together for the purpose of committing robberies within this State; and

WHEREAS, Said parties did, on or about the Eighth day of October, 1879, stop a train near Glendale, in the County of Jackson, in said State, and, with force and violence, take, steal and carry away the money and other express matter being carried thereon; and

WHEREAS, On the fifteenth day of July, 1881, said parties and their confederates did stop a train upon the line of the Chicago, Rock Island and Pacific Railroad, near Winston, in the County of Daviess, in said State, and, with force and violence, take, steal, and carry away the money and other express matter being carried thereon; and, in perpetration of the robbery last aforesaid, the parties engaged therein did kill and murder

Jesse James

COURTESY BETTMANN ARCHIVE

one WILLIAM WESTFALL, the conductor of the train together with one JOHN McCULLOCH, who was at the time in the employ of said company, then on said train; and WHEREAS, Frank James and Jesse W. James stand indicted in the Circuit Court of said Daviess County, for the murder of John W. Sheets, and the parties engaged in the rob-

beries and murders aforesaid have fled from justice and have absconded and secreted themselves:

Now, THEREFORE, in consideration of the premises and in lieu of all other rewards heretofore offered, for the arrest or conviction of the parties aforesaid, or either of them, by any person or corporatior, I, THOMAS T. CRITTENDEN, Governor of the State of Missouri, do hereby offer a reward of five thousand dollars ($5,000.00) for the arrest and conviction of each person participating in either of the robberies or murders aforesaid, excepting the said FRANK JAMES and JESSE W. JAMES; and for the arrest and delivery of said

FRANK JAMES and JESSE W. JAMES,

and each or either of them, to the sheriff of said Daviess County, I hereby offer a reward of five thousand dollars ($5,000.00) and for the conviction of either of the parties last aforesaid of participation in either of the murders or robberies above mentioned, I hereby offer a further reward of five thousand dollars ($5,000.00).

IN TESTIMONY WHEREOF, I have hereunto set my hand and caused to be affixed the GREAT SEAL of the State of Missouri. Done at the City of Jefferson on this 28th day of July, A. D. 1881.

(SEAL)   THOMAS T. CRITTENDEN
By the Governor:
MICHAL K. McGRATH, Sec'y of State.

33. Some Exploits of the James Brothers

BY J. W. BUEL

1. THE ATTACK ON THE SAMUELS RESIDENCE

WILLIAM PINKERTON, a brother of the chief detective, was sent to Kansas City immediately with five of the most trusted men in the force. Upon arriving at that place the sheriff of Clay county was sent for, after which twelve citizens of known pluck and reliability were engaged to watch the Samuels homestead and report from hour to hour by a rapid means of communication, which had been established. The greatest secrecy was enjoined upon all engaged in the undertaking and every possible precaution was taken to prevent any alarm reaching the bandits.

On the afternoon of January 25th, Jesse and Frank James were both seen in the yard fronting the Samuels residence and report of this quickly reached the sheriff and Mr. Pinkerton who were in Liberty. Arrangements were made for the immediate capture of the two bandits, who it was confidently supposed would spend the night in their mother's house. Accordingly the two officers rode to Kearney late in the afternoon, where they organized a party of twelve men who were to assist them, and preparing several balls of cotton saturated with turpentine and two hand-grenades, the well armed body of men proceeded to the Samuels residence, which they reached about midnight. A reconnoissance was first made with great care for indications of possible surprise, and after completely surrounding the house four of the men, with turpentine balls, were sent forward to open the attack. A window in the kitchen of the residence was stealthily approached, but in the act of raising it an old colored woman who had for many years been a house servant in the family, was awakened, and she at once gave the alarm. But the window was forced up and the two lighted balls were thrown into the room, and as the flames shot upward, threatening destruction to the house and its contents, the family were speedily aroused and efforts were made to extinguish the fire. At the moment every member of the household, consisting of Mr. and Mrs. Samuels, a son eight years of age, and the daughter, Miss Susie, and the old colored woman had partially subdued the flames, one of the detectives, or at least one of the party leading the attack, flung a hand-grenade into the room among the affrighted occupants, and a heavy explosion was the prelude to the dreadful havoc made by that instrument of death. A scream of anguish succeeded the report and groans from within, which, without any evidence of the outlaws' presence, convinced the detectives and citizen's posse that they had committed a grave and horrible crime; so, without examining the premises further the party withdrew, apparently with the fear that the inexcusable deed they had just committed would be avenged speedily if they tarried in the vicinity.

When the light was lighted by Dr. Samuels he found his little boy in the agonies of death, having received a terrible wound in the side from the exploded shell. Mrs. Samuels' right arm had been shattered, and hung helpless by her side; but she forgot her own misfortune in the anguish she suffered at seeing the dying struggles of her little boy. What a terrible night was that memorable 25th of January to the Samuels family! Alone with their dead boy, whom they worshipped, and with a desperately wounded mother, who would certainly have bled to death but for the thoughtfulness of the old colored servant who hastily bandaged the arm and staunched the flow of the crimson life-current.

The funeral of the innocent victim did not take place until the second day after the midnight attack, and then Mrs. Samuels, who had suffered an amputation of the injured member, was too greatly prostrated to attend and witness the last service over her darling boy, but the remains were accompanied to the grave by a very large body of sympathizing people of the neighborhood.

This unfortunate and indefensible attack, for a time allayed public animosity against the James Boys and turned the sympathy of people in western Missouri somewhat in their favor. Those who had been most earnest in their desire to see Jesse and Frank James brought to punishment, began to think more lightly of their crimes, attributing them partly, at least, to the manner in which they had been hunted and persecuted. It is a notorious fact that for some time this sentiment predominated in Clay and Jackson counties, and the same feeling extended to other parts of the State, and in March following led to the introduction of an amnesty bill in the Legislature, granting immunity for past offenses committed by

Jesse and Frank James, Coleman Younger, James Younger and Robert Younger. The bill was introduced by Gen. Jeff. Jones, of Callaway county, and contained a provisional clause that amnesty would be granted the parties named in the instrument for all offenses committed during the war, provided they would surrender to the lawful authorities and submit to such proceedings as might be brought against them in the several States for crimes charged against them since the war. After a stormy debate the bill was defeated, although had it passed none of the bandits named would have accepted the terms, for surrender meant either execution or life imprisonment. A rejection of the terms of surrender, by the Legislature, afforded a fresh pretext, however, to the bandits to pursue their crimes of blood and pillage, and it was not long before the country was again startled by the daring deeds of the outlaws.

2. ASSASSINATION OF DANIEL ASKEW

IMMEDIATELY after the defeat of the "outlaw amnesty bill," as it was called, the brigands planned the execution of new and direful schemes, one of which involved the assassination of a respectable citizen of Clay county.

The James Boys concluded, for reasons known only to themselves, that Mr. Daniel Askew was a member of the posse which made the attack on the Samuels residence, and this belief was justification sufficient, in their estimation, for murdering that gentleman; but the plan of its execution was equally as dastardly as the casting of the hand-grenade blindly and savagely among the several members of Dr. Samuels' family. The circumstances of the assassination were as follows: Mr. Askew was an unpretentious farmer, living about four miles from Kearney, in a neat frame house, but with no neighbors nearer than one mile. He had returned home from Liberty, late in the afternoon of April 12th, 1875, and after eating supper took a bucket and went to the spring, which was about fifty yards from the house, after water. This was about eight o'clock in the evening, but the moon was shining brightly and objects were plainly discernible. He returned from the spring with the water and sat the bucket upon a shelf on the porch, after which he proceeded to take a drink, but as he was in the act of lifting the cup to his mouth, three sharp shots rang out upon the still air and Mr. Askew plunged forward on his face dead, the three bullets having taken fatal effect upon his person, one entering the brain and the two others reaching vital spots in his body.

At the sound of the shots and the heavy fall on the porch, Mr. Askew's wife and daughter rushed out of the house just in time to see three men steal out from behind the cover of a large woodpile in front of the porch, and regain their horses and ride swiftly away. The three assassins were undoubtedly Jesse and Frank James and Clell Miller, for within an hour after the murder these three met a gentleman upon the highway and informed him of Mr. Askew's fate, and told him the murder was in consequence of the acts of Pinkerton's detectives.

This cowardly act, by which a peaceable citizen had been made to surrender up his life for the sake of a savage revenge, destroyed again every spark of sympathy for the desperadoes, and the determination for their capture was renewed. Armed posses of Clay county citizens set out in search of the assassins, but the pursuit was in vain, and after a week of earnest effort, finding no

trace of the brigands, the party returned to their homes, each one recking how soon his turn might come to add to the gory record of the remorseless freebooters.

3. THE SAN ANTONIO STAGE ROBBERY

AFTER the murder of Mr. Askew, the bandits, in anticipation of renewed efforts to effect their capture, left Missouri and visited their old haunts in the southwest. They spent several days in the Indian Territory for the purpose of learning with what persistency and the character of the search being made by the authorities. Finding that all effort at their apprehension was confined to western Missouri, the outlaws rode into Texas and soon formed a plan for robbing the stage running between San Antonio and Austin. To plan was to execute, and on the 12th of May, 1875, Jesse James, Clell Miller, Jim Reed and Cole and Jim Younger selected a spot on the highway, about twenty-three miles south-west of Austin, and there ambushed themselves to await the coming of the stage.

It was late in the evening, the sun just descending behind the hills and the chirrup of twilight insects had begun to echo in the solitude of the place. Eleven passengers, three of whom were ladies, were cheerily cracking jokes and relieving the discomforts of the journey by agreeable conversation. Suddenly the driver descried five horsemen riding out into the road one hundred yards ahead of the stage and advancing leisurely. Their appearance and conduct looked suspicious, but as no robberies had been perpetrated on the highway for many years, the driver did not realize what the act portended until, as the stage bowled up, the five men, drawing their pistols, commanded a halt. The order being accompanied by such persuasive authority of course the obedience of the driver was prompt. Then the passengers wondered what it meant, but before they could propound a question four of the brigands rode up on either side of the stage and ordered the inmates to get out. The women, seeing such cruel looking men and their fiercer looking pistols, screamed and scrambled over the male passengers with utter disregard of propriety, and created much confusion. Jesse James and Cole Younger did the talking for the bandits, and in courteous language assured the ladies they had nothing to fear provided the passengers acted with discretion. Soon the eleven but recently gay travelers were arranged in single file along the road behind the stage, and as not the slightest resistance was offered Frank James and Jim Younger had no difficulty in expeditiously relieving all the passengers of their money, watches and other valuables. Among the number was John Breckenridge, president of the First National Bank at San Antonio, from whom $1,000 were obtained; Bishop Gregg, of Austin, contributed his gold watch and nearly $50 in money, while from the other passengers sums from $25 to $50 were obtained.

Having completed the personal plunder, the bandits cut open the two mail bags from which a goodly sum of money was secured, but the amount has not been estimated. The haul aggregated, perhaps, $3,000, which they placed in a sack carried for the purpose, and then, bidding the passengers adieu, the border desperadoes rode swiftly into the shadows, leaving the surprised party to resume their journey in a less amiable mood.

4. THE GREAT TRAIN ROBBERY AT MUNCIE

NOTHING was heard of the bandits for several months after the stage robbery, and

their crimes were again relegated to partially forgotten incidents of the past. In December following, however, another attack by the outlaws refreshed the memory of their deeds and threw Missouri and Kansas into a fever of intense excitement.

The band of desperadoes, by some means known only to themselves, learned of an intended large shipment of gold-dust from Denver, via Kansas Pacific Railroad, and that it would be carried by a train arriving in Kansas City on a certain day. The place selected at which to intercept the train bearing the valuable shipment, was Muncie, a little station six miles west of Wyandotte, Kansas. There was a water tank near the place, at which the engines almost invariably stopped to take a fresh supply of water. At this point six bandits stationed themselves and awaited the train, which was not due until after nightfall. Prompt upon time the engine blew its shrill whistle, and then rolled up under the tank and stopped. In a moment the brigands left their place of concealment and boarded the train, one of them, Bill McDaniels, being deputed to cover and remain with the engineer and fireman. The robbers rushed through the cars and commanded every passenger to remain quiet under penalty of death. Two of them stood on the platform of the cars while the other three proceeded to the express car. The bandits presented their pistols at the head of the messenger and forced him to open the safe, from which the sum of $25,000 in money was taken and gold-dust valued at $30,000. This total sum secured was so large that no attempt was made to rob any of the passengers, and after the valuable plunder was placed in a sack, Jesse James blew a keen whistle and a moment after all the free-booters abandoned the train and regained their horses.

Soon as the passengers reached Wyandotte, which was speedily, the alarm was given, which spread to Kansas City, and another large body of men was sent in pursuit of the daring highwaymen. They chased the fugitives southward into Indian Territory, but the pursuit was abandoned in the Creek Nation, where all traces were blotted out.

About one month after this great robbery a police officer arrested Bill McDaniels in Kansas City, for drunkenness, his participation in the train plundering not then being suspected. But when searched at the police station a sheep-skin bag was found on his person filled with gold-dust. In addition to

this he had a large roll of money, and being known in Kansas City as a worthless fellow, suspicion was at once excited that he was a confederate of the train robbers. He was placed in the calaboose and allowed to sober up, and then taken upon a requisition to Lawrence, Kansas. On the following day after his arrest the city marshal and Con O'Hara, the detective, went into McDaniels' cell and spent two hours in a persistent endeavor to obtain a confession from him of his complicity in the robbery, or the names of those who committed the act. But he remained as silent as if he had lost the power of speech, and not a word concerning the

Jesse James Holding up a Train   COURTESY BETTMANN ARCHIVE

robbery did the officers ever hear from him. Two months after his apprehension, in taking him from the jail for trial, McDaniels broke from the deputy sheriff and escaped. After a week's search he was found, but resisting arrest, he was mortally wounded by a member of a citizens' posse named Bauermann. McDaniels died, however, refusing to reveal anything in regard to his confederates. It has since been ascertained, however, that those engaged in the Muncie robbery consisted of Jesse James, Arthur McCoy, Cole and Bob Younger, Clell Miller and McDaniels, the latter only being captured.

5. THE HUNTINGTON BANK ROBBERY

AFTER the train robbery the highwaymen separated, some going to Texas and others to Kentucky. In April, 1876, Frank James, Cole Younger, Tom McDaniels, a brother of Bill, and a small black-eyed fellow called Jack Keen, alias Tom Webb, confederated together for the purpose of perpetrating another bank robbery. Keen had been raised in the eastern part of Kentucky and was well acquainted with the mountainous regions of West Virginia and his native State. It was decided to attack and plunder the bank in Huntington, a town of 2,500 people, on the Ohio river, in West Virginia.

About the 1st of September the four bandits rode into the town under the leadership of Frank James and proceeded directly to the bank, which they reached at 2 P. M. Frank James and McDaniels dismounted, leaving Younger and Keen standing guard on the outside. When Frank and McDaniels entered the bank they found only R. T. Oney, the cashier, and a citizen who was making a deposit; these the robbers covered with their pistols and compelled the cashier to open the safe and deliver up all the money in the bank, amounting to $10,000. Having secured the booty the four outlaws rode rapidly out of town, not a single person in the place having the least suspicion of what occurred until Mr. Oney spread the news.

A posse of twenty-five citizens, headed by the sheriff, set out in pursuit of the bandits at three o'clock, one hour after the robbery was consummated, and followed the trail with the greatest persistency. The officers in other counties were notified by telegraph, and armed bodies of men were sent out from a dozen towns. One hundred miles southwest of Huntington the robbers were sighted and in an exchange of shots McDaniels was killed. This encouraged the pursuing party, who pressed the bandits so hard that they were forced to abandon their horses and take to the mountain fastnesses of Kentucky. The pursuit continued unabated for four weeks, and at length the outlaws were driven out of Kentucky and into Tennessee; here Keen was captured and taken back to Huntington, where he made a confession and was sentenced to eight years imprisonment in the penitentiary. Frank James and Cole Younger eluded pursuit and returned to the Indian Territory, where they met Jesse James and his band of highwaymen, and forthwith new plans were laid for another big robbery.

6. THE ROCKY CUT TRAIN ROBBERY

SEVEN months elapsed after the Muncie robbery before the desperate brigands, under the leadership of Jesse James, made another attempt to increase their ill-gotten gains. But in the meantime the band of highwaymen was increasing and organizing for another bold stroke. Many outlaws who had found safety in the Indian Nation were anxious to attach themselves to the James and Younger brothers, but very few were received. The noted bandits were excellent judges of human nature, and they were exceedingly careful not to repose confidence in any one who did not possess indisputable evidence of cunning and bravery; men who, in the event of capture, would not betray their comrades at any sacrifice. In July, 1876, arrangements were completed for rifling another treasure-laden train and the Missouri Pacific Railroad was chosen as the line for their operations. The reorganized party of highwaymen, consisting of Jesse and Frank James, Cole, Bob and Jim Younger, Clell Miller, Hobbs Kerry, Charlie Pitts and Bill Chadwell, nine in number, left their rendezvous in the Indian Territory and, riding separately, reached Otterville, Missouri, by a preconcerted understanding, on the 7th of July.

The capture and confession of Hobbs Kerry enables the giving of a minute narrative of all the circumstances connected with the robbery about to be related.

About one mile east of Otterville, a small station in Pittis county, is a place called Rocky Cut, which is a deep stone cleft, from which the train emerges only to strike the bridge across Otter creek. On the south side of the cut is a heavy wood, and in this the robbers concealed themselves to await the train which was not due there until nearly midnight. A watchman was stationed at the bridge, whom Charlie Pitts and Bob Younger arrested and, after taking his signal lantern and placing it in the track at the bridge approach, they securely tied the helpless fellow and then joined the main party. Hobbs Kerry and Bill Chadwell were detailed to watch the horses and keep them prepared for sudden flight.

As the train came dashing through the cut the engineer saw the danger signal and at once concluded something was wrong with the bridge, and he lost no time in having the brakes set and the engine reversed. The train came to a stop directly in the cut, and as it slowed up seven of the dare-devils leaped upon the cars and with one at each door, the robbers had no trouble in so intimidating the passengers as to prevent attack. Jesse James, the boldest of the bold, was the first to enter the express car, followed by Cole Younger. At the mouth of two heavy navy pistols the messenger was forced to open the safe, which contained fifteen thousand dollars in bank notes. This money was hastily thrown into a sack, and the shrill whistle was given by Jesse, which was the signal for the bandits to leave the train and mount. No effort was made to rob or harm any of the passengers, the single purpose of the bandits, agreed upon before the attack, was to secure only the valuables of the express.

When the train reached Tipton, report of the robbery was telegraphed to every station along the line, and also to St. Louis and Kansas City, and from these points all over the country.

Hobbs Kerry's statement is, that after the perpetration of the crime, the bandits rode southward together very rapidly until nearly daylight, when they entered a deep wood and there divided the money, after which the band rode off in pairs, except the James Boys and Cole Younger, who kept together. Kerry soon separated from Chadwell, who was his companion, and went to Fort Scott, and from there to Parsons, Kansas, thence to Joplin and then to Granby, where he remained for nearly a week, spending a great deal of money in gambling dens, and in his drunken moments let drop such remarks as led to the suspicion that he was a member of the gang that robbed the train. He next made a trip into Indian Territory, but after a short stay in that country he returned to Granby; there he was arrested in the latter part of August. The authorities had no difficulty in obtaining from Kerry the full particulars of the robbery and the names of his confederates. Detectives from all parts of the country, stimulated by the large rewards offered by the express company and Governor Hardin, set out in search of the bandits.

Every State was penetrated, every suspicious character put under surveillance, and all the ingenuity that could be devised by experienced hunters of criminals was exercised.

The James and Younger boys and Clell Miller, finding the pursuit at an end, returned from the Nation, whither they had first fled, and by stealthy night marches succeeded in reaching Jackson county, where they retired to the robbers' cave and were there safe from pursuit.

34. The Tragedy in Detail

A CONTEMPORARY NEWSPAPER ACCOUNT

SHOT

ST. JOSEPH, MO., April 3, 1882.—Between 8 and 9 o'clock this morning, Jesse James, the Missouri outlaw, before whose acts the deeds of Fra Diavolo, Dick Turpin, and Shinderbaunes dwindle into insignificance, was killed by a boy 20 years old, named Robert Ford, at his temporary residence at Thirteenth and Lafayette streets, in this city. In the light of all moral reasoning the shooting was wholly unjustifiable, but the law was vindicated. The large reward offered by the state for the body of the brigand, doubtless will go to the man who had the courage to draw a revolver on the notorious outlaw when his back was turned, as in this case. There is little doubt that the killing was a result of a premeditated plan formed by Robert and Charles Ford a few months ago. Charles had been an accomplice of Jesse James since the 3rd of last November, and entirely possessed his confidence. Robert, his brother, joined Jesse near Mrs. Samuels'

house, mother of the James boys, last Friday a week ago and accompanied Jesse and Charles to this city, Sunday, March 23. Jesse, his wife and two children removed from Kansas City, where they have lived several months, until they feared their whereabouts would be suspected, in a wagon to this city, arriving here November 8th, 1881, accompanied by Charles Ford, and rented a house on the corner of Lafayette and Twenty-first streets, where they stayed two months, when they secured the house at No. 1318 Lafayette street, formerly the property of Councilman Aylesbury, paying $14.00 a month for it, and giving the name of Thomas Howard.

THE HOUSE

is a one-story cottage, painted white, with green shutters, and romantically situated on the brow of a lofty eminence east of the city, commanding a fine view of the principal portions of the city, the river and railroads, and adapted as by nature for the perilous and desperate calling of James. Just east of the house is a deep gulch-like ravine, and beyond a broad expanse of open country backed by a belt of timber. The house, except from the west side, can be seen for several miles. There is a large yard attached to the cottage, and a stable where Jesse had been keeping two horses, which were found there this morning. Charles and Robert Ford have been occupying one of the rooms in the rear of the dwelling, and have secretly had an understanding to kill Jesse ever since last fall. A short time ago, before Robert had joined James, the latter proposed to rob the bank at Platte City. He said the Burgess murder trial would begin there today, and his plan was, if they could get another companion, to take a view of Platte City bank, and while arguments were being heard in the murder case, which would engage the attention of the citizens, boldly execute one of his favorite raids. Charles Ford approved of the plan and suggested his brother Robert as a companion worthy of sharing the enterprise with them. Jesse had met the boy at the latter's house, near Richmond, three years ago, and consented to see him. The two men accordingly went to where Robert was and arranged to have him accompany them to Platte City. As stated all three came to St. Joe a week ago Sunday. They remained at the house all week. Jesse thought it best Robert should not exhibit himself on the premises, lest the presence of three able-bodied men who were doing nothing should excite suspicion. They had fixed upon tonight to go to Platte City. Ever since the boys had been with Jesse, they had watched for

AN OPPORTUNITY TO SHOOT HIM,

but he was always so heavily armed that it was impossible to draw a weapon without

him seeing it. They declare they had no idea of taking him alive, considering the undertaking suicidal. The opportunity they had long wished for came this morning. Breakfast was over. Charles Ford and Jesse James had been in the stable currying their horses preparatory to their night ride. On returning to the room where Robert Ford was, Jesse said: "It's an awfully hot day." He pulled off his coat and vest and tossed them on the bed. Then he said, "I guess I'll take off my pistols for fear somebody will see them if I walk in the yard." He unbuckled the belt in which he carried two 45-caliber revolvers, one a Smith & Wesson, and the other a Colt, and laid them on the bed with his coat and vest. He then picked up a dusting brush with the intention of dusting some pictures which hung on the wall. To do this he got on a chair. His back was now turned to the brothers, who silently stepped between Jesse and his revolvers, and, at a motion from Charlie, they both drew their guns. Robert was the quickest of the two. In one instant he had the long weapon to a level with his eye with the muzzle no more than four feet from the back of the outlaw's head. Even in that motion, quick as thought, there was something that did not escape the acute ears of the hunted man. He made a motion as if to turn his head to ascertain the cause of that suspicious sound. But too late. A nervous pressure of the trigger, a quick flash, sharp report, and the well-directed ball CRASHED THROUGH THE OUTLAW'S SKULL.

There was no outcry, just a swaying of the body and it fell heavily back upon the carpet. The shot had been fatal and all the bullets in the chamber of Charley's revolver still directed at Jesse's head could not more effectually have decided the fate of the greatest bandit and free-booter that ever

Newspaper unidentified.

figured in the pages of the country's history. The ball had entered the base of the skull and made its way out through the forehead, over the left eye. It had been fired out of a Colt's 45, improved pattern, silver-mounted, and pearl-handled gun, presented by the dead man to his slayer only a few days ago. Mrs. James was in the kitchen when the shooting was done, divided from the room in which the bloody tragedy occurred by a dining room. She heard the shot, and dropping her household duties, ran into the front room. She saw her husband lying on his back, and his slayers each holding a revolver in hand, making for the fence in the rear of the house. Robert had reached the enclosure and was in the act of scaling it when she stepped to the door and called to him, "Robert, you have done this; come back." Robert answered, "I swear to God I did not." They then returned to where she stood. Mrs. James ran to the side of her husband and lifted up his head. Life was not extinct, and, when asked if he was hurt, it seemed to her that he wanted to say something, but couldn't. She tried to wash away the blood that was coursing over his face from the hole in his forehead, but it seemed to her that "the blood would come faster than she could wash it away," and in her hands Jesse James died. Charles Ford explained to Mrs. James that "a pistol had accidentally gone off." "Yes," said Mrs. James, "I guess it went off on purpose," and meanwhile Charley left the house. They went to the telegraph office and sent a message to Sheriff Timberlake, of this county, to Gov. Crittenden and other officers and then surrendered themselves to Marshal Craig and a posse who had gone in the direction of James' residence. They accompanied the officers to the house where they were furnished with a dinner, and about three o'clock were removed to the old circuit court room, where the inquest was held in the presence of an immense crowd. Mrs. James also accompanied the officers to the city hall, having previously left her two children aged 7 and 3, a boy and a girl, at the house of Mrs. Lurnal, who had known the Jameses under their assumed name of Howard ever since they had occupied the adjoining house. She was greatly affected by the tragedy and her heart-rending moans and expressions of grief were sorrowful evidence of the love she bore the desperado. The report of the killing of the notorious outlaw spread like wild fire through the city, and as usual the reports assumed every variety of form and color. Very few credited the news, however, and simply laughed at the idea that Jesse James was really the dead man. Nevertheless the excitement ran high and one confirming report succeeded another. Crowds of hundreds gathered at the undertaking establishment where lay the body, at the city hall, at the court house, and in fact, on every street corner, the almost incredible news constituting the sole object of conversation.

CORONER HEDDENS

was notified and Undertaker Sidenfader instructed to remove the body to his establishment. A large crowd accompanied the coroner to the morgue, but only a few, including a reporter were admitted. Nothing in the appearance of the remains indicated the desperate character of the man or the many bloody scenes in which he had been an actor. Only the lower part of the face, the square cheek bones, the stout prominent chin, covered with soft sandy beard, and thin, firmly closed lips, in a measure portrayed the determined will and courage of the dead man. A further inspection of the body revealed two large bullet holes on the right side of the breast, within three inches of the nipple, a bullet wound in the leg, and the absence of the middle finger of the left hand. After reviewing the remains the coroner repaired to the court, whither soon after Mrs. James, in the custody of Marshal Craig, and the two Ford boys, both heavily armed, followed. They were kept in separate apartments, until the jury announced themselves ready to hear testimony.

35. The Inquest

A CONTEMPORARY NEWSPAPER ACCOUNT

THE INQUEST

WHEN Charles Ford was called to the witness stand on Monday morning, he testified that he was about 24 years old, and had lived in Ray county near Richmond for about three years. He met and became acquainted with Jesse James soon after his residence began, and last November left the farm and went to Kansas City. While there he met Jesse James.

"Did he ask you to join him?"

"Jesse James asked me if I did not want to take a trip with him, and we would go and make a raise somewhere. He was living in Kansas City then. We left Kansas City on the 5th and arrived in St. Joe on the 8th, and went to Twenty-first and Lafayette streets where we lived until the day before Christmas, when he rented the house where he was killed and we lived there ever since. He said he wanted to take a trip out through Kansas and see how the banks were situated and said he would get the men, and wanted to know if I knew of any one we could get to help us. I told him I thought I could get my brother to help if I could go down and see him. So we went down there and we went to his mother's and stayed there until Friday night, and then went to my brother's and stayed until Saturday and started to St. Joe. On the way a storm came up and we stayed that night in a church. We stayed there until just before daylight and then we came on to within two miles east of St. Joe, where he said for us to stay until night and he went on in. He said there was going to be a murder trial in Platte City, and we would go up there and if the bank was all right we would rob it. He said when they were making the speeches everybody would be up to the court house and we would rob the bank."

"Well, now, explain how it was you came to kill him?"

"Well, we had come in from the barn where we had been feeding and currying the horses, and Jesse complained of being warm and pulled off his coat and threw it on the bed and opened the door, and said that he guessed he would pull off his belt as some person might see it. Then he went to brush off some pictures and when he turned his back I gave my brother the wink and we both pulled our pistols, but he, my brother, was the quickest and fired first. I had my finger on the trigger and was just going to fire, but I saw his shot was a death shot and did not fire. He heard us cock our pistols and turned his head. The ball struck him in the back of the head and he fell. Then I went out and got our hats, and we went and telegraphed Captain Craig and Sheriff Timberlake what we had done. Then we went to the marshal's office and asked a policeman that was there if he knew where the marshal was. He said that he did not, but that he would go with us to look him up. I asked a gentleman up town if he knew where the marshal was, he said he had just seen him get on a car going down in that direction. I said that was probably where they were going, and that we might as well go down there, and I told them who it was in the house and who it was that killed him, and how it took place and where his pistols, gun, and jewelry could be found and from there we came up here."

"How did you know it was James when he came to you?"

"He came to my house two years ago last summer; he was a sporting man and so was I; gambled and drank a little, so did I. I was acquainted with Miller, and he came with him and introduced him as Mr. Johnston. He stayed until the next day and he left, and after that Ed Miller told me it was Jesse James. I did not see him any more for some time, and when I did see him I asked him where Miller was, and he said that Miller was in bad health, and that he did not think he could live long. Then I did not see any thing more of him until the next spring. He was there two or three times last summer. Then he came down last fall."

"He asked you to do what?"

"To help rob trains and banks. I have been with him ever since."

"Had you any intention of leaving St. Joe soon?"

"Jesse said he would like to rob a bank and look around a little beforehand and I started out with him. He went first to Hia-

watha, then to Pawnee City, from there to Forrest City, then to White Cloud, Kansas, from there to Forrest City to see how the bank at that place was situated. He said that he liked the way the bank at Forrest City was situated, and said he wanted to take that bank, but I told him I did not want to go into that as I was sick then. We came up to Oregon. He said that he wanted to look at that bank, and from there we came down here, and that is the only trip I ever made with him. He would go into a bank with a large bill or several small ones to get changed and while the cashier was making the change he would take a look and see whether they were caged up, what sort of looking man it was, and whether they had a time lock or not."

"How did you get your living?"

"I was not at any expense. I did not spend any money. He had a good deal of money. He had some $1,500 or $1,600."

"Where did he keep it?"

"I don't know."

"Where did he get it?"

"I have no idea where he got it. I guess he must have got it robbing."

"Did Bob, your brother, come here to assist in robbing a bank?"

"Jesse had looked at a bank at Platte City. He said they were going to have a murder trial there this week, and while everybody would be at the court house, he would slip in and rob the bank, and if not he would come back to Forrest City and get that."

"What was your idea in that?"

"It was simply to get Bob here where one of us could kill him if once he took his pistols off. To try and do this with his pistols on would be useless, as I knew Jesse had often said he would not surrender to a hundred men, and if three men should step out

Newspaper unidentified.

in front of him and shoot him he could kill them before he fell."

Robert Ford, the young man who did the shooting, was then called, and as the individual who shot Jesse James walked forward he was the center of every eye in the room. He gave his evidence clearly, and stated that when he went to Ray County to live, he heard about the James boys, but did not meet Jesse until three years afterward. He came with Ed Miller. Witness had known Miller and he knew they were talking and planning a train robbery. Last January he went to Kansas City and had an interview with Governor Crittenden about capturing Jesse, at the St. James hotel.

"Did the governor tell you any thing about a reward?"

"He said $10,000 had been offered for Jesse or Frank dead or alive. I then entered into arrangements with Timberlake and Craig. I afterward told Charlie of the conversation I had with the officers and told him I would like to go with him. He said if I was willing to go, all right. We started that night, and went up to Mrs. Samuels and put the horses up.

"John Samuels (Jesse's half brother) was wounded, and they were expecting him to die. There were some friends of the family there whom Jesse did not wish to see him, so we stayed in the barn all night until they left, and that was pretty nearly daylight, and we stayed in the house all next day, and that night we started away. That was on Thursday night; Friday night we stayed at his brother-in-law's. We left Mrs. Samuels' and went about three miles into the woods for fear the officers would surprise us at her house. We started from the woods and came up to another of his brother-in-laws and got supper there and started from there here."

"This was last week?"

"Yes. We came at once to St. Joseph and then talked over the matter again, and how we could kill him."

"What have you been doing since you came here?"

"My brother and I go down town sometimes at night and get the papers."

"What did you tell Jesse you were with him for?"

"I told him I was going in with him."

"Had you any plans made to rob any bank?"

"He had spoken of several but had made no particular selection."

"Well, now will you give us the particulars of the killing and what time it occurred?"

"After breakfast, between 8 and 9 o'clock this morning, he, my brother and myself were in the room. He pulled off his pistols and got up on a chair to dust off some picture frames and I drew my pistol and shot him."

"How close were you to him?"

"About six feet away."

"How close was the hand to him which held the pistol?"

"About four feet I should think."

"Did he say any thing?"

"He started to turn his head but didn't say a word."

"How often has Charley been at home since he first went to Jesse's house to live?"

"Once during Christmas."

"Has he not been home since then?"

"No, sir; he came to my uncle's."

"How often has he been at your uncle's?"

"I saw him twice; once when he was there, I was in Kansas City."

"Was Jesse James unarmed when you killed him?"

"Yes, sir."

"Do you remember ever hearing any of the Samuels family calling him by name?"

"They always called him 'Dave'; that was the nick name. They never called him any thing but Dave."

"Did any one speak to him and call him by name?"

"Yes, I heard his mother speak to him and call him Dave and he called her mother."

"Do you know any one that can identify him?"

"Yes, sir, Sheriff Timberlake can when he comes; he was with him during the war."

This closed the testimony on Monday, and court adjourned to meet at 10 o'clock this morning, and at that hour an immense crowd filled the room. There was great excitement to see Little, Mrs. Samuels and Mrs. James, both of whom entered the court after the testimony was about half over.

Mr. Henry Craig, police commissioner of Kansas City, was the first witness examined, as follows: I was not acquainted with Jesse James personally, but am positive the body of the dead man is the outlaw, as it corresponds with the descriptions I have heard. I know Robert Ford, and for two months he has assisted Sheriff Timberlake and myself in the endeavor to capture Jesse James. He was not employed regularly by us, but acted in good faith, and according to our instructions, and assisted in every way he could to aid us. Charlie Ford I had never seen until I came to St. Joe, but understand he and Robert had some understanding."

Sheriff Timberlake of Clay county was next called, and said he was sheriff and was acquainted with Jesse James during life and recognized the body as that of Jesse. Had known him since 1864, and saw him the last time in 1870. Knew his face as well as any one. He had the second joint of his third finger shot off by which I also recognize him.

Ford was acting under my instructions and said if he could see Charlie Ford we could accomplish our end the sooner, and he acted squarely to all agreements.

Dick Little was then called and resumed his testimony; I have seen the body of the dead man and recognize it; I was with him a good deal last summer and know him perfectly; I also recognize him from the wounds on hand and on the right side.

Charles Alderman who keeps a livery stable in St. Joseph, testified that he was a trader; was not acquainted with Jesse James in life; have seen the body and recognize it as that of a man I traded horses with but did not know who he was, and last Saturday I got it back from Charles Ford, who has been at my place several times. He said he wanted a horse for his uncle, who I now presume was Jesse James.

Deputy Marshal Finley of St. Joseph said he resided in this city; I was not acquainted with Jesse James; went to the house where he was killed in answer to the telephone where the man was killed; found him on his back, and from Mrs. James got a description of the two men who killed the man and started out in search of them. She said one was her nephew and the other a young man, both named Johnson, but no relation. As we were going out we met the boys coming back. Bob said; I am the man who killed the person in the house. He is the notorious outlaw, Jesse James, or I am mistaken, and I can identify him. He described the wounds on Jesse James' body. He told us there were two watches and some diamonds in the house. We could not find them at first, but did find a necktie and a gold ring with the name of Jesse on the inside. Afterward we found two watches in the trunk. There was some small change in an old pocketbook, which I gave Mrs. James. On a $1 gold piece as a scarf pin were the initials J. W. J. Most of the property is now in the hands of the city marshal.

When the name of Mrs. Zerelda Samuels was called every man in the court room stood up for a good look at the mother of the dead bandit, and as she passed up the center aisle with the wife and the children of Jesse and a Mrs. Turner, the crowd parted right and left, and the party passed the reporters' table and took seats directly in front of the coroner. Her testimony was as follows: "I live in Clay county, and am the mother of Jesse James." Here she broke down and moaned several times "Oh, my poor boy. I have seen the body since my arrival and have recognized it as that of my son Jesse; the lady by my side is my daughter-in-law, and the children hers." (Mrs. Samuels again broke down at this point.) "He was a kind husband and son." Mrs. Jesse James was here asked if any valuables had been taken from the house at the time the officers arrived and she detailed the articles found by the city marshal.

This concluded the testimony, and it was announced that a recess would be taken, and the court room began to empty. Mrs. Samuels arose as did Mrs. James, and as the former turned and faced the crowd she spied Dick Little, and a most sensational scene occurred.

The coroner's jury then retired for deliberation, and in about half an hour returned the following verdict:

STATE OF MISSOURI ⎱ ss.
COUNTY OF BUCHANAN ⎰

An inquisition taken at St. Joseph, in the county of Buchanan, on the third day of April, 1882, before me, James W. Heddens, M. D., coroner of the county aforesaid, upon their view of the body of Jesse W. James, then and there lying dead, S. H. Sommers, W. H. Chouning, J. W. Moore, Thomas Norris, William Turner, W. H. George, good and lawful householders of the township of Washington, who, being duly sworn and charged diligently to enquire and true presentment make, how and in what manner, and by whom the said Jesse W. James came to his death, upon their oaths do say:

That the body of the deceased is that of Jesse W. James and that he came to his death by a wound in the back of his head, caused by a pistol shot fired intentionally by the hand of Robert Ford, in witness whereof as well the jurors aforesaid, have to this inquisition put their names at the place and on the day aforesaid.

JAMES W. HEDDENS, *Coroner*

S. H. SOMMERS, *Foreman*

W. H. CHOUNING,

J. W. MOORE,

THOS. NORRIS,

WM. TURNER,

W. H. GEORGE.

36. The Life and Adventures of Calamity Jane

BY HERSELF

EDITOR'S NOTE: In the last years of her life the woman born as Martha Cannary and widely known as Calamity Jane (1852-1903) was a pathetic figure, often staggering drunk, without a place to sleep. In better times she had been a living legend — supposedly the mistress of Wild Bill Hickok for a time, a scout for the U. S. army, and an excellent gunwoman. Near the close of her career she became an entertainer and for the purpose wrote a sketch of her life, which I have reprinted below. Although many people believed that she was a glamorous if not actually a heroic figure, others took a strongly dissenting view. A modern skeptic, Stewart H. Holbrook, has written:

"There are men alive today who will tell you in all seriousness that Calamity Jane was a plainswoman, scout, prospector and Indian fighter without peer. They will tell you that she was a trusted scout with General George Armstrong Custer. Others will swear she served, in the form and style of a *male* scout, with Crook, with Miles, with Terry. At least one windy old character of the West told me Jane was once a scout with the Negro cavalry commanded by the then Colonel (Pecos Bill) Shafter. There is no shred of evidence to show she ever served, either as man or woman, with any military body of the United States Army — that is, not in an official capacity. The Army did not carry camp followers on its muster rolls."

My maiden name was Martha Cannary, was born in Princeton, Missouri, May 1st, 1852. Father and mother natives of Ohio.

Had two brothers and three sisters, I being the oldest of the children. As a child I always had a fondness for adventure and out-door exercise and especial fondness for horses which I began to ride at an early age and continued to do so until I became an expert rider, being able to ride the most vicious and stubborn of horses, in fact the greater portion of my life in early times was spent in this manner.

In 1865 we emigrated from our homes in Missouri by the overland route to Virginia City, Montana, taking five months to make the journey. While on the way the greater portion of my time was spent in hunting along with the men and hunters of the party, in fact I was at all times with the men when there was excitement and adventures to be had. By the time we reached Virginia City I was considered a remarkable good shot and a fearless rider for a girl of my age. I remember many occurrences on the journey from Missouri to Montana. Many times in crossing the mountains the conditions of the trail were so bad that we frequently had to lower the wagons over ledges by hand with ropes, for they were so rough and rugged that horses were of no use. We also had many exciting times fording streams, for many of the streams in our way were noted for quicksand and boggy places, where, unless we were very careful, we would have lost horses and all. Then we had many dangers to encounter in the way of streams swelling on account of heavy rains. On occasions of that kind the men would usually select the best places to cross the streams, myself on more than one occasion have mounted my pony and swam across the stream several times merely to amuse myself and have had many narrow escapes from having both myself and pony washed away to certain death, but as the pioneers of those days had plenty of courage we overcome all obstacles, and reached Virginia City in safety.

Mother died at Black Foot, Montana, 1866, where we buried her. I left Montana in spring of 1866, for Utah, arriving at Salt Lake city during the summer. Remained in Utah until 1867, where my father died, then went to Fort Bridger, Wyoming Territory, where we arrived May 1, 1868. Remained around Fort Bridger during 1868, then went to Piedmont, Wyoming, with U. P. Railway. Joined General Custer as a scout at Fort Russell, Wyoming, in 1870, and started for Arizona for the Indian campaign. Up to this time I had always worn the costume of my sex. When I joined Custer I donned the uniform of a soldier. It was a bit awkward at first but I soon got to be perfectly at home in men's clothes.

Was in Arizona up to the winter of 1871 and during that time I had a great many adventures with the Indians, for as a scout I had a great many dangerous missions to perform and while I was in many close places always succeeded in getting away safely, for by this time I was considered the most reckless and daring rider and one of the best shots in the western country.

After that campaign I returned to Fort Sanders, Wyoming, remained there until spring of 1872, when we were ordered out to the Muscle Shell or Nursey Pursey* Indian outbreak. In that war Generals Custer, Miles, Terry and Cook were all engaged. This campaign lasted until fall of 1873.

It was during this campaign that I was christened Calamity Jane. It was on Goose creek, Wyoming, where the town of Sheridan is now located, Captain Egan was in command of the post. We were ordered out to quell an uprising of the Indians, and were out for several days, had numerous skirmishes during which six of the soldiers were killed and several severely wounded. When on returning to the post we were ambushed about a mile and a half from our destination. When fired upon Captain Egan was shot. I was riding in advance and on hearing the firing turned in my saddle and saw the captain reeling in his saddle as though about to fall. I turned my horse and galloped back with all haste to his side and got there in time to catch him as he was falling. I lifted him onto my horse in front of me and succeeded in getting him safely to the fort. Captain Egan, on recovering, laughingly said: "I name you Calamity Jane, the heroine of the plains." I have borne that name up to the present time. We were afterwards ordered to Fort Custer, where Custer City now stands, where we arrived in the spring of 1874; remained around Fort Custer all summer and were ordered to Fort Russell in fall of 1874, where we remained until spring of 1875; was then ordered to the Black Hills to protect miners, as that country was controlled by the Sioux Indians and the government had to send the soldiers to protect the lives of the miners and settlers in that section. Remained there until fall of 1875, and wintered at Fort Laramie. In spring of 1876, we were ordered north with General Cook to join Generals Miles, Terry and Custer at Big Horn river. During this march I swam the Platte river at Fort Fetterman as I was the bearer of important dispatches. I had a ninety mile ride to make,

* Nez Perce. The date was 1873.

being wet and cold, I contracted a severe illness and was sent back in Gen. Crook's ambulance to Fort Fetterman where I laid in the hospital for fourteen days. When able to ride I started for Fort Laramie where I met Wm. Hickock, better known as Wild Bill, and we started for Deadwood, where we arrived about June.

During the month of June I acted as a pony express rider carrying the U. S. mail between Deadwood and Custer, a distance of fifty miles, over one of the roughest trails in the Black Hills country. As many of the riders before me had been held up and robbed of their packages, mail and money that they carried, for that was the only means of getting mail and money between these points. It was considered the most dangerous route in the Hills, but as my reputation as a rider and quick shot was well known, I was molested very little, for the toll gatherers looked on me as being a good fellow, and they knew that I never missed my mark. I made the round trip every two days which was considered pretty good riding in that country. Remained around Deadwood during the summer visiting all the camps within an area of 100 miles. My friend, Wild Bill, remained in Deadwood during the summer with the exception of occasional visits to the camps. On the 2d of August, while setting at a gambling table in the Bell Union saloon, in Deadwood, he was shot in the back of the head by the notorious Jack McCall, a desperado. I was in Deadwood at the time and on hearing of the killing made my way at once to the scene of the shooting and found that my friend had been killed by McCall. I at once started to look for the assassin and found him at Shurdy's butcher shop and grabbed a meat cleaver and made him throw up his hands; through the excitement on hearing of Bill's death, having left

my weapons on the post of my bed. He was then taken to a log cabin and locked up, well secured as every one thought, but he got away and was afterwards caught at Fagan's ranch on Horse creek, on the old Cheyenne road, and was then taken to Yankton, Dakota, where he was tried, sentenced and hung.

I remained around Deadwood locating claims, going from camp to camp until the spring of 1877, when one morning I saddled my horse and rode towards Crook city. I had gone about 12 miles from Deadwood, at the mouth of Whitewood creek, when I met the overland mail running from Cheyenne to Deadwood. The horses on a run, about two hundred yards from the station; upon looking closely I saw they were pursued by Indians. The horses ran to the barn as was their custom. As the horses stopped I rode along the side of the coach and found the driver, John Slaughter, lying face downwards in the boot of the stage, he having been shot by the Indians. When the stage got to the station the Indians hid in the bushes. I immediately removed all baggage from the coach except the mail. I then took the driver's seat and with all haste drove to Deadwood, carrying the six passengers and the dead driver.

I left Deadwood in the fall of 1877 and went to Bear Butte Creek with the 7th Cavalry. During the fall and winter we built Fort Meade and the town of Sturgis. In 1878 I left the command and went to Rapid city and put in the year prospecting.

In 1879 I went to Fort Pierre and drove trains from Rapid city to Fort Pierce for Frank Witcher, then drove teams from Fort Pierce to Sturgis for Fred Evans. This teaming was done with oxen as they were better fitted for the work than horses, owing to the rough nature of the country.

In 1881 I went to Wyoming and returned in 1882 to Miles City and took up a ranch on the Yellowstone, raising stock and cattle, also kept a way-side inn, where the weary traveler could be accommodated with food, drink, or trouble, if he looked for it. Left the ranch in 1883, went to California, going through the states and territories, reached Ogden the latter part of 1883, and San Francisco in 1884. Left San Francisco in the summer of 1884 for Texas, stopping at Fort Yuma, Arizona, the hottest spot in the United States. Stopping at all points of interest until I reached El Paso in the fall. When in El Paso I met Mr. Clinton Burk, a native of Texas, who I married in August, 1885. As I thought I had traveled through life long enough alone and thought it was about time to take a partner for the rest of my days. We remained in Texas leading a quiet home life until 1889. On October 29th, 1887, I became the mother of a girl baby, the very image of its father, at least that is what he said, but who has the temper of its mother.

When we left Texas we went to Boulder, Colo., where we kept a hotel until 1893, after which we travelled through Wyoming, Montana, Idaho, Washington, Oregon, then back to Montana, then to Dakota, arriving in Deadwood October 9th, 1895, after an absence of seventeen years.

My arrival in Deadwood after an absence of so many years created quite an excitement among my many friends of the past, to such an extent that a vast number of the citizens who had come to Deadwood during my absence who had heard so much of Calamity Jane and her many adventures in former years were anxious to see me. Among the many whom I met were several gentlemen from eastern cities, who advised me to allow myself to be placed before the public in such a manner as to give the people of the eastern cities an opportunity of seeing the Woman Scout who was made so famous through her daring career in the west and Black Hills countries.

An agent of Kohl & Middleton, the celebrated museum men, came to Deadwood, through the solicitation of the gentlemen whom I had met there and arrangements were made to place me before the public in this manner. My first engagement began at the Palace museum, Minneapolis, January 20th, 1896, under Kohl & Middleton's management.

Hoping that this little history of my life may interest all readers, I remain as in the older days.

Yours,

MRS. M. BURK,
better known as Calamity Jane.

37. The Death Warrant of Billy the Kid

EDITOR'S NOTE: William Bonney, better known as Billy the Kid (1859-1881) was one of the most notorious outlaws which the old West produced, and by far the most colorful connected with the Territory of New Mexico. He was supposedly born in New York City. The facts about Billy the Kid are not always distinguishable from the many legends which originated soon after his death. There was something about his youth, the manner of his death, together with the time and place of his notoriety, which made him one of the likely subjects for a gunman's hall of fame. For many years after his death there were people who argued that he was still alive; or that he killed a man for every year of his age. Regardless of whether he is viewed as a Robin Hood or a hoodlum, two facts are incontrovertible: his personality and his career stimulated the folk imagination, and his legend is as alive now as it was shortly after his death. Billy was killed in New Mexico Territory by Sheriff Pat Garrett under the unusual circumstances described by Garrett in the account which follows.

To the Sheriff of Lincoln County, New Mexico, Greeting:

At the March term, A.D. 1881, of the District Court for the Third Judicial District of New Mexico, held at La Mesilla in the county of Doña Ana, William Bonny, *alias* Kid, *alias* William Antrim, was duly convicted of the crime of Murder in the First Degree; and on the fifteenth day of said term, the same being the thirteenth day of April, A.D. 1881, the judgment and sentence of said court were pronounced against the said William Bonny, *alias* Kid, *alias* William Antrim, upon said conviction according to law: whereby the said William Bonny, *alias* Kid, *alias* William Antrim, was adjudged and sentenced to be hanged by the neck until dead, by the Sheriff of the said county of Lincoln, within said county.

Therefore, you, the Sheriff of the said county of Lincoln, are hereby commanded that on Friday, the thirteenth day of May, A.D. 1881, pursuant to the said judgment and sentence of the said court, you take the said William Bonny, *alias* Kid, *alias* William Antrim, from the county jail of the county of Lincoln where he is now confined, to some safe and convenient place within the said county, and there, between the hours of ten o'clock, A.M., and three o'clock, P.M., of said day, you hang the said William Bonny, *alias* Kid, *alias* William Antrim by the neck until he is dead. And make due return of your acts hereunder.

Done at Santa Fé in the Territory of New Mexico, this 30th day of April, A.D. 1881. Witness my hand and the great seal of the Territory.

LEW. WALLACE,
Governor New Mexico.

By the Governor
W. G. Ritch
Secretary
N. M.

38. The Death Warrant Returned

TERRITORY
vs.
WM. BONNEY, *alias* KID

Death Warrant

Lincoln, Lincoln County New Mexico May 24th 1881 I hereby certify that the within

Warrant was not served owing to the fact that the within named prisoner escaped before the day set for serving said Warrant

PAT. F. GARRETT
Sheriff
Lincoln County
New Mexico

39. How I Killed Billy the Kid

BY PAT F. GARRETT

During the weeks following the Kid's escape, I was censured by some for my seeming unconcern and inactivity in the matter of his re-arrest. I was egotistical enough to think I knew my own business best, and preferred to accomplish this duty, if possible at all, in my own way. I was constantly, but quietly, at work, seeking sure information and maturing my plans of action. I did not lay about The Kid's old haunts, nor disclose my intentions and operations to any one. I stayed at home, most of the time, and busied myself about the ranch. If my seeming unconcern deceived the people and gave The Kid confidence in his security, my end was accomplished. It was my belief that The Kid was still in the country and haunted the vicinity of Fort Sumner; yet there was some doubt mingled wtih my belief. He was never taken for a fool, but was credited with the possession of extraordinary forethought and cool judgment, for one of his age. It seemed incredible that, in his situation, with the

extreme penalty of the law, the reward of detection, and the way of successful flight and safety open to him—with no known tie to bind him to that dangerous locality,—it seemed incredible that he should linger in the Territory. My first task was to solve my doubts.

Early in July I received a reply from a letter I had written to Mr. Brazil. I was at Lincoln when this letter came to me. Mr. Brazil was dodging and hiding from The Kid. He feared his vengeance on account of the part which he, Brazil, had taken in his capture. There were many others who "trembled in their boots" at the knowledge of his escape; but most of them talked him out of his resentment, or conciliated him in some manner.

Brazil's letter gave me no positive information. He said he had not seen The Kid since his escape, but, from many indications, believed he was still in the country. He offered me any assistance in his power to re-

Billy the Kid

from there. He consented. I then went to Poe, and, to him, I disclosed my business and all its particulars, showing him my correspondence. He, also, complied with my request that he should accompany me.

We three went to Roswell, and started up the Rio Pecos from there on the night of July 10th. We rode mostly in the night, followed no roads, but taking unfrequented routes, and arrived at the mouth of Tayban Arroyo, five miles south of Fort Sumner, one hour after dark, on the night of the 13th. Brazil was not there. We waited nearly two hours, but he did not come. We rode off a mile or two, staked our horses and slept until daylight. Early in the morning we rode up into the hills and prospected awhile with our field-glasses.

Poe was a stranger in the county and there was little danger that he would meet any one who knew him at Sumner. So, after an hour or two spent in the hills, he went into Sumner to take observations. I advised him, also, to go on to Sunnyside, seven miles above Sumner, and interview M. Rudolph, Esq., in whose judgment and discretion I had great confidence. I arranged with Poe to meet us that night at moonrise, at La Punta de la Glorietta, four miles north of Fort Sumner. Poe went on to the Plaza, and McKinney and myself rode down into the Pecos Valley, where we remained during the day. At night we started out circling around the town, and met Poe exactly on time at the trysting place.

Poe's appearance at Sumner had excited no particular observation, and he had gleaned no news there. Rudolph thought, from all indications, that The Kid was about; and yet, at times, he doubted. His cause for doubt seemed to be based on no evidence except the fact that The Kid was no fool, and no man in his senses, under the

capture him. I again wrote to Brazil, requesting him to meet me at the mouth of Tayban Arroyo, an hour after dark, on the night of the 13th day of July.

A gentleman named John W. Poe, who had superceded Frank Stewart, in the employ of the stockmen of the Canadian, was at Lincoln on business, as was one of my deputies, Thomas K. McKinney. I first went to McKinney, and told him I wanted him to accompany me on a business trip to Arizona; that we would go down home and start circumstances, would brave such danger.

I then concluded to go and have a talk with Peter Maxwell, Esq., in whom I felt sure I could rely. We had ridden to within a short distance of Maxwell's grounds, when we found a man in camp, and stopped. To Poe's surprise, he recognized in the camper an old friend and former partner, in Texas, named Jacobs. We unsaddled here, got some coffee, and, on foot, entered an orchard which runs from this point down to a row of old buildings, some of them occupied by Mexicans, not more than sixty yards from Maxwell's house. We approached these houses cautiously, and when within ear shot, heard the sound of voices conversing in Spanish. We concealed ourselves quickly and listened; but the distance was too great to hear words, or even distinguish voices. Soon a man arose from the ground, in full view, but too far away to recognize. He wore a broad-brimmed hat, a dark vest and pants, and was in his shirtsleeves. With a few words, which fell like a murmur on our ears, he went to the fence, jumped it, and walked down towards Maxwell's house.

Little as we then suspected it, this man was The Kid. We learned, subsequently, that when he left his companions that night, he went to the house of a Mexican friend, pulled off his hat and boots, threw himself on a bed and commenced reading a newspaper. He soon, however, hailed his friend, who was sleeping in the room, told him to get up and make some coffee, adding:—"Give me a butcher knife and I will go over to Pete's and get some beef; I'm hungry." The Mexican arose, handed him the knife, and The Kid, hatless and in his stocking-feet, started to Maxwell, which was but a few steps distant.

When the Kid, by me unrecognized, left the orchard, I motioned to my companions, and we cautiously retreated a short distance, and, to avoid the persons whom we had heard at the houses, took another route, approaching Maxwell's house from the opposite direction. When we reached the porch in front of the building, I left Poe and McKinney at the end of the porch, about twenty feet from the door of Pete's room, and went in. It was near midnight and Pete was in bed. I walked to the head of the bed and sat down on it, beside him, near the pillow. I asked him as to the whereabouts of The Kid. He said that The Kid had certainly been about, but he did not know whether he had left or not. At that moment a man sprang quickly into the door, looking back, and called twice in Spanish, "Who comes there?" No one replied and he came on in. He was bareheaded. From his step I could perceive he was either barefooted or in his stocking-feet, and held a revolver in his right hand and a butcher-knife in his left.

He came directly towards me. Before he reached the bed, I whispered: "Who is it, Pete?" but received no reply for a moment. It struck me that it might be Pete's brother-in-law, Manuel Abreu, who had seen Poe and McKinney, and wanted to know their business. The intruder came close to me, leaned both hands on the bed, his right hand almost touching my knee, and asked, in a low tone:—"Who are they Pete?"—at the same instant Maxwell whispered to me. "That's him!" Simultaneously The Kid must have seen, or felt, the presence of a third person at the head of the bed. He raised quickly his pistol, a self-cocker, within a foot of my breast. Retreating rapidly across the room he cried: "Quien es? Quien es?" (Who's that? Who's that?) All this occurred in a moment. Quickly as possible I drew my revolver and fired, threw my body aside and fired again. The second shot was useless;

The Kid fell dead. He never spoke. A struggle or two, a little strangling sound as he gasped for breath, and The Kid was with his many victims.

Maxwell had plunged over the foot of the bed on the floor, dragging the bed-clothes with him. I went to the door and met Poe and McKinney there. Maxwell rushed past me, out on the porch; they threw their guns down on him, when he cried: "Don't shoot, don't shoot." I told my companions I had got The Kid. They asked me if I had not shot the wrong man. I told them I had made no blunder; that I knew The Kid's voice too well to be mistaken. The Kid was entirely unknown to either of them. They had seen him pass in, and, as he stepped on the porch, McKinney, who was sitting, rose to his feet; one of his spurs caught under the boards, and nearly threw him. The Kid laughed, but, probably, saw their guns, as he drew his revolver and sprang into the door-way, as he hailed: "Who comes there?" Seeing a bareheaded, barefooted man, in his shirt-sleeves, with a butcher knife in his hand, and hearing his hail in excellent Spanish, they naturally supposed him to be a Mexican and an attaché of the establishment, hence their suspicion that I had shot the wrong man.

We now entered the room and examined the body. The ball struck him just above the heart, and must have cut through the ventricles. Poe asked me how many shots I fired; I told him two, but that I had no idea where the second one went. Both Poe and McKinney said The Kid must have fired then, as there were surely three shots fired. I told them that he had fired one shot, between my two. Maxwell said that The Kid fired; yet, when we came to look for bullet marks, none from his pistol could be found. We searched long and faithfully—found both my bullet marks and none other; so, against the impression and senses of four men, we had to conclude that The Kid did not fire at all. We examined his pistol—a self-cocker, calibre 41. It had five cartridges and one shell in the chambers, the hammer resting on the shell, but this proves nothing, as many carry their revolvers in this way for safety; besides, this shell looked as though it had been shot some time before.

It will never be known whether The Kid recognized me or not. If he did, it was the first time, during all his life of peril, that he ever lost his presence of mind, or failed to shoot first, and hesitate afterwards. He knew that a meeting with me meant surrender or fight. He told several persons about Sumner that he bore no animosity against me, and had no desire to do me injury. He also said that he knew, should we meet, he would have to surrender, kill me, or get killed himself. So, he declared his intention, should we meet, to commence shooting on sight.

On the following morning, the Alcalde, Alejandro Segura, held an inquest on the body. Hon. M. Rudolph, of Sunnyside, was foreman of the Coroner's Jury. They found a verdict that William H. Bonney came to his death from a gun-shot wound, the weapon in the hands of Pat. F. Garrett; that the fatal wound was inflicted by the said Garrett in the discharge of his official duty as Sheriff and that the homicide was justifiable.

The body was neatly and properly dressed and buried in the Military Cemetery at Fort Sumner, July 15, 1881. His exact age, on the day of his death, was 21 years, 7 months and 21 days.

I said that the body was buried in the cemetery at Fort Sumner; I wish to add that it is there to-day intact. Skull, fingers, toes, bones and every hair of the head that was buried with the body on that 15th day of

July, doctors, newspaper editors and para-
graphers to the contrary notwithstanding.
Some presuming swindlers have claimed to
have The Kid's skull on exhibition, or one
of his fingers, or some other portion of his
body, and one medical gentleman has persuaded credulous idiots that he has all the
bones strung upon wires. It is possible that
there is a skeleton on exhibition somewhere
in the States, or even in this Territory,
which was procured somewhere down the
Rio Pecos. We have them, lots of them, in
this section. The banks of the Pecos are
dotted from Fort Sumner to the Rio Grande
with unmarked graves, and the skeletons
are of all sizes, ages and complexions. Any
showman of ghastly curiosities can resurrect
one or all of them, and place them on exhibition as the remains of Dick Turpin,
Jack Shepherd, Cartouche, or The Kid, with
no one to say to him nay, so they don't ask
the people of the Rio Pecos to believe it.

Again I say that The Kid's body lies un-
disturbed in the grave,—and I speak of what
I know.

The Life of the Kid is ended and my history thereof is finished. Perhaps, however,
some of my readers will consent to follow
me through three or four additional pages,
which may be unnecessary and superfluous,
but which I insert for my own personal
gratification, and which I invite my friends
to read.

During the time occupied in preparing
the foregoing work for press, some circumstances have occurred, some newspaper articles have appeared, and many remarks have
been passed, referring to the disposal of The
Kid, his character, disposition and history,
and my contemplated publication of his life,
which I have resolved to notice, against the
advice of friends, who believe the proper

and more dignified plan would be to ignore
them altogether. But I have something to
say, and propose to say it.

A San Francisco daily, in an article which
I have never seen, but only comments
thereon in other journals, among other
strictures on my actions, questions my immunity from legal penalty for the slaying of
The Kid. I did think I was fully advised in
regard to this matter before I undertook the
dangerous task of his re-arrest, as I contemplated the possible necessity of having him
to kill. But I must acknowledge that I did
not consult with the San Francisco editor,
and can, at this late hour, only apologize,
humbly, for the culpable omission. The law
has decided as to my amenability to its re-
quirements, — should the opinion of the
scribbler be adverse, I can but abjectly crave
his mercy.

I have been portrayed in print and in illustrations, as shooting The Kid from behind a bed, from under a bed, and from
other places of concealment. After mature
deliberation I have resolved that honest confession will serve my purpose better than
prevarication. Hear!

I was not behind the bed, because, in the
first place, I could not get there. I'm not "as
wide as a church door," but the bed was so
close to the wall that a lath could scarce have
been introduced between. I was not under
the bed, and this fact will require a little
more complicated explanation. I *could* have
gotten under the bed; but, you see, I did not
know The Kid was coming. He took me by
surprise—gave me no chance on earth to
hide myself. Had I but suspected his proximity, or that he would come upon me in
that abrupt manner, I would have utilized
any safe place of concealment which might
have presented itself—under the bed, or under any article which I might have found

under the bed, large enough to cover me.

Scared? Suppose a man of The Kid's noted gentle and amiable disposition and temper, had warned you that when you two met you had better "come a shooting;" suppose he bounced in on you unexpectedly with a revolver in his hand, whilst yours was in your scabbard. Scared? Wouldn't you have been scared? I didn't dare to answer his hail:—"*Quien es?*" as the first sound of my voice, (which he knew perfectly well), would have been his signal to make a target of my physical personality, with his self-cocker, from which he was wont to pump a continuous stream of fire and lead, and in any direction, unerringly, which answered to his will. Scared, Cap? Well, I should say so. I started out on that expedition with the expectation of getting scared. I went out contemplating the probability of being shot at, and the possibility of being hurt, perhaps killed; but not if any precaution on my part would prevent such a catastrophe. The Kid got a very much better show than I had intended to give him.

Then, "the lucky shot," as they put it. It was not the shot, but the opportunity that was lucky, and everybody may rest assured I did not hesitate long to improve it. If there is any one simple enough to imagine that I did, or will ever, put my life squarely in the balance against that of The Kid, or any of his ilk, let him divest his mind of that absurd fallacy. It is said that Garrett did not give The Kid a fair show—did not fight him "on the square," etc. Whenever I take a contract to fight a man "on the square," as they put it, (*par* parenthesis—I am not on the fight), that man must bear the reputation, before the world and in my estimation, of an honorable man and respectable citizen; or, at least, he must be my equal in social standing, and I claim the right to place my

own estimate upon my own character, and my own valuation upon my own life. If the public shall judge that these shall be measured by the same standards as those of outlaws and murderers, whose lives are forfeit to the law, I beg the privilege of appeal from its decision.

I had a hope—a very faint hope—of catching The Kid napping, as it were, so that I might disarm and capture him. Failing in that, my design was to try and get "the drop" on him, with the, almost, certainty, as I believed, that he would make good his threat to "die fighting with a revolver at each ear;" so, with the drop, I would have been forced to kill him anyhow. I, at no time, contemplated taking any chances which I could avoid by caution or cunning. The only circumstances under which we could have met on equal terms, would have been accidental, and to which I would have been an unwilling party. Had we met unexpectedly, face to face, I have no idea that either one of us would have run away, and there is where the "square fight" would, doubtless, have come off. With one question I will dismiss the subject of taking unfair advantage, etc. What sort of "square fight," or "even show," would I have got, had one of The Kid's friends in Fort Sumner chanced to see me and informed him of my presence there, and at Pete Maxwell's room on that fatal night?

A few words in regard to criticisms from two isolated rural journals published, I think, somewhere in the hill-tops of the extreme northern counties of this Territory —at Guadalupitas, or Las Golondrinas, or La Cueva, or Vermejo. I have never seen a copy of either of them, and should have been ignorant of their existence had not a respectable newspaper copied their "puffs." These fellows object to my writing and

publishing a Life of The Kid. Their ex-
postulations come too late; it is written and
I will quarrel before I abandon the design
of publishing it.

One of these weekly emanations is called
"The Optician," or some similar name,
which would indicate that it is devoted to
the interests of an industry which is, or
should be, the exclusive prerogative of the
disciples of Paul Pry. Perhaps it is a medical
journal, edited by an M. D., who did *not* get
the skull, nor the finger, nor any of the bones
of The Kid's body, and is proportionately
incensed thereat.

The other, judging from the two or three
extracts I have seen from its columns, must,
also, be a medical journal, published in the
interests of an asylum for the imbeciles. I
would advise the manager to exercise more
vigilance in the absence of the editor, and
try to keep patients out of his chair. The
unfortunate moonling who scribbled that
"stickfull" which reflected upon me and my
book, judging from his peculiar phraseology, must be a demented fishmonger.

> You may spatter, you may soak him
>   With ink if you will,
> But the scent of stale cat-fish
>   Will cling 'round him still.

Both of these delectable hermits charge
me with intent to publish a Life of The Kid,
with the nefarious object of making money
thereby. O! asinine propellers of Faber's No.
2; O! ludificatory lavishers of Arnold's
night-tinted fluid; what the Hades else do
you suppose my object could be? Their phil-
osophy is that *I* must not attempt to make
any more money out of the result of my
"lucky shot," because, forsooth, "some men
would have been satisfied," etc. Anybody,
everybody else, authors who never were in
New Mexico and never saw The Kid, can
compile from newspaper rumors, as many
lives of him as they please, make all the
money out of their bogus, unreliable heroics
that can be extorted from a gullible public,
and these fellows will congratulate them;
but my truthful history should be sup-
pressed, because I got paid for ridding the
country of a criminal. How do these impertinent intermeddlers know how much
money I have made by this accident, or incident, or by whatever name they choose to
designate it? How do they know how much
it cost me to achieve the "accident"? How do
they know how many thousands of dollars
worth of stock and other property I have
saved to those who "rewarded" me, by the
achievement? Whose business is it if I choose
to publish a hundred books, and make
money out of them all, though I were as
rich as the Harper Brothers? Wonder if
either of these discontented fellows would
have refused to publish my book on shares.

Pat Garrett when he was 30, taken soon
after he shot Billy the Kid

Wonder what would have been the color of their notices, and when they would have "been satisfied." It's bile, Cully; nothing but bile. Take Indian Root Pills. And yet I thank you for your unsolicited, gratuitous notices, valueless as they are. They may help to sell a few copies of my work in your secluded locality. But, as I am no subject for charity, (though your articles would seem to say so), send in reasonable bills and I will pay them. I know the difficulties under which projectors of newspapers in isolated regions labor, and would have sent you each a liberal advertisement *without a hint*, had I known of your existence.

It is amusing to notice how brave some of The Kid's "ancient enemies," and, even, some who professed to be his friends, have become since there is no danger of their courage being put to the test by an interview with him. Some of them say that The Kid was a coward, (which is a cowardly lie), and anybody, with any nerve, could have arrested him without trouble, thus obviating the necessity of killing him. One has seen him slapped in the face when he had a revolver in his hand, and he did not resent it. One has seen a Mexican, over on the Rio Grande, choke him against the wall, The Kid crying and begging with a cocked pistol in his hand. These blowers are unworthy of notice. Most of them were vagabonds who had "slopped" over from one faction to the other during the war, regulating their maneuvers according to the prospect of danger or safety, always keeping in view their chances to steal a sore-back pony or a speckled calf, and aspiring to the appellation of stock-owners. There is not one of these brave mouth-fighters that would have dared to give voice to such lying bravado whilst The Kid lived, though he were chained in a cell; not one of them that, were he on their track, would not have set the prairie on fire to get out of his reach, and, in their fright, extinguished it again as they ran, leaving a wet trial behind. These silly vaporings are but repeated illustrations of that old fable, "The Dead Lion and the Live Ass."

I will now take leave of all those of my readers who have not already taken "French leave" of me. Whatever may be the cause of the effect, Lincoln county now enjoys a season of peace and prosperity to which she has ever, heretofore, been a stranger. No Indians, no desperadoes to scare our citizens from their labors, or disturb their slumbers. Stock wanders over the ranges in security, and vast fields of waving grain greet the eye, where, three years ago, not a stock of artificially-produced vegetation could be seen.

"Where late was barrenness and waste
The perfumed blossom, bud and blade,
Sweet, bashful pledges of approaching
 harvest,
Giving cheerful promise to the hope of
 industry,"

Gladden the eye, stamp contentment on happy faces and illustrate the pleasures of industry. The farmer to his plow, the stockman to his saddle, the merchant to his ledger, the blacksmith to his forge, the carpenter to his plane, the school-boy to his lass, and the shoemaker to his waxed-end, or, *vice versa*,

The shoemaker to   The schoolboy to
his   LAST   his whackst   END

40. The Body of Billy the Kid

A DOCUMENT

Territory of New Mexico ⎱
County of Miguel ⎰ Precinct No. 27.

To the District of the First Judicial District of the Territory of New Mexico.

Greetings:

On this the 15th day of July, A.D. 1881, I, the undersigned, Justice of the Peace of the above-named precinct, received information that a murder had taken place at Fort Sumner, in said precinct, and immediately upon receiving said information I proceeded to said place and named Milnor Rudolph, Jose Silva, Antonio Saavedra, Pedro Antonio Lucero, Lorenzo Jaramillo, and Sabal Gutierres a jury to investigate the case, and the above jury convened at the house of Luz B. Maxwell and proceeded to a room in said house, where they found the body of William Bonney, alias 'Kid,' with a shot on the left breast, and having examined the body they examined the evidence of Pedro Maxwell, which evidence is as follows:

'I being in bed in my room, at about midnight on the 14th day of July, Pat F. Garrett came into my room and sat at the end of my bed to converse with me. A short while after Garrett had sat down, William Bonney came in and got close to my bed with a gun in his hand and asked me, "Who is it? Who is it?" and then Pat F. Garrett fired two shots at the said William Bonney and the said William Bonney fell near my fireplace and I went out of the room, and when I came in again in about three or four minutes after the shots the said Bonney was dead.'

The jury found the following verdict:

'We of the jury unanimously find that William Bonney has been killed by a shot on the left breast near the region of the heart, the same having been fired with a gun in the hand of Pat F. Garrett, and our verdict is that the deed of said Garrett was justifiable homicide and we are unanimous on the opinion that the gratitude of all the community is due to the said Garrett for his deed and is worthy of being rewarded.'

M. Rudolph, President, Anto Saavedra, Pedro Anto Lucero, Jose X Silba, Sabal Gutierra X, Lorenzo X Jaramillo.

All said information I place to your knowledge.

ALEJANDRO SEGURA
Justice of Peace

III. Observers

41. Adventures on the Prairie

BY WASHINGTON IRVING

EDITOR'S NOTE: Washington Irving (1783-1859), frequently called the first American man of letters, was famous for his highly civilized and charming style. Born in New York City, he spent many years in Europe, as a traveler and in ministerial capacities. In 1832 he made a journey into the interior of the present state of Oklahoma, recording his impressions in a journal, and in 1835 published *A Tour on the Prairies*. The following is taken from the latter work.

After proceeding about two hours in a southerly direction, we emerged towards mid-day from the dreary belt of the Cross Timber, and to our infinite delight beheld "the great Prairie," stretching to the right and left before us. We could distinctly trace the meandering course of the Main Canadian, and various smaller streams, by the strips of green forest that bordered them. The landscape was vast and beautiful. There is always an expansion of feeling in looking upon these boundless and fertile wastes; but I was doubly conscious of it after emerging from our "close dungeon of innumerous boughs."

From a rising ground Beatte pointed out to the place where he and his comrades had killed the buffaloes; and we beheld several black objects moving in the distance, which he said were part of the herd. The Captain determined to shape his course to a woody bottom about a mile distant and to encamp there, for a day or two, by way of having a regular buffalo hunt, and getting a supply of provisions. As the troop defiled along the slope of the hill towards the camping ground, Beatte proposed to my mess-mates and myself, that we should put ourselves under his guidance, promising to take us where we should have plenty of sport. Leaving the line of march, therefore, we diverged towards the prairie; traversing a small valley, and ascending a gentle swell of land. As we reached the summit, we beheld a gang of wild horses about a mile off. Beatte was immediately on the alert, and no longer thought of buffalo hunting. He was mounted on his powerful half-wild horse, with a lariat coiled at the saddle bow, and set off in pursuit; while we remained on a rising ground watching his manoeuvres with great solicitude. Taking advantage of a strip of woodland, he stole quietly along, so as to get close to them before he was perceived. The moment they caught sight of him a grand scamper took place. We watched him skirting along the horizon like a privateer in full chase of a merchantman! at length he passed over the brow of a ridge, and down into a shallow valley; in a few moments he was on the opposite hill, and close upon one of the horses. He was soon head and head, and appeared to be trying to noose his prey; but they both disappeared again below the hill, and we saw no more of them. It turned out afterwards, that he had noosed a powerful horse, but could not hold him, and had lost his lariat in the attempt.

While we were waiting for his return, we

perceived two buffalo bulls descending a slope, towards a stream, which wound through a ravine fringed with trees. The young Count and myself endeavoured to get near them under covert of the trees. They discovered us while we were yet three or four hundred yards off, and turning about, retreated up the rising ground. We urged our horses across the ravine, and gave chase. The immense weight of head and shoulders causes the buffalo to labour heavily up hill; but it accelerates his descent. We had the advantage, therefore, and gained rapidly upon the fugitives, though it was difficult to get our horses to approach them, their very scent inspiring them with terror. The Count, who had a double barrelled gun loaded with ball, fired, but missed. The bulls now altered their course, and galloped down hill with headlong rapidity. As they

The Herd Leader

ran in different directions, we each singled one and separated. I was provided with a brace of veteran brass barrelled pistols, which I had borrowed at Fort Gibson, and which had evidently seen some service. Pistols are very effective in buffalo hunting, as the hunter can ride up close to the animal, and fire at it while at full speed; whereas the long heavy rifles used on the frontier, cannot be easily managed, nor discharged with accurate aim from horseback. My object, therefore, was to get within pistol shot of the buffalo. This was no very easy matter. I was well mounted on a horse of excellent speed and bottom, that seemed eager for the chase, and soon overtook the game; but the moment he came nearly parallel, he would keep sheering off with ears forked, and pricked forward, and every symptom of aversion and alarm. It was no wonder. Of all animals, a buffalo, when close pressed by the hunter, has an aspect the most diabolical. His two short black horns, curve out of a huge frontlet of shaggy hair; his eyes glow like coals; his mouth is open, his tongue parched and drawn up into a half crescent; his tail is erect, and tufted and whisking about in the air, he is a perfect picture of mingled rage and terror.

It was with difficulty I urged my horse sufficiently near, when, taking aim, to my chagrin, both pistols missed fire. Unfortunately the locks of these veteran weapons were so much worn, that in the gallop, the priming had been shaken out of the pans. At the snapping of the last pistol I was close upon the buffalo, when, in his despair, he turned round with a sudden snort and rushed upon me. My horse wheeled about as if on a pivot, made a convulsive spring, and, as I had been leaning on one side with pistol extended, I came near being thrown at the feet of the buffalo.

Three or four bounds of the horse carried us out of the reach of the enemy; who, having merely turned in desperate self defense, quickly resumed his flight. As soon as I could gather in my panic-stricken horse, and prime the pistols afresh, I again spurred in pursuit of the buffalo, who had slackened his speed to take breath. On my approach he again set off full tilt, heaving himself forward with a heavy rolling gallop, dashing with headlong precipitation through brakes and ravines, while several deer and wolves, startled from their coverts by his thundering career, ran helter skelter to right and left across the waste.

A gallop across the prairies in pursuit of game, is by no means so smooth a career as those may imagine, who have only the idea of an open level plain. It is true, the prairies of the hunting ground are not so much entangled with flowering plants and long herbage as the lower prairies, and are principally covered with short buffalo grass; but they are diversified by hill and dale, and where most level, are apt to be cut-up by deep rifts and ravines, made by torrents after rains; and which, yawning from an even surface, are almost like pitfalls in the way of the hunter, checking him suddenly, when in full career, or subjecting him to the risk of limb and life. The plains, too, are beset by burrowing holes of small animals, in which the horse is apt to sink to the fetlock, and throw both himself and his rider. The late rain had covered some parts of the prairie, where the ground was hard, with a thin sheet of water, through which the horse had to splash his way. In other parts there were innumerable shallow hollows, eight or ten feet in diameter, made by the buffaloes, who wallow in sand and mud like swine. These being filled with water, shone like mirrors, so that the horse was continually leaping over them or springing on one side. We had reached, too, a rough part of the prairie, very much broken and cut up; the buffalo, who was running for life, took no heed to his course, plunging down break-neck ravines, where it was necessary to skirt the borders in search of a safer descent. At length we came to where a winter stream had torn a deep chasm across the whole prairie, leaving open jagged rocks; and forming a long glen bordered by steep crumbling cliffs of mingled stone and clay. Down one of these the buffalo flung himself, half tumbling, half leaping, and then scuttled along the bottom; while I, seeing all further pursuit useless, pulled up, and gazed quietly after him from the border of the cliff, until he disappeared amidst the windings of the ravine.

Nothing now remained but to turn my steed and rejoin my companions. Here at first was some little difficulty. The ardour of the chase had betrayed me into a long, heedless gallop. I now found myself in the midst of a lonely waste, in which the prospect was bounded by undulating swells of land, naked and uniform, where, from the deficiency of landmarks and distinct features, an inexperienced man may become bewildered, and lose his way as readily as in the wastes of the ocean. The day too, was overcast, so that I could not guide myself by the sun; my only mode was to retrace the track my horse had made in coming, though this I would often lose sight of, where the ground was covered with parched herbage.

To one unaccustomed to it, there is something inexpressibly lonely in the solitude of a prairie. The loneliness of a forest seems nothing to it. There the view is shut in by trees, and the imagination is left free to picture some livelier scene beyond. But here we have an immense extent of landscape without a sign of human existence.

We have the consciousness of being far, far beyond the bounds of human habitation; we feel as if moving in the midst of a desert world. As my horse lagged slowly back over the scenes of our late scamper, and the delirium of the chase had passed away, I was peculiarly sensible to these circumstances. The silence of the waste was now and then broken by the cry of a distant flock of pelicans, stalking like spectres about a shallow pool; sometimes by the sinister croaking of a raven in the air, while occasionally a scoundrel wolf would scour off from before me; and, having attained a safe distance, would sit down and howl and wine with tones that gave a dreariness to the surrounding solitude.

After pursuing my way for some time, I descried a horseman on the edge of a distant hill, and soon recognized him to be the Count. He had been equally unsuccessful with myself; we were shortly afterwards rejoined by our worthy comrade, the Virtuoso, who, with spectacles on nose, had made two or three ineffectual shots from horseback.

We determined not to seek the camp until we had made one more effort. Casting our eyes about the surrounding waste, we descried a herd of buffalo about two miles distant, scattered apart, and quietly grazing near a small strip of trees and bushes. It required but little stretch of fancy to picture them so many cattle grazing on the edge of a common, and that the grove might shelter some lowly farm house.

We now formed our plan to circumvent the herd, and by getting on the other side of them, to hunt them in the direction where we knew our camp to be situated: otherwise, the pursuit might take us to such a distance as to render it impossible for us to find our way back before night-fall. Taking a wide circuit therefore, we moved slowly and cautiously, pausing occasionally, when we saw any of the herd desist from grazing. The wind fortunately set from them, otherwise they might have scented us and have taken the alarm. In this way, we succeeded in getting round the herd without disturbing it. It consisted of about forty head, bulls, cows and calves. Separating to some distance from each other, we now approached slowly in a parallel line, hoping by degrees to steal near without exciting attention. They began, however, to move off quietly, stopping at every step or two to graze, when suddenly a bull that, unobserved by us, had been taking his siesta under a clump of trees to our left, roused himself from his lair, and hastened to join his companions. We were still at a considerable distance, but the game had taken the alarm. We quickened our pace, they broke into a gallop, and now commenced a full chase.

As the ground was level, they shouldered along with great speed, following each other in a line; two or three bulls bringing up the rear, the last of whom, from his enormous size and venerable frontlet, and beard of sunburnt hair, looked like the patriarch of the herd; and as if he might long have reigned the monarch of the prairie.

There is a mixture of the awful and the comic in the look of these huge animals, as they bear their great bulk forwards, with an up and down motion of the unwieldy head and shoulders; their tail cocked up like the queue of pantaloon in a pantomime, the end whisking about in a fierce yet whimsical style, and their eyes glaring venomously with an expression of fright and fury.

For some time I kept parallel with the line, without being able to force my horse within pistol shot, so much had he been alarmed by the assault of the buffalo, in the preceding chase. At length I succeeded, but was again balked by my pistols missing fire. My companions, whose horses were less fleet, and more way-worn, could not overtake the herd; at length Mr. L. who was in the rear of the line, and losing ground, levelled his double barrelled gun, and fired a long raking shot. It struck a buffalo just above the loins, broke its back bone, and brought it to the ground. He stopped and alighted to despatch his prey, when borrowing his gun which had yet a charge remaining in it, I put my horse to his speed, again overtook the herd which was thundering along, pursued by the Count. With my present weapon there was no need of urging my horse to such close quarters; galloping along parallel, therefore, I singled out a buffalo, and by a fortunate shot brought it down on the spot. The ball had struck a vital part; it would not move from the place where it fell, but lay there struggling in mortal agony, while the rest of the herd kept on their headlong career across the prairie.

Dismounting, I now fettered my horse to prevent his straying, and advanced to contemplate my victim. I am nothing of a sportsman: I had been prompted to this unwonted exploit by the magnitude of the game, and the excitement of an adventurous chase. Now that the excitement was over, I could not but look with commiseration upon the poor animal that lay struggling and bleeding at my feet. His very size and importance, which had before inspired me with eagerness, now increased my compunction. It seemed as if I had inflicted pain in proportion to the bulk of my victim, and as if there were a hundred fold greater waste of life than there would have been in the destruction of an animal of inferior size.

To add to these after qualms of conscience, the poor animal lingered in his agony. He had evidently received a mortal wound, but death might be long in coming. It would not do to leave him here to be torn piecemeal, while yet alive, by the wolves that had already snuffed his blood, and were skulking and howling at a distance, and waiting for my departure, and by the ravens that were flapping about, croaking dismally in the air. It became now an act of mercy to give him his quietus, and put him out of his misery. I primed one of the pistols, therefore, and advanced close up to the buffalo. To inflict a wound thus in cool blood, I found a totally different thing from firing in the heat of the chase. Taking aim, however, just behind the fore-shoulder, my pistol for once proved true; the ball must have passed through the heart, for the animal gave one convulsive throe and expired.

While I stood meditating and moralizing over the wreck I had so wantonly produced, with my horse grazing near me, I was rejoined by my fellow sportsman, the Virtuoso; who, being a man of universal adroitness, and withal, more experienced and hardened in the gentle art of "venerie," soon managed to carve out the tongue of the buffalo, and delivered it to me to bear back to the camp as a trophy.

Our solicitude was now awakened for the young Count. With his usual eagerness and impetuosity he had persisted in urging his jaded horse in pursuit of the herd, unwilling to return without having likewise killed a buffalo. In this way he had kept on following them, hither and thither, and occasionally firing an ineffectual shot, until by degrees horseman and herd became indistinct in the distance, and at length swelling ground and strips of trees and thickets hid them from sight.

By the time my friend, the amateur, joined me, the young Count had been long lost to view. We held a consultation on the matter. Evening was drawing on. Were we to pursue him, it would be dark before we should overtake him, granting we did not entirely lose trace of him in the gloom. We should then be too much bewildered to find our way back to the encampment; even now, our return would be difficult. We determined, therefore, to hasten to the camp as speedily as possible, and sent out our half-breeds, and some of the veteran hunters, skilled in cruising about the prairies to search for our companion.

We accordingly set forward in what we supposed to be the direction of the camp. Our weary horses could hardly be urged beyond a walk. The twilight thickened upon us; the landscape grew gradually indistinct; we tried in vain to recognize various landmarks which we had noted in the morning. The features of the prairies are so similar as to baffle the eye of any but an Indian, or a practiced woodsman. At length night closed in. We hoped to see the distant glare of camp fires; we listened to catch the sound of the bells about the necks of the grazing horses. Once or twice we thought we distinguished them; we were mistaken. Nothing was to be heard but a monotonous concert of insects, with now and then the dismal howl of wolves mingling with the night breeze. We began to think of halting for the night, and bivouacking under the lee of some thicket. We had implements to strike a light; there was plenty of firewood at hand, and the tongues of our buffaloes would furnish us with a repast.

Just as we were preparing to dismount, we heard the report of a rifle, and shortly after, the notes of the bugle, calling up the night guard. Pushing forward in that direction, the camp fires soon broke on our sight, gleaming at a distance from among the thick groves of an alluvial bottom.

As we entered the camp, we found it a scene of rude hunters' revelry and wassail. There had been a grand day's sport, in which all had taken a part. Eight buffaloes had been killed; roaring fires were blazing on every side; all hands were feasting upon roasted joints, broiled marrow-bones, and the juicy hump, far-famed among the epicures of the prairies. Right glad were we to dismount and partake of the sturdy cheer, for we had been on our weary horses since morning without tasting food.

As to our worthy friend, the Commissioner, with whom we had parted company at the outset of this eventful day, we found him lying in a corner of the tent, much the worse for wear, in the course of a successful hunting match.

It seems that our man Beatte, in his zeal to give the Commissioner an opportunity of distinguishing himself, and gratifying his hunting propensities, had mounted him upon his half wild horse, and started him in pursuit of a huge buffalo bull, that had already been frightened by the hunters. The horse, which was fearless as his owner, and, like him, had a considerable spice of devil in his composition, and who, beside, had been made familiar with the game, no sooner came in sight and scent of the buffalo, than he set off like mad, bearing the involuntary hunter hither and thither, and whither he would not—up hill and down hill — leaping pools and brooks — dashing through glens and gullies, until he came up with the game. Instead of sheering off, he crowded upon the buffalo. The Commissioner, almost in self defence, discharged both barrels of a double barrelled gun into the enemy. The broadside took effect, but was not mortal. The buffalo turned furiously upon his pursuer; the horse, as he had been taught by his owner, wheeled off. The buffalo plunged after him. The worthy Commissioner, in great extremity, drew his sole pistol from his holster, fired it off as a stern chaser, shot the buffalo full in the breast, and brought him lumbering forward to the earth.

The Commissioner returned to camp, lauded on all sides for his signal exploit; but grievously battered and way-worn. He had been a hard rider per force, and a victor in spite of himself. He turned a deaf ear to all compliments and congratulations; had but little stomach for the hunter's fare placed before him, and soon retreated to stretch his limbs in the tent, declaring that nothing should tempt him again to mount

that half devil Indian horse, and that he had enough of buffalo hunting for the rest of his life.

It was too dark now to send any one in search of the young Count. Guns, however, were fired, and the bugle sounded from time to time, to guide him to the camp, if by chance he should straggle within hearing; but the night advanced without his making his appearance. There was not a star visible to guide him, and we concluded that wherever he was, he would give up wandering in the dark, and bivouack until daybreak.

It was a raw, overcast night. The carcasses of the buffaloes killed in the vicinity of the camp, had drawn about it an unusual number of wolves, who kept up the most forlorn concert of whining yells, prolonged into dismal cadences and inflexions, literally con-

Pawnee Breaking a Wild Horse.   *George Catlin*

verting the surrounding waste into a howling wilderness. Nothing is more melancholy than the midnight howl of a wolf on a prairie. What rendered the gloom and wildness of the night and the savage concert of the neighbouring waste the more dreary to us, was the idea of the lonely and exposed situation of our young and inexperienced comrade. We trusted, however, that on the return of daylight, he would find his way back to the camp, and then all the events of the night would be remembered only as so many savoury gratifications of his passion for adventure.

The morning dawned, and an hour or two passed without any tidings of the Count. We began to feel uneasiness lest, having no compass to aid him, he might perplex himself and wander in some opposite direction. Stragglers are thus often lost for days; what made us the more anxious about him was, that he had no provisions with him, was totally unversed in "wood craft," and liable to fall into the hands of some lurking or straggling party of savages.

As soon as our people, therefore, had made their breakfast, we beat up for volunteers for a cruise in search of the Count. A dozen of the rangers, mounted on some of the best and freshest horses, and armed with rifles, were soon ready to start; our half-breeds Beatte and Antoine also, with our little mongrel Frenchman, were zealous in the cause; so Mr. L. and myself, taking the lead, to show the way to the scene of our little hunt, where we had parted company with the Count, we all set out across the prairie. A ride of a couple of miles brought us to the carcasses of the two buffaloes we had killed. A legion of ravenous wolves were already gorging upon them. At our approach they reluctantly drew off, skulking with a caitiff look to the distance of a few hundred yards, and there awaiting our departure, that they might return to their banquet.

I conducted Beatte and Antoine to the spot from whence the young Count had continued the chase alone. It was like putting hounds upon the scent. They immediately distinguished the track of his horse amidst the trampings of the buffaloes, and set off at a round pace, following with the eye in nearly a straight course, for upwards of a mile, when they came to where the herd had divided, and run hither and thither about a meadow. Here the track of the horse's hoofs wandered and doubled and often crossed each other; our half-breeds were like hounds at fault. While we were all at a halt, waiting until they should unravel the maze, Beatte suddenly gave a short Indian whoop, or rather yelp, and pointed to a distant hill. On regarding it attentively, we perceived a horseman on the summit. "It is the Count!" cried Beatte, and set off at a full gallop, followed by the whole company. In a few moments he checked his horse. Another figure on horseback had appeared on the brow of a hill. This completely altered the case. The Count had wandered off alone; no other person had been missing from the camp. If one of these horsemen was indeed the Count, the other must be an Indian. If an Indian, in all probability a Pawnee. Perhaps they were both Indians; scouts of some party lurking in the vicinity. While these and other suggestions were hastily discussed, the two horsemen glided down from the profile of the hill, and we lost sight of them. One of the rangers suggested that there might be a straggling party of Pawnees behind the hill, and that the Count might have fallen into their hands. The idea had an electric effect upon the little troop. In an instant every horse was at full speed, the half-breeds leading the way; the young rangers as they rode set up wild yelps of exultation at the thoughts of having a brush with the Indians. A neck or nothing gallop brought us to the skirts of the hill, and revealed our mistake. In a ravine we found the two horsemen standing by a carcass of a buffalo which they had killed. They proved to be two rangers, who, unperceived, had left the camp a little before us, and had come here in a direct line, while we had made a wide circuit about the prairie.

This episode being at an end, and the sudden excitement being over, we slowly and coolly retraced our steps to the meadow; but it was some time before our half-breeds could again get on the track of the Count. Having at length found it, they succeeded in following it through all its doublings, until they came to where it was no longer mingled with the tramp of buffaloes, but became single and separate, wandering here and there about the prairies, but always tending in a direction opposite to that of the camp. Here the Count had evidently given up the pursuit of the herd, and had endeavoured to find his way to the encampment, but had become bewildered as the evening shades thickened around him, and had completely mistaken the points of the compass.

In all this quest our half-breeds displayed that quickness of eye, in following up a track, for which Indians are so noted. Beatte especially, was as staunch as a veteran hound. Sometimes he would keep forward on an easy trot; his eyes fixed on the ground a little ahead of his horse, clearly distinguishing prints in the herbage, which to me were invisible, excepting on the closest inspection. Sometimes he would pull up and walk his horse slowly, regarding the ground intensely; where to my eye nothing was apparent. Then he would dismount, lead his horse by the bridle, and advance cautiously step by step, with his face bent towards the earth, just catching, here and there, a casual indication of the vaguest kind to guide him onward. In some places where the soil was hard, and the grass withered, he would lose the track entirely, and wander backwards and forwards, and right and left, in search of it; returning occasionally to the place where he had lost sight of it, to take a new departure. If this failed he would examine the banks of the neighbouring streams, or the sandy bottoms of the ravines, in hopes of finding tracks where the Count had crossed. When he again came upon the track, he would remount his horse, and resume his onward course. At length, after crossing a stream, in the crumbling banks of which the hoofs of the horse were deeply dented, we came upon a high dry prairie, where our half-breeds were completely baffled. Not a foot print was to be discerned, though they searched in every direction; and Beatte at length coming to a pause, shook his head most despondingly.

Just then a small herd of deer, roused from a neighbouring ravine, came bounding by us. Beatte sprang from his horse, lev-

Keep Away!

elled his rifle, and wounded one slightly, but without bringing it to the ground. The report of the rifle was almost immediately followed by a long halloo from a distance. We looked around but could see nothing. Another long halloo was heard, and at length a horseman was descried, emerging out of a skirt of forest. A single glance showed him to be the young Count; there was a universal shout and scamper, every one setting off full gallop to greet him. It was a joyful meeting to both parties; for, much anxiety had been felt by us all on account of his youth and inexperience, and for his part, with all his love of adventure, he seemed right glad to be once more among his friends.

As we supposed, he had completely mistaken his course on the preceding evening, and had wandered about until dark, when he thought of bivouacking. The night was cold, yet he feared to make a fire, lest it might betray him to some lurking party of Indians. Hobbling his horse with his pocket handkerchief, and leaving him to graze on the margin of the prairie, he clambered into a tree, fixed his saddle in the fork of the branches, and placing himself securely with his back against the trunk, prepared to pass a dreary and anxious night, regaled occasionally with the howlings of the wolves. He was agreeably disappointed. The fatigue of the day soon brought on a sound sleep; he had delightful dreams about his home in Switzerland, nor did he wake until it was broad daylight.

He then descended from his roosting place, mounted his horse, and rode to the naked summit of a hill, from whence he beheld a trackless wilderness around him, but, at no great distance, the Grand Canadian, winding its way between borders of forest land. The sight of this river consoled him with the idea that, should he fail in finding his way back to the camp, or, in being found by some party of his comrades, he might follow the course of the stream, which could not fail to conduct him to some frontier post, or Indian hamlet. So closed the events of our hap-hazard buffalo hunt.

42. Ashore in California

BY RICHARD HENRY DANA

EDITOR'S NOTE: The long voyage which Dana (1815-1882) here partly describes in his justly famous narrative, *Two Years Before the Mast*, was a turning point in his life. Leaving Harvard because of difficulties with his eyesight, he shipped before the mast in an effort to regain his health, going to California via Cape Horn. He returned in 1836, healthy, energetic and with the raw materials for a classic about the sea. His reports of early California life are among the best that are extant.

OUR place of destination had been Monterey, but as we were to the northward of it when the wind hauled ahead, we made a fair wind for San Francisco. This large bay, which lies in latitude 37° 58', was discovered by Sir Francis Drake, and by him represented to be (as indeed it is) a magnificent bay, containing several good harbors, great depth of water, and surrounded by a fertile and finely wooded country. About thirty miles from the mouth of the bay, and on the southeast side, is a high point, upon which the Presidio is built. Behind this point is the little harbor, or bight, called Yerba Buena, in which trading-vessels anchor, and, near it, the Mission of Dolores. There was no other habitation on this side of the Bay, except a shanty of rough boards put up by a man named Richardson, who was doing a little trading between the vessels and the Indians.* Here, at anchor, and the only vessel, was a brig under Russian colors, from Sitka, in Russian America, which had come down to winter, and to take in a supply of tallow and grain, great quantities of which latter article are raised in the Missions at the head of the bay. The second day after our arrival we went on board the brig, it being Sunday, as a matter of curiosity; and there was enough there to gratify it. Though no larger than the Pilgrim, she had five or six officers, and a crew of between twenty and thirty; and such a stupid and greasy-looking set, I never saw before. Although it was quite comfortable weather and we had nothing on but straw hats, shirts, and duck trousers, and were barefooted, they had, every man of them, double-soled boots, coming up to the knees, and well greased; thick woollen trousers, frocks, waistcoats, pea-jackets, woollen caps, and everything in true Nova Zembla rig; and in the warmest days they made no change. The clothing of one of these men would weigh nearly as much as that of half our crew. They had brutish faces, looked like the antipodes of sailors, and apparently dealt in nothing but grease. They lived upon grease; ate it, drank it, slept in the midst of it, and their clothes were covered with it. To a Russian, grease is the greatest luxury. They looked with greedy eyes upon the tallow-bags as they were taken into the vessel, and, no doubt, would have eaten one up whole, had not the officer kept watch over it. The grease appeared to fill their pores, and to come out in their hair and on their faces. It seems as if it were this saturation which makes them stand cold and rain so well. If they were to go into a warm climate, they would melt and die of the scurvy.

The vessel was no better than the crew. Everything was in the oldest and most inconvenient fashion possible: running trusses and lifts on the yards, and large hawser cables, coiled all over the decks, and served and parcelled in all directions. The topmasts, top-gallant-masts, and studding-sail booms were nearly black for want of scraping, and the decks would have turned the stomach of a man-of-war's-man. The galley was down in the forecastle; and there the crew lived, in the midst of the steam and grease of the cooking, in a place as hot as an oven, and apparently never cleaned out. Five minutes in the forecastle was enough for us, and we were glad to get into the open air. We made some trade with them, buying Indian curiosities, of which they had a great number; such as bead-work, feathers of birds, fur moccasins, &c. I purchased a large robe, made of the skins of some animal, dried and sewed nicely together, and covered all over on the outside with thick downy feathers, taken from the breasts of various birds, and arranged with their different colors so as to make a brilliant show.

A few days after our arrival the rainy

* The next year Richardson built a one-story adobe house on the same spot, which was long afterwards known as the oldest house in the great city of San Francisco.

season set in, and for three weeks it rained almost every hour, without cessation. This was bad for our trade, for the collecting of hides is managed differently in this port from what it is in any other on the coast. The Mission of Dolores, near the anchorage, has no trade at all; but those of San José, Santa Clara, and others situated on the large creeks or rivers which run into the bay, and distant between fifteen and forty miles from the anchorage, do a greater business in hides than any in California. Large boats, or launches, manned by Indians, and capable of carrying from five to six hundred hides apiece, are attached to the Missions, and sent down to the vessels with hides, to bring away goods in return. Some of the crews of the vessels are obliged to go and come in the boats, to look out for the hides and goods. These are favorite expeditions with the sailors in fine weather; but now, to be gone three or four days, in open boats, in constant rain, without any shelter, and with cold food, was hard service. Two of our men went up to Santa Clara in one of these boats, and were gone three days, during all which time they had a constant rain, and did not sleep a wink, but passed three long nights walking fore and aft the boat, in the open air. When they got on board they were completely exhausted, and took a watch below of twelve hours. All the hides, too, that came down in the boats were soaked with water, and unfit to put below, so that we were obliged to trice them up to dry, in the intervals of sunshine or wind, upon all parts of the vessel. We got up tricing-lines from the jib-boom-end to each arm of the fore yard, and thence to the main and cross-jack yard-arms. Between the tops, too, and the mast-heads, from the fore to the main swifters, and thence to the mizzen rigging, and in all directions athwartships,

tricing-lines were run, and strung with hides. The head stays and guys, and the spritsail yard were lined, and, having still more, we got out the swinging-booms, and strung them and the forward and after guys with hides. The rail, fore and aft, the windlass, capstan, the sides of the ship, and every vacant place on deck, were covered with wet hides, on the least sign of an interval for drying. Our ship was nothing but a mass of hides, from the cat-harpins to the water's edge, and from the jib-boom-end to the taffrail.

One cold, rainy evening, about eight o'clock, I received orders to get ready to start for San José at four the next morning, in one of these Indian boats, with four days' provisions. I got my oil-cloth clothes, southwester, and thick boots ready, and turned into my hammock early, determined to get some sleep in advance, as the boat was to be alongside before daybreak. I slept on till all hands were called in the morning; for, fortunately for me, the Indians, intentionally, or from mistaking their orders, had gone off alone in the night, and were far out of sight. Thus I escaped three or four days of very uncomfortable service.

Four of our men, a few days afterwards, went up in one of the quarter-boats to Santa Clara, to carry the agent, and remained out all night in a drenching rain, in the small boat, in which there was not room for them to turn round; the agent having gone up to the Mission and left the men to their fate, making no provision for their accommodation, and not even sending them anything to eat. After this they had to pull thirty miles, and when they got on board were so stiff that they could not come up the gangway ladder. This filled up the measure of the agent's unpopularity, and never after this could he get anything done for him by the crew; and many a delay and vexation, and many a good ducking in the surf, did he get to pay up old scores, or "square the yards with the bloody quill-driver."

Having collected nearly all the hides that were to be procured, we began our preparations for taking in a supply of wood and water, for both of which San Francisco is the best place on the coast. A small island, about two leagues from the anchorage, called by us "Wood Island," and by the Mexicans "Isla de los Angeles," was covered with trees to the water's edge; and to this two of our crew, who were Kennebec men, and could handle an axe like a plaything, were sent every morning to cut wood, with two boys to pile it up for them. In about a week they had cut enough to last us a year, and the third mate, with myself and three others, were sent over in a large, schooner-rigged, open launch, which we had hired of the Mission, to take in the wood, and bring it to the ship. We left the ship about noon, but owing to a strong head wind, and a tide which here runs four or five knots, did not get into the harbor, formed by two points of the island, where the boats lie, until sundown. No sooner had we come-to, than a strong southeaster, which had been threatening us all day, set in, with heavy rain and a chilly air. We were in rather a bad situation: an open boat, a heavy rain, and a long night; for in winter, in this latitude, it was dark nearly fifteen hours. Taking a small skiff which we had brought with us, we went ashore, but discovered no shelter, for everything was open to the rain; and, collecting a little wood, which we found by lifting up the leaves and brush, and a few mussels, we put aboard again, and made the best preparations in our power for passing the night. We unbent

the mainsail, and formed an awning with it over the after part of the boat, made a bed of wet logs of wood, and, with our jackets on, lay down, about six o'clock, to sleep. Finding the rain running down upon us, and our jackets getting wet through, and the rough, knotty logs rather indifferent couches, we turned out; and, taking an iron pan which we brought with us, we wiped it out dry, put some stones around it, cut the wet bark from some sticks, and, striking a light, made a small fire in the pan. Keeping some sticks near to dry, and covering the whole over with a roof of boards, we kept up a small fire, by which we cooked our mussels, and ate them, rather for an occupation than from hunger. Still it was not ten o'clock; and the night was long before us, when one of the party produced an old pack of Spanish cards from his monkey-jacket pocket, which we hailed as a great windfall; and, keeping a dim, flickering light by our fagots, we played game after game, till one or two o'clock, when, becoming really tired, we went to our logs again, one sitting up at a time, in turn, to keep watch over the fire. Toward morning the rain ceased, and the air became sensibly colder, so that we found sleep impossible, and sat up, watching for daybreak. No sooner was it light than we went ashore, and began our preparations for loading our vessel. We were not mistaken in the coldness of the weather, for a white frost was on the ground, and — a thing we had never seen before in California — one or two little puddles of fresh water were skimmed over with a thin coat of ice. In this state of the weather, and before sunrise, in the gray of the morning, we had to wade off, nearly up to our hips in water, to load the skiff with the wood by armfuls. The third mate remained on board the launch, two more men stayed in the skiff to load and manage it, and all the water-work, as usual, fell upon the two youngest of us; and there we were with frost on the ground, wading forward and back, from the beach to the boat, with armfuls of wood, barefooted, and our trousers rolled up. When the skiff went off with her load, we could only keep our feet from freezing by racing up and down the beach on the hard sand, as fast as we could go. We were all day at this work, and toward sundown, having loaded the vessel as deep as she would bear, we hove up our anchor and made sail, beating out of the bay. No sooner had we got into the large bay than we found a strong tide setting us out to seaward, a thick fog which prevented our seeing the ship, and a breeze too light to set us against the tide, for we were as deep as a sand-barge. By the utmost exertions, we saved ourselves from being carried out to sea, and were glad to reach the leewardmost point of the island, where we came-to, and prepared to pass another night more uncomfortable than the first, for we were loaded up to the gunwale, and had only a choice among logs and sticks for a resting-place. The next morning we made sail at slack water, with a fair wind, and got on board by eleven o'clock, when all hands were turned-to to unload and stow away the wood, which took till night.

Having now taken in all our wood, the next morning a water-party was ordered off with all the casks. From this we escaped, having had a pretty good siege with the wooding. The water-party were gone three days, during which time they narrowly escaped being carried out to sea, and passed one day on an island, where one of them shot a deer, great numbers of which overrun the islands and hills of San Francisco Bay.

While not off on these wood and water parties, or up the rivers to the Missions, we had easy times on board the ship. We were moored, stem and stern, within a cable's length of the shore, safe from southeasters, and with little boating to do; and, as it rained nearly all the time, awnings were put over the hatchways, and all hands sent down between decks, where we were at work, day after day, picking oakum, until we got enough to calk the ship all over, and to last the whole voyage. Then we made a whole suit of gaskets for the voyage home, a pair of wheel-ropes from strips of green hide, great quantities of spun-yarn, and everything else that could be made between decks. It being now midwinter and in high latitude, the nights were very long, so that we were not turned-to until seven in the morning, and were obliged to knock off at five in the evening, when we got supper; which gave us nearly three hours before eight bells, at which time the watch was set.

As we had now been about a year on the coast, it was time to think of the voyage home; and, knowing that the last two or three months of our stay would be very busy ones, and that we should never have so good an opportunity to work for ourselves as the present, we all employed our evenings in making clothes for the passage home, and more especially for Cape Horn. As soon as supper was over and the kids cleared away, and each man had taken his smoke, we seated ourselves on our chests round the lamp, which swung from a beam, and went to work each in his own way, some making hats, others trousers, others jackets, &c., &c., and no one was idle. The boys who could not sew well enough to make their own clothes laid up grass into sinnet for the men, who sewed for them in return. Several of us clubbed together and bought a large piece of twilled cotton, which we made into trousers and jackets, and, giving them several coats of linseed oil, laid them by for Cape Horn. I also sewed and covered a tarpaulin hat, thick and strong enough to sit upon, and made myself a complete suit of flannel underclothing for bad weather. Those who had no southwester caps made them; and several of the crew got up for themselves tarpaulin jackets and trousers, lined on the inside with flannel. Industry was the order of the day, and every one did something for himself; for we knew that as the season advanced, and we went further south, we should have no evenings to work in.

Friday, December 25th. This day was Christmas; and, as it rained all day long, and there were no hides to take in, and nothing especial to do, the captain gave us a holiday (the first we had had, except Sundays, since leaving Boston), and plum-duff for dinner. The Russian brig, following the Old Style, had celebrated their Christmas eleven days before, when they had a grand blowout, and (as our men said) drank, in the forecastle, a barrel of gin, ate up a bag of tallow, and made a soup of the skin.

Sunday, December 27th. We had now finished all our business at this port, and, it being Sunday, we unmoored ship and got under way, firing a salute to the Russian brig, and another to the presidio, which were both answered. The commandante of the presidio, Don Guadalupe Vallejo, a young man, and the most popular, among the Americans and English, of any man in California, was on board when we got under way. He spoke English very well, and was suspected of being favorably inclined to foreigners.

We sailed down this magnificent bay with a light wind, the tide, which was running out, carrying us at the rate of four or five

knots. It was a fine day; the first of entire sunshine we had had for more than a month. We passed directly under the high cliff on which the presidio is built, and stood into the middle of the bay, from whence we could see small bays making up into the interior, large and beautifully wooded islands, and the mouths of several small rivers. If California ever becomes a prosperous country, this bay will be the centre of its prosperity. The abundance of wood and water; the extreme fertility of its shores; the excellence of its climate, which is as near to being perfect as any in the world; and its facilities for navigation, affording the best anchoring-grounds in the whole western coast of America — all fit it for a place of great importance.

The tide leaving us, we came to anchor near the mouth of the bay, under a high and beautifully sloping hill, upon which herds of hundreds and hundreds of red deer, and the stag, with his high branching antlers, were bounding about, looking at us for a moment, and then starting off, affrighted at the noises which we made for the purpose of seeing the variety of their beautiful attitudes and motions.

At midnight, the tide having turned, we hove up our anchor and stood out of the bay, with a fine starry heaven above us — the first we had seen for many weeks. Before the light northerly winds, which blow here with the regularity of trades, we worked slowly along, and made Point Año Nuevo, the northerly point of the Bay of Monterey, on Monday afternoon. We spoke, going in, the brig Diana, of the Sandwich Islands, from the Northwest Coast, last from Sitka. She was off the point at the same time with us, but did not get in to the anchoring-ground until an hour or two after us. It was ten o'clock on Tuesday morning when we came to anchor. Monterey looked just as it did when I saw it last, which was eleven months before, in the brig Pilgrim. The pretty lawn on which it stands, as green as sun and rain could make it; the pine wood on the south; the small river on the north side; the adobe houses, with their white walls and red-tiled roofs, dotted about on the green; the low, white presidio, with its soiled tri-colored flag flying, and the discordant din of drums and trumpets of the noon parade — all brought up the scene we had witnessed here with so much pleasure nearly a year before, when coming from a long voyage, and from our unprepossessing reception at Santa Barbara. It seemed almost like coming to a home.

43. A Day with the Cow Column

BY JESSE APPLEGATE

EDITOR'S NOTE: Jesse Applegate (1811-1888) was born in Kentucky and raised in Missouri. In 1843, with two brothers, Charles and Lindsay, he made a famous trek across the plains and mountains to the lower Willamette Valley in Oregon, of which his essay is a memorial. Jesse Applegate was a member of one of the earliest large emigrant groups to journey to the Oregon country. Many more were soon to follow. He had many pioneering gifts — was strong, adventurous, could survey, knew some law, and was fairly well-read. He could also write well when the occasion demanded, as his account testifies.

THE migration of a large body of men, women and children across the continent to Oregon was, in the year 1843, strictly an experiment; not only in respect to numbers, but to the outfit of the migrating party.

Before that date, two or three missionaries had performed the journey on horseback, driving a few cows with them. Three or four wagons drawn by oxen had reached Fort Hall, on Snake River, but it was the honest opinion of the most of those who had traveled the route down Snake River that no large number of cattle could be subsisted on its scanty pasturage, or wagons taken over a route so rugged and mountainous.

The emigrants were also assured that the Sioux would be much opposed to the passage of so large a body through their country, and would probably resist it on account of the emigrants destroying and frightening away the buffaloes, which had been diminishing in number.

The migrating body numbered over one thousand souls, with about one hundred and twenty wagons, drawn by six-ox teams, averaging about six yokes to the team, and several thousand loose horses and cattle.

The emigrants first organized and attempted to travel in one body, but it was soon found that no progress could be made with a body so cumbrous, and as yet as averse to all discipline. And at the crossing of the "Big Blue" it divided into two columns, which traveled in supporting distance of each other as far as Independence Rock, on the Sweet Water.

From this point, all danger from Indians being over, the emigrants separated into small parties better suited to the narrow mountain paths and small pastures in their front. Before the division on the Blue River there was some just cause for discontent in respect to loose cattle. Some of the emigrants had only their teams, while others had large herds in addition which must share the pastures and be guarded and driven by the whole body.

This discontent had its effect in the division on the Blue, those not encumbered with or having but few loose cattle attached themselves to the light column; those having more than four or five cows had of necessity to join the heavy or cow column. Hence the cow column, being much larger than the other and encumbered with its large herds had to use greater exertion and observe a more rigid discipline to keep pace with the more agile consort. It is with the cow or more clumsy column that I propose to journey with the reader for a single day.

It is four o'clock A. M.; the sentinels on duty have discharged their rifles—the signal that the hours of sleep are over; and every wagon and tent is pouring forth its night tenants, and slow-kindling smokes begin largely to rise and float away on the morning air. Sixty men start from the corral, spreading as they make through the vast herd of cattle and horses that form a semicircle around the encampment, the most distant perhaps two miles away.

The herders pass to the extreme verge and carefully examine for trails beyond, to see that none of the animals have strayed or been stolen during the night. This morning no trails lead beyond the outside animals in sight, and by five o'clock the herders begin to contract the great moving circle and the well-trained animals move slowly toward camp, clipping here and there a thistle or tempting bunch of grass on the way. In about an hour five thousand animals are close up to the encampment, and the teamsters are busy selecting their teams and driving them inside the "corral" to be yoked. The corral is a circle one hundred yards deep, formed with wagons connected strongly with each other, the wagon in the rear being connected with the wagon in front by its tongue and ox chains. It is a strong barrier that the most vicious ox cannot break, and in case of an attack of the Sioux would be no contemptible entrenchment.

From six to seven o'clock is a busy time; breakfast is to be eaten, the tents struck, the wagons loaded, and the teams yoked and brought up in readiness to be attached to their respective wagons. All know when, at seven o'clock, the signal to march sounds, that those not ready to take their proper places in the line of march must fall into the dusty rear for the day.

There are sixty wagons. They have been divided into fifteen divisions or platoons of four wagons each, and each platoon is entitled to lead in its turn. The leading platoon of today will be the rear one tomorrow, and will bring up the rear unless some teamster, through indolence or negligence, has lost his place in the line, and is condemned to that uncomfortable post. It is within ten minutes of seven; the corral but now a strong barricade is everywhere broken, the teams being attached to the wagons. The women and children have taken their places in them. The pilot (a borderer who has passed his life on the verge

Emigrants to the West

of civilization, and has been chosen to the post of leader from his knowledge of the savage and his experience in travel through roadless wastes) stands ready in the midst of his pioneers, and aids, to mount and lead the way. Ten or fifteen young men, not to-day on duty, form another cluster. They are ready to start on a buffalo hunt, are well mounted, and well armed as they need be, for the unfriendly Sioux have driven the buffalo out of the Platte, and the hunters must ride fifteen or twenty miles to reach them. The cow drivers are hastening, as they get ready, to the rear of their charge, to collect and prepare them for the day's march.

It is on the stroke of seven; the rushing to and fro, the cracking of the whips, the loud command to oxen, and what seems to be the inextricable confusion of the last ten minutes has ceased. Fortunately every one has been found and every teamster is at his post. The clear notes of the trumpet sound in the front; the pilot and his guards mount their horses, the leading division of wagons moves out of the encampment, and takes up the line of march, the rest fall into their places with the precision of clock work, until the spot so lately full of life sinks back into that solitude that seems to reign over the broad plain and rushing river as the caravan draws its lazy length toward the distant El Dorado. It is with the hunters we will briskly canter towards the bold but smooth and grassy bluffs that bound the broad valley, for we are not yet in sight of the grander but less beautiful scenery (of the Chimney Rock, Court House, and other bluffs, so nearly resembling giant castles and palaces) made by the passage of the Platte through the Highlands near Laramie. We have been traveling briskly for more than an hour. We have reached the top of the bluff, and now have turned to view the wonderful panorama spread before us. To those who have not been on the Platte my powers of description are wholly inadequate to convey an idea of the vast extent and grandeur of the picture, and the rare beauty and distinctness of its detail. No haze or fog obscures objects in the pure transparent atmosphere of this lofty region. To those accustomed only to the murky air of the sea-board, no correct judgment of distance can be formed by sight, and objects which they think they can reach in a two hours' walk may be a day's travel away; and though the evening air is a better conductor of sound, on the high plain during the day the report of the loudest rifle sounds little louder than the bursting of a cap; and while the report can be heard but a few hundred yards, the smoke of the discharge may be seen for miles. So extended is the view from the bluff on which the hunters stand that the broad river glowing under the morning sun like a sheet of silver, and the broader emerald valley that borders it stretch away in the distance until they narrow at almost two points in the horizon, and when first seen, the vast pile of the Wind River mountain, though hundreds of miles away, looks clear and distinct as a white cottage on the plain.

We are full six miles away from the line of march; though everything is dwarfed by distance, it is seen distinctly. The caravan has been about two hours in motion and is now extended as widely as a prudent regard for safety will permit. First, near the bank of the shining river, is a company of horsemen; they seem to have found an obstruction, for the main body has halted while

three or four ride rapidly along the bank of the creek or slough. They are hunting a favorable crossing for the wagons; while we look they have succeeded; it has apparently required no work to make it passable, for all but one of the party have passed on and he has raised a flag, no doubt a signal to the wagons to steer their course to where he stands. The leading teamster sees him though he is yet two miles off, and steers his course directly towards him, all the wagons following in his track. They (the wagons) form a line three quarters of a mile in length; some of the teamsters ride upon the front of their wagons, some walk beside their teams; scattered along the line companies of women and children are taking exercise on foot; they gather bouquets of rare and beautiful flowers that line the way; near them stalks a stately greyhound or an Irish wolf dog, apparently proud of keeping watch and ward over his master's wife and children.

Next comes a band of horses; two or three men or boys follow them, the docile and sagacious animals scarce needing this attention, for they have learned to follow in the rear of the wagons, and know that at noon they will be allowed to graze and rest. Their knowledge of time seems as accurate as of the place they are to occupy in the line, and even a full-blown thistle will scarcely tempt them to straggle or halt until the dinner hour has arrived. Not so with the large herd of horned beasts that bring up the rear; lazy, selfish and unsocial, it has been a task to get them in motion, the strong always ready to domineer over the weak, halt in the front and forbid the weaker to pass them. They seem to move only in fear of the driver's whip; though in the morning full to repletion, they have not been driven an hour before their hunger and thirst seem to indicate a fast of days' duration. Through all the long day their greed is never sated nor their thirst quenched, nor is there a moment of relaxation of the tedious and vexatious labors of their drivers, although to all others the march furnishes some season of relaxation or enjoyment. For the cow-drivers there is none.

But from the standpoint of the hunters the vexations are not apparent; the crack of the whips and loud objurgations are lost in the distance. Nothing of the moving panorama, smooth and orderly as it appears, has more attractions for the eye than that vast square column in which all colors are mingled, moving here slowly and there briskly, as impelled by horsemen riding furiously in front and rear.

But the picture, in its grandeur, its wonderful mingling of colors and distinctness of detail, is forgotten in contemplation of the singular people who give it life and animation. No other race of men with the means at their command would undertake so great a journey; none save these could successfully perform it with no previous preparation, relying only on the fertility of their invention to devise the means to overcome each danger and difficulty as it arose. They have undertaken to perform, with slow moving oxen, a journey of two thousand miles. The way lies over trackless wastes, wide and deep rivers, rugged and lofty mountains, and is beset with hostile savages. Yet, whether it were a deep river with no tree upon its banks, a rugged defile where even a loose horse could not pass, a hill too steep for him to climb, or a threatened attack of an enemy, they are always found ready and equal to the occasion, and always conquerors. May we not call them men of destiny? They are people changed in no essential particulars from their ancestors, who have followed closely on the footsteps of the receding savage, from the Atlantic sea-board to the valley of the Mississippi.

But while we have been gazing at the picture in the valley, the hunters have been examining the high plain in the other direction. Some dark moving objects have been discovered in the distance, and all are closely watching them to discover what they are, for in the atmosphere of the plains a flock of crows marching miles away, or a band of buffaloes or Indians at ten times the distance, look alike, and many ludicrous mistakes occur. But these are buffaloes, for two have stuck their heads together and are alternately pushing each other back. The hunters mount and away in pursuit, and I, a poor cow-driver, must hurry back to my daily toil, and take a scolding from my fellow herders for so long playing truant.

The pilot, by measuring the ground and timing the speed of the wagons and the walk of his horses, has determined the rate of each, so as to enable him to select the nooning place, as nearly as the requisite grass and water can be had at the end of five hours' travel of the wagons. Today, the ground being favorable, little time has been lost in preparing the road, so that he and his pioneers are at the nooning place an hour in advance of the wagons, which time is spent in preparing convenient watering places for the animals and digging little wells near the bank of the Platte. As the teams are not unyoked, but simply turned loose from the wagons, a corral is not formed at noon, but the wagons are drawn up in columns, four abreast, the leading wagon of each platoon on the left—the platoons being formed with that view. This brings friends together at noon as well as at night.

Today an extra session of the Council is being held, to settle a dispute that does not admit of delay, between a proprietor and a young man who has undertaken to do a man's service on the journey for bed and board. Many such engagements exist and much interest is taken in the manner this high court, from which there is no appeal, will define the rights of each party in such engagements. The Council was a high court in the most exalted sense. It was a Senate composed of the ablest and most respected fathers of the emigration. It exercised both legislative and judicial powers, and its laws and decisions proved it equal [to] and worthy of the high trust reposed in it. Its sessions were usually held on days when the caravan was not moving. It first took the state of the little commonwealth into consideration; revised or repealed rules defective or obsolete, and exacted such others as the exigencies seemed to require. The commonwealth being cared for, it next resolved itself into a court, to hear and settle private disputes and grievances. The offender and aggrieved appeared before it, witnesses were examined, and the parties were heard by themselves and sometimes by counsel. The judges thus being made fully acquainted with the case, and being in no way influenced or cramped by technicalities, decided all cases according to their merits. There was but little use for lawyers before this court, for no plea was entertained which was calculated to defeat the ends of justice. Many of these judges have since won honors in higher spheres. They have aided to establish on the broad basis of right and universal liberty two of the pillars of our great Republic in the Occident. Some of the young men who appeared before them as advocates have themselves sat upon the highest judicial tribu-

nals, commanded armies, been Governors of States, and taken high positions in the Senate of the nation.

It is now one o'clock; the bugle has sounded, and the caravan has resumed its westward journey. It is in the same order, but the evening is far less animated than the morning march; a drowsiness has fallen apparently on man and beast; teamsters drop asleep on their perches and even when walking by their teams, and the words of command are now addressed to the slowly creeping oxen in the softened tenor of women or the piping treble of children, while the snores of teamsters make a droning accompaniment.

But a little incident breaks the monotony of the march. An emigrant's wife whose state of health has caused Dr. Whitman to travel near the wagon for the day, is now taken with violent illness. The doctor has had the wagon driven out of the line, a tent pitched and a fire kindled. Many conjectures are hazarded in regard to this mysterious proceeding, and as to why this lone wagon is to be left behind.

And we too must leave it, hasten to the front and note the proceedings, for the sun is now getting low in the west, and at length the painstaking pilot is standing ready to conduct the train in the circle which he has previously measured and marked out, which is to form the invariable fortification for the night. The leading wagons follow him so nearly round the circle, that but a wagon length separates them. Each wagon follows in its track, the rear closing on the front, until its tongue and ox chains will perfectly reach from one to the other, and so accurate the measurement and perfect the practice, that the hindmost wagon of the train always precisely closes the gateway. As each wagon is brought into position it is dropped from its team (the teams being inside the circle), the team unyoked, and the yokes and chains are used to connect the wagon strongly with that in its front. Within ten minutes from the time the leading wagon halted, the barricade is formed, the teams unyoked and driven out to pasture.

Everyone is busy preparing fires of buffalo chips to cook the evening meal, pitching tents and otherwise preparing for the night. There are anxious watchers for the absent wagon, for there are many matrons who may be afflicted like its inmate before the journey is over; and they fear the strange and startling practice of this Oregon doctor will be dangerous. But as sun goes down, the absent wagon rolls into camp, the bright, speaking face and cheery look of the doctor, who rides in advance, declares without words that all is well, and both mother and child are comfortable. I would fain now and here pay a passing tribute to that noble, devoted man, Dr. Whitman. I will obtrude no other name upon the reader, nor would I his, were he of our party or even living, but his stay with us was transient, though the good he did us permanent, and he has long since died at his post.

From the time he joined us on the Platte until he left us at Fort Hall, his great experience and indomitable energy were of priceless value to the migrating column. His constant advice, which we knew was based upon a knowledge of the road before us, was — "travel, TRAVEL, TRAVEL — nothing else will take you to the end of your journey; nothing is wise that does not help you along, nothing is good for you that causes a moment's delay." His great authority as a physician and complete success in the case above referred to saved us many prolonged and perhaps ruinous delays from similar causes, and it is no disparagement to others to say, that to no other individual are the emigrants of 1843 so much indebted for the successful conclusion of their journey as to Dr. Marcus Whitman.

All able to bear arms in the party have been formed into three companies, and each of these into four watches. Every third night it is the duty of one of these companies to keep watch and ward over the camp, and it is so arranged that each watch takes its turn of guard duty through the different watches of the night. Those forming the first watch tonight will be second on duty, then third and fourth, which brings them through all the watches of the night. They begin at eight o'clock P.M. and end at four o'clock A.M.

It is not yet eight o'clock when the first watch is to be set; the evening meal is just over, and the corral now free from the intrusion of the cattle or horses, groups of children are scattered over it. The larger are taking a game of romps, "the wee toddling things" are being taught that great achievement that distinguishes man from the lower animals. Before a tent near the river a violin makes lively music, and some youths and maidens have improvised a dance upon the green; in another quarter a flute gives its mellow and melancholy notes to the still air, which as they float away over the quiet river seem a lament for the past rather than a hope for the future. It has been a prosperous day; more than twenty miles have been accomplished of the great journey. The encampment is a good one; one of the causes that threatened much future delay has just been removed by the skill and energy of "that good angel," Dr. Whitman, and it has lifted a load from the hearts of the elders. Many of **these are as-**

sembled around the good Doctor at the tent of the pilot (which is his home for the time being), and are giving grave attention to his wise and energetic counsel. The care-worn pilot sits aloof, quietly smoking his pipe, for he knows the brave Doctor is "strengthening his hands."

But time passes; the watch is set for the night, the council of old men has broken up and each has returned to his own quarter. The flute has whispered its last lament to the deepening night, the violin is silent and the dancers have dispersed. Enamored youth have whispered a tender "good night" in the ears of blushing maidens, or stolen a kiss from the lips of some future bride— for Cupid here as elsewhere has been busy bringing together congenial hearts, and among those simple people he alone is consulted in forming the marriage tie. Even the Doctor and the pilot have finished their confidential interview and have separated for the night. All is hushed and repose from the fatigue of the day, save the vigilant guard, and the wakeful leader who still has cares upon his mind that forbid sleep.

He hears the ten o'clock relief taking post and the "all well" report of the returned guard; the night deepens, yet he seeks not the needed repose. At length a sentinel hurries to him with the welcome report that a party is approaching—as yet too far away for its character to be determined, and he instantly hurries out in the direction seen. This he does both from inclination and duty, for in times past the camp had been unnecessarily alarmed by timid or inexperienced sentinels, causing much confusion and fright amongst women

Prairie Grave

and children, and it had been made a rule that all extraordinary incidents of the night should be reported directly to the pilot, who alone had the authority to call out the military strength of the column or so much of it as was in his judgment necessary to prevent a stampede or repel an enemy.

Tonight he is at no loss to determine that the approaching party are our missing hunters, and that they have met with success, and he only waits until by some further signal he can know that no ill has happened to them. This is not long wanting. He does not even await their arrival, but the last care of the day being removed, and the last duty performed, he too seeks the rest that will enable him to go through the same routine tomorrow. But here I leave him, for my task is also done, and unlike his, it is to be repeated no more.

44. A Buffalo Hunt

BY JOHN CHARLES FRÉMONT

EDITOR'S NOTE: John Charles Frémont (1813-1890) made three important expeditions to the Far West. In 1842 he made a scientific investigation of the Oregon Trail that took him to the Wind River chain of the Rocky Mountains and through South Pass. In 1843-44 he journeyed from the Missouri River to the Oregon country, thence to Pyramid Lake into present-day Nevada and across the Sierras in winter (see Part I) into California, where he spent the rest of the winter near Sutter's Fort. Frémont set out on his third expedition in the spring of 1845, with the professed purpose of further exploring the Great Basin and the Pacific Coast. He and his party of sixty-two reached California in January 1846 after a second winter crossing the Sierras.

Frémont's expeditions contributed valuable scientific observations and stimulated public interest in the Far West. Most of the territory he explored, however, had been previously discovered by fur traders and trappers. His description of the Golden Gate is included in the third expedition, of the Buffalo Hunt in the first expedition. Both are taken from Frémont's *Memoirs of My Life*.

July 1st.—Along our road to-day the prairie-bottom was more elevated and dry, and the hills which border the right side of the river higher and more broken and picturesque in the outline. The country, too, was better timbered. As we were riding quietly along the bank a grand herd of buffalo, some seven or eight hundred in number, came crowding up from the river, where they had been to drink, and commenced crossing the plain slowly, eating as they went. The wind was favorable; the coolness of the morning invited to exercise; the ground was apparently good, and the distance across the prairie (two or three miles) gave us a fine opportunity to charge them before they could get among the river-hills. It was too fine a prospect for a chase to be lost; and, halting for a few moments, the hunters were brought up and saddled, and Kit Carson, Maxwell, and I started together. They were now somewhat less than half a mile distant, and we rode easily along until within about three hundred yards, when a sudden agitation, a wavering in the band, and a galloping to and fro of some which were scattered along the skirts, gave us the intimation that we were discovered. We started together at a hand-gallop, riding steadily abreast of each other, and here the interest of the chase became so engrossingly intense that we were sensible to nothing else. We were now closing upon them rapidly, and the front of the mass was already in rapid motion for the hills, and in a few seconds the movement had communicated itself to the whole herd.

A crowd of bulls, as usual, brought up the rear, and every now and then some of them faced about, and then dashed on after the band a short distance, and turned and looked again, as if more than half inclined to stand and fight. In a few moments, however, during which we had been quickening our pace, the rout was universal, and we were going over the ground like a hurricane. When at about thirty yards, we gave the usual shout (the hunter's *pas de charge*) and broke into the herd. We entered on the side, the mass giving way in every di-

Among the Buffalo

rection in their heedless course. Many of the bulls, less active and less fleet than the cows, paying no attention to the ground, and occupied solely with the hunter, were precipitated to the earth with great force, rolling over and over with the violence of the shock, and hardly distinguishable in the dust. We separated on entering, each singling out his game.

My horse was a trained hunter, famous in the West under the name of Proveau, and, with his eyes flashing and the foam flying from his mouth, sprang on after the cow like a tiger. In a few moments he brought me alongside of her, and, rising in the stirrups, I fired at the distance of a yard, the ball entering at the termination of the long hair, and passing near the heart. She fell headlong at the report of the gun, and checking my horse, I looked around for my companions. At a little distance Kit was on the ground, engaged in tying his horse to the horns of a cow which he was preparing to cut up. Among the scattered bands, at some distance below, I caught a glimpse of Maxwell; and while I was looking a light wreath of white smoke curled away from his gun, from which I was too far to hear the report. Nearer, and between me and the hills toward which they were directing their course, was the body of the herd, and giving my horse the rein we dashed after them. A thick cloud of dust hung upon their rear, which filled my mouth and eyes and nearly smothered me. In the midst of this I could see nothing, and the buffalo were not distinguishable until within thirty feet. They crowded together more densely still as I came upon them, and rushed along in such a compact body that I could not obtain an entrance—the horse almost leaping upon them. In a few moments the mass divided to the right and left, the horns clattering with a noise heard above everything else, and my horse darted into the opening. Five or six bulls charged on us as we dashed along the line, but were left far behind; and, singling out a cow, I gave her my fire, but struck too high. She gave a tremendous leap, and scoured on swifter than before. I reined up my horse, and the band swept on like a torrent, leaving the place quiet and clear. Our chase had led us into dangerous ground. A prairie-dog village, so thickly settled that there were three or four holes in every twenty yards square, occupied the whole bottom for nearly two miles in length. Looking around, I saw only one of the hunters, nearly out of sight, and the long dark line of our caravan crawling along, three or four miles distant. After a march of twenty-four miles, we encamped at nightfall one mile and a half above the lower end of Brady's Island. The breadth of this arm of the river was eight hundred and eighty yards, and the water nowhere two feet in depth. The island bears the name of a man killed on this spot some years ago. His party had encamped here, three in company, and one of the number went off to hunt, leaving Brady and his companion together. These two had frequently quarreled, and on the hunter's return he found Brady dead, and was told that he had shot himself accidentally. He was buried here on the bank; but, as usual, the wolves had torn him out, and some human bones that were lying on the ground we supposed were his. Troops of wolves that were hanging on the skirts of the buffalo kept up an uninterrupted howling during the night, venturing almost into camp. In the morning they were sitting at a short distance, barking, and impatiently waiting our departure to fall upon the bones.

45. The Golden Gate

BY JOHN CHARLES FRÉMONT

The Bay of San Francisco has been celebrated, from the time of its first discovery, as one of the finest in the world, and is justly entitled to that character even under the seamen's view of a mere harbor. But when all the accessory advantages which belong to it—fertile and picturesque dependent country; mildness and salubrity of climate; connection with the great interior valley of the Sacramento and San Joaquin; its vast resources for ship timber, grain and cattle—when these advantages are taken into the account, with its geographical position on the line with Asia, it rises into an importance far above that of a mere harbor, and deserves a particular notice in any account of maritime California. Its latitudinal position is that of Lisbon; its climate is that of southern Italy; settlements upon it for more than half a century attest its healthfulness; bold shores and mountains give it grandeur; the extent and fertility of its dependent country give it great resources for agriculture, commerce, and population.

The Bay of San Francisco is separated by the sea by low mountain ranges. Looking from the peaks of the Sierra Nevada, the coast mountains present an apparently continuous line, with only a single gap, resembling a mountain pass. This is the entrance to the great bay, and is the only water communication from the coast to the interior country. Approaching from the sea, the coast presents a bold outline. On the south, the bordering mountains come down in a narrow ridge of broken hills, terminating in a precipitous point, against which the sea breaks heavily. On the northern side, the mountain presents a bold promontory, rising in a few miles to a height of two or three thousand feet. Between these points is the strait—about one mile broad in the narrowest part, and five miles long from the sea to the bay. To this Gate I gave the name of *Chrysopylæ*, or GOLDEN GATE; for the same reasons that the harbor of Byzantium (Constantinople afterwards), was called *Chrysoceras*, or GOLDEN HORN.* Passing through this gate, the bay opens to the right and left, extending in each direction about thirty-five miles, having a total length of more than seventy, and a coast of about two hundred and seventy-five miles. It is divided, by straits and projecting points, into three separates bays, of which the northern two are called San Pablo and Suisoon Bays. Within, the view presented is of a mountainous country, the bay resembling an interior lake of deep water, lying between parallel ranges of mountains. Islands, which have the bold character of the shores—some mere masses of rock, and others grass-covered, rising to the height of three and eight hundred feet—break its surface, and add to its picturesque appearance. Directly fronting the entrance, mountains a few miles from the shore rise about two thousand feet above the water, crowned by a forest of lofty cypress, which is visible from the sea, and makes a conspicuous landmark for vessels entering the bay. Behind, the rugged peak of Mount Diavolo, nearly four thousand feet high (three thousand seven hundred and seventy), overlooks the surrounding country of the bay and San Joaquin. The immediate shore of the bay derives, from its proximate and opposite relation to the sea, the name of *Contra-costa* (counter-coast, or opposite coast). It presents a varied character of rugged and broken hills, rolling and undulating land, and rich alluvial shores backed by fertile and wooded ranges, suitable for towns, villages, and farms, with which it is beginning to be dotted. A low alluvial-bottom land, several miles in breadth, with occasional open woods of oak, borders the foot of the mountains around the southern arm of the bay, terminating on a breadth of twenty miles in the fertile valley of San José, a narrow plain of rich soil, lying between ranges from two to three thousand feet high. The valley is openly wooded with groves of oak, free from underbrush, and after the spring rains covered with grass. Taken in connection with the valley of San Juan, with which it forms a continuous plain, it is fifty-five miles long and one to twenty broad, opening into smaller valleys among the hills. At the head of the bay it is twenty miles broad; and about the same at the southern end, where the soil is beautifully fertile, covered in summer

* NOTE.—The form of the harbor and its advantages for commerce, and that before it became an entrepot of Eastern commerce, suggested the name to the Greek founders of Byzantium. The form of the entrance into the Bay of San Francisco and its advantages for commerce, Asiatic inclusive, suggested to me the name which I gave to this entrance and which I put upon the map that accompanied a geographical Memoir addressed to the Senate of the United States in June, 1848.

with four or five varieties of wild clover, several feet high. In many places it is overgrown with wild mustard, growing ten or twelve feet high, in almost impenetrable fields, through which roads are made like lanes. On both sides the mountains are fertile, wooded, or covered with grasses and scattered trees. On the west it is protected from the chilling influence of the northwest winds by the *Cuesta de los Gatos* (wildcat ridge) which separates it from the coast. This is a grassy and timbered mountain, watered with small streams, and wooded on both sides with many varieties of trees and shrubbery, the heaviest forests of pine and cypress occupying the western slope. Timber and shingles are now obtained from this mountain; and one of the recently discovered quicksilver mines is on the eastern side of the mountain, near the Pueblo of San José. This range terminates on the south in the *Anno Nuevo* point of Monterey Bay, and on the north declines into a ridge of broken hills about five miles wide, between the bay and the sea, and having the town of San Francisco on the bay shore, near its northern extremity.

Sheltered from the cold winds and fogs of the sea, and having a soil of remarkable fertility, the valley of San José is capable of producing in great perfection many fruits and grains which do not thrive on the coast in its immediate vicinity. Without taking into consideration the extraordinary yields which have sometimes occurred, the fair average product of wheat is estimated at fifty fold, or fifty for one sown. The mission establishments of Santa Clara and San José, in the north end of the valley, were formerly, in the prosperous days of the missions, distinguished for the superiority of their wheat crops.

The slope of alluvial land continues en-

tirely around the eastern shore of the bay, intersected by small streams, and offering some points which good landing and deep water, with advantageous positions between the sea and interior country, indicate for furture settlement.

The strait of *Carquines,* about one mile wide and eight or ten fathoms deep, connects the San Pablo and Suisoon Bays. Around these bays smaller valleys open into the bordering country, and some of the streams have a short launch navigation, which serves to convey produce to the bay. Missions and large farms were established at the head of navigation on these streams, which are favorable sites for towns or villages. The country around the Suisoon Bay presents smooth, low ridges and rounded hills, clothed with wild oats, and more or less openly wooded on their summits. Approaching its northern shores from *Sonoma* it assumes, though in a state of nature, a cultivated appearance. Wild oats cover it in continuous fields, and herds of cattle and bands of horses are scattered over low hills and partly isolated ridges, where blue mists and openings among the abruptly terminating hills indicate the neighborhood of the bay.

The Suisoon is connected with an expansion of the river formed by the junction of the Sacramento and the San Joaquin, which enter San Francisco Bay in the same latitude, nearly, as the mouth of the Tagus at Lisbon. A delta of twenty-five miles in length, divided into islands by deep channels, connects the bay with the valley of the San Joaquin and Sacramento, into the mouths of which the tide flows, and which enter the bay together as one river.

Such is the bay, and the proximate country and shores of the bay of San Francisco. It is not a mere indention of the coast, but a little sea to itself, connected with the ocean by a defensible gate, opening out between seventy and eighty miles to the right and left, upon a breadth of ten to fifteen, deep enough for the largest ships, with bold shores suitable for towns and settlements, and fertile adjacent country for cultivation. The head of the bay is about forty miles from the sea, and there commences its connection with the noble valleys of San Joaquin and Sacramento.

46. The Platte and the Desert

BY FRANCIS PARKMAN

EDITOR'S NOTE: Francis Parkman (1823-1893) was one of America's leading historians. A New Englander by birth, his was a broad and sympathetic mind. Although afflicted by nervous ailments and ill-health during most of his life, he managed to live for almost seventy years despite the rigors of the American wilderness to which he sometimes exposed himself. These qualities are evident in the selections which I have made from *The Oregon Trail,* a classic of its kind, based on an extended journey to the Far West Parkman made in 1846.

WE were now at the end of our solitary journeyings along the St. Joseph trail. On the evening of the twenty-third of May we encamped near its junction with the old legitimate trail of the Oregon emigrants. We had ridden long that afternoon, trying in vain to find wood and water, until at length we saw the sunset sky reflected from a pool encircled by bushes and rocks. The water lay in the bottom of a hollow, the smooth prairie gracefully rising in ocean-like swells on every side. We pitched our tents by it; not however before the keen eye of Henry Chatillon had discerned some unusual object upon the faintly defined outline of the distant swell. But in the moist, hazy atmosphere of the evening, nothing could be clearly distinguished. As we lay around the fire after supper, a low and distant sound, strange enough amid the loneliness of the prairie, reached our ears, — peals of laughter, and the faint voices of men and women. For eight days we had not encountered a human being, and this singular warning of their vicinity had an effect extremely impressive.

About dark a sallow-faced fellow decended the hill on horseback, and splashing through the pool, rode up to the tents. He was enveloped in a huge cloak, and his broad felt hat was weeping about his ears with the drizzling moisture of the evening. Another followed, a stout, square-built, intelligent-looking man, who announced himself as the leader of an emigrant party, encamped a mile in advance of us. About twenty wagons, he said, were with him; the rest of his party were on the other side of the Big Blue, waiting for a woman who was in the pains of childbirth, and quarrelling meanwhile among themselves.

These were the first emigrants that we

had overtaken, although we had found abundant and melancholy traces of their progress throughout the course of the journey. Sometimes we passed the grave of one who had sickened and died on the way. The earth was usually torn up, and covered thickly with wolf-tracks. Some had escaped this violation. One morning, a piece of plank, standing upright on the summit of a grassy hill, attracted our notice, and riding up to it, we found the following words very roughly traced upon it, apparently with a red-hot iron: —

MARY ELLIS.
DIED MAY 7TH, 1845.
AGED TWO MONTHS.

Such tokens were of common occurrence. We were late in breaking up our camp on the following morning, and scarcely had we ridden a mile when we saw, far in advance of us, drawn against the horizon, a line of objects stretching at regular intervals along the level edge of the prairie. An intervening swell soon hid them from sight, until, ascending it a quarter of an hour after, we saw close before us the emigrant caravan, with its heavy white wagons creeping on in slow procession, and a large drove of cattle following behind. Half a dozen yellow-visaged Missourians, mounted on horseback, were cursing and shouting among them, their lank, angular proportions enveloped in brown homespun, evidently cut and adjusted by the hands of a domestic female tailor. As we approached, they called out to us: "How are ye, boys? Are ye for Oregon or California?"

As we pushed rapidly by the wagons, children's faces were thrust out from the white coverings to look at us; while the care-worn, thin-featured matron, or the buxom girl, seated in front, suspended the knitting on which most of them were engaged, to stare at us with wondering curiosity. By the side of each wagon stalked the proprietor, urging on his patient oxen, who shouldered heavily along, inch by inch, on their interminable journey. It was easy to see that fear and dissension prevailed among them; some of the men — but these, with one exception, were bachelors, — looked wistfully upon us as we rode lightly and swiftly by, and then impatiently at their own lumbering wagons and heavy-gaited oxen. Others were unwilling to advance at all, until the party they had left behind should have rejoined them. Many were murmuring against the leader they had chosen, and wished to depose him; and this discontent was fomented by some ambitious spirits, who had hopes of succeeding in his place. The women were divided between regrets for the homes they had left and fear of the deserts and savages before them.

We soon left them far behind, and hoped that we had taken a final leave; but our companions' wagon stuck so long in a deep muddy ditch, that before it was extricated the van of the emigrant caravan appeared again descending a ridge close at hand. Wagon after wagon plunged through the mud; and as it was nearly noon, and the place promised shade and water, we saw with satisfaction that they were resolved to encamp. Soon the wagons were wheeled into a circle; the cattle were grazing over the meadow, and the men, with sour, sullen faces, were looking about for wood and water. They seemed to meet but indifferent success. As we left the ground, I saw a tall, slouching fellow, with the nasal accent of "down east," contemplating the contents of his tin cup, which he had just filled with water.

"Look here, you," said he; "it's chock-full of animals!"

The cup, as he held it out, exhibited in fact an extraordinary variety and profusion of animal and vegetable life.

Riding up the little hill and looking back on the meadow, we could easily see that all was not right in the camp of the emigrants. The men were crowded together and an angry discussion seemed to be going forward. R____ was missing from his wonted place in the line, and the Captain told us that he had remained behind to get his horse shod by a blacksmith attached to the emigrant party. Something whispered in our ears that mischief was on foot; we kept on, however, and coming soon to a stream of tolerable water, we stopped to rest and dine. Still the absentee lingered behind. At last, as the distance of a mile, he and his horse suddenly appeared, sharply defined against the sky on the summit of a hill; and close behind, a huge white object rose slowly into view.

"What is that blockhead bringing with him now?"

A moment dispelled the mystery. Slowly and solemnly, one behind the other, four long trains of oxen and four emigrant wagons rolled over the crest of the hill and gravely descended, while R____ rode in state in the van. It seems that, during the process of shoeing the horse, the smothered dissensions among the emigrants suddenly broke into open rupture. Some insisted on pushing forward, some on remaining where they were, and some on going back. Kearsley, their captain, threw up his command in disgust. "And now, boys," said he, "if any of you are for going ahead, just you come along with me."

Four wagons, with ten men, one woman, and one small child, made up the force of

the "go-ahead" faction, and R____, with his usual proclivity toward mischief, invited them to join our party. Fear of the Indians — for I can conceive no other motive — must have induced him to court so burdensome an alliance. At all events the proceeding was a cool one. The men who joined us, it is true, were all that could be desired, — rude indeed in manners, but frank, manly, and intelligent. To tell them we could not travel with them was out of the question. I merely reminded Kearsley that if his oxen could not keep up with our mules he must expect to be left behind, as we could not consent to be farther delayed on the journey; but he immediately replied that his oxen *"should* keep up; and if they couldn't, why, he allowed, he'd find out how to make 'em."

On the next day, as it chanced, our English companions broke the axle-tree of their wagon, and down came the whole cumbrous machine lumbering into the bed of a brook. Here was a day's work cut out for us. Meanwhile our emigrant associates kept on their way, and so vigorously did they urge forward their powerful oxen that, what with the broken axle-tree and other mishaps, it was full a week before we overtook them; when at length we discovered them, one afternoon, crawling quietly along the sandy brink of the Platte. But meanwhile various incidents occurred to ourselves.

It was probable that at this stage of our journey the Pawnees would attempt to rob us. We began, therefore, to stand guard in turn, dividing the night into three watches, and appointing two men for each. Deslauriers and I held guard together. We did not march with military precision to and fro before the tents; our discipline was by no means so strict. We wrapped ourselves in our blankets and sat down by the fire; and Deslauriers, combining his culinary functions with his duties as sentinel, employed himself in boiling the head of an antelope for our breakfast. Yet we were models of vigilance in comparison with some of the party; for the ordinary practice of the guard was to lay his rifle on the ground, and, enveloping his nose in his blanket, meditate on his mistress, or whatever subject best pleased him. This is all well enough when among Indians who do not habitually proceed further in their hostility than robbing travellers of their horses and mules, though, indeed, a Pawnee's forbearance is not always to be trusted; but in certain regions farther to the west, the guard must beware how he exposes his person to the light of the fire, lest some keen-eyed skulking marksman should let fly a bullet or an arrow from the darkness.

Among various tales that circulated around our camp-fire was one told by Boisverd, and not inappropriate here. He was trapping with several companions on the skirts of the Blackfoot country. The man on guard, knowing that it behooved him to put forth his utmost precaution, kept aloof from the fire-light, and sat watching intently on all sides. At length he was aware of a dark, crouching figure, stealing noiselessly into the circle of the light. He hastily cocked his rifle, but the sharp click of the lock caught the ear of the Blackfoot, whose senses were all on the alert. Raising his arrow, already fitted to the string he shot it in the direction of the sound. So sure was his aim that he drove it through the throat of the unfortunate guard, and then, with a loud yell, bounded from the camp.

As I looked at the partner of my watch, puffing and blowing over his fire, it occurred to me that he might not prove the most efficient auxiliary in time of trouble.

"Deslauriers," said I, "would you run away if the Pawnees should fire at us?"

"Ah! oui, oui, Monsieur!" he replied very decisively.

At this instant a whimsical variety of voices, — barks, howls, yelps, and whines, all mingled together, — sounded from the prairie, not far off, as if a conclave of wolves of every age and sex were assembled there. Deslauriers looked up from his work with a laugh, and began to imitate this medley of sounds with a ludicrous accuracy. At this they were repeated with redoubled emphasis, the musician being apparently indignant at the successful efforts of a rival. They all proceeded from the throat of one little wolf, not larger than a spaniel, seated by himself at some distance. He was of the species called the prairie-wolf, — a grim-visaged, but harmless little brute, whose worst propensity is creeping among horses and gnawing the ropes of raw hide by which they are picketed around the camp. Other beasts roam the prairies far more formidable in aspect and in character. These are the large white and gray wolves, whose deep howl we heard at intervals from far and near.

At last I fell into a doze, and awaking from it found Deslauriers fast asleep. Scandalized by this breach of discipline, I was about to stimulate his vigilance by stirring him with the stock of my rifle; but compassion prevailing, I determined to let him sleep a while, and then arouse him to administer a suitable reproof for such forgetfulness of duty. Now and then I walked the rounds among the silent horses, to see that all was right. The night was chill, damp, and dark, the dank grass bending under the icy dew-drops. At the distance of a rod or two the tents were invisible, and nothing could be seen but the obscure figures of the horses deeply breathing, and restlessly starting as they slept, or still slowly champing the grass. Far off, beyond the black outline of the prairie, there was a ruddy light, gradually increasing, like the glow of a conflagration; until at length the broad disk of the moon, blood-red, and vastly magnified by the vapors, rose slowly upon the darkness, flecked by one or two little clouds, and as the light poured over the gloomy plain, a fierce and stern howl, close at hand, seemed to greet it as an unwelcome intruder. There was something impressive and awful in the place and the hour; for I and the beasts were all that had consciousness for many a league around.

Some days elapsed, and brought us near the Platte. Two men on horseback approached us one morning, and we watched them with the curiosity and interest that, upon the solitude of the plains, such an encounter always excites. They were evidently whites, from their mode of riding, though, contrary to the usage of that region, neither of them carried a rifle.

"Fools!" remarked Henry Chatillon, "to ride that way on the prairie; Pawnee find them — then they catch it."

Pawnee *had* found them, and they had come very near "catching it;" indeed nothing saved them but the approach of our party. Shaw and I knew one of them, — a man named Turner whom we had seen at Westport. He and his companion belonged to an emigrant party encamped a few miles in advance, and had returned to look for some stray oxen, leaving their rifles, with characteristic rashness or ignorance, behind them. Their neglect had nearly cost them dear; for, just before we came up,

half a dozen Indians approached, and seeing them apparently defenceless, one of the rascals seized the bridle of Turner's horse and ordered him to dismount. Turner was wholly unarmed; but the other jerked a pistol out of his pocket, at which the Pawnee recoiled; and just then some of our men appearing in the distance, the whole party whipped their rugged little horses and made off. In no way daunted, Turner foolishly persisted in going forward.

Long after leaving him, and late that afternoon, in the midst of a gloomy and barren prairie, we came suddenly upon the great trail of the Pawnees, leading from their villages on the Platte to their war and hunting grounds to the southward. Here every summer passes the motley concourse: thousands of savages, men, women, and children, horses and mules, laden with their weapons and implements, and an innumerable multitude of unruly wolfish dogs, who have not acquired the civilized accomplishment of barking, but howl like their wild cousins of the prairie.

The permanent winter villages of the Pawnees stand on the lower Platte, but throughout the summer the greater part of the inhabitants are wandering over the plains, — a treacherous, cowardly banditti, who, by a thousand acts of pillage and murder, have deserved chastisement at the hands of government. Last year a Dakota warrior performed a notable exploit at one of these villages. He approached it alone, in the middle of a dark night, and clambering up the outside of one of the lodges, which are in the form of a half-sphere, looked in at the round hole made at the top for the escape of smoke. The dusky light from the embers showed him the forms of the sleeping inmates; and dropping lightly through the opening, he unsheathed his knife, and stirring the fire, coolly selected his victims. One by one he stabbed and scalped them; when a child suddenly awoke and screamed. He rushed from the lodge, yelled a Sioux war-cry, shouted his name in triumph and defiance, and darted out upon the dark prairie, leaving the whole village behind him in a tumult, with the howling and baying of dogs, the screams of women, and the yells of the enraged warriors.

Our friend Kearsley, as we learned on rejoining him, signalized himself by a less bloody achievement. He and his men were good woodsman, well skilled in the use of the rifle, but found themselves wholly out of their element on the prairie. None of them had ever seen a buffalo; and they had very vague conceptions of his nature and appearance. On the day after they reached the Platte, looking towards a distant swell they beheld a multitude of little black specks in motion upon its surface.

"Take your rifles, boys," said Kearsley, "and we'll have fresh meat for supper." This inducement was quite sufficient. The ten men left their wagons, and set out in hot haste, some on horseback and some on foot, in pursuit of the supposed buffalo. Meanwhile a high grassy ridge shut the game from view; but mounting it after half an hour's running and riding, they found themselves suddenly confronted by about thirty mounted Pawnees. Amazement and consternation were mutual. Having nothing but their bows and arrows, the Indians thought their hour was come, and the fate that they were conscious of richly deserving about to overtake them. So they began, one and all, to shout forth the most cordial salutations, running up with extreme earnestness to shake hands with the Missourians, who were as much rejoiced as they were to escape the expected conflict.

A low, undulating line of sand-hills bounded the horizon before us. That day we rode ten hours, and it was dusk before we entered the hollows and gorges of these gloomy little hills. At length we gained the summit, and the long-expected valley of the Platte lay before us. We all drew rein, and sat joyfully looking down upon the prospect. It was right welcome, — strange, too, and striking to the imagination; and yet it had not one picturesque or beautiful feature; nor had it any of the features of grandeur, other than its vast extent, its solitude, and its wildness. For league after league, a plain as level as a lake was outspread beneath us; here and there the Platte, divided into a dozen thread-like sluices, was traversing it, and an occasional clump of wood, rising in the midst like a shadowy island, relieved the monotony of the waste. No living thing was moving throughout the vast landscape, except the lizards that darted over the sand and through the rank grass and prickly pears at our feet.

We had passed the more tedious part of the journey; but four hundred miles still intervened between us and Fort Laramie; and to reach that point cost us the travel of three more weeks. During the whole of this

time we were passing up the middle of a long, narrow, sandy plain, reaching like an outstretched belt nearly to the Rocky Mountains. Two lines of sandhills, broken often into the wildest and most fantastic forms, flanked the valley at the distance of a mile or two on the right and left; while beyond them lay a barren trackless waste, extending for hundreds of miles to the Arkansas on the one side and the Missouri on the other. Before and behind us the level monotony of the plain was unbroken as far as the eye could reach. Sometimes it glared in the sun, an expanse of hot, bare sand; sometimes it was veiled by long coarse grass. Skulls and whitening bones of buffalo were scattered everywhere; the ground was tracked by myriads of them, and often covered with the circular indentations where the bulls had wallowed in the hot weather. From every gorge and ravine opening from the hills, descended deep, well-worn paths, where the buffalo issue twice a day in regular procession to drink in the Platte. The river itself runs through the midst, a thin sheet of rapid, turbid water, half a mile wide, and scarcely two feet deep. Its low banks, for the most part without a bush or a tree, are of loose sand, with which the stream is so charged that it grates on the teeth in drinking. The naked landscape is, of itself, dreary and monotonous enough; and yet the wild beasts and wild men that frequent the valley of the Platte make it a scene of interest and excitement to the traveller. Of those who have journeyed there, scarcely one, perhaps, fails to look back with fond regret to his horse and his rifle.

Early in the morning after we reached the Platte, a long procession of squalid savages approached our camp. Each was on foot, leading his horse by a rope of bull-hide.

His attire consisted merely of a scanty cincture, and an old buffalo robe, tattered and begrimed by use, which hung over his shoulders. His head was close shaven, except a ridge of hair reaching over the crown from the middle of the forehead, very much like the long bristles on the back of a hyena, and he carried his bow and arrows in his hand, while his meagre little horse was laden with dried buffalo meat, the produce of his hunting. Such were the first specimens that we met — and very indifferent ones they were — of the genuine savages of the plains.

They were the Pawnees whom Kearsley had encountered the day before, and belonged to a large hunting party, known to be ranging the prairie in the vicinity. They strode rapidly by, within a furlong of our tents, not pausing or looking towards us, after the manner of Indians when meditating mischief or conscious of ill desert. I went out to meet them, and had an amicable conference with the chief, presenting him with half a pound of tobacco, at which unmerited bounty he expressed much gratification. These fellows, or some of their companions, had committed a dastardly outrage upon an emigrant party in advance of us. Two men, at a distance from the rest, were seized by them, but, lashing their horses, they broke away and fled. At this the Pawnees raised the yell and shot at them, transfixing the hindmost through the back with several arrows, while his companion galloped away and brought in the news to his party. The panic-stricken emigrants remained for several days in camp, not daring even to go out in quest of the dead body.

Our New England climate is mild and equable compared with that of the Platte. This very morning, for instance, was close and sultry, the sun rising with a faint oppressive heat; when suddenly darkness gathered in the west, and a furious blast of sleet and hail drove full in our faces, icy cold, and urged with such demoniac vehemence that it felt like a storm of needles. It was curious to see the horses; they faced about in extreme displeasure, holding their tails like whipped dogs, and shivering as the angry gusts, howling louder that a concert of wolves, swept over us. Wright's long train of mules came sweepng round before the storm, like a flight of snow-birds driven by a winter tempest. Thus we all remained stationary for some minutes, crouching close to our horses' necks, much too surly to speak, though once the Captain looked up from between the collars of his coat, his face blood-red, and the muscles of his mouth contracted by the cold into a most ludicrous grin of agony. He grumbled something that sounded like a curse, directed, as we believed, against the unhappy hour when he had first thought of leaving home. The thing was too good to last long; and the instant the puffs of wind subsided we pitched our tents, and remained in camp for the rest of a gloomy and lowering day. The emigrants also encamped near at hand. We being first on the ground, had appropriated all the wood within reach; so that our fire alone blazed cheerily. Around it soon gathered a group of uncouth figures, shivering in the drizzling rain. Conspicuous among them were two or three of the half-savage men who spend their reckless lives in trapping among the Rocky Mountains, or in trading for the Fur Company in the Indian villages. They were all of Canadian extraction; their hard, weather-beaten faces and bushy moustaches looked out from beneath the hoods of their white capotes with a bad and brutish expression, as if their owners might be the willing agents of any villany. And such in fact is the character of many of these men.

On the day following we overtook Kearsley's wagons, and thenceforward for a week or two, we were fellow-travellers. One good effect, at least, resulted from the alliance; it materially diminished the fatigues of standing guard; for the party being now more numerous, there were longer intervals between each man's turns of duty.

47. The Black Hills

BY FRANCIS PARKMAN

WE travelled eastward for two days, and then the gloomy ridges of the Black Hills rose before us. The village passed along for some miles beneath their declivities, trailing out to a great length over the arid prairie, or winding among small detached hills of distorted shapes. Turning sharply to the left, we entered a wide defile of the mountains, down the bottom of which a brook came winding, lined with tall grass and dense copses, amid which were hidden many beaver dams and lodges. We passed along between two lines of high precipices and rocks piled in disorder one upon another, with scarcely a tree, a bush, or a clump of grass. The restless Indian boys wandered along their edges and clambered up and down their rugged sides, and sometimes a group of them would stand on the verge of a cliff and look down on the procession as it passed beneath. As we advanced, the passage grew more narrow; then it suddenly expanded into a round grassy meadow, completely encompassed by mountains; and here the families stopped as they came up in turn, and the camp rose like magic.

The lodges were hardly pitched when, with their usual precipitation, the Indians set about accomplishing the object that had brought them there; that is, obtaining poles for their new lodges. Half the population, men, women, and boys, mounted their horses and set out for the depths of the mountains. It was a strange cavalcade, as they rode at full gallop over the shingly rocks and into the dark opening of the defile beyond. We passed between precipices, sharp and splintering at the tops, their sides beetling over the defile or descending in abrupt declivities, bristling with fir-trees. On our left they rose close to us like a wall, but on the right a winding brook with a narrow strip of marshy soil intervened. The stream was clogged with old beaver-dams and spread frequently into wide pools. There were thick bushes and many dead and blasted trees along its course, though frequently nothing remained but stumps cut close to the ground by the beaver, and marked with the sharp chisel-like teeth of those indefatigable laborers. Sometimes we dived among trees, and then emerged upon open spots, over which, Indian-like, all galloped at full speed. As Pauline bounded over the rocks I felt her saddle-girth slipping, and alighted to draw it tighter; when

the whole cavalcade swept by me in a moment, the women with their gaudy ornaments tinkling as they rode, the men whooping, laughing, and lashing forward their horses. Two black-tailed deer bounded away among the rocks; Raymond shot at them from horseback; the sharp report of his rifle was answered by another equally sharp from the opposing cliffs, and then the echoes, leaping in rapid succession from side to side died away rattling far amid the mountains.

After having ridden in this manner six or eight miles the scene changed, and all the declivities were covered with forests of tall, slender spruce and pine trees. The Indians began to fall off to the right and left, dispersing with their hatchets and knives to cut the poles which they had come to seek. I was soon left almost alone; but in the stillness of those lonely mountains, the stroke of hatchets and the sound of voices might be heard from far and near.

Reynal, who imitated the Indians in their habits as well as the worst features of their character, had killed buffalo enough to make a lodge for himself and his squaw, and now he was eager to get the poles necessary to complete it. He asked me to let Raymond go with him, and assist in the work. I assented, and the two men immediately entered the thickest part of the wood. Having left my horse in Raymond's keeping, I began to climb the mountain. I was weak and weary, and made slow progress, often pausing to rest; but after an hour I gained a height whence the little valley out of which I had climbed seemed like a deep, dark gulf, though the inaccessible peak of the mountain was still towering to a much greater distance above. Objects familiar from childhood surrounded me, — crags and rocks, a black and sullen brook that gurgled with a hollow voice deep among the crevices, a wood of mossy, distorted trees and prostrate trunks flung down by age and storms, scattered among the rocks, or damming the foaming waters of the brook.

Wild as they were, these mountains were thickly peopled. As I climbed farther, I found the broad, dusty paths made by the elk, as they filed across the mountain side. The grass on all the terraces was trampled down by deer; there were numerous tracks of wolves, and in some of the rougher and more precipitous parts of the ascent I found footprints different from any that I had ever seen, and which I took to be those of the Rocky Mountain sheep. I sat down on a rock; there was a perfect stillness. No wind was stirring, and not even an insect could be heard. I remembered the danger of becoming lost in such a place, and fixed my eye upon one of the tallest pinnacles of the opposite mountain. It rose sheer upright from the woods below, and, by an extraordinary freak of nature, sustained aloft on its very summit a large, loose rock. Such a landmark could never be mistaken, and feeling once more secure, I began again to move forward. A white wolf jumped up from among some bushes and leaped clumsily away; but he stopped for a moment and turned back his keen eye and grim, bristling muzzle. I longed to take his scalp and carry it back with me as a trophy of the Black Hills, but before I could fire, he was gone among the rocks. Soon after I heard a rustling sound, with a cracking of twigs at a little distance, and saw moving above the tall bushes the branching antlers of an elk. I was in a hunter's paradise.

Such are the Black Hills, as I found them in July; but they wear a different garb when winter sets in, when the broad boughs of the fir-trees are bent to the ground by the load of snow, and the dark mountains are white with it. At that season the trappers, returned from their autumn expeditions, often build their cabins in the midst of these solitudes, and live in abundance and luxury on the game that harbors there. I have heard them tell how, with their tawny mistresses, and perhaps a few young Indian companions, they had spent months in total seclusion. They would dig pitfalls, and set traps for the white wolves, sables, and martens, and though through the whole night the awful chorus of the wolves would resound from the frozen mountains around them, yet within their massive walls of logs they would lie in careless ease before the blazing fire, and in the morning shoot the elk and deer from their very door.

48. The Diary of John Sutter

EDITOR'S NOTE: The name of John A. Sutter (1803-1880) stands very prominent in the history of California. Few men of the Far West rose to such prominence, wealth and power, only to have their empire shattered. Born in Germany of Swiss parents, he journeyed to the United States in 1834. After living in St. Louis and visiting Oregon and Hawaii, he settled in 1839 in the Sacramento Valley of California. He built a colony, New Helvetia, and a fort, Sutter's Fort. With the American annexation of the state, in which he played a role favorable to the United States, he became extremely wealthy. But in 1848 gold was discovered by Sutter's employee, Marshall, near Sutter's mill and as a result the gold rushers swarmed over Sutter's land, leaving him ruined and helpless. In 1873 he moved to Pennsylvania, where he lived on a pension from California and where he vainly begged Congress to reimburse him for his services. The U. S. Supreme Court disallowed his claims to his land.

His diary appeared in four issues of the San Francisco *Argonaut* in January and February of 1878. The *Argonaut*'s editor wrote:

"The following rough notes of narrative in the hand of the venerable General Sutter, the discoverer of gold in California, were found amongst the papers of an eminent citizen of this State, recently deceased, through the kindly courtesy of whose widow we are enabled to give them to the public. As a relation of incidents in the life of a man held in respect by every Californian, and as a record of events closely associated with, and largely contributing to, the foundation of American Empire on the Pacific Coast, these hasty and imperfect memoranda will, it is believed, have a double interest and lasting value. We have thought it best to preserve, as nearly as was practicable, the quaint phraseology, erroneous orthography, and imperfect punctuation of the manuscript; these peculiarities being obviously only the failures of an intelligent foreigner struggling with the difficulties of an unfamiliar tongue, and giving, in our judgment, an added charm to the narrative."

Sutter wrote the diary in May or June of 1856. The entries end long before his death.

I LEFT the State of Missouri (where I has resided for a many years) on the 11th April, 1838, and travelled with the party of Men under Capt Tripps, of the Amer. fur Compy, to their Rendezvous in the Rocky Mountains (Wind River Valley); from there I travelled with 6 brave Men to Oregon, as I considered myself not strong enough to cross the Sierra Nevada and go direct to California (which was my intention from my first Start on having got some informations from a Gent'n in New Mexico, who has been in California).

Under a good Many Dangers and other troubles I have passed the Different forts or trading posts of the Hudson Bay Compy. and arrived at the Mission at the Dalls on Columbia River. From this place I crossed right strait through thick & thin and arrived to the great astonishment of the inhabitants. I arrived in 7 days in the Valley of the Willamette, while others with good guides arrived only in 17 days previous my Crossing. At fort Vancouver I has been very hospitably received and invited to pass the Winter with the Gentlemen of the Company, but as a Vessel of the Compy was ready to sail for the Sandwich Islands, I took a passage in her, in hopes to get Soon a Passage from there to California, but 5 long Months I had to wait to find an Opportunity to leave, but not direct to California, except far out of the Way to the Russian American Colonies of the North West Coast, to Sitka the Residence of the Gov'r, (Lat. 57). I remained one Month there and delivered the Cargo of the Brig Clementine, as I had Charge of the Vessel, and then sailed down the Coast in heavy Gales, and entered in Distress in the Port of San Francisco, on the 2d of July 1839. An Officer and 15 Soldiers came on board and ordered me out, saying that Monterey is the Port of entry, & at last I could obtain 48 hours to get provisions (as we were starving) and some repairing done on the Brig.

In Monterey I arranged my affairs with the Custom House, and presented myself to Govr. Alvarado, and told him my intention to Settle here in this Country, and that I have brought with me 5 White Men and 8 Kanacas (two of them married). 3 of the Whitemen were Mechanics, he was very glad to hear that, and particularly when I told him, that I intend to Settle in the interior on the banks of the river Sacramento, because the Indians then at this time would not allow white Men and particularly of the Spanish Origin to come near them, and was very hostile, and stole the horses from the inhabitants, near San Jose. I got a General passport for my small Colony and permission to select a Territory where ever I would find it convenient, and to come in one Years time again in Monterey to get my Citizenship and the title of the Land, which I have done so, and not only this, I received a high civil Office ("Representante del Govierno en las fronteras del Norte, y Encargado de la Justicia").

When I left Yerbabuena (now San Francisco) after having leaved the Brig and dispatched her back to the S. J.* I bought several small Boats (Launches) and Chartered the Schooner "Isabella" for my Exploring Journey to the inland Rivers and particularly to find the Mouth of the River Sacramento, as I could find Nobody who could give me information, only that they Knew that some very large Rivers are in the interior.

It took me eight days before I could find the entrance of the Sacramento, as it is very deceiving and very easy to pass by, how it happened to several Officers of the Navy afterwards which refused to take a pilot. About 10 miles below Sacramento City I fell in with the first Indians which was all armed & painted & looked very hostile; they was about 200 Men, as some of them understood a little Spanish I could make a Kind

of treaty with them, and the two which understood Spanish came with me, and made me a little better acquainted with the Country. All other Indians on the up River hided themselves in the Bushes, and on the Mouth of Feather River they runned all away so soon they discovered us. I was examining the Country a little further up with a Boat, while the larger Crafts let go their Ankers. On my return all the white Men came to me and asked me how much longer I intended to travell with them in such a Wilderness. I saw plain that it was a Mutiny. I answered them that I would give them an answer the next Morning and left them and went in the Cabin.

The following Morning I gave Orders to return, and entered in the American River, landed at the former Tannery on the 12th Augt. 1839. Gave Orders to get every thing on Shore, pitch the tents and mount the 3 Cannons, called the white Men, and told them that all those which are not contented could leave on board the Isabella next Morning and that I would settle with them imediately and remain alone with the Canacas, of 6 Men 3 remained, and 3 of them I gave passage to Yerbabuena.

The Indians was first troublesome, and came frequently, and would it not have been for the Cannons they would have Killed us for sake of my property, which they liked very much, and this intention they had very often, how they have confessed to me afterwards, when on good terms. I had a large Bull Dog which saved my life 3 times, when they came slyly near the house in the Night: he got hold of and marked them most severely. In a short time removed my Camps on the very spot where now the Ruins of Sutters fort stands, made acquaintance with a few Indians which came to work for a

* Sandwich Islands.

short time making Adobes, and the Canacas was building 3 grass houses, like it is customary on the Sandwich Islands. Before I came up here, I purchased Cattle & Horses on the Rancho of Senor Martinez and had great difficulties & trouble to get them up, and had to wait for them long time, and received them at least on the 22d October 1839. Not less then 8 Men wanted to be in the party, as they were afraid of the Indians and had good reason to be so.

Before I got the Cattle we was hunting Deer & Elk etc and so afterwards to safe the Cattle as I had then only about 500 head, 50 horses & a manada* of 25 mares. One Year, that is in the fall 1840, I bought 1000 head of Cattle of Don Antonio Sunol and a many horses more of Don Joaquin Gomez and others. In the fall 1839 I have built an Adobe house, covered with Tule and two other small buildings in the middle of the fort; they was afterwards destroyed by fire. At the same time we cut a Road through the Woods where the City of Sacramento stand, then we made the New Embarcadero, where the old Zinkhouse stands now. After this it was time to make a Garden, and to sow some Wheat &c. We broke up the soil with poor Californian ploughs, I had a few Californians employed as Baqueros, and 2 of them making Cal. Carts & stocking the ploughs etc.

In the Spring 1840. the Indians began to be troublesome all around me, Killing and Wounding Cattle, stealing horses, and threatening to attack us en Mass I was obliged to make Campaigns against them and punish them severely, a little later about 2 a 300 was aproching and got United on Cosumne River, but I was not waiting for them. Left a small Garrison at home, Canons & other Arms loaded, and left with 6 brave men & 2 Baquero's in the night, and took them by surprise at Day light. The fighting was a little hard, but after having lost about 30 men, they was willing to make a treaty with me, and after this lecon they behaved very well, and became my best friends and Soldiers, with which I has been assisted to conquer the whole Sacramento and a part of the San Joaquin Valley.

They became likewise tolerable good laborers and the boys had to learn mechanical trades; teamster's, Vaquero's, etc. At the time the Communication with the Bay was very long and dangerous, particularly in open Boats; it is a great Wonder that we got not swamped a many times, all time with an Indian Crew and a Canaca at the helm. Once it took me (in December 1839.) 16 days to go down to Yerbabuena and to return. I went down again on the 22d Xber 39. to Yerbabuena and on account of the inclemency of the Weather and the strong current in the River I need a whole month (17 days coming up) and nearly all the provisions spoiled.

March the 18th dispatched a party of White men and Indians in serch for pine timber and went not further up on the Amer. River as about 25 miles, found and cut some but not of a good quality and rafted it down the River. On the end of the month of March there was an other conspiracy of some Indians, but was soon quelled when I succeeded to disarm them. *August 17th.* The men who crossed with me the Rocky Mountains with two others had a chance to come from Oregon on board an Amer. Vessel which landed them at Bodega, at the time occupied by the Russians. When they told the Russian Governor that they wanted to join me, he received them very kindly and hospitable, furnished them with fine horses, new Saddles etc. at a very

* Drove or herd.

low rate and· gave them direction whereabout they would have to travell, without being seen by some Spaniards, which would have them brought to Sonoma in the prison and after a many difficulties they found me at last. I was of Course very glad having these brave men again with me, and employed them, and so I became strong at once.

August 23d. Capt. Ringold of Comadore Wilkes' Exploring Squadron arrived on the Embarcadero, piloted by one of the Launches Indian crew; without this they would not have found so easy the entrance of the Sacramento. They had 6 Whaleboats & 1 Launch, 7 Officers and about 50 men in all. I was very glad indeed to see them, sent immediately saddled horses for the Officers, and my Clerk with an invitation to come and see me. At their arrival I fired a salut, and furnished them what they needed. They was right surprised to find me up here in this Wilderness, it made a very good impression upon the Indians to see so many whites are coming to see me, they surveyed the River as far as the Butes.

September 4th. Arrived the Russian Govr Mr. Alexander Rottcheff on board the Schooner Sacramento, and offered me their whole Establishment at Bodega & Ross for sale, and invited me to come right of with him, as there is a Russian Vessel at Bodega, and some Officers with plein power, to transact this business with me, and particularly they would give me the preference, as they became all acquainted with me, during a months stay at Sitka. I left and went with him down to the Bay in Company with Capt. Ringold's Expedition. What for a fleet we thought then, is on the River. Arriving at Bodega, we came very soon to terms, from there we went to fort Ross where they showed me everything and re-

turned to Bodega again, and before the Vessel sailed we dined on board the Helena, and closed the bargain for $30,000, which has been paid. And other property, was a separate account which has been first paid.

September 28th. I dispatched a number of men and my Clerk by Land to Bodega, to receive the Cattle, Horses, Mules & Sheep, to bring them up to Sutter's fort, called then New Helvetia, by crossing the Sacramento they lost me from about 2000 head about a 100, which drowned in the River, but of most of them we could safe the hides, our Cal. Banknotes at the time.

I did send a Clerk with some men in charge of these Establishments and left the necessary horses and Cattle there. The Schooner Sacramento keept up the communication between the Coast and here, and brought me as freight the Lumber, to finish the House in the fort. I was just building and errecting the fort at the time in Aug. & Sept. for protection of the Indians and of the Californians which became bery jealous seeing these fortifications and 12 Canons and a field piece mounted, and two other brass pieces unmounted at the time.

October 18th. A party of Comodore Wilkes' Exploring Squadron, arrived from Oregon by land, consisting of the Scientific Corps, a few Naval Officers, Marine Soldiers and Mountaineers as Guides under Command of Lieut. Emmons. I received them so well as I could, and then the Scientific Corps left by Land for San Jose and the Naval Officers & Marines I dispatched them on board of one of my Vessels.

*March 6th.** Capt. Fremont arrived at the fort with Kit Carson, told me that he was an officer of the U. S. and left a party behind in Distress and on foot, the few surviving

* 1844

Mules was packed only with the most necessary. I received him politely and his Company likewise as an old acquaintance. The next Morning I furnished them with fresh horses, & a Vaquero with a pack Mule loaded with Necessary Supplies for his Men. Capt Fremont found in my Establishment every thing what he needed, that he could travell without Delay. He could have not found it so by a Spaniard, perhaps by a great Many and with loosing a great deal of time. I sold him about 60 Mules & about 25 horses, and fat young Steers or Beef Cattle, all the Mules & horses got Shoed. On the 23d March, all was ready and on the 24th he left with his party for the U. States.

As an Officer of the Govt. it was my duty to report to the Govt., that Capt. Fremont arrived. Genl. Micheltorena dispatched Lieut. Col. Telles (afterwards Gov. of Sinaloa) with Capt., Lieut. and 25 Dragoons, to inquire what Captain Fremonts business was here; but he was en route as they arrive only on the 27th. From this time on Exploring, Hunting & Trapping parties has been started, at the same time Agricultural & Mechanical business was progressing from Year to year, and more Notice has been taken of my establishment. It became even a fame, and some early Distinguished Travellers like Doctor Sandells, Wasnesensky & others, Captains of Trading Vessels & SuperCargos, & even Californians (after the Indians was subdued) came and paid me a visit, and was astonished to see what for Work of all kinds has been done. Small Emigrant parties arrived, and brought me some very valuable Men, with one of those was Major Bidwell (he was about 4 Years in my employ). Major Reading & Major Hensley with 11 other brave Men arrived alone, both of those Gentlemen has been 2 Years in my employ, with these parties

excellent Mechanics arrived which was all employed by me, likewise good farmers. We made imediately Amer. ploughs in my Shops and all kind of work done. Every year the Russians was bound to furnish me with good iron & Steel & files, Articles which could not be got here, likewise Indian Beeds and the most important of all was 100 lb of fine Rifle & 100 lb of Canon powder, and several 100 lb of Lead (every year). With these I was carefull like with Gold.

From the Hudsons Bay Company I received likewise great supplies, and particularly Powder, lead, and Shot, Beaver Trapps and Clothing (on Credit, to be paid for in Beaver and Otter Skins). They would not have done this to everyone; but as I has been highly recommended to these gentlemen from England and personally acquainted, they have done so. Once I received a visit of Mr. Douglas, who was the Commander in Chief of the establishments on the Pacific & the mountains, after Dr. McLaughlin resigned. With such a supply of Powder, Amunition & Arms, I made a bold appearance. The fort was built in about 4 years of time, as it was very difficult to get the necessary lumber we was sawing by hand Oak timber. Under Gen'l Micheltorena our Govr. I received the rank and Title Capt. of the Mexican Army. He found it his Policy to be friend with me, as he was all time threatened with a Revolution of the Californians notwithstanding having about 1000 troups (Mexicans). Having the rank as Capt. and Military Comander of the Northern frontieres, I began to drill the Indians, with the assistance of two good Non Commissioned Officers from my Country, which I promoted to Capt & first Lieut't & got their Comissions and from the time I had a self-made Garrison, but the Soldiers to earn for their Uniforms & food etc. had to work when they was not on Duty. During this time my Stock was increasing; had about then 8000 head of Cattle and 2000 horses and breeding Mares and about 4000 Sheep. Of the Wool we made our own Plankets, as we established under great Difficulties a factory. Plankets, like nearly all other articles was very scarce and sold to very high prices at the time.

Emigration continued in small parties, just strong enough to protect themselves travelling through a Country of hostile Indians, all of them was allways hospitably received under my roof and all those who could or would not be employed, could stay with me so long as they liked, and when leaving, I gave them Passports which was everywhere respected. Was some trouble below, all came immediately to me for protection. Of the different unfortunate Emigrations which suffered so much in the Snow, it is unnecessary to speak of, as it was published in the papers throughout the States.

In the fall 1844, I went to Monterey with Major Bidwell and a few armed men (Cavallada & Servants); how it was customary to travell at these times, to pay a Visit to Gen'l Micheltorrena. I has been received with the greatest Civil and Military honors. One day he gave a great Diner, after Diner all the Troupes were parading, and in the evening a balloon was sent to the higher regions, etc, etc.

At the time it looked very gloomy; the people of the Country was arming and preparing to make a Revolution, and I got some sure and certain information, of the British Consul and other Gentlemen of my acquaintance which I visited on my way to Monterey. They did not know that the General and myself were friends, and told and discovered me the whole plan, that in

a short time the people of the Country will be ready to blockade the General and his troupes in Monterey, and then take him prisoner and send him and his Soldiers back to Mexico, and make a Gov'r of their own people etc. I was well aware what we could expect should they succeed to do this; they would drive us foreigners all very soon out of the Country, how they have done it once, in the winter 1839. Capt. Vioget has already been engaged by Castro & Alvarado to be ready with his vessel to take the Gen'l and his Soldiers to Mexico.

I had a confidential Conversation with Genl. Micheltorena who received me with great honors and Distinction in Monterey. After having him informed of all what is going on in the Country, he took his measures in a Counsel of war in which I has been present. I received my Orders to raise such a large auxiliary force as I possibly could, and to be ready at his Order, at the same time I received some Cartridges and some small Arms which I had shiped on board the Alert, and took a Passage myself for San francisco (or then Yerba buena). If I had travelled by land, Castro would have taken me a Prisoner in San Juan, where he was laying in Ambush for me. In Yerba buena I remained only a few hours as my Schooner was ready to receive me on board, having waited for me at Ya. Ba.* I visited the Officers of the Custom house and Castro's Officer, which immediately after I left received an Order to arrest me, but I was under fair Way to Sacramento.

After my Arrival at the fort, I began to organize a force for the General, regular Drill of the Indian Infanterie took place, the Mounted Rifle Company about 100 Men of all Nations was raised, of which Capt. Gantt was the Commander; as all was under

* Yerba Buena.

fair way and well organized, and joint with a Detachment of California Cavallry (which deserted from Vallejo) we left the fort with Music and flying Colors on the 1th January 1845, to join the General, and comply with his Orders. Major Reading was left with a small Garrison of Frenchmen, Canadians and Indians, as Commander of the upper Country.

Castro had his Headquarters then in the Mission of San Jose. He did not expect us so soon, as he was just commencing to fortify himself, he ran away with his Garrison, was collecting a stronger force, and want to trouble us on our March, but as he saw that I was on good Qui Vive for him, he left for Monterey to unite with the forces that was blockading the General and his troops in Monterey, and advanced or runed for the lower Country, to call or force the people there to take Arms against the Government. On the Salinas River near Monterey the Genl. was encamped, and with our united force, about 600 Men (he left a Garrison in Monterey) we pursued the enemy, and had to pursue him down to Los Angeles. The first encounter we had with the enemy was at Buenaventura, where we attacked him and drove them out their comfortable quarters. While at and near Santa Barbara, a great Many of Soldiers of my Division Deserted, over 50 men of the Mounted Rifles, the Detachment of Cala. Cavalry deserted and joined their Countrymen the Rebells, likewise a good number of the Mexican Dragoons.

Near San Fernando (Mission) the enemy occupied a fine position, and appeared in full strength, joined by a company of American Traders coming from Sonora and another Company of the same consisting of Traders and Trappers and the whole force of the enemy was over thousand Men, well provided with everything, and our force has been no more as about 350 or 375 Men, and during the battle of Cahuenga near San Fernando, the balance of the Mounted Riflemen, and the Artillerie deserted, and myself fell in the hands of the enemy and was taken prisoner and transported to Los Angeles.

A few days after this, the General, surrounded by the enemy, so that he could get nothing more to eat, capitulated, and after the necessary Documents was signed by both parties, the Genl. was allowed to march with Music and flying colours to San Pedro, where some vessels was ready to take him and his troops on board, and after having delivered their arms etc. proceeded up to Monterey to take the remaining Garrison, the family of the General and his privat property, likewise the families of some of the officers. This was the End of the reign of Genl. Govr. Manl. Micheltorena.

The new Govt. under Gov. Pio Pico, and General Castro, etc. had the intention to shoot me. They was of the Oppinion, that I had joined Genl. Micheltorena Voluntarely, but so soon as I could get my Baggage and my papers, I could prove and show by the Orders of my General that I have obeied his Orders, and done my Duty to the legal Governmt. And so I was acquitted with all honors, and confirmed in my former Offices as Military Commander of the Northern frontier, and encharged with the Justice, with the expressed wish that I might be so faithful to the new Govt. as I had been to Genl. Micheltorena.

While I was in Santa Barbara had a Conversation with Genl. Micheltorena, in reference of the expense, etc., because at the time I had already an Account of about $8000, without counting a cent for my own services, and for my whole rendered services from beginning of my different Offices which I held under Alvarado & the Genl. never they have paid me, even for a Courier, and never furnished me with a Govts. horse. The General told me that he knew this very well, and as he had no money, he would let me have some land, and even if I should like the sobrante* for which I applied when last in Monterey, and which Document was mislaid or destroyed by Dn. Manuel Timeno. I told him that I would be contented, and as we are in Campaign and might be killed by the enemy I wish that the Document would be written in the name of my eldest Son and my whole family.

The Genl. did send for one of his Aid-de-Camp Capt. Castaneda, who was acting Secretary. This Gentleman wrote the Document (he is alife yet), he has given his testimony before the Land Commission about 2 years ago. This Document with a many others has been given to John S. Fowler in Care while he was acting as my Agent, and was afterwards destroyed by fire.

After a return of hardship from San Fernando through Tulare Valley, we turned all out again to our former Occupations, and arrived at the fort on the 1th April 1845.

September 27th. A large party of emigrants arrived. On the 30th dispatched a party of men to assist them.

October 7th. Another large party arrived (about 60 Wagons). Visitors and letters from the U. States.

October 21st. Received Bandas (Proclamations) and Orders of Governor Pio Pico and Genl. Castro. This was on account rumors was circulating that war had been declared between the U. States and Mexico. On the 23d a Meeting was held of the Emigrants at the Fort (Thursday). After the Proclamations had been translated to the

Meeting, they adjourned over until Monday next.

November 11th. was the Day when the Commissioner from Mexico, Don Andres Castillero arrived at the Fort in Company with Genl. Dn. Jose Castro, Col. Prudon, Ma. Lees,** staff and Escort of Castro. A salut was fired.

After having refused to let them have the fort for $100,000, or for Castros offer for the Mission of San Jose etc, etc, they left the next day. Salut fired.

December 10th. Capt. J. C. Fremont arrived again.

December 12th. Delivered him 14 mules.

December 13th. Left for the South to meet Capt. J. Walker.† On the same day, two Blacksmiths of Fremonts arrived, to take charge of one of the Blacksmith Shops, to make Horse Shoes Nails etc.

December 23d. Indians was driving of Stock, some of it we got back again.

December 25th. Arrived Capt. W. L. Hastings direct from the U. States crossing the Mountains with 11 men, among them was Doctor Semple, if they had arrived one day later they would have been cut of by the immense quantity of Snow. I keept the whole party over winter, some of them I employed.

January 14th.†† Capt. Leidesdorff U. S. vice Consul & Capt. Hinckley, Capt. of the Port of San francisco, arrived on a friendly Visit. On the 15th January Capt Fremont returned, not beeing able to find Capt. Walker. As we were two officers of the Mex. Govt. with the Vice Consul of the U. S. we put ourselves in Uniform, and visited Fremont in his Camp, and invited him to dine with us at the Fort, which he accepted,

* An extension of a land grant.
** Major J. P. Leese.
†Joseph Reddeford Walker.
††1846.

Sutter's Fort on the Sacramento. *From a contemporary drawing.*

put himself in Uniform and joint us, as we approached the Fort a salut was fired.

January 17th. Supplied Fremonts Camp with Provisions.

January 19th. Capt. Fremont with 8 of his men took passage on board my Schooner for Yerba buena.

January 30th. Received a Visit of Major Snyder and Mr. Sublette, they brought the News of War being declared between the U. S. & England.

February 19th. News was sent to me that no Mexican Troopes has arrived, which were daily expected in the Country, and that probably California is about to be delivered up to the U. S.

March 14th. Doctor Marsh sent an Express with information of Fremonts Difficulties with Castro. Capt. Fremont was blockaded near Monterey by Castro and his Troopes, and refused him to proceed to the South through the Country on the Coste, etc. The foreign Residents wanted to assist Fremont, but he refused their aid.

March 21st. Capt. Fremont returned and camped on the other side of the Amer. Fork, and looking out for the Californiens, and in a few days left for the upper Sacramento, and for Oregon.

April 28th. Arrived Lieut. A. Gillespie of the U. States Marine Corps, who had secret Dispatches for Fremont, and wanted to overtake him on his route to Oregon. I furnished him with Animals, he went up to Peter Lassens with my Guide. At P. Lassens he hired Men and bought Animals to overtake Fremont. After a sharp riding he succeeded to overtake him, and returned with him to the Sacramento Valley.

May 25th. Saml. Neal passed on a secret errant for Monterey.

May 30th. Lieut. A. Gillespie arrived from the Upper Sacramento Valley, and left on the 1st June on board my Schooner for Yerba buena.

June 3d. I left in Company of Major Reading, and most all of the Men in my employ, for a Campaign with the Mukelemney Indians, which has been engaged by Castro and his Officers to revolutionize all the Indians against me, to Kill all the foreigners, burn their houses and Wheat fields etc. These Mukelemney Indians had great promesses and some of them were finely dressed and equiped, and those came apparently on a friendly visit to the fort and Vicinity and had long Conversation with the influential Men of the Indians, and one Night a Number of them entered in my Potrero (a kind of closed pasture) and was Ketching horses to drive the whole Cavallada away with them. The Sentinel at the fort heart the distant Noise of these Horses, and gave due notice, & imediately I left with about 6 well armed Men and attacked them, but they could make their escape in the Woods (where Sac. City stands now) and so I left a guard with the horses. As we had to cross the Mukelemney River on rafts, one of those rafts capsized with 10 Rifles, and 6 prs of Pistols, a good supply of Amunition, and the Clothing of about 24 Men, and Major Reading & another Man nearly drowned.

Some Men remained on the dry places as they had no Clothing nor Arms, the remaining Arms and amunitions has been divided among the whole, and so we marched the whole Night on the Calaveras, and could not find the enemy. In the Morning by Sunrise we took a little rest, and soon dispatched a party to discover and reconnoitre the enemy. A Dog came to our Camp which was a well known dog of the Mukelemneys, a sign that they are not very far from us; at the same time a Courier of the party came on galloping, telling us that the party fell already in an engagemt with the enemy. Imediately we left galloping to join in the fight; already some of our Men was wounded and unable to fight. We continued the fighting until they retired and fled in a large hole like a Cellar in the bank of the Calaveras, covered with brushes and trees, firing and shooting with their bows and arrows, but we had them blockaded, and killed them a good many of their Men, but on account of having no more powder and balls, we found it very prudent to leave the Scene slowly, so that it appeared as we wanted to Camp, and so we made a forced March and Crossed the Mukelemney, and returned from this Campaign on the 7th June.

June 8th. Arrived Lieut. Francisco Arce with 8 Soldiers & Govt. horses from Sonoma for Genl. Castro.

June 9th. Departed Lieutenant Arce for Monterey.

June 10th. A party of Americans under Command of E. Merritt, took all the horses from Arce at Murphey's.

June 13th. The Portsmouths Launch arrived under Command of Lieut. Hunter, in Company with Lieut. Gillespie, Purser Waldron & Doctor Duvall.

June 14th. Lieut. Gillespie & Hensley left for Fremont's Camp near Hock farm.

June 16th. Merritt & Kitt Carson arrived with News of Sonoma beeing occupied by the Americans, and the same evening arrived as prissoners Genl. Vallejo, Don Salvador Vallejo, Lt. Col. Prudon & M. Leese, and given under my charge and Care, I have treated them with kindness and so good as I could, which was reported to Fremont, and he then told me that prissoners ought not to be treated so, then I told him, if it

is not right how I treat them, to give them in charge of somebody else.

June 17th. Departed the Portsmouth Launch for Yerba buena. Capt. Fremont moved Camp up to the Amer. fork, a good many people joining Fremonts Camp.

June 18th. Arrived Express from Sonoma with letter from Capt. Montgomery.

June 19th. Arrived Capt. Fremont with about 20 Men from Camp. Jose Noriega was detained prissoner. Fremonts Blacksmiths were busily engaged. Vicente Peralta, who was up in the Valley on a visit, was detained prissoner.

June 21st. Capt. Fremont & Camp deposited the Packs and then camped across Amer. fork. Major Reading and my Trappers joined the Camp, and left for Sonoma as a strong Detachment of Californians crossed the Estrecho de Carqinas at Benicia.

June 26th. Lieut. Revere & Dr. Henderson of the Portsmouth with a party of Men arrived in a Man of War Boat. A party of Men arrived from Oregon by land, which joined Fremont.

June 28th. Arrived Lieut. Bartlett of the Portsmouth and organized a Garrison.

July 10th. [Fremont] Arrived or returned from Sonoma with his Company. On this trip or Campaign to Sonoma some cruel actions has been done on both sides.

Capt. Montgomery did send an Amer. flag by Lieut. Revere then in Command of Sonoma, and some dispatches to Fremont, I received the Order to hist the flag by Sunrise from Lt. Revere. Long time before daybreak, I got ready with loading the Canons and when it was day the roaring of the Canons got the people all stirring. Some them made long faces, as they thought if the Bear flag would remain there would be a better chance to rob and plunder. Capt.

Fremont received Orders to proceed to Monterey with his forces, Capt. Montgomery provided for the upper Country, established Garrisons in all important places, Yerba buena, Sonoma, San Jose, and fort Sacramento. Lieut. Missroon came to organize our Garrison better and more Numbers of white Men and Indians of my former Soldiers, and gave me the Command of this Fort. The Indians have not yet received their pay yet for their services, only each one a shirt and a pre.* of pants, & abt. 12 men got Coats. So went the War on in California. Capt. Fremont was nearly all time engaged in the lower Country and made himself Governor, until Genl. Kearny arrived, when an other Revolution took place. And Fremont for disobeying Orders was made prissoner by Genl. Kearny, who took him afterwards with him to the U. States by Land across the Mountains. After

the War I was anxious that Business should go on like before, and on the 28th May, 1847, Marshall & Gingery, two Millwrights, I employed to survey the large Millraise for the Flour Mill at Brighton.

May 24th. Lieut't Anderson arrived with a Detachment of Stevenson's Regiment of N. Y. Volunteers for a Garrison, and to relieve my Indian Soldiers from their Service.

May 31st. Mr. Marshall commenced the great work of the large Millraise, with ploughs and scrapers.

June 13th. A visit of Genl Kearny and his Staff and a few other Gentlemen. A salut was fired and the Garrison was parading.

June 14th. A diner given to Gen'l Kearny and Staff. Capt. Fremont a prisoner of Gen'l Kearny. Walla Walla Indian Chiefs and people visited Fremont and wanted their

* French abbreviation of *une paire*, pair.

Sacramento in 1850

pay for Services rendered in the Campaign when they was with Fremonts Battaillon, he then ordered one of his officers to pay them with Govt's horses (Horses which has been taken from the people of the Country was called Govt. horses and war horses) .

June 16th. Gen'l Kearny, Staff & Escort etc. left for the U. States across the Mountains.

June 22nd. The Walla Walla Indians have done a great deal of Depredations on their return march to Oregon, stole horses of mine and other people, stole from a many Indian tribes and maltreated them. They are a very bad Tribe of Indians and very warlike.

July 20th. Got all the necessary timber for the frame of the millbuilding.

July 21st. Left with Marshall and an Indian Chief in search for a Mill site in the Mountains.

July 17th. 18th & 19th. Went on a visit to Comodore Stockton in his Camp on Bear creek. The Comodore left with a Strong party for the U. States across the Mountains. Made a present to the Comodore with my best and finest horse of my Cavallada. Great Sickness and diseases amongst the Indian tribes, and a great Number of them were dying notwithstanding of having employed a Doctor to my hospital.

August 2d. Major Cloud, paymaster & Capt Folsom quartermaster arrived; the former paid off the Garrison at the fort. On the 4th, these two Gentlemen left on Horseback. I accompanied them, and we was only but only ½ mile from the fort Major Cloud fell from his horse senseless and died in the evening. The Surgeon of the Garrison & my own Doctor have done what could be done to safe him. On the 6th, Major Cloud was burried with military honors. Capt. Folsom commanded the Troops, as Lieut't Anderson was sick.

August 25th. Capt Hart of the Mormon Battaillon arrived, with a good many of his Men on their Way to great Salt Lake. They had Orders for Govt. Horses, which I delivered to them, (War Horses) *not paid for yet.* They bought provisions and got Blacksmith work done. I employed about Eighty Men of them, some as Mechanics, some as laborers, on the Mill and Millraise at Brighton; some as laborers at the Sawmill at Columa.

August 28th. Marshall moved, with P. Wimmer family and the working hands to Columa, and began to work briskly on the sawmill.

September 10th. Mr. Sam'l Brannan returned from the great Salt Lake, and announced a large Emigration by land. On the 19th the Garrison was removed, Lieut't Per Lee took her down to San francisco.

September 21st. Employed more Carpenters to assist Brouett on the Grist Mill.

October 3d. A great many Emigrants arrived, and so it continued through the whole of the month.

October 12th. A small Store was established by S'l Brannan & Smith in one of the houses near the fort.

November 1st. Getting with a great deal of trouble and with breaking wagons the four Runs of Millstones, to the Mill Site (Brighton) from the Mountains.

December 22d. Received about 2000 fruit trees with great expenses from Fort Ross, Napa Valley and other places, which was given in Care of men who called themselves Gardeners, and nearly all of the trees was neglected by them and died.

*January 28th.** Marshall arrived in the evening, it was raining very heavy, but he told me he came on important business. After

---

* 1848. Marshall discovered gold at the Coloma sawmill January 24, 1848.

we was alone in a private Room he showed me the first Specimens of Gold, that is he was not certain if it was Gold or not, but he thought it might be; immediately I made the proof and found that it was Gold. I told him even that most of all is 23 Carat Gold; he wished that I should come up with him immediately, but I told him that I have to give first my orders to the people in all my factories and shops.

February 1st. Left for the Sawmill attended by a Baquero (Olimpio). Was absent 2d, 3d, 4th, & 5th. I examined myself everything and picked up a few Specimens of Gold myself in the tail race of the Sawmill; this Gold and others which Marshall and some of the other laborers gave to me (it was found while in my employ and Wages) I told them that I would a Ring got made of it so soon as a Goldsmith would be here. I had a talk with my employed people all at the Sawmill. I told them that as they do know now that this Metal is Gold, I wished that they would do me the great favor and keep it secret only 6 weeks, because my large Flour Mill at Brighton would have been in Operation in such a time, which undertaking would have been a fortune to me, and unfortunately the people would not keep it secret, and so I lost on this Mill at the lowest calculation about $25,000.

March 7th. The first party of Mormons, employed by me left for washing and digging Gold and very soon all followed, and left me only the sick and the lame behind. And at this time I could say that every body left me from the Clerk to the Cook. What for great Damages I had to suffer in my tannery which was just doing a profitable and extensive business, and the Vatts was left filled and a quantity of half finished leather was spoiled, likewise a large quantity of raw hides collected by the farmers and

of my own killing. The same thing was in every branch of business which I carried on at the time. I began to harvest my wheat, while others was digging and washing Gold, but even the Indians could not be keeped longer at Work. They was impatient to run to the mines, and other Indians had informed them of the Gold and its Value; and so I had to leave more as ⅔ of my harvest in the fields.

March 21st. Threatened by a band of Robbers, from the Red Woods at San Francisquito near Santa Clara.

April 2d. Mr. Humphrey a regular Miner arrived, and left for Columa with Wimmer & Marshall. Entered with them in Mining, furnished Indians, teams and provisions to this Company, and as I was loosing instead making something, I left this Company as a Partner. Some of the neighbors, while the Mormons left, became likewise the Goldfever and went to the Mountains prospecting and soon afterwards moved up to digg and wash Gold, and some of them with great success.

April 16th. Mr. Gray (from Virginia) who purchased Silver Mines in the San Jose Valley for a Compy and was interested himself. At the fort he learned the news of the Gold discovery. I presented him some Speciments of Gold. He left for the States across the Mountains. Some families are moving in the Mountains to camp and settle there.

April 18th. More curious people arrived, bound for the Mountains. I left for Columa, in Company with Major P. B. Reading and Mr. Kembel (Editor of the Alta-California) we were absent 4 Days. We was prospecting and found Silver and iron ore in abundance.

April 28th. A great many people more went up to the Mountains. This day the Saw mill was in Operation and the first Lumber has been sawed in the whole upper Country. *May 1st.* Saml Brannan was building a store at Natoma, Mormon Islands, and have done a very large and heavy business.

May 15th. Paid off all the Mormons which has been employed by me, in building these Mills and other Mechanical trades, all of them made their pile, and some of them became rich & wealthy, but all of them was bound to the great Salt Lake, and spent there their fortunes to the honor and Glory of the Lord!

May 19th. The great Rush from San Francisco arrived at the fort, all my friends and acquaintances filled up the houses and the whole fort, I had only a little Indian boy, to make them roasted Ripps etc. as my Cooks left me like every body else. The Merchants, Doctors, Lawyers, Sea Captains, Merchants etc. all came up and did not know what to do, all was in a Confusion, all left their wives and families in San francisco,

John Sutter

and those which had none locked their Doors, abandoned their houses, offered them for sale cheap, a few hundred Dollars House & Lot (Lots which are worth now $100,000 and more), some of these men were just like greazy. Some of the Merchants has been the most prudentest of the Whole, visited the Mines and returned immediately and began to do a very profitable business, and soon Vessels came from every where with all Kind of Merchandise, the whole old thrash which was laying for Years unsold, on the Coasts of South & Central America, Mexico, Sandwich Islands etc. All found a good Market here.

Mr. Brannan was erecting a very large Warehouse, and have done an immense business, connected with Howard & Green; S. Francisco.

May 21st. Saml Kyburg errected or established the first Hotel in the fort in the larger building, and made a great deal of Money. A great Many traders deposited a great deal of goods in my Store (an Indian was the Key Keeper and performed very well). Afterwards every little Shanty became a Warehouse and Store; the fort was then a veritable Bazaar. As white people would not be employed at the Time I had a few good Indians attending to the Ferry boat, and every night came up, and delivered the received Money for ferryage to me, after deductions for a few bottles of brandy, for the whole of them. Perhaps some white people at the time would not have acted so honestly. *May 25th.* The travelling to the Mines was increasing from day to day, and no more Notice was taken, as the people arrived from South America, Mexico, Sandwich Islands, Oregon, etc. All the Ships Crews, and Soldiers deserted. In the beginning of July, Col. Mason our Military Governor, with Capt. Sherman (Secretary of State) **Capt. Folsom,**

Quartermstr, and an Escort, of which some deserted, and some other Gentlemen, travelled in Company with the Governor.

As we wanted to celebrate the 4th of July we invited the Governor and his suite to remain with us, and he accepted. Kyburg gave us a good Diner, every thing was pretty well arranged. Pickett was the Orator. It was well done enough for such a new Country and in such an excitement and Confusion. And from this time on you know how every thing was going on here. One thing is certain that the people looked on my property as their own, and in the Winter of 1849 to 1850, a great Number of horses has been stolen from me, whole Manadas of Mares driven away and taken to Oregon etc. Nearly my whole Stock of Cattle has been Killed, several thousands, and left me a very small Quantity. The same has been done with my large stock of Hogs, which was running like ever under nobodies care and so it was easy to steal them. I had not an Idea that people could be so mean, and that they would do a Wholesale business in Stealing.

On the upper Sacramento, that is, from the Buttes downward to the point or Mouth of feather River, there was most all of my Stock running and during the Overflow the Cattle was in a many bands on high spots like Islands. There was a fine chance to approach them in small Boats and shoot them. This business has been very successfully done by one party of 5 Men (partners) which had besides hired people, and Boats Crews, which transported the beef to the Market at Sacramento City and furnished that City with my own beef, and because these Men was nearly alone, on account of the Overflow, and Monopolized the Market.

In the Spring of 1850, these 5 men divided their Spoil of $60,000 clear profits made of Cattle. All of them left for the Atlantic State; one of them returned again in the Winter from 1850 to 51, hired a new band of Robers to follow the same business and kill of the balance or the few that was left. My Baqueros found out this Nest of thiefs in their Camp butchering just some heads of my Cattle. On their return they informed me what they have seen. In the neighborhood of the same Camp they saw some more cows shot dead, which the Rascal then butchered. Immediately I did send to Nicolaus for the Sheriff (Jas. Hopkins) as then at the time we had laws in force?!? After all was stolen and destroyed the Sheriff arrived at Hock farm. I furnished him a Posse of my employed Men. They proceeded over on the Sacramento to where the thiefs were encamped. As the Sheriff wanted to arrest them they just jumped in their Boats and off they went, the Sheriff threatened them to fire at them, but that was all, and laughing they went at large.

One day my Son was riding after Stock a few miles below Hock farm. He found a Man (his name was Owens) butchering one of our finest milch Cows (of Durham stock of Chile, which cost $300.) He told the Man that he could not take the Meat, that he would go home and get people, and so he has done, and he got people and a Wagon and returned to the Spot but Owens found it good to clear out. Two brothers of this Man was respectable Merchants in Lexington Mo. and afterwards in Westport well acquainted with me. He came one day in my house and brought me their compliments, I received him well, and afterwards turned out to be a thief. How many of this kind came to California which loosed their little honor by crossing the Istmus or the plains. I had nothing at all to do with speculations, but stuck by the plough, but by paying such high Wages, and particularly under Ky-

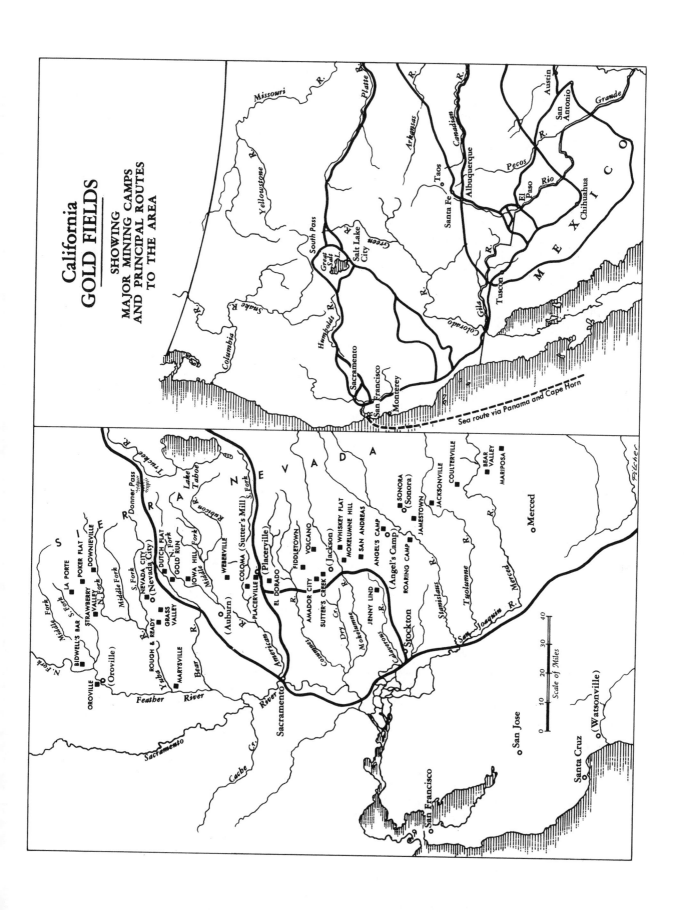

California
GOLD FIELDS

SHOWING
MAJOR MINING CAMPS
AND PRINCIPAL ROUTES
TO THE AREA

burg's management, I have done this business with a heavy loss as the produce had no more the Value like before, and from the time on Kyburg left I curtailed my business considerable, and so far that I do all at present with my family and a few Indian Servants. I did not speculate, only occupied my land, in the hope that it would be before long decided and in my favor by the U.S. Land Commission; but now already 3 years & two months have elapsed, and I am waiting now very anxiously for the Decission, which will revive or bring me to the untimely grave.

All the other Circumstances you know all yourself, perhaps I have repeated many things which I wrote in the 3 first sheets, because I had them not to see what I wrote, and as it is now several months I must have forgotten. Well it is only a kind of memorandum, and not a History at all, Only to remember you on the different periods when such and such things happened.

I need not mention again, that all the Visitors has allways been hospitably received and treated. That all the sick and wounded found allways Medical Assistance, Gratis, as I had nearly all the time a Physician in my employ. The Assistance to the Emigrants, that is all well known. I dont need to write anything about this.

I think now from all this you can form some facts, and that you can mention how thousands and thousands made their fortunes, from this Gold Discovery produced through my industry and energy, (some wise merchants and others in San francisco called the building of this Sawmill, another of Sutter's folly) and this folly saved not only the Mercantile World from Bankruptcy, but even our General Gov't. but for me it has turned out a folly, then without having discovered the Gold, I would have become the richest wealthiest man on the Pacific Shore.

49. Looking for Gold

BY J. D. BORTHWICK

EDITOR'S NOTE: J. D. Borthwick was an Edinburgh artist who happened to be in New York in 1851, at the height of the gold rush. He caught the California fever and sailed for Panama, where he crossed the Isthmus and proceeded toward his goal. He became a miner and had a fair share of luck. But he never stopped drawing and painting, and earned a good deal of money drawing portraits of the men around him, their diggings, their stakes, and whatever else they wanted

to record or felt proud of. His book, *Three Years in California*, is one of the best eyewitness accounts of the place and time, as much for its style as for its lively matter. It was published in Edinburgh in 1857. I have drawn upon it for the following three accounts.

THE town of Placerville—or Hangtown, as it was commonly called—consisted of one long straggling street of clapboard houses and log cabins, built in a hollow at the side of a creek, and surrounded by high and steep hills.

The diggings here had been exceedingly rich—men used to pick the chunks of gold out of the crevices of the rocks in the ravines with no other tool than a bowie-knife; but these days had passed, and now the whole surface of the surrounding country showed the amount of real hard work which had been done. The beds of the numerous ravines which wrinkle the faces of the hills, the bed of the creek, and all the little flats alongside of it, were a confused mass of heaps of dirt and piles of stones lying around the innumerable holes, about six feet square and five or six feet deep, from which they had been thrown out. The original course of the creek was completely obliterated, its waters being distributed into numberless little ditches, and from them conducted into the "long toms" of the miners through canvas hoses, looking like immensely long slimy sea-serpents.

The number of bare stumps of what had once been gigantic pine trees, dotted over the naked hill-sides surrounding the town, showed how freely the ax had been used, and to what purpose was apparent in the extent of the town itself, and in the numerous log-cabins scattered over the hills, in situations apparently chosen at the caprice of the owners, but in reality with a view to be near to their diggings, and at the same time to be within a convenient distance of water and firewood.

Along the whole length of the creek, as far as one could see, on the banks of the creek, in the ravines, in the middle of the principal and only street of the town, and even inside some of the houses, were parties of miners, numbering from three or four to a dozen, all hard at work, some laying into it with picks, some shoveling the dirt into the "long toms," or with long-handled shovels washing the dirt thrown in, and throwing out the stones, while others were working pumps or baling water out of the holes with buckets. There was a continual noise and clatter, as mud, dirt, stones, and water were thrown about in all directions; and the men, dressed in ragged clothes and big boots, wielding picks and shovels, and rolling big rocks about, were all working as if for their lives, going into it with a will, and a degree of energy, not usually seen amoung laboring men. It was altogether a scene which conveyed the idea of hard work in the fullest sense of the words, and in comparison with which a gang of railway navvies would have seemed to be merely a party of gentlemen amateurs playing at working *pour passer le temps.*

A stroll through the village revealed the extent to which the ordinary comforts of life were attainable. The gambling-houses, of which there were three or four, were of course the largest and most conspicuous buildings; their mirrors, chandeliers, and other decorations, suggesting a style of life totally at variance with the outward indications of everything around them.

The street itself was in many places knee-deep in mud, and was plentifully strewed with old boots, hats, and shirts, old sardine-boxes, empty tins of preserved oysters, empty bottles, worn-out pots and kettles, old ham-bones, broken picks and shovels, and other rubbish too various to particularize. Here and there, in the middle of the street, was a square hole about six feet deep, in which one miner was digging, while another was baling the water out with a bucket, and a third, sitting alongside the heap of dirt which had been dug up, was washing it in a rocker. Wagons, drawn by six or eight mules or oxen, were navigating along the street, or discharging their strangely-assorted cargoes at the various stores; and men in picturesque rags, with large muddy boots, long beards, and brown faces, were the only inhabitants to be seen.

There were boarding-houses on the *table-d'hôte* principle, in each of which forty or fifty hungry miners sat down three times a day to an oilcloth-covered table, and in the course of about three minutes surfeited themselves on salt pork, greasy steaks, and pickles. There were also two or three "hotels," where much the same sort of fare was to be had, with the extra luxuries of a table-cloth and a superior quality of knives and forks.

The stores were curious places. There was no specialty about them—everything was to be found in them which it could be supposed that any one could possibly want, excepting fresh beef (there was a butcher who monopolized the sale of that article).

On entering a store, one would find the storekeeper in much the same style of costume as the miners, very probably sitting on an empty keg at a rickety little table,

Gold Hunters

playing "seven up" for "the liquor" with one of his customers.

The counter served also the purpose of a bar, and behind it was the usual array of bottles and decanters, while on shelves above them was an ornamental display of boxes of sardines, and brightly-colored tins of preserved meats and vegetables with showy labels, interspersed with bottles of champagne and strangely-shaped bottles of exceedingly green pickles, the whole being arranged with some degree of taste.

Goods and provisions of every description were stowed away promiscuously all round the store, in the middle of which was invariably a small table with a bench, or some empty boxes and barrels for the miners to sit on while they played cards, spent their money in brandy and oysters, and occasionally got drunk.

During the week, and especially when the miners were all at work, Hangtown was comparatively quiet; but on Sundays it was a very different place. On that day the miners living within eight or ten miles all flocked in to buy provisions for the week—to spend their money in the gambling-rooms—to play cards—to get their letters from home—and to refresh themselves, after a week's labor and isolation in the mountains, in enjoying the excitement of the scene according to their tastes.

The gamblers on Sundays reaped a rich harvest; their tables were thronged with crowds of miners betting eagerly, and of course losing their money. Many men came in, Sunday after Sunday, and gambled off all the gold they had dug during the week, having to get credit at a store for their next week's provisions, and returning to their diggings to work for six days in getting more gold, which would all be transferred the next Sunday to the gamblers, in the vain hope of recovering what had been already lost.

The street was crowded all day with miners loafing about from store to store, making their purchases and asking each other to drink, the effects of which began to be seen at an early hour in the number of drunken men, and the consequent frequency of rows and quarrels. Almost every man wore a pistol or a knife—many wore both—but they were rarely used. The liberal and prompt administration of Lynch law had done a great deal towards checking the wanton and indiscriminate use of these weapons on any slight occasion. The utmost latitude was allowed in the exercise of self-defense. In the case of a row, it was not necessary to wait till a pistol was actually leveled at one's head—if a man made even a motion towards drawing a weapon, it was considered perfectly justifiable to shoot him first, if possible. The very prevalence of the custom of carrying arms thus in a great measure was a cause of their being seldom used. They were never drawn out of bravado, for when a man once drew his pistol, he had to be prepared to use it, and to use it quickly, or he might expect to be laid low by a ball from his adversary; and again, if he shot a man without sufficient provocation, he was pretty sure of being accommodated with a hempen cravat by Judge Lynch.

The storekeepers did more business on Sundays than in all the rest of the week; and in the afternoon crowds of miners could be seen dispersing over the hills in every direction, laden with the provisions they had been purchasing, chiefly flour, pork and beans, and perhaps a lump of fresh beef.

Gold Mining

There was only one place of public worship in Hangtown at that time, a very neat wooden edifice, which belonged to some denomination of Methodists, and seemed to be well attended.

There was also a newspaper published two or three times a week, which kept the inhabitants "posted up" as to what was going on in the world.

The richest deposits of gold were found in the beds and banks of the rivers, creeks, and ravines, in the flats on the convex side of the bends of the streams, and in many of the flats and hollows high up in the mountains. The precious metal was also abstracted from the very hearts of the mountains, through tunnels drifted into them for several hundred yards; and in some places real mining was carried on in the bowels of the earth by means of shafts sunk to the depth of a couple of hundred feet.

The principal diggings in the neighborhood of Hangtown were surface diggings; but, with the exception of river diggings, every kind of mining operation was to be seen in full force.

The gold is found at various depths from the surface; but the dirt on the bed-rock is the richest, as the gold naturally in time sinks through earth and gravel, till it is arrested in its downward progress by the solid rock.

The diggings here were from four to six or seven feet deep; the layer of "pay-dirt" being about a couple of feet thick on the top of the bed-rock.

I should mention that "dirt" is the word universally used in California to signify the substance dug, earth, clay, gravel, loose slate, or whatever other name might be more appropriate. The miners talk of rich dirt and poor dirt, and of "stripping off" so many feet of "top dirt" before getting to "pay-dirt," the latter meaning dirt with so much gold in it that it will pay to dig it up and wash it.

The apparatus generally used for washing was a "long tom," which was nothing more than a wooden trough from twelve to twenty-five feet long, and about a foot wide. At the lower end it widens considerably, and on the floor there is a sheet of iron pierced with holes half an inch in diameter, under which is placed a flat box a couple of inches deep. The long tom is set at a slight inclinataion over the place which is to be worked, and a stream of water is kept running through it by means of a hose, the mouth of which is inserted in a dam built for the purpose high enough up the stream to gain the requisite elevation; and while some of the party shovel the dirt into the tom as fast as they can dig it up, one man stands at the lower end stirring up the dirt as it is washed down, separating the stones and throwing them out, while the earth and small gravel falls with the water through the sieve into the "ripple-box." This box is about five feet long, and is crossed by two partitions. It is also placed at an inclination, so that the water falling into it keeps the dirt loose, allowing the gold and heavy particles to settle to the bottom, while all the lighter stuff washes over the end of the box along with the water. When the day's work is over, the dirt is taken from the "ripple-box" and is "washed out" in a "wash-pan," a round tin dish, eighteen inches in diameter, with shelving sides three or four inches deep. In washing out a panful of dirt, it has to be placed in water deep enough to cover it over; the dirt is stirred up with the hands, and the gravel thrown out; the pan is then taken in both hands, and by an indescribable series of maneuvers all the dirt is gradually washed out of it, leaving nothing but the gold and a small quantity of black sand. This black sand is mineral (some oxide or other salt of iron), and is so heavy that it is not possible to wash it all out; it has to be blown out of the gold afterwards when dry.

Another mode of washing dirt, but much more tedious, and consequently only resorted to where a sufficient supply of water for a long tom could not be obtained, was by means of an apparatus called a "rocker" or "cradle." This was merely a wooden cradle, on the top of which was a sieve. The dirt was put into this, and a miner, sitting alongside of it, rocked the cradle with one hand, while with a dipper in the other he kept baling water on to the dirt. This acted on the same principle as the "tom," and had formerly been the only contrivance in use; but it was now seldom seen, as the long tom effected such a saving of time and labor. The latter was set immediately over the claim, and the dirt was shoveled into it at once, while a rocker had to be set alongside of the water, and the dirt was carried to it in buckets from the place which was being worked. Three men working together with a rocker—one digging, another carrying the dirt in buckets, and the third rocking the cradle—would wash on an average a hundred bucketfuls of dirt to the man in the course of the day. With a "long tom" the dirt was so easily washed that parties of six or eight could work together to advantage, and four or five hundred bucketfuls of dirt a day to each one of the party was a usual day's work.

I met a San Francisco friend in Hangtown practising his profession as a doctor, who very hospitably offered me quarters in his cabin, which I gladly accepted. The accommodation was not very luxurious, being merely six feet of the floor on which

to spread my blankets. My host, however, had no better bed himself, and indeed it was as much as most men cared about. Those who were very particular preferred sleeping on a table or a bench when they were to be had; bunks and shelves were also much in fashion; but the difference in comfort was a mere matter of imagination, for mattresses were not known, and an earthen floor was quite as soft as any wooden board. Three or four miners were also inmates of the doctor's cabin. They were quondam New South Wales squatters, who had been mining for several months in a distant part of the country, and were now going to work a claim about two miles up the creek from Hangtown. As they wanted another hand to work their long tom with them, I very readily joined their party. For several days we worked this place, trudging out to it when it was hardly daylight, taking with us our dinner, which consisted of beefsteaks and bread, and returning to Hangtown about dark; but the claim did not prove rich enough to satisfy us, so we abandoned it, and went "prospecting," which means looking about for a more likely place.

A "prospector" goes out with a pick and shovel, and a wash-pan; and to test the richness of a place he digs down till he reaches the dirt in which it may be expected that the gold will be found; and washing out a panful of this, he can easily calculate, from the amount of gold which he finds in it, how much could be taken out in a day's work. An old miner, looking at the few specks of gold in the bottom of his pan, can tell their value within a few cents; calling it a twelve or a twenty cent "prospect," as it may be. If, on washing out a panful of dirt, a mere speck of gold remained, just enough to swear by, such dirt was said to have only "the color," and was not worth digging. A twelve-cent

Out Prospecting

prospect was considered a pretty good one; but in estimating the probable result of a day's work, allowance had to be made for the time and labor to be expended in removing top-dirt, and in otherwise preparing the claim for being worked.

To establish one's claim to a piece of ground, all that was requisite was to leave upon it a pick or shovel, or other mining tool. The extent of ground allowed to each individual varied in different diggings from ten to thirty feet square, and was fixed by the miners themselves, who also made their own laws, defining the rights and duties of those holding claims; and any dispute on such subjects was settled by calling together a few of the neighboring miners, who would enforce the due observance of the laws of the diggings. After prospecting for two or three days we concluded to take up a claim near a small settlement called Middletown, two or three miles distant from Hangtown. It was situated by the side of a small creek, in a rolling hilly country, and consisted of about a dozen cabins, one of which was a store supplied with flour, pork, tobacco, and other necessaries.

We found near our claim a very comfortable cabin, which the owner had deserted, and in which we established ourselves. We had plenty of firewood and water close to us, and being only two miles from Hangtown, we kept ourselves well supplied with fresh beef. We cooked our "dampers" in New South Wales fashion, and lived on the fat of the land, our bill of fare being beefsteaks, damper, and tea for breakfast, dinner, and supper. A damper is a very good thing, but not commonly seen in California, excepting among men from New South Wales. A quantity of flour and water, with a pinch or two of salt, is worked into a dough, and, raking down a good hardwood fire, it is placed on the hot ashes, and then smothered in more hot ashes to the depth of two or three inches, on the top of which is placed a quantity of the still burning embers. A very little practice enables one to judge from the feel of the crust when it is sufficiently cooked. The great advantage of a damper is, that it retains a certain amount of moisture, and is as good when a week old as when fresh baked. It is very solid and heavy, and a little of it goes a great way, which of itself is no small recommendation when one eats only to live.

Another sort of bread we very frequently made by filling a frying-pan with dough, and sticking it upon end to roast before the fire.

The Americans do not understand dampers. They either bake bread, using saleratus to make it rise, or else they make flapjacks, which are nothing more than pancakes made of flour and water, and are a very good substitute for bread when one is in a hurry, as they are made in a moment.

As for our beefsteaks, they could not be beat anywhere. A piece of an old iron-hoop, twisted into a serpentine form and laid on the fire, made a first-rate gridiron, on which every man cooked his steak to his own taste. In the matter of tea I am afraid we were dreadfully extravagant, throwing it into the pot in handfuls. It is a favorite beverage in the mines—morning, noon, and night—and at no time is it more refreshing than in the extreme heat of midday.

In the cabin two bunks had been fitted up, one above the other, made of clapboards laid crossways, but they were all loose and warped. I tried to sleep on them one night, but it was like sleeping on a gridiron; the smooth earthen floor was a much more easy couch.

50. Miners' Law

BY J. D. BORTHWICK

THE miners on the creek were nearly all Americans, and exhibited a great variety of mankind. Some, it was very evident, were men who had hitherto only worked with their heads; others one would have set down as having been mechanics of some sort, and as having lived in cities; and there were numbers of unmistakable backwoodsmen and farmers from the Western States. Of these a large proportion were Missourians, who had emigrated across the plains. From the State of Missouri the people had flocked in thousands to the gold diggings, and particularly from a county in that state called Pike County.

The peculiarities of the Missourians are very strongly marked, and after being in the mines but a short time, one could distinguish a Missourian, or a "Pike," or "Pike County," as they are called, from the natives of any other western State. Their costume was always exceedingly old and greasy-looking; they had none of the occasional foppery of the miner, which shows itself in brilliant red shirts, boots with flaming red tops, fancy-colored hats, silver-handled

bowie-knives, and rich silk sashes. It always seemed to me that a Missourian wore the same clothes in which he had crossed the plains, and that he was keeping them to wear on his journey home again. Their hats were felt, of a dirty-brown

Crossing the Plain in a Hand Cart

color, and the shape of a short extinguisher. Their shirts had perhaps, in days gone by, been red, but were now a sort of purple; their pantaloons were generally of a snuffy-brown color, and made of some woolly home-made fabric. Suspended at their back from a narrow strap buckled round the waist they carried a wooden-handled bowie-knife in an old leathern sheath, not stitched, but riveted with leaden nails; and over their shoulders they wore strips of cotton or cloth as suspenders—mechanical contrivances never thought of by any other men in the mines. As for their boots, there was no peculiarity about them, excepting that they were always old. Their coats, a garment not frequently seen in the mines for at least six months of the year, were very extraordinary things—exceedingly tight, short-waisted, long-skirted surtouts of homemade frieze of a greyish-blue color.

As for their persons, they were mostly long, gaunt, narrow-chested, round-shouldered men, with long, straight, light-colored, dried-up-looking hair, small thin sallow faces, with rather scanty beard and moustache, and small grey sunken eyes, which seemed to be keenly perceptive of everything around them. But in their movements the men were slow and awkward, and in the towns especially they betrayed a childish astonishment at the strange sights occasioned by the presence of the divers nations of the earth. The fact is, that till they came to California many of them had never in their lives before seen two houses together, and in any little village in the mines they witnessed more of the wonders of civilization than ever they had dreamed of.

In some respects, perhaps, the mines of California were as wild a place as any part of the Western States of America; but they were peopled by a community of men of all classes, and from different countries, who though living in a rough backwoods style, had nevertheless all the ideas and amenities of civilized life; while the Missourians, having come direct across the plains from their homes in the backwoods, had received no preparatory education to enable them to show off to advantage in such company.

And in this they labored under a great disadvantage, as compared with the lower classes of people of every country who came to San Francisco by way of Panama or Cape Horn. The men from the interior of the States learned something even on their journey to New York or New Orleans, having their eyes partially opened during the few days they spent in either of those cities en route; and on the passage to San Francisco they naturally received a certain degree of polish from being violently shaken up with a crowd of men of different habits and ideas from their own. They had to give way in many things to men whose motives of action were perhaps to them incomprehensible, while of course they gained a few new ideas from being brought into close contact with such sorts of men as they had hitherto only seen at a distance, or very likely had never heard of. A little experience of San Francisco did them no harm, and by the time they reached the mines they had become very superior men to the raw bumpkins they were before leaving their homes.

It may seem strange, but it is undoubtedly true, that the majority of men in whom such a change was most desirable became in California more humanized, and acquired a certain amount of urbanity; in fact, they came from civilized countries in the rough state, and in California got licked into shape, and polished.

A View of San Francisco in 1851

I had subsequently, while residing on the Isthmus of Nicaragua, constant opportunities of witnessing the truth of this, in contrasting the outward-bound emigrants with the same class of men returning to the States after having received a California education. Every fortnight two crowds of passengers rushed across the Isthmus, one from New York, the other from San Francisco. The great majority in both cases were men of the lower ranks of life, and it is of course to them alone that my remarks apply. Those coming from New York—who were mostly Americans and Irish—seemed to think that each man could do just as he pleased, without regard to the comfort of his neighbors. They showed no accommodating spirit, but grumbled at everything, and were rude and surly in their manners; they were very raw and stupid, and had no genius for doing anything for themselves or each other to assist their progress, but perversely delighted in acting in opposition to the regulations and arrangements made for them by the Transit Company. The same men,

however, on their return from California, were perfect gentlemen in comparison. They were orderly in their behavior; though rough, they were not rude, and showed great consideration for others, submitting cheerfully to any personal inconvenience necessary for the common good, and showing by their conduct that they had acquired some notion of their duties to balance the very enlarged idea of their rights which they had formerly entertained.

The Missourians, however, although they acquired no new accomplishments on their journey to California, lost none of those which they originally possessed. They could use an ax or a rifle with any man. Two of them would chop down a few trees and build a log cabin in a day and a half, and with their long five-foot-barrel rifle, which was their constant companion, they could "draw a bead" on a deer, a squirrel, or the white of an Indian's eye, with equal coolness and certainty of killing.

Though large-framed men, they were not remarkable for physical strength, nor were they robust in constitution; in fact, they were the most sickly set of men in the mines, fever and ague and diarrhoea being their favorite complaints.

We had many pleasant neighbors, and among them were some very amusing characters. One man who went by the name of the "Philosopher," might possibly have earned a better right to the name, if he had had the resolution to abstain from whisky. He had been, I believe, a farmer in Kentucky, and was one of a class not uncommon in America, who, without much education, but with great ability and immense command of language, together with a very superficial knowledge of some science, hold forth on it most fluently, using such long words, and putting them so well together, that, were it not for the crooked ideas they enunciated, one might almost suppose they knew what they were talking about.

Phrenology was this man's hobby, and he had all the phrenological phraseology at his finger-ends. His great delight was to paw a man's head and to tell him his character. One Sunday morning he came into our cabin as he was going down to the store for provisions, and after a few minutes' conversation, of course he introduced phrenology; and as I knew I should not get rid of him till I did so, I gave him my permission to feel my head. He fingered it all over, and gave me a very elaborate synopsis of my character, explaining most minutely the consequences of the combination of the different bumps, and telling me how I would act in a variety of supposed contingencies. Having satisfied himself as to my character, he went off, and I was in hopes I was done with him, but an hour or so after dark, he came rolling into the cabin just as I was going to turn in. He was as drunk as he well could be; his nose was swelled and bloody,

his eyes were both well blackened, and altogether he was very unlike a learned professor of phrenology. He begged to be allowed to stay all night; and as he would most likely have broken his neck over the rocks if he had tried to reach his own home that night, I made him welcome, thinking that he would immediately fall asleep without troubling me further. But I was very much mistaken; he had no sooner lain down, than he began to harangue me as if I were a public meeting or a debating society, addressing me as "gentlemen," and expatiating on a variety of topics, but chiefly on phrenology, the Democratic ticket, and the great mass of the people. He had a bottle of brandy with him, which I made him finish in hopes it might have the effect of silencing him; but there was unfortunately not enough of it for that—it only made him worse; for he left the debating society and got into a barroom, where, when I went to sleep, he was playing "poker" with some imaginary individual whom he called Jim.

In the morning he made most ample apologies, and was very earnest in expressing his gratitude for my hospitality. I took the liberty of asking him what bumps he called those in the neighborhood of his eyes. "Well, sir," he said, "you ask me a plain question, I'll give you a plain answer. I got into a 'muss' down at the store last night, and was whipped; and I deserved it too." As he was penitent, I did not press him for further particulars; but I heard from another man the same day that when at the store he had taken the opportunity of an audience to lecture them on his favorite subject, and illustrated his theory by feeling several heads, and giving very full descriptions of the characters of the individuals. At last he got hold of a man who must have had something peculiar in the formation of his cranium, for he gave him a most dreadful character, calling him a liar, a cheat, and a thief, and winding up by saying that he was a man who would murder his father for five dollars.

The natural consequence was that the owner of this enviable character jumped up and pitched into the phrenologist, giving him the whipping which he had so candidly acknowledged, and would probably have murdered him without the consideration of the five dollars, if the bystanders had not interfered.

Very near where we were at work, a party of half-a-dozen men held a claim in the bed of the creek, and had as usual dug a race through which to turn the water, and so leave exposed the part they intended to work. This they were now anxious to do, as the creek had fallen sufficiently low to admit of it; but they were opposed by a number of miners whose claims lay so near the race that they would have been swamped had the water been turned into it.

They could not come to any settlement of the question among themselves; so, as was usual in such cases, they concluded to leave it to a jury of miners; and notice was accordingly sent to all the miners within two or three miles up and down the creek, requesting them to assemble on the claim in question the next afternoon. Although a miner calculates an hour lost as so much money out of his pocket, yet all were interested in supporting the laws of the diggings; and about a hundred men presented themselves at the appointed time. The two opposing parties then having tossed up for the first pick, chose six jurymen each from the assembled crowd.

When the jury had squatted themselves all together in an exalted position on a heap of stones and dirt, one of the plaintiffs,

as spokesman for his party, made a very pithy speech, calling several witnesses to prove his statements, and citing many of the laws of the diggings in support of his claims. The defendants followed in the same manner, making the most of their case; while the general public, sitting in groups on the different heaps of stones piled up between the holes with which the ground was honeycombed, smoked their pipes and watched the proceedings.

After the plaintiff and defendant had said all they had to say about it, the jury examined the state of the ground in dispute; they then called some more witnesses to give further information, and having laid their shaggy heads together for a few minutes, they pronounced their decision; which was, that the men working on the race should be allowed six days to work out their claims before the water should be turned in upon them.

Neither party was particularly well pleased with the verdict—a pretty good sign that it was an impartial one; but they had to abide by it, for had there been any resistance on either side, the rest of the miners would have enforced the decision of this august tribunal. From it there was no appeal; a jury of miners was the highest court known, and I must say I never saw a court of justice with so little humbug about it.

The laws of the creek, as was the case in all the various diggings in the mines, were made at meetings of miners held for the purpose. They were generally very few and simple. They defined how many feet of ground one man was entitled to hold in a ravine—how much in the bank, and in the bed of the creek; how many such claims he could hold at a time; and how long he could absent himself from his claim without forfeiting it. They declared what was necessary

Returning from a Miner's Meeting

to be done in taking up and securing a claim which, for want of water, or from any other cause, could not be worked at the time; and they also provided for various contingencies incidental to the peculiar nature of the diggings.

Of course, like other laws they required constant revision and amendment, to suit the progress of the times; and a few weeks after this trial, a meeting was held one Sunday afternoon for legislative purposes. The miners met in front of the store to the number of about two hundred; a very respectable-looking old chap was called to the chair; but for want of that article of furniture he mounted an empty pork-barrel, which gave him a commanding position; another man was appointed secretary, who placed his writing materials on some empty boxes piled up alongside of the chair. The chairman then, addressing the crowd, told them the object for which the meeting had been called, and said he would be happy to hear any gentleman who had any remarks to offer; whereupon some one proposed an amendment of the law relating to a certain description of claim, arguing the point in a very neat speech. He was duly seconded, and there was some slight opposition and discussion; but when the chairman declared it carried by the ayes, no one called for a division, so the secretary wrote it all down, and it became law.

Two or three other acts were passed, and when the business was concluded, a vote of thanks to the chairman was passed for his able conduct on the top of the pork-barrel. The meeting was then declared to be dissolved, and accordingly dribbled into the store, where the legislators, in small detachments, pledged each other in cocktails as fast as the storekeeper could mix them. While the legislature was in session, however, everything was conducted with the utmost formality, for Americans of all classes are particularly *au fait* at the ordinary routine of public meetings.

After working our claim for a few weeks, my partner left me to go to another part of the mines, and I joined two Americans in buying a claim five or six miles up the creek. It was supposed to be very rich, and we had to pay a long price for it accordingly, although the men who had taken it up, and from whom we bought it, had not yet even prospected the ground. But the adjoining claims were being worked, and yielding largely, and from the position of ours, it was looked on as an equally good one.

There was a great deal to be done, before it could be worked, in the way of removing rocks and turning the water; and as three of us were not sufficient to work the place properly, we hired four men to assist us, at the usual wages of five dollars a-day. It took about a fortnight to get the claim into order before we could begin washing, but we then found that our labor had not been expended in vain, for it paid uncommonly well.

When I bought this claim, I had to give up my cabin, as the distance was so great, and I now camped with my partners close to our claim, where we had erected a brush house. This is a very comfortable kind of abode in summer, and does not cost an hour's labor to erect. Four uprights are stuck in the ground, and connected with cross pieces, on which are laid heaps of leafy brushwood, making a roof completely impervious to the rays of the sun. Sometimes three sides are filled in with a basketwork of brush, which gives the edifice a more compact and comfortable appearance. Very frequently a brush shed of this sort was erected over a tent, for the thin material of which tents were usually made offered but poor shelter from the burning sun.

When I left my cabin, I handed it over to a young man who had arrived very lately in the country, and had just come up to the mines. On meeting him a few days afterwards, and asking him how he liked his new abode, he told me that the first night of his occupation he had not slept a wink, and had kept candles burning till daylight, being afraid to go to sleep on account of the rats.

Rats, indeed! poor fellow! I should think there were a few rats, but the cabin was not worse in that respect than any other in the mines. The rats were most active colonizers. Hardly was a cabin built in the most out-of-the-way part of the mountains, before a large family of rats made themselves at home in it, imparting a humanized and inhabited air to the place. They are not supposed to be indigenous to the country. They are a large black species, which I believe those who are learned in rats call the Hamburg breed. Occasionally a pure white one

is seen, but more frequently in the cities than in the mines; they are probably the hoary old patriarchs, and not a distinct species.

They are very destructive, and are such notorious thieves, carrying off letters, newspapers, handkerchiefs, and things of that sort, with which to make their nests, that I soon acquired a habit, which is common enough in the mines, of always ramming my stockings tightly into the toes of my boots, putting my neckerchief into my pocket, and otherwise securing all such matters before turning in at night. One took these precautions just as naturally, and as much as a matter of course, as when at sea one fixes things in such manner that they shall not fetch way with the motion of the ship. As in civilized life a man winds up his watch and puts it under his pillow before going to bed; so in the mines, when turning in, one just as instinctively sets to work to circumvent the rats in the manner described, and, taking off his revolver, lays it under his pillow, or at least under the coat or boots, or whatever he rests his head on.

I believe there are individuals who faint or go into hysterics if a cat happens to be in the same room with them. Any one having a like antipathy to rats had better keep as far away from California as possible, especially from the mines. The inhabitants generally, however, have no such prejudices; it is a free country—as free to rats as to Chinamen; they increase and multiply and settle on the land very much as they please, eating up your flour, and running over you when you are asleep, without ceremony.

No one thinks it worth while to kill individual rats—the abstract fact of their existence remains the same; you might as well wage war upon mosquitoes. I often shot rats, but it was for the sport, not for the mere object of killing them. Rat-shooting is capital sport, and is carried on in this wise: The most favorable place for it is a log cabin in which the chinks have not been filled up, so that there is a space of two or three inches between the logs; and the season is a moonlight night. Then when you lie down for the night (it would be absurd to call it "going to bed" in the mines), you have your revolver charged, and plenty of ammunition at hand. The lights are of course put out, and the cabin is in darkness; but the rats have a fashion of running along the tops of the logs, and occasionally standing still, showing clearly against the moonlight outside; then is your time to draw a bead upon them and knock them over—if you can. But it takes a good shot to do much at this sort of work, and a man who kills two or three brace before going to sleep has had a very splendid night's shooting.

51. Gold is Where You Find It

BY J. D. BORTHWICK

WE worked our claim very successfully for about six weeks, when the creek at last became so dry that we had not water enough to run our long tom, and the claim was rendered for the present unavailable. It, of course, remained good to us for next season; but as I had no idea of being there to work it, I sold out my interest to my partners, and, throwing mining to the dogs, I broke out in a fresh place altogether.

I had always been in the habit of amusing myself by sketching in my leisure moments, especially in the middle of the day, for an hour or so after dinner, when all hands were taking a rest—"nooning" as the miners call it—lying in the shade, in the full enjoyment of their pipes, or taking a nap. My sketches were much sought after, and on Sundays I was beset by men begging me to do something for them. Every man wanted a sketch of his claim, or his cabin, or some spot with which he identified himself; and as they offered to pay very handsomely, I was satisfied that I could make paper and pencil much more profitable tools to work with than pick and shovel.

My new pursuit had the additional attraction of affording me an opportunity of gratifying the desire which I had long felt of wandering over the mines, and seeing

Gold Hunter's Camp

all the various kinds of diggings, and the strange specimens of human nature to be found in them.

I sent to Sacramento for a fresh supply of drawing paper, for which I had only to pay the moderate sum of two dollars and a half (ten shillings sterling) a sheet; and finding my old brother-miners very liberal patrons of the fine arts, I remained some time in the neighborhood actively engaged with my pencil.

I then had occasion to return to Hang-town. On my arrival there, I went as usual to the cabin of my friend the doctor, which I found in a pretty mess. The ground on which some of the houses were built had turned out exceedingly rich; and thinking that he might be as lucky as his neighbors, the doctor had got a party of six miners to work the inside of his cabin on half shares. He was to have half the gold taken out, as the rights of property in any sort of house or habitation in the mines extend to the mineral wealth below it. In his cabin were two large holes, six feet square and about seven deep; in each of these were three miners, picking and shoveling, or washing the dirt in rockers with the water pumped out of the holes. When one place had been worked out, the dirt was all shoveled back into the hole, and another one commenced alongside of it. They took about a fort-night in this way to work all the floor of the cabin, and found it very rich.

There was a young Southerner in Hang-town at this time, who had brought one of his slaves with him to California. They worked and lived together, master and man sharing equally the labors and hardships of the mines.

One night the slave dreamed that they had been working the inside of a certain cabin in the street, and had taken out a great pile of gold. He told his master in the morning, but neither of them thought much of it, as such golden dreams are by no means uncommon among the miners. A few nights afterwards, however, he had precisely the same dream, and was so convinced that their fortune lay waiting for them under this particular cabin, that he succeeded at last in persuading his master to believe it also. The master said nothing to any one about the dream, but made some pretext for wishing to become the owner of the cabin, and finally succeeded in buying it. He and his slave immediately moved in, and set to work digging up the earthen floor, and the dream proved to be so far true that before they had worked all the ground they had taken out twenty thousand dollars.

There were many slaves in various parts of the mines working with their masters, and I knew frequent instances of their receiving their freedom. Some slaves I have also seen left in the mines by their masters, working faithfully to make money enough wherewith to buy themselves. Of course, as California is a free State, a slave, when once taken there by his master, became free by law; but no man would bring a slave to the country unless one on whose fidelity he could depend.

Niggers, in some parts of the mines, were pretty numerous, though by no means form-ing so large a proportion of the population as in the Atlantic States. As miners they were proverbially lucky, but they were also inveterate gamblers, and did not long re-main burdened with their unwonted riches.

In the mines the Americans seemed to exhibit more tolerance of negro blood than is usual in the States—not that negroes were allowed to sit at table with white men, or considered to be at all on an equality, but, owing partly to the exigencies of the unsettled state of society, and partly, no doubt, to the important fact that a nigger's dollars were as good as any others, the Americans overcame their prejudices so far that negroes were permitted to lose their money in the gambling rooms; and in the less frequented drinking-shops they might be seen receiving drink at the hands of white barkeepers. In a town or camp of any size there was always a "nigger boarding-house," kept, of course, by a darky, for the special accommodation of colored people; but in places where there was no such institution, or at wayside houses, when a negro wanted accommodation, he waited till the company had finished their meal and left the table before he ventured to sit down. I have often, on such occasions, seen the white waiter, or the landlord, when he filled that office himself, serving a nigger with what he wanted without apparently doing any violence to his feelings.

A very striking proof was seen, in this matter of waiting, of the revolution which California life caused in the feelings and occupations of the inhabitants. The Americans have an intense feeling of repugnance to any kind of menial service, and consider waiting at table as quite degrading to a free and enlightened citizen. In the United States there is hardly such a thing to be found as a native-born American waiting at table. Such service is always performed by negroes, Irishmen, or Germans; but in California, in the mines at least, it was very different. The almighty dollar exerted a still more powerful influence than in the old States, for it overcame all pre-existing false notions of dignity. The principle was universally admitted, and acted on, that no honest occupation was derogatory, and no questions of dignity interfered to prevent a man from employing himself in any way by which it suited his conveni-

San Francisco Street Scene

ence to make his money. It was nothing uncommon to see men of refinement and education keeping restaurants or roadside houses, and waiting on any ragamuffin who chose to patronize them, with as much *empressement* as an English waiter who expects his customary coppers. But as no one considered himself demeaned by his occupation, neither was there any assumption of a superiority which was not allowed to exist; and whatever were their relative positions, men treated each other with an equal amount of deference.

After being detained a few days in Hangtown waiting for letters from San Francisco, I set out for Nevada City, about seventy miles north, intending from there to travel up the Yuba River, and see what was to be seen in that part of the mines.

My way lay through Middletown, the scene of my former mining exploits, and from that through a small village, called Cold Springs, to Caloma, the place where gold was first discovered. It lies at the base of high mountains, on the south fork of the American River. There were a few very neat well-painted houses in the village; but as the diggings in the neighborhood were not particularly good, there was little life or animation about the place; in fact, it was the dullest mining town in the whole country.

The first discovery of gold was accidentally made at this spot by some workmen in the employment of Colonel Sutter, while digging a race to convey water to a saw-mill. Colonel Sutter, a Swiss by birth, had, some years before, penetrated to California, and there established himself. The fort which he built for protection against the Indians, and in which he resided, is situated a few miles from where Sacramento City now stands.

I dined at Caloma, and proceeded on my way, having a stiff hill to climb to gain the high land lying between me and the middle fork of the American River. Crossing the rivers is the most laborious part of California traveling; they flow so far below the average level of the country, which, though exceedingly rough and hilly, is comparatively easy to travel; but on coming to the brink of this high land, and looking down upon the river thousands of feet below one, the summit of the opposite side appears almost nearer than the river itself, and one longs for the loan of a pair of wings for a few moments to save the toil of descending so far, and having again to climb an equal height to gain such an apparently short distance.

Some miles from Caloma is a very pretty place called Greenwood Valley—a long, narrow, winding valley, with innumerable ravines running into it from the low hills on each side. For several miles I traveled down this valley: the bed of the creek which flowed through it, and all the ravines, had been dug up, and numbers of cabins stood on the hillsides; but at this season the creek was completely dry, and consequently no mining operations could be carried on. The cabins were all tenantless, and the place looked more desolate than if its solitude had never been disturbed by man.

At the lower end of Greenwood Valley was a small village of the same name, consisting of half-a-dozen cabins, two or three stores, and a hotel. While stopping here for the night, I enjoyed a great treat in the perusal of a number of late newspapers—among others the *Illustrated News*, containing accounts of the Great Exhibition. In the mines one was apt to get sadly behind in modern history. The express men in the towns made a business of selling editions of the leading papers of the United States, containing the news of the fortnight, and expressly got up for circulation in California. Of these the most popular with northern men was the *New York Herald,* and with the southerners the *New Orleans Delta.* The *Illustrated News* was also a great favorite, being usually sold at a dollar, while other papers only fetched half that price. But unless one happened to be in some town or village when the mail from the States arrived, there was little chance of ever seeing a paper, as they were all bought up immediately.

I struck the middle fork of the American River at a place called Spanish Bar. The scenery was very grand. Looking down on the river from the summit of the range, it seemed a mere thread winding along the deep chasm formed by the mountains, which were so steep that the pine trees clinging to their sides looked as though they would slip down into the river. The face of the mountain by which I descended was covered with a perfect trellis-work of zigzag trails, so that I could work my way down by long or short tacks as I felt inclined. On the mountain on the opposite side I could see the faint line of the trail which I had to follow; it did not look by any means inviting; and I was thankful that, for the present at any rate, I was going downhill. Walking down a long hill, however, so steep that one dare not run, though not quite such hard work at the time as climbing up, is equally fatiguing in its results, as it shakes one's knees all to pieces.

I reached the river at last, and crossing over in a canoe, landed on the "Bar."

What they call a Bar in California is the flat which is usually found on the convex side of a bend in a river. Such places have nearly always proved very rich, that being the side on which any deposit carried down by the river will naturally lodge, while the opposite bank is generally steep and precipitous, and contains little or no gold. Indeed, there are not many exceptions to the rule that, in a spot where one bank of a river affords good diggings, the other side is not worth working.

The largest camps or villages on the rivers are on the bars, and take their name from them.

The nomenclature of the mines is not very choice or elegant. The rivers all retain the names given to them by the Spaniards, but every little creek, flat, and ravine, besides of course the towns and villages which have been called into existence, have received their names at the hands of the first one or two miners who have happened to strike the diggings. The individual pioneer has seldom shown much invention or originality in his choice of a name; in most cases he has either immortalized his own by tacking "ville" or "town" to the end of it, or has more modestly chosen the name of some place in his native State; but a vast number of places have been absurdly named from some trifling incident connected with their first settlement; such as Shirt Tail Cañon, Whisky Gulch, Port Wine Diggins, Humbug Flat, Murderer's Bar, Flapjack Cañon, Yankee Jim's, Jackass Gulch, and hundreds of others with equally ridiculous names.

Spanish Bar was about half a mile in length, and three or four hundred yards wide. The whole place was honeycombed with the holes in which the miners were at work; all the trees had been cut down, and there was nothing but the red shirts of the miners to relieve the dazzling whiteness of the heaps of stones and gravel which reflected the fierce rays of the sun and made the extreme heat doubly severe.

At the foot of the mountain, as if they had been pushed back as far as possible off the diggings, stood a row of booths and tents, most of them of a very ragged and worn-out appearance. I made for the one which looked most imposing—a canvas edifice, which, from the huge sign all along the front, assumed to be the "United States" Hotel. It was not far from twelve o'clock, the universal dinner-hour in the mines; so I lighted my pipe, and lay down in the shade to compose myself for the great event.

The American system of using hotels as regular boarding-houses prevails also in California. The hotels in the mines are really boarding-houses, for it is on the number of their boarders they depend. The transient custom of travelers is merely incidental. The average rate of board per week at these institutions was twelve or fifteen dollars, and the charge for a single meal was a dollar, or a dollar and a half.

The "United States" seemed to have a pretty good run of business. As the hour of noon (feeding time) approached, the miners began to congregate in the bar-room; many of them took advantage of the few minutes before dinner to play cards, while the rest looked on, or took gin cocktails to whet their appetites. At last there could not have been less than sixty or seventy miners assembled in the bar-room, which was a small canvas enclosure about twenty feet square. On one side was a rough wooden door communicating with the *salle à manger;* to get as near to this as possible was the great object, and there was a press against it like that at the pit door of a theatre on a benefit night.

As twelve o'clock struck the door was drawn aside, displaying the banqueting hall, an apartment somewhat larger than the bar-room, and containing two long tables well supplied with fresh beef, potatoes, beans, pickles, and salt pork. As soon as the door was opened there was a shout, a rush, a scramble, and a loud clatter of knives and forks, and in the course of a very few minutes fifty or sixty men had finished their dinner. Of course many more rushed into the dining-room than could find seats, and the disappointed ones came out again looking rather foolish, but they "guessed there would be plenty to eat at the second table."

Having had some experience of such places, I had intended being one of the second detachment myself, and so I guessed likewise that there would be plenty to eat at the second table, and "cal'lated" also that I would have more time to eat it in than at the first.

San Francisco Saloon

We were not kept long waiting. In an incredibly short space of time the company began to return to the bar-room, some still masticating a mouthful of food, others picking their teeth with their fingers, or with sharp-pointed bowie-knives, and the rest, with a most provokingly complacent expression about their eyes, making horrible motions with their jaws, as if they were wiping out their mouths with their tongues, determined to enjoy the last lingering after-taste of the good things they had been eating—rather a disgusting process to a spectator at any time, but particularly aggravating to hungry men waiting for their dinner.

When they had all left the dining-room, the door was again closed while the table was being relaid. In the meantime there had been constant fresh arrivals, and there were now almost as many waiting for the second table as there had been for the first. A crowd very quickly began to collect round the door and I saw that to dine at number two, as I had intended, I must enter into the spirit of the thing; so I elbowed my way into the crowd, and secured a pretty good position behind a tall Kentuckian, who I knew would clear the way before me. Very soon the door was opened, when in we rushed pell-mell. I labored under the disadvantage of not knowing the diggings; being a stranger, I did not know the lay of the tables, or whereabouts the joints were placed; but immediately on entering I caught sight of a good-looking roast of beef at the far end of one of the tables, at which I made a desperate charge. I was not so green as to lose time in trying to get my legs over the bench and sit down, and in so doing perhaps be crowded out altogether; but I seized a knife and fork, with which

I took firm hold of my prize, and occupying as much space as possible with my elbows, I gradually insinuated myself into my seat. Without letting go the beef, I then took a look around, and had the gratification of seeing about a dozen men leaving the room, with a most ludicrous expression of disappointment and hope long deferred. I have no doubt that when they got into the bar-room they guessed there would be lots to eat at the table number three; I hope there was. I know there was plenty at number two; but it was a "grab game"—every man for himself. If I had depended on the waiter getting me a slice of roast beef, I should have had the hungry number threes down upon me before I had commenced my dinner.

Good-humor, however, was the order of the day; conversation, of course, was out of the question; but if you asked a man to pass you a dish, he did do so with pleasure, devoting one hand to your service, while with his knife or fork, as it might be, in the other, he continued to convey the contents of his plate to their ultimate destination. I must say that a knife was a favorite weapon with my *convives,* and in wielding it they displayed considerable dexterity, using it to feed themselves with such things as most people would eat with a spoon, if eating for a wager, or with a fork if only eating for ordinary purposes.

After dinner a smart-looking young gentleman opened a monte bank in the bar-room, laying out five or six hundred dollars on the table as his bank. For half an hour or so he did a good business, when the miners began to drop off to resume their work.

52. Western Characters

BY HORACE GREELEY

EDITOR'S NOTE: Horace Greeley (1811-1872) was born in Amherst, New Hampshire. He came to New York City in 1831, and in 1841 he founded the New York *Tribune* which was influential in shaping political opinion in the Northern and Western areas of the United States, and served as a vehicle for Greeley's social and economic views. Greeley was the originator of the phrase, "Go West, young man". As one of the founders of the Republican party, Greeley supported Lincoln's nomination in 1860. During the war he aligned himself with the radical anti-slavery faction, but after the war he favored a liberal policy towards the South. In 1872, as the Liberal-Republican Candidate for the Presidency, he was defeated by Grant. The following selection is taken from *Overland Journey to San Francisco* in which Greeley tells of his trip to the West in 1859.

Horace Greeley

Denver, June 21, 1859

I KNOW it is not quite correct to speak of this region as "Western," seeing that it is in fact the center of North America and very close to its backbone. Still, as the terms "Eastern" and "Western" are conventional and relative—Castine being "Western" to a Bluenose and Carson Valley, "Eastern" to a Californian—I take the responsibility of grouping certain characters I have noted on the plains and in or about the mountains as "Western," begging that most respectable region which lies east of the buffalo-range —also that portion which lies west of the Colorado—to excuse the liberty.

The first circumstance that strikes a stranger traversing this wild country is the vagrant instincts and habits of the great majority of its denizens—perhaps I should say, of the American people generally, as exhibited here. Among any ten whom you successively meet, there will be natives of New England, New York, Pennsylvania, Virginia or Georgia, Ohio or Indiana, Kentucky or Missouri, France, Germany, and perhaps Ireland. But, worse than this; you cannot enter a circle of a dozen persons of whom at least three will not have spent some years in California, two or three have made claims and built cabins in Kansas or Nebraska, and at least one spent a year or so in Texas. Boston, New York, Philadel-

379

phia, New Orleans, St. Louis, Cincinnati, have all contributed their quota toward peopling the new gold region. The next man you meet driving an ox-team, and white as a miller with dust, is probably an ex-banker or doctor, a broken merchant or manufacturer from the old states, who has scraped together candle-ends charitably or contemptuously allowed him by his creditors on settlement, and risked them on a last desperate cast of the dice by coming hither. Ex-editors, ex-printers, ex-clerks, ex-steamboat men, are here in abundance—all on the keen hunt of the gold which only a few will secure. One of the stations at which we slept on our way up—a rough tent with a cheering hope (since blasted) of a log house in the near future—was kept by an ex-lawyer of Cincinnati and his wife, an ex-actress from our New York Bowery—she being cook. Omnibus-drivers from Broadway repeatedly handled the ribbons; ex-border ruffians from civilized Kansas—some of them of unblessed memory—were encountered on our way, at intervals none too long. All these, blended with veteran Mountain men, Indians of all grades from the tamest to the wildest, half-breeds, French trappers and *voyageurs* (who have generally two or three Indian wives apiece) and an occasional negro, compose a medley such as hardly another region can parallel. Honolulu, or some other port of the South Sea Islands, could probably match it most nearly.

The old mountaineers form a caste by themselves, and they prize the distinction. Some of them are Frenchmen, or Franco-Americans, who have been trapping or trading in and around these mountains for a quarter of a century, have wives and children here, and here expect to live and die. Some of these have accumulated property and cash to the value of two hundred thousand dollars, which amount will not easily be reduced, as they are frugal in everything (liquor sometimes excepted), spend but a pittance on the clothing of their families, trust little, keep small stocks of goods, and sell at large profits. Others came years ago from the states, some of them on account each of a "difficulty" wherein they severally killed or savagely maimed their respective antagonists under circumstances on which the law refuses to look leniently; whence their pilgrimage to and prolonged sojourn here, despite enticing placards offering five hundred dollars or perhaps one thousand dollars for their safe return to the places that knew them once, but shall know them no more. This class is not numerous, but is more influential than it should be in giving tone to the society of which its members form a part. Prone to deep drinking, soured in temper, always armed, bristling at a word, ready with the rifle, revolver or bowie-knife, they give law and set fashions which, in a country where the regular administration of justice is yet a matter of prophecy, it seems difficult to overrule or disregard. I apprehend that there have been, during my two weeks sojourn, more brawls, more fights, more pistol-shots with criminal intent in this log city of one hundred and fifty dwellings, not three-fourths completed nor two-thirds inhabited, nor one-third fit to be, than in any community of no greater numbers on earth. This will be changed in time—I trust within a year, for the empty houses are steadily finding tenants from the two streams of emigration rolling in daily up the Platte on the one hand, down Cherry Creek on the other, including some scores of women and children, who generally stop here, as all of them should; for life in the mountains is yet horribly rough. Public religious worship, a regular mail and other civilizing influences, are being established; there is a gleam of hope that the Arapahoes—who have made the last two or three nights indescribably hideous by their infernal war-whoops, songs and dances—will at last clear out on the foray against the Utes they have so long threatened, diminishing largely the aggregate of drunkenness and riot, and justifying expectations of comparative peace. So let me close up my jottings from this point—which circumstances beyond my control have rendered so voluminous—with a rough ambrotype of

LIFE IN DENVER.

The rival cities of Denver and Auraria front on each other from either bank of Cherry Creek, just before it is lost in the South Platte. The Platte has its sources in and around the South Park of the Rocky Mountains, a hundred miles south-west of this point; but Cherry Creek is headed off from them by that river, and, winding its northward course of forty or fifty miles over the plains, with its sources barely touching the Mountains, is a capricious stream, running quite smartly when we came here, but whose broad and thirsty sands have since drank it all up at this point, leaving the log foot-bridges which connect the two large cities as useless as an ice-house in November. The Platte, aided by the melting of the snows on the higher mountains, runs nearly full-banked, though the constant succession of hot suns and dry winds begins to tell upon it; while Clear Creek (properly Vasquer's Fork), which issues directly from the Mountains just above its crossing on the way to the Gregory diggings, is nearly at its highest, and will so remain till the inner mountains are mainly denuded of their snowy mantles. But, within a few days, a foot-bridge has been completed over the Platte, virtually abolishing the ferry and saving considerable time and money to gold-seekers and travelers; while another over Clear Creek precludes not only delay but danger—several wagons having been wrecked and two or three men all but drowned in attempts to ford its rapid, rocky current. Thus the ways of the adventurous grow daily smoother; and they who visit this region ten years hence, will regard as idle tales the stories of privation, impediment, and "hair-breadth 'scapes" which are told, or might be, by the gold-seekers of 1859.

Of these rival cities, Auraria is by far the more venerable—some of its structures being, I think, fully a year old, if not more. Denver, on the other hand, can boast of no antiquity beyond September or October last. In the architecture of the two cities there is, notwithstanding, a striking similarity—cotton-wood logs, cut from the adjacent bottom of the Platte, roughly hewed on the upper and under sides, and chinked with billets of split cotton-wood on the inner, and with mud on the outer side, forming the walls of nearly or quite every edifice which adorns either city. Across the center of the interior, from shorter wall to wall, stretches a sturdy ridge-pole, usually in a state of nature, from which "shooks," or split saplings of cotton-wood, their split sides down, incline gently to the transverse or longer sides; on these (in the more finished structures) a coating of earth is laid; and, with a chimney of mud-daubed sticks in one corner, a door nearly opposite, and a hole beside it representing or prefiguring a window, the edifice is complete. Of course, many have no earth on their covering of shooks, and so are liable to gentle inundation in the rainy season; but, though we have had thunder and lightning almost daily, with a brisk gale in most instances, there has been no rain worth naming such here for weeks, and the unchinked, barely shook-covered houses, through whose sides and roofs you may see the stars as you lie awake nights, are decidedly the cooler and airier. There is a new hotel nearly finished in Auraria, which has a second story (but no first story) floor; beside this, mine eyes have never yet been blessed with the sight of any floor whatever in either Denver or Auraria. The last time I slept or ate with a floor under me (our wagon-box and mother earth excepted) was at Junction-City, nearly four weeks ago. The "Denver House," which is the Astor House of the gold region, has walls of logs, a floor of earth, with windows and roof of rather flimsy cotton-sheeting; while every guest is allowed as good a bed as his blankets will make. The charges are no higher than at the Astor and other first-class hotels, except for liquor—twenty-five cents a drink for dubious whisky, colored and nicknamed to suit the taste of customers—being the regular rate throughout this region. I had the honor to be shaved there by a nephew (so he assured me) of Murat, Bonaparte's king of Naples —the honor and the shave together costing but a paltry dollar. Still, a few days of such luxury surfeited me, mainly because the main or drinking-room was also occupied

Denver City

by several blacklegs as a gambling-hall, and their incessant clamor of "Who'll go me twenty? The ace of hearts is the winning card. Whoever turns the ace of hearts wins the twenty dollars," etc. etc., persisted in at all hours up to midnight, became at length a nuisance, from which I craved deliverance at any price. Then the visitors of that drinking and gambling-room had a careless way, when drunk, of firing revolvers, sometimes at each other, at other times quite miscellaneously, which struck me as inconvenient for a quiet guest with only a leg and a half, hence in poor condition for dodging bullets. So I left.

"How do you live in Denver?" I inquired of a New York friend some weeks domiciled here, in whose company I visited the mines. "O, I've jumped a cabin," was his cool, matter-of-course reply. As jumping a cabin was rather beyond my experience, I inquired further, and learned that, finding an uninhabited cabin that suited him, he had quietly entered and spread his blankets, eating at home or abroad as opportunity might suggest. I found, on further inquiry, that at least one-third of the habitations in Denver and Auraria were desolate when we came here (they have been gradually filling up since), some of the owners having gone into the mountains, digging or prospecting, and taken their limited supply of household goods along with them; while others, discouraged by the poor show of mining six weeks ago, when even the nearer mountains were still covered with snow and ice, rushed pell-mell down the Platte with the wild reflux of the spring emigration, abandoning all but what they could carry away. It is said that lots and cabins together sold

for twenty-five dollars—so long as there were purchasers; but these soon failing, they were left behind like campfires in the morning, and have since been at the service of all comers.

So, in company with a journalizing friend, I, too, have "jumped a cabin," and have kept to it quite closely, under a doctor's care, for the last week or ten days. It is about ten feet square, and eight feet high, rather too well chinked for summer, considering that it lacks a window, but must be a capital house for this country in winter. I board with the nearest neighbor; and it is not my landlady's fault that the edible resources of Denver are decidedly limited. But even these are improving. To the bread, bacon, and beans, which formed the staple of every meal a short time ago, there have been several recent additions; milk, which was last week twenty-five cents per quart, is now down to ten, and I hear a rumor that eggs, owing to a recent increase in the number of hens, within five hundred miles, from four or five to twelve or fifteen, are about to fall from a dollar a dozen to fifty cents a dozen. On every side, I note signs of progress—improvement—manifest destiny:—there was a man about the city yesterday with lettuce to sell—and I am credibly assured that there will be green peas next month—actually peas!—provided it should rain soakingly meantime—whereof a hazy, lowering sky would seem just now to afford some hope. (P.S. The hope has vanished.) But I—already sadly behind, and nearly able to travel again—must turn my back on this promise of luxuries, and take the road to Laramie to-day, or at furthest to-morrow.

53. Portrait of a Desperado

BY MARK TWAIN

EDITOR'S NOTE: Soon after the beginning of the Civil War Mark Twain (1835-1910) — Samuel Langhorne Clemens — set out with his brother Orion for the great West. Orion had been appointed territorial secretary of Nevada and Twain went along, the Mississippi river trade, in which he was engaged as a pilot, having come to an end due to the hostilities. In Nevada and in other parts of the West he obtained a great deal of interesting material, most of which he incorporated into an account of his travels, *Roughing It,* selections from which follow.

REALLY and truly, two thirds of the talk of drivers and conductors had been about this man Slade, ever since the day before we reached Julesburg. In order that the eastern reader may have a clear conception of what a Rocky Mountain desperado is, in his highest state of development, I will reduce all this mass of overland gossip to one straightforward narrative, and present it in the following shape:

Slade was born in Illinois, of good parentage. At about twenty-six years of age he killed a man in a quarrel and fled the country. At St. Joseph, Missouri, he joined one of the early California-bound emigrant trains, and was given the post of train-master. One day on the plains he had an angry dispute with one of his wagon-drivers, and both drew their revolvers. But the driver was the quicker artist, and had his weapon cocked first. So Slade said it was a pity to waste life on so small a matter, and proposed that the pistols be thrown on the ground and the quarrel settled by a fist-fight.

The unsuspecting driver agreed, and threw down his pistol—whereupon Slade laughed at his simplicity, and shot him dead!

He made his escape, and lived a wild life for awhile, dividing his time between fighting Indians and avoiding an Illinois sheriff, who had been sent to arrest him for his first murder. It is said that in one Indian battle he killed three savages with his own hand, and afterward cut their ears off and sent them, with his compliments, to the chief of the tribe.

Slade soon gained a name for fearless resolution, and this was sufficient merit to procure for him the important post of overland division-agent at Julesburg, in place of Mr. Jules, removed. For some time previously, the company's horses had been frequently stolen, and the coaches delayed, by gangs of outlaws, who were wont to laugh at the idea of any man's having the temerity to resent such outrages. Slade resented them promptly. The outlaws soon found that the new agent was a man who did not fear anything that breathed the breath of life. He made short work of all offenders. The result was that delays ceased, the company's property was let alone, and no matter what happened or who suffered, Slade's coaches went through, every time! True, in order to bring about this wholesome change, Slade had to kill several men—some say three, others say four, and others six—but the world was the richer for their loss. The first prominent difficulty he had was with the ex-agent Jules, who bore the reputation of being a reckless and desperate man himself. Jules hated Slade for supplanting him, and a good fair occasion for a fight was all he was waiting for. By and by Slade dared to employ a man whom Jules had once discharged. Next, Slade seized a team of stage-horses which he accused Jules of having driven off and hidden somewhere for his own use. War was declared, and for a day or two the two men walked warily about the streets, seeking each other, Jules armed with a double-barreled shot gun, and Slade with his history-creating revolver. Finally, as Slade stepped into a store, Jules poured the contents of his gun into him from behind the door. Slade was pluck, and Jules got several bad pistol wounds in return. Then both men fell, and were carried to their respective lodgings, both swearing that better aim should do deadlier work next time. Both were bedridden a long time, but Jules got on his feet first, and gathering his possess-

The Magic of the "Drop."
Frederick Remington

ions together, packed them on a couple of mules, and fled to the Rocky Mountains to gather strength in safety against the day of reckoning. For many months he was not seen or heard of, and was gradually dropped out of the remembrance of all save Slade himself. But Slade was not the man to forget him. On the contrary, common report said that Slade kept a reward standing for his capture, dead or alive!

After awhile, seeing that Slade's energetic administration had restored peace and order to one of the worst divisions of the road, the overland stage company transferred him to the Rocky Ridge division in the Rocky Mountains, to see if he could perform a like miracle there. It was the very paradise of outlaws and desperadoes. There was absolutely no semblance of law there. Violence was the rule. Force was the only recognized authority. The commonest misunderstandings were settled on the spot with the revolver or the knife. Murders were done in open day, and with sparkling frequency, and nobody thought of inquiring into them. It was considered that the parties who did the killing had their private reasons for it; for other people to meddle would have been looked upon as indelicate. After a murder, all that Rocky Mountain etiquette required of a spectator was, that he should help the gentleman bury his game—otherwise his churlishness would surely be remembered against him the first time he killed a man himself and needed a neighborly turn in interring him.

Slade took up his residence sweetly and peacefully in the midst of this hive of horse-thieves and assassins, and the very first time one of them aired his insolent swaggerings in his presence he shot him dead! He began a raid on the outlaws, and in a singularly short space of time he had completely stopped their depredations on the stage stock, recovered a large number of stolen horses, killed several of the worst desperadoes of the district, and gained such a dread ascendancy over the rest that they respected him, admired him, feared him, obeyed him! He wrought the same marvelous change in the ways of the community that had marked his administration at Overland City. He captured two men who had stolen overland stock, and with his own hands he hanged them. He was supreme judge in his district, and he was jury and executioner likewise —and not only in the case of offences against his employers, but against passing emigrants as well. On one occassion some emigrants had their stock lost or stolen, and told Slade, who chanced to visit their camp. With a single companion he rode to a ranch, the owners of which he suspected, and opening the door, commenced firing, killing three, and wounding the fourth.

From a bloodthirstily interesting little Montana book* I take this paragraph:

While on the road, Slade held absolute sway. He would ride down to a station, get into a quarrel, turn the house out of windows, and maltreat the occupants most cruelly. The unfortunates had no means of redress, and were compelled to recuperate as best they could. On one of these occasions, it is said he killed the father of the fine little half-breed boy Jemmy, whom he adopted, and who lived with his widow after his execution. Stories of Slade's hanging men, and of innumerable assaults, shootings, stabbings and beatings, in which he was a principal actor, form part of the legends of the stage line. As for minor quarrels and shootings, it is absolutely certain that a minute history of Slade's life would be one long record of such practices.

Slade was a matchless marksman with a navy revolver. The legends say that one morning at Rocky Ridge, when he was feel-

ing comfortable, he saw a man approaching who had offended him some days before— observe the fine memory he had for matters like that—and, "Gentlemen," said Slade, drawing, "it is a good twenty-yard shot—I'll clip the third button on his coat!" Which he did. The bystanders all admired it. And they all attended the funeral, too.

On one occasion a man who kept a little whisky-shelf at the station did something which angered Slade—and went and made his will. A day or two afterward Slade came in and called for some brandy. The man reached under the counter (ostensibly to get a bottle—possibly to get something else), but Slade smiled upon him that peculiarly bland and satisfied smile of his which the neighbors had long ago learned to recognize as a death-warrant in disguise, and told him to "none of that!—pass out the high-priced article." So the poor bar-keeper had to turn his back and get the high-priced brandy from the shelf; and when he faced around again he was looking into the muzzle of Slade's pistol. "And the next instant," added my informant, impressively, "he was one of the deadest men that ever lived."

The stage-drivers and conductors told us that sometimes Slade would leave a hated enemy wholly unmolested, unnoticed and unmentioned, for weeks together—had done it once or twice at any rate. And some said they believed he did it in order to lull the victims into unwatchfulness, so that he could get the advantage of them, and others said they believed he saved up an enemy that way, just as a schoolboy saves up a cake, and made the pleasure go as far as it would by gloating over the anticipation. One of these cases was that of a Frenchman who had offended Slade. To the surprise of every-

*"The Vigilantes of Montana," by Prof. Thos. J. Dimsdale.

body Slade did not kill him on the spot, but let him alone for a considerable time. Finally, however, he went to the Frenchman's house very late one night, knocked, and when his enemy opened the door, shot him dead—pushed the corpse inside the door with his foot, set the house on fire and burned up the dead man, his widow and three children! I heard this story from several different people, and they evidently believed what they were saying. It may be true, and it may not. "Give a dog a bad name," etc.

Slade was captured, once, by a party of men who intended to lynch him. They disarmed him, and shut him up in a strong log-house, and placed a guard over him. He prevailed on his captors to send for his wife, so that he might have a last interview with her. She was a brave, loving, spirited woman. She jumped on a horse and rode for life and death. When she arrived they let her in without searching her, and before the door could be closed she whipped out a couple of revolvers, and she and her lord marched forth defying the party. And then, under a brisk fire, they mounted double and galloped away unharmed!

In the fulness of time Slade's myrmidons captured his ancient enemy Jules, whom they found in a well-chosen hiding-place in the remote fastnesses of the mountains, gaining a precarious livelihood with his rifle. They brought him to Rocky Ridge, bound hand and foot, and deposited him in the middle of the cattle-yard with his back against a post. It is said that the pleasure that lit Slade's face when he heard of it was something fearful to contemplate. He examined his enemy to see that he was securely tied, and then went to bed, content to wait till morning before enjoying the luxury of killing him. Jules spent the night in the cattle-yard, and it is a region where warm nights are never known. In the morning Slade practised on him with his revolver, nipping the flesh here and there, and occasionally clipping off a finger, while Jules begged him to kill him outright and put him out of his misery. Finally Slade reloaded, and walking up close to his victim, made some characteristic remarks and then dispatched him. The body lay there half a day, nobody venturing to touch it without orders, and then Slade detailed a party and assisted at the burial himself. But he first cut off the dead man's ears and put them in his vest pocket, where he carried them for some time with great satisfaction. That is the story as I have frequently heard it told and seen it in print in California newspapers. It is doubtless correct in all essential particulars.

In due time we rattled up to a stage-station, and sat down to breakfast with a half-savage, half-civilized company of armed and bearded mountaineers, ranchmen and station employees. The most gentlemanly-appearing, quiet and affable officer we had yet found along the road in the Overland Company's service was the person who sat at the head of the table, at my elbow. Never youth stared and shivered as I did when I heard them call him SLADE!

Here was romance, and I sitting face to face with it!—looking upon it—touching it—hobnobbing with it, as it were! Here, right by my side, was the actual ogre who, in fights and brawls and various ways, *had taken the lives of twenty-six human beings,* or all men lied about him! I suppose I was the proudest stripling that ever traveled to see strange lands and wonderful people.

He was so friendly and so gentle-spoken that I warmed to him in spite of his awful history. It was hardly possible to realize that this pleasant person was the pitiless scourge of the outlaws, the raw-head-and-bloody-bones the nursing mothers of the mountains terrified their children with. And to this day I can remember nothing remarkable about Slade except that his face was rather broad across the cheek bones, and that the cheek bones were low and the lips peculiarly thin and straight. But that was enough to leave something of an effect upon me, for since then I seldom see a face possessing those characteristics without fancying that the owner of it is a dangerous man.

The coffee ran out. At least it was reduced to one tincupful, and Slade was about to take it when he saw that my cup was empty. He politely offered to fill it, but although I wanted it, I politely declined. I was afraid he had not killed anybody that morning, and might be needing diversion. But still with firm politeness he insisted on filling my cup, and said I had traveled all night and better deserved it than he—and while he talked he placidly poured the fluid, to the last drop. I thanked him and drank it, but it gave me no comfort, for I could not feel sure that he would not be sorry, presently, that he had given it away, and proceed to kill me to distract his thoughts from the loss. But nothing of the kind occurred. We left him with only twenty-six dead people to account for, and I felt a tranquil satisfaction in the thought that in so judiciously taking care of No. 1 at that breakfast-table I had pleasantly escaped being No. 27. Slade came out to the coach and saw us off, first ordering certain reärrangements of the mail-bags for our comfort, and then we took leave of him, satisfied that we should hear of him again, some day, and wondering in what connection.

And sure enough, two or three years afterward, we did hear of him again. News came to the Pacific coast that the Vigilance Committee in Montana (whither Slade had removed from Rocky Ridge) had hanged him. I find an account of the affair in the thrilling little book I quoted a paragraph from in the last chapter—"The Vigilantes of Montana; being a Reliable Account of the Capture, Trial and Execution of Henry Plummer's Notorious Road Agent Band: By Prof. Thos. J. Dimsdale, Virginia City, M. T." Mr. Dimsdale's chapter is well worth reading, as a specimen of how the people of the frontier deal with criminals when the courts of law prove inefficient. Mr. Dimsdale makes two remarks about Slade, both of which are accurately descriptive, and one of which is exceedingly picturesque: "Those who saw him in his natural state only, would pronounce him to be a kind husband, a most hospitable host and a courteous gentleman; on the contrary, those who met him when maddened with liquor and surrounded by a gang of armed roughs, would pronounce him a fiend incarnate." And this: "From Fort Kearney, west, he was feared *a great deal more than the Almighty.*" For compactness, simplicity and vigor of expression, I will "back" that sentence against anything in literature. Mr. Dimsdale's narrative is as follows. In all places where italics occur, they are mine:

After the execution of the five men on the 14th of January, the Vigilantes considered that their work was nearly ended. They had freed the country of highwaymen and murderers to a great extent, and they determined that in the absence of the regular civil authority they would establish a People's Court where all offenders should be tried by judge and jury. This was the nearest approach to social order that the circumstances permitted, and, though strict legal authority was wanting, yet the people were firmly determined to maintain its efficiency, and to enforce its decrees. It may here be mentioned that the overt act which was the last round on the fatal ladder leading to the scaffold on which Slade perished, *was the tearing in pieces and stamping upon a writ of this court, followed by his arrest of the Judge, Alex. Davis, by authority of a presented Derringer, and with his own hands.*

J. A. Slade was himself, we have been informed, a Vigilante; he openly boasted of it, and said he knew all that they knew. He was never accused, or even suspected, of either murder or robbery, committed in this Territory (the latter crime was never laid to his charge, in any place); but that he had killed several men in other localities was notorious, and his bad reputation in this respect was a most powerful argument in determining his fate, when he was finally arrested for the offence above mentioned. On returning from Milk River he became more and more addicted to drinking, until at last it was a common feat for him and his friends to "take the town." He and a couple of his dependents might often be seen on one horse, galloping through the streets, shouting and yelling, firing revolvers, etc. On many occasions he would ride his horse into stores, break up bars, toss the scales out of doors and use most insulting language to parties present. Just previous to the day of his arrest, he had given a fearful beating to one of his followers; but such was his influence over them that the man wept bitterly at the gallows, and begged for his life with all his power. *It had become quite common, when Slade was on a spree, for the shop-keepers and citizens to close the stores and put out all the lights;* being fearful of some outrage at his hands. For his wanton destruction of goods and furniture, he was always ready to pay, when sober, if he had money; but there were not a few who regarded payment as small satisfaction for the outrage, and these men were his personal enemies.

From time to time Slade received warnings from men that he well knew would not deceive him, of the certain end of his conduct. There

was not a moment, for weeks previous to his arrest, in which the public did not expect to hear of some bloody outrage. The dread of his very name, and the presence of the armed band of hangers-on who followed him alone prevented a resistance which must certainly have ended in the instant murder or mutilation of the opposing party.

Slade was frequently arrested by order of the court whose organization we have described, and had treated it with respect by paying one or two fines and promising to pay the rest when he had money; but in the transaction that occurred at this crisis, he forgot even this caution, and goaded by passion and the hatred of restraint, he sprang into the embrace of death.

Slade had been drunk and "cutting up" all night. He and his companions had made the town a perfect hell. In the morning, J. M. Fox, the sheriff, met him, arrested him, took him into court and commenced reading a warrant that he had for his arrest, by way of arraignment. He became uncontrollably furious, and *seizing the writ, he tore it up, threw it on the ground and stamped upon it.* The clicking of the locks of his companions' revolvers was instantly heard, and a crisis was expected. The sheriff did not attempt his retention; but being at least as prudent as he was valiant, he succumbed, leaving Slade the *master of the situation and the conqueror and ruler of the courts, law and law-makers.* This was a declaration of war, and was so accepted. The Vigilance Committee now felt that the question of social order and the preponderance of the law-abiding citizens had then and there to be decided. They knew the character of Slade, and they were well aware that they must submit to his rule without murmur, or else that he must be dealt with in such fashion as would prevent his being able to wreak his vengeance on the committee, who could never have hoped to live in the Territory secure from outrage or death, and who could never leave it without encountering his friends, whom his victory would have emboldened and stimulated to a pitch that would have rendered them reckless of consequences. The day previous he had ridden into Dorris's store, and on being requested to leave, he drew his revolver and threatened to kill the gentleman who spoke to him. Another saloon he had led his horse into, and buying a bottle of wine, he tried to make the animal drink it. This was not considered an uncommon performance, as he had often entered saloons and commenced firing at the lamps, causing a wild stampede.

A leading member of the committee met Slade, and informed him in the quiet, earnest manner of one who feels the importance of what he is saying: "Slade, get your horse at once, and go home, or there will be ——— to pay." Slade started and took a long look, with his dark and piercing eyes, at the gentleman. "What do you mean?" said he. "You have no right to ask me what I mean," was the quiet reply, "get your horse at once, and remember what I tell you." After a short pause he promised to do so, and actually got into the saddle; but, being still intoxicated, he began calling aloud to one after another of his friends, and at last seemed to have forgotten the warning he had received and became again uproarious, shouting the name of a well-known courtezan in company with those of two men whom he considered heads of the committee, as a sort of challenge; perhaps, however, as a simple act of bravado. It seems probable that the intimation of personal danger he had received had not been forgotten entirely; though fatally for him, he took a foolish way of showing his remembrance of it. He sought out Alexander Davis, the Judge of the Court, and drawing a cocked Derringer, he presented it at his head, and told him that he should hold him as a hostage for his own safety. As the judge stood perfectly quiet, and offered no resistance to his captor, no further outrage followed on this score. Previous to this, on account of the critical state of affairs, the committee had met, and at last resolved to arrest him. His execution had not been agreed upon, and, at that time, would

have been negatived, most assuredly. A messenger rode down to Nevada to inform the leading men of what was on hand, as it was desirable to show that there was a feeling of unanimity on the subject, all along the gulch.

The miners turned out almost *en masse,* leaving their work and forming in solid column, about six hundred strong, armed to the teeth, they marched up to Virginia. The leader of the body well knew the temper of his men on the subject. He spurred on ahead of them, and hastily calling a meeting of the executive, he told them plainly that the miners meant "business," and that, if they came up, they would not stand in the street to be shot down by Slade's friends; but that they would take him and hang him. The meeting was small, as the Virginia men were loath to act at all. This momentous announcement of the feeling of the Lower Town was made to a cluster of men, who were deliberating behind a wagon, at the rear of a store on Main street.

The committee were most unwilling to proceed to extremities. All the duty they had ever performed seemed as nothing to the task before them; but they had to decide, and that quickly. It was finally agreed that if the whole body of the miners were of the opinion that he should be hanged, that the committee left it in their hands to deal with him. Off, at hot speed, rode the leader of the Nevada men to join his command.

Slade had found out what was intended, and the news sobered him instantly. He went into P.S. Pfouts' store, where Davis was, and apologized for his conduct, saying that he would take it all back.

The head of the column now wheeled into Wallace street and marched up at quick time. Halting in front of the store, the executive officer of the committee stepped forward and arrested Slade, who was at once informed of his doom, and inquiry was made as to whether he had any business to settle. Several parties spoke to him on the subject; but to all such inquiries he turned a deaf ear, being entirely absorbed in the terrifying reflections on his own awful position. He never ceased his entreaties for life, and to see his dear wife. The unfortunate lady referred to, between whom and Slade there existed a warm affection, was at this time living at their ranch on the Madison. She was possessed of considerable personal attractions; tall, well-formed, of graceful carriage, pleasing manners, and was, withal, an accomplished horsewoman.

A messenger from Slade rode at full speed to inform her of her husband's arrest. In an instant she was in the saddle, and with all the energy that love and despair could lend to an ardent temperament and a strong physique, she urged her fleet charger over the twelve miles of rough and rocky ground that intervened between her and the object of her passionate devotion.

Meanwhile a party of volunteers had made the necessary preparations for the execution, in the valley traversed by the branch. Beneath the site of Pfouts and Russell's stone building there was a corral, the gate-posts of which were strong and high. Across the top was laid a beam, to which the rope was fastened, and a dry-goods box served for the platform. To this place Slade was marched, surrounded by a guard, composing the best armed and most numerous force that has ever appeared in Montana Territory.

The doomed man had so exhausted himself by tears, prayers and lamentations, that he had scarcely strength left to stand under the fatal beam. He repeatedly exclaimed, "My God! my God! must I die? Oh, my dear wife!"

On the return of the fatigue party, they encountered some friends of Slade, staunch and reliable citizens and members of the committee, but who were personally attached to the condemned. On hearing of his sentence, one of them, a stout-hearted man, pulled out his handkerchief and walked away, weeping like a child. Slade still begged to see his wife, most piteously, and it seemed hard to deny his request; but the bloody consequences that were sure to follow the inevitable attempt at a rescue, that her

presence and entreaties would have certainly incited, forbade the granting of his request. Several gentlemen were sent for to see him, in his last moments, one of whom (Judge Davis) made a short address to the people; but in such low tones as to be inaudible, save to a few in his immediate vicinity. One of his friends, after exhausting his powers of entreaty, threw off his coat and declared that the prisoner could not be hanged until he himself was killed. A hundred guns were instantly leveled at him; whereupon he turned and fled; but, being brought back, he was compelled to resume his coat, and to give a promise of future peaceable demeanor.

Scarcely a leading man in Virginia could be found, though numbers of the citizens joined the ranks of the guard when the arrest was made. All lamented the stern necessity which dictated the execution.

Everything being ready, the command was given, "Men, do your duty," and the box being instantly slipped from beneath his feet, he died almost instantaneously.

The body was cut down and carried to the Virginia Hotel, where, in a darkened room, it was scarcely laid out, when the unfortunate and bereaved companion of the deceased arrived, at headlong speed, to find that all was over, and that she was a widow. Her grief and

"I've been looking for You."

heart-piercing cries were terrible evidences of the depth of her attachment for her lost husband, and a considerable period elapsed before she could regain the command of her excited feelings.

There is something about the desperado-nature that is wholly unaccountable—at least it looks unaccountable. It is this. The true desperado is gifted with splendid courage, and yet he will take the most infamous advantage of his enemy; armed and free, he will stand up before a host and fight until he is shot all to pieces, and yet when he is under the gallows and helpless he will cry and plead like a child. Words are cheap, and it is easy to call Slade a coward (all executed men who do not "die game" are promptly called cowards by unreflecting people), and when we read of Slade that he "had so exhausted himself by tears, prayers and lamentations, that he had scarcely strength left to stand under the fatal beam," the disgraceful word suggests itself in a moment—yet in frequently defying and inviting vengeance of banded Rocky Mountain cut-throats by shooting down their comrades and leaders, and never offering to hide or fly, Slade showed that he was a man of peerless bravery. No coward would dare that. Many a notorious coward, many a chicken-livered poltroon, coarse, brutal, degraded, has made his dying speech without a quaver in his voice and been swung into eternity with what looked like the calmest fortitude, and so we are justified in believing, from the low intellect of such a creature, that it was not *moral* courage that enabled him to do it. Then, if moral courage is not the requisite quality, what could it have been that this stout-hearted Slade lacked? —this bloody, desperate, kindly-mannered, urbane gentleman, who never hesitated to warn his most ruffianly enemies that he would kill them whenever or wherever he came across them next! I think it is a conundrum worth investigating.

54. The Pony Express

BY MARK TWAIN

IN a little while all interest was taken up in stretching our necks and watching for the "pony-rider"—the fleet messenger who sped across the continent from St. Joe to Sacramento, carrying letters nineteen hundred miles in eight days! Think of that for perishable horse and human flesh and blood to do! The pony-rider was usually a little bit of a man, brimful of spirit and endurance. No matter what time of the day or night his watch came on, and no matter whether it was winter or summer, raining, snowing, hailing, or sleeting, or whether his "beat" was a level straight road or a crazy trail over mountain crags and precipices, or whether it led through peaceful regions or regions that swarmed with hostile Indians, he must be always ready to leap into the saddle and be off like the wind! There was no idling-time for a pony-rider on duty. He rode fifty miles without stopping, by daylight, moonlight, starlight, or through the blackness of darkness—just as it happened. He rode a splendid horse that was born for a racer and fed and lodged like a gentleman; kept him at his utmost speed for ten miles, and then, as he came crashing up to the station where stood two men holding fast a fresh, impatient steed, the transfer of rider and mail-bag was made in the twinkling of an eye, and away flew the eager pair and were out of sight before the spectator could get hardly the ghost of a look. Both rider and horse went "flying light." The rider's dress was thin, and fitted close; he wore a "round-about," and a skull-cap, and tucked his pantaloons into his boot-tops like a race-rider. He carried no arms —he carried nothing that was not absolutely necessary, for even the postage on his literary freight was worth *five dollars a letter*. He got but little frivolous correspondence to carry—his bag had business letters in it, mostly. His horse was stripped of all unnecessary weight, too. He wore a little wafer of a racing-saddle, and no visible blanket. He wore light shoes, or none at all. The little flat mail-pockets strapped under the rider's thighs would each hold about the bulk of a child's primer. They held many and many an important business chapter and newspaper letter, but these were written on paper as airy and thin as gold-leaf, nearly, and thus bulk and weight were economized. The stage-coach traveled about a hundred to a hundred and twenty-five miles a day

Pony Express Rider. *Frederick Remington*

(twenty-four hours), the pony-rider about two hundred and fifty. There were about eighty pony-riders in the saddle all the time, night and day, stretching in a long, scattering procession from Missouri to California, forty flying eastward, and forty toward the west, and among them making four hundred gallant horses earn a stirring livelihood and see a deal of scenery every single day in the year.

We had had a consuming desire, from the beginning, to see a pony-rider, but somehow or other all that passed us and all that met us managed to streak by in the night, and so we heard only a whiz and a hail, and the swift phantom of the desert was gone before we could get our heads out of the windows. But now we were expecting one along every moment, and would see him in broad daylight. Presently the driver exclaims:

"HERE HE COMES!"

Every neck is stretched further, and every eye strained wider. Away across the endless dead level of the prairie a black speck appears against the sky, and it is plain that it moves. Well, I should think so! In a second or two it becomes a horse and rider, rising and falling, rising and falling—sweeping toward us nearer and nearer—growing more and more distinct, more and more sharply defined—nearer and still nearer, and the flutter of the hoofs comes faintly to the ear—another instant a whoop and a hurrah from our upper deck, a wave of the rider's hand, but no reply, and man and horse burst past our excited faces, and go winging away like a belated fragment of a storm!

So sudden is it all, and so like a flash of unreal fancy, that but for the flake of white foam left quivering and perishing on a mailsack after the vision had flashed by and disappeared, we might have doubted whether we had seen any actual horse and man at all, maybe.

We rattled through Scott's Bluffs Pass, by and by. It was along here somewhere that we first came across genuine and unmistakable alkali water in the road, and we cordially hailed it as a first-class curiosity, and a thing to be mentioned with eclat in letters to the ignorant at home. This water gave the road a soapy appearance, and in many places the ground looked as if it had been whitewashed. I think the strange alkali water excited us as much as any wonder we had come upon yet, and I know we felt very complacent and conceited, and better satisfied with life after we had added it to our list of things which *we* had seen and some other people had not. In a small way we were the same sort of simpletons as those who climb unnecessarily the perilous peaks of Mont Blanc and the Matterhorn, and derive no pleasure from it except the reflection that it isn't a common experience. But once in a while one of those parties trips and comes darting down the long mountain-crags in a sitting posture, making the crusted snow smoke behind him, flitting from bench to bench, and from terrace to terrace, jarring the earth where he strikes, and still glancing and flitting on again, sticking an iceberg into himself every now and then, and tearing his clothes, snatching at things to save himself, taking hold of trees and fetching them along with him, roots and all, starting little rocks now and then, then big boulders, then acres of ice and snow and patches of forest, gathering and still gathering as he goes, adding and still adding to his massed and sweeping grandeur as he nears a three thousand-foot precipice, till at last he waves his hat magnificently and rides into eternity on the back of a raging and tossing avalanche!

This is all very fine, but let us not be carried away by excitement, but ask calmly, how does this person feel about it in his cooler moments next day, with six or seven thousand feet of snow and stuff on top of him?

We crossed the sand hills near the scene of the Indian mail robbery and massacre of 1856, wherein the driver and conductor perished, and also all the passengers but one, it was supposed; but this must have been a mistake, for at different times afterward on the Pacific coast I was personally acquainted with a hundred and thirty-three or four people who were wounded during that massacre, and barely escaped with their lives. There was no doubt of the truth of it—I had it from their own lips. One of these parties told me that he kept coming across arrow-heads in his system for nearly seven years after the massacre; and another of them told me that he was stuck so literally full of arrows that after the Indians were gone and he could raise up and examine himself, he could not restrain his tears, for his clothes were completely ruined.

The most trustworthy tradition avers, however, that only one man, a person named

The Attack

Babbitt, survived the massacre, and he was desperately wounded. He dragged himself on his hands and knee (for one leg was broken) to a station several miles away. He did it during portions of two nights, lying concealed one day and part of another, and for more than forty hours suffering unimaginable anguish from hunger, thirst and bodily pain. The Indians robbed the coach of everything it contained, including quite an amount of treasure.

55. Virginia City Revisited

BY J. ROSS BROWNE

EDITOR'S NOTE: J. Ross Browne was a frequent contributor to *Harper's* magazine. His lively interest in the West of the sixties is exemplified by the following article, which appeared in *Harper's* in 1865. It is a humorous and stimulating portrait of one of the "bad towns" of the West.

I WAS prepared to find great changes on the route from Carson to Virginia City. At Empire City—which was nothing but a sage-desert inhabited by Dutch Nick on the occasion of my early explorations—I was quite bewildered with the busy scenes of life and industry. Quartz-mills and saw-mills had completely usurped the valley along the head of the Carson River; and now the hammering of stamps, the hissing of steam, the whirling clouds of smoke from tall chimneys, and the confused clamor of voices from a busy multitude, reminded one of a manufacturing city. Here, indeed, was progress of a substantial kind.

Further beyond, at Silver City, there were similar evidences of prosperity. From the descent into the cañon through the Devil's Gate, and up the grade to Gold Hill, it is almost a continuous line of quartz-mills, tunnels, dumps, sluices, water-wheels, frame shanties, and grog-shops.

Gold Hill itself has swelled into the proportions of a city. It is now practically a continuation of Virginia. Here the evidences of busy enterprise are peculiarly striking. The whole hill is riddled and honey-combed with shafts and tunnels. Engine-houses for hoisting are perched on points apparently inaccessible; quartz-mills of various capacities line the sides of the cañon; the main street is well flanked by brick stores, hotels, express-offices, saloons, restaurants, groggeries, and all those attractive places of resort which go to make up a flourishing mining town. Even a newspaper is printed here, which I know to be a spirited and popular institution, having been viciously assailed by the same. A runaway team of horses, charging full tilt down the street, greeted our arrival in a lively and characteristic manner, and came very near capsizing our stage. One man was run over some distance below, and partially crushed; but as somebody was killed nearly every day, such a meagre result afforded no general satisfaction.

Descending the slope of the ridge that divides Gold Hill from Virginia City a strange scene attracts the eye. He who gazes upon it for the first time is apt to doubt if it be real. Perhaps there is not another spot upon the face of the globe that presents a scene so weird and desolate in its natural aspect, yet so replete with busy life, so animate with human interest. It is as if a wondrous battle raged, in which the combatants were man and earth. Myriads of swarthy, bearded, dust-covered men are piercing into the grim old mountains, ripping them open, thrusting murderous holes through their naked bodies; piling up engines to cut out their vital arteries; stamping and crushing up with infernal machines their disemboweled fragments, and holding fiendish revels amidst the chaos of destruction; while the mighty earth, blasted, barren, and scarred by the tempests of ages, fiercely affronts the foe—smiting him with disease and death; scoffing at his puny assaults with a grim scorn; ever grand in his desolation, ever dominant in the infinity of his endurance. "Come!" he seems to mutter, "dig, delve, pierce, and bore, with your picks, your shovels, and your infernal machines; wring out of my veins a few globules of the precious blood; hoard it, spend it, gamble for it, bring perdition to your souls with it —do what you will, puny insects! Sooner or later the death-blow smites you, and Earth swallows you! From earth you came—to earth you go again!"

The city lies on a rugged slope, and is singularly diversified in its uprisings and downfallings. It is difficult to determine, by any system of observation or measurement, upon what principle it was laid out. My impression is that it was never laid out at all, but followed the dips, spurs, and angles of the immortal Comstock. Some of the streets run straight enough; others seem to dodge about at acute angles in search of an

Virginia City. *Harper's Magazine*

open space, as miners explore the subterranean regions in search of a lead. The cross-streets must have been forgotten in the original plan—if ever there was a plan about this eccentric city. Sometimes they happen accidentally at the most unexpected points; and sometimes they don't happen at all where you are sure to require them. A man in a hurry to get from the upper slope of the town to any opposite point below must try it under-ground or over the roofs of the houses, or take the customary circuit of half a mile. Every body seems to have built wherever he could secure a lot. The two main streets, it must be admitted, are so far regular as to follow pretty nearly the direction of the Comstock lead. On the lower slope, or plateau, the town, as viewed from any neighboring eminence, presents much the appearance of a vast number of shingle-roofs shaken down at random, like a jumbled pack of cards. All the streets are narrow, except where there are but few houses, and there they are wide enough at present. The business part of the town has been built up with astonishing rapidity. In the spring of 1860 there was nothing of it save a few frame shanties and canvas tents, and one or two rough stone cabins. It now presents some of the distinguishing features of a metropolitan city. Large and substantial brick houses, three or four stories high, with ornamental fronts, have filled up most of the gaps, and many more are still in progress of erection. The oddity of the plan, and variety of its architecture—combining most of the styles known to the ancients, and some but little known to the moderns—give this famous city a grotesque, if not picturesque, appearance, which is rather increased upon a close inspection.

Immense freight-wagons, with ponderous wheels and axles, heavily laboring under prodigious loads of ore for the mills, or groaning with piles of merchandise in boxes, bales, bags, and crates, block the narrow streets. Powerful teams of horses, mules, or oxen, numbering from eight to sixteen animals to each wagon, make frantic efforts to drag these land schooners over the ruts, and up the sudden rises, or through the sinks of this rut-smitten, ever-rising, ever-sinking city. A pitiable sight it is to see them! Smoking hot, reeking with sweat, dripping with liquefied dust, they pull, jerk, groan, fall back, and dash forward, tumble down, kick, plunge, and bite; then buckle to it again, under the galling lash; and so live and so struggle these poor beasts, for

their pittance of barley and hay, till they drop down dead. How they would welcome death if they had souls! Yet men have souls, and work hard too for their miserable pittance of food. How many of the countless millions of the earth yearn for death or welcome its coming? Even the teamsters that drive these struggling labor-worn brutes seem so fond of life that they scorn eternity. Brawny, bearded fellows they are; their faces so ingrained with the dust and grit of earth, and tanned to such an uncertain hue by the scorching suns and dry winds of the road, that for the matter of identity they might as well be Hindoos or Belooches. With what malignant zeal they crack their leather-thonged whips, and with what ferocious vigor they rend the air with their imprecations! O Plutus! such swearing—a sliding scale of oaths to which swearing in all other parts of the world is as the murmuring of a gentle brook to the volume and rush and thunder of a cataract. The fertility of resource displayed by these reckless men; their ready command of metaphor; their marvelous genius for strange, startling, and graphic combination of slang and profanity; their grotesque originality of inflexion and climax; their infatuated credulity in the understanding of dumb animals; would in the pursuit of any nobler art elevate them to a niche in the temple of fame. Surely if murder be deemed one of the Fine Arts in Virginia City, swearing ought not to be held in such common repute.

Entering the main street you pass on the upper side huge piles of earth and ore, hoisted out of the shafts or run out of the tunnels, and cast over the "dumps." The hill-sides, for a distance of more than a mile, are perfectly honeycombed. Steam-engines are puffing off their steam; smoke-stacks are blackening the air with their thick volumes of smoke; quartz-batteries are battering; hammers are hammering; subterranean blasts are bursting up the earth; picks and crow-bars are picking and crashing into the precious rocks; shanties are springing up, and carpenters are sawing and ripping and nailing; store-keepers are rolling their merchandise in and out along the way-side; fruit vendors are peddling their fruits; wagoners are tumbling out and piling in their freights of dry goods and ore; saloons are glittering with their gaudy bars and fancy glasses, and many-colored liquors, and thirsty men are swilling the burning poison; auctioneers, surrounded by eager and gaping crowds of speculators, are shouting off the stocks of delinquent stock-holders; organ-grinders are grinding their organs and torturing consumptive monkeys; hurdy-gurdy girls are singing bacchanalian songs in bacchanalian dens; Jew clothiers are selling off prodigious assortments of worthless garments at ruinous prices; billstickers are sticking up bills of auctions, theatres, and new saloons; newsboys are crying the city papers with the latest telegraphic news; stages are dashing off with passengers for "Reese;" and stages are dashing in with passengers from "Frisco;" and the inevitable Wells, Fargo, and Co. are distributing letters, packages, and papers to the hungry multitude, amidst tempting piles of silver bricks and wonderful complications of scales, letter-boxes, clerks, account-books, and twenty-dollar pieces. All is life, excitement, avarice, lust, deviltry, and enterprise. A strange city truly, abounding in strange exhibitions and startling combinations of the human passions. Where upon earth is there such another place?

One of the most characteristic features of Virginia is the inordinate passion of the inhabitants for advertising. Not only are the columns of the newspapers filled with every possible species of advertisement, but the streets and hill-sides are pasted all over with flaming bills. Says the proprietor of a small shanty, in letters that send a thrill of astonishment through your brain:

"LOOK HERE! *For fifty cents* YOU CAN GET A GOOD SQUARE MEAL at the HOWLING WILDERNESS SALOON!"

A square meal is not, as may be supposed, a meal placed upon the table in the form of a solid cubic block, but a substantial repast of pork and beans, onions, cabbage, and other articles of sustenance that will serve to fill up the corners of a miner's stomach.

The Jew clothing-stores present the most marvelous fertility of invention in this style of advertising. Bills are posted all over the doorways, in the windows, on the pavements, and on the various articles of clothing hung up for sale. He who runs may read:

"NOW OR NEVER! *Cheapest coats in the world!!* PANTS GIVEN AWAY!!! WALK IN, GENTS."

And so on without limit. New clothes and clothes doubtful are offered for sale at these prolific establishments, which are always selling off at cost or suicidal prices, yet never seem to be reduced in stock. I verily believe I saw hanging at the door of one of these shops the identical pair of stockings stolen from me several years ago at Strawberry.

Drinking establishments being rather numerous, the competition in this line of business gives rise to a very persuasive and attractive style of advertising. The bills are usually printed in florid and elaborately gilt letters, and frequently abound in pictures of an imaginative character. "Cosy Home," "Miner's Retreat," "Social Hall," "Empire," "Indication," "Fancy-Free,"

"Snug," "Shades," etc., are a few of the seductive names given to these places of popular resort; and the announcements are generally followed by a list of "choice liquors" and the gorgeous attractions of the billiard department, together with a hint that Dick, Jack, Dan, or Jerry "is always on hand, and while grateful for past favors will spare no pains to merit a continuance of the same. By catering to the public taste he hopes to make his house in the future, as it has been in the past, a real HOME for the Boys!" Nice homes these, and a nice family of boys that will come out of them! Where will they live when they grow to be men? A good idea it was to build a stone penitentiary.

"Oh yes! Oh yes! Oh yes!"
"AUCTION SALES EVERY DAY!"

This is another form of advertisement for a very prolific branch of trade. Day and night auctions are all the rage in Virginia as in San Francisco. Every thing that can't go any other way, and many things that can, go by auction. Stocks, horses, mules, boots, groceries, tinware, drugs and medicines, and rubbish of all kinds are put in flaming bills and auctioned off to the highest bidder for cash. "An'af! an'af! an'af! shall I have it?" is a part of the language popularly spoken on the principal streets.

A cigar store not much bigger than a dry-goods box must have its mammoth posters out over the town and hill-sides, displaying to the public eye the prodigious assortments of Regalias, Principes, Cheroots, etc., and choice brands of "Yellow-leaf," "Honey-dew," "Solace," and "Eureka," to be had within the limits of their cigar and tobacco emporium. If Archimedes were to rush from the solace of a bath and run naked through the streets of Virginia, shouting "Eureka! Eureka!" it would merely be regarded as a dodge to dispose of an invoice of Fine-Cut.

Quack pills, sirups, tonics, and rectifiers stare you in the face from every mud-bank, rock, post, and corner, in red, black, blue, and white letters; in hieroglyphics, in cadaverous pictures of sick men, and astounding pictures of well men.

Every branch of trade, every conceivable species of amusement, is forced upon the public eye in this way. Bill-posting is one of the fine arts. Its professors are among the most notable characters in Virginia. They have a specific interest in certain corners, boards, boxes, and banks of earth and rock, which, with the brush and pot of paste, yield them a handsome revenue. To one who witnesses this bill-mania for the first time the effect is rather peculiar. He naturally imagines that the whole place is turned inside out. Every man's business fills his eye from every point of view, and he can not conceive the existence of a residence unless it be that where so much of the inside is out some portion of the outside may be in. With the exception of the silver mines this is, to a casual observer, an inverted city, and may well claim to be a city of anomalies.

I had occasion, during my stay, to avail myself of the services of a professional bill-sticker. For the sum of six dollars he agreed to make me notorious. The bills were printed in the approved form: "A Trip to Iceland," etc. Special stress was given to the word "ICELAND," and my name was printed in extravagantly conspicuous letters. In the course of a day or two I was shocked at the publicity the Professor of Bill-Posting had given me. From every rock, corner, dry-goods box, and awning post; from every screen in every drinking saloon, I was confronted and brow-beaten by my own name. I felt disposed to shrink into my boots. Had any body walked up to me and said, "Sir, you are a humbug!'' it would have been an absolute relief. I would have grasped him by the hand, and answered, "I know it, my dear fellow, and honor you for your frankness!" But there was one consolation: I was suffering in company. A lady, popularly known as "The Menken," had created an immense sensation in San Francisco, and was about to favor the citizens of Virginia with a classical equestrian exhibition entitled "Mazeppa." She was represented as tied in an almost nude state to the back of a wild horse, which was running away with her at a fearful rate of speed. My friend the Professor was an artist in the line of bill-sticking, and carefully studied effects. He evidently enjoyed Mazeppa. It was a flaming and a gorgeous bill. Its colors were of the most florid character; and he posted accordingly. First came Mazeppa on the mustang horse; then came the Trip to Iceland and myself. If I remember correctly we (that is to say "The Menken" and I) were followed by "Ayer's Tonic Pills," "Brown's Bronchial Troches," and "A good Square Meal at the Howling Wilderness Saloon." Well, I suppose it was all right, though it took me rather aback at the first view. If the lady had no reason to complain, it was not for me, an old traveler, to find fault with the bill-sticker for placing me prominently before the public. Perhaps the juxtaposition was unfortunate in a pecuniary point of view; perhaps the citizens of Virginia feel no great interest in icy regions. Be that as it may, never again so long as I live will I undertake to run "Iceland" in the vicinity of a beautiful woman tied to the back of a wild horse.

But I anticipate my story. Scarcely had I descended from the stage when I was greeted by several old friends, who expressed themselves highly gratified at my arrival.

Their remarks, indeed, were so complimentary that I hesitate to repeat them. Truth, however, must be regarded, even at the expense of modesty. "Your sketch of Washoe," said they, "was a capital burlesque. It was worthy of Phœnix or Artemus Ward! A great many people thought it was true! Of course we understood it, but you know one-half of mankind doesn't know a joke from a demonstration in Euclid!" Here was glory! Here was a reward for all my past sufferings! An unfortunate gentleman walks all the way over from Placerville to Washoe, with his blankets on his back; endures the most extraordinary privations; catches the rheumatism, tic-douloureux, and dysentery; invests in the Dead Broke; fails to make an agency pay; drags his weary limbs back again, and writes out what he conceives to be a truthful account of his experiences, and is then complimented upon having made a capital hit, perpetrated a most admirable burlesque, worthy the distinguished humorists of the age! It was a sorry joke for me..I was terribly in earnest about it, at all events.

"You will admit," said these excellent friends, "that the richness of this country surpasses any thing ever known in the world before; that you were altogether mistaken about the silver leads?"

"No, gentlemen," was my answer, "I can't admit any such thing. I said the Comstock was wonderfully rich, so far as any body could judge from the specimens of ore taken out; but I thought there was considerable doubt as to where the most valuable running feet might run. That doubt is not yet removed from my mind. I advised people not to invest in the ten thousand outside leads that were then in existence. Where are your Flowery Diggings now? What is your Desert worth per running foot? How much will you give me for my Scandalous

Wretch, or Bobtail Horse, or Root Hog or Die—all first-class leads in the neighborhood of the Devil's Gate? Show me a single lead that pays assessments, or pays any thing at all, or is likely ever to pay fifty cents per acre, outside of the main lead in Gold Hill and Virginia City; show me how many of your best mines pay dividends, and I will take back all I said."

At this there was a general look of blankness, as if the facts had not occurred to them before in that point of view.

"But you'll admit that a man can't see much of a mineral district in a few days. You ought to spend a week or two in each mine; then you would be prepared to say something about it."

Strange, isn't it, that people will never get over this idea! Wherever I travel I am told that nothing can be seen short of a few weeks or a few months or a few years! If I undertake to look at a potatoe-patch or a cabbage-garden, it is urgently represented that I can "form no conception how potatoes and cabbages grow in this section" without a month's careful examination of the roots or fibers. I am occasionally so bothered in this way as to feel tempted to offer rather a rude reply, viz.: that one who makes it his business to observe things around him can, with an ordinary share of penetration and some common-sense, see as much in a day as many people who live on the spot see in a lifetime. It might be effrontery to tell these Virginians, upon so brief an inspection, that I knew more of their city and its resources than they did; but I would even venture something on that point.

"You did us great injury," said they, "by so casual a glance at our mines. For example, you cast contempt upon the whole Comstock lead by representing its dips, spurs, and angles in a sort of burlesque map resembling a bunch of straw."

Alas, poor human nature! These very parties, who complained of my map because it resembled a bunch of straw—illustrating the assertion that every body's dips, spurs, and angles were running into every body else's—were at that very moment, and doubtless are yet, at daggers' points of litigation with other parties who had run into their dips, spurs, and angles. I don't know of a mine on the Comstock which does not infringe upon the alleged rights of some other mine. The results of an actual survey are precisely the same as those produced by a bundle of straw well inked and pressed upon a sheet of paper. To call a map so accurately truthful as mine a burlesque calculated to throw contempt upon the subject, manifests a degree of visual obliquity, if not moral assurance, absolutely refreshing.

The citizens of Virginia, like the citizens of Timbuctoo in Africa and Reykjavik in Iceland, are enthusiastic admirers of their own place of residence. Not satisfied with the praise usually bestowed upon the city by every stranger who enters it and who desires to maintain friendly relations with the inhabitants, they are exacting to a degree bordering on the despotic. A visitor is required to go into ecstasies over the climate, should there chance to occur, during his sojourn, a passably fine day. He is called upon at every turn to do homage to the wonderful progress of improvement, which they consider far ahead of any thing ever achieved by human beings constructed in the usual form. He is expected to pay the tribute of admiration to the magnificence of the buildings and the sumptuous accommodations of the hotels. If he does not boldly, firmly, and without reservation, express the opinion that the mines are richer by a thousand to one than those of Mexico or South America, he is at once set down as a man whose opinion is worth nothing. Should a stray bullet whiz by his head and kill some equally innocent party within a distance of three paces, he is gravely assured and required to believe that there is as much respect paid to life and limb in Virginia City as there is in any city in the Union. At any hour of the night, when the noise around his lodgings would shame Bedlam, his attention is exultingly directed to the elysian repose of this delectable metropolis. Passing those dens of infamy that abound on every street, he is invited, with an assurance almost incredible, to render homage to the exalted condition of public morals. In full view of the most barren, blasted, and horribly desolate country that perhaps the light of heaven ever shone upon, he is appealed to, as a lover of nature, to admire the fertility of the soil, the luxuriance of the vegetation, and the exquisite beauty of the scenery. Surrounded by an enthusiastic dozen of citizens, most of whom are afflicted with sore throat, mountain fever, erysipelas, bleeding of the nose, shortness of breath, heart disease, diarrhea, and loss of appetite, he is urged to observe the remarkable salubrity of the climate, and to disabuse his mind of those prejudices against it arising from the misrepresentations of interested parties.

"Oh wad some power the giftie gie us—"
But what's the use? It would only make us miserable. We are better off as it is. Men who can see heaven in Virginia City are to be envied. Their condition is such that a change to a better world would not seem materially necessary to their exaltation; and I am sure the worst that could happen them

would be borne with as much fortitude as lost sinners are permitted to exercise.

Making due allowance for the atmosphere of exaggeration through which a visitor sees every thing in this wonderful mining metropolis, its progress has been sufficiently remarkable to palliate in some measure the extraordinary flights of fancy in which its inhabitants are prone to indulge. I was not prepared to see so great a change within the brief period of three years; for when people assure me "the world never saw any thing like it," "California is left in the shade," "San Francisco is eclipsed" "Montgomery Street is nowhere now," my incredulity is excited, and it takes some little time to judge of the true state of the case without prejudice. Speaking then strictly within bounds, the growth of this city is remarkable. When it is considered that the surrounding country affords but few facilities for the construction of houses; that lumber has to be hauled a considerable distance at great expense; that lime, bricks, iron-work, sashes, doors, etc., cost three or four times what similar articles do in San Francisco; that much indispensable material can only be had by transporting it over the mountains a distance of more than a hundred and fifty miles; and that the average of mechanical labor, living, and other expenses is correspondingly higher than in California, it is really wonderful how much has been done in so short a space of time.

Yet, allowing all this, what would be the impressions of a Fejee Islander sent upon a mission of inquiry to this strange place? His earliest glimpse of the main street would reveal the curious fact that it is paved with a conglomerate of dust, mud, splintered planks, old boots, clippings of tinware, and playing-cards. It is especially prolific in the matter of cards. Mules are said to fatten on them during seasons of scarcity when the straw gives out. The next marvelous fact that would strike the observation of this wild native is that so many people live in so many saloons, and do nothing from morning till night, and from night till morning again, but drink fiery liquids and indulge in profane language. How can all these able-bodied men afford to be idle? Who pays their expenses? And why do they carry pistols, knives, and other deadly weapons, when no harm could possibly befall them if they went unarmed and devoted themselves to some useful occupation? Has the God of the white men done them such an injury in furnishing all this silver for their use that they should treat His name with contempt and disrespect? Why do they send missionaries to the Fejee Islands and leave their own country in such a dreadful state of neglect? The Fejeeans devour their enemies occasionally as a war measure; the white man swallows his enemy all the time without regard to measure. Truly the white man is a very uncertain native! Fejeeans can't rely upon him.

When I was about to start on my trip to Washoe, friends from Virginia assured me I would find hotels there almost, if not quite, equal to the best in San Francisco. There was but little difference, they said, except in the matter of extent. The Virginia hotels were quite as good, though not quite so large. Of course I believed all they told me. Now I really don't consider myself fastidious on the subject of hotels. Having traveled in many different countries I have enjoyed an extensive experience in the way of accommodations, from my mother-earth to the foretop of a whale-ship, from an Indian wigwam to a Parisian hotel, from an African palm-tree to an Arctic snowbank.

I have slept in the same bed with two donkeys, a camel, half a dozen Arabs, several goats, and a horse. I have slept on beds alive with snakes, lizards, scorpions, centipeds, bugs, and fleas—beds in which men stricken with the plague had died horrible deaths—beds that might reasonably be suspected of small-pox, measles, and Asiatic cholera. I have slept in beds of rivers and beds of sand, and on the bare bed rock. Standing, sitting, lying down, doubled up, and hanging over; twisted, punched, jammed and elbowed by drunken men; snored at in the ears; sat upon and smothered by the nightmare; burnt by fires, rained upon, snowed upon, and bitten by frost—in all these positions, and subject to all these discomforts, I have slept with comparative satisfaction. There are pleasanter ways of sleeping, to be sure, but there are times when any way is a blessing. In respect to the matter of eating I am even less particular. Frogs, horse-leeches, snails, and grasshoppers are luxuries to what I have eaten. It has pleased Providence to favor me with appetites and tastes appropriate to a great variety of circumstances and many conditions of life. These facts serve to show that I am not fastidious on the subject of personal accommodations.

Perhaps my experience in Virginia was exceptional; perhaps misfortune was determined to try me to the utmost extremity. I endeavored to find accommodations at a hotel recommended as the best in the place, and was shown a room over the kitchen stove, in which the thermometer ranged at about 130 to 150 degrees of Fahrenheit. To be lodged and baked at the rate of $2 per night, cash in advance, was more than I could stand, so I asked for another room. There was but one more, and that was preempted by a lodger who might or might not

The Hurdy-Gurdy Girls

come back and claim possession in the middle of the night. It had no window except one that opened into the passage, and the bed was so arranged that every other lodger in the house could take a passing observation of the sleeper and enjoy his style of sleeping. Nay, it was not beyond the resources of the photographic art to secure his negative and print his likeness for general distribution. It was bad enough to be smothered for want of light and air; but I had no idea of paying $2 a night for the poor privilege of showing people how I looked with my eyes shut, and possibly my mouth open. A man may have an attack of nightmare, his countenance may be distorted by horrible dreams; he may laugh immoderately at a very bad pun made in his sleep—in all which conditions of body and mind he doubtless presents an interesting spectacle to the critical eyes of a stranger, but he doesn't like to wake up suddenly and be caught in the act.

The next hotel to which I was recommended was eligibly located on a street composed principally of grog-shops and gambling-houses. I was favored with a front-room about eight feet square. The walls were constructed of boards fancifully decorated with paper, and afforded this facility to a lodger—that he could hear all that was going on in the adjacent rooms. The partitions might deceive the eye, but the ear received the full benefit of the various oaths, ejaculations, conversations, and perambulations in which his neighbors indulged. As for the bed, I don't know how long it had been in use, or what race of people had hitherto slept in it, but the sheets and blankets seemed to be sadly discolored by age—or lack of soap and water. It would be safe to say washing was not considered a paying investment by the managers of this establishment. Having been over twenty-four hours without sleep or rest I made an attempt to procure a small supply, but miserably failed in consequence of an interesting conversation carried on in the passage between the chamber-maids, waiters, and other ladies and gentlemen respecting the last free fight. From what I could gather this was considered the best neighborhood in the city for free fights. Within the past two weeks three or four men had been shot, stabbed, or maimed close by the door. "Oh, it's a lively place, you bet!" said one of the ladies (the chamber-maid, I think), "an oncommon lively place—reely hexcitin'. I look out of the winder every mornin' jist to see how many dead men are layin' around. I declare to gracious the bullets flies around here sometimes like hailstones!" "An' shur," said a voice in that rich brogue which can never be mistaken, "it's no wondher the boys shud be killin' an' murtherin' themselves forninst the door, whin they're all just like me, dyin' in love wid yer beau-

teeful self!" A smart slap and a general laugh followed this suggestion. "Git away wid ye, Dinnis; yer always up to yer mischief! As I was sayin', no later than this mornin', I see two men a poppin' away at each other wid six-shooters—a big man an' a little man. The big man he staggered an' fell right under the winder, wid his head on the curb-stone, an' his legs a stickin' right up in the air. He was all over blood, and when the boys picked him up he was dead as a brickbat. 'Tother chap he run into a saloon. You better b'leeve this is a lively neighborhood. I tell you hailstones is nothink to the way the bullets flies a-round." "That's so," chimes in another female voice; "I see myself, with my own eyes, Jack's corpse an' two more carried away in the last month. If I'd a had a six-shooter then you bet they'd a carried away the fellow that nipped Jack!"

Now taking into view the picturesque spectacle that a few dead men dabbled in blood must present to the eye on a fine morning, and the chances of a miscellaneous ball carrying away the top of one's cranium, or penetrating the thin board wall and ranging upward through his body as he lies in bed, I considered it best to seek a more secluded neighborhood, where the scenery was of a less stimulating character and the hail-storms not quite so heavy. By the kind aid of a friend I secured comparatively agreeable quarters in a private lodging-house kept by a widow lady. The rooms were good and the beds clean, and the price not extravagant for this locality—$12 a week without board.

So much for the famous hotels of Virginia. If there are any better, neither myself, nor some fellow-travelers who told me their experiences, succeeded in finding them. The concurrent testimony was that they are dirty, ill-kept, badly attended by rough, ill-mannered waiters—noisy to such a degree that a sober man can get but little rest, day or night, and extravagantly high in proportion to the small comfort they afford. One of the newspapers published a statement which the author probably intended for a joke, but which is doubtless founded upon fact—namely, that a certain hotel advertised for 300 chickens to serve the same number of guests. Only one chicken could be had for love or money—a very ancient rooster, which was made into soup and afterward served up in the form of a fricasee for the 300 guests. The flavor was considered extremely delicate—what there was of it; and there was plenty of it such as it was.

Still if we are to credit what the Virginia newspapers say—and it would be dangerous to intimate that they ever deal in any thing save the truth—there are other cities on the eastern slope of the Sierras which afford equally attractive accommodations. On the occasion of the recent Senatorial contest at Carson City, the prevailing rates charged for lodgings, according to the Virginia *Enterprise,* were as follows: "For a bed in a house, barn, blacksmithshop, or hay-yard (none to be had—all having been engaged shortly before election) ; horse-blanket in an old sugar hogshead per night, $10; crockery-crate, with straw, $7.50; without straw, $5.75; for cellar-door, $4; for roosting on a smooth pole, $3.50; pole, common, rough, $3; plaza fence, $2.50; walking up and down the Warm Springs road—if cloudy, $1.50; if clear, $1.25. (In case the clouds are very thick and low $1.75 is generally asked.)

Very good roosting in a pine-tree, back of Camp Nye, may still be had free, but we understand that a company is being formed to monopolize all the more accessible trees. We believe they propose to improve by putting two pins in the bottom of each tree, or keep a man to boost regular customers. They talk of charging six bits."

I could scarcely credit this, if it were not that a friend of mine, who visited Reese River last summer, related some experiences of a corroborative character. Unable to secure lodgings elsewhere, he undertook to find accommodations in a vacant sheep corral. The proprietor happening to come home about midnight found him spread out under the lee of the fence. "Look-a-here, stranger!" said he, gruffly, "that's all well enough, but I gen'rally collect in advance. Just fork over four bits or mizzle!" My friend indignantly mizzled. Cursing the progressive spirit of the age, he walked some distance out of town, and was about to finish the night under the lee of a big quartz boulder, when a fierce-looking speculator, with a six-shooter in his hand, suddenly appeared from a cavity in the rock, saying, "No yer don't! Take a fool's advice now, and git! When you go a prospectin' around ov nights agin, jest steer ov this boulder ef you please!" In vain my friend attempted to explain. The rising wrath of the squatter was not to be appeased by soft words, and the click of the trigger, as he raised his pistol and drew a bead, warned the trespasser that it was time to be off. He found lodgings that night on the public highway to Virginia City and San Francisco.

56. Hunting Big Redwoods

BY JOHN MUIR

EDITOR'S NOTE: John Muir (1838-1914) is among the greatest of the American naturalists. He made many nature studies in California and Alaska, and was one of the early explorers of what is now Sequoia National Park, King's Canyon National Park and Yosemite National Park. To his efforts are largely due the establishment of these and other areas as national parks.

THE Big Tree (*Sequoia gigantea*) is nature's forest masterpiece, and, as far as I know, the greatest of living things. It belongs to an ancient stock, as its remains in old rocks show, and has a strange air of other days about it, a thoroughbred look inherited from the long ago, the auld lang syne of trees. Once the genus was common, and with many species flourished in the now desolate Arctic regions, the interior of North America, and in Europe; but in long eventful wanderings from climate to climate only two species have survived the hardships they had to encounter, the *gigantea* and *sempervirens:* the former now restricted to the western slopes of the Sierra, the other to the Coast Mountains, and both to California, excepting a few groves of redwood which extend into Oregon. The Pacific coast in general is the paradise of conifers. Here nearly all of them are giants, and display a beauty and magnificence unknown elsewhere. The climate is mild, the ground never freezes, and moisture and sunshine abound all the year. Nevertheless, it is not easy to account for the colossal size of the Sequoias. The largest are about three hundred feet high, and thirty feet in diameter.

Who of all the dwellers of the plains and prairies and fertile home forests of round-headed oak and maple, hickory and elm, ever dreamed that earth could bear such growths?—trees that the familiar pines and firs seem to know nothing about, lonely, silent, serene, with a physiognomy almost godlike, and so old, thousands of them still living had already counted their years by tens of centuries when Columbus set sail from Spain, and were in the vigor of youth or middle age when the star led the Chaldean sages to the infant Saviour's cradle. As far as man is concerned, they are the same yesterday, to-day, and forever, emblems of permanence.

No description can give any adequate idea of their singular majesty, much less of their beauty. Excepting the sugar pine, most of its neighbors with pointed tops seem to be forever shouting "Excelsior!" while the Big Tree, though soaring above them all, seems satisfied, its rounded head poised lightly as a cloud, giving no impression of trying to go higher. Only in youth does it show, like other conifers, a heavenward yearning, keenly aspiring with a long quick-growing top. Indeed, the whole tree, for the first century or two, or until a hundred to a hundred and fifty feet high, is arrowhead in form, and, compared with the solemn rigidity of age, is as sensitive to the wind as a squirrel tail. The lower branches are gradually dropped, as it grows older, and the upper ones thinned out, until comparatively few are left. These, however, are developed to great size, divide again and again, and terminate in bossy rounded masses of leafy branchlets, while the head becomes dome-shaped. Then, poised in fullness of strength and beauty, stern and solemn in mien, it glows with eager, enthusiastic life, quivering to the tip of every leaf and branch and far-reaching root, calm as a granite dome, — the first to feel the touch of the rosy beams of the morning, the last to bid the sun good-night.

Perfect specimens, unhurt by running fires or lightning, are singularly regular and symmetrical in general form, though not at all conventional, showing infinite variety in sure unity and harmony of plan. The immensely strong, stately shafts, with rich purplish-brown bark, are free of limbs for a hundred and fifty feet or so, though dense

The Big Trees

tufts of sprays occur here and there, producing an ornamental effect, while long parallel furrows give a fluted, columnar appearance. The limbs shoot forth with equal boldness in every direction, showing no weather side. On the old trees the main branches are crooked and rugged, and strike rigidly outward, mostly at right angles from the trunk, but there is always a certain measured restraint in their reach which keeps them within bounds. No other Sierra tree has foliage so densely massed, or outlines so finely, firmly drawn, and so obediently subordinate to an ideal type. A particularly knotty, angular, ungovernable-looking branch, five to eight feet in diameter, and perhaps a thousand years old, may occasionally be seen pushing out from the trunk, as if determined to break across the bounds of the regular curve; but, like all the others, as soon as the general outline is approached, the huge limb dissolves into massy bosses of branchlets and sprays, as if the tree were growing beneath an invisible bell glass, against the sides of which the branches were moulded, while many small varied departures from the ideal form give the impression of freedom to grow as they like.

Except in picturesque old age, after being struck by lightning and broken by a thousand snowstorms, this regularity of form is one of the Big Tree's most distinguishing characteristics. Another is the simple sculptural beauty of the trunk, and its great thickness as compared with its height and the width of the branches; many of them being from eight to ten feet in diameter at a height of two hundred feet from the ground, and seeming more like finely modeled and sculptured architectural columns than the stems of trees, while the great strong limbs are like rafters supporting the magnificent dome head.

The root system corresponds in magnitude with the other dimensions of the tree, forming a flat, far-reaching, spongy network, two hundred feet or more in width, without any taproot; and the instep is so grand and fine, so suggestive of endless strength, it is long ere the eye is released to look above it. The natural swell of the roots, though at first sight excessive, gives rise to buttresses no greater than are required for beauty as well as strength, as at once appears when you stand back far enough to see the whole tree in its true proportions. The fineness of the taper of the trunk is shown by its thickness at great heights, — a diameter of ten feet at a height of two hundred being, as we have seen, not uncommon. Indeed, the boles of but few trees hold their thickness so well as Sequoia. Resolute, consummate, determined in form, always beheld with wondering admiration, the Big Tree always seems unfamiliar, standing alone, unrelated, with peculiar physiognomy, awfully solemn and earnest. Nevertheless, there is nothing alien in its looks. The madroña, clad in thin smooth red and yellow bark and big glossy leaves, seems, in the dark coniferous forests of Washington and Vancouver Island, like some lost wanderer from the magnolia groves of the South, while Sequoia, with all its strangeness, seems more at home than any of its neighbors, holding the best right to the ground as the oldest, strongest inhabitant. One soon becomes acquainted with new species of pine and fir and spruce as with friendly people, shaking their outstretched branches like shaking hands, and fondling their beautiful little ones; while the venerable aboriginal Sequoia, ancient of other days, keeps you at a distance, taking no notice of you, speaking only to the winds, thinking only of the sky, looking as strange in aspect and behavior among the neighboring trees as would the mastodon or hairy elephant among the homely bears and deer. Only the Sierra juniper is at all like it, standing rigid and unconquerable on glacial pavements for thousands of years, grim, rusty, silent, uncommunicative, with an air of antiquity about as pronounced as that so characteristic of Sequoia.

The bark of full-grown trees is from one to two feet thick, rich cinnamon-brown, purplish on young trees and shady parts of the old, forming magnificent masses of color with the underbrush and beds of flowers. Toward the end of winter the trees themselves bloom, while the snow is still eight or ten feet deep. The pistillate flowers are about three eighths of an inch long, pale green, and grow in countless thousands on the ends of the sprays. The staminate are still more abundant, pale yellow, a fourth of an inch long, and when the golden pollen is ripe they color the whole tree, and dust the air and the ground far and near.

The cones are bright grass-green in color, about two and a half inches long, one and a half wide, and are made up of thirty or forty strong closely packed rhomboidal scales, with four to eight seeds at the base of each. The seeds are extremely small and light, being only from an eighth to a fourth of an inch long and wide, including a filmy surrounding wing, which causes them to glint and waver in falling, and enables the wind to carry them considerable distances from the tree.

The faint lisp of snowflakes, as they alight, is one of the smallest sounds mortal can hear. The sound of falling Sequoia seeds, even when they happen to strike on flat leaves or flakes of bark, is about as faint. Very different are the bumping and thudding of the falling cones. Most of them are cut off by the Douglas squirrel, and stored for the sake of the seeds, small as they are. In the calm Indian summer these busy harvesters with ivory sickles go to work early in the morning, as soon as breakfast is over, and nearly all day the ripe cones fall in a steady pattering, bumping shower. Unless harvested in this way, they discharge their seeds, and remain on the tree for many years. In fruitful seasons the trees are fairly laden. On two small specimen branches, one and a half and two inches in diameter, I counted four hundred and eighty cones. No other California conifer produces nearly so many seeds, excepting perhaps its relative, the redwood of the Coast Mountains. Millions are ripened annually by a single tree, and the product of one of the main groves in a fruitful year would suffice to plant all the mountain ranges of the world.

The dense tufted sprays make snug nesting places for birds, and in some of the loftiest, leafiest towers of verdure thousands of generations have been reared, the great solemn trees shedding off flocks of merry singers every year from nests like the flocks of winged seeds from the cones.

The Big Tree keeps its youth far longer than any of its neighbors. Most silver firs are old in their second or third century, pines in their fourth or fifth, while the Big Tree, growing beside them, is still in the bloom of its youth, juvenile in every feature, at the age of old pines, and cannot be said to attain anything like prime size and beauty before its fifteen hundredth year, or, under favorable circumstances, become old before its three thousandth. Many, no doubt, are much older than this. On one of the Kings River giants, thirty-five feet and eight inches in diameter, exclusive of bark, I counted upwards of four thousand annual wood rings, in which there was no trace of decay

after all these centuries of mountain weather. There is no absolute limit to the existence of any tree. Their death is due to accidents, not, as of animals, to the wearing out of organs. Only the leaves die of old age, — their fall is foretold in their structure; but the leaves are renewed every year, and so also are the other essential organs, wood, roots, bark, buds. Most of the Sierra trees die of disease. Thus the magnificent silver firs are devoured by fungi, and comparatively few of them live to see their three hundredth birth year. But nothing hurts the Big Tree. I never saw one that was sick or showed the slightest sign of decay. It lives on through indefinite thousands of years, until burned, blown down, undermined, or shattered by some tremendous lightning stroke. No ordinary bolt ever seriously hurts Sequoia. In all my walks I have seen only one that was thus killed outright. Lightning, though rare in the California lowlands, is common on the Sierra. Almost every day in June and July small thunderstorms refresh the main forest belt. Clouds like snowy mountains of marvelous beauty grow rapidly in the calm sky about midday, and cast cooling shadows and showers that seldom last more than an hour. Nevertheless, these brief, kind storms wound or kill a good many trees. I have seen silver firs, two hundred feet high, split into long peeled rails and slivers down to the roots, leaving not even a stump; the rails radiating like the spokes of a wheel from a hole in the ground where the tree stood. But the Sequoia, instead of being split and slivered, usually has forty or fifty feet of its brash knotty top smashed off in short chunks about the size of cord wood, the beautiful rosy-red ruins covering the ground in a circle a hundred feet wide or more. I never saw any that had been cut down to the ground, or even to below the branches, except one in the Stanislaus Grove, about twelve feet in diameter, the greater part of which was smashed to fragments, leaving only a leafless stump about seventy-five feet high. It is a curious fact that all the very old Sequoias have lost their heads by lightning. "All things come to him who waits;" but of all living things Sequoia is perhaps the only one able to wait long enough to make sure of being struck by lightning. Thousands of years it stands ready and waiting, offering its head to every passing cloud as if inviting its fate, praying for heaven's fire as a blessing; and when at last the old head is off, another of the same shape immediately begins to grow on. Every bud and branch seems excited, like bees that have lost their queen, and tries hard to repair the damage. Branches that for many centuries have been growing out horizontally at once turn upward, and all their branchlets arrange themselves with reference to a new top of the same peculiar curve as the old one. Even the small subordinate branches halfway down the trunk do their best to push up to the top and help in this curious head-making.

The great age of these noble trees is even more wonderful than their huge size, standing bravely up, millennium in, millennium out, to all that fortune may bring them; triumphant over tempest and fire and time, fruitful and beautiful, giving food and shelter to multitudes of small fleeting creatures dependent upon their bounty. Other trees may claim to be about as large or as old; Australian gums, Senegal baobabs, Mexican taxodiums, English yews, and venerable Lebanon cedars, trees of renown, some of which are from ten to thirty feet in diameter. We read of oaks that are supposed to have existed ever since the creation, yet, strange to say, I can find no definite accounts of the age of any of these trees, but only estimates based on tradition and assumed average rates of growth. No other known tree approaches the Sequoia in grandeur, height and thickness being considered, and none, as far as I know, has looked down on so many centuries, or opens such impressive and suggestive views into history. The majestic monument of the Kings River Forest is, as we have seen, fully four thousand years old, and, measuring the rings of annual growth, we find it was no less than twenty-seven feet in diameter at the beginning of the Christian era, while many observations lead me to expect the discovery of others ten or twenty centuries older. As to those of moderate age, there are thousands, mere youths as yet, that

"saw the light that shone
On Mahomed's uplifted crescent,
On many a royal gilded throne
And deed forgotten in the present,
. . . saw the age of sacred trees
And Druid groves and mystic larches,
And saw from forest domes like these
The builder bring his Gothic arches."

Great trees and groves need to be venerated as sacred monuments and halls of council and worship. But soon after the discovery of the Calaveras Grove one of the grandest trees was cut down for the sake of the stump! The laborious vandals had seen "the biggest tree in the world;" then, forsooth, they must try to see the biggest stump and dance on it.

The growth in height for the first two centuries is usually at the rate of eight to ten inches a year. Of course all very large trees are old, but those equal in size may vary greatly in age, on account of variations in soil, closeness or openness of growth, etc.

Thus, a tree about ten feet in diameter that grew on the side of a meadow was, according to my own count of the wood rings, only two hundred and fifty-nine years old at the time it was felled, while another in the same grove, of almost exactly the same size, but less favorably situated, was fourteen hundred and forty years old. The Calaveras tree cut for a dance floor was twenty-four feet in diameter, and only thirteen hundred years old; another, about the same size, was a thousand years older.

One of my own best excursions among the Sequoias was made in the autumn of 1875, when I explored the then unknown or little-known Sequoia region south of the Mariposa Grove for comprehensive views of the belt, and to learn what I could of the peculiar distribution of the species and its history in general. In particular, I was anxious to try to find out whether it had ever been more widely distributed since the glacial period; what conditions, favorable or otherwise, were affecting it; what were its relations to climate, topography, soil, and the other trees growing with it, etc.; and whether, as was generally supposed, the species was nearing extinction. I was already acquainted in a general way with the northern groves, but, excepting some passing glimpses gained on excursions into the high Sierra about the head waters of Kings and Kern rivers, I had seen nothing of the south end of the belt.

Nearly all my mountaineering has been done on foot, carrying as little as possible, depending on camp fires for warmth, that so I might be light and free to go wherever my studies might lead. But on this Sequoia trip, which promised to be long, I was persuaded to take a small wild mule with me, to carry provisions and a pair of blankets. The friendly owner of the animal, having noticed that I sometimes looked tired when I came down from the peaks to replenish my bread sack, assured me that his "little Brownie mule" was just what I wanted, — tough as a knot, perfectly untirable, low and narrow, just right for squeezing through brush, able to climb like a chipmunk, jump from boulder to boulder like a wild sheep, and go anywhere a man could go. But tough as he was, and accomplished as a climber, many a time in the course of our journey, when he was jaded and hungry, wedged fast in rocks or struggling in chaparral like a fly in a spider web, his troubles were sad to see, and I wished he would leave me and find his way home alone.

We set out from Yosemite about the end of August, and our first camp was made in the well-known Mariposa Grove. Here and in the adjacent pine woods I spent nearly a week, carefully examining the boundaries of the grove for traces of its greater extension without finding any. Then I struck out into the majestic trackless forest to the southeastward, hoping to find new groves or traces of old ones in the dense silver fir and pine woods about the head of Big Creek, where soil and climate seemed most favorable to their growth; but not a single tree or old monument of any sort came to light until I climbed the high rock called Wamellow by the Indians. Here I obtained telling views of the fertile forest-filled basin of the upper Fresno. Innumerable spires of the noble yellow pine were displayed rising one above another on the braided slopes, and yet nobler sugar pines with superb arms outstretched in the rich autumn light, while away toward the southwest, on the verge of the glowing horizon, I discovered the majestic domelike crowns of Big Trees towering high over all, singly and in close grove congregations. There is something wonderfully attractive in this king tree, even when beheld from afar, that draws us to it with indescribable enthusiasm,—its superior height and massive smoothly rounded outlines proclaiming its character in any company; and when one of the oldest of them attains full stature on some commanding ridge, it seems the very god of the woods. I ran back to camp, packed Brownie, and steered over the divide and down into the heart of the Fresno Grove. Then choosing a camp on the side of a brook where the grass was good, I made a cup of tea, and set off free among the brown giants, glorying in the abundance of new work about me. One of the first special things that caught my attention was an extensive landslip. The ground on the side of a stream had given way to a depth of about fifty feet, and with all its trees had been launched into the bottom of the stream ravine. Most of the trees — pines, firs, incense cedar, and Sequoia — were still standing erect and uninjured, as if unconscious that anything out of the common had happened. Tracing the ravine alongside the avalanche, I saw many trees whose roots had been laid bare, and in one instance discovered a Sequoia, about fifteen feet in diameter, growing above an old prostrate trunk that seemed to belong to a former generation. This slip had occurred seven or eight years ago, and I was glad to find not only that most of the Big Trees were uninjured, but that many companies of hopeful seedlings and saplings were growing confidently on the fresh soil along the broken front of the avalanche. These young trees were already eight or ten feet high, and were shooting up vigorously, as if sure of eternal life, though young pines, firs, and libocedrus were running a race with them for the sunshine, with an even start. Farther down the ravine I counted five hundred and

thirty-six promising young Sequoias on a bed of rough bouldery soil not exceeding two acres in extent.

The Fresno Big Trees covered an area of about four square miles, and while wandering about, surveying the boundaries of the grove, anxious to see every tree, I came suddenly upon a handsome log cabin, richly embowered, and so fresh and unweathered it was still redolent of gum and balsam, like a newly felled tree. Strolling forward, wondering who could have built it, I found an old, weary-eyed, unspeculative, gray-haired man on a bark stool by the door, reading a book. The discovery of his hermitage by a stranger seemed to surprise him; but when I explained that I was only a tree lover sauntering along the mountains to study Sequoia, he bade me welcome, and made me bring my mule down to a little slanting meadow before his door and camp with him, promising to show me his pet trees and many curious things bearing on my studies.

After supper, as the evening shadows were falling, the good hermit sketched his life in the mines, which, in the main, was like that of most other pioneer gold hunters, — a succession of intense experiences, full of big ups and downs, like the mountain topography. Since "'49" he had wandered over most of the Sierra, sinking innumerable prospect holes like a sailor making soundings, digging new channels for streams, sifting gold-sprinkled boulder and gravel beds with unquenchable energy, — life's noon, the meanwhile, passing unnoticed into late afternoon shadows. Then, health and gold gone, the game played and lost, like a wounded deer creeping into this forest solitude, he awaits the sundown call. How sad the undertones of many a life here, now the noise of the first big gold battles has died away! How many interesting wrecks lie drifted and stranded in hidden nooks of the gold region! Perhaps no other range contains the remains of so many rare and interesting men. The name of my hermit friend is John A. Nelder, a fine, kind man, who in going into the woods has at last gone home; for he loves nature truly, and realizes that these last shadowy days, with scarce a glint of gold in them, are the best of all. Birds, squirrels, plants, get loving natural recognition, and delightful it was to see how sensitively he responded to the silent influences of the woods. His eyes brightened as he gazed on the trees that stand guard around his little home; squirrels and mountain quails came at his call to be fed; and he tenderly stroked the little snow-bent sapling Sequoias, hoping they might yet grow straight to the sky and rule the grove. One of the greatest of his trees stands a little way back of his cabin, and he proudly led me to it, bidding me admire its colossal proportions and measure it, to see if in all the forest there could be another so grand. It proved to be only twenty-six feet in diameter, and he seemed distressed to learn that the Mariposa Grizzly Giant was larger. I tried to comfort him by observing that his was the taller, finer formed, and perhaps the more favorably situated. Then he led me to some noble ruins, remnants of gigantic trunks of trees that he supposed must have been larger than any now standing; and though they had lain on the damp ground, exposed to fire and the weather for centuries, the wood was perfectly sound. Sequoia timber is not only beautiful in color, — rose-red when fresh, and as easily worked as pine, — but it is almost absolutely unperishable. Build a house of Big Tree logs on granite, and that house will last about as long as its foundation. Indeed, fire seems

to be the only agent that has any appreciable effect on it. From one of these ancient trunk remnants I cut a specimen of the wood, which neither in color, strength, nor soundness could be distinguished from specimens cut from living trees, although it had certainly lain on the damp forest floor for more than three hundred and eighty years; probably more than thrice as long. The time in this instance was determined as follows: when the tree from which the specimen was derived fell, it sunk itself into the ground, making a ditch about two hundred feet long and five or six feet deep; and in the middle of this ditch, where a part of the fallen trunk had been burned out of the way, a silver fir, four feet in diameter and three hundred and eighty years old, was growing; showing that the Sequoia trunk had lain on the ground three hundred and eighty years plus the unknown time that it lay before the part whose place had been taken by the fir was burned out of the way, and that which had elapsed ere the seed from which the monumental fir sprang fell into the prepared soil and took root. Now, because Sequoia trunks are never wholly consumed in one forest fire, and these fires recur only at considerable intervals, and because Sequoia ditches, after being cleared, are often left unplanted for centuries, it becomes evident that the trunk remnant in question may have been on the ground a thousand years or more. Similar vestiges are common, and, together with the root bowls and long straight ditches of the fallen monarchs, throw a sure light back on the postglacial history of the species, bearing on its distribution. One of the most interesting features of this grove is the apparent ease and strength and comfortable independence in which the trees occupy their place in the general forest. Seedlings, saplings, young and middle-aged trees, are grouped promisingly around the old patriarchs, betraying no sign of approach to extinction. On the contrary, all seem to be saying, "Everything is to our mind, and we mean to live forever." But, sad to tell, a lumber company was building a large mill and flume near by, assuring widespread destruction.

Day after day, from grove to grove, cañon to cañon, I made a long wavering way; terribly rough in some places for Brownie, but cheery for me, for Sequoias were seldom out of sight. We crossed the rugged, picturesque basins of Redwood Creek, the North Fork of the Kaweah, and Marble Fork, gloriously forested, and full of beautiful cascades and falls, sheer and slanting, infinitely varied with broad curly foam fleeces and strips of embroidery in which the sunbeams revel. Thence we climbed into the noble forest on the Marble and Middle Fork divide. After a general exploration of the Kaweah basin this part of the Sequoia belt seemed to me the finest, and I then named it the Giant Forest. It extends, a magnificent growth of giants, grouped in pure temple groves, ranged in colonnades along the sides of meadows, or scattered among the other trees, from the granite headlands overlooking the hot foothills and plains of the San Joaquin back to within a few miles of the old glacier fountains, at an elevation of five thousand to eight thousand four hundred feet above the sea.

When I entered this sublime wilderness the day was nearly done; the trees, with rosy glowing countenances, seemed to be hushed and thoughtful, as if waiting in conscious religious dependence on the sun, and one naturally walked softly and awestricken among them. I wandered on, meeting nobler trees where all are noble, subdued in the general calm, as if in some vast hall pervaded by the deepest sanctities and solemnities that sway human souls. At sundown the trees seemed to cease their worship and breathe free. I heard the birds going home. I too sought a home for the night on the edge of a level meadow, where there is a long open view between the evenly ranked trees standing guard along its sides. Then, after a good place was found for poor Brownie, who had had a hard, weary day, sliding and scrambling across the Marble cañon, I made my bed and supper, and lay on my back, looking up to the stars through pillared arches finer far than the pious heart of man telling its love ever reared. Then I took a walk up the meadow to see the trees in the pale light. They seemed still more marvelously massive and tall than by day, heaving their colossal heads into the depths of the sky among the stars, some of which seemed to be sparkling on their branches like flowers. I built a big fire, that vividly illumined the huge brown boles of the nearest trees, and the little plants and cones and fallen leaves at their feet; keeping up the show until I fell asleep to dream of boundless forests and trail-building for Brownie.

Joyous birds welcomed the dawn, and the squirrels, now their food cones were ripe, and had to be quickly gathered and stored for winter, began their work before sunrise. My tea-and-bread-crumb breakfast was soon done, and leaving jaded Brownie to feed and rest, I sauntered forth to my studies. In every direction Sequoia ruled the woods. Most of the other big conifers were present here and there, but not as rivals or companions. They only served to thicken and enrich the general wilderness. Trees of every age cover craggy ridges as well as the deep moraine-soiled slopes, and plant their magnificent shafts along every brookside and meadow. Bogs and meadows are rare or entirely awanting in the isolated groves north of Kings River; here there is a beautiful series of them lying on the broad top of the main dividing ridge, imbedded in the very heart of the mammoth woods, as if for ornament, their smooth plushy bosoms kept bright and fertile by streams and sunshine.

Resting awhile on one of the most beautiful of them, when the sun was high, it seemed impossible that any other forest picture in the world could rival it. There lay the grassy, flowery lawn, three fourths of a mile long, smoothly outspread, basking in mellow autumn light, colored brown and yellow and purple, streaked with lines of green along the streams, and ruffled here and there with patches of ledum and scarlet vaccinium. Around the margin there is first a fringe of azalea and willow bushes, colored orange-yellow and enlivened with vivid dashes of red cornel, as if painted. Then up spring the mighty walls of verdure, three hundred feet high, the brown fluted pillars so thick and tall and strong they seem fit to uphold the sky; the dense foliage, swelling forward in rounded bosses on the upper half, variously shaded and tinted, — that of the young trees dark green, of the old yellowish. An aged lightning-smitten patriarch, standing a little forward beyond the general line, with knotty arms outspread, was covered with gray and yellow lichens, and surrounded by a group of saplings whose slender spires seemed to lack not a single leaf or spray in their wondrous perfection.

Such was the Kaweah meadow picture that golden afternoon; and as I gazed every color seemed to deepen and glow, as if the progress of the fresh sun work were visible from hour to hour, while every tree seemed religious and conscious of the presence of God. A freeman revels in a scene like this, and time goes by unmeasured. I stood fixed in silent wonder, or sauntered about, shifting my points of view, studying the physiognomy of separate trees, and going out to the different color patches to see how they were put on and what they were made of; giving free expression to my joy, exulting in nature's wild immortal vigor and beauty, never dreaming any other human being was near. Suddenly the spell was broken by dull bumping, thudding sounds, and a man and horse came in sight at the farther end of the meadow, where they seemed sadly out of place. A good big bear or mastodon or megatherium would have been more in keeping with the old mammoth forest. Nevertheless, it is always pleasant to meet one of our own species, after solitary rambles, and I stepped out where I could be seen and shouted, when the rider reined in his galloping mustang and waited my approach. He seemed too much surprised to speak, until, laughing in his puzzled face, I said I was glad to meet a fellow mountaineer in so lonely a place. Then he abruptly asked: "What are you doing? How did you get here?" I explained that I came across the cañons from Yosemite, and was only looking at the trees. "Oh, then I know," he said, greatly to my surprise. "You must be John Muir." He was herding a band of horses that had been driven up a rough trail from the lowlands to feed on these forest meadows. A few handfuls of crumb detritus was all that was left in my bread sack, so I told him that I was nearly out of provisions, and asked whether he could spare me a little flour. "Oh yes, of course you can have anything I've got," he said. "Just take my track, and it will lead you to my camp in a big hollow log on the side of a meadow two or three miles from here. I must ride after some strayed horses, but I'll be back before night; in the meantime make yourself at home." He galloped away to the northward. I returned to my own camp, saddled Brownie, and by the middle of the afternoon discovered his noble den in a fallen Sequoia hollowed by fire, — a spacious log house of one log, carbon-lined, centuries old, yet sweet and fresh, weather-proof, earthquake-proof, likely to outlast the most durable stone castle, and commanding views of garden and grove grander far than the richest king ever enjoyed. Brownie found plenty of grass, and I found bread, which I ate, with views from the big, round, ever open door. Soon the Good Samaritan mountaineer came in, and I enjoyed a famous rest, listening to his observations on trees, animals, adventures, etc., while he was busy preparing supper. In answer to inquiries concerning the distribution of the Big Trees he gave a good deal of information of the forest we were in, with little in general. He had heard that the species extended a long way south, — he knew not how far.

In the forest between the Middle and East Fork of the Kaweah I met a grand fire; and as fire is the master scourge and controller of the distribution of trees, I stopped to watch it and learn what I could of its works and ways with the giants. It came racing up the steep chaparral-covered slopes of the East Fork cañon with passionate enthusiasm in a broad cataract of flames: now bending down low to feed on the green bushes, devouring acres of them at a breath; now towering high in the air, as if looking abroad to choose a way; then stooping to feed again, — the lurid flapping surges and the smoke and terrible rushing and roaring hiding all that is gentle and orderly in the work. But as soon as the deep forest was

reached the ungovernable flood became calm, like a torrent entering a lake; creeping and spreading beneath the trees, where the ground was level or sloped gently, slowly nibbling the cake of compressed needles and scales with flames an inch high, rising here and there to a foot or two on dry twigs and clumps of small bushes and brome grass. Only at considerable intervals were fierce bonfires lighted, where heavy branches broken off by snow had accumulated, or around some venerable giant whose head had been stricken off by lightning.

I tethered Brownie on the edge of a little meadow beside a stream, a good safe way off, and then cautiously chose a camp for myself in a big stout hollow trunk, not likely to be crushed by the fall of burning

John Muir

trees, and made a bed of ferns and boughs in it. The night, however, and the strange wild fireworks were too beautiful and exciting to allow much sleep. There was no danger of being chased and hemmed in; for in the main forest belt of the Sierra, even when swift winds are blowing, fires seldom or never sweep over the trees in broad all-embracing sheets, as they do in the dense Rocky Mountain woods and in those of the Cascade Mountains of Oregon and Washington. Here they creep from tree to tree with tranquil deliberation, allowing close observation, though caution is required, in venturing around the burning giants, to avoid falling limbs and knots and fragments from dead shattered tops. Though the day was best for study, I sauntered about night after night, learning what I could, and admiring the wonderful show vividly displayed in the lonely darkness: the ground fire advancing in long crooked lines, gently grazing and smoking on the close-pressed leaves, springing up in thousands of little jets of pure flame on dry tassels and twigs, and tall spires and flat sheets with jagged flapping edges dancing here and there on grass tufts and bushes; big bonfires blazing in perfect storms of energy, where heavy branches mixed with small ones lay smashed together in hundred-cord piles; big red arches between spreading root swells and trees growing close together; huge fire-mantled trunks on the hill slopes glowing like bars of hot iron; violet-colored fire running up the tall trees, tracing the furrows of the bark in quick-quivering rills, and lighting magnificent torches on dry shattered tops; and ever and anon, with a tremendous roar and burst of light, young trees clad in low-descending feathery branches vanishing in one flame two or three hundred feet high.

One of the most impressive and beautiful sights was made by the great fallen trunks lying on the hillsides, all red and glowing like colossal iron bars fresh from a furnace; two hundred feet long, some of them, and ten to twenty feet thick. After repeated burnings have consumed the bark and sapwood, the sound charred surface, being full of cracks and sprinkled with leaves, is quickly overspread with a pure rich furred ruby glow, almost flameless and smokeless, producing a marvelous effect in the night. Another grand and interesting sight are the fires on the tops of the largest living trees, flaming above the green branches at a height of perhaps two hundred feet, entirely cut off from the ground fires, and looking like signal beacons on watch towers. From one standpoint I sometimes saw a dozen or more, those in the distance looking like great stars above the forest roof. At first I could not imagine how these Sequoia lamps were lighted, but the very first night, strolling about, waiting and watching, I saw the thing done again and again. The thick fibrous bark of old trees is divided by deep, nearly continuous furrows, the sides of which are bearded with the bristling ends of fibres broken by the growth swelling of the trunk; and when the fire comes creeping around the foot of the tree, it runs up these bristly furrows in lovely pale blue quivering, bickering rills of flame, with a low, earnest, whispering sound, to the lightning-shattered top of the trunk, which, in the dry Indian summer, with perhaps leaves and twigs and squirrel-gnawed cone scales and seed wings lodged on it, is readily ignited. These lamp-lighting rills, the most beautiful fire streams I ever saw, last only a minute or two; but the big lamps burn with varying brightness for days and weeks, throwing off sparks like the spray of a fountain, while ever and anon a shower of red coals comes sifting down through the branches, followed at times, with startling effect, by a big burned-off chunk weighing perhaps half a ton.

The immense bonfire, where fifty or a hundred cords of peeled, split, smashed wood have been piled around some old giant by a single stroke of lightning, is another grand sight in the night. The light was so great I found I could read common print three hundred yards from them, and the illumination of the circle of on-looking trees is indescribably impressive. Other big fires, roaring and booming like waterfalls, were blazing on the upper sides of trees on hill slopes against which limbs broken off by heavy snow had rolled, while branches high overhead, tossed and shaken by the ascending air current, seemed to be writhing in pain. Perhaps the most startling phenomenon of all was the quick death of childlike Sequoias only a century or two of age. In the midst of the other comparatively slow and steady fire work, one of these tall beautiful saplings, leafy and branchy, would be seen blazing up suddenly all in one heaving, booming, passionate flame reaching from the ground to the top of the tree, and fifty to a hundred feet or more above it, with a smoke column bending forward and streaming away on the upper free-flowing wind. To burn these green trees, a strong fire of dry wood beneath them is required to send up a current of air hot enough to distill inflammable gases from the leaves and sprays; then, instead of the lower limbs gradually catching fire and igniting the next and next in succession, the whole tree seems to explode almost simultaneously, and with awful roaring and throbbing a round tapering flame shoots up two or three hundred feet, and in a second or two is quenched, leaving the green spire a black dead mast, bristled and roughened with down-curling boughs. Nearly all the trees that have been burned down are lying with their heads uphill, because they are burned far more deeply on the upper side, on account of broken limbs rolling down against them to make hot fires, while only leaves and twigs accumulate on the lower side, and are quickly consumed without injury to the tree. But green resinless Sequoia wood burns very slowly, and many successive fires are required to burn down a large tree. Fires can run only at intervals of several years, and when the ordinary amount of firewood that has rolled against the gigantic trunk is consumed, only a shallow scar is made, which is slowly deepened by recurring fires until far beyond the centre of gravity; and when at last the tree falls, it of course falls uphill. The healing folds of wood layers on some of the deeply burned trees show that centuries have elapsed since the last wounds were made.

When a great Sequoia falls, its head is smashed into fragments about as small as those made by lightning, and are mostly devoured by the first running hunting fire that finds them, while the trunk is slowly wasted away by centuries of fire and weather. One of the most interesting fire actions on the trunk is the boring of those great tunnel-like hollows through which horsemen may gallop. All of these famous hollows are burned out of the solid wood, for no Sequoia is ever hollowed by decay. When the tree falls, the brash trunk is often broken straight across into sections, as if sawed; into these joints the fire creeps, and, on account of the great size of the broken ends, burns for weeks or even months without being much influenced by the weather. After the great glowing ends fronting each other have burned so far apart that their rims cease to burn, the fire continues to work on in the centres, and the ends become deeply concave. Then, heat being radiated from side to side, the burning goes on in each section of the trunk independent of the other, until the diameter of the bore is so great that the heat radiated across from side to side is not sufficient to keep them burning. It appears, therefore, that only very large trees can receive the fire auger and have any shell rim left.

Of all the Tule basin forest the section on the North Fork seemed the finest, surpassing, I think, even the Giant Forest of the Kaweah. Southward from here, though the width and general continuity of the belt is well sustained, I thought I could detect a slight falling off in the height of the trees and in closeness of growth. All the basin was swept by swarms of hoofed locusts, the southern part over and over again, until not a leaf within reach was left on the wettest bogs, the outer edges of the thorniest chaparral beds, or even on the young conifers, which, unless under the stress of dire famine, sheep never touch. Of course Brownie suffered, though I made diligent search for grassy sheep-proof spots. When I turned him loose one evening on the side of a carex bog, he dolefully prospected the desolate neighborhood without finding anything that even a starving mule could eat. Then, utterly discouraged, he stole up behind me while I was bent over on my knees making a fire for tea, and in a pitiful mixture of bray and neigh begged for help. It was a mighty touching prayer, and I answered it as well as I could with half of what was left of a cake made from the last of the flour given me by the Indians; hastily

passing it over my shoulder, and saying: "Yes, poor fellow, I know, but soon you'll have plenty. To-morrow down we go to alfalfa and barley," — speaking to him as if he were human, as through stress of trouble plainly he was. After eating his portion of bread he seemed content, for he said no more, but patiently turned away to gnaw leafless ceanothus stubs. Such clinging, confiding dependence, after all our scrambles and adventures together, was very touching, and I felt conscience-stricken for having led him so far in so rough and desolate a country. "Man," says Lord Bacon, "is the god of the dog." So also he is of the mule and many other dependent fellow mortals.

Next morning I turned westward, determined to force a way straight to pasture, letting Sequoia wait. Fortunately, ere we had struggled down through half a mile of chaparral we heard a mill whistle, for which we gladly made a bee line. At the sawmill we both got a good meal; then, taking the dusty lumber road, pursued our way to the lowlands. The nearest good pasture, I counted, might be thirty or forty miles away. But scarcely had we gone ten when I noticed a little log cabin, a hundred yards or so back from the road, and a tall man, straight as a pine, standing in front of it, observing us as we came plodding down through the dust. Seeing no sign of grass or hay, I was going past without stopping, when he shouted, "Travelin'?" Then, drawing nearer: "Where have you come from? I didn't notice you go up." I replied I had come through the woods from the north, looking at the trees. "Oh, then you must be John Muir. Halt; you're tired; come and rest, and I'll cook for you." Then I explained that I was tracing the Sequoia belt; that on account of sheep my mule was starving, and therefore I must push on to the lowlands. "No, no," he said. "That corral over there is full of hay and grain. Turn your mule into it. I don't own it, but the fellow who does is hauling lumber, and it will be all right. He's a white man. Come and rest. How tired you must be! The Big Trees don't go much farther south, nohow. I know the country up there; have hunted all over it. Come and rest, and let your little doggone rat of a mule rest. How in heavens did you get him across the cañons? Roll him, or carry him? He's poor, but he'll get fat; and I'll give you a horse, and go with you up the mountains, and while you're looking at the trees I'll go hunting. It will be a short job, for the end of the Big Trees is not far." Of course I stopped. No true invitation is ever declined. He had been hungry and tired himself many a time in the Rocky Mountains as well as in the Sierra. Now he owned a band of cattle, and lived alone. His cabin was about eight by ten feet; the door at one end, a fireplace at the other, and a bed on one side, fastened to the logs. Leading me in without a word of mean apology, he made me lie down on the bed; then reached under it, brought forth a sack of apples, and advised me to keep "chawing" at them until he got supper ready. Finer, braver hospitality I never found in all this good world, so often called selfish.

Next day, with hearty, easy alacrity, the mountaineer procured horses, prepared and packed provisions, and got everything ready for an early start the following morning. Well mounted, we pushed rapidly up the South Fork of the river, and soon after noon were among the giants once more. On the divide between the Tule and Deer Creek a central camp was made, and the mountaineer spent his time in deer-hunting, while, with provisions for two or three days, I explored the woods, and, in accordance with what I had been told, soon reached the southern extremity of the belt on the South Fork of Deer Creek. To make sure, I searched the woods a considerable distance south of the last Deer Creek grove, passed over into the basin of the Kern, and climbed several high points commanding extensive views over the sugar-pine woods, without seeing a single Sequoia crown in all the wide expanse to the southward. On the way back to camp, however, I was greatly interested in a grove I discovered on the east side of the Kern River divide, opposite the North Fork of Deer Creek. The height of the pass where the species crossed over is about seven thousand feet, and I heard of still another grove whose waters drain into the upper Kern, opposite the Middle Fork of the Tule. It appears, therefore, that though the Sequoia belt is two hundred and sixty miles long most of the trees are on a section to the south of Kings River, only about seventy miles in length. But though the area occupied by the species increases so much to the southward, there is but little difference in the size of the trees. A diameter of twenty feet and height of two hundred and seventy-five is perhaps about the average for anything like mature and favorably situated trees. Specimens twenty-five feet in diameter are not rare, and a good many approach a height of three hundred feet. Occasionally one meets a specimen thirty feet in diameter, and rarely one that is larger. The majestic stump on Kings River is the largest I saw and measured on the entire trip. Careful search around the boundaries of the forests and groves and in the gaps of the belt failed to discover any trace of the former existence of the species beyond its present limits. On the contrary, it seems to be slightly extending its boundaries; for the outstanding stragglers, occasionally met a mile or two from the main bodies, are young instead of old monumental trees. Ancient ruins and the ditches and root bowls the big trunks make in falling were found in all the groves, but none outside of them. We may therefore conclude that the area covered by the species has not been diminished during the last eight or ten thousand years, and probably not at all in postglacial times. For admitting that upon those areas supposed to have been once covered by Sequoia every tree may have fallen, and that fire and the weather had left not a vestige of them, many of the ditches made by the fall of the ponderous trunks, weighing five hundred to nearly a thousand tons, and the bowls made by their upturned roots would remain visible for thousands of years after the last remnant of the trees had vanished. Some of these records would doubtless be effaced in a comparatively short time by the inwashing of sediments, but no inconsiderable part of them would remain enduringly engraved on flat ridge tops, almost wholly free from such action.

In the northern groves, the only ones that at first came under the observation of students, there are but few seedlings and young trees to take the places of the old ones. Therefore the species was regarded as doomed to speedy extinction, as being only an expiring remnant, vanquished in the so-called struggle for life, and shoved into its last strongholds in moist glens where conditions are exceptionally favorable. But the majestic continuous forests of the south end of the belt create a very different impression. Here, as we have seen, no tree in the forest is more enduringly established. Nevertheless, it is oftentimes vaguely said that the Sierra climate is drying out, and that this on-coming, constantly increasing drought

Sequoias

will of itself surely extinguish King Sequoia, though sections of wood rings show that there has been no appreciable change of climate during the last forty centuries. Furthermore, that Sequoia *can* grow and *is* growing on as dry ground as any of its neighbors or rivals we have seen proved over and over again. "Why, then," it will be asked, "are the Big Tree groves always found on well-watered spots?" Simply because Big Trees give rise to streams. It is a mistake to suppose that the water is the cause of the groves being there. On the contrary, the groves are the cause of the water being there. The roots of this immense tree fill the ground, forming a sponge, which hoards the bounty of the clouds, and sends it forth in clear perennial streams instead of allowing it to rush headlong in short-lived, destructive floods. Evaporation is also checked and the air kept still in the shady Sequoia depths, while thirsty robber winds are shut out.

Since, then, it appears that Sequoia can and does grow on as dry ground as its neighbors, and that the greater moisture found with it is an effect rather than a cause of its presence, the notions as to the former greater extension of the species and its near approach to extinction, based on its supposed dependence on greater moisture, are seen to be erroneous. Indeed, all my observations go to show that in case of prolonged drought the sugar pines and firs would die before Sequoia. Again, if the restricted and irregular distribution of the species be interpreted as the result of the desiccation of the range, then, instead of increasing in individuals toward the south, where the rainfall is less, it should diminish.

If, then, its peculiar distribution has not been governed by superior conditions of soil and moisture, by what has it been governed? Several years before I made this trip, I noticed that the northern groves were located on those parts of the Sierra soil belt that were first laid bare and opened to pre-emption when the ice sheet began to break up into individual glaciers. And when I was examining the basin of the San Joaquin, and trying to account for the absence of Sequoia where every condition seemed favorable for its growth, it occurred to me that this remarkable gap in the belt is located in the channel of the great ancient glacier of

the San Joaquin and Kings River basins which poured its frozen floods to the plain, fed by the snows that fell on more than fifty miles of the summit peaks of the range. Constantly brooding on the question, I next perceived that the great gap in the belt to the northward, forty miles wide, between the Stanislaus and Tuolumne groves, occurs in the channel of the great Stanislaus and Tuolumne glacier, and that the smaller gap between the Merced and Mariposa groves occurs in the channel of the smaller Merced glacier. The wider the ancient glacier, the wider the gap in the Sequoia belt, while the groves and forests attain their greatest development in the Kaweah and Tule River basins; just where, owing to topographical conditions, the region was first cleared and warmed, while protected from the main ice rivers that flowed past to right and left down the Kings and Kern valleys. In general, where the ground on the belt was first cleared of ice, there the Sequoia now is; and where, at the same elevation and time, the ancient glaciers lingered, there the Sequoia is not. What the other conditions may have been which enabled the Sequoia to establish itself upon these oldest and warmest parts of the main soil belt I cannot say. I might venture to state, however, that since the Sequoia forests present a more and more ancient and long-established aspect to the southward, the species was probably distributed from the south toward the close of the glacial period, before the arrival of other trees. About this branch of the question, however, there is at present much fog, but the general relationship I have pointed out between the distribution of the Big Tree and the ancient glacier system is clear. And when we bear in mind that all the existing forests of the Sierra are growing on comparatively fresh moraine soil, and that the range itself has been recently sculptured and brought to light from beneath the ice mantle of the glacial winter, then many lawless mysteries vanish, and harmonies take their places.

But notwithstanding all the observed phenomena bearing on the postglacial history of this colossal tree point to the conclusion that it never was more widely distributed on the Sierra since the close of the glacial epoch; that its present forests are scarcely past prime, if indeed they have reached prime; that the postglacial day of the species is probably not half done; yet when, from a wider outlook, the vast antiquity of the genus is considered, and its ancient richness in species and individuals, — comparing our Sierra giant and Sequoia sempervirens of the coast, the only other living species, with the many fossil species already discovered, and described by Heer and Lesquereux, some of which flourished over large areas around the Arctic Circle, and in Europe and our own territories, during tertiary and cretaceous times, — then indeed it becomes plain that our two surviving species, restricted to narrow belts within the limits of California, are mere remnants of a genus both as to species and individuals, and that they probably are verging to extinction. But the verge of a period beginning in cretaceous times may have a breadth of tens of thousands of years, not to mention the possible existence of conditions calculated to multiply and reëxtend both species and individuals. No unfavorable change of climate, so far as I can see, no disease, but only fire and the axe and the ravages of flocks and herds threaten the existence of these noblest of God's trees. In nature's keeping they are safe, but through man's agency destruction is making rapid progress, while in the work

of protection only a beginning has been made. The Mariposa Grove belongs to and is guarded by the state; the General Grant and Sequoia National Parks, established ten years ago, and efficiently guarded by a troop of cavalry under the direction of the Secretary of the Interior; so also are the small Tuolumne and Merced groves, which are included in the Yosemite National Park; while a few scattered patches and fringes, scarce at all protected, though belonging to the national government, are in the Sierra Forest Reservation.

Perhaps more than half of all the Big Trees have been sold, and are now in the hands of speculators and millmen. Even the beautiful little Calaveras Grove of ninety trees, and so historically interesting from its being the first discovered, is now owned, together with the much larger South or Stanislaus Grove, by a lumber company.

Far the largest and most important section of protected Big Trees is in the grand Sequoia National Park, now easily accessible by stage from Visalia. It contains seven townships, and extends across the whole breadth of the magnificent Kaweah basin. But, large as it is, it should be made much larger. Its natural eastern boundary is the high Sierra, and the northern and southern boundaries the Kings and Kern rivers; thus including the sublime scenery on the head waters of these rivers, and perhaps nine tenths of all the Big Trees in existence. Private claims cut and blotch both of the Sequoia parks as well as all the best of the forests, every one of which the government should gradually extinguish by purchase, as it readily may, for none of these holdings is of much value to the owners. Thus, as far as possible, the grand blunder of selling would be corrected. The value of these forests in storing and dispensing the bounty of the mountain clouds is infinitely greater than lumber or sheep. To the dwellers of the plain, dependent on irrigation, the Big Tree, leaving all its higher uses out of the count, is a tree of life, a never failing spring, sending living water to the lowlands all through the hot, rainless summer. For every grove cut down a stream is dried up. Therefore all California is crying, "Save the trees of the fountains!" Nor, judging by the signs of the times, is it likely that the cry will cease until the salvation of all that is left of *Sequoia gigantea* is sure.

57. The Emigrant Train

BY ROBERT LOUIS STEVENSON

EDITOR'S NOTE: In the fall of 1879 Robert Louis Stevenson (1850-1894) journeyed from Europe to California in order to join the American woman he was soon to marry, Fanny Osbourne. His health was very poor (he was tubercular) and he was low in pocket but in spirit he was as undaunted as ever. He described his transcontinental journey in *Across the Plains,* from which I have taken the following passages.

ALL this while I had been travelling by mixed trains, where I might meet with Dutch widows and little German gentry fresh from table. I had been but a latent emigrant; now I was to be branded once more, and put apart with my fellows. It was about two in the afternoon of Friday that I found myself in front of the Emigrant House, with more than a hundred others, to be sorted and boxed for the journey. A white-haired official, with a stick under one arm, and a list in the other hand, stood apart in front of us, and called name after name in the tone of a command. At each name you would see a family gather up its brats and bundles and run for the hindmost of the three cars that stood awaiting us, and I soon concluded that this was to be set apart for the women and children. The second or central car, it turned out, was devoted to men travelling alone, and the third to the Chinese. The official was easily moved to anger at the least delay; but the emigrants were both quick at answering their names, and speedy in getting themselves and their effects on board.

The families once housed, we men carried the second car without ceremony by simultaneous assault. I suppose the reader has some notion of an American railroad-car, that long, narrow wooden box, like a flat-roofed Noah's ark, with a stove and a convenience, one at either end, a passage down the middle, and transverse benches upon either hand. Those destined for emigrants on the Union Pacific are only remarkable for their extreme plainness, nothing but wood entering in any part into their constitution, and for the usual inefficacy of the lamps, which often went out and shed but a dying glimmer even while they burned. The benches are too short for anything but a young child. Where there is scarce elbow-room for two to sit, there will not be space enough for one to lie. Hence the company, or rather, as it appears from certain bills about the Transfer Station, the company's servants, have conceived a plan for the better accommodation of travellers. They prevail on every two to chum together. To each of the chums they sell a board and three square cushions stuffed with straw, and covered with thin cotton. The benches can be made to face each other in pairs, for the backs are reversible. On the approach of night the boards are laid from bench to bench, making a couch wide enough for two, and long enough for a man of the middle height; and the chums lie down side by side upon the cushions with the head to the conductor's van and the feet to the engine. When the train is full, of course this plan is impossible, for there must not be more than one to every bench, neither can it be carried out unless the chums agree. It was to bring about this last condition that our white-haired official now bestirred himself. He made a most active master of ceremonies, introducing likely couples, and even guaranteeing the amiability and honesty of each. The greater the number of happy couples the better for his pocket, for it was he who sold the raw material of the beds. His price for one board and three straw cushions began with two dollars and a half; but before the train left, and, I am sorry to say, long after I had purchased mine, it had fallen to one dollar and a half.

The match-maker had a difficulty with me; perhaps, like some ladies, I showed myself too eager for union at any price; but certainly the first who was picked out to be my bedfellow, declined the honour without thanks. He was an old, heavy, slow-spoken man, I think from Yankeeland, looked me all over with great timidity, and then began to excuse himself in broken phrases. He didn't know the young man, he said. The young man might be very honest, but how was he to know that? There was another young man whom he had met already in the train; he guessed *he* was honest, and would prefer to chum with *him* upon the whole. All this without any sort of excuse, as though I had been inanimate or absent. I began to tremble lest everyone should refuse my company, and I be left rejected. But the next in turn was a tall, strapping, long-limbed, small-headed, curly-haired Pennsylvania Dutchman, with a soldierly smartness in his manner. To be exact, he had acquired it in the navy. But that was all one; he had at least been trained to desperate resolves, so he accepted the match, and the white-haired swindler pronounced the connubial benediction, and pocketed his fees.

The rest of the afternoon was spent in making up the train. I am afraid to say how many baggage-waggons followed the engine, certainly a score; then came the Chinese, then we, then the families, and the rear was brought up by the conductor in what, if I have it rightly, is called his caboose. The class to which I belonged was of course far the largest, and we ran over, so to speak, to both sides; so that there were some Caucasians among the Chinamen, and some bachelors among the families. But our own car was pure from admixture, save for one little boy of eight or nine, who had the whooping-cough. At last, about six, the long train crawled out of the Transfer Station and across the wide Missouri river to Omaha, westward bound.

It was a troubled uncomfortable evening

in the cars. There was thunder in the air, which helped to keep us restless. A man played many airs upon the cornet, and none of them were much attended to, until he came to "Home, sweet home." It was truly strange to note how the talk ceased at that, and the faces began to lengthen. I have no idea whether musically this air is to be considered good or bad; but it belongs to that class of art which may be best described as a brutal assault upon the feelings. Pathos must be relieved by dignity of treatment. If you wallow naked in the pathetic, like the author of "Home, sweet home," you make your hearers weep in an unmanly fashion; and even while yet they are moved, they despise themselves and hate the occasion of their weakness. It did not come to tears that night, for the experiment was interrupted. An elderly, hard-looking man, with a goatee beard and about as much appearance of sentiment as you would expect from a retired slaver, turned with a start and bade the performer stop that "damned thing." "I've heard about enough of that," he added; "give us something about the good country we're going to." A murmur of adhesion ran round the car; the performer took the instrument from his lips, laughed and nodded, and then struck into a dancing measure; and, like a new Timotheus, stilled immediately the emotion he had raised.

The day faded; the lamps were lit; a party of wild young men, who got off next evening at North Platte, stood together on the stern platform, singing "The Sweet By-and-bye" with very tuneful voices; the chums began to put up their beds; and it seemed as if the business of the day were at an end. But it was not so; for, the train stopping at some station, the cars were instantly thronged with the natives, wives and fathers, young men and maidens, some of them in little more than nightgear, some with stable lanterns, and all offering beds for sale. Their charge began with twenty-five cents a cushion, but fell, before the train went on again, to fifteen, with the bed-board gratis, or less than one fifth of what I had paid for mine at the Transfer. This is my contribution to the economy of future emigrants.

A great personage on an American train is the newsboy. He sells books (such books!), papers, fruit, lollipops, and cigars; and on emigrant journeys, soap, towels, tin washing dishes, tin coffee pitchers, coffee, tea, sugar, and tinned eatables, mostly hash or beans and bacon. Early next morning the newsboy went around the cars, and chumming on a more extended principle became the order of the hour. It requires but a copartnery of two to manage beds; but washing and eating can be carried on most economically by a syndicate of three. I myself entered a little after sunrise into articles of agreement, and became one of the firm of Pennsylvania, Shakespeare, and Dubuque. Shakespeare was my own nickname on the cars; Pennsylvania that of my bedfellow; and Dubuque, the name of a place in the State of Iowa, that of an amiable young fellow going west to cure an asthma, and retarding his recovery by incessantly chewing or smoking, and sometimes chewing and smoking together. I have never seen tobacco so sillily abused. Shakespeare bought a tin washing-dish, Dubuque a towel, and Pennsylvania a brick of soap. The partners used these instruments, one after another, according to the order of their first awaking; and when the firm had finished there was no want of borrowers. Each filled the tin dish at the water filter opposite the stove, and retired with the whole stock in trade to the platform of the car. There he knelt down, supporting himself by a shoulder against the woodwork or one elbow crooked about the railing, and made a shift to wash his face and neck and hands; a cold, an insufficient, and, if the train is moving rapidly, a somewhat dangerous toilet.

On a similar division of expense, the firm of Pennsylvania, Shakespeare, and Dubuque supplied themselves with coffee, sugar, and necessary vessels; and their operations are a type of what went on through all the cars. Before the sun was up the stove would be brightly burning; at the first station the natives would come on board with milk and eggs and coffee cakes; and soon from end to end the car would be filled with little parties breakfasting upon the bedboards. It was the pleasantest hour of the day.

There were meals to be had, however, by the wayside: a breakfast in the morning, a dinner somewhere between eleven and two, and supper from five to eight or nine at night. We had rarely less than twenty minutes for each; and if we had not spent many another twenty minutes waiting for some express upon a side track among miles of desert, we might have taken an hour to each repast and arrived at San Francisco up to time. For haste is not the foible of an emigrant train. It gets through on sufferance, running the gauntlet among its more considerable brethren; should there be a block, it is unhesitatingly sacrificed; and they cannot, in consequence, predict the length of the passage within a day or so. Civility is the main comfort that you miss. Equality, though conceived very largely in America, does not extend so low down as to an emigrant. Thus in all other trains, a warning cry of "All aboard!" recalls the passengers to take their seats; but as soon as I was alone with emigrants, and from the Transfer all the way to San Francisco, I found this ceremony was pretermitted; the train stole from the station without note of warning, and you had to keep an eye upon it even while you ate. The annoyance is considerable, and the disrespect both wanton and petty.

Many conductors, again, will hold no communication with an emigrant. I asked a conductor one day at what time the train would stop for dinner; as he made no answer I repeated the question, with a like result; a third time I returned to the charge, and then Jack-in-office looked me coolly in the face for several seconds and turned ostentatiously away. I believe he was half ashamed of his brutality; for when another person made the same inquiry, although he still refused the information, he condescended to answer, and even to justify his reticence in a voice loud enough for me to hear. It was, he said, his principle not to tell people where they were to dine; for one answer led to many other questions, as what o'clock it was? or, how soon should we be there? and he could not afford to be eternally worried.

As you are thus cut off from the superior authorities, a great deal of your comfort depends on the character of the newsboy. He has it in his power indefinitely to better and brighten the emigrant's lot. The newsboy with whom we started from the Transfer was a dark, bullying, contemptuous, insolent scoundrel, who treated us like dogs. Indeed, in his case, matters came nearly to a fight. It happened thus: he was going his rounds through the cars with some commodities for sale, and coming to a party who were at *Seven-up* or *Cascino* (our two games), upon a bed-board, slung down a cigar-box in the middle of the cards, knocking one man's hand to the floor. It was the last straw. In a moment the whole party were upon their feet, the cigars were upset, and he was ordered to "get out of that directly, or he would get more than he reckoned for." The fellow grumbled and muttered, but ended by making off, and was less openly insulting in the future. On the other hand, the lad who rode with us in this capacity from Ogden to Sacramento made himself the friend of all, and helped us with information, attention, assistance, and a kind countenance. He told us where and when we should have our meals, and how long the train would stop; kept seats at table for those who were delayed, and watched that we should neither be left behind nor yet unnecessarily hurried. You, who live at home at ease, can hardly realise the greatness of this service, even had it stood alone. When I think of that lad coming and going, train after train, with his bright face and civil words, I see how easily a good man may become the benefactor of his kind. Perhaps he is discontented with himself, perhaps troubled with ambitions; why, if he but knew it, he is a hero of the old Greek stamp; and while he thinks he is only earning a profit of a few cents, and that perhaps exorbitant, he is doing a man's work, and bettering the world.

I must tell here an experience of mine with another newsboy. I tell it because it gives so good an example of that uncivil kindness of the American, which is perhaps their most bewildering character to one newly landed. It was immediately after I had left the emigrant train; and I am told I looked like a man at death's door, so much had this long journey shaken me. I sat at the end of a car, and the catch being broken, and myself feverish and sick, I had to hold the door open with my foot for the sake of air. In this attitude my leg debarred the newsboy from his box of merchandise. I made haste to let him pass when I observed that he was coming; but I was busy with a book, and so once or twice he came upon me unawares. On these occasions he most rudely struck my foot aside; and though I myself apologised, as if to show him the way, he answered me never a word. I chafed furiously, and I fear the next time it would have come to words. But suddenly I felt a touch upon my shoulder, and a large juicy pear was put into my hand. It was the newsboy, who had observed that I was looking ill and so made me this present out of a tender heart. For the rest of the journey I was petted like a sick child; he lent me newspapers, thus depriving himself of his legitimate profit on their sale, and came repeatedly to sit by me and cheer me up.

THE PLAINS OF NEBRASKA

It had thundered on the Friday night, but the sun rose on Saturday without a cloud. We were at sea—there is no other adequate expression—on the plains of Nebraska. I made my observatory on the top of a fruit-waggon, and sat by the hour upon that perch to spy about me, and to spy in vain for something new. It was a world almost without a feature; an empty sky, an empty earth; front and back, the line of railway stretched from horizon to horizon, like a cue across a billiard-board; on either hand, the green plain ran till it touched the skirts of heaven. Along the track innumerable wild sunflowers, no bigger than a crown-piece, bloomed in a continuous flower-bed; grazing beasts were seen upon the prairie at all degrees of distance and diminution; and, now and again we might perceive a few dots beside the railroad which grew more and more distinct as we drew nearer till they turned into wooden cabins, and then dwindled and dwindled in our wake until they melted into their surroundings, and we were once more alone upon the billiard-board. The train toiled over this infinity like a snail; and being the one thing moving, it was wonderful what huge proportions it began to assume in our regard. It seemed miles in length, and either end of it within but a step of the horizon. Even my own body or my own head seemed a great thing in that emptiness. I note the feeling the more readily as it is the contrary of what I have read of in the experience of others. Day and night, above the roar of the train, our ears were kept busy with the incessant chirp of grasshoppers— a noise like the winding up of countless clocks and watches, which began after a while to seem proper to that land.

To one hurrying through by steam there was a certain exhilaration in this spacious vacancy, this greatness of the air, this discovery of the whole arch of heaven, this straight, unbroken, prison-line of the horizon. Yet one could not but reflect upon the weariness of those who passed by there in old days, at the foot's pace of oxen, painfully urging their teams, and with no landmark but that unattainable evening sun for which they steered, and which daily fled them by an equal stride. They had nothing, it would seem, to overtake; nothing by which to reckon their advance; no sight for repose or for encouragement; but stage after stage, only the dead green waste under foot, and the mocking, fugitive horizon. But the eye, as I have been told, found differences even here; and at the worst the emigrant came, by perseverance, to the end of his toil. It is the settlers, after all, at whom we have a right to marvel. Our consciousness, by which we live, is itself but

the creature of variety. Upon what food does it subsist in such a land? What livelihood can repay a human creature for a life spent in this huge sameness? He is cut off from books, from news, from company, from all that can relieve existence but the prosecution of his affairs. A sky full of stars is the most varied spectacle that he can hope. He may walk five miles and see nothing; ten, and it is as though he had not moved; twenty, and still he is in the midst of the same great level, and has approached no nearer to the one object within view, the flat horizon which keeps pace with his advance. We are full at home of the question of agreeable wall-papers, and wise people are of opinion that the temper may be quieted by sedative surroundings. But what is to be said of the Nebraskan settler? His is a wall-paper with a vengeance—one quarter of the universe laid bare in all its gauntness. His eye must embrace at every glance the whole seeming concave of the visible world; it quails before so vast an outlook, it is tortured by distance; yet there is no rest or shelter, till the man runs into his cabin, and can repose his sight upon things near at hand. Hence, I am told, a sickness of the vision peculiar to these empty plains.

Yet perhaps with sunflowers and cicadæ, summer and winter, cattle, wife and family, the settler may create a full and various existence. One person at least I saw upon the plains who seemed in every way superior to her lot. This was a woman who boarded us at a way station, selling milk. She was largely formed; her features were more than comely; she had that great rarity —a fine complexion which became her; and her eyes were kind, dark, and steady. She sold milk with patriarchal grace. There was not a line in her countenance, not a note in her soft and sleepy voice, but spoke of an entire contentment with her life. It would have been fatuous arrogance to pity such a woman. Yet the place where she lived was to me almost ghastly. Less than a dozen wooden houses, all of a shape and all nearly of a size, stood planted along the railway lines. Each stood apart in its own lot. Each opened direct off the billiard-board, as if it were a billiard-board indeed, and these only models that had been set down upon it ready made. Her own, into which I looked, was clean but very empty, and showed nothing homelike but the burning fire. This extreme newness, above all in so naked and flat a country, gives a strong impression of artificiality. With none of the litter and discolouration of human life; with the paths unworn, and the houses still sweating from the axe, such a settlement as this seems purely scenic. The mind is loth to accept it for a piece of reality; and it seems incredible that life can go on with so few properties, or the great child, man, find entertainment in so bare a playroom.

And truly it is as yet an incomplete society in some points; or at least it contained, as I passed through, one person incompletely civilised. At North Platte, where we supped that evening, one man asked another to pass the milk-jug. This other was well-dressed and of what we should call a respectable appearance; a darkish man, high spoken, eating as though he had some usage of society; but he turned upon the first speaker with extraordinary vehemence of tone———

"There's a waiter here!" he cried.

"I only asked you to pass the milk," explained the first.

Here is the retort verbatim———

"Pass! Hell! I'm not paid for that business; the waiter's paid for it. You should use civility at table, and, by God, I'll show you how!"

The other man very wisely made no answer, and the bully went on with his supper as though nothing had occurred. It pleases me to think that some day soon he will meet with one of his own kidney; and that perhaps both may fall.

THE DESERT OF WYOMING

To cross such a plain is to grow homesick for the mountains. I longed for the Black Hills of Wyoming, which I knew we were soon to enter, like an ice-bound whaler for the spring. Alas! and it was a worse country than the other. All Sunday and Monday we travelled through these sad mountains, or over the main ridge of the Rockies, which is a fair match to them for misery of aspect. Hour after hour it was the same unhomely and unkindly world about our onward path; tumbled boulders, cliffs that drearily imitate the shape of monuments and fortifications—how drearily, how tamely, none can tell who has not seen them; not a tree, not a patch of sward, not one shapely or commanding mountain form; sage-brush, eternal sage-brush; over all, the same weariful and gloomy colouring, grays warming into brown, grays darkening towards black; and for sole sign of life, here and there a few fleeing antelopes; here and there, but at incredible intervals, a creek running in a cañon. The plains have a grandeur of their own; but here there is nothing but a contorted smallness. Except for the air, which was light and stimulating, there was not one good circumstance in that God-forsaken land.

I had been suffering in my health a good deal all the way; and at last, whether I was exhausted by my complaint or poisoned in some wayside eating-house, the evening we left Laramie, I fell sick outright. That was a night which I shall not readily forget. The lamps did not go out; each made a faint shining in its own neighborhood, and the shadows were confounded together in the long, hollow box of the car. The sleepers lay in uneasy attitudes; here two chums alongside, flat upon their backs like dead folk; there a man sprawling on the floor, with his face upon his arm; there another half seated with his head and shoulders on the bench. The most passive were continually and roughly shaken by the movement of the train; others stirred, turned, or stretched out their arms like children; it was surprising how many groaned and murmured in their sleep; and as I passed to and fro, stepping across the prostrate, and caught now a snore, now a gasp, now a half-formed word, it gave me a measure of the worthlessness of rest in that unresting vehicle. Although it was chill, I was obliged to open my window, for the degradation of the air soon became intolerable to one who was awake and using the full supply of life. Outside, in a glimmering night, I saw the black, amorphous hills shoot by unweariedly into our wake. They that long for morning have never longed for it more earnestly than I.

And yet when day came, it was to shine upon the same broken and unsightly quarter of the world. Mile upon mile, and not a tree, a bird, or a river. Only down the long, sterile cañons, the train shot hooting and awoke the resting echo. That train was the one piece of life in all the deadly land; it was the one actor, the one spectacle fit to be observed in this paralysis of man and nature. And when I think how the railroad has been pushed through this unwatered wilderness and haunt of savage tribes, and now will bear an emigrant for some £12 from the Atlantic to the Golden Gates; how

at each stage of the construction, roaring, impromptu cities, full of gold and lust and death, sprang up and then died away again, and are now but wayside stations in the desert; how in these uncouth places pig-tailed Chinese pirates worked side by side with border ruffians and broken men from Europe, talking together in a mixed dialect, mostly oaths, gambling, drinking, quarrelling and murdering like wolves; how the plumed hereditary lord of all America heard, in this last fastness, the scream of the "bad medicine waggon" charioting his foes; and then when I go on to remember that all this epical turmoil was conducted by gentlemen in frock coats, and with a view to nothing more extraordinary than a fortune and a subsequent visit to Paris, it seems to me, I own, as if this railway were the one typical achievement of the age in which we live, as if it brought together into one plot all the ends of the world and all the degrees of social rank, and offered to some great writer the busiest, the most extended, and the most varied subject for an enduring literary work. If it be romance, if it be contrast, if it be heroism that we require, what was Troy town to this? But, alas! it is not these things that are necessary —it is only Homer.

Here also we are grateful to the train, as to some god who conducts us swiftly through these shades and by so many hidden perils. Thirst, hunger, the sleight and ferocity of Indians are all no more feared, so lightly do we skim these horrible lands; as the gull, who wings safely through the hurricane and past the shark. Yet we should not be forgetful of these hardships of the past; and to keep the balance true, since I have complained of the trifling discomforts of my journey, perhaps more than was enough, let me add an original document. It was

not written by Homer, but by a boy of
eleven, long since dead, and is dated only
twenty years ago. I shall punctuate, to make
things clearer, but not change the spelling.

"*My dear sister Mary,—I am afraid you
will go nearly crazy when you read my letter. If Jerry*" (the writer's eldest brother)
"*has not written to you before now, you
will be surprised to heare that we are in
California, and that poor Thomas*" (another
brother, of fifteen) "*is dead. We started
from ——— in July, with plenty of provisions and too yoke oxen. We went along
very well till we got within six or seven
hundred miles of California, when the Indians attacked us. We found places where
they had killed the emigrants. We had one
passenger with us, too guns, and one revolver; so we ran all the lead We had into
bullets (and) hung the guns up in the wagon
so that we could get at them in a minit. It
was about two o'clock in the afternoon;
droave the cattel a little way; when a prairie
chicken alited a little way from the wagon.*

"*Jerry took out one of the guns to shoot
it, and told Tom to drive the oxen. Tom
and I drove the oxen, and Jerry and the
passenger went on. Then, after a little, I
left Tom and caught up with Jerry and the
other man. Jerry stopped for Tom to come
up; me and the man went on and sit down
by a little stream. In a few minutes, we
heard some noise; then three shots (they
all struck poor Tom, I suppose); then they
gave the war hoop, and as many as twenty
of the red skins came down upon us. The
three that shot Tom was hid by the side
of the road in the bushes.*

"*I thought the Tom and Jerry were shot;
so I told the other man that Tom and Jerry
were dead, and that we had better try to
escape, if possible. I had no shoes on; having*

a sore foot, I thought I would not put them
on. The man and me run down the road,
but We was soon stopt by an Indian on a
pony. We then turend the other way, and
run up the side of the Mountain, and hid
behind some cedar trees, and stayed there
till dark. The Indians hunted all over after
us, and verry close to us, so close that we
could here there tomyhawks Jingle. At dark
the man and me started on, I stubing my
toes against sticks and stones. We traveld
on all night; and next morning, Just as it
was getting gray, we saw something in the
shape of a man. It layed Down in the grass.
We went up to it, and it was Jerry. He
thought we ware Indians. You can imagine
how glad he was to see me. He thought we
was all dead but him, and we thought him
and Tom was dead. He had the gun that
he took out of the wagon to shoot the prairie
Chicken; all he had was the load that was
in it.*

"*We traveld on till about eight o'clock,
We caught up with one wagon with too
men with it. We had traveld with them before one day; we stopt and they Drove on;
we knew that they was ahead of us, unless
they had been killed to. My feet was so sore
when we caught up with them that I had
to ride; I could not step. We traveld on
for too days, when the men that owned the
cattle said they would (could) not drive
them another inch. We unyoked the oxen;
we had about seventy pounds of flour; we
took it out and divided it into four packs.
Each of the men took about 18 pounds
apiece and a blanket. I carried a little bacon,
dried meat, and little quilt; I had in all
about twelve pounds. We had one pint of
flour a day for our alloyance. Sometimes
we made soup of it; sometimes we (made)
pancakes; and sometimes mixed it up with
cold water and eat it that way. We traveld*

twelve or fourteen days. The time came at last when we should have to reach some place or starve. We saw fresh horse and cattle tracks. The morning come, we scraped all the flour out of the sack, mixed it up, and baked it into bread, and made some soup, and eat everything we had. We traveld on all day without anything to eat, and that evening we Caught up with a sheep train of eight wagons. We traveld with them till we arrived at the settlements; and know I am safe in California, and got to good home, and going to school.

"Jerry is working in ——— *. It is a good country. You can get from 50 to 60 and 75 Dollars for cooking. Tell me all about the affairs in the States, and how all the folks get along."*

And so ends this artless narrative. The little man was at school again, God bless him, while his brother lay scalped upon the deserts.

58. The Yellowstone

BY RUDYARD KIPLING

EDITOR'S NOTE: Between 1887 and 1889 Rudyard Kipling (1865-1936) traveled through India, China, Japan and the United States. Later he lived for a few years in the United States. The essay which follows is from *American Notes* (1891).

ONCE upon a time there was a carter who brought his team and a friend into the Yellowstone Park without due thought. Presently they came upon a few of the natural beauties of the place, and that carter turned his team into his friend's team, howling:—

"Get out o' this, Jim. All hell's alight under our noses!"

And they called the place Hell's Half-Acre to this day to witness if the carter lied.

We, too, the old lady from Chicago, her husband, Tom, and the good little mares, came to Hell's Half-Acre, which is about sixty acres in extent, and when Tom said:—

"Would you like to drive over it?"

We said:—

"Certainly not, and if you do we shall report you to the park authorities."

There was a plain, blistered, peeled, and abominable, and it was given over to the sportings and spoutings of devils who threw mud, and steam, and dirt at each other with whoops, and halloos, and bellowing curses.

The places smelled of the refuse of the pit, and that odor mixed with the clean, wholesome aroma of the pines in our nostrils throughout the day.

This Yellowstone Park is laid out like Ollendorf, in exercises of progressive difficulty. Hell's Half-Acre was a prelude to ten or twelve miles of geyser formation.

We passed hot streams boiling in the forest; saw whiffs of steam beyond these, and yet other whiffs breaking through the misty green hills in the far distance; we trampled on sulphur in crystals, and sniffed things much worse than any sulphur which is known to the upper world; and so journeying, bewildered with the novelty, came upon a really park-like place where Tom suggested we should get out and play with the geysers on foot.

Imagine mighty green fields splattered with limebeds, all the flowers of the summer growing up to the very edge of the lime. That was our first glimpse of the geyser basins.

The buggy had pulled up close to a rough, broken, blistered cone of spelter stuff between ten and twenty feet high. There was trouble in that place—moaning, splashing, gurgling, and the clank of machinery. A spurt of boiling water jumped into the air, and a wash of water followed.

I removed swiftly. The old lady from Chicago shrieked. "What a wicked waste!" said her husband.

I think they call it the Riverside Geyser. Its spout was torn and ragged like the mouth of a gun when a shell has burst there. It grumbled madly for a moment or two, and then was still. I crept over the steaming lime—it was the burning marl on which Satan lay—and looked fearfully down its mouth. You should never look a gift geyser in the mouth.

I beheld a horrible, slippery, slimy funnel with water rising and falling ten feet at a time. Then the water rose to lip level with a rush, and an infernal bubbling troubled this Devil's Bethesda before the sullen heave of the crest of a wave lapped over the edge and made me run.

Mark the nature of the human soul! I had begun with awe, not to say terror, for this was my first experience of such things. I stepped back from the banks of the Riverside Geyser, saying:—

"Pooh! Is that all it can do?"

Yet for aught I knew, the whole thing might have blown up at a minute's notice,

she, he, or it being an arrangement of uncertain temper.

We drifted on, up that miraculous valley. On either side of us were hills from a thousand or fifteen hundred feet high, wooded from crest to heel. As far as the eye could range forward were columns of steam in the air, misshapen lumps of lime, mist-like preadamite monsters, still pools of turquoise-blue stretches of blue corn-flowers, a river that coiled on itself twenty times, pointed bowlders of strange colors, and ridges of glaring, staring white.

A moon-faced trooper of German extraction — never was park so carefully patrolled — came up to inform us that as yet we had not seen any of the real geysers; that they were all a mile or so up the valley, and tastefully scattered round the hotel in which we would rest for the night.

America is a free country, but the citizens look down on the soldier. I had to entertain that trooper. The old lady from Chicago would have none of him; so we loafed alone together, now across half-rotten pine logs sunk in swampy ground, anon over the ringing geyser formation, then pounding through river-sand or brushing knee-deep through long grass.

"And why did you enlist?" said I.

The moon-faced one's face began to work. I thought he would have a fit, but he told me a story instead — such a nice tale of a naughty little girl who wrote pretty love letters to two men at once. She was a simple village wife, but a wicked "family novelette" countess couldn't have accomplished her ends better. She drove one man nearly wild with the pretty little treachery, and the other man abandoned her and came West to forget the trickery.

Moon-face was that man.

We rounded and limped over a low spur

of hill, and came out upon a field of aching, snowy lime rolled in sheets, twisted into knots, riven with rents, and diamonds, and stars, stretching for more than half a mile in every direction.

On this place of despair lay most of the big, bad geysers who know when there is trouble in Krakatoa, who tell the pines when there is a cyclone on the Atlantic seaboard, and who are exhibited to visitors under pretty and fanciful names.

The first mound that I encountered belonged to a goblin who was splashing in his tub.

I heard him kick, pull a shower-bath on his shoulders, gasp, crack his joints, and rub himself down with a towel; then he let the water out of the bath, as a thoughtful man should, and it all sunk down out of sight till another goblin arrived.

So we looked and we wondered at the Beehive, whose mouth is built up exactly like a hive, at the Turban (which is not in the least like a turban), and at many, many other geysers, hot holes, and springs. Some of them rumbled, some hissed, some went off spasmodically, and others lay dead still in sheets of sapphire and beryl.

Would you believe that even these terrible creatures have to be guarded by the troopers to prevent the irreverent Americans from chipping the cones to pieces, or, worse still, making the geyser sick? If you take a small barrel full of soft-soap and drop it down a geyser's mouth, that geyser will presently be forced to lay all before you, and for days afterward will be of an irritated and inconstant stomach.

When they told me the tale I was filled with sympathy. Now I wish that I had soft-soap and tried the experiment on some lonely little beast far away in the woods. It sounds so probable and so human.

Yet he would be a bold man who would administer emetics to the Giantess. She is flat-lipped, having no mouth; she looks like a pool, fifty feet long and thirty wide, and there is no ornamentation about her. At irregular intervals she speaks and sends up a volume of water over two hundred feet high to begin with, then she is angry for a day and a half — sometimes for two days.

Owing to her peculiarity of going mad in the night, not many people have seen the Giantess at her finest; but the clamor of her unrest, men say, shakes the wooden hotel, and echoes like thunder among the hills.

The congregation returned to the hotel to put down their impressions in diaries and note-books, which they wrote up ostentatiously in the verandas. It was a sweltering hot day, albeit we stood somewhat higher than the level of Simla, and I left that raw pine creaking caravansary for the cool shade of a clump of pines between whose trunks glimmered tents.

A batch of United States troopers came down the road and flung themselves across the country into their rough lines. The Melican cavalryman can ride, though he keeps his accoutrements pig-fashion and his horse cow-fashion.

I was free of that camp in five minutes — free to play with the heavy, lumpy carbines, have the saddles stripped, and punch the horses knowingly in the ribs. One of the men had been in the fight with "Wrap-up-his-Tail," and he told me how that great chief, his horse's tail tied up in red calico, swaggered in front of the United States cavalry, challenging all to single combat. But he was slain, and a few of his tribe with him.

"There's no use in an Indian, anyway," concluded my friend.

A couple of cow-boys — real cow-boys — jingled through the camp amid a shower of mild chaff. They were on their way to Cook City, I fancy, and I know that they never washed. But they were picturesque ruffians exceedingly, with long spurs, hooded stirrups, slouch hats, fur weather-cloth over their knees, and pistol-butts just easy to hand.

"The cow-boy's goin' under before long," said my friend. "Soon as the country's settled up he'll have to go. But he's mighty useful now. What would we do without the cow-boy?"

"As how?" said I, and the camp laughed.

"He has the money. We have the skill. He comes in winter to play poker at the military posts. We play poker — a few. When he's lost his money we make him drunk and let him go. Sometimes we get the wrong man."

And he told me a tale of an innocent cow-boy who turned up, cleaned out, at an army post, and played poker for thirty-six hours. But it was the post that was cleaned out when that long-haired Caucasian removed himself, heavy with everybody's pay and declining the proffered liquor.

"Noaw," said the historian, "I don't play with no cow-boy unless he's a little bit drunk first."

Ere I departed I gathered from more than one man the significant fact that up to one hundred yards he felt absolutely secure behind his revolver.

"In England, I understand," quoth the limber youth from the South, — "in England a man is n't allowed to play with no fire-arms. He's got to be taught all that when he enlists. I did n't want much teaching how to shoot straight 'fore I served Uncle Sam. And that's just where it is. But you was talking about your Horse Guards now?"

I explained briefly some peculiarities of equipment connected with our crackest crack cavalry. I grieve to say the camp roared.

"Take 'em over swampy ground. Let 'em run around a bit an' work the starch out of 'em, an' then, Almighty, if we would n't plug 'em at ease I'd eat their horses."

There was a maiden — a very little maiden — who had just stepped out of one of James's novels. She owned a delightful mother and an equally delightful father — a heavy-eyed, slow-voiced man of finance. The parents thought that their daughter wanted change.

She lived in New Hampshire. Accordingly, she had dragged them up to Alaska and to the Yosemite Valley, and was now returning leisurely, via the Yellowstone, just in time for the tail-end of the summer season at Saratoga.

We had met once or twice before in the park, and I had been amazed and amused at her critical commendation of the wonders that she saw. From that very resolute little mouth I received a lecture on American literature, the nature and inwardness of Washington society, the precise value of Cable's works as compared with Uncle Remus Harris, and a few other things that had nothing whatever to do with geysers, but were altogether pleasant.

Now, an English maiden who had stumbled on a dust-grimed, lime-washed, sun-peeled, collarless wanderer come from and going to goodness knows where, would, her mother inciting her and her father brandishing his umbrella, have regarded him as a dissolute adventurer — a person to be disregarded.

Not so those delightful people from New Hampshire. They were good enough to treat him — it sounds almost incredible — as a human being, possibly respectable, probably not in immediate need of financial assistance.

Papa talked pleasantly and to the point. The little maiden strove valiantly with the accent of her birth and that of her rearing, and mamma smiled benignly in the background.

Balance this with a story of a young English idiot I met mooning about inside his high collar, attended by a valet. He condescended to tell me that "you can't be too careful who you talk to in these parts." And stalked on, fearing, I suppose, every minute for his social chastity.

That man was a barbarian (I took occasion to tell him so), for he comported himself after the manner of the headhunters and hunted of Assam who are at perpetual feud one with another.

You will understand that these foolish stories are introduced in order to cover the fact that this pen cannot describe the glories of the Upper Geyser Basin. The evening I spent under the lee of the Castle Geyser, sitting on a log with some troopers and watching a baronial keep forty feet high spouting hot water. If the Castle went off first, they said the Giantess would be quiet, and *vice versâ,* and then they told tales till the moon got up and a party of campers in the woods gave us all something to eat.

Then came soft, turfy forest that deadened the wheels, and two troopers on detachment duty stole noiselessly behind us. One was the Wrap-up-his-Tail man, and they talked merrily while the half-broken horses bucked about among the trees. And so a cavalry escort was with us for a mile, till we got to a mighty hill all strewn with moss agates, and everybody had to jump out and pant in that thin air. But how intoxicating it was! The old lady from Chicago ducked like an emancipated hen as she scuttled about the road, cramming pieces of rock into her reticule. She sent me fifty yards down to the hill-side to pick up a piece of broken bottle which she insisted was moss agate.

"I've some o' that at home, an' they shine. Yes, you go get it, young man."

As we climbed the long path the road grew viler and viler till it became, without disguise, the bed of a torrent; and just when things were at their rockiest we nearly fell into a little sapphire lake — but never sapphire was so blue — called Mary's Lake; and that between eight and nine thousand feet above the sea.

Afterward, grass downs, all on a vehement slope, so that the buggy, following the new-made road, ran on the two off-wheels mostly till we dipped head-first into a ford, climbed up a cliff, raced along down, dipped again, and pulled up dishevelled at "Larry's" for lunch and an hour's rest.

Then we lay on the grass and laughed with sheer bliss of being alive. This have I known once in Japan, once on the banks of the Columbia, what time the salmon came in and California howled, and once again in the Yellowstone by the light of the eyes of the maiden from New Hampshire. Four little pools lay at my elbow, one was of black water (tepid), one clear water (cold), one clear water (hot), one red water (boiling). My newly washed handkerchief covered them all, and we two marvelled as children marvel.

"This evening we shall do the Grand Canyon of the Yellowstone," said the maiden.

"Together?" said I; and she said, "Yes."

The sun was beginning to sink when we heard the roar of falling waters and came to a broad river along whose banks we ran.

And then — I might at a pinch describe the infernal regions, but not the other place. The Yellowstone River has occasion to run through a gorge about eight miles long. To get to the bottom of the gorge it makes two leaps, one of about one hundred and twenty and the other of three hundred feet. I investigated the upper or lesser fall, which is close to the hotel.

Up to that time nothing particular happens to the Yellowstone — its banks being only rocky, rather steep, and plentifully adorned with pines.

At the falls it comes round a corner, green, solid, ribbed with a little foam, and not more than thirty yards wide. Then it goes over, still green, and rather more solid than before. After a minute or two, you, sitting upon a rock directly above the drop, begin to understand that something has occurred; that the river has jumped between solid cliff walls, and that the gentle froth of water lapping the sides of the gorge below is really the outcome of great waves.

And the river yells aloud; but the cliffs do not allow the yells to escape.

That inspection began with curiosity and finished in terror, for it seemed that the whole world was sliding in chrysolite from under my feet. I followed with the others round the corner to arrive at the brink of the canyon. We had to climb up a nearly perpendicular ascent to begin with, for the ground rises more than the river drops. Stately pine woods fringe either lip of the gorge, which is the gorge of the Yellowstone. You'll find all about it in the guide books.

All that I can say is that without warning or preparation I looked into a gulf seventeen hundred feet deep, with eagles and fish-hawks circling far below. And the sides of that gulf were one wild welter of color — crimson, emerald, cobalt, ochre, amber, honey splashed with port wine, snow white, vermilion, lemon, and silver gray in wide washes. The sides did not fall sheer, but were graven by time, and water, and air into monstrous heads of kings, dead chiefs — men and women of the old time. So far below that no sound of its strife could reach us, the Yellowstone River ran a finger-wide strip of jade green.

The sunlight took those wondrous walls and gave fresh hues to those that nature had already laid there.

Evening crept through the pines that shadowed us, but the full glory of the day flamed in that canyon as we went out very cautiously to a jutting piece of rock — blood-red or pink it was — that overhung the deepest deeps of all.

Now I know what it is to sit enthroned amid the clouds of sunset as the spirits sit in Blake's pictures. Giddiness took away all sensation of touch or form, but the sense of blinding color remained.

When I reached the mainland again I had sworn that I had been floating.

The maid from New Hampshire said no word for a very long time. Then she quoted poetry, which was perhaps the best thing she could have done.

"And to think that this show-place has been going on all these days an' none of we ever saw it," said the old lady from Chicago, with an acid glance at her husband.

"No, only the Injians," said he, unmoved; and the maiden and I laughed.

Inspiration is fleeting, beauty is vain, and the power of the mind for wonder limited. Though the shining hosts themselves had risen choiring from the bottom of the gorge, they would not have prevented her papa and one baser than he from rolling stones down those stupendous rainbow-washed slides. Seventeen hundred feet of steepest pitch and rather more than seventeen hundred colors for log or bowlder to whirl through!

So we heaved things and saw them gather way and bound from white rock to red or yellow, dragging behind them torrents of color, till the noise of their descent ceased and they bounded a hundred yards clear at the last into the Yellowstone.

"I've been down there," said Tom, that evening. "It's easy to get down if you're careful — just sit an' slide; but getting up is worse. An' I found down below there two stones just marked with a picture of the canyon. I would n't sell these rocks not for fifteen dollars."

And papa and I crawled down to the Yellowstone — just above the first little fall — to wet a line for good luck. The round moon came up and turned the cliffs and pines into silver; and a two-pound trout came up also, and we slew him among the rocks, nearly tumbling into that wild river.

* * * * *

Then out and away to Livingstone once more. The maiden from New Hampshire disappeared, papa and mamma with her. Disappeared, too, the old lady from Chicago, and the others.

59. The Round-Up

BY EMERSON HOUGH

EDITOR'S NOTE: Emerson Hough (1857-1923) was the author of several best-selling novels, among them *The Covered Wagon,* which was made into a motion picture in the twenties. He was on intimate terms with many cowboys and with the various aspects of their life. A friend of Pat Garrett, the sheriff who killed Billy the Kid, he accompanied Garrett on a long horseback trip in New Mexico while gathering material for his *The Story of the Outlaw* — this not long before Garrett was killed. Hough's account of the roundup is the best I have ever seen. It is taken from his *The Story of the Cowboy.*

SINCE the beginning of mankind's struggle with Nature the harvest season has been a time of victory and rejoicing. At that time man unbends his back and gives thanks for the reaping. Then come the days of final activity, of supreme exertion, the climax of all that has a material, an allegorical, or spectacular interest in the yearly war for existence. The round-up is the harvest of the range. Therefore it is natural that its customs should offer more of interest than those of any other part of the year. It were matter of course, also, that features so singular and stirring in their intense action as those of the cowman's harvest should be known and blazoned about for the knowledge of those living elsewhere than upon the cattle fields. Writers and artists have seized upon this phase of the cattle man's life, and given it so wide a showing that the public might well have at least a general idea of the subject. Yet perhaps this general idea would be a more partial and less ac-

"Cutting Out"

curate notion than is deserved by the complicated and varied business system of the cattle harvest. If we would have a just idea of the life and character of the man who makes the round-up, we should approach the subject rather with a wish to find its fundamental principles than a desire to see its superficial pictures.

The system of the round-up, while it retains the same general features over the whole of the cow country, and has done so for years, is none the less subject to considerable local modifications, and it has in many respects changed with the years as other customs of the industry have changed; for not even the ancient and enduring calling of the cowman could be free from the law of progress. The Western traveller who first saw a round-up twenty years ago would not be in position to describe one of to-day. Sectional differences make still other changes which should be regarded. Yet all these round-ups, of the past and of the present, of the North and of the South, ground themselves upon a common principle— namely, upon that desire for absolute jus-

tice which has been earlier mentioned as a distinguishing trait of the cowman and the trade he follows.

Reverting, as we must continually do, to the early times of the cattle industry, we shall find ourselves back in the days of water fronts in the dry Southwest. Here the round-up depended upon local conditions, just as it has ever since. If the *ranchero* had practically all the water near him, he had also practically all the cattle, and the harvest of the calves was merely a large going forth on his part and marking his own increase without being troubled with that of others. This feature would be apt to continue more in a wide and sparsely pastured country than in one where the cattle of many owners were mingled together on the range. Again, if we follow up the history of the range until we come upon the time of large individual holdings of land under fence, we must see how similar was the round-up then to that of the dry country; for here man had done what Nature had done in the other case, and had separated the owner's cattle from those of his neighbours. It remained, therefore, much a matter of an individual and not a community harvest; whereas the community harvest is the one which the average man has in mind when speaking of a round-up. The free-grass round-up is the one where the ingenuity, the energy, and the resources of the cowman are best to be seen, his way of carrying out his fundamental purpose of justice to all men on the vast, unfenced, and undefined farm of the range, where the thousands of cattle, belonging to dozens of owners, each animal wild as a deer and half as fleet, are all gathered, counted, separated, and identified with a system and an accuracy little short of the marvellous. Until one has seen such a round-up on the open plains he has neither seen the cowboy at his best nor seen the fruition of the system that he represents.

The time of the calf round-up is in the spring, after the grass has become good and after the calves have grown large enough for the branding, this time being later in the North than in the South by perhaps thirty days. Naturally, upon a country where the open range is common property there can not be a round-up for each man who owns cattle running at large. Naturally, also, there must be more than one round-up to gather all the cattle over the vast extent of a cattle region. Here the system of the cowman is at once in evidence. The State cattle association divides the entire State range into a number of round-up districts—let us say into a dozen or two dozen districts. Each district conducts its own round-up, this under the working supervision of some experienced man who goes by the name of the round-up captain or round-up boss, and who is elected by vote of the cowmen of his district. Under this general officer are all the bosses in charge of the different ranch outfits sent by men having cattle in the round-up. In the very outset of the levy for these troops of the range the idea of justice is apparent. Not all men own equal numbers of the cattle, so it would be obviously unfair to ask all to furnish an equal amount of the expense and labour in the total of the round-up duties. The small outfits send a few men, the large ones more, the aim being that of fairness to all and hardship to none. The whole force of a small modern round-up may not exceed thirty men. In one of the large Southern round-ups there once met at the Double Forks of the Brazos nearly three hundred men. All these men met at one ranch, and it is proof of the largeness of the cattle life

and its methods that they were all well fed and entertained by the owner of the ranch. Nowadays perhaps a ranch of ordinary size will send two messes of men of half a dozen or more men each as its *pro rata* in the round-up, each mess with its own cook, and perhaps with two wagons to each mess to carry along the tents and supplies. In the old days no tents were taken, and the life was rougher than it is now, but of late years the cowboy has grown sybaritic. With each ranch outfit there must of course be the proper horse herd, "cavoy," or "cavvieyah." Each man will have eight or ten horses for his own use, for he has now before him the hardest riding of the year. All these horses, some of them a bit gay and frisky in the air of spring, are driven along with the ranch outfit as its own horse herd, the total usually split into two herds, each under the charge of one or more herders, known as "horse wranglers"—an expression confined to the Northern ranges, and bearing a certain collegiate waggishness of flavour, though the origin of the term is now untraceable. There are, of course, night wranglers and day wranglers, it being the duty of these men to see to it that the horse herd is kept together and at hand when wanted for the work.

Sometime toward the middle of May, let us say, all these different outfits leave their home ranches and head for the rendezvous of the round-up. The opening date of the round-up is known, and the different outfits, big and little, move in so as to be on hand a few days before the beginning of the work. It may be imagined what a scene must be this general gathering of the cow clans, how picturesque this assemblage of hardy, rugged men fresh from their wild life and ready for the still wilder scenes of activity which are before them!

There may be fifty men, perhaps five hundred horses at the main camp, and of the total there is not one animal which does not boil over with the energy of full-blooded life. The men rejoice as those should rejoice who go forth to the harvest, the horses exult because spring has come, with its mysterious stirring airs. The preliminary days are passed in romp and frolic, perhaps at cards and games. Each man, however, has his own work outlined, and makes his preparations for it. His personal outfit is overhauled and put in repair. His rope has a touch to "limber it up," his straps are softened, his clothing put in order. If he has a wild horse in his string, he takes the opportunity of giving it a few lessons of the sort which make up the cow pony's education. Swiftly the grand camp of the round-up settles into the system of veterans, and all is rapidly made ready for the exacting duties which are to follow.

The total country to be covered by the round-up is perhaps a strip forty by one hundred miles in extent. The direction in which the round-up will work will depend

Branding a Calf

upon the habits and the ranging of the cattle at that time, there being no hard and fast rules possible. Local conditions determine also the location of the several round-up camps, which of course must be where grass and water are abundant and where there is room to handle the herds. At times there may perhaps be five thousand or more head of cattle in one body, though the numbers are more likely to run not over fifteen hundred or two thousand at a time. The tendency nowadays is all in favour of smaller round-ups, other herds being gathered after the first is worked, and the size of each assembling depending of course upon local circumstances. It may be better to drive in all the cattle from a large strip of country to a good working ground, or it may be more convenient to make several herds and frequent changes of camp.

The round-up captain knows the men who are to work under him, and from among these he appoints lieutenants who shall have each a certain band of men under him while covering the country. Advice is given to each party as to what direction it shall take after the start is made, all these arrangements being made so as not to give special inconvenience to the men of the respective ranch outfits, who will naturally wish to camp with their own mess wagon. On the day before the start the little army of the plains has its campaign all planned and lying out before it, and each man knows about what he is to do. On the night before the opening day the cowpuncher, if he be wise, goes to bed early and gets a full night's sleep, for not another will he have now for many a night to come. The flickerings of the cooks' fires, confined in their trenches so that they may not spread and so that their heat may be well utilized, rise and fall, casting great shadows upon the tent walls where the cowboys unroll their blankets and prepare for rest. The wind sighs and sings in the way the wind has upon the plains. The far-off neigh of a restless pony, the stamp of a horse picketed near by, the shrilling yell of the coyote, and all those further vague and nameless noises which pass in the air at night over the wild range come to the cowboy as unneeded and un-noted lullaby. His sleep is deep and untroubled, and to him it seems scarce begun when it is suddenly ended amid the chorus of calls, groans, and shoutings of his companions answering at the gray of dawn the call of the uneasy round-up boss, who sings out his long cry of "Roll out! roll out!" followed by the shrill call of the cook, "Grub pi-i-i-le!" The cook has been up for an hour, and has made his fire perhaps of cottonwood limbs, perhaps of the *bois des vaches* —natural fuel, of the buffalo on the cattle range. This early morning summons the cowpuncher dare not disobey, for the etiquette of the round-up is strict enough in its way. It is but dim daylight at best when the camp has kicked off its blankets and risen up shoutingly. In a few moments it has broken into a scene of wild but methodical activity. In much less than an hour after the first call for boots and saddles the whole strange cavalcade is under way, and behind it the cooks are breaking camp and pitching the plunder into the wagons for the move.

Through the wet grass at break of dawn come the rush and pounding of many hoofs, and ahead of the swinging ropes of the wranglers gallops the horse herd as it is brought in for the morning saddling. To receive it a hasty corral is made, after the rude but efficient ways of the range. This corral is but a single rope stretched about the sides of an irregular parrallelogram, or rather it is made of several single ropes united end to end. Sometimes the corral runs out from the wheels of two wagons, the ropes being supported at their outer ends by two men, who swing out and act as living gateposts, leaving open a gap into which the horses are driven. The latter will not attempt to break over this single strand, though they might well do so had they not learned the lesson of not running against rope. Sometimes this strange corral is made by stringing the rope from the saddle horns of several of the laziest and solemnest of the old saddle horses, which thus serve as the fence posts, this way being more common at midday or out in the open country, where a short pause is made by the outfit. Sometimes a wagon wheel, a horse, and a man or two may all be doing duty as posts for the corral, it being the peculiarity of the cowman to use what means are best and nearest to his hand in all his operations. The handling of the horse herd offers some of the most picturesque features of the round-up, and the first morning of the round-up is apt to furnish some thrilling bits of action at the horse corrals when the men are roping their mounts, pulling them unwilling forth and cinching the great saddles firmly upon their bulging and protesting sides. In the early times the cow horse was a wilder animal that he is to-day, but in these degenerate days a wild horse is not thought desirable, and indeed many or most of the cow horses are not roped at all for their saddling. The cowboy simply goes into the corral, picks out his horse, and throws his bridle over its neck with a most civilized disregard for the spectacular.

After the handling of the horse herd and the saddling up, the little army swiftly gets into motion and wings out widely over the plains, the men sometimes shouting and running their horses in prodigal waste of energy, for all is exuberance and abounding vigour on these opening days in spring. Each little party spreads out under its commander until each man becomes a commander for himself, imposing upon himself the duty of driving before him to the agreed meeting place ahead all the cattle that may come in his line of march. As the cowpuncher thus rides out into his great gray harvest field he sees no great wealth of horned herds about him or before him. It is a big country, and the many thousands of cattle make but a small showing upon it. Did they seem numerous as in an Eastern pasture, the range must surely be a depastured and impoverished one. Here and there, scattered about, out beyond where the horse herds have been feeding, there may be a few little groups of cattle. Out farther, upon some hogback or along the side of some *coulee,* a horned head is lifted high, gazing in astonishment at this strange invasion of the range. The animal may be a grade longhorn, though now the old Texas stock has practically vanished from the range. The shorthorn is valued, the white-faced Hereford still more popular, since it is hardy and quick to mature. All these, one by one, by twos and threes, and finally in fifties and hundreds, the keen-eyed and hard-riding cowpuncher starts out and away from their feeding ground and drives on ahead of him toward the meeting place. The string of other animals running ahead, perhaps half a mile to one side, where some other cowpuncher is driving, is sure to be noted by the cattle near to him. He gives a shout and starts toward them, and, true to their gregarious habits, they start on the run for their companions on ahead, this being just what it is wished they should do. This herding habit of the range cattle is

the basis of many of the operations of handling them. Thus each little *coulee* and draw, each ridge and little flat is swept of its inhabitants, which all go on forward toward where the long lines of dust are beginning to converge and mingle. As a matter of course, all the cattle, big and little, cows, calves, and steers, are included in the assembling, and are driven in together. The driving is not the work of a novice, but yet is not so difficult, for most of the cattle are so wild that they run at the sight of a horseman, more especially if they be of the old longhorn breed, and all the cowboy needs to do is to ride hard to one side and so direct their flight. Other cattle join those running, so that the whole horned populace goes in and along, but a small per cent being missed in the round-up, though of course it is not possible to gather up every individual that may be ranging wild and unobserved in the vast expanses of the open plains.

Thus, later in the day, the gatherings of the individuals and of the separate parties meet in a vast, commingling multitude of cattle. The place is in some valley or upon some plain offering room for handling the herd. Clouds of dust arise. The sun shines hot. Above the immediate shuffle and clacking of the nearby cattle comes a confused and tremendous tumult, the lowing of cows, the bawling of calves, the rumbling bellows of other animals protesting at this unusual situation. The whirling flight of the cowboys on their many different quests, the neighing of horses, the shouts of command or of exultation—all these wild sounds beat upon the air in a medley apparently arising out of bedlam, and all these sights arise from what seems to the unskilled observer a hopeless and irremediable disorder. Yet as matter of fact each rider of all this

Cowboys of Colorado

little army knows exactly what he is about. Each is working for a definite and common purpose, and the whole is progressing under a system of singular perfection. This confusion is that of chaos falling into order. The guiding and controlling mind of man will subject all this mighty disorder to his own ends. These great horned creatures, outnumbering a hundred to one their human guards, are helpless to escape from the living cordon of fearless horse and daring rider. Out of the dust and heat and turmoil one gathers a single definite thought, evolves a single character. The yearly climax of his calling has brought into vivid view the cowboy in that position which shows himself and his profession in their most unique and striking form.

Perhaps a couple of thousand of cattle are gathered in this herd here upon a little flat valley a mile or so across. On the other side of the valley are lines of willows and low trees, and on beyond, in the direction of the sun, runs the shining thread of a river. Toward the shelter of the trees the thin blue smoke of the camp fires is arising. Possibly some of the cowpunchers run over to the camp to snatch a bite to eat, for the work of the cutting out has not yet begun. The milling of the cattle has thrown them into confusion, and the calves are separated from their mothers, so that a little time must be allowed. A calf does not always know its own mother, but no mother mistakes her own offspring. This is the second basis of the cunning handling of the wild herds.

The cowman has the cattle of the range all together now, and knows they will tend to hang together for a time and not separate. He knows also that the calves will run with their mothers, so that the brand of the mother will prove the ownership of the calf. Presently the intense, trying work of the cutting out will begin, in which all these calves will be sorted out and labelled in the great joint inventory of the range.

At this stage of the round-up operations there again comes into play the question of local conditions. It is all a matter of locality what shall be the description of the cattle to be separated, and this again is a matter which has been subject to change of custom in the trade. If this round-up be, for instance, in one of the thickly settled districts of Montana, no attention is paid to any but the calves and unbranded cattle. There is no attempt to sort or separate the different herds of branded cattle belonging to different owners, or to drive back a given owner's cattle toward his range. All the cows and calves are cut out from the general herd, and are held in a separate body, the rest of the entire herd being allowed to scatter and depart at will over the common range. The calves are then taken indiscriminately from this cow herd and branded duly according to their mothers' brands.

On yet other portions of the range the ranchmen may not be so numerous or the ranges may be larger. Perhaps there are a few owners whose interests are practically the same, by reason of the ranging habits of their cattle. They know that their cattle are not apt to go off a certain range, and therefore they do not trouble themselves to keep track of them. But they would not like these cattle to wander, say, one hundred miles from home. If in a round-up there should be found cattle, say, of five or six different

brands, all pretty well within the country where they belonged, no effort would be made to separate these. But if on the same country there should be found a number of cattle of some outfit, known to be perhaps a hundred miles from the range where they belonged, it would be part of the duty of the round-up to cut out these cattle and "throw them over" to the proper range. In all things the common sense of the cowman governs. Thus it may happen that the entire herd of a certain outfit is thus cut out and thrown over without a single calf being branded, because the cowman knows it would not be good for these calves to be driven perhaps fifty miles or so immediately after the branding and other operations of the round-up. All the time there are numbers of these round-ups and subround-ups going on, as the necessities of the situation demand. Sometimes the big corrals of a convenient ranch are used. It is a singular fact that corral work was once more common, for instance, in certain parts of Wyoming that it is to-day. It was known that organized bands of cattle thieves, characterized by the cowmen as "some boys who were a little on the rustle," had a habit of using these corrals at night to hold together the bunches of calves they were running out of the country, the rustlers being shrewd enough to know that they could in no better way render tractable a bunch of calves than by keeping them a few nights away from their mothers, who would surely run them off during the night if all were left out in the open together. It thus seeming that the ranch corrals were being used in the robbery of the men who built them, the latter tore them down and after that relied upon the open round-up. The latter form of the round-up work is, of course, the more interesting, and we shall suppose that the herd is made out on the open range and held together simply by the force of horsemanship.

It having been agreed, then, what sort of cattle are to be cut out, the work of separation begins, perhaps two or three different "cuts" being in progress at the same time, each of these "cuts" being held at a distance from the main herd. As it is difficult to overcome the disposition of an animal to break back and join its fellows in the main herd when it is singled out and driven, it is customary to start the "cut" with some sober-minded old cattle which are willing to stand where they are placed, and so serve as a nucleus for the growing band, the cowboy here again calling to his aid the habit of gregariousness among the cattle.

The calf branding is the chief work of the round-up, and it would be difficult to find work more exacting and exhausting. The cowpuncher prepares for this deliberately. When he goes into the herd to cut out calves he mounts a fresh horse, and every few hours he again changes horses, for, though some horses are better than others in cutting out, there is no horse which can long endure the fatigue of the rapid and intense work of cutting. Before the rider stretches a sea of interwoven horns, waving and whirling as the densely packed ranks of cattle close in or sway apart. It is no prospect for a weakling, but into it goes the cowpuncher on his determined little horse, heeding not the plunging and crushing and thrusting of the excited cattle. Down under the heels of the herd, half hid in the whirl of dust, he spies a little curly calf running, dodging, and twisting, always at the heels of its mother. The cowpuncher darts in and after, following the two through the thick of surging and plunging beasts. The sharp-eyed pony sees almost as soon as his rider which cow is wanted, and he needs small

guidance from that time on. He follows hard at her heels, edging her constantly toward the flank of the herd, at times nipping her hide as a reminder of his own superiority. In spite of herself the cow gradually turns out toward the edge, and at last is rushed clear of the crush, the calf following close behind her. Very often two cowpunchers work together in the operation of cutting out, this facilitating matters somewhat.

Already preparations have been made for the animals cut out. The branding men have fire and fuel, and irons are heated to a cherry red. All the irons of the outfits represented are on hand at the fire, a great many of them, and easily to be confused withal. A "tally man," to keep record of the calves branded to each outfit, has been appointed by the captain to serve as general clerk of the round-up. This man, of course, has opportunity to favour one outfit or another by falsifying his scores, but this contingency is never considered in the rude ethics of the range, where civilized suspicion, known as conservatism, has not yet fully entered. The tally man is usually chosen for his fitness to keep these accounts, or perhaps for his unfitness to do other work at the time. Perhaps there is some oldish cowman, or some one who has been sick, or who has been hurt in the riding of the previous day, and who, though not fit for the saddle, will do for the book. This man acts as the agent of all the outfits, and upon his count depends each owner's estimate of his season's profits.

As the cowpuncher rushes his first cow and calf clear of the herd, the tally man stands near the fire, sharpening his pencil with a knife disproportionately large. Even as he looks over toward the herd there is a swirl of the long loop which has hung just clear of the ground as the cowpuncher rode out into the open after his quarry. The loop spreads and hisses out into a circle as it flickers and curves about the cowpuncher's head, and then it darts out and down like the stoop of a hawk. The unfortunate calf is laid by the heels. The pony stops and squats, flaring back upon its haunches, its mane falling forward over its gleaming eyes, its sides heaving, its quarters already gray with the dust of the herd. There is a twist of the rope about the horn of the saddle, and all is over with the wild life of the curly, bawling calf. It is flipped lightly upon its side, and away it goes, skating along over the sagebrush, regardless of cuts or bruises, up to the fire where the irons glow and where the tally man now has his pencil sharpened. Two men seize it as it comes into their field of operations. One catches it by the ears and twists its head sideways, sitting down upon it so that the little creature can not move. Another man casts free the rope and lays hold of its hind legs, pushing one far forward with his own foot, and pulling the other back at full length with both his brawny hands. Helpless, the calf lies still, panting. A man approaches with a glowing iron fresh from the fire, and claps this, hissing and seething, upon the shrinking hide. A malodorous cloud of smoke arises from the burning hair. The iron cuts quite through the hair and full into the hide, so that the mark shall never grow over again with hair. A piteous bawl arises from the little animal—a protest half drowned by the rush of mingled sounds about. Meantime a third man trims out with a sharp knife the required slice, if any, which is to be taken from the ear or dewlap to complete the registered mark of the owner. In a moment the calf is released and shoved to one side to rejoin its mother, who mutters at its injuries, and licks it soothingly. The

calf stands with legs spread wide apart, sick and dizzy, indisposed to move, and shorn for many days of much of its friskiness. Mother and calf alike are hustled out of the way. The tally man calls out, "Bar Y, one calf." Another calf is by this time coming skating up to the fire, and again the iron is hissing. Meantime the hubbub and the turmoil increase, until all seems again lost to chaos. Taut ropes cross the ground in many directions. The cutting ponies pant and sweat, rear and plunge. The garb of the cowpuncher now is one of white alkali, which hangs gray in his eyebrows and mustache. Steers bellow and run to and fro. Cows charge on their persecutors, amid confusion and great laughings. Fleet yearlings and young cows break away and run for the open, pursued by cowboys who care not how or where they ride. The dust and the lowings and bellowings and runnings wax until all seems hopeless. Yet all the time the irons are busy, all the time the calves are sliding up to the fire, all the time the voice of the tally man is chanting, and all the time the lines of figures are growing longer on his grimy pages. The herd lessens. The number of calves visible among the cattle becomes small. Finally the last calf is cut out and branded. The cowpunchers pull up their heaving ponies. The branding men wipe their faces. The tally man again sharpens his pencil. The herd is "worked." It may scatter now as it wills. This field has been reaped. It remains now to go on to other fields.

At the close of the day's work the men have less disposition to romp and play pranks than they had at the start of the morning. They are weary, but weary with that fatigue readily shaken off by a man in fine health and good condition. The cooks and teamsters have prepared the camp, and the professional duties of the cowpuncher close when he takes off his saddle. Until bedtime, which comes soon after the evening meal, he may lounge and smoke. The cook has prepared abundance of food for these hard-working men, whose constant exercise in the fresh air gives them good appetites. In the *menu* of the round-up fresh beef is sure to figure, and beef of the best sort running in the herd. It makes no difference whose brand is on the animal desired for the mess; if wanted, it is forthwith roped, thrown, and butchered. In the old days no account was kept of the round-up beef, but of later days the owner of an animal killed for beef is usually credited with it on the round-up books. Sometimes, when time and opportunity offer, the cowpuncher has for his dinner a dish probably unknown elsewhere than on the range, and not common there. A choice bit of "porterhouse" steak, cut thick, is placed between two steaks of similar size and excellence, and the whole buried under a bed of hot coals. In this way the middle steak retains all the juices of its double envelope, and offers a morsel which might well be appreciated by a man less hungry or more particular than the tired cowpuncher. A pound or so of beef, with some tinned vegetables, taken with a quart or so of coffee, and the cowpuncher is ready to hunt his blankets and make ready for another day. He does not work on the eight hours a day schedule, but works during the hours when it is light enough to see. The end of the day may find him some miles from where the cook's fires are gleaming, and the swift chill of the night of the plains may have fallen before his jogging pony, which trots now with head and ears down, brings him up to the camp which for him, as much as any place on earth, is home.

Such is something of the routine of the round-up, and one day, barring the weather conditions, is like another throughout the long and burning summer, one round-up following another closely all through the season. The work is a trifle monotonous to the cowboy, perhaps, in spite of its exciting features, and is to-day more monotonous than it was in the past, before the good old days had left the plains forever. In those times the country was wilder, and there was more of novelty and interest in the operations of the range. To-day the great plains are but a vast pasture ground for the cattle belonging to the community of cowmen, and the highly differentiated system of the round-up progresses as a purely business operation, whose essential object is the establishment of the individual rights of each member of that community. The methods of the round-up seem of necessity rude and inaccurate, but really they are singularly efficient and precise. The skilled labour of the cowpuncher gives to each man that which belongs to him, and nothing more.

It is a curious review, that which passes under the eyes of the tally men and branders during the calf harvesting. Sometimes a calf comes up with a cow whose hide is a network of confused and conflicting brands, so that it is impossible to tell justly whose property she is. In such a case the calf is not branded at all to any owner, but is thrown into the association credit, where it belongs equally to all, and where its value will be equally divided. Sometimes in the hurry of the work a calf is branded with the wrong iron, and is thus given the sign of a man to whom it does not belong. This would seem to be a puzzling proposition to the cowpuncher, for the brand is something which, to use the cowpuncher's phrase, does not "come out in the washin'." Yet the remedy is very simple. Another calf is "traded back" for the calf wrongly branded, the proper brand of the former calf being placed upon the "traded" calf. Of course, this leaves two mismatched calves on the range, whose brands do not tally with those of their mothers, but within the year time will have equalized the error, for the calves will have left their mothers, and the one will probably be worth about as much as the other.

Mingled with such questions as these during the branding operations are always the complex ones of strays and Mavericks. Sometimes a stray cow is found during the round-up bearing the brand of a man foreign to that round-up district, or one not represented in the round-up. The increase of this animal is branded with the brand of its owner, who has been no party to the transaction at all, but who has been safe under the system of the round-up. In the case of Mavericks found during the round-up, a like intelligent and just method obtains. Roughly speaking, an animal must be a yearling to be a Maverick, and on some ranges this rule is laid down, though really a Maverick becomes such at the time when it ceases to follow the cow and begins to shift for itself. If it is missed in the first round-up of its life, it falls under the rules or laws governing the handling of Mavericks, such rules offering considerable local variations. On some ranges of Wyoming, for instance, the cowmen have agreed lines establishing the borders of their respective ranges, and a cowman may brand for his own a calf running on his range and not following any cow. This right is merely one of comity among the local ranchers, and one which it is not expected will be abused. Indeed, the comity goes still further, showing yet more clearly the interdependence

and mutual confidence of the cowmen. If after the round-up a rancher finds a neighbour's calf unbranded, but following the cow upon his own range, he brands the calf with the owner's proper brand, and not with his own. This is simply a matter of individual honesty. The cowman knows that his neighbour will do as much for him. Each ranch keeps its own separate tally-book in this way, and these are exchanged at the end of the season, so that each man gets what belongs to him, no matter where it may have wandered, and no matter whether he ever sees it again or not. It has been elsewhere mentioned that on some parts of the range all the Mavericks are sold at auction before the beginning of the round-up (always to some resident cowman who is known to be responsible). In this case, when a Maverick is found in the round-up it is dragged to the fire—perhaps by two ropes, for it is big and lusty—and has put upon it the "vent brand" of the association, thus securing an abstract of title which it is to carry with it through life, and which will hold good in any cattle market of the land.

It may readily be seen how honest and how expert must be the men who carry out so intricate a system. It should be borne in mind that brands do not show so distinctly upon hide as they do upon paper, and, of course, it must be remembered that a range cow may carry more than one brand, and perhaps a "vent brand" or so, if she has changed ownership before. Here again there may be exceptions arising out of local conditions. For instance, if a herd of cattle is brought from a far Southern range to one in the North, where that brand is not met and is not recorded, it is not always the case that the owner will have these animals counterbranded; for it is known that no confusion will arise if they are left as they are, and, of course, the fewer brands an animal carries the easier it is to tell whose it is. It is justice, and justice by the shortest and most practical route, which is the desire of the cowman, whether that imply the branding of a Maverick or the hanging of a cattle thief.

After the calf round-up comes the beef round-up, and this, too, may be called the cowman's harvest, or his final harvest. The beef round-up may begin in July or August, and perhaps it may be conducted by the joint efforts of two districts instead of one. The joint outfit acts under much the same system of gathering up the cattle as has been described for the calf round-up. All the cattle of the range are gathered in great herds, and the latter are handled as during the calf round-up, though the operation is somewhat simpler. Only the mature or fatted animals are cut out from the herd, the rest being left to scatter as they like. The separated number goes under the name of the "beef cut," and this "cut" is held apart and driven on ahead from place to place as the round-up progresses, the beef herd thus growing from day to day until all the range has been worked. The herd is then driven in by easy stages to the shipping point on the railroad, where it is perhaps held until the arrival of the herd from the adjoining district, so that the shippers may be reasonably sure they have in all the beef fit for shipment from their ranges. Then the long train loads of cattle go on to the great markets, and the work of the ranchman proper is done for the season. Perhaps in the shipment of beef there may be a few animals picked up on the range during the beef drive which belong to some owner or owners not represented in the outfits. Such animals, if fit for shipment as beef, are

driven along with the main herd and shipped and sold without the owners' knowledge, the money being returned to the owners in due time through the inspectors at the markets. Obviously this is better than allowing these animals to run wild and unutilized as strays upon the range, of no profit to the owners or any one else. The common sense and the fairness of the cowman's system prevail on the beef round-up as in the harvesting of the calves.

So perfect is this great interdependent system of the round-up on the main cattle ranges of to-day that the ranchmen trust to it almost entirely for the determining and the handling of their yearly product. Range riding is now nearly done away with in some of the more populous districts, the cattle ranging in common over the country as they like, with no efforts made to confine them to any given range. All these things are modified by local conditions, and the whole system of ranching cattle is becoming modified by the advance of time. To-day the rancher uses more and more feed about his ranch. He raises hay for his stock, a bit of grain for his horses in winter time, or perhaps he buys hay or grain of the "grangers" who are moving in about him. Speaking in the original and primitive sense, this is not range work at all. The cowman proper depended solely upon the standing grass for his cattle food, upon the saddle for the assembling of his wealth, upon his own iron for the marking of it.

If it be now obvious what is the intention of the cowman in the round-up and what the method by which he obtains his purposes, we shall none the less fail of a fair review of this business system if we lose sight of the chief actor in all these operations, the cowpuncher himself. His is the tireless form that rides day after day in rain or shine throughout the long season, collecting the cattle upon their wild pasture ground, and his the undaunted heart to meet all the hardships of one of the hardest callings known to men. From May until November he may be in the saddle, each week growing gaunter and grimmer and more bronzed, his hair and mustache becoming more and more bleached and burned, his eye perhaps more hollow though not less bright and keen. If he be tired, none may know it; if he be sick, it shall not appear; if he be injured, it must not be confessed until confession is unnecessary. His creed is one of hardihood, his shibboleth is to dare, his etiquette is not to complain. Such doctrine is not for the weak. It is no place for a timid man, this grinding crush in the middle of the herd, and the cowardly or considerate horseman would better ride elsewhere than in the mad and headlong cross-country chases of the round-up. The goring of a steer, the fall from a pitching horse, the plunge over a cut bank, the crushing of a limb in the press, or the trampling under a thousand hoofs—such possibilities face the cowpuncher on the round-up not part of the time, but all the time. He accepts them as matter of course and matter of necessity, and with the ease of custom. Yet he is mortal and may suffer injury. If the injury be not fatal, he accepts it calmly, and waits till he is well again. If a round-up knows a burial, it is not the first one which has been known. Men of action must meet fatality at times, and other men of action will have small time to mourn them. The conditions of life upon the range are severe, so severe that had they been known in advance they would have been shunned by hundreds of men who in their ignorance thought themselves fit for cowboys and learned later that they were not.

It goes without saying that so hardy and healthy a creature as this cowpuncher must have his amusements, even at his times of hardest work. The round-up is by no means a succession of dreary experiences, for it is there that one will find the most grotesque exhibitions of cowpuncher vitality and cowpuncher merriment. There probably never was a round-up where the boys did not rope a steer for some ambitious cowpuncher to ride bareback for a wager. This feat is not so easy as it looks, for the hide of a steer, or, worse yet, the hide of a big fat bull, is loose and rolling, so that, as the cowpuncher would say, it "turns plum over between a feller's legs." Sometimes a yearling or a runty little "dogy" is roped for this form of sport, the cowpuncher wreathing his long legs under its belly to its intense disgust and fright, though he probably sits it safely when the ropes are "turned loose" in spite of its antics, for it is the boast of a first-class cowpuncher that he can "ride ary thing that wears ha'r." Sometimes the cowboys enter into competitive tests of skill, trying to see which man can, alone and unassisted, in the shortest space of time, "rope, throw, and tie" a full-grown steer. It would seem almost impossible for one man to perform this feat, yet a good cowpuncher will do it so smoothly and swiftly that neither the steer nor the spectator can tell just how it happened. Yet another little sport on the round-up is sometimes to hitch up a cow and a broncho or "mean" horse together to a wagon, the horse jumping and plunging over the cow to the intense delight of these rough souls, to whom the wildest form of action is the most congenial.

It is taken for granted that all the men engaging in a round-up are good riders, and if it should chance that any one becomes entangled in an argument with a pitching pony, the event is one of great pleasure to his friends, who gather about him and give him encouragement of the cowpuncher sort, with abundant suggestions as to how he shall ride and much insistence that he must "ride him fair." If the cowpuncher is thrown, he is sure to get more jeers than sympathy, but it is his business not to be thrown. Nowadays the horse herd, always one of the picturesque features about the round-up, is losing some of its old interest with the gradual passing away of the habit of bucking or pitching among the range horses. The horse herd is to-day much graded up, as are the herds of cattle, and the modern cow pony may be quite a respectable bit of horseflesh. It is apt to be a more solid and "chunky" animal than the old Spanish pony, just as the cowboy himself is apt to be a more bulky man than the first cowpunchers who came up the Trail. One may note yet other changes. At the strictly modern round-up of to-day one will see few leather "chaps," few heavy hats with wide leather bands, few bucking horses, and no "guns." If we would study the cowpuncher we must do so soon, if we wish ever to see him as he once was at his best; and if we would see a round-up on the range we should not tarry too long, for yearly it becomes more and more restricted, modified, and confined, less and less a wild gathering of the plains, more and more a mere barnyard fixture. The days of the commonplace have come, and well may we mourn the past that has gone by.

The stirring scenes of the round-up, the rush and whirl of the cutting out, the hurry and noise of the branding, the milling of the main herds, and all the gusty life of the wild *mêlée* are things to remember as long as one lives, and they readily invite the multifold descriptive efforts that have been

given them. Yet aside from the common or conventional pictures there may arise detached ones, some perhaps from out of the past, perhaps wilder and more picturesque than those we may easily find to-day at the focus of affairs upon the range. Memory brings up a little scene far down in the dry and desert region of the Neutral Strip, where once our party of antelope hunters crossed the range where a round-up was in progress. We had noticed the many hoof prints of cattle and horses, all trending in a certain direction, and guessed the cause when we saw the long lines of dust rising and stringing out on the hazy and trembling horizon. In that barren and flinty-soiled region water is a rare thing, and he who does not know the water holes for the country a hundred miles about would far better do his antelope hunting elsewhere. Yet we knew we were near the line of the old cattle trails, and indeed just before noon one day fell upon the wide parallel lines ground out of the hard, gray soil by the thousands of hoofs that had crossed the country in earlier years. Thinking that we should thus come upon water at some time either that day or the next, we followed along the trail, and, as luck had it, within a couple of hours we fell upon a little pool of water by the wayside. It was a very baddish bit of water, muddy, discoloured, trampled, shallow at best, and now hardly sufficient to fill the hoof marks with its greenish-yellow fluid that fairly boiled under the downright rays of the sun. Yet it was water, and such as it was we were glad to find it, since it was the first for more than twenty-four hours. We camped beside it joyfully, feeling that now all the trials of life were past. As we lay there, under such shade as the wagon offered on the blindingly hot day, we saw a trail of dust coming from the line of hills about us, and with the glasses soon made out a squad of mounted men. These came on down to the water hole, and in time were joined there by other men who came from various directions. The party was the mess of a Strip outfit that had been out all day rounding up cattle back of the watering place. The men were hot and tired and covered with dust, but if any one was disposed to grumble he kept it to himself. The cook unfastened the tail-gate of his wagon, and in a twinkling had a kitchen table and pantry right at hand, with flour and meat within reach. Some of the boys kicked together enough of the abundant prairie chips—the only fuel within sixty miles of that point—and soon the preparations for the hurried meal were in progress. When the cook wanted water for his coffee he walked to the pool—in which, by the way, several dead carcasses were lying—and, picking out the point where the water seemed clearest, he calmly dipped up his coffeepot full and returned without comment to the fire. No one said a word about the quality of the water, which really was of a sort to make one shudder at the memory years later, and if the coffee was not good no one complained of it. From the mess box the cook produced his tin dishes, his knives and forks, and table was spread without cloth flat on the dusty and hoof-beaten soil. The heat was glaring, and in it, without suspicion of shade, the men sat, their flannel shirts covered over the shoulders with the white dust of the plains, their broad hats pushed back upon their foreheads as they ate. It was a scene for some better painter or writer than has yet appeared, this dusty, weather-beaten, self-reliant little body of men. Each face of the circle comes to mind clearly even after years of time. They were silent, dignified fellows,

these men, not talking much among themselves or with us, though they offered us of what they had, we having apparently convinced them that we were not "on the rustle," we in turn sharing with them what our mess box offered, as it happened some fresh game, which was much appreciated.

Before the meal began each man unsaddled his horse and turned it loose upon the prairie, where it first went to water and then set to feeding on the short sun-burned grass. When it came time to leave camp, the horses were rounded up by the herder, a young boy not over fifteen years of age, whom all the men called "Kid." In their rough way they seemed fond of the boy, who had evidently shown the quality demanded on the plains, and as the boy gathered up his horses into the rope corral made by two or three cow ponies and a couple of men as supports, the round-up boss looked on at his businesslike movements with approval, and remarked aside to one of the men, "That's a d—n good kid all right." To which the other replied with an approving grunt. The Kid rounded up

Range Rider.   *Harper's Magazine*

his charges swiftly, and got them into a many-coloured mass of mingling heads and tossing manes within the confines of the rope corral, after which the work of roping the mounts followed. The Kid begged of the foreman the privilege of doing the roping, and the latter, smiling in rough fashion, gave him what he asked, not laughing at his failures, but giving him a bit of advice about his work now and then when he had a specially wily pony to capture from out the moving and plunging bunch of wild range horses. It was a good instance of the chivalry sometimes shown by stronger natures to ones weaker or less skilled, and it afforded also a good example of the development of the cowboy from youth to manhood, from inexperience to skill.

Presently each man had out his mount, and had saddled the grunting and complaining beast in the effective fashion of the plains. There was a little mild pitching, but not enough to interest the tired cowpunchers. In a trice the rope corral was down and the ropes coiled at the saddle horns of their owners. The cook had his mess wagon slapped shut, and the teamster his team "hooked up." The men rode away as silent as they came, the foreman and some of those passing most closely to us saying as they rode by, "So long, fellers." No one looked back as he rode away, for this would have been a bit of curiosity not in good form on the range. They passed away into the edge of the rim of hills, and we saw them no more.

Such is one picture of the range, and it shows the cowboy not as a devil-may-care, roistering fellow, full of strange oaths and uncouth conduct, but, as he should perhaps better be seen, as a steady, hard-working, methodical man, able in his calling, faithful in his duties, and prompt in their fulfilment. These men were grimy with toil of a most exacting sort. Their fare was coarse and common, and even the first necessary of comfort was denied them. They were rudely clad, and all armed to the last item, for that was a country where arms were at times needful. Yet hard as was their apparent lot, and rude as they who shared it, their simple and uncomplaining hardihood and self-control, their dignity, and their generous conduct to the younger member of the party left a lasting impression—perhaps a good one of its kind—of the cowboy as he is in actual life upon the range.

Other titles of interest

THE GREAT SIOUX UPRISING
C. M. Oehler
292 pp., 6 illus., 6 maps
80759-9 $14.95

COMANCHES
The Destruction of a People
T. R. Fehrenbach
596 pp., 43 illus., 2 maps
80586-3 $16.95

CRIMSONED PRAIRIE
The Indian Wars
S.L.A. Marshall
270 pp., 20 photos
80226-0 $12.95

THE DISCOVERY AND
CONQUEST OF MEXICO
Bernal Díaz del Castillo
Translated by A. P. Maudslay
New introduction by
Hugh Thomas
512 pp., 33 illus., 2 maps
80697-5 $16.95

ENCYCLOPEDIA OF WESTERN
LAWMEN & OUTLAWS
Jay Robert Nash
581 pp., 530 illus.
80591-X $25.95

FIRE AND BLOOD
A History of Mexico
Updated Edition
T. R. Fehrenbach
687 pp., 1 map
80628-2 $18.95

GERONIMO
Alexander B. Adams
381 pp., 18 illus.
80394-1 $14.95

GREAT DOCUMENTS IN
AMERICAN INDIAN HISTORY
Edited by Wayne Moquin with
Charles Van Doren
New foreword by Dee Brown
458 pp., 20 illus. & 5 maps
80659-2 $16.95

PERSONAL MEMOIRS OF
P. H. SHERIDAN
New introduction by
Jeffry D. Wert
560 pp., 16 illus., 16 maps
80487-5 $15.95

POCAHONTAS
The Life and the Legend
Frances Mossiker
424 pp., 28 illus.
80699-1 $15.95

WIND ON THE
BUFFALO GRASS
Native American Artist-Historians
Edited by Leslie Tillett
176 pp., 111 illus.
80357-7 $18.95

Available at your bookstore

OR ORDER DIRECTLY FROM

DA CAPO PRESS, INC.

1-800-321-0050